JUST BETWEEN THE LAW AND US

Obligations

Edited by

Neil Sargent

and

Logan Atkinson

Department of Law
Carleton University

CANADIAN LEGAL STUDIES SERIES

Captus Press

Canadian Legal Studies Series
Just Between the Law and Us: Obligations

Captus Press Inc.
Units 14 & 15, 1600 Steeles Avenue West
Concord, Ontario, L4K 4M2, Canada
Telephone: (416) 736–5537
Fax: (416) 736–5793
Email: Info@captus.com
Internet: http://www.captus.com

Canada *We acknowledge the financial support of the Government of Canada through the Canada Book Fund for our publishing activities.*

Library and Archives Canada Cataloguing in Publication

    Just between the law and us : obligations / edited by Neil Sargent and Logan Atkinson.

(Canadian legal studies series)
Previously published as part of Just between the law and us : introductory
    readings in private law. First eds. published under title:
Introduction to private law relationships.
Includes bibliographical references.
ISBN 978-1-55322-233-0

1. Civil law — Canada — Textbooks. 2. Civil law — Canada — Cases.
I. Sargent, N. (Neil)   II. Atkinson, Logan, date   III. Series: Canadian legal studies series

KE495.J875 2010   346.71   C2010-907070-4
KF385.ZA2J875 2010

0 9 8 7 6 5 4 3 2 1
Printed and bound in Canada

Table of Contents

Preface

This is the first publication of *Just Between the Law and Us: Volume II — Obligations*, at least in this format. It is one of two successor volumes to *Just Between the Law and Us: Introductory Readings in Private Law* (published by Captus Press in 2005), which in turn succeeded the third edition of *Introduction to Private Law Relationships* (published by Captus in 1999 and edited by M.J. Mac Neil, N. Sargent, T.B. Dawson, and M.A. Nixon). The present volume continues the development of reading materials for undergraduate students of private law theory and doctrine, capitalizing on the wholesale re-organization of those materials represented in the 2005 volume.

The students in our second year survey courses in private law have been the impetus for the development and re-development of these materials. Their persistent questions and challenges force us to continually re-consider the value of these materials to their learning experience, and that re-consideration in turn generates additional reflection on our teaching and learning goals more broadly conceived. By its very nature, private law transforms itself as the generations pass, most often quite subtly, but occasionally in a dramatic way. Our students' expectations change, too — their interests shifting in collaboration with other, more general shifts in the world around us. Our task is to ensure that the materials from which our students gain what is likely their first thorough exposure to the problems of private law remain relevant, challenging, and vital to them, while at the same time focusing on historical patterns and foundational philosophical assumptions. Our hope is that the current volume is a success in this respect.

We owe a large debt to the editors of the three editions of *Introduction to Private Law Relationships*, all of whom are current or former members of the Department of Law at Carleton University. Their work set a very high standard for us to follow, especially in the attempt to orient our students to the interconnections between private law rules and ordinary social experience. This is always a difficult challenge, and the readings collected in the editions of *Introduction to Private Law Relationships* and the work done in editing and teaching from those editions all functioned as inspiration for us in collecting the materials appearing in the current volume.

As is always the case in the production of volumes in the "Canadian Legal Studies Series", personnel at Captus Press have been a tremendous help in seeing this volume through. Special mention ought to be made of Pauline Lai and Lily Chu, both of whom have been very supportive and energetic as the project unfolded.

Neil Sargent
Logan Atkinson

1 Contract and Voluntary Obligation

(a) The Essence of Contract†

Brian Coote

The Will Theory

Under the will theory, contracts are seen as expressions of the human will and, for that reason, as being inherently worthy of respect. In that premise are found both the justification of contract law and the basis of many of its incidents. The theory asserts the liberal principle of individual self-determination and the value of individual judgment and volition. Both are thought to be enhanced when two or more wills meet in agreement.

The idea of contract as an expression of will or intention can be traced back at least to classical Greece and Rome. Later it was developed particularly by the Pandectists, the scholars who reintroduced the duty of Roman law to Europe from the Renaissance onwards. Through them the theory influenced provisions of the French and German Civil Codes as well as of Scottish law. In turn, it influenced the development of the common law in the nineteenth century, through the writings of such European theorists as Pothier and Savigny.

Associated with the will theory, or derived from it, have been the concepts of contract as agreement, of consensus *ad idem*, offer and acceptance, intention to contract, privity and the *vinculum juris*, and construction and interpretation by reference to the intention of the parties. The theory has also lent support to defences such as mistake, misrepresentation, duress and undue influence and hence to the idea that consent to a contract should be full, free and true. In the common law of the classical period, perhaps its best-known manifestation was freedom of contract, a doctrine which both reinforced, and was itself reinforced by, the then-prevailing philosophy of laissez faire. So pervading did that doctrine become that it found its way into the constitutions of both the United States and Germany.

Subject to a limited number of restrictions, the law of contract could be seen to have delegated to individual citizens a form of legislative authority. While this could mean that one party could place him or herself to some degree under the control of another, the power to do so was itself an expression of individual autonomy and an incident of freedom. The most often-quoted judicial statement of the freedom of contract doctrine was that of Sir George Jessel in the 1875 case of *Printing and Numerical Registering Co v Sampson* where he said:

> if there is one thing which more than another public policy requires it is that men of full age and competent understanding shall have the utmost liberty of contracting, and that their contracts when entered into freely and voluntarily shall be held sacred and shall be enforced by Courts of Justice.

---

† Extract from (1988) 1 Journal of Contract Law 91 at 99–106. [Notes and/or References omitted.] Reproduced with permission of Brian Coote (author) and LexisNexis Australia. The author of this article has proposed an alternative theory of the nature of contract, a summary statement of which appears on p. 195 of the original work.

In the common law context, however, the will theory has its weaknesses, both as a justification for the enforcement of contracts and as a basis for prediction. Under the postal rule, for example, it is clear that an offeror could be bound to an offer he had already attempted to withdraw. The theory is also *prima facie* incompatible with the existence of implied-by-law terms. The most obvious weakness is the impossibility in practice of determining what the will of the parties might be, even supposing an exact concurrence of wills could ever exist about all aspects of any particular contract. The common law response has, of course, been to apply objective tests of will and intention. The parties are bound, not by what they actually intended, but by the inferences to be drawn from what they said and did. This objective approach has meant that a search for the apparent intentions of the parties has been a practical possibility. But it also means that the existence of contract law can hardly be justified by reference to some mystical need to give effect to the human will, since it is not necessarily the actual will which is the determinant.

The use of standard forms which gained momentum in the nineteenth century and which has accelerated since, has also undermined the idea of consensus *ad idem*. There has, too, been a retreat from the notion of freedom of contract, coinciding with a retreat from laissez-faire economics which has only recently been reversed. These matters will be adverted to again in due course.

The Bargain Theory

The bargain theory is a common law development from the notion of contract as agreement. It incorporates what has been called the bargain theory of consideration, attributed in the United States to O.W. Holmes, which sees consideration in terms of reciprocal conventional inducement. The distinguishing feature of a contract at common law is said to be a bargain or exchange between the parties. As a theory it is necessarily confined to the common law system, which is the only one to contain, through the doctrine of consideration, any requirement of reciprocity between the parties.

As we have seen, *Cheshire & Fifoot* subscribe to this theory. They are seemingly not alone. Professor C.J. Hamson, for example, has suggested that "consideration, offer and acceptance are an indissoluble trinity, facets of one identical notion which is that of notion bargain." The requirement of reciprocal consideration ensures that the parties

make their undertakings to each other and that, since each makes a "payment", each desires those undertakings to be made. The bargain theory, therefore, reinforces the ideas of privity, request and mutuality.

An obvious drawback to the theory is its exclusiveness. Not only has it to be confined to contracts at common law. Within the common law it fails to include contracts by deed made without consideration. On the other hand, it can also be argued in its favour that it does not exclude the possibility of gratuitous contracts. Even if simple contracts must be bargains, the common law does not require any equivalence of exchange. If the promise of a peppercorn can be a sufficient consideration, the bargain theory could be said to include the possibility of a contract being made by way of gift, otherwise then by use of a deed.

The Promise Theory

The promise theory says in effect that contracts are promises, that promises should be kept, and that it is therefore appropriate that the law should enforce them.

The idea of a promise as something to be kept is an ancient one and has drawn support from the Jewish, Christian and Muslim religions. The nearest Roman law came to a general type of contract and took the form of a ritual promise. In Roman times and since, the bindingness of promises has been seen to be required by natural law. In England, promises were important to the Anglo-Saxons. For centuries they were also enforced by the ecclesiastical courts. In the King's courts, the writ of assumpsit was, in form, an action on the case for damage caused by breach of promise. In more recent times, as we have already seen, text-book definitions of contract have frequently been cast in terms of promise, as was the definition in the Restatement of Contracts.

The promise theory, then, has the advantage of reflecting a practice of some antiquity and of giving legal expression to widely held intuitions of what is fair and right. It is not confined to agreements. But as a theory of contract it, too, has its drawbacks. It assumes that contracts are enforced because they are promises but, in practice, no legal system has ever enforced every promise and life would be intolerable under any system which did so, human nature being what it is. On the other hand, as has already been pointed out, some promises are nowadays enforceable which would not have been recognised as contracts under classical common law. There are problems too about what comprises a promise, why promises should be kept and why the law should intervene to enforce them.

It seems generally to be agreed that promisors place themselves under obligation to their promisees and in that sense surrender a measure of autonomy to them. Promises are seen as voluntary acts and the resultant obligation as being in some sense or another voluntarily incurred by the promisor. There is less agreement as to what constitutes a promise. Some regard it as merely an emphatic expression of intent, a statement of resolve or commitment, or a prediction. For others, it depends on an intention by the promisor to accept obligation in respect of whatever he or she has undertaken. The problem of futurity has already been mentioned.

As to why promises should be kept and, in particular, why the law should intervene to enforce them, there is again an absence of agreement. In the past, morality and religion have been accepted reasons. Professor Roscoe Pound argued that the extensive modern use of common forms had, in itself, "relaxed" the claims of morality for the enforcement of contracts. Even so, Professor Fried has recently argued the moral basis of contracts. More widely acceptable nowadays might be claims of utility and convenience. Promising can be regarded as a socially useful practice which it is in the interests of society to foster and protect. It could be said to provide facilities for its members in the form of systems of rules which give them the power, at their choice, to place themselves under the obligation.

This latter view of promises, too, has its detractors, principally on the ground that it presupposes an intention to be bound on the part of the promisor. If promises depend on intention, argued Adam Smith, a promise made without an intention to perform it would never be binding. Other commentators would claim that the search for intention is an unnecessary fiction. In practice, of course, the common law derives intention objectively, on the basis of the appearance of what the promisor has said and done.

For himself, Adam Smith preferred to found obligation on the reasonable expectations induced in the promisee. Some later commentators have taken the argument a step further by basing obligation on reliance by the promisee in pursuance of his or her reasonable expectations. These approaches have both been sufficiently important in contract theory to justify separate treatment here.

The Reasonable Expectations Theory

Adam Smith's theory of the foundation of contract law has come down to us in transcripts made by his students of his lectures in Jurisprudence. He based the obligation to perform a contract on the reasonable expectations induced by a promise and the disappointment of those obligations occasioned by breach.

In the classical period and since, views similar to those seem to have been shared very widely. In England, for example, they have appeared in such textbooks as *Pollock, Holland, Salmond, Anson*, and *Cheshire and Fifoot* and to have had the endorsement of Austin and Goodhart. In the United States, they were supported by *Corbin* and were incorporated by Roscoe Pound into one of his jural postulates. In Canada they have the support of contributors to *Studies in Contract Law* and are endorsed, for example, in Professor Waddams' *Contract* text. So widespread has been their acceptance that they have been described by Professor Atiyah as being now traditional.

It is not immediately obvious why the reasonable expectations theory should have held so much appeal, for so long. No doubt, promises and contracts do usually raise expectations and in most cases are intended to do so. But in practice, the raising of reasonable expectations is neither sufficient nor necessary for the existence of a promise or contract. A statement that I am likely to call at your home on Saturday afternoon may well raise expectations of a visit but it would not be a promise. On the other hand a statement would not be any less a promise merely because the promisee did not believe it could or would be performed. And a promise made by deed can be a binding contract even through the beneficiary is unaware of its existence. Then, too, there is a certain circularity in the theory. What marks it as especially reasonable to base expectations on a promise or contract if not that it is regarded as binding?

There is a further problem in the nature of expectation itself. Life is full of disappointments but we do not ordinarily expect the law to make provision for them to be compensated, even when the expectations themselves are reasonable. And if contract law exists to protect reasonable expectations, how are we to explain the decision of the

3

House of Lords in *Addis v. Gramophone Co. Ltd.*, the effect of which in most cases is to deny compensation for the "disappointment of mind" caused by breach of contract?

It was doubtless reasons of this kind, at least in part, which led to the development of the reliance theory.

The Reliance Theory

This theory, in its strongest form, is that a contract arises (or should arise) whenever a promisee has relied upon a promise in a way which would cause detriment if it were not kept. Writing in 1933 about justifications for contract liability, Professor M.R. Cohen described it as the "favourite theory today". Since then, it has attracted strong support from Fuller and Perdue in their famous 1937 article on "The Reliance Interest in Damages" and, in more recent times, from Professors Horwitz and Atiyah in particular.

Since it is based on loss or injury to the promisee, the theory has the advantage of appearing both objective (in not depending upon the intentions of the promisor) and fair (in visiting liability on the one who by inviting reliance has caused loss or injury). It appears, too, to draw some historical justification from the earliest actions in assumpsit, which could be said to have been based on loss or damage suffered as the result of reliance on the defendant's promise. Professor Cohen recognised that in basing liability on loss or damage the theory would appeal to those who wished to see contract integrated with other forms of obligation and particularly with tort.

Nevertheless, as a theory of contract it has serious limitations. For example, damages in contract characteristically are measured not by the loss suffered by the promisee in reliance on the promise but by the loss resulting from the promisor's failure to perform. The promisee is entitled in general to be put in the position he or she would have occupied had the contract been performed, the so-called "expectation" measure. Fuller and Perdue's answer to this objection was to extend their concept of "reliance" to include failure by the promisee to make alternative contractual arrangements in reliance on the promise (lost opportunity costs). On that basis, they suggested, the expectation measure was essentially a rule-of-thumb means of assessing reliance loss, followed by the courts for the sake of efficiency and convenience.

The reliance theory also seemingly fails to explain why, as is the case, executory contracts are binding from the moment of their formation and are enforceable independently of whether either party has acted to his or her detriment. Professor Atiyah would answer that the law has been wrong in this respect. A less drastic answer might be to say that, in enforcing wholly executory contracts, the object of the law is to protect not only particular acts of reliance but also the practice of relying on contracts generally.

A third difficulty is that neither reliance nor a tendency to induce reliance is either sufficient or necessary for the existence of a contract. Promises made in a social context, such as an invitation to dinner, may induce reliance but are not contracts. The same can be true of invitations to treat, such as advertisements for the holding of an auction, or offers such as tenders, which may induce reliance before being withdraw. On the other hand, a contract by deed can bind even though it has not been communicated to, let alone been relied upon by, the promisee. Like the reasonable expectations theory the reliance theory also contains an element of circularity.

Finally, the reliance theory bases contractual obligation, not on what a promisor said or did, but on the reactions of another to those things. As such it would be a potential instrument for the imposition of obligations for which the promisor has not contracted.

(b)   Contracts, Promises and the Law of Obligations†

P.S. Atiyah

For at least 100 years — and in many respects for more like twice that time — common lawyers have operated within a particular conceptual framework governing the law of obligations. Within this framework, the fundamental distinction has been that between obligations which are voluntarily assumed, and obligations which are imposed by law. The former constitutes the law of contract, the latter falls within the purview of the law of tort. There is, in addition, that somewhat anomalous body of law which came to be known as the law of quasi-contract, or in more modern times, as the law of restitution. This body of law was accommodated within the new conceptual framework by the academic lawyers and jurists from the 1860's onwards, and, after a considerable time lag, their ideas came to be part of the accepted orthodoxies. The law of quasi-contract, it came to be said, was part of the law of obligations which did not arise from voluntary acts of the will, but from positive rules of law. Quasi-contract thus took its place alongside tort law on one side of the great divide. Contract alone remained on the other side. Nobody ever paid much attention to the place of the law of trusts in this scheme of things. Equity, after all, was a peculiarly English invention and theorising about the law of obligations was very much a Roman and subsequently a Continental fashion. ... [N]obody seems to have troubled overmuch about the place of equitable obligations in the great divide between voluntarily assumed and legally imposed obligations.

These broad distinctions reflected a set of values, and ways of thought which also exercised a most profound influence on the conceptual pattern which was imposed on Contract law itself. Contractual obligations came to be treated as being almost exclusively about promises, agreements, intentions, acts of will. The function of the law came to be seen as that of merely giving effect to the private autonomy of contracting parties to make their own legal arrangements. It is, of course, well known

[and,] indeed, has become part of the modern orthodoxy, that the private autonomy, this extreme freedom of contract, came to be abused by parties with greater bargaining power, and has been curtailed in a variety of ways, both by legislative activity and by the judges themselves. ... I ... wish to discuss ... the conceptual framework of Contract and its place in the law of obligations as a whole. I want to suggest that, despite the increasing attacks upon freedom of contract, and the great divide between Contract and Tort, the conceptual apparatus which still dominates legal thinking on these issues is the apparatus of the nineteenth century.... I want to suggest, further, that this conceptual apparatus is not based on any objective truths, it does not derive from any eternal verities. It is the result, quite specifically of a nineteenth-century heritage, an amalgam of classical economics, of Benthamite radicalism, of liberal political ideals and of the law, itself created and moulded in the shadow of these movements. The result, I will argue, is that our basic conceptual apparatus, the fundamental characterisations and divisions which we impose on the phenomena with which we deal, do not reflect the values of our own times, but those of the last century. ... [T]o argue the case for revising our concepts so that they conform more closely to the values of today involves no judgment that those values are better than the values of yesterday. Indeed, the revision may prove useful to those who think otherwise, for it will bring into greater relief precisely what is involved in today's values.

It is time to turn away from these generalities, and I propose to begin by spending a few moments on the paradigm of modern contract theory. ... A typical contract is, first, a bilateral executory agreement. It consists of an exchange of promises; the exchange is deliberately carried through, by the process of offer and acceptance, with the intention of creating a binding deal. When the offer is accepted, the agreement is consummated, and a

---

† (1978) 94 L.Q. Rev. 193 at 193–97, 204–205, 208–209, 222–23. Reproduced with permission of Sweet & Maxwell Limited, Hampshire, U.K..

contract comes into existence before anything is actually *done* by the parties. No performance is required, no benefit has to be rendered, no act of detrimental reliance is needed, to create the obligation. The contract is binding because the parties intend to be bound; it is their will, or intention, which creates the liability. It is true that the law has this technical requirement known as the doctrine of consideration, but except in rare and special cases, mutual promises are consideration for each other, and therefore the model, by definition, complies with the requirement of consideration. When the contract is made, it binds each party to performance, or, in default, to a liability to pay damages in lieu. Prima facie these damages will represent the value of the innocent party's disappointed expectations. The plaintiff may, therefore, bring suit on a wholly executory contract, for example, because the defendant has attempted to cancel his offer or acceptance, or withdraw from the contract, and may recover damages for his disappointed expectations even though he has not relied upon the contract in any way, and even though the defendant has received no benefit under it. The whole model is suffused with the idea that the fundamental purpose of contract law is to give effect — within limits of course — to the intentions of the parties. It is their decision, and their free choice, which makes the contract binding, and determines its interpretation, and its result in the event of breach. It is, of course, a commonplace today that all legal obligations are, in the last resort, obligations created or at least recognised by the law, but the classical model of contract is easily enough adjusted to take account of this truism. The law of contract, it is said, consists of power-conferring rules. The law provides facilities for private parties to make use of them if they so wish. Those who wish to create legal obligations have only to comply with a simple set of rules and the result will be recognised by the law.

There is no doubt that this model has been of astonishing power. For 100 years it has had no serious rival. Today many lawyers would probably want to qualify it, or modify it in a variety of respects. Many would admit, perhaps insist, that the model is primarily useful in connection with the business transaction, and it does not fit the consumer transaction, or the family arrangement, or other agreements which cannot be characterised as business deals. ... But making all allowances for the necessary qualifications, I do not think it would be seriously disputed that this is the paradigm model of contract which we have inherited from

nineteenth-century lawyers. Indeed, a glance at the Contract textbooks will confirm that the model is still alive and well.

. . . .

Before proceeding further to examine the reality of this model of contract, it is worth pausing to consider some of its underlying presuppositions.... The first of these is that the classical model assumes that contract law is fundamentally about what parties *intend*, and not about what they *do*. ... The classical model is thus concerned with executory arrangements, with forward-looking planning. Contracts have a chronology, a time sequence, as can be seen by looking at the Table of Contents of any Contract textbook published in the last 100 years. They are created first, and performed (or not performed) thereafter. In this respect, of course, contractual obligations necessarily differ from those on the other side of the great divide. The law of torts, and the law of quasi-contract are concerned with what parties *do*. It is human action, or inaction, which creates liability in tort, or in restitution. Among other results, this means that Contract lawyers focus on a different time sequence. In tort, or in restitutionary claims, it is the causing of damage or injury on the one hand, or the rendering of benefits on the other, which is the immediate object of interest. In contract, likewise, damage or injury may be caused, or benefits rendered, but it is not these consequences, or the actions giving rise to them which are the focus of attention of the classical model. It is the intention of the parties which (it is assumed) must necessarily precede the causing of the damage or the rendering of the benefits, and which is therefore the source of the obligations. ...

The second presupposition of the classical model of contract is that a contract is a *thing*, which has some kind of objective existence prior to any performance or any act of the parties. Of all the examples of legal reification, none is surely more powerful than this. A contract is a thing which is "made," is "broken," is "discharged." ... The tendency to reify legal concepts is, in the case of contract, given powerful impetus by the fact that so many contractual arrangements are in written form. Even today, lawyers constantly use the words "the contract" to signify both the legal relations created by the law, and the piece of paper in which those relations (or some of them) are expressed. Here again, there is a profound difference in the lawyer's way of looking at legal obligations on the other side of the great divide. A contract may be a "thing" but nobody would conceptualise a quasi-contract or a tort as a thing. One reason why the tendency to reify the concept of contract has had important results is that it has reinforced the respect for the private autonomy of the contractual relationship. If a contract is a thing created by the contracting parties, it is easier to see it as a relationship within defined and limited parameters. Within these parameters, concepts such as fairness, justice, reasonableness have far less room to operate than they do with diffuse concepts like tort or quasi-contract.

. . . .

The fourth presupposition of the classical model of Contract is that there is indeed *one* model, that it is possible and useful to think still in terms of general principles of Contract.... We know, of course, that most contracts fall into particular categories which have their own rules and qualifications derogating from the general law. There are, for example, special rules applicable to contracts of employment, consumer credit contracts, consumer sales, leases, mortgages, insurance contracts, house purchase, matrimonial agreements and many others. Indeed, there are few contracts today which are *not* governed by specific rules which in some measure derogate from the general law. But none of this has shaken the power of the classical model of Contract. This model is, without doubt, based on an economic model, that of the free market. ...

. . . .

What I suggest then, is that wherever benefits are rendered, wherever acts of reasonable reliance take place, obligations may arise, both morally and in law. These obligations are by no means confined to cases where explicit promises are given, for they may arise in cases where we would imply a promise, but they also arise in many cases where any attempt to imply a promise would be nothing but a bare fiction. The man who boards a bus without any intention of paying for his fare is bound to pay it though it is difficult to see what reality there can be in claiming that he impliedly promises to pay. The man who signs a document without reading it does not make an implied any more than an express promise in any genuine sense.

Now I want next to suggest that these cases of benefits rendered or of action in reliance, are

more common than is suggested by our conventional image of the legal world. In conventional contract theory, the paradigm of contract is the executory arrangement. Executory contract theory has totally subsumed liabilities and obligations which arise from the receipt of benefits or from acts of reasonable reliance. But in practice, the whole executory transaction is nothing like such a paradigm as it appears in the books. I have already said something of the difficulties involved in the very concept of a paradigm in this context, but the most cursory look at the world and at the law will reveal that many types of transactions do not fit the model of the wholly executory arrangement at all. Vast numbers of transactions are not in any real sense binding prior to something being *done* by one or both of the parties. ... The language of consumer transactions, in particular, is not couched in terms of promises. People "book" holidays, or air reservations, they "order" goods, they "accept" estimates, and so on. Even in business circles this sort of terminology is more common than the express language of promises and undertakings. Whether language of this kind is treated as creating an obligation is traditionally thought of as depending upon whether the language is tantamount to being promissory. But it is at least arguable that in many cases of this nature the reality is otherwise. Frequently, both in law and in moral discourse we appear to determine whether there should be an obligation first, and then decide how the language should be construed afterwards. And it follows that the existence or non-existence of the obligation is then being decided independently of the existence of any promise.

. . . .

... ([I]t may be urged) the whole point of contractual liability is to permit parties to determine conclusively their own obligations. The promise creates the liability, and does not merely evidence it. In non-contractual cases, *per contra*, the duty is in the first instance created by the law; and the promise cannot be treated as creating the obligation. But I suggest that this analysis is the result of treating the executory contract as the paradigm of contract, the heritage of the classical law which I have already criticised. In the part-executed transaction ... it is in fact frequently the case that there would be a liability even apart from any express or implied promise. Promises are not a necessary condition of the existence of a liability or the creation of an obligation. The performance by one party of

7

acts which are beneficial to the other, the rendering of services to another, for instance, would normally be thought of as creating some sort of obligation even in the absence of a promise. Similarly, acts of reasonable reliance would often create liability in tort, or by way of trust, or other equitable obligation, even where there is no express or implied promise. Indeed, did not the whole law of trusts arise because property was entrusted to other hands, usually no doubt because of some understanding that the trustee would behave in a certain fashion? In circumstances of this kind, therefore, where obligations would normally be thought of as arising from what has been done, rather than from what has been said, there seems to me no difficulty in regarding promises as having primarily an evidentiary role.

. . . .

I do not, of course, want to suggest that the whole law of obligation can be rewritten in terms of a few simple principles drawn from the notions of benefit and reliance. Society and social and economic relationships are too complex in the modern industrial world for oversimplifications of this nature. But what I do want to suggest is that the great divide between duties which are voluntarily assumed, and duties which are imposed by law is itself one of these oversimplifications. A more adequate and more unifying conceptual structure for the law of obligations can be built around the inter-relationship between the concepts of reciprocal benefits, acts of reasonable reliance, and voluntary human conduct.

(c) *Carlill v. Carbolic Smoke Ball Co.*†

[LINDLEY L.J.:]

This is an appeal by the defendants against a decision of HAWKINS, J, rendering them liable to pay the plaintiff 100 pounds under the circumstances to which I will allude presently. The defendants are interested in selling as largely as possible an article they call the "Carbolic smoke ball." What that is I do not know. But they have great faith in it as an effectual preventive against influenza and colds, or any diseases caused by taking cold, and as also useful in a great variety of other complaints. They are so confident in the merits of this thing that they say in one leaflet that the carbolic smoke ball never fails to cure all the diseases therein mentioned when used strictly according to these directions. Like other tradespeople they want to induce the public to have sufficient confidence in their preparation to buy it largely. That being the position they put this advertisement into various newspapers. It is printed in black-faced type, that is to say, the striking parts of it are. It is, therefore, put

in a form to attract attention, and they mean that it should attract attention for the purposes to which I have already alluded.

[His LORDSHIP read the advertisement.] The plaintiff is a lady who, upon the faith of one of these advertisements, went and bought at a chemist's in Oxford Street one of these smoke balls. She used it three times daily for two weeks according to the printed directions supplied. But before she had done using it she was unfortunate enough to contract influenza, so that in her case this ball did not produce the desired effect. Whereupon she says to the Carbolic Smoke Ball Co: "Pay me this reward of 100 pounds." "Oh no," they respond, "We will not pay you the 100 pounds." She then brings an action, and HAWKINS, J, has held that the defendants must pay her the 100 pounds. Then they appeal to us and say that that judgment is erroneous. The appeal has been argued with great ingenuity by the defendants' counsel, and his contentions are reduced in substance to this — that, put it as you will, this is not a binding promise.

---

† [1891–1894] All ER Rep 127.

. . . .

... The first observation I would make upon this is that we are not dealing with any inference of fact. We are dealing with an express promise to pay 100 pounds in certain events. There can be no mistake about that at all. Read this how you will, and twist it about as you will, here is a distinct promise, expressed in language which is perfectly unmistakeable, that 100 pounds reward will be paid by the Carbolic Smoke Ball Co to any person who contracts influenza after having used the ball three times daily, and so on. One must look a little further and see if this is intended to be a promise at all; whether it is a mere puff — a sort of thing which means nothing. Is that the meaning of it? My answer to that question is "No," and I base my answer upon this passage: "1,000 pounds is deposited with the Alliance Bank, Regent Street, showing our sincerity in the matter." What is that money deposited for? What is that passage put in for, except to negative the suggestion that this is a mere puff, and means nothing at all? The deposit is called in aid by the advertisers as proof of their sincerity in the matter. What do they mean? It is to show their intention to pay the 100 pounds in the events which they have specified. I do not know who drew the advertisement, but he has distinctly in words expressed that promise. It is as plain as words can make it.

Then it is said that it is a promise that is not binding. In the first place it is said that it is not made with anybody in particular. The offer is to anybody who performs the conditions named in the advertisement. Anybody who does perform the conditions accepts the offer. I take it that if you look at this advertisement in point of law, it is an offer to pay 100 pounds to anybody who will perform these conditions, and the performance of these conditions is the acceptance of the offer. That rests upon a string of authorities, the earliest of which is that celebrated advertisement case of *Williams v Carwardine* which has been followed by a good many other cases concerning advertisements of rewards. But then it is said: "Supposing that the performance of the conditions is an acceptance of the offer, that acceptance ought to be notified." Unquestionably as a general proposition when an offer is made, you must have it not only accepted, but the acceptance notified. But is that so in cases of this kind? I apprehend that this is rather an exception to the rule, or, if not an exception, it is open to the observation that the notification of the

acceptance need not precede the performance. This offer is a continuing offer. It was never revoked, and if notice of acceptance is required (which I doubt very much, for I rather think the true view is that which is as expressed and explained by **LORD BLACKBURN** in *Brogden v Metropolitan Rail Co*) the person who makes the offer receives the notice of acceptance contemporaneously with his notice of the performance of the conditions. Anyhow, if notice is wanted, he gets it before his offer is revoked, which is all you want in principle. But I doubt very much whether the true view is not, in a case of this kind, that the person who makes the offer shows by his language and from the nature of the transaction that he does not expect and does not require notice of the acceptance apart from notice of the performance.

We have, therefore, all the elements which are necessary to form a binding contract enforceable in point of law subject to two observations. First of all, it is said that this advertisement is so vague that you cannot construe it as a promise; that the vagueness of the language, to which I will allude presently, shows that a legal promise was never intended nor contemplated. No doubt the language is vague and uncertain in some respects, and particularly in that the 100 pounds is to be paid to any person who contracts influenza after having used the ball three times daily, and so on. It is said, "When are they to be used?" According to the language of the advertisement no time is fixed, and, construing the offer most strongly against the person who has made it, one might infer that any time was meant. I doubt whether that was meant, and I doubt whether that would not be pushing too far the doctrine as to construing language most strongly against the person using it. I doubt whether business people, or reasonable people would understand that if you took a smoke ball and used it three times daily for the time specified — two weeks — you were to be guaranteed against influenza for the rest of your life. I do not think the advertisement means that, to do the defendants justice. I think it would be pushing their language a little too far. But if it does not mean that, what does it mean? ...

... And it strikes me, I confess, that the true construction of this is that 100 pounds will be paid to anybody who uses this smoke ball three times daily, for two weeks according to the printed directions, and who gets influenza, or a cold, or some other disease caused by taking cold, within a reasonable time after so using it. I think that that is the fair and proper business construction of it.

If that is the true construction, it is enough for the plaintiff. Therefore, I say no more about the vagueness of the document.

I come now to the last point, which I think requires attention, [i.e], the question of the consideration. Counsel for the defendants has argued with great skill that this is a nudum pactum — that there is no consideration. We must apply to that argument the usual legal tests. Let us see whether there is no advantage to the defendants. Counsel says it is no advantage to them how much the ball is used. What is an advantage to them and what benefits them is the sale, and he has put the ingenious case that a lot of these balls might be stolen, and that it would be no advantage to them if the thief or other people used them. The answer to that I think is this. It is quite obvious that, in the view of the defendants, the advertisers, a use of the smoke balls by the public, if they can get the public to have confidence enough to use them, will react and produce a sale which is directly beneficial to them, the defendants. Therefore it appears to me that out of this transaction emerges an advantage to them which is enough to constitute a consideration. But there is another view of it. What about the person who acts upon this and accepts the offer? Does not that person put himself to some inconvenience at the request of the defendants? Is it nothing to use this ball three times daily at the request of the defendants for two weeks according to the directions? Is that to go for nothing? It appears to me that that is a distinct inconvenience, if not a detriment, to any person who uses the smoke ball. When, therefore, you come to analyze this argument of want of consideration, it appears to me that there is ample consideration for the promise.

. . . .

It appears to me, therefore, that these defendants must perform their promise, and if they have been so unguarded and so unwary as to expose themselves to a great many actions, so much the worse for them. For once in a way the advertiser has reckoned too much on the gullibility of the public. It appears to me that it would be very little short of a scandal if we said that no action would lie on such a promise as this, acted upon as it has been. The appeal must be dismissed with costs.

(d) *Gilbert Steel Ltd. v. University Construction Ltd.*†

[WILSON J.A.:]

This is an appeal from the order of Mr. Justice Pennell dismissing the plaintiff's action for damages for breach of oral agreement for the supply of fabricated steel bars to be incorporated into apartment buildings being constructed by the defendant. The case raises some fundamental principles of contract law.

The circumstances giving rise to the action are as follows. On September 4, 1968, the plaintiff entered into a written contract to deliver to the defendant fabricated steel for apartment buildings to be erected at three separate sites referred to in the contract as the "Flavin, Tectate and University projects". The price fixed by that contract was $153 per ton for "Hard Grade" and $159 per ton for "Grade 60,000." Deliveries for the Flavin and Tectate projects were completed in August, 1969, and October, 1969, respectively, and paid for at the agreed-upon prices.

Two apartment buildings calling for the supply of 3,000 tons of fabricated steel were to be erected at the University site. However, prior to the defendant's notifying the plaintiff of its intention to commence construction on the first of these two

---

† (1976), 12 O.R. (2d) 19 (C.A.).

buildings, the owners of the steel mill announced an increase in the price of unfabricated steel. They also gave warning of a further increase to come. The plaintiff approached the defendant about a new contract for the University project and a written contract dated October 22, 1969, was entered into for the supply of fabricated steel for the first building. The new price was $156 per ton for "Hard grade" and $165 per ton for "Grade 60,000." In fact this increase in price did not reflect the full amount of the initial increase announced by the mill owners.

On March 1, 1970, while the building under construction was still far from completion, the mill owners announced the second increase in price and a further discussion took place between John Gilbert and his brother Harry representing the plaintiff and Mendel Tenenbaum and Hersz Tenenbaum representing the defendant with respect to the price to be paid for the steel required to complete the first building. It is this discussion which the plaintiff alleges resulted in a binding oral agreement that the defendant would pay $166 per ton for "Hard grade" and $178 per ton for "Grade 60,000." Although the plaintiff submitted to the defendant a written contract embodying these revised prices following their meeting, the contract was not executed. It contained, in addition to the increased prices, two new clauses which the trial Judge found had not been the subject of any discussion with the defendant but were unilaterally imported into the document by the plaintiff. The trial Judge also found, however, that the defendant agreed at the meeting to pay the increased price.

From March 12, 1970, until the completion of the first building the defendant accepted deliveries of the steel against invoices which reflected the revised prices but, in making payments on account, it remitted cheques in rounded amounts which at the date of the issuance of the writ resulted in a balance owing to the plaintiff in accordance with the invoices.

Having found on the evidence that the defendant had orally agreed to pay the increased prices, the legal issue confronting Mr. Justice Pennell was whether that agreement was legally binding upon the defendant or whether it failed for want of consideration. Counsel for the defendant submitted at the trial that past consideration is no consideration and that the plaintiff was already obliged before the alleged oral agreement was entered into to deliver the steel at the original prices agreed to in the written contract of October 22, 1969. Where

then was the *quid pro quo* for the defendant's promise to pay more?

Counsel for the plaintiff sought to supply this omission from the evidence of Hersz Tenenbaum who, during the course of discussions which took place in September, 1970, with a view to a contract for the supply of steel for the second building at the University site, asked whether the plaintiff would give him "a good price" on steel for this building. Plaintiff's counsel argued that the promise of a good price on the second building was the consideration the defendant received for agreeing to pay the increased price on the first. The trial Judge rejected this submission and found the oral agreement unenforceable for want of consideration. In the course of his reasons for judgment the trial Judge adverted briefly to an alternate submission made by the plaintiff's counsel. He said:

> I should, in conclusion, mention a further point which was argued with ingenuity by Mr. Morphy. His contention was that the consideration for the oral agreement was the mutual abandonment of right under the prior agreement in writing. I must say, with respect, that this argument is not without its attraction for me.

On the appeal Mr. Morphy picked up and elaborated upon this submission which had intrigued the trial Judge. In launching his main attack on the trial Judge's finding that the oral agreement was unenforceable for want of consideration, he submitted that the facts of this case evidenced not a purported oral variation of a written contract which failed for want of consideration but an implied rescission of the written contract and the creation of a whole new contract, albeit oral, which was subsequently reneged on by the defendant. The consideration for this new oral agreement, submitted Mr. Morphy, was the mutual agreement to abandon the previous written contract and to assume the obligations under the new oral one. Mr. Morphy submitted to the Court for its consideration two lines of authority, the first line illustrated by the leading case of *Stilk v. Myrick* (1809), in which the subsequent agreement was held to be merely a variation of the earlier agreement and accordingly failed for want of consideration, and the other line illustrated by *Morris v. Baron & Co.*, in which the subsequent agreement was held to have rescinded the former one and was therefore supported by the mutual agreement to abandon the old obligations and substitute the new. Mr. Morphy invited us to find that the oral agreement to pay the increased price for steel fell into the second category. There was, he acknowledged, no express rescission of the written contract but price is such a fundamental term of a contract for the supply of goods that the substitution of a new price must connote a new contract and impliedly rescind the old.

It is impossible to accept Mr. Morphy's submission in face of the evidence adduced at the trial. It is clear that the sole reason for the discussions between the parties in March, 1970, concerning the supply of steel to complete the first building at the University site was the increase in the price of steel by the mill owners. No changes other than the changes in price were discussed. The trial Judge found that the other two changes sought to be introduced into the written document submitted by the plaintiff to the defendant for signature following the discussions had not even been mentioned at the meeting. Moreover, although repeated references were made at trial by the Gilbert brothers to the fact that the parties had made a "new contract" in March, 1970, it seems fairly clear from the evidence when read as a whole that the "new contract" referred to was the agreement to pay the increased price for the steel, *i.e.*, the agreement which effected the variation of the written contract and not a new contract in the sense of a contract replacing *in toto* the original contract of October 22, 1969.

I am not persuaded that either of the parties intended by their discussions in March, 1970, to rescind their original contract and replace it with a new one. Indeed, it is significant that no such plea was made in the statement of claim which confined itself to an allegation that "it was orally agreed in March 1970 that the prices as set forth in the said contract [*i.e.*, of October 22, 1969] would be varied...". Accordingly, consideration for the oral agreement is not to be found in a mutual agreement to abandon the earlier written contract and assume the obligations under the new oral one.

Nor can I find consideration in the vague references in the evidence to the possibility that the plaintiff would give the defendant "a good price" on the steel for the second building if it went along with the increased prices on the first. The plaintiff, in my opinion, fell far short of making any commitment in this regard.

Counsel for the appellant put before us as an alternate source of consideration for the agreement to pay the increased price, the increased credit afforded by the plaintiff to the defendant as a result of the increased price. The argument went

something like this. Whereas previously the defendant had credit outstanding for 60 days in the amount owed on the original prices, after the oral agreement was made he had credit outstanding for 60 days in the amount owed on the higher prices. Therefore, there was consideration flowing from the promisee and the law does not inquire into its sufficiency. Reliance was placed by counsel on the decision of Chief Justice Meredith in *Kilbuck Coal Co. v. Turner & Robinson*. This case, however, is clearly distinguishable from the case at bar, as Mr. Justice Pennell pointed out in his reasons, on the basis of the *force majeure* clause which had relieved the plaintiff of its obligations under the original contract. In undertaking to supply coal despite the strike the plaintiff was unquestionably providing consideration of real substance in that case. I cannot accept counsel's contention, ingenious as it is, that the increased credit inherent in the increased price constituted consideration flowing from the promisee for the promisor's agreement to pay the increased price.

The final submission put forward by counsel for the appellant was that the defendant, by his conduct in not repudiating the invoices reflecting the increase in price when and as they were received, had in effect acquiesced in such increase and should not subsequently be permitted to repudiate it. There would appear to be two answers to this submission. The first is summed up in the maxim that estoppel can never be used as a sword but only as a shield. A plaintiff cannot found his claim in estoppel. Secondarily, however, it should perhaps be pointed out that in order to found an estoppel the plaintiff must show, not only that the conduct of the defendant was clearly referable to the defendant's having given up its right to insist on the original prices, but also that the plaintiff relied on the defendant's conduct to its detriment. I do not think the plaintiff can discharge either of these burdens on the facts of this case.

In summary, I concur in the findings of the trial Judge that the oral agreement made by the parties in March, 1970, was an agreement to vary the written contract of October 22, 1969, and that it must fail for want of consideration.

Argument was directed on the appeal to the question of interest, a matter not dealt with by the trial Judge. The written contract of October 22, 1969, is silent on the subject of interest although it specifies in the terms of payment "net 60 days from date of invoice". I have considered whether it is to be implied from these words that interest will be exigible if the amount owing is not paid within the 60-day period. Such meager authority as exists on the meaning of "net" in different contexts does not appear to be helpful. Generally it has reference to the amount established after all proper expenses or deductions have been allowed for. However, it is also commonly used to mean the "rock-bottom price" from which no discount will be given. "Net" may not be an apt word to use in connection with an extension of credit but I have concluded that this is what the parties had in mind in this case. Payment could be deferred by the defendant for the 60-day period free of any sanction but after the expiry of that period, interest would be exigible. Since no rate is specified I find that interest is payable on overdue amounts at the statutory rate of 5 per cent per annum. I attach no significance to the notation "1 per cent per month interest on overdue accounts" on the invoices received by the defendant at the increased prices on the basis that interest cannot be imposed unilaterally in this manner.

The judgment of Pennell J., should be varied to provide that the plaintiff shall have judgment for interest at the rate of 5 per cent on the payments which were overdue for more than 60 days under the contract dated October 22, 1969. Subject to this variation the appeal should be dismissed with costs.

The respondent cross-appealed on the subject of costs. The trial Judge made no order as to costs although the defendant was successful in the action. Mr. Starkman submits that, in failing to award costs to his successful client, Mr. Justice Pennell did not exercise his discretion with respect to costs judicially. A review of Mr. Justice Pennell's reasons for judgment indicates that he was motivated to withhold costs by his assessment of the conduct of the defendant which led up to this litigation and, since he was in a better position than this Court to make such an assessment, I see no reason to interfere with his disposition as to the costs at trial.

The cross-appeal should accordingly be dismissed. There will be no order as to costs of the cross-appeal.

Appeal and cross-appeal dismissed.

(e)   Non-Contractual Relationships in Business: A Preliminary Study†

Stewart Macaulay

TENTATIVE FINDINGS

. . . .

The Adjustment of Exchange Relationships and the Settling of Disputes

While a significant amount of creating business exchanges is done on a fairly noncontractual basis, the creation of exchanges usually is far more contractual than the adjustment of such relationships and the settlement of disputes. Exchanges are adjusted when the obligations of one or both parties are modified by agreement during the life of the relationship. For example, the buyer may be allowed to cancel all or part of the goods he has ordered because he no longer needs them; the seller may be paid more than the usual contract price by the buyer because of unusual changed circumstances. Dispute settlement involves determining whether or not a party has performed as agreed and, if he has not, doing something about it. For example, a court may have to interpret the

---

† (1963) 28 American Sociological Rev. 55 at 60–67. [Notes and/or References omitted.]

meaning of a contract, determine what the alleged defaulting party has done and determine what, if any, remedy the aggrieved party is entitled to. Or one party may assert that the other is in default, refuse to proceed with performing the contract and refuse to deal ever again with the alleged defaulter. If the alleged defaulter, who in fact may not be in default, takes no action, the dispute is then "settled."

Business exchanges in non-speculative areas are usually adjusted without dispute. Under the law of contracts, if B orders 1,000 widgets from S at $1.00 each, B must take all 1,000 widgets or be in breach of contract and liable to pay S his expenses up to the time of the breach plus his lost anticipated profit. ... A lawyer with many large industrial clients said,

> Often businessmen do not feel they have "a contract" — rather they have "an order." They speak of "cancelling the order" rather than "breaching our contract." When I began practice I referred to order cancellations as breaches of contract, but my clients objected since they do not think of cancellation as wrong. Most clients, in heavy industry at least, believe that there is a right to cancel as part of the buyer-seller relationship. There is a widespread attitude that one can back out of any deal within some very vague limits. Lawyers are often surprised by this attitude.

Disputes are frequently settled without reference to the contract or potential or actual legal sanctions. There is a hesitancy to speak of legal rights or to threaten to sue in these negotiations. Even where the parties have a detailed and carefully planned agreement which indicates what is to happen if, say, the seller fails to deliver on time, often they will never refer to the agreement but will negotiate a solution when the problem arises apparently as if there had never been any original contract. One purchasing agent expressed a common business attitude when he said,

> if something comes up, you get the other man on the telephone and deal with the problem. You don't read legalistic contract clauses at each other if you ever want to do business again. One doesn't run to lawyers if he wants to stay in business because one must behave decently.

Or as one businessman put it, "You can settle any dispute if you keep the lawyers and accountants out of it. They just do not understand the give-and-take needed in business." All of the house counsel interviewed indicated that they are called into the dispute settlement process only after the businessmen have failed to settle matters in their own way. Two indicated that after being called in house counsel at first will only advise the purchasing agent, sales manager or other official involved; not even the house counsel's letterhead is used on communications with the other side until all hope for a peaceful resolution is gone.

Law suits for breach of contract appear to be rare. ... A law firm with more than 40 lawyers and a large commercial practice handles in a year only about six trials concerned with contract problems. Less than 10 per cent of the time of this office is devoted to any type of work related to contracts disputes. Corporations big enough to do business in more than one state tend to sue and be sued in the federal courts. Yet only 2,779 out of 58,293 civil actions filed in the United States District Courts in fiscal year 1961 involved private contracts. During the same period only 3,447 of the 61,138 civil cases filed in the principal trial courts of New York State involved private contracts. The same picture emerges from a review of appellate cases. Mentschikoff has suggested that commercial cases are not brought to the courts either in periods of business prosperity (because buyers unjustifiably reject goods only when prices drop and they can get similar goods elsewhere at less than the contract price) or in periods of deep depression (because people are unable to come to court or have insufficient assets to satisfy any judgment that might be obtained). Apparently, she adds, it is necessary to have "a kind of middle-sized depression" to bring large numbers of commercial cases to the courts. However, there is little evidence that in even "a kind of middle-sized depression" today's businessmen would use the courts to settle disputes.

At times relatively contractual methods are used to make adjustments in ongoing transactions and to settle disputes. Demands of one side which are deemed unreasonable by the other occasionally are blocked by reference to the terms of the agreement between the parties. The legal position of the parties can influence negotiations even though legal rights or litigation are never mentioned in their discussions; it makes a difference if one is demanding what both concede to be a right or begging for a favour. Now and then a firm may threaten to turn matters over to its attorneys, threaten to sue, commence a suit or even litigate and carry an appeal to the highest court which will hear the matter. Thus, legal sanctions, while not an everyday affair, are not unknown in business.

One can conclude that while detailed planning and legal sanctions play a significant role in some exchanges between businesses, in many business exchanges their role is small.

TENTATIVE EXPLANATIONS

Two questions need to be answered: (A) How can business successfully operate exchange relationships with relatively so little attention to detailed planning or to legal sanctions, and (B) Why does business ever use contract in light of its success without it?

Why are Relatively Non-contractual Practices so Common?

In most situations contract is not needed. Often its functions are served by other devices. Most problems are avoided without resort to detailed planning or legal sanctions because usually there is little room for honest misunderstandings or good faith differences of opinion about the nature and quality of a seller's performance. Although the parties fail to cover all foreseeable contingencies, they will exercise care to see that both understand the primary obligation on each side. Either products are standardized with an accepted description or specifications are written calling for production to certain tolerances or results. Those who write and read specifications are experienced professionals who will know the customs of their industry and those of the industries with which they deal. Consequently, these customs can fill gaps in the express agreements of the parties. Finally, most products can be tested to see if they are what was ordered; typically in manufacturing industry we are not dealing with questions of taste or judgment where people can differ in good faith.

When defaults occur they are not likely to be disastrous because of techniques of risk avoidance or risk spreading. One can deal with firms of good reputation or he may be able to get some form of security to guarantee performance. One can insure against many breaches of contract where the risks justify the costs. Sellers set up reserves for bad debts on their books and can sell some of their accounts receivable. Buyers can place orders with two or more suppliers of the same item so that a default by one will not stop the buyer's assembly lines.

Moreover, contract and contract law are often thought unnecessary because there are many effective non-legal sanctions. Two norms are widely accepted. (1) Commitments are to be honored in almost all situations; one does not welsh on a deal. (2) One ought to produce a good product and stand behind it. Then, too, business units are organized to perform commitments, and internal sanctions will induce performance. For example, sales personnel must face angry customers when there has been a late or defective performance. The salesmen do not enjoy this and will put pressure on the production personnel responsible for the default. If the production personnel default too often, they will be fired. At all levels of the two business units personal relationships across the boundaries of the two organizations exert pressures for conformity to expectations. Salesmen often know purchasing agents well. The same two individuals occupying these roles may have dealt with each other [for] from five to 25 years. Each has something to give the other. Salesmen have gossip about competitors, shortages and price increases to give purchasing agents who treat them well. Salesmen take purchasing agents to dinner, and they give purchasing agents Christmas gifts hoping to improve the chances of making sale. The buyer's engineering staff may work with the seller's engineering staff to solve problems jointly. The seller's engineers may render great assistance, and the buyer's engineers may desire to return the favour by drafting specifications which only the seller can meet. The top executives of the two firms may know each other. They may sit together on government or trade committees. They may know each other socially and even belong to the same country club. The interrelationships may be more formal. Sellers may hold stock in corporations which are important customers; buyers may hold stock in important suppliers. Both buyer and seller may share common directors on their boards. They may share a common financial institution which has financed both units.

The final type of non-legal sanction is the most obvious. Both business units involved in the exchange desire to continue successfully in business and will avoid conduct which might interfere with attaining this goal. One is concerned with both the reaction of the other party in the particular exchange and with his own general business reputation. Obviously, the buyer gains sanctions insofar as the seller wants the particular exchange to be completed. Buyers can withhold part or all of their payments until sellers have performed to their satisfaction. If a seller has a great deal of money tied up in his performance which he must recover quickly, he will go a long way to please the buyer in order to be paid. Moreover, buyers who are dissatisfied may cancel and cause sellers to lose the cost of what they have done up to cancellation. Furthermore, sellers hope for repeat [] orders, and one gets few of these from unhappy customers. Some industrial buyers go so far as to formalize this sanction by issuing "report cards" rating the performance of each supplier. The supplier rating goes to the top management of the seller organization, and these men can apply internal sanctions to salesmen, production supervisors or product designers if there are too many "D's" or "F's" on the report card.

While it is generally assumed that the customer is always right, the seller may have some counterbalancing sanctions against the buyer. The seller may have obtained a large downpayment from the buyer which he will want to protect. The seller may have an exclusive process which the buyer needs. The seller may be one of the few firms which has the skill to make the item to the tolerances set by the buyer's engineers and within the time available. There are costs and delays involved in turning from a supplier one has dealt with in the past to a new supplier. Then, too, market conditions can change so that a buyer is faced with shortages of critical items. The most extreme example is the post World War II gray market conditions when sellers were rationing goods rather than selling them. Buyers must build up some reserve of good will with suppliers if they face the risk of such shortage and desire good treatment when they occur. Finally, there is reciprocity in buying and selling. A buyer cannot push a supplier too far if that supplier also buys significant quantities of the product made by the buyer.

Not only do the particular business units in a given exchange want to deal with each other again, they also want to deal with other business units in the future. And the way one behaves in a particular transaction, or a series of transactions, will colour his general business reputation. Blacklisting can be formal or informal. Buyers who fail to pay their bills on time risk a bad report in credit rating services such as Dun and Bradstreet. Sellers who do not satisfy their customers become the subject of discussion in the gossip exchanged by purchasing agents and salesmen, at meetings of purchasing agents' associations and trade associations, or even at country clubs or social gatherings where members of top management meet. The

American male's habit of debating the merits of new cars carries over to industrial items. Obviously, a poor reputation does not help a firm make sales and may force it to offer great price discounts or added services to remain in business. Furthermore, the habits of unusually demanding buyers become known, and they tend to get no more than they can coerce out of suppliers who choose to deal with them. Thus often contract is not needed as there are alternatives.

Not only are contract and contract law not needed in many situations, their use may have, or may be thought to have, undesirable consequences. Detailed negotiated contracts can get in the way of creating good exchange relationships between business units. If one side insists on a detailed plan, there will be delay while letters are exchanged as the parties try to agree on what should happen if a remote and unlikely contingency occurs. In some cases they may not be able to agree at all on such matters and as a result a sale may be lost to the seller and the buyer may have to search elsewhere for an acceptable supplier. Many businessmen would react by thinking that had no one raised the series of remote and unlikely contingencies all this wasted effort could have been avoided.

Even where agreement can be reached at the negotiation stage, carefully planned arrangements may create undesirable exchange relationships between business units. Some businessmen object that in such a carefully worked out relationship one gets performance only to the letter of the contract. Such planning indicates a lack of trust and blunts the demands of friendship, turning a cooperative venture into an antagonistic horse trade. Yet the greater danger perceived by some businessmen is that one would have to perform his side of the bargain to its letter and thus lose what is called "flexibility." Businessmen may welcome a measure of vagueness in the obligations they assume so that they may negotiate matters in light of the actual circumstances.

Adjustment of exchange relationships and dispute settlement by litigation or the threat of it also has many costs. The gain anticipated from using this form of coercion often fails to outweigh these costs, which are both monetary and non-monetary. Threatening to turn matters over to an attorney may cost no more money than postage or a telephone call; yet few are so skilled in making such a threat that it will not cost some deterioration of the relationship between the firms. One businessman said that customers had better not rely on legal rights or threaten to bring a breach of contract law suit against him since he "would not be treated like a criminal" and would fight back with every means available. Clearly actual litigation is even more costly than making threats. Lawyers demand substantial fees from larger business units. A firm's executives often will have to be transported and maintained in another city during the proceedings if, as often is the case, the trial must be held away from the home office. Top management does not travel by Greyhound and stay at the Y.M.C.A. Moreover, there will be the cost of diverting top management, engineers, and others in the organization from their normal activities. The firm may lose many days work from several key people. The non-monetary costs may be large too. A breach of contract law suit may settle a particular dispute, but such an action often results in a "divorce" ending the "marriage" between the two businesses, since a contract action is likely to carry charges with at least overtones of bad faith. Many executives, moreover, dislike the prospect of being cross-examined in public. Some executives may dislike losing control of a situation by turning the decision-making power over to lawyers. Finally, the law of contract damages may not provide an adequate remedy even if the firm wins the suit; one may get vindication but not much money.

Why Do Relatively Contractual Practices Ever Exist?

Although contract is not needed and actually may have negative consequences, businessmen do make some carefully planned contracts, negotiate settlements influenced by their legal rights and commence and defend some breach of contract law suits or arbitration proceedings. In view of the findings and explanation presented to this point, one may ask why. Exchanges are carefully planned when it is thought that planning and a potential legal sanction will have more advantages than disadvantages. Such a judgment may be reached when contract planning serves the internal needs of an organization involved in a business exchange. For example, a fairly detailed contract can serve as a communication device within a large corporation. While the corporation's sales manager and house counsel may work out all the provisions with the customer, its production manager will have to make the product. He must be told what to do and how to handle at least the most obvious contingencies. Moreover, the sales manager may want to remove certain issues from future negotiation by

his subordinates. If he puts the matter in the written contract, he may be able to keep his salesmen from making concessions to the customer without first consulting the sales manager. Then the sales manager may be aided in his battles with his firm's financial or engineering departments if the contract calls for certain practices which the sales manager advocates but which the other departments resist. Now the corporation is obligated to a customer to do what the sales manager wants to do; how can the financial or engineering departments insist on anything else?

Also one tends to find a judgment that the gains of contract outweigh the costs where there is a likelihood that significant problems will arise. One factor leading to this conclusion is complexity of the agreed performance over a long period. Another factor is whether or not the degree of injury in case of default is thought to be potentially great. This factor cuts two ways. First, a buyer may want to commit a seller to a detailed and legally binding contract, where the consequence of a default by the seller would seriously injure the buyer. For example, the airlines are subject to law suits from the survivors of passengers and to great adverse publicity as a result of crashes. One would expect the airlines to bargain for carefully defined and legally enforceable obligations on the part of the airframe manufacturers when they purchase aircraft. Second, a seller may want to limit his liability for a buyer's damages by a provision in their contract. For example, a manufacturer of air conditioning may deal with motels in the South and Southwest. If this equipment fails in the hot summer months, a motel may lose a great deal of business. The manufacturer may wish to avoid any liability for this type of injury to his customers and may want a contract with a clear disclaimer clause.

Similarly, one uses or threatens to use legal sanctions to settle disputes when other devices will not work and when the gains are thought to outweigh the costs. For example, perhaps the most common type of business contracts case fought all the way through to the appellate courts today is an action for an alleged wrongful termination of a dealer's franchise by a manufacturer. Since the franchise has been terminated, factors such as personal relationships and the desire for future business will have little effect; the cancellation of the franchise indicates they have already failed to maintain the relationship. Nor will a complaining dealer worry about creating a hostile relationship between himself and the manufacturer. Often the dealer has suffered a great financial loss both as to his investment in building and equipment and as to his anticipated future profits. A cancelled automobile dealer's lease on his showroom and shop will continue to run, and his tools for servicing, say, Plymouths cannot be used to service other makes of cars. Moreover, he will have no more new Plymouths to sell. Today there is some chance of winning a law suit for terminating a franchise in bad faith in many states and in the federal courts. Thus, often the dealer chooses to risk the cost of a lawyer's fee because of the chance that he may recover some compensation for his losses.

An "irrational" factor may exert some influence on the decision to use legal sanctions. The man who controls a firm may feel that he or his organization has been made to appear foolish or has been the victim of fraud or bad faith. The law suit may be seen as a vehicle "to get even" although the potential gains, as viewed by an objective observer, are outweighed by the potential costs.

The decision whether or not to use contract — whether the gain exceeds the costs — will be made by the person within the business unit with the power to make it, and it tends to make a difference who he is. People in a sales department oppose contract. Contractual negotiations are just one more hurdle in the way of a sale. Holding a customer to the letter of a contract is bad for "customer relations." Suing a customer who is not bankrupt and might order again is poor strategy. Purchasing agents and their buyers are less hostile to contracts but regard attention devoted to such matters as a waste of time. In contrast, the financial control department — the treasurer, controller or auditor — leans toward more contractual dealings. Contract is viewed by these people as an organizing tool to control operations in a large organization. It tends to define precisely and to minimize the risks to which the firm is exposed. Outside lawyers — those with many clients — may share this enthusiasm for a more contractual method of dealing. These lawyers are concerned with preventive law — avoiding any possible legal difficulty. They see many unstable and unsuccessful exchange transactions, and so they are aware of, and perhaps overly concerned with, all of the things which can go wrong. Moreover, their job of settling disputes with legal sanctions is much easier if their client has not been overly casual about transaction planning. The inside lawyer, or house counsel, is harder to classify. He is likely to have some sympathy with a more contractual method of dealing. He shares the outside lawyer's "craft urge" to see exchange transactions neat and tidy from a legal standpoint. Since he is more concerned with avoiding and settling disputes than selling goods, he is likely to be less willing to rely on a man's word as the sole sanction than is a salesman. Yet the house counsel is more a part of the organization and more aware of its goals and subject to its internal sanctions. If the potential risks are not too great, he may hesitate to suggest a more contractual procedure to the sales department. He must sell his services to the operating departments, and he must hoard what power he has, expending it on only what he sees as significant issues.

The power to decide that a more contractual method of creating relationships and settling disputes shall be used will be held by different people at different times in different organizations. In most firms the sales department and the purchasing department have a great deal of power to resist contractual procedures or to ignore them if they are formally adopted and to handle disputes their own way. Yet in larger organizations the treasurer and the controller have increasing power to demand both systems and compliance. Occasionally, the house counsel must arbitrate the conflicting positions of these departments; in giving "legal advice" he may make the business judgment necessary regarding the use of contract. At times he may ask for an opinion from an outside law firm to reinforce his own position with the outside firm's prestige.

Obviously, there are other significant variables which influence the degree that contract is used. One is the relative bargaining power or skill of the two business units. Even if the controller of a small supplier succeeds within the firm and creates a contractual system of dealing, there will be no contract if the firm's large customer prefers not to be bound to anything. Firms that supply General Motors deal as General Motors wants to do business, for the most part. Yet bargaining power is not size or share of the market alone. Even a General Motors may need a particular supplier, at least temporarily. Furthermore, bargaining power may shift as an exchange relationship is first created and then continues. Even a giant firm can find itself bound to a small supplier once production of an essential item begins for there may not be time to turn to another supplier. Also, all of the factors discussed in this paper can be viewed as *components* of bargaining power — for example, the personal relationship between the presidents of the buyer and the seller firms may give a sales manager great power over a purchasing agent who has been instructed to give the seller "every consideration." Another variable relevant to the use of contract is the influence of third parties. The federal government, or a lender of money, may insist that a contract be made in a particular transaction or may influence the decision to assert one's legal rights under a contract.

Contract, then, often plays an important role in business, but other factors are significant. To understand the functions of contract the whole system of conducting exchanges must be explored fully. More types of business communities must be studied, contract litigation must be analyzed to see why the non-legal sanctions fail to prevent the use of legal sanctions and all of the variables suggested in this paper must be classified more systematically.

(f)   *Balfour v. Balfour*†

NOTE

This case involves the issue of intention to create legal relations. A married couple who had been living in Ceylon returned to England when the husband had leave. The wife suffered from rheumatoid arthritis, and it was agreed that she should stay in England until she was well enough to rejoin her husband in Ceylon. As he was leaving, they agreed that he would pay her £30 per month, and she would not pledge his credit. This arrangement was confirmed by subsequent letters. Difficulties arose in the relationship, and they subsequently separated. The wife brought an action against the husband to recover money that she claimed was due under the agreement.

The issue before the judges of the Court of Appeal was whether there was a legally binding contract. All three judges offered the opinion that there was no contract. Representative excerpts of their reasoning taken from the judgments of Duke L.J. and Atkin L.J. are reproduced below.

When you read this case, consider the policy choices made by the judges. Why do you think they refused the claim? Can you think of other ways the issues could have been approached? What is the significance of this case in understanding contract law?

EXTRACT

[DUKE L.J.:]

... [The real question] is whether there is evidence of any such exchange of promises as would make the promise of the husband the basis of an agreement. It was strongly urged by [counsel for the wife] that the promise being absolute in form ought to be construed as one of the mutual promises which make an agreement. It was said that a promise and an implied undertaking between strangers, such as the promise and implied undertaking alleged in this case would have founded an action on contract. That may be so, but it is impossible to disregard in this case what was the basis of the whole communications between the parties under which the alleged contract is said to have been formed. The basis of their communications was their relationship of husband and wife, a relationship which creates obligations.... There was a discussion between the parties while they were absent from one another, whether they should agree upon a separation.... [In the present] case there was no agreement at all. The parties were husband and wife, and subject to all the conditions, in point of law, involved in that relationship. It is possible to say that where the relationship of husband and wife exists, and promises are

---

† [1919] 2 K.B. 571 at 576–80. [Court of Appeal (WARRINGTON, DUKE and ATKIN L.JJ.), January 24, 25, 1919].

exchanged, they must be deemed to be promises of a contractual nature. In order to establish a contract there ought to be something more than mere mutual promises having regard to the domestic relations of the parties. It is required that the obligations arising out of that relationship shall be discharged before either of the parties can found a contract upon such promises. ... What is said on the part of the wife in this case is that her arrangement with her husband that she should assent to that which was in his discretion to do or not to do was the consideration moving from her to her husband. The giving up of that which was not a right was not a consideration. The proposition that the mutual promises made in the ordinary domestic relationship of husband and wife of necessity give cause for action on a contract seems to me to go to the very root of the relationship, and to be a possible fruitful source of dissension and quarrelling. I cannot see that any benefit would result from it to either of the parties, but on the other hand it would lead to unlimited litigation in a relationship which should be obviously as far as possible protected from possibilities of that kind. I think, therefore, that in point of principle there is no foundation for the claim which is made here, and I am satisfied that there was no consideration moving from the wife to the husband or promise by the husband to the wife which was sufficient to sustain this action founded on contract. I think, therefore, that the appeal must be allowed.

[ATKIN L.J.:]

... It is quite common, and it is the natural and inevitable result of the relationship of husband and wife, that the two spouses should make arrangements between themselves — agreements such as are in dispute in this action — agreements for allowances, by which the husband agrees that he will pay to his wife a certain sum of money, per week, or per month, or per year, to cover either her own expenses or the necessary expenses of the household and of the children of the marriage, and in which the wife promises either expressly or impliedly to apply the allowance for the purpose for which it is given. To my mind those agreements, or many of them, do not result in contracts at all, and they do not result in contracts even though there may be what as between other parties would constitute consideration for the agreement. The consideration, as we know, may consist either in some right, interest, profit or benefit accruing to one party, or some forbearance, detriment, loss or

responsibility given, suffered or undertaken by the other. That is a well-known definition, and it constantly happens, I think, that such arrangements made between husband and wife are arrangements in which there are mutual promises, or in which there is consideration in form within the definition that I have mentioned. Nevertheless they are not contracts, and they are not contracts because the parties did not intend that they should be attended by legal consequences. To my mind it would be of the worst possible example to hold that agreements such as this resulted in legal obligations which could be enforced in the Courts. It would mean this, that when the husband makes his wife a promise to give her an allowance of 30s. or 2l. a week, whatever he can afford to give her, for the maintenance of the household and children, and she promises so to apply it, not only could she sue him for his failure in any week to supply the allowance, but he could sue her for non-performance of the obligation, express or implied, which she had undertaken upon her part. ... They are not sued upon, not because the parties are reluctant to enforce their legal rights when the agreement is broken, but because the parties, in the inception of the arrangement, never intended that they should be sued upon. Agreements such as these are outside the realm of contracts altogether. The common law does not regulate the form of agreements between spouses. Their promises are not sealed with seals and sealing wax. The consideration that really obtains for them is that natural love and affection which counts for so little in these cold Courts. The terms may be repudiated, varied or renewed as performance proceeds or as disagreements develop, and the principles of the common law as to exoneration and discharge and accord and satisfaction are such as find no place in the domestic code. The parties themselves are advocates, judges, Courts, sheriff's officer and reporter. In respect of these promises each house is a domain into which the King's writ does not seek to run, and to which his officers do not seek to be admitted. The only question in this case is whether or not this promise was of such a class or not. For the reasons given by my brethren it appears to me to be plainly established that the promise here was not intended by either party to be attended by legal consequences. I think the onus was upon the plainitiff [i.e., the wife], and the plaintiff has not established any contract. The parties were living together, the wife intending to return [to Ceylon]. The suggestion is that the husband bound himself to pay 30l. a month under all circumstances, and she bound herself to be satisfied with that sum under all circumstances, and, although she was in ill-health and alone in this country, that out of that sum she undertook to defray the whole of the medical expenses that might fall upon her, whatever might be the development of her illness, and in whatever expenses it might involve her. To my mind neither party contemplated such a result. I think that the parol evidence upon which the case turns does not establish a contract. I think that the letters do not evidence such a contract, or amplify the the oral evidence which was given by the wife, which is not in dispute. For these reasons I think the judgment of the Court was wrong and that this appeal should be allowed.

Appeal allowed.

(g) *Family Law Act*†

1.(1) In this Act,

. . . .

"domestic contract" means a domestic contract as defined in Part IV (Domestic Contracts);

. . . .

2.(9) A provision of a domestic contract in respect of a matter that is dealt with in this Act may be incorporated in an order made under this Act.

(10) A domestic contract dealing with a matter that is also dealt with in this Act prevails unless this Act provides otherwise.

. . . .

51. In this Part,

"cohabitation agreement" means an agreement entered into under section 53;

"domestic contract" means a marriage contract, separation agreement or cohabitation agreement;

"marriage contract" means an agreement entered into under section 52;

"paternity agreement" means an agreement entered into under section 59;

"separation agreement" means an agreement entered into under section 54.

52.(1) Two persons who are married to each other or intend to marry may enter into an agreement in which they agree on their respective rights and obligations under the marriage or on separation, on the annulment or dissolution of the marriage or on death, including,

(a) ownership in or division of property;

(b) support obligations;

(c) the right to direct the education and moral training of their children, but not the right to custody of or access to their children; and

(d) any other matter in the settlement of their affairs.

(2) A provision in a marriage contract purporting to limit a spouse's rights under Part II (Matrimonial Home) is unenforceable.

53.(1) Two persons who are cohabiting or intend to cohabit and who are not married to each other may enter into an agreement in which they agree on their respective rights and obligations during cohabitation, or on ceasing to cohabit or on death, including,

(a) ownership in or division of property;

(b) support obligations;

(c) the right to direct the education and moral training of their children, but not the right to custody of or access to their children; and

(d) any other matter in the settlement of their affairs.

---

† R.S.O., 1990, c. F.3. as am. by S.O. 2005, c. 5, s. 27.

(2) If the parties to a cohabitation agreement marry each other, the agreement shall be deemed to be a marriage contract.

54. Two persons who cohabited and are living separate and apart may enter into an agreement in which they agree on their respective rights and obligations, including,

(a) ownership in or division of property;

(b) support obligations;

(c) the right to direct the education and moral training of their children;

(d) the right to custody of and access to their children; and

(e) any other matter in the settlement of their affairs.

55.(1) A domestic contract and an agreement to amend or rescind a domestic contract are unenforceable unless made in writing, signed by the parties and witnessed.

(2) A minor has capacity to enter into a domestic contract, subject to the approval of the court, which may be given before or after the minor enters into the contract.

. . . .

56.(1) In the determination of a matter respecting the education, moral training or custody of or access to a child, the court may disregard any provision of a domestic contract pertaining to the matter where, in the opinion of the court, to do so is in the best interests of the child.

(h)   Contract Marriage — The Way Forward or Dead End?†

David McLellan

HISTORICAL BACKGROUND

In general, the Victorian feminist movement attacked the common law doctrine of coverture by demanding that the same principles which underlay public law should also apply to domestic law. They insisted on individual rights and equality before the law for women as well as men. In this area they achieved substantial success. The disappointing Divorce Act 1857 did at least concede the possibility of civil action for divorce on the egregious grounds of incest, bigamy, or gross physical cruelty — though it confirmed the double standard that only a wife's (and not a husband's) adultery justified the severing of a marriage. More importantly, the Married Women's Property Act of 1870 removed some of a wife's property from her husband's control, though only by a fictional trust which adopted the protective language of equity: the loss of independent legal personality on marriage was left untouched. The Married Women's

Property Act 1883 gave women control over property brought into a marriage, but still refused to treat married women on an equal footing with those unmarried, by granting them *femme sole* status with respect to their property and contracts.

John Stuart Mill and Victorian feminists in general paid more attention to married women's lack of economic and contractual rights and less to considering the disempowering effects of the economic dependency of most wives on their husbands. In so doing, they were, in effect, carrying the liberal tradition as founded by Hobbes and Locke to its most progressive limit. As the twentieth century has advanced, approximate legal equality in marriage has been achieved with easy divorce, legal access to jobs, and control by both men and women separately or together, of their fertility. Yet the practical division of labour in the household and the grossly disproportionate share falling on women when both partners work full-time, the continuing effective inequality of jobs

---

† (1996) 23:2 Journal of Law and Society 234 at 234–41. [Notes and/or References omitted.] Copyright © by David McLellan. Reproduced with permission Blackwell Publishers, Ltd.

and wages available to women, the unfairness of divorce settlements, and so on, indicates that something more is needed. One reaction is to say that the individualistic side of Mill's agenda needs to be pushed further:

> ... although we are more receptive to the ideal, we are nowhere achieving in practice the kind of equality between the sexes that Mill looks forward to. It will be a good day when *The Subjection of Women* is outdated, but it is not yet.

Another approach is to say that the fault lies precisely in Mill's individualistic conceptual approach: his nineteenth-century liberalism was adequate to the first wave of feminist demands, but now what is needed is the abolition of the sex-bound stereotypes in marriage and that this is impossible within a classical liberal framework, though some who follow this line generously allow that there are aspects of Mill's thought which put it beyond a simple demand for the equal entry of women into male offices and privileges. In the contemporary world, these radically different approaches come into sharp focus in the debate about the contractualization of marriage.

Those who wish to push the liberal individualistic aspects of Mill (and Locke) argue that marriage should become a contractual relationship like any other. At the present time it is clear that marriage is a peculiar form of contract. It is true that marriage has been a contractual relationship since at least the fourteenth century — though usually as a vehicle for family control over property arrangements. And Blackstone declared that 'our law considers marriage in no other light than as a civil contract'. But, following Locke, it is still taken by most liberal theory to be inappropriate to apply to marriage the general principles of liberty and equality that are held to operate in political and legal institutions. In other forms of contract, the substantive decisions about the relationship are left to the parties. But in the marriage contract, no such bargaining is possible and those involved in it will find they cannot vary its terms: agreement about, for example, inter-spousal payments or planning for the termination of marriage will be unenforceable. Not being a written contract, something which the parties could read and on which they could seek legal independent advice, it is difficult to see how those involved could be said genuinely to consent. This is in conflict with the standard liberal legal principle that a contract may be void unless the parties have read it (or had it read

to them) before signing, because the free and informed consent of the parties is a necessary condition for the contract's validity. Unlike contracts about property, the marriage contract is easy to make, but comparatively difficult to dissolve. Moreover, there are restrictions on the capacity to form a marriage which are uncharacteristic of other types of contract: the parties must be of the opposite sex, not already married, and not closely related to each other. And until recently, it was held, with marital immunity from rape, that the marriage contract involved the relinquishing of the right to self-protection by one party. It would thus seem that marriage is not a contract in the ordinary sense of the word, but a status-contract: it is a contract grounded in and maintaining status or ascription. Individuals deciding to marry may have the same freedom of choice that governs other contractual relations; but once entered into, the terms and conditions of the contractual relationship are dictated by the State.

THE ARGUMENT FOR CONTRACT MARRIAGE

This state of affairs is widely regarded as unsatisfactory: the marital partners have lost those principles associated with status, while not gaining the freedom associated with contract. The continued existence of the traditional marriage contract tends to treat the family as a unit and thus allows vital decisions about names, domicile, and finance to be made by the husband. One proposed solution is the full contractualization of marriage. In the formulation of one of its leading exponents, the proposal is that:

> ... the state could leave most substantive marital rights and obligations to be defined privately, but make the legal system available to resolve disputes arising under the privately created 'legislation'.

It is argued, first, that such a reform is in line with the way in which society is moving. There is a growing emphasis on individual happiness and fulfilment in marriage which mirrors the emphasis on pluralism and private choice in society at large. More specifically, recent practice has been to encourage the control of certain divorce terms by private agreement, following mediation and the consent of the parties, a trend which has influenced the proposed Parts I and II of the proposed Family Law Bill. In many areas of the law — tax, criminal, property, tort, and evidence — marital partners are increasingly treated as separate individuals with distinct aims, interests, and intentions. The possibility of the contractual ordering of non-marital relationships, highlighted in the United States of America by the *Marvin* case, is being greatly strengthened. The lessening of the differentiation between married and unmarried couples, the almost complete removal of sex discrimination from family law, and the ease with which marriage can be contracted — all these factors, it is said, mean that the contractualization of marriage would be going with the grain of social development. This is not to suggest that the contract view of marriage is as yet the dominant one — even in the United States, let alone the United Kingdom. But given the recent rise in the popularity of the idea of freedom of contract its application to marriage is worth considering.

As well as being in tune with the *Zeitgeist*, it is also argued that the contractualization of marriage would bring with it clear advantages to the parties. First, it would facilitate communication between them, would identify potential conflicts in advance, encourage the sort of planning that is increasingly necessary in an era of disposable relationships, and even — paradoxically — give couples a greater sense of security. Second, it would allow couples to escape from an outmoded legal tradition through an agreement especially tailored to fit their needs, thus respecting the values of privacy and freedom in the ordering of personal relationships; it would give added authority to an anti-patriarchal and egalitarian stance; and it could be used to confer legitimation and structure on other forms of relationships — homosexual, polygamous, and so on. This accommodation of diversity, together with the clarification of expectations offered by prenuptial contracting, the advance identification of problems, the creation of a normative blue-print by which to resolve conflicts in an ongoing relationship would, it is claimed, offer increased security and predictability and thus enhance the stability of sexual relationships. It is not, of course, being suggested that *all* aspects of such relationships are patient of contractual regulation: even its most ardent supporters concede that contracts to respect, honour, and love would be difficult to specify as to performance and breach. And, clearly, contractualization would be wise to begin at least with the most economic aspects of marriage. Moreover, contracting would not be imposed on couples, but simply be an option that they could choose: a standard package of marital obligations could be laid down by statute

with model contracts developed by various groups, publications, or individuals. But the main point insisted on by the proponents of contracting in marriage is that contract here would be filling an increasingly empty space since there has been a withdrawal of public policy and state control over marriage. Furthermore, social institutions such as church, extended family, and community, which used to play an important part in defining and supporting marital norms, have declined in influence. As Mary Ann Glendon writes:

> ... the lack of firm and fixed ideas about what marriage is and should be is but an aspect of the alienation of modern man. And in this respect the law seems truly to reflect the fact that in modern society more and more is expected of human relationships while at the same time social conditions have rendered these relationships increasingly fragile.

Without the introduction of any easily cognizable private contract, a certain 'lawlessness' will ensue. The state should therefore allow marital partners to define and plan their relationships with the character, content, duration, and structure that they wish and afford legal enforcement to their contractual provisions.

THE ARGUMENT AGAINST CONTRACT MARRIAGE

It is difficult to deny some validity to the above arguments. But a little reflection indicates that there are powerful theoretical, practical, and ethical problems involved. Most of the objections considered by the proponents of the contractualization of marriage are relatively superficial and easily answered. On the psychological level it is not difficult to argue against the view that the contractualization of marriage would undermine its emotional basis, foster negative attitudes, destroy trust, import the morals of the market place, create impoverished consent, and foster instability. But at a more profound level, the demand that marriage should become, in John Stuart Mill's words, a 'true contract' reveals difficulties that are not so easily answered.

Inevitably, there is the whole question of the status of contract. As Durkheim remarked, the scope of contract and its very meaning is controlled by implicit social understandings:

> ... everything in the contract is not contractual
> ... wherever a contract exists, it is submitted to

24

regulation which is the work of society and not that of individuals.

If there are as many types of contract as there are societies, our focus should be on the type of society we want rather than on contract itself. For to concentrate on contract can be seen as constraining the scope of our imagining possible relations with others — a large issue to which I will return in my conclusion. More specifically, there is widespread disagreement over the concept of contract: is it to do with form or substance? Is it subjective or objective? The proposals to contractualize marriage seem to rely on the will theory of contract which dominated nineteenth-century discussion and maintained the view that contract was a private matter. But the realist critique of this theory claims that the public aspects of contract dominate the private aspects. In the words of one of its most trenchant critics:

> ... the law of contract may be viewed as a subsidiary branch of public law, as a body of rules according to which the sovereign power of the state will be exercised as between the parties to a more or less voluntary transaction.

Or again:

> ... in enforcing contracts, the government does not merely allow two individuals to do what they have found pleasant in their eyes — enforcement, in fact, puts the machinery of the law in the service of one party against the other. When that is worthwhile and how that should be done are important questions of public policy.

Thus, questions of public policy loom large and public policy limitations on contractual freedom [have] expanded dramatically in recent decades, including limits to do with good faith and unconscionability. Contract is extremely indeterminate in that the range of intention-based or policy-based arguments makes virtually any decision possible. In a slightly different vein, it is not so long since the imminent 'death' of contract was proclaimed. Developments in, for example, labour law or commercial law mean that contract law is in danger of dissolving into a series of discrete bodies of law which diminish the substance of contract by moving it towards a subsidiary role within a set of relationships which are essentially ones of status involving packages of rights and duties.

Even if we abstract from the above conceptual uncertainties, the proposals for the contractualization of marriage still involve difficulties of a much more empirical nature which cast doubt on whether contract can ever be the royal road to freedom and equality. Indeed, its proponents have not taken to heart the warning of the patriarchal Fitzjames Stephen in his reply to Mill:

> ... submission and protection are correlative; withdraw the one and the other is lost, and force will assert itself a hundred times more harshly through the law of contract than it ever did through the law of status.

In a society where power is systematically distributed asymmetrically, contract is likely simply to reinforce such an asymmetry. After all, the thoroughly egalitarian principles of such avatars of the liberal contractarian approach as Hobbes and Locke end up by justifying absolutist rule and a landed oligarchy respectively. The problems encountered by women in domestic relationships are inadequate child support, a weak position in the labour market, and male violence. The position of many women in society makes the possession of equal rights virtually meaningless or even counterproductive. Consider the case of a battered wife who, for economic reasons, is disinclined to press criminal charges and have her husband sent to jail and is blamed for allowing herself to be a victim. Although it is only too obvious a point, it cannot be repeated too often that inequality of bargaining power means that the construction and enforcement of contracts are liable to be symptoms of such inequality rather than its remedy. And this repetition is justified when we look at the attitude to such considerations in the work of the proponents of the contractualization of marriage. Weitzman, for example, considers the idea that:

> ... men who typically have more power, will use that power to impose a contract that is even more unfavourable than traditional legal marriage.

In reply, all she can offer is the:

> assumption that even though men have more power, they nevertheless share an egalitarian ideology and will not think it 'fair' or 'just' to try to impose an exploitative contract on the women they love.

And she refuses to countenance the kind of restrictions on freedom of contract that operate in other areas to protect weaker parties such as consumers or tenants on the grounds that:

... it seems appropriate to assume that the type of overreaching that is profitable in the market sector would be neither profitable nor possible in an intimate contract. This is because parties to an intimate contract are much more likely to begin with norms of fairness and a genuine concern for the welfare of the other party.

And when she does explicitly discuss social policy issues, this whole vital area is dealt with under the rubric of 'concern for the weak-minded woman in love'. It is not weak-mindedness that is the enemy of equality in marriage; it is actual or threatened economic deprivation. Again, Marjorie Schultz, at the very end of her long and detailed article advocating the contractual ordering of marriage, raises the question of 'wrong' choices arising from 'the tendency of private ordering to reflect and reinforce power disparities in existing relationships'. This does indeed go to the heart of the matter. But her reply simply sidesteps the issue:

> ... any system which attempted to impose standardised rules, even where those rules reflected more modern and desirable goals, like sexual equality, would not sufficiently respect the pluralism and privacy of intimate values nor allow for the planning and self-definition of goals posited by this Article as vital to an effective system of marriage regulation. The essential point is that in intimacy no-one can say what is 'right' except the parties involved.

This is woefully inadequate. For one thing, the 'parties involved' are many. Marriages result in children and their upbringing is, properly, the concern of others: neighbour, society, the State, and so on. Further, at the beginning of her article, Schultz had stressed that such ideas as reciprocity, party capacity, equality, and consent were all necessary conditions of the validity of her proposals. Finally, take Will Kymlicka's sharp article on 'Rethinking the Family': in discussing what he calls 'reproductive contract', he airily confines to a mere bracket the words 'assuming the parties are fully informed, have equal bargaining power and so on'. Under current social and economic arrangements, such an assumption is utopian. There is indeed scope for utopian thinking (compare Oscar Wilde) but we should be aware that it is precisely that.

A note of realism may be injected into discussion of the contractualization of marriage by the results of liberalization at the other end of the process — divorce. This is, of course, a complex phenomenon, but it is clear that men have been in a better position than women to recover from the effects of a broken marriage. Men's earning power typically increases during marriage, while a woman's remains constant, or decreases. On divorce, according to Weitzman's well-known findings in California, men's income rises by about 70 per cent while women's decreases by about 40 per cent. The much-discussed feminization of 'poverty', or at least the higher visibility of female poverty, is undoubtedly connected with the increase in divorce. The pioneering reforms in Geneva involving no-fault divorces with the parties writing their own settlements, have been much criticized for their inequality of outcome — as have the recent innovations in this country concerning the role of mediators in favouring the stronger party. Even the concepts evolved by contract law to protect the vulnerable, such as duress and unconscionability, would be extremely hard to specify in intimate relations, subject to widely differing interpretations, and thus likely to be ignored by the courts as not following the traditional rubrics.

Even such a clear and incisive thinker as Okin is ambivalent, not to say ambiguous, about the role of contract. As a liberal, she is obviously in favour of contract, but remains in the abstract realm of Rawlsian social contract theory. Although individual contracts might be appropriate for her 'genderless' society, she does not confront the problems involved in present society by the realities of the inequality of bargaining power. These ambiguities are not accidental: as Kymlicka says: 'Liberals believe in freedom of contract within the constraint of justice' and presuppose universal 'equality of opportunity'. But a moment's thought about the kind of measures that would need to be implemented to ensure *real* equality of opportunity shows that all present thought about private contracting should be postponed until that profound transformation of society which is its necessary precondition has been accomplished. Until then, it should be realized that the 'contract marriage' as a means for women to negotiate a mutually advantageous relationship with men is open only to a few well-educated and economically independent women — such as the writers of many of the above pieces. For the majority, fairness is more likely to be improved by current proposals for splitting pensions after divorce or the reforms of the property rights of non-married cohabitants now being considered by the Law Commission along the lines of, for example, the New South Wales De Facto Relationships Act 1984.

(i) *In Re Baby M*[†]

NOTE

This case concerned who should have parental rights in relation to a baby girl born to Mary Beth Whitehead (Gould) after insemination with the sperm of William Stern. Whitehead had agreed to be paid to bear the child for the Sterns, who were a childless couple. The Sterns were highly educated individuals. William Stern had obtained his PhD and worked as a biochemist. Elizabeth Stern had an M.D. and worked as a pediatrician. Neither was infertile, but Elizabeth Stern suffered from mild multiple sclerosis, which she feared would be exacerbated by pregnancy. The two couples had a reasonably amicable relationship until the birth of the child, although it had progressively deteriorated. Elizabeth Stern insisted that Mary Beth Whitehead undergo amniocentesis and take a prescription drug to control the effects of a difference in blood group between Mary Beth Whitehead and William Stern. The Whiteheads also delayed signing certain papers related to the contract. Mary Beth Whitehead refused to give up the child after her birth. She named the child, begged to have the child with her, and fled to Florida with the child for over three months despite a court order obtained by William Stern that the child be in his custody pending determination of the validity of the contract. Much was made in the trial of evidence evaluating the parenting abilities and personalities of Mary Beth Whitehead and the Sterns. She was said to be impulsive, manipulative, over-invested in the child and prone to lie in crisis situations. The Whitehead marriage was portrayed as unstable and "plagued" by a history of financial and alcohol related problems and domestic violence. The Sterns were said to be rational, caring and well-educated, and with a stable marriage and a supportive community.

The well known legal and media battle that ensued, concerning the validity of the so-called surrogacy contract and determinations of custody, is a fascinating and important example of differing approaches to contract law and policy. The issues discussed at length included the validity of the surrogacy contract and the appropriateness of specific performance as a remedy to enforce the contract, the conditions on which parental rights could be terminated, the best interests of the child and who should have custody. Although not excerpted in the material that follows, the judges also considered a constitutional right to procreation and explored an analogy to adoption. The judgments of Sorkow J., who was the trial judge, and of Wilentz C.J., who delivered the decision of the appellate court, contrast markedly with each other on matters of the nature and scope of contracting in such circumstances and the effect of public policy considerations. They are excerpted below together with an edited version of the contract signed by Whitehead and her husband Richard and William Stern.

EXTRACT

Baby M: Surrogacy Contract[‡]

This AGREEMENT is made this 6th day of February 1985 by and between MARY BETH WHITEHEAD, a married woman (herein referred to as "Surrogate"), RICHARD WHITEHEAD, her husband (herein referred to as "Husband"), and WILLIAM STERN, (herein referred to as "Natural Father").

. . . .

Now therefore, in consideration of the mutual promises contained herein and the intentions of being legally bound hereby, the parties agree as follows:

1. MARY BETH WHITEHEAD, Surrogate, represents that she is capable of conceiving children. MARY BETH WHITEHEAD understands and agrees that in

---

[†] 525 A.2d 1128 (N.J. Super.Ch. 1987); 537 A.2d 1227 (N.J. 1988).
[‡] *Matter of Baby M*, 537 A.2d 1227 (N.J. 1988), Appendix A.

the best interest of the child, she will not form or attempt to form a parent-child relationship with any child or children she may conceive, carry to term and give birth to, pursuant to the provisions of this Agreement, and shall freely surrender custody to WILLIAM STERN, Natural Father, immediately upon birth of the child; and terminate all parental rights to said child pursuant to this Agreement.

2. MARY BETH WHITEHEAD, Surrogate, and RICHARD WHITEHEAD, her husband, have been married since 12/2/73, and RICHARD WHITEHEAD is in agreement with the purposes, intents and provisions of this Agreement and acknowledges that his wife, MARY BETH WHITEHEAD, Surrogate, shall be artificially inseminated pursuant to the provisions of this Agreement. RICHARD WHITEHEAD agrees that in the best interest of the child, he will not form or attempt to form a parent-child relationship with any child or children MARY BETH WHITEHEAD, Surrogate, may conceive by artificial insemination as described herein, and agrees to freely and readily surrender immediate custody of the child to WILLIAM STERN, Natural Father; and terminate his parental rights; RICHARD WHITEHEAD further acknowledges he will do all acts necessary to rebut the presumption of paternity of any offspring conceived and born pursuant to aforementioned agreement as provided by law, including blood testing and/or HLA testing.

3. WILLIAM STERN, Natural Father, does hereby enter into this written contractual Agreement with MARY BETH WHITEHEAD, Surrogate, where MARY BETH WHITEHEAD shall be artificially inseminated with the semen of WILLIAM STERN by a physician. MARY BETH WHITEHEAD, Surrogate, upon becoming pregnant, acknowledges that she will carry said embryo/fetus(s) until delivery. MARY BETH WHITEHEAD, Surrogate, and RICHARD WHITEHEAD, her husband, agree that they will cooperate with any background investigation into the Surrogate's medical, family and personal history and warrants the information to be accurate to the best of their knowledge. MARY BETH WHITEHEAD, Surrogate, and RICHARD WHITEHEAD, her husband, agree to surrender custody of the child to WILLIAM STERN, Natural Father, immediately upon birth, acknowledging that it is the intent of this Agreement in the best interests of the child to do so; as well as institute and cooperate in proceedings to terminate their respective parental rights to said child and sign any and all necessary affidavits, documents, and the like, in order to further the

intent and purposes of this Agreement. It is understood by MARY BETH WHITEHEAD, and RICHARD WHITEHEAD, that the child to be conceived is being done so for the sole purpose of giving said child to WILLIAM STERN, its natural and biological father. MARY BETH WHITEHEAD and RICHARD WHITEHEAD agree to sign all necessary affidavits prior to and after the birth of the child and voluntarily participate in any paternity proceedings necessary to have WILLIAM STERN'S name entered on said child's birth certificate as the natural or biological father.

4. That the consideration for this Agreement, which is compensation for services and expenses, and in no way is to be construed as a fee for termination of parental rights or a payment in exchange for a consent to surrender the child for adoption, in addition to other provisions contained herein shall be as follows:

(A) $10,000 shall be paid to MARY BETH WHITEHEAD, Surrogate, upon surrender of custody to WILLIAM STERN, the natural and biological father of the child born pursuant to the provisions of this Agreement for surrogate services and expenses in carrying out her obligations under this Agreement;

(B) The consideration to be paid to MARY BETH WHITEHEAD, Surrogate, shall be deposited with the infertility center of New York (hereinafter ICNY), the representative of WILLIAM STERN, at the time of the signing of this Agreement, and held in escrow until completion of the duties and obligations of MARY BETH WHITEHEAD, Surrogate, as herein described.

(C) WILLIAM STERN, Natural Father, shall pay the expenses incurred by MARY BETH WHITEHEAD, Surrogate, pursuant to her pregnancy, more specifically defined as follows:
(1) all medical, hospitalization, and pharmaceutical, laboratory and therapy expenses incurred as a result of MARY BETH WHITEHEAD'S pregnancy, not covered or allowed by her present health and major medical insurance, including all extraordinary medical expenses and all reasonable expenses for treatment of any emotional or mental conditions or problems related to said pregnancy, but in no case shall any such expenses be paid or reimbursed after a period of six (6) months have elapsed since

the date of the termination of the pregnancy, and this Agreement specifically excludes any expenses for lost wages or other non-itemized incidentals related to said pregnancy.

(2) WILLIAM STERN, Natural Father, shall not be responsible for any latent medical expenses occurring six (6) weeks subsequent to the birth of the child, unless the medical problem or abnormality incident thereto was known and treated by a physician prior to the expiration of said six (6) week period and in written notice of the same sent to ICNY, as representative of WILLIAM STERN by certified mail, return receipt requested, advising of this treatment.

(3) WILLIAM STERN, Natural Father, shall be responsible for the total costs of all paternity testing. Such paternity testing may, at the option of WILLIAM STERN, Natural Father, be required prior to release of the surrogate fee from escrow. In the event WILLIAM STERN, Natural Father, is conclusively determined not to be the biological father of the child as a result of an HLA test, this agreement will be deemed breached and MARY BETH WHITEHEAD, Surrogate, shall not be entitled to any fee. WILLIAM STERN, Natural Father, shall be entitled to reimbursement of all medical and related expenses from MARY BETH WHITEHEAD, Surrogate, and RICHARD WHITEHEAD, her husband.

. . . .

(5) MARY BETH WHITEHEAD, Surrogate, and RICHARD WHITEHEAD, her husband, understand and agree to assume all risks, including the risk of death, which are incidental to conception, pregnancy, childbirth, including but not limited to postpartum complications.

(6) MARY BETH WHITEHEAD, Surrogate, and RICHARD WHITEHEAD, her husband, hereby agree to undergo psychiatric evaluation by JOAN EINWOHNER, a psychiatrist as designated by WILLIAM STERN or an agent thereof. WILLIAM STERN shall pay for the cost of said psychiatric evaluation. MARY BETH

WHITEHEAD and RICHARD WHITEHEAD shall sign, prior to the their evaluations, a medical release permitting dissemination of the report prepared as a result of said psychiatric evaluations to ICNY or WILLIAM STERN and his wife.

(7) MARY BETH WHITEHEAD, Surrogate, and RICHARD WHITEHEAD, her husband, hereby agree that it is the exclusive and sole right of WILLIAM STERN, Natural Father, to name said child.

(8) "Child" as referred to in this Agreement shall include all children born simultaneously pursuant to the insemination contemplated herein.

(9) In the event of the death of WILLIAM STERN, prior or subsequent to the birth of said child, it is hereby understood and agreed by MARY BETH WHITEHEAD, Surrogate, and RICHARD WHITEHEAD, her husband, that the child will be placed in the custody of WILLIAM STERN'S wife.

(10) In the event that the child is miscarried prior to the fifth (5th) month of pregnancy, no compensation, as enumerated in paragraph 4(a), shall be paid to MARY BETH WHITEHEAD, Surrogate. However, the expenses enumerated in paragraph 4(c) shall be paid or reimbursed to MARY BETH WHITEHEAD, Surrogate. In the event the child is miscarried, dies or is stillborn subsequent to the fourth (4th) month of pregnancy and said child does not survive, the surrogate shall receive $1,000.00 in lieu of the compensation enumerated in paragraph 4(a). In the event of a miscarriage or stillbirth as described above, this Agreement shall terminate and neither MARY BETH WHITEHEAD, Surrogate, nor WILLIAM STERN, Natural Father, shall be under any further obligation under this Agreement.

(11) MARY BETH WHITEHEAD, Surrogate, and WILLIAM STERN, Natural Father, shall have undergone complete physical and genetic evaluation, under the direction and supervision of a licensed physician, to determine whether the physical health and well-being of each is satisfactory. Said physical examination shall include testing for venereal

diseases, specifically including but not limited to, syphilis, herpes and gonorrhea. Said venereal disease testing shall be done prior to, but not limited to, each series of insemination.

(12) In the event that pregnancy has not occurred within a reasonable time, in the opinion of WILLIAM STERN, Natural Father, this Agreement shall terminate by written notice to MARY BETH WHITEHEAD, Surrogate at the residence provided to the ICNY by the Surrogate, from ICNY, as representative of WILLIAM STERN, Natural Father.

(13) MARY BETH WHITEHEAD, Surrogate, agrees that she will not abort the child once conceived except, if in the professional medical opinion of the inseminating physician, such action is necessary for the physical health of MARY BETH WHITEHEAD or the child has been determined by said physician to be physiologically abnormal. MARY BETH WHITEHEAD further agrees, upon the request of said physician to undergo amniocentesis or similar tests to detect genetic and congenital defects. In the event said test reveals that the fetus is genetically or congenitally abnormal, MARY BETH WHITEHEAD, Surrogate, agrees to abort the fetus upon demand of WILLIAM STERN, Natural Father, in which event, the fee paid to the surrogate will be in accordance to paragraph 10. If MARY BETH WHITEHEAD refuses to abort the fetus upon demand of WILLIAM STERN, his obligations as stated in this Agreement shall cease forthwith, except as to obligations of paternity imposed by statute.

(14) Despite the provisions of Paragraph 13, WILLIAM STERN, Natural Father, recognizes that some genetic and congenital abnormalities may not be detected by amniocentesis or other tests, and therefore, if proven to be the biological father of the child, assumes the legal responsibility for any child who may possess genetic or congenital abnormalities.

(15) MARY BETH WHITEHEAD, Surrogate, further agrees to adhere to all medical instructions given to her by the inseminating physician as well as her independent obstetrician. MARY BETH WHITEHEAD also agrees not to smoke cigarettes, drink alcoholic beverages, use illegal drugs, or take non-prescription medications or prescribed medications without written consent from her physician. MARY BETH WHITEHEAD agrees to follow a prenatal medical examination schedule to consist of no fewer visits than: one visit per month during the first seven (7) months of pregnancy, two visits (each to occur at two-week intervals) during the eighth and ninth month of pregnancy.

. . . .

(17) Each party acknowledges that he or she fully understands this Agreement and its legal effect, and that they are signing the same freely and voluntarily and that neither party has any reason to believe that the other(s) did not freely and voluntarily execute said Agreement.

(18) In any event any of the provisions of this Agreement are deemed to be invalid or unenforceable, the same shall be deemed severable from the remainder of this Agreement and shall not cause the invalidity or unenforceability of the remainder of this Agreement. If such provisions shall be deemed invalid due to its scope or breadth, then said provisions shall be deemed valid to the extent of the scope or breadth permitted by law.

(19) The original of this Agreement, upon execution, shall be retained by the Infertility Center of New York, with photocopies being distributed to MARY BETH WHITEHEAD, Surrogate, and WILLIAM STERN, Natural Father, having the same legal effect as the original.

[Signed etc....]

BABY M: TRIAL DECISION†

[SORKOW P.J.F.P.:]

. . . .

The Issue

The primary issue to be determined by this litigation is what are the best interests of a child until now called "Baby M." All other concerns raised by counsel constitute commentary.

That commentary includes the need to determine if a unique arrangement between a man and woman, unmarried to each other, creates a contract. If so, is the contract enforceable; and if so, by what criteria, means and manner. If not, what are the rights and duties of the parties with regard to custody, visitation and support.

Jurisdiction

There can be no solution satisfactory to all in this kind of case. Justice, our desired objective, to the child and the mother, to the child and the father, cannot be obtained for both parents. The court will seek to achieve justice for the child. This court's fact finding and application of relevant law must mitigate against the heartfelt desires of one or other of the natural parents.

Where courts are forced to choose between a parent's rights and a child's welfare, the choice is and must be the child's welfare and best interest by virtue of the court's responsibility as *parens patriae*....

. . . .

The development of new techniques and alternatives for non-coital reproduction have given society awesome opportunities. The transformation of the family will continue in the coming years because of these new techniques. As Doctor Judith Greif testified, "We are already dealing with a new family form." Unfortunately, the law is slow to react to the rapid advance of science and changing human behavior. This minimal pace is made apparent when it is realized that as of this date not one state in this nation has adopted a law that specifically addresses either affirmatively or negatively the concept of surrogate parenting although many studies are in process and legislation has been introduced. There are two bills pending in the New Jersey Legislature.

It took years of legislative debate and judicial inquiry to define and develop today's laws of abortion and artificial insemination. The issues and dimensions of surrogacy are still evolving, but it is necessary that laws be adopted to give our society a sense of definition and direction if the concept is to be allowed to further develop. With an increasing number of surrogate births, legislation can avoid harm to society, the family and the child. Some of the issues that need legislation are: establishing standards for sperm donors, legitimacy of the child, rights of the biological father's spouse, rights of the biological mother's spouse, rights of the two biological actors as to each other and to the child, qualifications for the surrogate, the allowance of compensation to the surrogate and concerns regarding the imperfect child. Many questions must be answered; answers must come from legislation. If there is no law then society will suffer the negative aspects of this alternative reproduction vehicle that appears to hold out so much hope to the childless who make up a substantial segment of our society.

Today, however, this court can only decide what is before it. It will decide on legal principles alone. This court must not manage morality or temper theology. Its charge is to examine what law there is and apply it to the facts proven in this cause.

. . . .

And so it will be as the court makes its conclusions. It will not slavishly parrot this opinion or that conclusion but will weigh the expert testimony and use it where appropriate to reach its decision.

This court is confronted with circumstances in which on February 6, 1985, the parties to this litigation, with great joy and expectation, entered into a surrogate arrangement. It was an arrangement where both — the prospective family and the surrogate mother — wanted the child; albeit, for different purposes. Even though the insemination is artificial, the parental attitude is real. The couple sought to bring into existence a child by conscious pre-arrangement which, as far as biologically possi-

---

† 525 A.2d 1128 (1987) (N.J.Super.Ch.) at 1132, 1137–37, 1156–60, 1163, 1167–71.

ble, would be genetically their own. The surrogate consciously chose to bear a child for another couple with the understanding that she would not contest but would consent to their adoption to it.

The adverse pressure and exploitation of the unplanned pregnancy is not present. When the child arrives, it has a home waiting for it with a biological father and his wife.

Concerns have been expressed about the efficacy of surrogate arrangements. They are:

1. that the child will not be protected;
2. the potential for exploitation of the surrogate mother;
3. the alleged denigration of human dignity by recognizing any agreement in which a child is produced for money;
4. surrogacy is invalid because it is contrary to adoption statutes and other child benefit laws such as statutes establishing standards for termination of parental rights;
5. it will undermine traditional notions of family; and
6. surrogacy allows an elite economic group to use a poorer group of people to achieve their purposes.

It is argued that the child will not be protected. So long as there is no legislation and some court action in surrogacy arrangements is required, the child born of surrogacy will be protected in New Jersey. If there is compliance with the contract terms, adoption will be necessary; hence, court inquiry about best interests must take place. If there is non-compliance with the contract, as in this case, best interests is still litigated with protection to the child, with its own guardian and experts retained to aid the court in its best interests determination.

The second argument against surrogacy is that the surrogate mother will be exploited. To the contrary. It is the private adoption that has that great potential for, if not actual, exploitation of the mother. In the private adoption, the woman is already pregnant. The biological father may be unknown or at best uninterested in his obligations. The woman may want to keep the child but cannot do so for financial reasons. There is the risk of illegal consideration being paid to the mother. In surrogacy, none of these "downside" elements appear. The arrangement is made when the desire and intention to have a family exist on the couple's part. The surrogate has an opportunity to consult,

take advice and consider her act and is not forced into the relationship. She is not yet pregnant.

The third argument is that to produce or deal with a child for money denigrates human dignity. With that premise this court urgently agrees. The 13th Amendment to the United States Constitution is still valid law. The law of adoption in New Jersey does prohibit the exchange of any consideration for obtaining a child. The fact is, however, that the money to be paid to the surrogate is not being paid for the surrender of the child to the father. And that is just the point — at birth, mother and father have equal rights to the child absent any other agreement. The biological father pays the surrogate for her willingness to be impregnated and carry his child to term. At birth, the father does not purchase the child. It is his own biological genetically related child. He cannot purchase what is already his.

The fourth argument against surrogacy is that it is a concept running contrary to the laws of adoption in New Jersey. It is in this court's view that the laws of adoption in this State do not apply to surrogacy contracts. Adoption is a concept unknown at common law. It is a statutory remedy and must be strictly construed. It is submitted that at the time that even the most current adoption laws were adopted, no thought or consideration was given to the law's effect or relevance to surrogacy. Surrogacy was not a viable procreation alternative and was unknown when the laws of adoption were passed.... The same rationale must attach to laws dealing with termination of parental rights. Indeed, it is held that the only concept of law that can presently attach to surrogacy arrangements [is] contract law principles and *parens patriae* concepts for the benefit of the child. These are the only polestars available for this court to chart its course on the issues of surrogacy.

. . . .

The fifth argument against surrogacy is that it will undermine traditional notions of family. How can that be when the childless husband and wife so very much want a child? They seek to make a family. They intend to have a family. The surrogate mother could not make a valid contract without her husband's consent to her act. This statement should not be construed as antifeminist. It means that if the surrogate is married, her husband will, in all probability, have to sign the contract to establish his non-paternity pursuant to the New

Jersey Parentage Law. Both sides of the equation must agree.

The sixth and final argument suggests that an elite upper economic group of people will use the lower economic group of woman to "make their babies." This argument is insensitive and offensive to the intense drive to procreate naturally and when that is impossible, to use what lawful means are possible to gain a child. This intense desire to propagate the species is fundamental. It is within the soul of all men and women regardless of economic status.

During the course of the testimony offered by the principals to this writing, the court was told on several occasions that a writing was executed by them. Indeed, that writing was marked into evidence. The court was further told by the parties that they all understood their obligations under the contract. Specifically, it was understood by all that Mr. Stern's sperm would be used to artificially inseminate Mrs. Whitehead. Upon conception, Mrs. Whitehead would carry the child and when she gave birth, she would then surrender the infant to the biological father and his wife. Mrs. Whitehead would also voluntarily renounce her parental rights to permit Mrs. Stern to adopt the infant. Mrs. Stern, it must be noted, is not a party to the contract. This was to avoid any possible inference that there is a violation of *N.J.S.A.* 9:3–54 (which prohibits giving a consideration to obtain an adoptable child). Mr. Whitehead signed a certification pursuant to *N.J.S.A.* 9:17–44 establishing his non-paternity. Mr. Stern agreed to pay Mrs. Whitehead $10,000 for conceiving and bearing his child.

Fundamentally, when there were no time constraints, when Mrs. Whitehead was not pregnant, when each party had the opportunity to obtain advice (legal, medical and/or psychological), the parties expressed their respective offers and acceptances to each other and reduced their understanding to a writing. If the mutual promises were not sufficient to establish a valid consideration, then certainly there was consideration when there was conception. The male gave his sperm; the female gave her egg in their pre-planned effort to create a child — thus, a contract.

For the past year, there has been a child in being. She is alive and well. She is tangible proof of that which the Whiteheads and Mr. Stern in concert agreed to do. The child was conceived with mutual understanding by the parties of her future life. Except now, Mrs. Whitehead has failed to perform one of her last promises, which was to surrender the child and renounce parental rights. She

has otherwise performed the personal service that she had undertaken — conception and carrying the child to term. The terms of the contract have been executed but for the surrender.

It is argued that Mrs. Whitehead should have a time period after delivery to determine if she wants to surrender the child. Such a rule has been developed in Kentucky by the use of Kentucky's private placement adoption statute. Use of laws not intended for their intended purpose creates forced and confusing results. There should be no use of the New Jersey adoption statutes to accommodate or deny surrogacy contracts.... The sole legal concepts that control are *parens patriae* and best interests of the child. To wait for birth, to plan, pray and dream of the joy it will bring and then be told that the child will not come home, that a new set of rules applies and to ask a court to approve such a result deeply offends the conscience of this court. A person who has promised is entitled to rely on the concomitant promise of the other promisor. This court holds therefore that in New Jersey, although the surrogacy contract is signed, the surrogate may nevertheless renounce and terminate the contract until the time of conception. She may be subject then for such monetary damages as may be proven. Specific performance to compel the promised conception, gestation, and birth shall not be available to the male promisor. However, once conception has occurred the parties['] rights are fixed, the terms of the contract are firm and performance will be anticipated with the joy that only a newborn can bring.

Having defined a new rule of law, this court hastens to add an exception. After conception, only the surrogate shall have the right, to the exclusion of the sperm donor, to decide whether to abort the fetus. Her decision to abort must comply with the guidelines set forth in *Roe v. Wade*, 410 U.S. 113, 93 S. Ct. 705, 35 L. Ed. 2d 147 (1973).

. . . .

It is argued that the contract in this case is one of adhesion. It was a writing printed by and supplied by ICNY. That its terms were not immutable is shown by the testimony of the attorney, Saul Radow, who by deposition reported negotiating changes to the written contract; albeit, minor changes. By definition, a contract of adhesion is one in which one party has no alternative but to accept or reject the other party's terms and there are no options by which the party may obtain the product or service. Here, neither party has a superior bargaining position. Each had what the other wanted. A price for the service each was to perform was struck and a bargain reached. One did not force the other. Neither had expertise that left the other at a disadvantage. Neither had disproportionate bargaining power. Although the contract was a form, there is no proof that it was absolute and could not be altered. Defendant offered no proof to this end. Mrs. Whitehead[] acknowledged that minor changes were bargained for. There is no evidence of any absence of good faith or fair dealing. This is not a contract of adhesion....

Defendants argue unconscionability. They claim the terms are manifestly unfair or oppressive. These terms were known to Mrs. Whitehead from her earlier surrogate contracting experience. She read the second contract, albeit briefly, prior to signing it. She was aware of her compensation. She had been pregnant before and had to be aware of the risks of pregnancy. Her obligation included physical examination for her own welfare as well as the welfare of the fetus. Mrs. Whitehead says that Mr. Stern undertook no risks. To compare the risk of pregnancy in a woman to the donation of sperm by the man would be unconscionable. This, however, is the bargain Mrs. Whitehead sought and obtained. Mr. Stern did take a risk, however[. W]hether the child would be normal or abnormal, whether accepted or rejected he would have a lifetime obligation and responsibility to the child as its natural and biological father.

To the issue of unconscionability, defendants fail to show proof of overreaching or disproportionate bargaining that result[s] in an unfair contract. Mrs. Whitehead was anxious to contract. At the New Brunswick meeting, she pressed for a definitive statement by the Sterns. She knew just what she was bargaining for. This court finds that she has changed her mind, reneged on her promise and now seeks to avoid her obligations. Unconscionability claims arise, more often than not, in consumer contracts for products or services. The seller is in the dominant position and the buyer must comply or there is no deal. Not so here — either party could have walked away from the other. Either party would then have continued on ICNY's roster of available surrogates and childless families seeking a surrogate. They chose not to do so. The bargain here was one for totally personal service. It was a very scarce service Mrs. Whitehead was providing. Indeed, it might even be said she had the dominant bargaining position for without her Mr. Stern had no other immediate source

available. Each party sought [the] other to fulfill their needs.

It is argued by *amicus* that the $10,000 to be paid Mrs. Whitehead is so low as to be unconscionable. In counterpoint, it is stated that not all services can be compensated by money. Millions of men and women work for each other in their marital relationship. There may even be mutual inequality in the value of the work performed but the benefits obtained from the relationship serve to reject the concept of equating societal acts to a monetary balancing. Perhaps the risk was great for the money to be paid but the risk was what Mrs. Whitehead chose to assume and at the agreed upon fee. And it is assumed she received other intangible benefits and satisfaction from doing what she did. Her original application set forth her highly altruistic purpose. Notwithstanding *amicus'* position, all in this world cannot be equated to money.

It is defendants' claim of unconscionability. They must show such unfairness, overreaching, bargaining disparity or patent unfairness that no reasonable person acting without duress would accept the contract terms. This, defendants have failed to do.

Defendants next claim relief from the contract because the Whiteheads had no attorney at the time they entered the contract. It is hornbook law that any person who possesses legal capacity may be bound by a contract even when it is entered without representation unless there is fraud, overreaching or undue influence which caused the party to enter the contract.

It was Dr. Vetter, one of defendants' own psychiatrists, who testified unequivocally that the Whiteheads had legal capacity to contract. There were no mental disabilities. They understood what they were doing. They understood the contract terms. That there was capacity to contract was proven by a preponderance of the credible evidence. ... Their prior counsel was available to them. They chose not to call him. ... It is well settled that disparity of education or sophistication is not considered grounds for avoidance of a contract. ...

. . . .

It is further argued that the contract is illusory; that is to say, that only one of the parties has an obligation, the other only benefits, that there is no mutuality of obligation. This does not mean equality of obligation. Such is not the case.

Mr. Stern gave his sperm; Mrs. Whitehead gave her egg. Together the miracle of a new life was obtained. Mrs. Whitehead argues Mr. Stern does not have to take the child under certain circumstances which have not happened and are not before this court. She is arguing, hypothetically, "if." It is suggested again that this court is dealing with the facts before it. Even assuming *arguendo*, that the court were to address the issue of the illusory contract as stated by defendants, the conclusion would be the same. The Whiteheads argue that Mr. Stern does not have to take the baby if it is imperfect; but the fact is the contract does provide that there is an obligation and responsibility, and there is a life long responsibility by Mr. Stern for the child's support and welfare. The contract is not illusory.

. . . .

For the foregoing reasons, this court concludes and holds that the surrogate-parenting agreement is a valid and enforceable contract pursuant to the laws of New Jersey. The rights of the parties to contract are constitutionally protected under the 14th Amendment of the United States Constitution. This court further finds that Mrs. Whitehead has breached her contract in two ways: 1) by failing to surrender to Mr. Stern the child born to her and Mr. Stern and 2) by failing to renounce her parental rights to that child.

What are the remedies available to the plaintiff? The remedies that exist for breach of a contract are an award of money damages or specific enforcement of the terms of the contract. There are, of course, other remedies but they are neither relevant nor applicable here. Monetary damages cannot possibly compensate plaintiff for the loss of his bargain because of defendant's breach. The singular subject of the contract further mitigates against an award of damages.

Plaintiff acknowledges that before the remedy of specific performance can be used it must be shown that the contract was entered into with understanding and free will. ... It must also be shown that the contract was entered in good faith, without fraud and is not unenforceable because of public policy. By reason of the findings heretofore made, to wit: there is no evidence of fraud and the parties voluntarily entered the agreement, indeed they were all very anxious to do so, such contracts are not contrary to public policy. ... There is no reason why this court should not order specific performance.

Specific performance is a discretionary remedy. It should only be exercised in accordance with principles of equity. In each case the evaluation of the equities must be left to the judgment and good conscience of the trial court. This means that the court must adjudge and weigh whether the parties' conduct was fair and reasonable. Will the relief afforded by the remedy be unreasonable? If specific performance is ordered, the result will be just what the parties bargained for and the contract contemplated. Mr. Stern wanted progeny, a child. Mrs. Whitehead wanted to give the child she would bear to a childless couple. His sperm fertilized her egg. A child was born. Until the child was placed in his home he never knew the stress and bliss, the responsibilities and rewards of a child. The Whiteheads have two children. They did not want any more. Theirs was the perfect family, Mr. Whitehead testified. The Whiteheads agreed that Mr. Whitehead should get a vasectomy to prevent further conception. It is suggested that Mrs. Whitehead wanted a baby, now that she is older than when her first two children were born, to experience and fulfill herself again as a woman. She found the opportunity in a newspaper advertisement. She received her fulfillment. Mr. Stern did not.

At this point the court would enter its order for specific performance, but an additional inquiry is necessary. Since we here deal with a human life of only one year, since we treat with, as the guardian *ad litem* has said "the most precious and unique thing on this earth, a small vulnerable and lovable child," inquiry must be made to determine if the result of such an order for specific performance would be in the child's best interest. This court holds that whether there will be specific performance of this surrogacy contract depends on whether doing so is in the child's best interest. Again, as the guardian *ad litem* has asserted "the child's best interest is the only aspect of man's law that must be applied in fashioning a remedy for this contract ... for any contract that deals with the children of our society...." Any other result would indeed conflict with the court's role as *parens patriae*. Thus, in the absence of a public policy regarding surrogacy in New Jersey, with the rule as aforesaid that the laws of adoption, custody and parental termination were never intended to apply and do not apply to surrogacy, the only rule of law by which this court may be guided is the application of the doctrine of a child's best interests in the exercise of its *parens patriae* jurisdiction.

. . . .

What does "best interests of the child" mean? The concept is the most important one to be addressed herein. Its meaning is amorphous. It has many meanings for it is a concept general in meaning but specific in application. It is more than a child's happiness, physical, mental and moral welfare. ...

Best interests has been variously defined by expert witnesses in this case as follows:

Dr. H. Koplewicz: The best interest is the best placement, the best custody.

Dr. B. Sokoloff: Everything that is most suitable for a child's proper growth, development with a minimum amount of disability.

Dr. A. Levine: A psychological milieu and environment best conducive to healthy normal relationships.

Dr. J. Greif: Best interests are two basic needs, themes interwoven during the developmental stage. They are a closeness to be loved and to love — to feel nurtured and a sense of oneness with the opportunity to be separate — to develop one's own ideas and feeling, to be independent.

But perhaps *Dr. Salk* gives the most quantified definition. He establishes nine criteria in defining "best interests of a child."

1. Was the child wanted and planned for? We now know the Sterns desperately wanted a child. They intended by the contract to have a child. They previously planned for the child by considering Mrs. Stern's own capability inquiring about adoption and exploring surrogacy. They resolved in favor of surrogacy as the only viable vehicle for them to have a family. Mr. and Mrs. Stern contracted for Mrs. Whitehead's services. They created a nursery and made new wills to provide for the expected child. Mrs. Whitehead wanted to carry a child for a childless couple. It is clear that the Sterns planned for and wanted the child. Mrs. Whitehead did not. ...

2. What is the emotional stability of the people in the child's home environment? The Sterns are found to have a strong and mutually supportive relationship. Any familial difficulties are handled through rational decision making. This is good evidence of mutual respect and empathy. Each recognizes and respects the other's needs, desires and goals. There is evi-

dence of successful cooperative parenting of the infant child.

The Whiteheads appear to have a stable marriage now. It was earlier plagued with separations, domestic violence and severe financial difficulties requiring numerous house moves. There was a bankruptcy. Mrs. Whitehead dominates the family. Mr. Whitehead is clearly in a subordinate role. He had little to do with the subject child. Mrs. Whitehead is found to be thoroughly enmeshed with Baby M, unable to separate her own needs from the baby's. This overbearing could inhibit the child's development of independence. The mental health professionals called by the guardian *ad litem* agree that Mrs. Whitehead may have trouble subordinating her own needs to the child's needs. Mrs. Whitehead has been shown, by clear and convincing proof to this court's satisfaction, to be impulsive, as shown by her unplanned future when dropping out of high school and the removal of her son from a second grade classroom without first making inquiry of the teacher and principal. Another example of impulsiveness is her flight to Florida in violation of a court order. She has been shown, by clear and convincing proof to this court's satisfaction, to be manipulative. Reference need only be made to the tapes of July 15 and 16, 1986. If she was not suicidal, she was certainly manipulative in making the threat to take her life and the baby's life. She has been shown by clear and convincing proof to this court's satisfaction, to be exploitive also. She uses her children for her own ends: witness the bringing of her older daughter to court where the child was terrorized by the crush of media and her fawning use of the media to her own narcissistic ends. It appears she totally failed to consider the impact of the false sex abuse charge on her daughter. The placement of an infant's crib in Tuesday's room is without sensitivity or regard to Tuesday's feelings.

3. What is the stability and peacefulness of the families? Again, the Sterns are found to be living private unremarkable lives. The Whiteheads have known marital discord, domestic violence and many residential moves, although things are tranquil now.

4. What is the ability of the subject adults to recognize and respond to the child's physical and emotional needs? This court finds

from clear and convincing proofs presented to it that Mrs. Whitehead has been shown to impose herself on her children. Her emphasis with the infant may impair the parenting of her other two children for whom she has been, with limited exception until now, a good mother. She exhibits an emotional over-investment. It was argued by defendant's counsel that Mrs. Whitehead loved her children too much. This is not necessarily a strength. Too much love can smother a child's independence. Even an infant needs her own space.

. . . .

5. What are the family attitudes towards education and their motivation to encourage curiosity and learning? The Sterns have demonstrated the strong role that education has played in their lives. They both hold doctoral degrees in the sciences. Mrs. Stern is a medical doctor. Mrs. Whitehead dropped out of the tenth grade in high school. Mr. Whitehead graduated high school doing enough, as he said "to get by." Mrs. Whitehead has interposed herself in her son's education, denying the finding of a professional child study team and rejecting their recommendations.

6. What is the ability of the adults to make rational judgments? Mr. Whitehead permits his wife to make most of the important decisions in their family. His active participation in the May 5, 1986 elopement is hardly evidence of cogent thought. Mrs. Whitehead is found to be impulsive especially in crisis circumstances or moments of heightened concern. She doesn't think of the consequences: at age 15 1/2 she dropped out of school; she withdrew her son from second grade for what she perceived to be an affront to him without first inquiring of the teacher or principal; she eloped to Florida in direct violation of a court order, without considering the economic and emotional consequences. She impulsively, not to say maliciously, made an untruthful allegation about Mr. Stern. Mr. and Mrs. Stern have shown a capability to make logical reasoned decisions in all circumstances.

7. What is the capacity of the adults in the child's life to instill positive attitudes about matters concerning health? It is already noted that Mrs. Stern is a pediatrician. The court assumes her skill can but benefit the child. Other than failing to have the child vaccinated when Mrs. Whitehead was in Florida for the first few months of the child's life, which is not to be minimized, there is no evidence that she would convey poor health habits to the child. Mr. Whitehead has been shown to be an episodic alcoholic "binging" for two week periods approximately every six months. He is doing nothing to eliminate this concern. To infuse a child into such a milieu is problematic.

8. What is the capacity of the adults in the baby's life to explain the circumstances of origin with least confusion and greatest emotional support? Mrs. Whitehead being the parent most invested with the infant's care, in all likelihood would be charged with the task of telling the child of her origin. This court doubts her capability to truthfully report Baby M's origin. She has shown little empathy for the Sterns and their role and even less ability to acknowledge the facts surrounding the original contract. Insofar as emotional support is concerned, the court doubts Mrs. Whitehead could or would subordinate herself for the child' benefit when there is a conflictual circumstance such as relating the child's origin to her. To this day she still appears to reject any role Mr. Stern played in the conception. She chooses to forget that but for him there would be no child. The quality of her reporting capabilities have been tested in these proceedings and are found generally wanting. The Sterns have indicated a willingness to obtain professional advice on how and when to tell his daughter. Important in this equation is the child's trust that will have been constructed between custodial parent and child.

9. Which adults would better help the child cope with her own life? It has been shown that Mrs. Whitehead has trouble coping in crisis. She can manage the routine. The Sterns have shown no aberration in either circumstance.

The court also evaluates the climate in which the child may be exposed with the Whiteheads. In addition to a history of economic and domestic instability with another house move imminent, the reduced level of importance given to education in the Whitehead home and the character trait problems defined by almost all the mental health professionals including Mrs. Whitehead's own chosen experts, Mrs. Whitehead has a genuine problem in recognizing and reporting the truth.

. . . .

... The court is satisfied that based on the details above, Mrs. Whitehead is manipulative, impulsive and exploitive. She is also for the most part, untruthful, choosing only to remember what may enhance her position, or altering the facts about which she is testifying or intentionally not remembering. Education plays a subordinate role in the [Whiteheads'] milieu. The judgment-making ability of Mrs. Whitehead is sorely tested. One outstanding example was her decision to run away in the face of a court order. While she claims fear of the system made her do it this court sees it, minimally, as a disregard of her legal and civic obligation to respond to a court's order, and, maximally, as a contempt of the court order. She does not concern herself with consequences of her acts. Her lack of candour makes her a poor candidate to report to the child in an age appropriate manner and time, the facts of the child's origin. She is a woman without empathy. She expresses none for her husband's problems with alcohol and her infusion of her other children into this process, exposing them rather than protecting them from the searing scrutiny of the media, mitigates against her claim for custody. She is a good mother for and to her older children. She would not be a good custodian for Baby M.

This court is satisfied by clear and convincing proof that Mr. and Mrs. Stern wanted and planned for this child. They intended to be parents of the child. They have a strong and mutually supportive relationship wherein each respects the other and there is a balancing of obligations. There is proof of a successful cooperative parenting effort. The Sterns have a private, quiet and unremarkable life which [augurs] well for a stable household environment. Mr. and Mrs. Stern show sensitivity to the child's physical and emotional needs. They would be supportive of education and have shown, at least in their own lives, a motivation for learning. It can be concluded that they would initiate and encourage intellectual curiosity and learning for the child. They have shown an ability to make rational judgments in the face of most trying emotional circumstances. They have obeyed the law.

With the health and medical education of Mrs. Stern and the scientific training of Mr. Stern, the child's health will not be jeopardized. Mr. and Mrs. Stern have been presented as credible, sincere and truthful people. They have expressed a willingness, and a history of obtaining professional help, to address the child's unique problems. Finally, they have shown no difficulty in coping with crisis. It may be anticipated that because the child is unique and at risk, crisis for the next several years will be part of their lives. Mr. and Mrs. Stern have shown an ability to deal with such exigencies. It is for all these reasons and because of all of the facts found by this court as the trier of fact that we find by clear and convincing evidence, indeed by a measure of evidence, reaching beyond reasonable doubt, that Melissa's best interests will be served by being placed in her father's sole custody.

... Enforcing the contract will leave Mr. and Mrs. Whitehead in the same position that they were in when the contract was made. To not enforce the contract will give them the child and deprive Mr. Stern of his promised benefits. This court therefore will specifically enforce the surrogate-parenting agreement to compel delivery of the child to the father and to terminate the mother's parental rights.

ON APPEAL[†]

[WILENTZ C.J.:]

In this matter the Court is asked to determine the validity of a contract that purports to provide a new way of bringing children into a family. For a fee of $10,000, a woman agrees to be artificially inseminated with the semen of another woman's husband; she is to conceive a child, carry it to term, and after its birth surrender it to the natural father and his wife. The intent of the contract is that the child's natural mother will thereafter be forever separated from her child. The wife is to adopt the child, and she and the natural father are to be regarded as its parents for all purposes. The contract providing for this is called a "surrogacy contract," the natural mother inappropriately called the "surrogate mother."

We invalidate the surrogacy contract because it conflicts with the law and public policy of this

---

[†] *In the Matter of Baby M*, 537 A.2d 1227 (N.J. 1988) at 1234–35, 1238, 1240, 1242–44, 1246–53, 1255–56, 1259, 1264.

State. While we recognize the depth of the yearning of infertile couples to have their own children, we find the payment of money to a "surrogate" mother illegal, perhaps criminal, and potentially degrading to women. Although in this case we grant custody to the natural father, the evidence having clearly proved such custody to be in the best interests of the infant, we void both the termination of the surrogate mother's parental rights and the adoption of the child by the wife/stepparent. We thus restore the "surrogate" as the mother of the child. We remand the issue of the natural mother's visitation rights to the trial court, since that issue was not reached below and the record before us is not sufficient to permit us to decide it *de novo*.

We find no offense to our present laws where a woman voluntarily and without payment agrees to act as a "surrogate" mother, provided that she is not subject to a binding agreement to surrender her child. Moreover, our holding today does not preclude the legislature from altering the current statutory scheme, within the constitutional limits, so as to permit surrogacy contracts. Under current law, however, the surrogacy agreement before us is illegal and invalid.

FACTS

. . . .

Although clearly expressing its view that the surrogacy contract was valid, the trial court devoted the major portion of its opinion to the question of the baby's best interests. The inconsistency is apparent. The surrogacy contract calls for the surrender of the child to the Sterns, permanent and sole custody in the Sterns, and termination of Mrs. Whitehead's parental rights, all without qualification, all regardless of any evaluation of the best interests of the child. As a matter of fact the contract recites (even before the child was conceived) that it is in the best interests of the child to be placed with Mr. Stern. In effect, the trial court awarded custody to Mr. Stern, the natural father, based on the same kind of evidence and analysis as might be expected had no surrogacy contract existed. Its rationalization, however, was that while the surrogacy contract was valid, specific performance would not be granted unless that remedy was in the best interests of the child. The factual issues confronted and decided by the trial court are the same as if Mr. Stern and Mrs. Whitehead had

had the child out of wedlock, intended or unintended, and then disagreed about custody. The trial court's awareness of the irrelevance of the contract in the court's determination of custody is suggested by its remark that beyond the question of the child's best interests, "[a]ll other concerns raised by counsel constitute commentary." (217 N.J. *supra* at 323, 525 A. 2d 1128.)

On the question of best interests — and we agree, but for different reasons, that custody was the critical issue — the court's analysis of the testimony was perceptive, demonstrating both its understanding of the case and its considerable experience in these matters. We agree substantially with both its analysis and conclusions on the matter of custody.

The court's review and analysis of the surrogacy contract, however, is not at all in accord with ours. ...

. . . .

INVALIDITY AND UNENFORCEABILITY OF SURROGACY CONTRACT

We have concluded that this surrogacy contract is invalid. Our conclusion has two bases: direct conflict with existing statutes and conflict with the public policies of this State, as expressed in its statutes and decisional law.

One of the surrogacy contract's basic purposes, to achieve the adoption of a child through private placement, though permitted in New Jersey "is very much disfavored." Its use of money for this purpose — and we have no doubt whatsoever that the money is being paid to obtain an adoption and not, as the Sterns argue, for the personal services of Mary Beth Whitehead — is illegal and perhaps criminal. In addition to the inducement of money, there is the coercion of contract: the natural mother's irrevocable agreement, prior to birth, even prior to conception, to surrender the child to the adoptive couple. Such an agreement is totally unenforceable in private placement adoption. Even where the adoption is through an approved agency, the formal agreement to surrender occurs only *after* birth, and, then by regulation, only after the birth mother has been offered counselling. Integral to these invalid provisions of the surrogacy contract is the related agreement, equally invalid, on the part of the natural mother to cooperate with, and not to contest, proceedings to terminate her parental rights, as well as her contractual concession, in aid of the adoption, that the child's best interests would be served by awarding custody to the natural father and his wife — all of this before she has even conceived, and, in some cases, before she has the slightest idea of what the natural father and adoptive mother are like.

The foregoing provisions not only directly conflict with New Jersey statutes, but also offend long-established State policies. These critical terms, which are at the heart of the contract, are invalid and unenforceable; the conclusion therefore follows, without more, that the entire contract is unenforceable.

Conflict with Statutory Provisions

The surrogacy contract conflicts with:

1. laws prohibiting the use of money in connection with adoptions;
2. laws requiring proof of parental unfitness or abandonment before termination of parental rights is ordered or an adoption is granted; and
3. laws that make surrender of custody and consent to adoption revocable in private placement adoptions.

. . . .

2. The termination of Mrs. Whitehead's parental rights, called for by the surrogacy contract and actually ordered by the court, fails to comply with the stringent requirements of New Jersey law. Our law, recognizing the finality of any termination of parental rights, provides for such termination only where there has been a voluntary surrender of a child to an approved agency or to the division of youth and family services ("DYFS"), accompanied by a formal document acknowledging termination of parental rights ... or where there has been a showing of parental abandonment or unfitness. ...

... [I]n order for DYFS to terminate parental rights it must prove, by clear and convincing evidence, that "(t)he child's health and development have been or will be seriously impaired by the parental relationship," that "(t)he parents are unable or unwilling to eliminate the harm and delaying permanent placement will add to the harm," that "(t)he court has considered alternatives to termination," and that "(t)he termination of parental rights will not do more harm than good." This interpretation of the statutory language requires a most substantial showing of harm to the

child if the parental relationship were to continue, far exceeding anything that a "best interests" test connotes.

In order to terminate parental rights under the private placement adoption statute, there must be a finding of "intentional abandonment or a very substantial neglect of parental duties without a reasonable expectation of a reversal of that conduct in the future." ...

. . . .

In this case a termination of parental rights was obtained not by proving the statutory prerequisites but by claiming the benefit of contractual provisions. From all that has been stated above, it is clear that a contractual agreement to abandon one's parental rights, or not to contest a termination action, will not be enforced in our courts. The Legislature would not have so carefully, so consistently, and so substantially restricted termination of parental rights if it had intended to allow termination to be achieved by one short sentence in a contract.

Since the termination was invalid, it follows, as noted above, that adoption of Melissa by Mrs. Stern could not properly be granted.

. . . .

The provision in the surrogacy contract whereby the mother irrevocably agrees to surrender custody of her child and to terminate her parental rights conflicts with the settled interpretation of New Jersey statutory law. There is only one irrevocable consent, and that is one explicitly provided for by statute: A consent to surrender of custody and a placement with an approved agency or with DYFS. The provision in the surrogacy contract, agreed to before conception, requiring the natural mother to surrender custody of the child without any right of revocation is one more indication of the essential nature of this transaction: The creation of a contractual system of termination and adoption designed to circumvent our statutes.

Public Policy Considerations

The surrogacy contract's invalidity, resulting from its direct conflict with the above statutory provisions is further underlined when its goals and means are measured against New Jersey's public policy. The contract's basic premise, that the natural parents can decide in advance of birth which one is to have custody of the child, bears no relationship to the settled law that the child's best interests shall determine custody....

The surrogacy contract guarantees permanent separation of the child from one of its natural parents. Our policy, however, has long been that to the extent possible, children should remain with and be brought up by both of their natural parents.... This is not simply some theoretical ideal that in practice has no meaning. The impact of failure to follow that policy is nowhere better shown than in the results of this surrogacy contract. A child, instead of starting off its life with as much peace and security as possible, finds itself immediately in a tug-of-war between contending mother and father.

. . . .

Under the contract, the natural mother is irrevocably committed before she knows the strength of her bond with her child. She never makes a totally voluntary, informed decision, for quite clearly any decision prior to the baby's birth is, in the most important sense, uninformed, and any decision after that, compelled by a pre-existing contractual commitment, the threat of a lawsuit, and the inducement of a $10,000 payment, is less than totally voluntary. Her interests are of little concern to those who controlled this transaction.

Although the interest of the natural father and adoptive mother is certainly the predominant interest, realistically the *only* interest served, even they are left with less than what public policy requires. ...

Worst of all, however, is the contract's total disregard of the best interests of the child. There is not the slightest suggestion that any inquiry will be made at any time to determine the fitness of the Sterns as custodial parents, of Mrs. Stern as an adoptive parent, their superiority to Mrs. Whitehead or the effect on the child of not living with her natural mother.

This is the sale of a child, or, at the very least, the sale of a mother's right to her child, the only mitigating factor being that one of the purchasers is the father. Almost every evil that prompted prohibition of the payment of money in connection with adoptions exists here.

. . . .

The point is made that Mrs. Whitehead *agreed* to the surrogacy arrangement, supposedly fully understanding the consequences. Putting aside the issue of how compelling her need for money may have been, and how significant her understanding of the consequences, we suggest that her consent is irrelevant. There are, in a civilized society, some things that money cannot buy. In America, we decided long ago that merely because conduct purchased by money was "voluntary" did not mean that it was good or beyond regulation and prohibition. Employers can no longer buy labor at the lowest price they can bargain for, even though that labor is "voluntary," or buy women's labor for less money than paid to men for the same job, or purchase the agreement of children to perform oppressive labor or purchase the agreement of workers to subject themselves to unsafe or unhealthful working conditions. There are, in short, values that society deems more important than granting to wealth whatever it can buy, be it labor, love, or life. Whether this principle recommends prohibition of surrogacy, which presumably sometimes results in great satisfaction to all of the parties, is not for us to say. We note here only that, under existing law, the fact that Mrs. Whitehead "agreed" to the arrangement is not dispositive.

The long-term effects of surrogacy contracts are not known, but feared — the impact on the child who learns her life was bought. That she is the offspring of someone who gave birth to her only to obtain money; the impact on the natural mother as the full weight of her isolation is felt along with the full reality of the sale of her body and her child; the impact on the natural father and adoptive mother once they realize the consequences of their conduct. Literature in related areas suggests these are substantial considerations, although, given the newness of surrogacy, there is little information. ...

The surrogacy contract is based on principles that are directly contrary to the objectives of our laws. It guarantees the separation of a child from its mother; it looks to adoption regardless of suitability; it totally ignores the child; it takes the child from the mother regardless of her wishes and her maternal fitness; and it does all of this, it accomplishes all of its goals, through the use of money.

Beyond that is the potential degradation of some women that may result from this arrangement. In many cases, of course, surrogacy may bring satisfaction, not only to the infertile couple, but to the surrogate mother herself. The fact, however, that many women may not perceive surrogacy negatively but rather see it as an opportunity does not diminish its potential for devastation to other women.

In sum, the harmful consequences of this surrogacy arrangement appear to us all too palpable. In New Jersey the surrogate mother's agreement to sell her child is void. Its irrevocability infects the entire contract, as does the money that purports to buy it.

TERMINATION

We have already noted that under our laws termination of parental rights cannot be based on contract, but may be granted only on proof of the statutory requirements. That conclusion was one of the bases for invalidating the surrogacy contract. Although excluding the contract as a basis for parental termination, we did not explicitly deal with the question of whether the statutory bases for termination existed. We do so here.

As noted before, if termination of Mrs. Whitehead's parental rights is justified, Mrs. Whitehead will have no further claim either to custody or to visitation, and adoption by Mrs. Stern may proceed pursuant to the private placement adoption statute. If termination is not justified, Mrs. Whitehead remains the legal mother, and even if not entitled to custody, she would ordinarily be expected to have some rights of visitation....

. . . .

Nothing in this record justifies a finding that would allow a court to terminate Mary Beth Whitehead's parental rights under the statutory standard. It is not simply that obviously there was no "intentional abandonment or very substantial neglect of parental duties without a reasonable expectation of reversal of that conduct in the future," quite the contrary, but furthermore that the trial court never found Mrs. Whitehead an unfit mother and indeed affirmatively stated that Mary Beth Whitehead had been a good mother to her other children.

Although the question of best interests of the child is dispositive of the custody issue in a dispute between natural parents, it does not govern the question of termination. It has long been decided that the mere fact that a child would be better off with one set of parents than with another is an insufficient basis for terminating the natural parent's rights. Furthermore, it is equally well settled that surrender of a child and a consent to

adoption through private placement do not alone warrant termination. It must be noted, despite some language to the contrary, that the interests of the child are not the only interests involved when termination issues are raised. The parent's rights, both constitutional and statutory, have their own independent vitality....

. . . .

A significant variation on these facts, however, occurred in *Sorentino II*. The surrender there was not through private placement but through an approved agency. Although the consent to surrender was held invalid due to coercion by the agency, the natural parents failed to initiate the lawsuit to reclaim the child for over a year after relinquishment. By the time this Court reached the issue of whether the natural parents' rights could be terminated, the adoptive parents had had custody for three years. These circumstances ultimately persuaded this Court to permit termination of the natural parents' rights and to allow a subsequent adoption. The unique facts of *Sorentino II* were found to amount to a forsaking of parental obligations....

. . . .

... We therefore conclude that the natural mother is entitled to retain her rights as a mother.

. . . .

CUSTODY

Having decided that the surrogacy contract is illegal and unenforceable, we now must decide the custody question without regard to the provisions of the surrogacy contract that would give Mr. Stern sole and permanent custody. ... [T]he legal framework becomes a dispute between two couples over the custody of a child produced by the artificial insemination of one couple's wife by the other's husband.... The applicable rule given these circumstances is clear: The child's best interests determine custody.

. . . .

It seems to us that given her predicament, Mrs. Whitehead was rather harshly judged — both by the trial court and by some of the experts. She was guilty of a breach of contract, and indeed,

Consensus ad idem is as much a part of the law of written contracts as it is of oral contracts. The signature to a contract is only one way of manifesting assent to contractual terms. However, in the case of *L'Estrange v. F. Graucob, Ltd.*, there was in fact no *consensus ad idem*. Miss L'Estrange was a proprietor of a café. Two salesmen of the defendant company persuaded her to order a cigarette machine to be sold to her by their employer. They produced an order form which Miss L'Estrange signed without reading all of its terms. Amongst the many clauses in the document signed by her, there was included a paragraph, with respect to which she was completely unaware, which stated "any express or implied condition, statement, or warranty, statutory or otherwise not stated herein is hereby excluded". In her action against the company she alleged that the article sold to her was unfit for the purposes for which it was sold and contrary to the *Sale of Goods Act*. The company successfully defended on the basis of that exemption clause.

Although the subject of critical analysis by learned authors (see, for example, J.R. Spencer, "Signature, Consent, and the Rule in *L'Estrange v. Graucob*", [1973] C.L.J. 104), the case has survived, and it is now said that it applies to all contracts irrespective of the circumstances under which they are entered into, if they are signed by the party who seeks to escape their provisions.

Thus, it was submitted that the ticket cases, which in the circumstances of this case would afford a ready defence for the hirer of the automobile are not applicable.

As is pointed out in Waddams, *The Law of Contracts*, at p. 191:

From the 19th century until recent times an extraordinary status has been accorded to the signed document that will be seen in retrospect, it is suggested, to have been excessive.

The justification for the rule in *L'Estrange v. Graucob, Ltd.*, appears to have been founded the objective theory of contracts, by which parties are bound to a contract in writing by their conduct by outward appearance than what the parties inwardly meant to this, in turn, stems from the classic statement of Blackburn, J., in *Smith v. Hughes* (1871), ...B. 597 at p. 607:

...hend that if one of the parties intends e a contract on one set of terms, other intends to make a contract on

another set of terms, or, as it is sometimes expressed, if the parties are not ad idem, there is no contract, unless the circumstances are such as to preclude one of the parties from denying that he has agreed to the terms of the other. The rule of law is that stated in *Freeman v. Cooke* (1848), 2 Ex. 654, 154 E.R. 652. *If, whatever a man's real intention may be, he so conducts himself that a reasonable man would believe that he was assenting to the terms proposed by the other party, and that other party upon that belief enters into the contract with him, the man thus conducting himself would be equally bound as if he had intended to agree to the other party's terms.* (Emphasis added.)

Even accepting the objective theory to determine whether Mr. Clendenning had entered into a contract which included all the terms of the written instrument, it is to be observed that an essential part of that test is whether the other party entered into the contract in the belief that Mr. Clendenning was assenting to all such terms. In the instant case, it was apparent to the employee of Tilden Rent-A-Car that Mr. Clendenning had not in fact read the document in its entirety before he signed it. It follows under such circumstances that Tilden Rent-A-Car cannot rely on provisions of the contract which it had no reason to believe were being assented to by the other contracting party.

As stated in Waddams, *The Law of Contracts*, p. 191:

One who signs a written document cannot complain if the other party reasonably relies on the signature as a manifestation of assent to the contents, or ascribes to words he uses their reasonable meaning. But the other side of the same coin is that only a reasonable expectation will be protected. If the party seeking to enforce the document knew or had reason to know of the other's mistake the document should not be enforced.

In ordinary commercial practice and where there is frequently a sense of formality in the transaction, and where there is a full opportunity for the parties to consider the terms of the proposed contract submitted for signature, it might well be safe to assume that the party who attaches his signature to the contract intends by so doing to acknowledge his acquiescence to its terms, and that the other party entered into the contract upon that belief. This can hardly be said, however, where the contract is entered into in circumstances such as were present in this case.

she did break a very important promise, but we think it is expecting something well beyond normal human capabilities to suggest that this mother should have parted with her newly born infant without a struggle. Other than survival, what stronger force is there? We do not know of, and cannot conceive of, any other case where a perfectly fit mother was expected to surrender her newly born infant, perhaps forever, and was then told she was a bad mother because she did not. We know of no authority suggesting that the moral quality of her act in those circumstances should be judged by referring to a contract made before she became pregnant. We do not countenance, and would never countenance, violating a court order as Mrs. Whitehead did, even a court order that is wrong; but her resistance to an order that she surrender her infant, possibly forever, merits a measure of understanding. We do not find it so clear that her efforts to keep her infant, when measured against the Sterns' efforts to take her away, make one, rather than the other, the wrongdoer. ...

[After reviewing the expert evidence the court was prepared to uphold the order of sole custody to William Stern. Rights to visitation were remanded for a rehearing....]

CONCLUSION

This case affords some insight into a new reproductive arrangement: the artificial insemination of a surrogate mother. The unfortunate events that have unfolded illustrate that its unregulated use can bring suffering to all involved. Potential victims include the surrogate mother and her family, the natural father and his wife, and most importantly, the child. Although surrogacy has apparently provided positive results for some infertile couples, it can also, as this case demonstrates, cause suffering to participants, here essentially innocent and well-intended.

We have found that our present laws do not permit the surrogacy contract used in this case. Nowhere, however, do we find any legal prohibition against surrogacy when the surrogate mother volunteers, without any payment, to act as a surrogate and is given the right to change her mind and to assert her parental rights. Moreover, the legislature remains free to deal with this most sensitive issue as it sees fit, subject only to constitutional constraints.

If the Legislature decides to address surrogacy, consideration of this case will highlight many of its potential harms. We do not underestimate the difficulties of legislating on this subject. In addition to the inevitable confrontation with the ethical and moral issues involved, there is the question of the wisdom and effectiveness of regulating a matter so private, yet of such public interest. Legislative consideration of surrogacy may also provide the opportunity to begin to focus on the overall implications of the new reproductive biotechnology — *in vitro* fertilization, preservation of sperm and eggs, embryo implantation and the like. The problem is how to enjoy the benefits of the technology — especially for infertile couples — while minimizing the risk of abuse. The problem can be addressed only when society decides what its values and objectives are in this troubling, yet promising, area.

The judgment is affirmed in part, reversed in part, and remanded for further proceedings consistent with this opinion.

2 Judicial Intervention in Contract

(a) *Tilden Rent-A-Car Co. v. Clendenning*†

[DUBIN J.A.:]

Upon his arrival at Vancouver airport, Mr. Clendenning, a resident of Woodstock, Ontario, attended upon the office of Tilden Rent-A-Car Company for the purpose of renting a car while he was in Vancouver. He was an experienced traveller and had used Tilden Rent-A-Car Company on many prior occasions. He provided the clerk employed at the airport office of Tilden Rent-A-Car Company with the minimum information which was asked of him, and produced his American Express credit card. He was asked by the clerk whether he desired additional coverage, and, as was his practice, he said "yes". A contract was submitted to him for his signature, which he signed in the presence of the clerk, and he returned the contract to her. She placed his copy of it in an envelope and gave him the keys to the car. He then placed the contract in the glove compartment of the vehicle. He did not read the terms of the contract before signing it, as was readily apparent to the clerk, and in fact he did not read the contract until his litigation was commenced, nor had he read a copy of a similar contract on any prior occasion.

The issue on the appeal is whether the defendant is liable for the damage caused to the automobile while being driven by him by reason of the exclusionary provisions which appear in the contract.

On the front of the contract are two relevant clauses set forth in box form. They are as follows:

15. COLLISION DAMAGE WAIVER BY CUSTOMERS INITIALS "J.C." *In consideration of the payment of $2.00 per day [customer's] liability for damage to rented vehicle including windshield is limited to NIL.* But notwithstanding payment of said fee, customer shall be fully liable for all collision damage if vehicle is used, operated or driven in violation of any of the provisions of this rental agreement or off highways serviced by federal, provincial, or municipal governments, and for all damages to vehicle by striking overhead objects.

16. I, the undersigned have read and received a copy of above and reverse side of this contract.

Signature of customer or employee of customer "John T. Clendenning" (Emphasis added.)

On the back of the contract in particularly small type and so faint in the customer's copy as to be hardly legible, there are a series of conditions, the relevant ones being as follows:

6. The customer agrees not to use the vehicle in violation of any law, ordinance, rule or regulation of any public authority.

7. The customer agrees that the vehicle will not be operated: (a) By any person who has drunk or consumed any intoxicating liquor, whatever be the quantity, or who is under the influence of drugs or narcotics;

The rented vehicle was damaged while being driven by Mr. Clendenning in Vancouver. His evidence at trial, which was accepted by the trial Judge, was to the effect that in endeavouring to avoid a collision with another vehicle and acting out a sudden emergency, he drove the car into a pole. He stated that although he had pleaded guilty to a charge of driving while impaired in Vancouver, he did so on the advice of counsel, and at the time of the impact he was capable of the proper control of the motor vehicle. This evidence was also accepted by the trial Judge.

Mr. Clendenning testified that on earlier occasions when he had inquired as to what added coverage he would receive for the payment of $2 per day, he had been advised that "such payment provided full non-deductible coverage". It is to be observed that the portion of the contract reproduced above does provide that "In consideration of the payment of $2.00 per day customers liability for damage to rented vehicle including windshield is limited to NIL".

A witness called on behalf of the plaintiff gave evidence as to the instructions given to its employees as to what was said to be by them to their customers about the conditions in the contract. He stated that unless inquiries were made, nothing was to be said by its clerks to the customer with respect to the exclusionary conditions. He went on to state that if inquiries were made, the clerks were instructed to advise the customer that by the payment of the $2 additional fee the customer had complete coverage "unless he were intoxicated, or unless he committed an offence under the *Criminal Code* such as intoxication".

Mr. Clendenning acknowledged that he had assumed, either by what had been told to him in the past or otherwise, that he would not be responsible for any damage to the vehicle on payment of the extra premium unless such damage was caused by reason of his being so intoxicated as to be incapable of proper control of the vehicle, a provision with which he was familiar as being a statutory provision in his own insurance contract.

The provisions fastening liability for damage to the vehicle on the hirer, as contained in the clauses hereinbefore referred to, are completely inconsistent with the express terms which purport to provide complete coverage for damage to the vehicle in exchange for the additional premium. It is to be noted, for example, that if the driver of the vehicle exceeded the speed-limit even by one mile per hour, or parked the vehicle in a no-parking area, or even had one glass of wine or one

bottle of beer, the contract purports to make the hirer completely responsible for all damage to the vehicle. Indeed, if the vehicle at the time of any damage to it was being driven off a federal, provincial or municipal highway, such as a shopping plaza for instance, the hirer purportedly would be responsible for all damage to the vehicle.

Mr. Clendenning stated that if he had known of the full terms of the written instrument, he would not have entered into such a contract. Having regard to the findings made by the trial Judge it is apparent that Mr. Clendenning had not in fact acquiesced to such terms.

It was urged that the rights of the parties were governed by what has come to be known as the rule in *L'Estrange v. F. Graucob, Ltd.*", [19 K.B. 394, and in particular the following from the judgment of Scrutton, L.J., at p.

> In cases in which the contract is contained in a railway ticket or other unsigned document, it is necessary to prove that an alleged was aware, or ought to have been aware of its terms and conditions. These cases have no application when the document has been signed. *When a document containing contractual terms is signed, then, in the absence of fraud, I will add, misrepresentation, the party who it is bound, and it is wholly immaterial whether he has read the document or not.* (Emphasis added.)

In the same case MAUGHAM, L.J. at p. 406: —

> There can be no dispute as to the law in of the statement of the law by *Parker v. South Eastern Ry. Co.*, [19 421, which has been read by my brother, to the effect that where the person signed a written agreement it is immaterial to the question of his liability under it that he has not read it and does not know its contents. That is true in any case in which the agreement is held to be an agreement in writing. There are, however, two possibilities to be kept in view. The first is that it might be proved that the document, though signed by the plaintiff, was signed in circumstances which made it not her act. This is the case of *Non est factum*.

And at p. 407:

> Another possibility is that the plaintiff might have been induced to sign by a misrepresentation

A transaction, such as this one, is invariably carried out in a hurried, informal manner. The speed with which the transaction is completed is said to be one of the attractive features of the services provided.

The clauses relied on in this case, as I have already stated, are inconsistent with the over-all purpose for which the contract is entered into by the hirer. Under such circumstances, something more should be done by the party submitting the contract for signature than merely handing it over to be signed.

. . . .

In modern commercial practice, many standard form printed documents are signed without being read or understood. In many cases the parties seeking to rely on the terms of the contract know or ought to know that the signature of a party to the contract does not represent the true intention of the signer, and that the party signing is unaware of the stringent and onerous provisions which the standard form contains. Under such circumstances, I am of the opinion that the party seeking to rely on such terms should not be able to do so in the absence of first having taken reasonable measures to draw such terms to the attention of the other party, and, in the absence of such reasonable measures, it is not necessary for the party denying knowledge of such terms to prove either fraud, misrepresentation or *non est factum*.

In the case at bar, Tilden Rent-A-Car took no steps to alert Mr. Clendenning to the onerous provisions in the standard form of contract presented by it. The clerk could not help but have known that Mr. Clendenning had not in fact read the contract before signing it. Indeed the form of the contract itself with the important provisions on the reverse side and in very small type would discourage even the most cautious customer from endeavouring to read and understand it. Mr. Clendenning was in fact unaware of the exempting provisions. Under such circumstances, it was not open to Tilden Rent-A-Car to rely on those clauses, and it was not incumbent on Mr. Clendenning to establish fraud, misrepresentation or *non est factum*. Having paid the premium, he

was not liable for any damage to the vehicle while being driven by him.

As Lord Denning stated in *Neuchatel Asphalte Co. Ltd. v. Barnett*, [1957] 1 W.L.R. 356 at p. 360: "We do not allow printed forms to be made a trap for the unwary."

In this case the trial Judge held that "the rule in *L'Estrange v. Graucob*" governed. He dismissed the action, however, on the ground that Tilden Rent-A-Car had by their prior oral representation misrepresented the terms of the contract. He imputed into the contract the assumption of Mr. Clendenning that by the payment of the premium he was "provided full non-deductible coverage unless at the time of the damage he was operating the automobile while under the influence of intoxicating liquor to such an extent as to be for the time incapable of the proper control of the automobile". Having found that Mr. Clendenning had not breached such a provision, the action was dismissed.

For the reasons already expressed, I do not think that in the circumstances of this case "the rule in *L'Estrange v. Graucob*" governed, and it was not incumbent upon Mr. Clendenning to prove misrepresentation.

In any event, if "the rule in *L'Estrange v. Graucob*" were applicable, it was in error, in my respectful opinion, to impute into the contract a provision which Tilden Rent-A-Car had not in fact represented as being a term of the contract.

As was stated in *Canadian Indemnity Co. v. Okanagan Mainline Real Estate Board et al.*, [1971] S.C.R. 493 at p. 500, 16 D.L.R. (3d) 715 at p. 720, [1971] 1 W.W.R. 289:

> A party who misrepresents, albeit innocently, the contents or effect of a clause inserted by him into a contract cannot rely on the clause in the face of his misrepresentation:
>
> Under such circumstances, absent the exclusionary provisions of the contract, the defendant was entitled to the benefit of the contract in the manner provided without the exclusionary provisions, and the action, therefore, had to fail.

In the result, therefore, I would dismiss the appeal with costs.

47

(b)   Culpable Silence: Liability for Non-disclosure in the Contractual Arena†

Shannon Kathleen O'Byrne

This article is concerned with the extent to which one party has a common law duty to disclose information to another, either antecedent to or during the life of a commercial contract. Though the general rule for contractual negotiations is that there is no duty of disclosure, such an unqualified statement is misleading since there are numerous instances of liability being founded for a failure to disclose. Similarly, a duty to disclose during the performance of a contract can exist — even absent an express promise — as a result of the nature of the relationship between the parties, the nature of the contract in question, or the occurrence of material events concurrent with or subsequent to the contract's formation. In short, the existence of a duty to disclose in the contractual arena can escape general detection because it is implicit in or absorbed by a variety of other legal rubrics.

·   ·   ·   ·

III.   DUTY TO DISCLOSE IN CONTRACT LAW, RESTITUTION, ESTOPPEL, AND MISTAKE

1.   Duty to Disclose as an Implied Term

In *Opron*, Justice Feehan reviewed the circumstances in which the court will imply a contractual term, including a term to disclose. Before turning to this analysis, a brief account of the facts in *Opron* is in order.

Opron Construction Co. was the successful tenderer for a construction contract related to a provincial dam project. The tender information provided to it by the province was inaccurate — Alberta had withheld certain information and even concealed other data which came to light later. These inaccuracies occasioned cost overruns by the plaintiff and it sued for breach of contract, deceit and negligent misrepresentation. The province relied, *inter alia*, on a series of exclusionary clauses to shelter itself from liability.

In response to the plaintiff's allegation that Alberta was in breach of an implied term that "there were no facts within the knowledge of the defendant or its agents which had not been disclosed to the plaintiff which were inconsistent with or contradicted the contractual warranties and representations ... made by the defendant", Feehan J. observed that implying terms into a contract involves a two-part analysis. First, it had to be decided whether the term to be implied was "inconsistent with or in conflict with any express term or disclaimer clause in the contract". If not, the court would be entitled to imply the term if it: (a) arose out of established custom or usage; (b) was necessary so as to give business efficacy to the contract; or (c) arose as a legal incident of the particular class and kind of contract at issue.

After a detailed analysis, Feehan J. ruled that the contract contained an implied term that the owner would "disclose relevant information in its possession which contradicts its express representations". This was because first, there was no "entire contract" or merger clause; second, implying such an obligation would not fly in the face of the "investigation" clause; third, a term to disclose would give the contract business efficacy; and fourth, such a term is a legal incident of construction contracts, absent a clause forbidding this kind of reliance, due, *inter alia*, to the short amount of time tenderers are typically given to prepare their tenders. In plaintiff counsel's words, "[t]o permit an owner such as the government to disclose infor-

---

† (1998) 30 Can. Bus. L.J. 239 at 239–40, 248–254, 257–60. [Notes and/or References omitted.] Reproduced with permission of the author and The Canadian Business Law Journal.

mation which it knows is contradicted by other information in its possession, is to subvert the contract itself". The exclusion clauses did not assist Alberta's defence because the court also made a finding of fraudulent misrepresentation. Though it was, therefore, not necessary to consider whether the "investigation clause" and other clauses effectively absolved the defendant's liability, Justice Feehan did make a determination on this point as well. On the "investigation" clause, for example, he concluded that it:

> ... merely requires the tenderer "to investigate and satisfy himself of everything and of every condition affecting the works to be performed and the labour and material to be provided"; it does not specify what information he may have [with] regard to in conducting this investigation. In particular, neither this clause nor any other forbid the plaintiff from considering and relying on the soils information conveyed in the tender package.

Similarly, clauses which disclaimed responsibility for interpretations of information in the tender documents were also insufficient to exclude liability for Alberta. According to Feehan J., such clauses only excluded liability for inferences which the contractor draws, not for reliance on the basic information contained therein. Feehan J. also distinguished the clause disclaiming the accuracy of the information provided in the tender because it was not drafted broadly enough.

The exceedingly strict interpretation which Feehan J. brought to his analysis of the exclusion clauses is consistent with the operation of the *contra proferentem* rule but may also manifest the court's distaste for the objectionable "veil of secrecy" which Alberta maintained at Opron's expense during the course of the entire project.

2. Duty to Disclose as an Obligation Mandated by Good Faith

Another argument successfully advanced by counsel for the plaintiff in *Opron* was that Alberta had an obligation to disclose material information as part of an implied covenant of good faith and fair dealing. More specifically, the defendant was said to be contractually obliged to disclose information to the plaintiff which was "inconsistent with or contradicted the information provided in the tender documents".

Mr Justice Feehan acceded to this argument, while acknowledging that implying good faith obli-

gations was in its infancy in Canada in 1994. Fortified by certain statements of the Supreme Court of Canada regarding civil law contracts, as well as by the leading decision of *Gateway Realty Ltd. v. Arton Holdings Ltd.(No. 3)*, he held that such an obligation should be inferred. To reach this conclusion, he noted that in the construction industry, tenderers will reasonably expect that the owner, having provided information, will not withhold information which would "materially affect the prospective tenderers' bids". As a result:

> [T]here is a covenant implied by law that the parties will deal fairly and in good faith with one another in the exchange of information. It is reasonable, where the owner or its agents impart critical information in the tender documents which form part of the contract, that there is an implied covenant that such information has been furnished in good faith, in the honest and reasonable belief that it is complete and accurate, with all material information provided, in the sense that there is no inconsistent information within the owner's knowledge bearing upon the tender or the performance of the contract.

In the end, the government was found liable, *inter alia*, for a failure to disclose, both precontractually and during the course of the contract.

3. Duty to Disclose as an Incident of the Law of Mistake, Estoppel, Unconscionability and Unjust Enrichment

(a) Law of Mistake

While the law does not ordinarily impose a duty to disclose prior to the execution of a contract, a *de facto* duty to disclose may arise for the party wishing to create an enforceable contract. This is because silence, which produces a unilateral mistake in the innocent party, will result in the contract being rescinded, rectified, or otherwise being subject to equitable intervention. In *Bank of British Columbia v. Wren Development Ltd.*, for example, the defendant's guarantee was set aside because the bank did not provide him with the information he requested on the state of the collateral security supporting the primary debt. Even though the defendant purportedly waived his request by immediately signing the guarantee without waiting for the bank to gather the data he had asked for, the court ruled that "there was a unilateral mistake on the part of the defendant ... which was induced by the misrepresentation of the plaintiff in failing to disclose material facts to him". The court's approach thereby imposed on the bank what amounts — in practice if not in law — to a positive duty to disclose.

According to the recent decision of the Saskatchewan Court of Appeal in *Montreal Trust v. Maley*, to succeed in an action based on unilateral mistake the plaintiff must establish:

(1) that a mistake occurred;
(2) that there was a fraud or the equivalent on the [defendant's] part in that she knew or must ... have known when the agreement was executed that the [plaintiff] misunderstood its significance and that she did nothing to enlighten the [plaintiff] ...

The rationale for such a rule is incontrovertible, namely a refusal by equity to tolerate unconscionable conduct, misrepresentation, sharp practice, fraud or its equivalent.

In *Maley*, the defendant Maley had received as part of his termination settlement the right to purchase land which acquisition was intended to be subject to the plaintiff's well-known policy of retaining all surface leases. When it became clear that the leases had not been excluded in the conveyancing documents — because of a number of errors "encouraged and fostered by Maley" — the plaintiff (Montreal Trust) brought an action to secure a rectification order.

Not surprisingly, the court was receptive to the plaintiff's prayer for relief since the defendant knowingly took advantage of the plaintiff's mistake. Indeed, Wakeling J.A. ultimately agreed with Professor Waddams' assertion that: "[w]here there is a mistake as to contractual terms the courts have characterized such conduct as 'equivalent to fraud' and there is no doubt that relief is available". He also agreed with the proposition that whether the unmistaken party created the mistake or not was irrelevant. Rather, it was the defendant's failure to point out the error that founded liability.

Though the court ultimately resolved the dispute in Montreal Trust's favour on a narrower

point of employment law, it also affirmed the law of mistake referred to in the preceding paragraph. Furthermore, the law of mistake governed the result because, in the court's view, Maley's conduct was "sufficiently reprehensible" to justify an order of rectification. In short, "it would be inequitable or unconscionable for a party to be permitted to take advantage of another's mistake, even if not induced by him".

That the law has set its face against "snapping up" an offer, as in *Maley*, is equivalent to saying that the unmistaken party owes a duty to disclose a material error in the offer if he or she wishes to secure an enforceable contract. The conclusion has been affirmed often. A recent example is when McLachlin C.J.S.C. (as she then was) in *First City Capital v. British Columbia Building Corp.*, observed that:

[T]he equitable jurisdiction of the courts to relieve against mistake in contract comprehends situations where one party, who knows or ought to know of another's mistake in a fundamental term, remains silent and snaps at the offer, seeking to take advantage of the other's mistake. In such cases, it would be unconscionable to enforce the bargain and equity will set aside the contract.

In *Can-Dive Services Ltd. v. Pacific Coast Energy Corp.*, Shaw J. agreed with this exposition of law and extended it also to cover a situation where,

... although there was no actual knowledge of the mistake, circumstances were such that a reasonable person in the position of the party wishing to enforce the written contract ought to have known of the mistake. Thus, constructive notice will suffice.

Hence, whether the mistake is unilateral (as in *Maley*) or mutual (as in *Can-Dive*), the courts will order rectification where "it would be against conscience to allow the written agreement to prevail".

(c)   *Sevidal v. Chopra*†

[OYEN J.:]

The plaintiffs, Soliman and Eleanor Sevidal, claim they suffered damages as a result of a series of events which took place at the time of their purchase of a home which had radioactive material in the backyard.

The Sevidals decided to buy their first home in March, 1981. The consulted the defendant, Antonietta Antonio, a real estate agent employed by the defendant, Northgate Realty Ltd. With her help their search led them to 63 McClure Cres. in Scarborough, which was owned by the defendants, Chand Kirshan Chopra and Asha Chopra.

After some negotiations the Sevidals entered into an agreement to purchase with the Chopras in April, 1981. The Chopras did not disclose to the Sevidals that radioactive soil had been found in the McClure Cres. area and that there was a "hot spot" across the street.

Although the agreement was conditional upon mortgage financing, Antonio had the Sevidals waive the condition before they had applied for the mortgage.

.   .   .   .

LIABILITY OF THE CHOPRAS

The issues with respect to the Chopras relate to disclosure. Did the Chopras owe a duty to the Sevidals to disclose the presence of radioactive material in the McClure Cres. area before the agreement to purchase was signed, or to disclose the discovery of radioactive material in the backyard of 63 McClure Cres. before the closing?

Here we are dealing with a latent defect. Latent defects with respect to the sale of land, have been described succinctly in 42 *Hals.*, 4th ed., p. 47, para. 51: "latent defects are such as would not be revealed by any inquiry which a purchaser is in a position to make before entering into the contract for purchase".

Redican v. Nesbitt, stands for the proposition that the doctrine of *caveat emptor* does not apply to fraud, error *in substantialibus* or where there is a warranty, contractual condition or collateral contract.

In reviewing whether a cause of action existed in the case of *McGrath v. MacLean*, Dubin J.A., quoted favourably from a lecture by Professor Bora Laskin, as he then was, entitled "Defects of Title and Quality: Caveat Emptor and the Vendor's Duty of Disclosure", *Special Lectures of the Law Society of Upper Canada* (1960), p. 389 at pp. 403–4:

> Does the vendor have any duty of disclosure in matters of quality and fitness which do not constitute defects of title? Here we deal with the classical notion of *caveat emptor* as applied to the physical amenities and condition of the property unrelated to any outstanding claims of third parties or public authorities such as would impinge on the title. *Absent fraud, mistake or misrepresentation, a purchaser takes existing property as he finds it*, whether it be dilapidated, bug-infested or otherwise uninhabitable or deficient in expected amenities, unless he protects himself by contract terms....
>
> *I do not propose to dwell on fraud, mistake or misrepresentation save to make a few observations about the way in which, if established, they relieve a purchaser from the binding effect of caveat emptor. Fraud can be a rather elastic conception, and there are cases which show a tendency to find fraud when there has been concealment by the vendor of latent defects. Rowley v. Isley*, a British Columbia decision entitling a purchaser to rescind (even after paying the price and taking possession) where there was a failure to disclose infestation by roaches, illustrates the proposition, and goes quite far in allowing rescission after the transaction had been closed. *On the other hand, a latent defect of quality going to fitness for habitation and which is either unknown to the vendor or such as not to make him chargeable with concealment or reckless disregard of its truth or falsity will not support any claim of redress by the purchaser. He must find his protection in warranty.* (Emphasis added.)

---

† (1987), 64 O.R. (2d) 169 (H.C.) at 171, 183–84, 187–89.

At p. 792, Dubin J.A. went on to state with respect to *Rowley v. Isley*:

> It is to be observed that Coady J., in the case of *Rowley v. Isley et al.*, found against the vendor in the following language:
>
> > *The failure to disclose* to the plaintiff, however, the true condition of the house, as to the infestation by cockroaches and to the prior fumigation, rendered necessary by reason of the prior excessive cockroach infestation, *was I think, a fraudulent misrepresentation arising from a suppression of the truth.* This condition, under the circumstances, it was the agent's duty to disclose. (Emphasis added.)

An exception to the general rule of *caveat emptor* will be found where there is fraud or fraudulent misrepresentation and, where there is such a finding, failure on the part of the vendor to disclose will give rise to a cause of action.

Fraud arises when a statement is made "knowingly, or without belief in its truth, or recklessly, careless whether it be true or false": *per* Lord Herschell in *Derry v. Peek* (1889). Fraud can also arise where there is active concealment: *Able v. McDonald, infra.* Finally, fraud arises where there is failure to disclose a potential danger: *Rivtow Marine, McGrath v. MacLean, C.R.F. Holdings, Ford v. Schmitt,* all *infra.*

Counsel for the Sevidals argued that failure to disclose the presence of radioactive contamination both in the area and later on the property itself amounted to a fraudulent misrepresentation, and that the Chopras intended to deceive the Sevidals.

It appears that many of the cases turn on their particular facts. It would be useful, therefore, to review them.

. . . .

To return to the case before me, and dealing first with the issue of whether the Chopras should have disclosed the existence of radioactive material in the area prior to entering into the agreement of purchase and sale, I find, based on the principles enunciated in the cases to which I have referred, that they should have. They knew about the potentially dangerous latent defect prior to the signing of the agreement. The fact that at the time the agreement was signed the latent defect was only known to be on property in the immediate area and not on the property itself, provides no excuse for non-

disclosure. The Chopras were guilty of concealment of facts so detrimental to the Sevidals that it amounted to a fraud upon them, and, therefore, the Chopras are liable in deceit.

In considering the second issue of whether the Chopras should have disclosed the discovery of radioactive material on their property prior to closing, the principles enunciated in the cases would apply equally but even more forcefully to them when the discovery was made on their property a week prior to closing but there is one further aspect which must be addressed before I make my finding: whether there is a duty to disclose a change of circumstance after the agreement is signed but before closing.

In the cases already set out, the vendor knew of the latent defect prior to the signing of the agreement. In this case, I have found as well that the Chopras knew of the latent defect in the immediate area prior to the signing of the agreement but I want to deal separately with whether they should have disclosed the latent defect on their property which they knew nothing about when they signed the agreement but which they discovered was there at least a week prior to closing.

The Sevidals' counsel referred me to the case of *With v. O'Flanagan*, for the proposition that where a representation is true at the time when it is made, but owing to a change of circumstances becomes untrue before or at the time of completion, it is the vendor's duty to disclose the change of circumstances. That case is distinguishable because the statement made by the vendor about the income if a medical practice, though true when made, became untrue due to the illness of the doctor *before* the contract was signed. In this case, a change of circumstance occurred *after* the signing of the agreement and before closing.

In *Abel v. McDonald*, (C.A.), when the purchasers moved in they discovered that the basement floor had dropped several inches from the time they had inspected the property before signing the offer. Aylesworth J.A. found fraud through active non-disclosure on the part of the vendors. He indicated that active non-disclosure meant that with the knowledge that the damage to the premises had occurred after the agreement was signed, the vendors actively prevented that knowledge from coming to the notice of the purchasers.

In the case before me, while there may not have been quite the same non-disclosure in the *Able* case, the comments of McFarlane J.A. in *Sorensen v. Kaye Holdings, supra,* apply:

... where, as here, the claim is for damages for fraud, it is my opinion that the court must consider the whole of the dealings between the parties from [the first meeting] until their contract was carried through to completion ...

In all the circumstances of this case, I find that the Chopras had a duty to disclose the change in circumstances to the Sevidals prior to closing. Accordingly, with regard to the second issue, I find that the Chopras should have disclosed the discovery of radioactive material on their property, and I find the Chopras were guilty of concealment of facts so detrimental to the Sevidals that it amounted to a fraud upon them. Therefore, the Chopras are liable in deceit.

(d) *Geffen v. Goodman Estate*†

[WILSON J.:]

The respondent, Stacy Randall Goodman, as executor of his mother's estate and on his own behalf, commenced an action claiming that he and his siblings were entitled to certain property left to his mother, Tzina Goodman, by his grandmother, Annie Sanofsky. The appellants, Sam, William and Ted Geffen are the brothers and nephew of Stacy's mother. They are the trustees of a certain trust agreement in which Stacy's mother is named as the settlor and under which the trust property is to be distributed amongst all of Annie Sanofsky's grandchildren. This appeal concerns the validity of the trust agreement.

1. THE FACTS

Annie Sanofsky had four children, Sam, Ted, Jack and Tzina. Sam and Ted Geffen are both successful businessmen currently living in the United States. Their brother Jack is an insurance underwriter who lives in Edmonton. Their sister Tzina, (Mrs. Goodman) now deceased, had a less than trouble-free life. She first came under the care of a psychiatrist while a teenager. Psychiatric intervention became a common feature of her existence. She was hospitalized many times over the years and was eventually diagnosed as suffering from bipolar affective disorder, formerly known as manic depressive disorder, and immature personality. Tzina's illness caused strain in her family relationships. Her disorder tended to drive people away from her. Although she married and had children she did not have much contact with her children after her separation from her husband. Her contact with them was purely casual.

In 1968, with the help of her son Jack, Annie Sanofsky executed a will providing for a life estate to her daughter Tzina and directing that on Tzina's death her estate should be distributed to all of her (Annie's) grandchildren. At the time of their mother's death the four children were surprised to learn that a new will had been executed in 1975 which superseded the 1968 will. Under the new will Annie Sanofsky left the property which had been her home outright to her daughter Tzina, provided bequests of $1000 each to her sons, and directed that the residue of her estate be held in trust for Tzina during her lifetime and pass on Tzina's death to her (Tzina's) children.

The three Geffen brothers, not surprisingly, were unhappy with the way in which their mother had disposed of her estate. They thought it unfair that their children had been cut out of the will. Their sister agreed. They were especially concerned, however, with their mother's decision to bequeath her home in Calgary outright to their sister. Tzina had a history of mental illness and they feared that her disability would interfere with her capacity to act responsibly in relation to the prop-

† [1991] 2 S.C.R. 353.

erty she had inherited. They were particularly concerned that Tzina might divest herself of the assets she needed for her own support. If this happened they might be called upon to contribute to her support. They, along with their sister, decided to seek legal advice as to whether or not the second will was valid.

They retained the services of Mr. Pearce, a Calgary lawyer, and explained the situation to him. Jack Geffen acted as spokesman for the family. The options open to Tzina were canvassed. It was suggested that the house be transferred by Tzina to her brothers' children. A disagreement ensued between Tzina and her brother Jack. She did not like the idea of transferring title to the house immediately, leaving herself with only a life interest in it. Mr. Pearce suggested that she take some time to think things over. The meeting disbanded, the brothers paid for the consultation and all concerned returned to their respective homes.

Mrs. Goodman thereafter had only casual contact with her brothers but continued to seek the advice of counsel and communicated with Mr. Pearce on several occasions. As a result of these consultations it was suggested to Mrs. Goodman that the Calgary residence be put into a trust for her for life with her brothers as trustees but that she would retain the right to dispose of the property by will. This suggestion was vehemently rejected by Jack but accepted by Ted and Sam Geffen. Jack indicated that he would have nothing further to do with the trust and it was agreed that Ted's son William would replace him as a trustee.

Mr. Pearce then went ahead and prepared the trust deed. The trust property was conveyed to the trustees on terms that Mrs. Goodman retained a life interest in the Calgary residence and that on her request the trustees would consider a sale of the property so long as the sale was in Mrs. Goodman's best interests. The trust deed further provided that upon Mrs. Goodman's death the trust property would be divided equally among her surviving children, nephews and nieces, i.e., all Annie Sanofsky's grandchildren.

After the deed was executed Mrs. Goodman was apparently not too sure of the effect of what she had done. She attempted twice to put the property on the market. Her attempts were thwarted by Mr. Pearce. Mrs. Goodman died in May of 1984, leaving a last will and testament in which she left her entire estate to her children.

. . . .

4. ANALYSIS

The Presumption of Undue Influence

. . . .

The equitable doctrine of undue influence was developed, as was pointed out by Lindley L.J. in *Allcard v. Skinner* (1887), 36 Ch. D. 145, not to save people from the consequences of their own folly but to save them from being victimized by other people (at pp. 182–83). In the context of gifts and other transactions, equity will intervene and set aside such arrangements if procured by undue influence. Over the years it became accepted that equitable protection could be invoked in two ways.

In *Allcard v. Skinner*, supra, the plaintiff joined a sisterhood devoted to charitable works under the auspices of a clergyman of the Church of England. Upon becoming a full member of the sisterhood she made the requisite vows of poverty, chastity and obedience. In accordance with these vows she from time to time handed over to the mother superior income and capital to which she was entitled under her father's will. Several years later the plaintiff left the sisterhood and joined the Roman Catholic Church. She then sued for the return of the stock she had given away, claiming that she had been induced by undue influence to turn the property over to the mother superior.

Cotton L.J. began by setting out the doctrine of undue influence in broad terms. At page 171 he said:

> Does the case fall within the principles laid down by the decisions of the Court of Chancery in setting aside voluntary gifts executed by parties who at the time were under such influence as, in the opinion of the Court, enabled the donor afterwards to set the gift aside? These decisions may be divided into two classes — First, where the court has been satisfied that the gift was the result of influence expressly used by the donee for the purpose; second, where the relations between the donor and donee have at or shortly before the execution of the gift been such as to raise a presumption that the donee had influence over the donor.

Lindley L.J. commented to similar effect on the state of the law at that time. He said at p. 181:

> The doctrine relied upon by the Appellant is the doctrine of undue influence expounded and

enforced in *Huguenin v. Baseley*, and other cases of that class. These cases may be subdivided into two groups, which, however, often overlap.

First, there are the cases in which there has been some unfair and improper conduct, some coercion from outside, some overreaching, some form of cheating, and generally, though not always, some personal advantage obtained by a donee placed in some close and confidential relation to the donor....

The second group consists of cases in which the position of the donor to the donee has been such that it has been the duty of the donee to advise the donor, or even to manage his property for him. In such cases the Court throws upon the donee the burden of proving that he has not abused his position, and of proving that the gift made to him has not been brought about by any undue influence on his part. In this class of cases it has been considered necessary to shew that the donor had independent advice, and was removed from the influence of the donee when the gift to him was made.

In the present case there was no evidence of undue influence as such and it therefore remains to consider whether the relationship between the parties gave rise to a presumption of undue influence.

What are the factors that go to establishing a presumption of undue influence? This question has been the focus of much debate in recent years. Equity has recognized that transactions between persons standing in certain relationships with one another will be presumed to be relationships of influence until the contrary is shown. These include the relationship between trustee and beneficiary; solicitor and client; doctor and patient; parent and child; guardian and ward; and future husband and fiancee. Beginning, however, with *Zamet v. Hyman*, it came to be accepted that the relationships in which undue influence will be presumed are not confined to fixed categories and that each case must be considered on its own facts. Since then it has been generally agreed that the existence of some "special" relationship must be shown in order to support the presumption although what constitutes such a "special" relationship is a matter of some doubt. In Snell's *Principles of Equity* (1982), for instance, it is stated at p. 540 that the presumption applies when the transaction has been effected between parties in a fiduciary relationship to one another. Others suggest that influence flows naturally from confidential relationships: see *Cana-*

dian Encyclopedic Digest (Western). In *Lloyds Bank Ltd. v. Bundy*, this issue was canvassed in some detail by Sir Eric Sachs who indicated that the existence of an advisory relationship is relevant to the determination. He went on to say at p. 767:

Such cases tend to arise where someone relies on the guidance or advice of another, where the other is aware of that reliance and where the person on whom reliance is placed obtains, or may well obtain, a benefit from the transaction or has some other interest in it being concluded.

Sir Eric's comments were approved in *National Westminster Bank Plc. v. Morgan, supra*, a case raising the propriety of a bank's involvement in securing a transaction with one of its customers. Lord Scarman explained his difficulty with the existing state of the law at p. 703. To him, words and phrases such as "confidence", "confidentiality" and "fiduciary duty" were inadequate concepts to guide the inquiry and often led justices into a misinterpretation of facts:

There are plenty of confidential relationships which do not give rise to the presumption of undue influence ... and there are plenty of non-confidential relationships in which one person relies upon the advice of another....

In expressing his approval of Sir Eric's words, Lord Scarman noted at p. 709 that relationships in which one party develops a dominating influence over another are "infinitely various" and there was no substitute for a "meticulous examination of the facts".

. . . .

In my view, neither the result nor process focused approach to the doctrine of undue influence fully captures the true purport of this equitable rule. I say this primarily because the doctrine applies to a wide variety of transactions from pure gifts to classic contracts. In the case of the former it seems to make sense that the process leading up to the gifting should be subject to judicial scrutiny because there is something so completely repugnant about the judicial enforcement of coerced or fraudulently induced generosity. With respect to contractual relations, however, it has long been the view of the courts that the sanctity of bargains should be protected unless they are patently unfair. I cannot think of any situation in which a contract has been rescinded on the sole basis that the process leading up to the bargain was somehow tainted. Something more, such as detrimental reliance, must be shown. It seems to me, therefore, that whatever the measure of undue influence this Court adopts, it must be sufficiently flexible to account for a wide variety of transactions.

What then is the nature of the relationship that must exist in order to give rise to a presumption of undue influence? Bearing in mind the decision in *Morgan*, its critics and the divergence in the jurisprudence which it spawned, it is my opinion that concepts such as "confidence" and "reliance" do not adequately capture the essence of relationships which may give rise to the presumption. I would respectfully agree with Lord Scarman that there are many confidential relationships that do not give rise to the presumption just as there are many non-confidential relationships that do. It seems to me rather that when one speaks of "influence" one is really referring to the ability of one person to dominate the will of another, whether through manipulation, coercion, or outright but subtle abuse of power. I disagree with the Court of Appeal's decision in *Goldsworthy v. Brickell*, *supra*, that it runs contrary to human experience to characterize relationships of trust or confidence as relationships of dominance. To dominate the will of another simply means to exercise a persuasive influence over him or her. The ability to exercise such influence may arise from a relationship of trust or confidence but it may arise from other relationships as well. The point is that there is nothing per se reprehensible about persons in a relationship of trust or confidence exerting influence, even undue influence, over their beneficiaries. It depends on their motivation and the objective they seek to achieve thereby.

What of the controversial requirement of "manifest disadvantage" articulated in *Morgan*? In my view, the critics were correct in pointing out that this test, while perhaps appropriate in a purely commercial setting, limits the doctrine of undue influence too much. In the case of gifts or bequests, for example, it makes no sense to insist that the donor or testator prove that their generosity placed them at a disadvantage. While one could say that giving away anything is in a literal sense ipso facto disadvantageous, it seems to me that this is a wholly unrealistic test to apply to a gift. A donor who wishes to make a gift is not really disadvantaged by doing so. On the contrary, his or her own purpose is served by doing so. Disadvantage is accordingly, to my mind, not a particularly appropriate concept for general application to the

wide variety of situations to which the doctrine of undue influence could conceivably apply.

What then must a plaintiff establish in order to trigger a presumption of undue influence? In my view, the inquiry should begin with an examination of the relationship between the parties. The first question to be addressed in all cases is whether the potential for domination inheres in the nature of the relationship itself. This test embraces those relationships which equity has already recognized as giving rise to the presumption, such as solicitor and client, parent and child, and guardian and ward, as well as other relationships of dependency which defy easy categorization.

Having established the requisite type of relationship to support the presumption, the next phase of the inquiry involves an examination of the nature of the transaction. When dealing with commercial transactions, I believe that the plaintiff should be obliged to show, in addition to the required relationship between the parties, that the contract worked unfairness either in the sense that he or she was unduly disadvantaged by it or that the defendant was unduly benefited by it. From the court's point of view this added requirement is justified when dealing with commercial transactions because, as already mentioned, a court of equity, even while tempering the harshness of the common law, must accord some degree of deference to the principle of freedom of contract and the inviolability of bargains. Moreover, it can be assumed in the vast majority of commercial transactions that parties act in pursuance of their own self-interest. The mere fact, therefore, that the plaintiff seems to be giving more than he is getting is insufficient to trigger the presumption.

By way of contrast, in situations where consideration is not an issue, e.g., gifts and bequests, it seems to me quite inappropriate to put a plaintiff to the proof of undue disadvantage or benefit in the result. In these situations the concern of the court is that such acts of beneficence not be tainted. It is enough, therefore, to establish the presence of a dominant relationship.

Once the plaintiff has established that the circumstances are such as to trigger the application of the presumption, i.e., that apart from the details of the particular impugned transaction the nature of the relationship between the plaintiff and defendant was such that the potential for influence existed, the onus moves to the defendant to rebut it. As Lord Evershed M.R. stated in *Zamet* v. *Hyman*, *supra*, at p. 938, the plaintiff must be shown to have entered into the transaction as a result of his own "full, free and informed thought". Substantively, this may entail a showing that no actual influence was deployed in the particular transaction, that the plaintiff had independent advice, and so on. Additionally, I agree with those authors who suggest that the magnitude of the disadvantage or benefit is cogent evidence going to the issue of whether influence was exercised.

In the present case neither the trial judge nor the Court of Appeal went into very much detail as to why the presumption of undue influence was properly applicable given the nature of the relationship between Mrs. Goodman and her older brothers. They focused instead on the details of the execution of the trust agreement itself. A review of the circumstances between the deceased and her brothers at the relevant time does, however, disclose that the relationship between them was such that a potential existed for the brothers to exercise a persuasive influence over their sister. *Halsbury's Laws of England* (4th ed.) designates the relevant time when it identifies the class of case in which a presumption of undue influence arises:

> **330.** ... Secondly, there are those cases in which the relationship between the donor and the donee at the time of or shortly before the making of the gift has been such as to raise a presumption that the donee had influence over the donor. In this second class of case the onus is on the donee to rebut the presumption by showing that the donor made the gift only after full, free and informed thought about it.... [Emphasis added.]

It is true that the trial judge found as a fact that there was very little contact between Mrs. Goodman and her brothers over the years prior to the death of their mother. Uncontradicted evidence disclosed that Mrs. Goodman had a history of mental health problems and that she suffered from both bipolar affective disorder and a personality disorder which at times made her domineering and aggressive but at other times withdrawn and helpless depending on her mood swings. The brothers were aware that their sister's condition made her a difficult person to deal with and affected her ability to act responsibly on her own behalf and to make an adequate living for herself. They knew that their mother had shouldered the bulk of responsibility for their sister and that without her help they would likely have to step in to assist. Even although the brothers were successful businessmen who were significantly better off than their sister, they regarded her as a potential liability and sought

to avoid any financial responsibility for her. Indeed, it was the suspicion that they might be placed in a position of responsibility for their sister that prompted Jack to play a role in assisting their mother in the preparation of her first will the terms of which ensured that this would not happen.

It was when the mother died and the brothers discovered that she had executed a second will which removed the protections contained in the first one that the real potential for the brothers to influence their sister arose. The evidence discloses that Mrs. Goodman had sought the assistance of her brothers to see her through the emotional crisis of the death of her mother, her primary caregiver. Communications between Mrs. Goodman and her brothers increased during this period. They knew she needed support and protection. She consulted with them as to what the best arrangement would be. The brothers were well aware that their sister had reposed her trust and confidence in them to help her straighten out her legal and financial affairs. It was a situation where the brothers knew their sister was vulnerable, knew that she was relying upon them to help her and knew that they had interests of their own which did not necessarily coincide with hers. Thus, apart from the particular circumstances surrounding the execution of the trust agreement, the relationship between the deceased and the appellants was such that it could have afforded them the potential to exercise undue influence over her.

. . . . .

DISPOSITION

I would allow the appeal, set aside the decision of the Court of Appeal, and restore the decision of the trial judge.

[La FOREST J.:]

. . . .

In another situation, the relationship of brother and sister might well support a presumption of undue influence. Given these findings of fact by the trial judge, however, it is difficult to accept that the relationship between Mrs. Goodman and her brothers was one where the potential for a dominating influence existed. In so holding, I am not insensitive to the fact that the trust agreement was first proposed during the difficult period immediately following their mother's death. However, the facts as found by the trial judge simply do not bear out the view that Mrs. Goodman was relying upon her brothers for assistance even during this troubled time. I accordingly conclude that there could be no presumption of undue influence at that time.

The facts are even stronger as they relate to the subsequent period. In this regard, it must be remembered that the trust arrangement was not finalized until several months after the death of Mrs. Goodman's mother. It was only entered into by Mrs. Goodman after numerous independent consultations with her attorney, Mr. Pearce, and "following periods of independent thought by her". In the words of the trial judge, at p. 228:

> By the time Mrs. Goodman had decided to include all of the grandchildren, that is to say, to include her own children as beneficiaries as well as all of her nieces and nephews, <u>contact between herself and her three brothers no longer existed.</u> [Emphasis added.]

(e) *Lloyds Bank Ltd. v. Bundy*[†]

[LORD DENNING M.R..:]

Broadchalke is one of the most pleasing villages in England. Old Herbert Bundy was a farmer there. His home was at Yew Tree Farm. It went back for 300 years. His family had been there for generations. It was his only asset. But he did a very foolish thing. He mortgaged it to the bank. Up to the very hilt. Not to borrow money for himself, but for the sake of his son. Now the bank have come down on him. They have foreclosed. They want to get him out of Yew Tree Farm and to sell it. They have brought this action against him for possession. Going out means ruin for him. He was granted legal aid. His lawyers put in a defence. They said that when he executed the charge to the bank he did not know what he was doing; or at any rate the circumstances were such that he ought not to be bound by it. At the trial his plight was plain. The judge was sorry for him. He said he was a 'poor old gentleman'. He was so obviously incapacitated that the judge admitted his proof in evidence. He had a heart attack in the witness box. Yet the judge felt he could do nothing for him. There is nothing, he said, 'which takes this out of the vast range of commercial transactions'. He ordered Herbert Bundy to give up possession of Yew Tree Farm to the bank.

Now there is an appeal to this court. The ground is that the circumstances were so exceptional that Herbert Bundy should not be held bound.

THE EVENTS BEFORE DECEMBER 1969

Herbert Bundy had only one son, Michael Bundy. He had great faith in him. They were both customers of Lloyds Bank at the Salisbury branch. They had been customers for many years. The son formed a company called MJB Plant Hire Ltd. It hired out earth-moving machinery and so forth. The company banked at Lloyds too at the same branch.

In 1961 the son's company was in difficulties. The father on 19th September 1966 guaranteed the company's overdraft for £1,500 and charged Yew Tree Farm to the bank to secure the £1,500. Afterwards the son's company got further into difficulties. The overdraft ran into thousands. In May 1967 the assistant bank manager, Mr. Bennett, told the son the bank must have further security. The son said his father would give it. So Mr. Bennett and the son went together to see the father. Mr. Bennett produced the papers. He suggested that the father should sign a further guarantee for

---

† [1974] 3 All E.R. 757 (C.A.).

£5,000 and to execute a further charge for £6,000. The farther said that he would help his son as far as he possibly could. Mr. Bennett did not ask the father to sign the papers there and then. He left them with the father so that he could consider them overnight and take advice on them. The father showed them to his solicitor, Mr. Trethowan, who lived in the same village. The solicitor told the father the £5,000 was the utmost that he could sink in his son's affairs. The house was worth about £10,000 and this was half his assets. On that advice the father on 27th May 1969 did execute the further guarantee and the charge, and Mr. Bennett witnessed it. So at the end of May 1967 the father had charged the house to secure £7,500.

THE EVENTS OF DECEMBER 1969

During the next six months the affairs of the son and his company went from bad to worse. The bank had granted the son's company an overdraft up to a limit of £10,000, but this was not enough to meet the outgoings. The son's company drew cheques which the bank returned unpaid. The bank were anxious. By this time Mr. Bennett had left to go to another branch. He was succeeded by a new assistant manager, Mr. Head. In November 1969 Mr. Head saw the son and told him that the account was unsatisfactory and that he considered that the company might have to cease operations. The son suggested that the difficulty was only temporary and that his father would be prepared to provide further money if necessary.

On 17th December 1969 there came the occasion which, in the judge's words, was important and disastrous for the father. The son took Mr. Head to see his father. Mr. Head had never met the father before. This was his first visit. He went prepared. He took with him a form of guarantee and a form of charge filled in with the father's name ready for signature. There was a family gathering. The father and mother were there. The son and the son's wife. Mr. Head said that the bank had given serious thought whether they could continue to support the son's company. But that the bank were prepared to do so in this way. (i) The bank would continue to allow the company to draw money on overdraft up to the existing level of £10,000, but the bank would require the company to pay ten per cent of its incomings into a separate account. So that ten per cent would not go to reduce the overdraft. Mr. Head said that this would have the effect 'of reducing the level of borrowing'. In other words, the bank was cutting down the overdraft. (ii) The bank would require the father to give a guarantee of the company's account in a sum of £11,000 and to give the bank a further charge on the house of £3,500, so as to bring the total charge to £11,000. The house was only worth about £10,000, so this charge for £11,000 would sweep up all that the father had.

On hearing the proposal, the father said that Michael was his only son and that he was 100 per cent behind him. Mr. Head produced the forms that had already been filled in. The father signed them and Mr. Head witnessed them there and then. On this occasion, Mr. Head, unlike Mr. Bennett, did not leave the forms with the father; nor did the father have any independent advice.

It is important to notice the state of mind of Mr. Head and of the father. Mr. Head said in evidence:

> [The father] asked me what in my opinion Company was doing wrong and Company's position. I told him. I did not explain Company's accounts very fully as I had only just taken over.... [The son] said Company had a number of bad debts. I wasn't entirely satisfied with this. I thought the trouble was more deep-seated.... I thought there was no conflict of interest. I would think the [father] relied on me implicitly to advise him about the transaction as Bank Manager.... I knew he had no other assets except Yew Tree Cottage.

The father said in evidence:

> 'Always thought Mr. Head was genuine. I have always trusted him.... No discussion how business was doing that I can remember. I simply sat back and did what they said.'

The solicitor, Mr. Trethowan, said of the father:

> [The father] is straightforward. Agrees with anyone.... Doubt if he understood all that Mr. Head explained to him.

So the father signed the papers. Mr. Head witnessed them and took them away. The father had charged the whole of his remaining asset, leaving himself with nothing. The son and his company gained a respite. But only for a short time. Five months later, in May 1970, a receiving order was made against the son. Thereupon the bank stopped all overdraft facilities for the company. It ceased to trade. The father's solicitor, Mr. Trethowan, at once went to see Mr. Head. He said he was concerned that the father had signed the guarantee.

In due course the bank insisted on the sale of the house. In December 1971 they agreed to sell it for £7,500 with vacant possession. The family were very disappointed with this figure. It was, they said, worth much more. Estate agents were called to say so. But the judge held that it was a valid sale and that the bank can take all the proceeds. The sale has not been completed, because the father is still in possession. The bank have brought these proceedings to evict the father.

THE GENERAL RULE

Now let me say at once that in the vast majority of cases a customer who signs a bank guarantee or a charge cannot get out of it. No bargain will be upset which is the result of the ordinary interplay of forces. There are many hard cases which are caught by this rule. Take the case of a poor man who is homeless. He agrees to pay a high rent to a landlord just to get a roof over his head. The common law will not interfere. It is left to Parliament. Next take the case of a borrower in urgent need of money. He borrows it from the bank at high interest and it is guaranteed by a friend. The guarantor gives his bond and gets nothing in return. The common law will not interfere. Parliament has intervened to prevent moneylenders charging excessive interest. But it has never interfered with banks.

Yet there are exceptions to this general rule. There are cases in our books in which the courts will set aside a contract, or a transfer of property, when the parties have not met on equal terms, when the one is so strong in bargaining power and the other so weak that, as a matter of common fairness, it is not right that the strong should be allowed to push the weak to the wall. Hitherto those exceptional cases have been treated each as a separate category in itself. But I think the time has come when we should seek to find a principle to unite them. I put on one side contracts or transactions which are voidable for fraud or misrepresentation or mistake. All those are governed by settled principles. I go only to those where there has been inequality of bargaining power, such as to merit the intervention of the court.

THE CATEGORIES

The first category is that of 'duress of goods'. A typical case is when a man is in a strong bargaining position by being in possession of the goods of another by virtue of a legal right, such as, by way of pawn or pledge or taken in distress. The owner is in a weak position because he is in urgent need of the goods. The stronger demands of the weaker more than is justly due, and he pays it in order to get the goods. Such a transaction is voidable. He can recover the excess: see *Astley v. Reynolds* and *Green v. Duckett*. To which may be added the cases of 'colore officii', where a man is in a strong bargaining position by virtue of his official position or public profession. He relies on it so as to gain from the weaker — who is urgently in need — more than is justly due: see *Pigot's Case* cited by Lord Kenyon C.J.; *Parker v. Bristol and Exeter Railway Co.* and *Steele v. Williams*. In such cases the stronger may make his claim in good faith honestly believing that he is entitled to make his demand. He may not be guilty of any fraud or misrepresentation. The inequality of bargaining power — the strength of the one versus the urgent need of the other — renders the transaction voidable and the money paid to be recovered back: see *Maskell v. Horner*.

The second category is that of the 'unconscionable transaction'. A man is so placed as to be in need of special care and protection and yet his weakness is exploited by another far stronger than himself so as to get his property at a gross undervalue. The typical case is that of the 'expectant heir'. But it applies to all cases where a man comes into property, or is expected to come into it, and then being in urgent need another gives him ready cash for it, greatly below its true worth, and so gets the property transferred to him: see *Evans v. Llewellin*. Even though there be no evidence of fraud or misrepresentation, nevertheless the transaction will be set side: see *Fry v. Lane* where Kay J. said:

> The result of the decisions is that where a purchase is made from a poor and ignorant man at a considerable undervalue, the vendor having no independent advice, a Court of Equity will set aside the transaction.

This second category is said to extend to all cases where an unfair advantage has been gained by an unconscientious use of power by a stronger party against a weaker: see the cases cited in Halsbury's Law of England and in Canada, *Morrison v. Coast Finance Ltd.* and *Knupp v. Bell*.

The third category is that of 'undue influence' usually so called. These are divided into two classes as stated by Cotton L.J. in *Allcard v. Skinner*. The first are these where the stronger has been guilty of some fraud or wrongful act — expressly so as to gain some gift or advantage from the weaker. The second are those where the stronger has not been guilty of any wrongful act, but has, through the relationship which existed between him and the weaker, gained some gift or advantage for himself. Sometimes the relationship is such as to raise a presumption of undue influence, such as parent over child, solicitor over client, doctor over patient, spiritual adviser over follower. At other times a relationship of confidence must be proved to exist. But to all of them the general principle obtains which was stated by Lord Chelmsford L.C. in *Tate v. Williamson*:

> Wherever the persons stand in such a relation that, while it continues, confidence is necessarily reposed by one, and the influence which naturally grows out of that confidence is possessed by the other, and this confidence is abused, or the influence is exerted to obtain an advantage at the expense of the confiding party, the person so availing himself of his position will not be permitted to retain the advantage, although the transaction could not have been impeached if no such confidential relation had existed.

Such a case was *Tufton v. Sperni*.

The fourth category is that of 'undue pressure'. The most apposite of that is *Williams v. Bayley* where a son forged his father's name to a promissory note, and, by means of it, raised money from the bank of which they were both customers. The bank said to the father, in effect: 'Take your choice — give us security for your son's debt. If you do take that on yourself, then it will all go smoothly; if you do not, we shall be bound to exercise pressure.' Thereupon the father charged his property to the bank with payment of the note. The House of Lords held that the charge was invalid because of undue pressure exerted by the bank. Lord Westbury said:

> A contract to give security for the debt of another, which is a contract without consideration, is, above all things, a contract that should be based upon the free and voluntary agency of the individual who enters into it.

Other instances of undue pressure are where one party stipulates for an unfair advantage to which the other has no option but to submit. As where an employer — the stronger party — had employed a builder — the weaker party — to do work for him. When the builder asked for payment of sums properly due (so as to pay his workmen) the employer refused to pay unless he was given some added advantage. Stuart V-C said:

> 'Where an agreement, hard and inequitable in itself, has been exacted under circumstances of pressure on the part of the person who exacts it this Court will set it aside': see *Ormes v. Beadel*; *D & C Builders Ltd. v. Rees*.

The fifth category is that of salvage agreements. When a vessel is in danger of sinking and seeks help, the rescuer is in a strong bargaining position. The vessel in distress is in urgent need. The parties cannot be truly said to be on equal terms. The Court of Admiralty have always recognised that fact. The fundamental rule is:

> If the parties have made an agreement, the Court will enforce it, unless it be manifestly unfair and unjust; but if it be manifestly unfair and unjust, the Court will disregard it and decree what is fair and just.

See *Akerblom v. Price*, *per* Brett L.J. applied in a striking case, *The Port Caledonia and The Anna*, when the rescuer refused to help with a rope unless he was paid £1,000.

THE GENERAL PRINCIPLES

Gathering all together, I would suggest that through all these instances there runs a single thread. They rest on 'inequality of bargaining power'. By virtue of it, the English law gives relief to one who, without independent advice, enters into a contract of terms which are very unfair or transfers property for a consideration which is grossly inadequate, when his bargaining power is grievously impaired by reason of his own needs or desires, or by his own ignorance or infirmity, coupled with undue influences or pressures brought to bear on him by or for the benefit of the other. When I use the word 'undue' I do not mean to suggest that the principle depends on proof of any wrongdoing. The one who stipulates for an unfair advantage may be moved solely by his own self-interest, unconscious of the distress he is bringing to the other. I have also avoided any reference to the will of the one being 'dominated' or 'overcome' by the other. One who is in extreme need may knowingly consent to a most improvident bargain, solely to relieve the straits in which he finds himself. Again, I do not mean to suggest that every transaction is saved by independent advice. But the absence of it may be fatal. With these explanations, I hope this principle will be found to reconcile the cases. Applying it to the present case, I would notice these points.

1. The consideration moving from the bank was grossly inadequate. The son's company was in serious difficulty. The overdraft was at its limit of £10,000. The bank considered that their existing security was insufficient. In order to get further security, they asked the father to charge the house — his sole asset — to the uttermost. It was worth £10,000. The charge was for £11,000. That was for the benefit of the bank. But not at all for the benefit of the father, or indeed for the company. The bank did not promise to continue the overdraft or to increase it. On the contrary, they required the overdraft to be reduced. All that the company gained was a short respite from impending doom.
2. The relationship between the bank and the father was one of trust and confidence. The bank knew that the father relied on them implicitly to advise him about the transaction. The father trusted the bank. This gave the bank much influence on the father. Yet the bank failed in that trust. They allowed the father to charge the house to his ruin.
3. The relationship between the father and the son was one where the father's natural affection had much influence on him.

4. He would naturally desire to accede to his son's request. He trusted his son. There was a conflict of interest between the bank and the father. Yet the bank did not realise it. Nor did they suggest that the father should get independent advice. If the father had gone to his solicitor — or to any man of business — there is no doubt that any of them would say: 'You must not enter into this transaction. You are giving up your house, your sole remaining asset, for no benefit to you. The company is in such a parlous state that you must not do it.'

These considerations seem to me to bring this case within the principles I have stated. But, in case that principle is wrong, I would also say that the case falls within the category of undue influence of the second class stated by Cotton L.J. in *Allcard v. Skinner*. I have no doubt that the assistant bank manager acted in the utmost good faith and was straightforward and genuine. Indeed the father said so. But beyond doubt he was acting in the interests of the bank — to get further security for a bad debt. There was such a relationship of trust and confidence between them that the bank ought not to have swept up his sole remaining asset into their hands — for nothing — without his having independent advice. I would therefore allow this appeal.

(f) *Pelech v. Pelech*†

[WILSON J.:]

Section 11(2) of the *Divorce Act*, R.S.C. 1970, c. D-8, confers on the court the power to vary a previous order for maintenance "having regard to the conduct of the parties since the making of the order or any change in the condition, means or other circumstances of either of them". This appeal specifically addresses the extent of the constraints, if any, imposed on that power by the existence of

---

† [1987] 1 S.C.R. 801.

a valid and enforceable maintenance agreement. Should the parties be held to the terms of their contract or should the court intervene to remedy the inequities now alleged by one of the parties to be flowing from the bargain previously entered into freely and [in] full knowledge and with the advice of counsel?

. . . . . .

I.   THE FACTS

The parties were married in 1954. They had two children. The respondent, Mr. Pelech, ran a general contracting business which later expanded and diversified. The appellant assisted her husband by acting as a receptionist and bookkeeper until the mid-1960's. The parties were divorced on May 1, 1969. Wilson C.J. of the British Columbia Supreme Court who presided at the petition for divorce found that Mrs. Pelech had serious psychological problems and awarded custody of the children to Mr. Pelech. He also awarded Mrs. Pelech permanent maintenance and referred the case to the Registrar for recommendations in this regard.

The parties, after obtaining the advice of counsel, entered into a maintenance agreement on September 15, 1969 which was approved by the Registrar. The agreement provided for a total payment of $28,760 over a period of thirteen months. Clause (b) of the agreement stated:

> (b) The Petitioner agrees to accept the foregoing periodic payments in full satisfaction of all claim she now has or may have in the future for maintenance from the Respondent.

Mrs. Pelech also agreed to transfer to Mr. Pelech one share which she held in a business operated by him. The agreement, on the recommendation of the Registrar and with the consent of the parties, was confirmed and incorporated into an order of the court. Mrs. Pelech subsequently transferred the share to Mr. Pelech and Mr. Pelech paid the maintenance monies as agreed. Mrs. Pelech was 37 years old at the time of the divorce and Mr. Pelech 44.

At the time of the divorce in 1969 Mr. Pelech's net worth was $128,000. Fifteen years later, when the current application to vary the original order was heard, that net worth had increased to $1,800,000. The intervening years were not so kind to Mrs. Pelech. She invested most of the money she received for maintenance and

endeavoured to live on the interest from it supplemented by income she was able to earn from temporary work as a bookkeeper and sales clerk. However, over the years her psychological problems increased and were compounded by severe physical problems. Because of her bad health she was often unable to work and she encroached on the capital of her maintenance fund in order to survive. In April 1982 the fund was depleted and Mrs. Pelech applied for social assistance. Later that same year she received an inheritance which enabled her to make a $15,000 down payment on a bachelor apartment. The balance of the purchase price was financed with a $16,000 mortgage. The judge at first instance summarized the state of Mrs. Pelech's affairs at the time of this application as follows:

> The wife currently receives monthly welfare payments of $430, from which she pays all her living expenses. Other than the mortgage, she has no other debt. At present, this woman is definitely living at a poverty existence level. The medical prognosis for her future ability to undertake gainful employment appears to be guarded. In view of the wife's history of ongoing disabilities together with her inability to either obtain or retain gainful employment for any appreciable period of time, I think the realistic prospects of this 53-year-old woman to obtain any type of future gainful employment will be most unlikely.

Mrs. Pelech is now 54 years old and Mr. Pelech 61. The two children are grown up and fend for themselves.

. . . .

V.   PRELIMINARY OBSERVATIONS

The central issue in this case concerns the effect of a valid and enforceable antecedent settlement agreement on the court's discretionary power under s. 11(2) to vary maintenance orders. Some preliminary observations might be helpful.

The first observation concerns the principle that a maintenance agreement can never totally extinguish the jurisdiction of the court to impose its own terms on the parties. This principle derives from the House of Lords' decision in *Hyman v. Hyman*, [1929] A.C. 601. In that case, Lord Hailsham L.C. stated at p. 614:

> However this may be, it is sufficient for the decision of the present case to hold, as I do, that the power of the Court to make provision

for a wife on the dissolution of her marriage is a necessary incident of the power to decree such a dissolution, conferred not merely in the interests of the wife, but of the public, and that the wife cannot by her own covenant preclude herself from invoking the jurisdiction of the Court or preclude the Court from the exercise of that jurisdiction.

The view that a freely negotiated and informed waiver of legal rights cannot oust the jurisdiction of the court is supported by the language of s. 11(2) and by the case law. Although the recent decision of this Court in *Messier v. Delage*, [1983] 2 S.C.R. 401, did not involve a maintenance agreement, the *Hyman* principle underlies the view expressed by Chouinard J., speaking for the majority of the Court, that s. 11(1) orders can never be truly final. Chouinard J. described the implications of the scheme in s. 11 in the following passage at pp. 411–12:

> In the case at bar the issue turned exclusively on s. 11 of the *Divorce Act*. Subsection (2) of that section is concerned with four factors:
> (a) the conduct of the parties;
> (b) their respective conditions;
> (c) their means;
> (d) the other circumstances of either of them.

Section 11(2) states that an order may be varied from time to time or rescinded in light of the foregoing factors, which the Court must weigh against each other. In my opinion what is significant about this subsection is that an order is never final. It may be varied from time to time or rescinded if the Court thinks it fit and just to do so, taking these factors into consideration.

Hyman and *Messier* settle the narrow issue of the court's jurisdiction to intervene. However, they do not answer the broader question of when it is fit and just to exercise that jurisdiction having regard to the enumerated factors. Accordingly, the second observation I would make concerns the change in emphasis which has occurred since the enactment of the current legislation in 1968. The jurisprudence discloses a distinct movement away from the concept of moral blameworthiness or "fault" and towards a search for what is fair and reasonable having regard to all the circumstances of the parties including their means and needs.

. . . .

The change in focus from apportionment of blame to an assessment of what is reasonable

based on the needs and means of the parties applies both to orders made under s. 11(1) as in *Connelly* and variation orders made under s. 11(2) as in *Katz*. In the latter context the added criterion of change can thus be viewed in terms of changes in circumstance which make the original order no longer fair and reasonable.

The third and final observation I want to make concerns the significance under s. 11 of the fact that the parties have themselves agreed on the issue of maintenance. It is clear from the case law that this has to be an important factor in the court's consideration under either subs. (1) or (2). It is clear also that it has a significant impact on the degree or nature of the change in circumstances required to trigger the s. 11(2) discretion. Unfortunately, the extent of this impact has eluded definition. Blair J.A. in *Webb v. Webb* (1984), 39 R.F.L. (2d) 113 (Ont. C.A.), summarizes at p. 131 the various attempts to do so:

> Canadian courts have recognized, when making or varying maintenance orders pursuant to s. 11 of the Divorce Act, that a pre-existing agreement cannot be "lightly disregarded", as Morden J.A. said in *Harrington v. Harrington* (1981), 33 O.R. (2d) 150 at 154, 22 R.F.L. (2d) 40 at 45, 123 D.L.R. (3d) 689 (C.A.). A more rigorous test applies to the change of circumstances justifying a departure from the terms of an agreement, upon which a divorce decree is based, than applies to ordinary applications for variation under s. 11(2). A variety of words, phrases and epithets have been used to describe this higher standard including a "very significant change (of) circumstances" in *Bjornson v. Bjornson* (1970), 2 R.F.L. 414 at 415 (B.C.C.A.), Davey C.J.B.C; a "gross" change in *Ditullio v. Ditullio* (1974), 3 O.R. (2d) 519, 16 R.F.L. 148 at 151, 46 D.L.R. (3d) 66 (H.C.), DuPont L.J.S.C; an "unexpected change ... quite outside the realization of expectations" in *Burns v. Burns*, [1963] 2 O.R. 142 at 146, 38 D.L.R. (2d) 572 (H.C.), Gale J; and "not only some change in circumstances but conditions which arouse the conscience of the court, and call for action" in *Poste v. Poste*, [1973] 2 O.R. 674 at 676, 11 R.F.L. 264, 35 D.L.R. (3d) 71 (H.C.) Wright J.

The inevitable imprecision of such a standard has created great uncertainty and lies at the heart of the divergence of views expressed by the parties and by the courts below in the present appeal. An examination of the case law reveals that the spectrum of opinion ranges from an extremely restrictive approach, which would allow intervention only where children are at risk or where the agreement is unconscionable, to a very broad approach which gives the parties' agreement very little weight and affirms the position of the court as the arbiter of what is fair and reasonable.

These preliminary observations may be summed up as follows:

1) It is a well established principle that the court's supervisory jurisdiction over maintenance cannot be extinguished by contract.
2) The general trend of the case law in fashioning maintenance orders has been to move away from "fault" and achieve an arrangement that is fair and reasonable in light of all the circumstances of the parties including their means and needs.
3) While it is generally accepted that the existence of an antecedent settlement agreement made by the parties is an important fact, there is a wide range of views as to how this affects the legal principles governing the exercise of the discretion conferred in s. 11.

VI. ALTERNATIVE VIEWS

Lambert J.A.'s decision in the Court of Appeal reflects the view that an antecedent settlement agreement effectively restricts the power of the court under s. 11 of the *Divorce Act*. The clearest expression of this view is to be found in the judgment of the Ontario Court of Appeal in *Farquar v. Farquar, supra,* in which Zuber J.A. held that the courts should overturn a valid and enforceable maintenance agreement only in "a narrow range of cases".

A very different and arguably more paternalistic philosophy is manifest in judgments of the Manitoba Court of Appeal such as *Newman v. Newman* (1980), 4 Man. R. (2d) 50 which minimize the importance of freedom of contract and impose on the parties a judicial standard of reasonableness notwithstanding their agreement to the contrary.

A third "compromise" view emerges from *Webb* where Blair J.A. suggests that the change in circumstances which triggers the court's discretionary power in s. 11(2) must be a "gross" or "catastrophic" change.

Finally, a fourth possibility is suggested by recurrent references in the case-law to specific categories of change as a justification for judicial intervention rather than simply change of a certain magnitude.

A. The "Private Choice" Approach

In *Farquar* the respondent wife expressly waived her right to maintenance in the minutes of settlement which were incorporated in the divorce decree. A year later she applied for a s. 11(2) variation and was granted a lump sum order. The husband appealed. Zuber J.A., for a unanimous court, agreed that the maintenance provisions imposed by the trial judge were much more appropriate than those arrived at by the parties in the minutes of settlement. However, he found that that was not the issue before him; the issue before him was whether the settlement should be respected and precluded judicial intervention.

Zuber J.A. started with the proposition that it is preferable for parties to settle their own affairs. He gave a number of reasons for this including that (1) the parties are more likely to accept and live with an arrangement they have made themselves as opposed to one imposed upon them; (2) the administrative burden of the courts is relieved by respecting the parties' freedom of contract; and (3) treating the agreement reached by the parties as final allows them to plan their separate futures with relative peace of mind. In this last regard Zuber J.A. quoted from Anderson J.'s decision in *Dal Santo v. Dal Santo, supra,* at p. 120:

> It is of great importance not only to the parties but to the community as a whole that contracts of this kind should not be lightly disturbed. Lawyers must be able to advise their clients in respect of their future rights and obligations with some degree of certainty. Clients must be able to rely on these agreements and know with some degree of assurance that once a separation agreement is executed their affairs have been settled on a permanent basis. The courts must encourage parties to settle their differences without recourse to litigation. The modern approach in family law is to mediate and conciliate so as to enable the parties to make a fresh start in life on a secure basis. If separation agreements can be varied at will, it will become much more difficult to persuade the parties to enter into such agreements.

Zuber J.A. also observed that property issues and maintenance issues are nowadays frequently intertwined in the terms of a settlement. Thus, it might be quite unfair to alter the provisions for maintenance without also altering the division of property.

Zuber J.A. acknowledged that there were nevertheless two kinds of circumstance in which a settlement is not binding. The first is where the settlement is invalid according to traditional common law or equitable doctrines. The second is [composed] of "that narrow range of cases where a court will relieve against a matrimonial settlement even though the contract is valid" (p. 252). Unfortunately, Zuber J.A. did not find it necessary to elaborate on this "narrow range of cases" other than to reject the notion that change by itself is a determining factor. In this regard he said at p. 253:

> In my respectful view, changed circumstances, even substantially changed circumstances, are not a sufficient basis for avoiding the minutes of settlement. It is inevitable that the circumstances of the contracting parties will change following the agreement. If the change of circumstances would allow a party to avoid an otherwise enforceable agreement, then it is apparent that no separation agreement or minutes of settlement can ever finally resolve anything. If the parties agree to settle their affairs, then their affairs should be regarded as settled. Changed circumstances, however, are not irrelevant. If the agreement is vulnerable on some other basis the new circumstances of the parties will be a factor in the determination of the amount of maintenance.

Zuber J.A. applied these principles to the case before him and concluded that the Court had no basis on which to intervene and that the settlement freely negotiated by the parties should be respected.

B. The Court's Overriding Power

The core values underlying the approach in *Farquar* are those of individual responsibility and freedom of contract. An opposing view is to be found in the judgments of the Manitoba Court of Appeal in *Newman v. Newman, supra, Katz v. Katz, supra,* and *Ross v. Ross* (1984), 39 R.F.L. (2d) 51. In this line of cases the Court asserts its supervisory role and finds that it is not significantly constrained by the presence of a binding agreement. Although the Court often acknowledges that the existence of an agreement is an important circumstance to be considered and that finality in the ordering of post-marital obligations is a laudable objective, a finding that the agreement does not meet the court's standard of fairness or reasonableness justifies an exercise of the s. 11(2) power.

In *Newman*, Monnin J.A. (as he then was), Matas J.A. concurring considered the relevance of a prior separation agreement to a s. 11(1) order for maintenance and stated at p. 52:

> I have always been and still am of the view that under Sec. 11 of the *Divorce Act*, a court can do what it thinks proper under the circumstances with respect to maintenance for the wife and children and the hands of the court cannot be fettered by a written agreement executed by the parties. It is clear though that, in order to encourage at all times this type of settlement, rather than to encourage litigation between the spouses, the court should not lightly disturb the terms of a duly negotiated contract. But if the court feels that there is need for change, it allows it.

. . . .

In *Katz*, Monnin J.A. and Hall J.A. in separate reasons both acknowledged that the agreement entered into by the parties was a factor to be considered but went on to suggest that, where the dependent spouse can demonstrate a need, a variation could be granted. Hall J.A. rejected the trial judge's test of "moving hardship" in the following passage at p. 422:

> With great respect, it is my opinion that it is both fit and just to grant the wife a variation, having regard to the change in her circumstances and the presumed financial ability of the husband to afford those changes. Indeed, I am sure he would want to make them if the law so provides, notwithstanding that the settlement agreement is being varied. In my view, the test is what is reasonable rather than one of moving hardship. What is the just course for the husband to follow? The settlement agreement is only a factor to be taken into account and is not conclusive of the issue of variation.

This broad approach to the court's discretion under s. 11 has recently been affirmed in *Ross*. In that case the parties negotiated a settlement which in the court's view did not reflect the husband's relatively extensive financial resources. There was evidence that during the negotiations the husband pressured the wife with threats into accepting his offer. However, the wife did have assistance from independent counsel before executing the contract and in fact a certificate of independent legal advice was attached to the agreement. Hall J.A., with whom Monnin C.J.M. and O'Sullivan J.A. concurred, after stating that the contract was an "important circumstance" and should not be "lightly disturbed", went on to hold at p. 54:

> But where, as here, there exists an unfair and unbalanced settlement arrived at in the circumstances described, I think the learned trial judge was justified in making the award which he did. In other words, it was reasonable in the circumstances for him to have added a lump sum award maintenance to that provided in the separation agreement.

Matas J.A. also approved of the trial judge's test of what is fair and reasonable. His reasons, however, are especially useful in that he discussed the underlying rationale for advocating a larger role for the courts. At page 64 he wrote:

> In my opinion, we have not yet reached the stage where we can safely say that generally husbands and wives are equal or nearly so, in earning capacity, or where we can necessarily say that generally the responsibilities of marriage have not disadvantaged the earning potential of the wife. In many cases, especially of more recent marriages, the courts could rely on the fairness of imposing an obligation on the wife to quickly become self-supporting. In some cases, the court could not.

Only Huband J.A. in dissent took issue with the broad flexible approach of the majority. He wrote at p. 68:

> I subscribe to the general statement in the reasons of Hall J.A. that the court has the right to depart from the terms of a separation agreement under certain circumstances. Differences, however, arise in attempting to determine those proper circumstances. As Hall J.A. has noted, the presence of a separation agreement is an important circumstance for the court to take into account when exercising jurisdiction under s. 11(1) of the *Divorce Act*, R.S.C. 1970, c. D-8. The question is no longer what is reasonable maintenance, but, rather, what is reasonable maintenance, given that the parties have executed an agreement to determine that issue? Normally, a separation agreement constitutes a formidable limitation on the court's discretion. If it were not so, there would be no point in parties bothering to negotiate an out-of-court maintenance agreement. What is reasonable maintenance must be determined in light of a valid, voluntary separation agreement. Conversely, it is prima facie unreasonable for a party to such an agreement to take benefits under the contract and then seek court assistance to obtain more favourable maintenance arrangements.

And later at pp. 73–74:

> With respect, I do not think that the fact that a separation agreement is, or seems to be, unfair to one of the parties, is a sufficient foundation for the court to vary the terms of a separation agreement. There are many contracts which, in retrospect, may be viewed as "unfair" to one of the contracting parties, but that is not, of itself, in law or in equity, a basis for altering the agreement.

Huband J.A. went on to find that the application to vary should be dismissed.

In summary, the Manitoba decisions do not distinguish in any significant manner between applications for maintenance in the face of an antecedent agreement and applications in which there is no such agreement. The court exercises its discretion on the basis of what it considers fair and reasonable whether or not the parties have, in effect, settled their own financial affairs.

. . . .

VII.   CONCLUSIONS

The need to compensate for systemic gender-based inequality advanced by Matas J.A. in *Ross* forms a counterpoint to the need for finality identified by Anderson J. in *Dal Santo* and approved by Zuber J.A. in *Farquar* and Lambert J.A. in the present appeal. The Alberta Court of Appeal in *Jull* describes the tension in terms of the competing values of fairness and freedom. While I am in sympathy with Matas J.A.'s concern, I believe that the case by case approach and the continuing surveillance by the courts over the consensual arrangements of former spouses which he advocates will ultimately reinforce the very bias he seeks to counteract. In addition, I believe that every encouragement should be given to ex-spouses to settle their financial affairs in a final way so that they can put their mistakes behind them and get on with their lives. I would, with all due respect, reject the Manitoba Court of Appeal's broad and unrestricted interpretation of the court's jurisdiction in maintenance matters. It seems to me that it goes against the main stream of recent authority, both legislative and judicial, which emphasizes mediation, conciliation and negotiation as the appropriate means of settling the affairs of the spouses when the marriage relationship dissolves.

However, as I stated at the outset, the *Hyman* principle that parties cannot by contract oust the jurisdiction of the court in matters of spousal maintenance is an established tenet of Canadian law. The question thus becomes the nature and extent of the constraint imposed on the courts by the presence of an agreement which was intended by the parties to settle their affairs in a final and conclusive manner. The *Webb* standard of catastrophic change (by which is meant, I believe, that the change must be "dramatic" or "radical" or "gross", not that it must be the result of a catastrophy [*sic*]) is one attempt to reconcile the competing values represented by *Farquar* and *Ross* and still remain within the ambit of the *Hyman* principle and the language of the statute. However, although I agree that radical change should be an important factor in a court's decision to interfere with freely negotiated minutes of settlement, by itself it provides too imprecise a standard. It fails to relate the change in any way to the fact of the marriage so as to justify attributing responsibility for it to the former spouse. Moreover, the legitimation offered in *Webb* and by Wong L.J.S.C. in the present appeal in terms of a change which negates a fundamental premise of the contract provides no guidance whatsoever in cases of totally unexpected and unanticipated misfortunes.

The approach taken by Zuber J.A. in *Farquar* also falls short of articulating a workable criterion by failing to identify the requisites of the "narrow range of cases". I do, however, agree with Zuber J.A.'s emphasis on the importance of finality in the financial affairs of former spouses and that considerable deference should be paid to the right and the responsibility of individuals to make their own decisions.

It seems to me that where the parties have negotiated their own agreement, freely and on the advice of independent legal counsel, as to how their financial affairs should be settled on the breakdown of their marriage, and the agreement is not unconscionable in the substantive law sense, it should be respected. People should be encouraged to take responsibility for their own lives and their own decisions. This should be the overriding policy consideration.

. . . .

Absent some causal connection between the changed circumstances and the marriage, it seems to me that parties who have declared their relationship at an end should be taken at their word.

They made the decision to marry and they made the decision to terminate their marriage. Their decisions should be respected. They should thereafter be free to make new lives for themselves without an ongoing contingent liability for future misfortunes which may befall the other. It is only, in my view, where the future misfortune has its genesis in the fact of the marriage that the court should be able to override the settlement of their affairs made by the parties themselves. Each marriage relationship creates its own economic pattern from which the self-sufficiency or dependency of the partners flows. The assessment of the extent of that pattern's post-marital impact is essentially a matter for the judge of first instance. The causal connection between the severe hardship being experienced by the former spouse and the marriage provides, in my view, the necessary legal criterion for determining when a case falls within the "narrow range of cases" referred to by Zuber J.A. in *Farquar*. It is this element which is missing in *Webb*. Accordingly, where an applicant seeking maintenance or an increase in the existing level of maintenance establishes that he or she has suffered a radical change in circumstances flowing from an economic pattern of dependency engendered by the marriage, the court may exercise its relieving power. Otherwise, the obligation to support the former spouse should be, as in the case of any other citizen, the communal responsibility of the state.

VIII. DISPOSITION OF THE APPEAL

The dependency of the appellant Mrs. Pelech on social assistance is evidence of the extremity of her need. In addition, there are the observations of Wong L.J.S.C. at trial that her impoverishment is dire and her future prospects limited if not non-existent. However, although I agree with him that her present state evidences "a gross change in circumstances" since the time of the original order incorporating the minutes of settlement in 1969, no link is found by the trial judge between the change of circumstances and her former marriage to Mr. Pelech. Indeed, quite the contrary. Wong L.J.S.C. found that the psychological problems which have resulted in her inability to care for herself predated the marriage and contributed to its failure. He specifically rejected the submission that they stemmed from the marriage or from the behaviour of the respondent during it.

Wong L.J.S.C. also rejected the submission that the agreement was improvident and unconscionable. He found that it was entered into freely by Mrs. Pelech on the advice of counsel and was perfectly fair at the time it was made. He found, however, that the basic premise on which it was entered into, namely that Mrs. Pelech would be able to work and support herself, had not materialized.

While I realize that Mrs. Pelech's present hardship is great, to burden the respondent with her care fifteen years after their marriage has ended for no other reason than that they were once husband and wife seems to me to create a fiction of marital responsibility at the expense of individual responsibility. I believe that the courts must recognize the right of the individual to end a relationship as well as to begin one and should not, when all other aspects of the relationship have long since ceased, treat the financial responsibility as continuing indefinitely into the future. Where parties, instead of resorting to litigation, have acted in a mature and responsible fashion to settle their financial affairs in a final way and their settlement is not vulnerable to attack on any other basis, it should not, in my view, be undermined by courts concluding with the benefit of hindsight that they should have done it differently.

For these reasons I would dismiss the appeal. I would make no award as to costs.

Consequences of Non-Performance in Contract

(a) *Hadley v. Baxendale*†

[ALDERSON, BARON for the Court:]

We think that there ought to be a new trial in this case, but, in so doing, we deem it to be expedient and necessary to state explicitly the rule which the Judge, at the next trial, ought, in our opinion, to direct the jury to be governed by when they estimate the damages....

Now we think the proper rule in such a case as the present is this: Where two parties have made a contract which one of them has broken, the damages which the other party ought to receive in respect of such breach of contract should be such as may fairly and reasonably be considered either arising naturally, *i.e.*, according to the usual course of things, from such breach of contract itself, or such as may reasonably be supposed to have been in the contemplation of both parties, at the time they made the contract, as the probable result of the breach of it. Now, if the special circumstances under which the contract was actually made were communicated by the plaintiffs to the defendants, and thus known to both parties, the damages resulting from the breach of such a contract, which they would reasonably contemplate, would be the amount of injury which would ordinarily follow from a breach of contract under these special circumstances so known and communicated. But, on the other hand, if these special circumstances were wholly unknown to the party breaking the contract, he, at the most, could only be supposed to have had in his contemplation the amount of injury which would arise generally, and in the great multitude of cases not affected by any special circumstances, from such a breach of contract. For, had the special circumstances been known, the parties might have specially provided for the breach of contract by special terms as to the damages in that case; and of this advantage it would be very unjust to deprive them.

[A new trial was ordered.]

---

† (1854), 9 Exch. 341, 156 E.R. 145.

(b) *Hadley v. Baxendale*, A Study in the Industrialization of the Law†

Richard Danzig

II.

The novelty of the changes effected in procedural and substantive law by *Hadley v. Baxendale* suggests that the opinion may be examined as an invention. The innovation effected in the law is here unusually stark. Baron Alderson, in support of the central proposition he advanced, cited no precedent and invoked no British legislative or academic authority in favor of the rule he articulated. Nor was this due to oversight. The opinion broke new ground by establishing a rule for decision by judges in an area of law — the calculation of damages in contracts suits — which had previously been left to almost entirely unstructured decision by English juries.

. . . .

III.

To understand the origins and the limitations of the rule in *Hadley v. Baxendale* we must appreciate the industrial and legal world out of which it came and for which it was designed. In 1854 Great Britain was in a state of extraordinary flux. Between 1801 and 1851 its population rose from 10.6 to 20.9 million people and its gross national product increased from £10.7 to £523.3 million. By 1861 its population was 23.2 million and its GNP £668.0 million. Contemporaries saw the magnitude of this change and were aware of its impact on the law. As one writer, surveying the scene in 1863, put it:

> What our Law was then [in 1828], it is not now; and what it is now, can best be understood by seeing what it was, then. It is like the comparison between England under former, and present, systems of transit, for persons, property, and intelligence: between the days of lumbering wagons, stage coaches, and a creeping post — and of swift, luxurious rail-

roads and [lightning] telegraphs. All is altered: material, inducing corresponding moral and social changes.

Arising squarely in the middle of the "industrial revolution" and directly in the midst of the "Great Boom" of 1842–1874, *Hadley v. Baxendale* was a product of these times. The case was shaped by the increasing sophistication of the economy and the law — and equally significantly by the gaps, the naiveté, and the crudeness of the contemporary system.

The raw facts of the case should alert the reader to the half-matured and unevenly developing nature of the economy in which the decision was rendered. For example, the Hadley mill was steam-powered. While it was not hand-run, animal-driven, wind-powered, or water-powered, as in an earlier age, it was also not powered by electricity as it would be in the next century. So with the now famous broken shaft. It was a complicated piece of machinery, manufactured by a specialized company on the other side of England. But it was neither a standardized nor a mass-produced machine. It was handcrafted. Thus, the transaction in *Hadley v. Baxendale*: the old shaft had to be brought to eastern England as the "model" for the new one.

The circumstances of the breach similarly reflect a half-way modernized society. The breach occurred because the shaft was sent by canal, the early industrial transport form, rather than by rail, the mature industrial transport form. That both co-existed as significant means of shipment suggests the transitional nature of the period. The ready acceptance of the notion that delay gave rise to damages, that time meant money, suggests the affinity of the modes of thought of this age to our own. But the units of account for measuring time in *Hadley v. Baxendale* suggest the distance between our period and this one: speed for a trip across England was measured in days, not hours.

---

† (1975) 4 Journal of Legal Studies 249 at 254–55, 259–64. [Notes and/or References omitted.] Reproduced with permission of University of Chicago Press via RightsLink.

If the facts of the case offer us a glimpse of an economic world in transition, what of the legal system which had to deal with that transition? This system was also modernizing, but, at the time of *Hadley v. Baxendale*, it was still strikingly underdeveloped. The case itself indicates the rudimentary and uneven development of the commercial law of the period. *Hadley v. Baxendale* is frequently described as a case involving a claim for damages consequent on a breach of a negotiated contract for especially quick delivery of a consigned package; but in fact, although this was the first of two counts on which the Hadleys initially pressed their suit, both the official and the contemporary press reports make it clear that before going to trial against Baxendale they abandoned all claim to damages based on a specific contract. Instead their pleadings claimed damages arising as a consequence of Pickford's failure to effect delivery "within a reasonable time" as it was obliged to do because of its status as a common carrier. If, as Maine posited ten years after *Hadley v. Baxendale*, the process of modernization involves a movement from status to contract, this most famed of modern contract cases is peculiarly antiquarian!

The pleadings' emphasis on status rather than contract appears to have been related to the underdeveloped nature of the law of agency in England at the time. The *Gloucester Journal* report of the Assize trial comments:

> The declaration had originally contained two counts; the first charging the defendants with having contracted to deliver the crank within the space of two days, which they did in truth do, but there was a doubt how far Mr. Perrett, the agent of the defendants, had authority to bind them by any special contract which would vary their ordinary liability. It was therefore thought not prudent to proceed upon that count, but upon the count of not delivering within a reasonable time.

The Hadleys' counsel apparently reasoned that a jury verdict against Baxendale predicated on what was said to or by the Pickfords' clerk might be upset by an appellate court on a theory that personal liability could not be imputed to Baxendale through comment to or by an agent. The situation was summarized by Baxendale's counsel in the argument on appeal:

> Here the declaration is founded upon the defendants' duty as common carriers, and indeed there is no pretense for saying that they entered into a special contract to bear all

the consequences of the non-delivery of the article in question. They were merely bound to carry it safely, and to deliver it within a reasonable time. The duty of the clerk, who was in attendance at the defendants' office, was to enter the article, and to take the amount of the carriage; but a mere notice to him, such as was here given, could not make the defendants, as carriers, liable as upon a special contract. Such matters, therefore, must be rejected from the consideration of the question.

Baxendale's counsel here overstates the case, but at the least it appears that there was an uncertainty in the rudimentary law of agency as it existed at the time.

This uncertainty may explain Baron Alderson's surprising assertion that the Hadleys failed to serve notice that the mill operations were dependent on the quick return of the shaft. It may be that as a factual matter the Hadleys never served notice on the Pickfords' clerk of their extreme dependence on the shaft, and that the Court reporter simply erred in asserting that notice had been served to this effect. But it is also possible that Baron Alderson saw the case as the Pickfords' counsel urged: "... a mere notice ... was here given ... [but it] could not make the defendants liable ... [and therefore it was to] be rejected from the consideration of the question."

This agency problem underscores the fact that the case is *Hadley v. Baxendale*, not *Hadley v. Pickford's Moving Co.*; in other words, that the opinion was handed down at a time and in a situation in which principals were personally liable for the misfeasance of their companies. Although the principle of limited liability was already recognized in England for exceptional "chartered" companies, it was not until 1855 that Parliament extended the right to ordinary entrepreneurs, and it was not until 1901 that Pickfords (and many other companies) incorporated. In 1854 the desirability of limiting personal liability for corporate debts was a major item of parliamentary debate and the legal world's most hotly disputed subject. This contemporary ferment was fed by, and in turn reinforced, related areas of concern about the run of liability: a Royal Commission was meeting in 1854 to consider expanding the right to petition for bankruptcy; the right to limit liability for torts by means of a prior contract was being pondered in the courts; and the alleged right of common carriers to limit liability for property loss by mere prior notification was being keenly debated.

Under these conditions the concept of a severe restriction on the scope of damages in contract actions must have seemed both less alien than it would have appeared to a judge a decade earlier, and more important than it would have seemed to a judge a decade later. For in 1854 judges were, at one and the same time, confronted with a growing acceptance of the idea of limited liability and yet with a situation of unlimited personal liability for commercial misfeasance. This was a time, moreover, when commercial interactions involved increasing agglomerations of capital and a pyramiding and interlocking of transactions, so that any error might lead to damages that could significantly diminish annual profits or even destroy the personal fortunes of those sharing in thinly financed ventures.

(c) *Peevyhouse v. Garland Coal & Mining Company*†

[JACKSON J.:]

In the trial court, plaintiffs Willie and Lucille Peevyhouse sued the defendant, Garland Coal and Mining Company, for damages for breach of contract. Judgment was for plaintiffs in an amount considerably less than was sued for. Plaintiffs appeal and defendant cross-appeals.

In the briefs on appeal, the parties present their argument and contentions under several propositions; however, they all stem from the basic question of whether the trial court properly instructed the jury on the measure of damages.

Briefly stated, the facts are as follows: plaintiffs owned a farm containing coal deposits, and in November, 1954, leased the premises to defendant for a period of five years for coal mining purposes. A "strip-mining" operation was contemplated in which the coal would be taken from pits on the surface of the ground, instead of from underground mine shafts. In addition to the usual covenants found in a coal mining lease, defendant specifically agreed to perform certain restorative and remedial work at the end of the lease period. It is unnecessary to set out the details of the work to be done, other than to say that it would involve the moving of many thousands of cubic yards of dirt, at a cost estimated by expert witnesses at about $29,000.00. However, plaintiffs sued for only $25,000.00.

During the trial, it was stipulated that all covenants and agreements in the lease contract had been fully carried out by both parties, except the remedial work mentioned above; defendant conceded that this work had not been done.

Plaintiffs introduced expert testimony as to the amount and nature of the work to be done, and its estimated cost. Over plaintiffs' objections, defendant thereafter introduced expert testimony as to the "diminution in value" of plaintiffs' farm resulting from the failure of defendant to render performance as agreed in the contract — that is, the difference between the present value of the farm, and what its value would have been if defendant had done what it agreed to do.

At the conclusion of the trial, the court instructed the jury that it must return a verdict for plaintiffs, and left the amount of damages for jury determination. On the measure of damages, the court instructed the jury that it might consider the cost of performance of the work defendant agreed to do, "together with all of the evidence offered on behalf of either party".

It thus appears that the jury was at liberty to consider the "diminution in value" of plaintiffs' farm as well as the cost of "repair work" in determining the amount of damages.

It returned a verdict for plaintiffs for $5,000.00 — only a fraction of the "cost of performance", *but*

---

† (1963), 382 P. (2d) 109 (Okla. S.C.).

more than the total value of the farm even after the remedial work is done.

On appeal, the issue is sharply drawn. Plaintiffs contend that the true measure of damages in this case is what it will cost plaintiffs to obtain performance of the work that was not done because of defendant's default. Defendant argues that the measure of damages is the cost of performance "limited, however, to the total difference in the market value before and after the work was performed".

It appears that this precise question has not heretofore been presented to this court. In *Ardizonne v. Archer*, 72 Okl. 70, 178 P. 263, this court held that the measure of damages for breach of a contract to drill an oil well was the reasonable cost of drilling the well, but here a slightly different factual situation exists. The drilling of an oil well will yield valuable geological information, even if no oil or gas is found, and of course if the well is a producer, the value of the premises increases. In the case before us, it is argued by defendant with some force that the performance of the remedial work defendant agreed to do will add at the most only a few hundred dollars to the value of plaintiffs' farm, and that the damages should be limited to that amount because that is all plaintiffs have lost.

Plaintiffs rely on *Groves v. John Wunder Co.* In that case, the Minnesota court, in a substantially similar situation, adopted the "cost of performance" rule as opposed to the "value" rule. The result was to authorize a jury to give plaintiff damages in the amount of $60,000, where the real estate concerned would have been worth only $12,160, even if the work contracted for had been done.

It may be observed that *Groves v. John Wunder Co., supra*, is the only case which has come to our attention in which the cost of performance rule has been followed under circumstances where the cost of performance greatly exceeded the diminution in value resulting from the breach of contract. Incidentally, it appears that this case was decided by a plurality rather than a majority of the members of the court.

Defendant relies principally upon *Sandy Valley & E.R. Co. v. Hughes*; *Bigham v. Wabash-Pittsburg Terminal Ry. Co.*; and *Sweeney v. Lewis Const. Co.* These were all cases in which, under similar circumstances, the appellate courts followed the "value" rule instead of the "cost of performance" rule. Plaintiff points out that in the earliest of these cases (*Bigham*) the court cites as authority on

the measure of damages an earlier Pennsylvania *tort* case, and that the other two cases follow the first, with no explanation as to why a measure of damages ordinarily followed in cases sounding in tort should be used in contract cases. Nevertheless, it is of some significance that three out of four appellate courts have followed the diminution in value rule under circumstances where, as here, the cost of performance greatly exceeds the diminution in value.

The explanation may be found in the fact that the situations presented are artificial ones. It is highly unlikely that the ordinary property owner would agree to pay $29,000 (or its equivalent) for the construction of "improvements" upon his property that would increase its value only about ($300) three hundred dollars. The result is that we are called upon to apply principles of law theoretically based upon reason and reality to a situation which is basically unreasonable and unrealistic.

In *Groves v. John Wunder Co., supra*, in arriving at its conclusions, the Minnesota court apparently considered the contract involved to be analogous to a building and construction contract, and cited authority for the proposition that the cost of performance or completion of the building as contracted is ordinarily the measure of damages in actions for damages for the breach of such a contract.

In an annotation following the Minnesota case beginning at 123 A.L.R. 515, the annotator places the three cases relied on by defendant (*Sandy Valley, Bigham* and *Sweeney*) under the classification of cases involving "grading and excavation contracts".

We do not think either analogy is strictly applicable to the case now before us. The primary purpose of the lease contract between plaintiffs and defendant was neither "building and construction" nor "grading and excavation". It was merely to accomplish the economical recovery and marketing of coal from the premises, to the profit of all parties. The special provisions of the lease contract pertaining to remedial work were incidental to the main object involved.

Even in the case of contracts that are unquestionably building and construction contracts, the authorities are not in agreement as to the factors to be considered in determining whether the cost of performance rule or the value rule should be applied. The American Law Institute's *Restatement of the Law, Contracts*, Volume 1, Sections 346(1)(*a*)(*i*) and (*ii*) submits the proposition that the cost of performance is the proper measure of damages "if this is possible and does not involve *unreasonable economic waste*"; and that the diminution in value caused by the breach is the proper measure "if construction and completion in accordance with the contract would involve *unreasonable economic waste*". (Emphasis supplied). In an explanatory comment immediately following the text, the Restatement makes it clear that the "economic waste" referred to consists of the destruction of a substantially completed building or other structure. Of course no such destruction is involved in the case now before us.

On the other hand, in McCormick, *Damages*, Section 168, it is said with regard to building and construction contracts that "... in cases where the defect is one that can be repaired or cured without *undue expense*" the cost of performance is the proper measure of damages, but where "... the defect in material or construction is one that cannot be remedied without an *expenditure for reconstruction disproportionate to the end to be attained*" (emphasis supplied) the value rule should be followed. The same idea was expressed in *Jacob & Youngs, Inc. v. Kent*, as follows:

> The owner is entitled to the money which will permit him to complete, unless the cost of completion is grossly and unfairly out of proportion to the good to be attained. When that is true, the measure is the difference in value.

It thus appears that the prime consideration in the *Restatement* was "economic waste"; and that the prime consideration in McCormick, *Damages*, and in *Jacob & Youngs, Inc. v. Kent, supra*, was the relationship between the expense involved and the "end to be attained" — in other words, the "relative economic benefit".

In view of the unrealistic fact situation in the instant case, and certain Oklahoma statutes to be hereinafter noted, we are of the opinion that the "relative economic benefit" is a proper consideration here. This is in accord with the recent case of *Mann v. Clowser*, where, in applying the cost rule, the Virginia court specifically noted that "... the defects are remediable from a practical standpoint and the costs *are not grossly disproportionate to the results to be obtained*" ([e]mphasis supplied).

23 O.S. 1961 §§ 96 and 97 provide as follows:

> **96.** ... Notwithstanding the provisions of this chapter, no person can recover a greater amount in damages for the breach of an obligation, than he would have gained by the full performance thereof on both sides....

> **97.** ... Damages must, in all cases, be reasonable, and where an obligation of any kind appears to create a right to unconscionable and grossly oppressive damages, contrary to substantial justice no more than reasonable damages can be recovered.

Although it is true that the above sections of the statute are applied most often in tort cases, they are by their own terms, and the decisions of this court, also applicable in actions for damages for breach of contract. It would seem that they are peculiarly applicable here where, under the "cost of performance" rule, plaintiffs might recover an amount about nine times the total value of their farm. Such would seem to be "unconscionable and grossly oppressive damages, contrary to substantial justice" within the meaning of the statute. Also, it can hardly be denied that if plaintiffs here are permitted to recover under the "cost of performance" rule, they will receive a greater benefit from the breach than could be gained from full performance, contrary to the provisions of Sec. 96.

An analogy may be drawn between the cited sections, and the provisions of 15 O.S. 1961 §§ 214 and 215. These sections tend to render void any provisions of a contract which attempt to fix the amount of stipulated damages to be paid in case of a breach, except where it is impracticable or extremely difficult to determine the actual damages. This results in spite of the agreement of the parties, and the obvious and well known rationale is that insofar as they exceed the actual damages suffered, the stipulated damages amount to a penalty or forfeiture which the law does not favor.

23 O.S. 1961 §§ 96 and 97 have the same effect in the case now before us. *In spite of the agreement of the parties*, these sections limit the damages recoverable to a reasonable amount not "contrary to substantial justice"; they prevent plaintiffs from recovering a "greater amount in damages for the breach of an obligation" than they would have "gained by the full performance thereof".

We therefore hold that where, in a coal mining lease, lessee agrees to perform certain remedial work on the premises concerned at the end of the lease period, and thereafter the contract is fully performed by both parties except that the remedial work is not done, the measure of damages in an action by lessor against lessee for damages for breach of contract is ordinarily the reasonable cost of performance of the work; however, where the contract provision breached was merely incidental to the main purpose in view, and where the economic benefit which would result to lessor by full performance of the work is grossly disproportionate to the cost of performance, the damages which lessor may recover are limited to the diminution in value resulting to the premises because of the non-performance.

We believe the above holding is in conformity with the intention of the Legislature as expressed in the statutes mentioned, and in harmony with the better-reasoned cases from the other jurisdictions where analogous fact situations have been considered. It should be noted that the rule as stated does not interfere with the property owner's right to "do what he will with his own" *Chamberlain v. Parker*, or his right, if he chooses, to contract for "improvements" which will actually have the effect of reducing his property's value. Where such result is in fact contemplated by the parties, and is a main or principal purpose of those contracting, it would seem that the measure of damages for breach would ordinarily be the cost of performance.

The above holding disposes of all of the arguments raised by the parties on appeal.

Under the most liberal view of the evidence herein, the diminution in value resulting to the premises because of non-performance of the remedial work was $300.00. After a careful search of the record, we have found no evidence of a higher figure, and plaintiffs do not argue in their briefs that a greater diminution in value was sustained. It thus appears that the judgment was clearly excessive, and that the amount for which judgment should have been rendered is definitely and satisfactorily shown by the record.

We are asked by each party to modify the judgment in accordance with the respective theories advanced, and it is conceded that we have authority to do so. 12 O.S. 1961 § 952; *Busboom v. Smith*; *Stumpf v. Stumpf*.

We are of the opinion that the judgment of the trial court for plaintiffs should be, and it is hereby, modified and reduced to the sum of $300.00, and as so modified it is affirmed.

. . . .

[IRWIN J. (dissenting):]

By the specific provisions in the coal mining lease under consideration, the defendant agreed as follows:

. . . .

7b. Lessee agrees to make fills in the pits dug on said premises on the property line in such manner that fences can be placed thereon and access had to opposite sides of the pits.

7c. Lessee agrees to smooth off the top of the spoil banks on the above premises.

7d. Lessee agrees to leave the creek crossing the above premises in such a condition that it will not interfere with the crossings to be made in pits as set out in 7b.

...

7f. Lessee further agrees to leave no shale or dirt on the high wall of said pits....

Following the expiration of the lease, plaintiffs made demand upon defendant that it carry out the provisions of the contract and to perform those covenants contained therein.

Defendant admits that it failed to perform its obligations that it agreed and contracted to perform under the lease contract and there is nothing in the record which indicates that defendant could not perform its obligations. Therefore, in may opinion defendant's breach of the contract was wilful and not in good faith.

Although the contract speaks for itself, there were several negotiations between the plaintiffs and defendant before the contract was executed. Defendant admitted in the trial of the action, that plaintiffs insisted that the above provisions be included in the contract and that they would not agree to the coal mining lease unless the above provisions were included.

In consideration for the lease contract, plaintiffs were to receive a certain amount as royalty for the coal produced and marketed and in addition thereto their land was to be restored as provided in the contract.

Defendant received as consideration for the contract, its proportionate share of the coal produced and marketed and in addition thereto, the *right to use* plaintiffs' land in the furtherance of its mining operations.

The cost for performing the contract in question could have been reasonably approximated when the contract was negotiated and executed and there are no conditions now existing which could not have been reasonably anticipated by the parties. Therefore, defendant had knowledge, when it prevailed upon the plaintiffs to execute the lease, that the cost of performance might be disproportionate to the value or benefits received by plaintiff for the performance.

Defendant has received its benefits under the contract and now urges, in substance, that plaintiffs' measure of damages for its failure to perform should be the economic value of performance to the plaintiffs and not the cost of performance.

If a peculiar set of facts should exist where the above rule should be applied as the proper measure of damages, (and in my judgment those facts do not exist in the instant case) before such rule should be applied, consideration should be given to the benefits received or contracted for by the party who asserts the application of the rule.

Defendant did not have the right to mine plaintiffs' coal or to use plaintiffs' property for its mining operations without the consent of plaintiffs. Defendant had knowledge of the benefits that it would receive under the contract and the approximate cost of performing the contract. With this knowledge, it must be presumed that defendant thought that it would be to its economic advantage to enter into the contract with plaintiffs and that it would reap benefits from the contract, or it would have not entered into the contract.

Therefore, if the value of the performance of a contract should be considered in determining the measure of damages for breach of a contract, the value of the benefits received under the contract by a party who breaches a contract should also be considered. However, in my judgment, to give consideration to either in the instant action, completely rescinds and holds for naught the solemnity of the contract before us and makes an entirely new contract for the parties.

In *Goble v. Bell Oil & Gas Co.*, we held:

> Even though the contract contains harsh and burdensome terms which the court does not in all respects approve, it is the province of the parties in relation to lawful subject matter to fix their rights and obligations, and the court will give the contract effect according to its expressed provisions, unless it be shown by competent evidence proof that the written agreement as executed is the result of fraud, mistake, or accident.

In *Cities Service Oil Co. v. Geolograph Co. Inc.*, we said:

> While we do not agree that the contract as presently written is an onerous one, we think the short answer is that the folly or wisdom of a contract is not for the court to pass on.

In *Great Western Oil & Gas Company v. Mitchell*, we held:

The law will not make a better contract for parties than they themselves have seen fit to enter into, or alter it for the benefit of one party and to the detriment of the others; the judicial function of a court of law is to enforce a contract as it is written.

I am mindful of Title 23 O.S. 1961 § 96, which provides that no person can recover a greater amount in damages for the breach of an obligation than he could have gained by the full performance thereof on both sides, except in cases not applicable herein. However, in my judgment, the above statutory provision is not applicable here.

In my judgment, we should follow the case of *Groves v. John Wunder Company*, which defendant agrees "that the fact situation is apparently similar to the one in the case at bar", and where the Supreme Court of Minnesota held:

> The owner's or employer's damages for such a breach (i.e., breach hypothesized in 2d syllabus) are to be measured, not in respect to the value of the land to be improved, but by the reasonable cost of doing that which the contractor promised to do and which he left undone.

The hypothesized breach referred to states that where the contractor's breach of a contract is wilful, that is, in bad faith, he is not entitled to any benefit of the equitable doctrine of substantial performance.

In the instant action defendant has made no attempt to even substantially perform. The contract in question is not immoral, is not tainted with fraud, and was not entered into through mistake or accident and is not contrary to public policy. It is clear and unambiguous and the parties understood the terms thereof, and the approximate cost of fulfilling the obligations could have been approximately ascertained. There are no conditions existing now which could not have been reasonably anticipated when the contract was negotiated and executed. The defendant could have performed the contract if it desired. It has accepted and reaped the benefits of its contract and now urges that plaintiffs' benefits under the contract be denied. If plaintiffs' benefits are denied, such benefits would inure to the direct benefit of the defendant.

Therefore, in my opinion, the plaintiffs were entitled to specific performance of the contract and since defendant has failed to perform, the proper measure of damages should be the cost of performance. Any other measure of damage would be holding for naught the express provisions of the contract; would be taking from the plaintiffs the benefits of the contract and placing those benefits in defendant which has failed to perform its obligations; would be granting benefits to defendant without a resulting obligation; and would be completely

rescinding the solemn obligation of the contract for the benefit of the defendant to the detriment of the plaintiffs by making an entirely new contract for the parties.

I therefore respectfully dissent [from] the opinion promulgated by a majority of my associates.

(d) *Wallace v. United Grain Growers Ltd.*†

NOTE

W. worked as a printer for a competitor of R., (a wholly owned subsidiary of United Grain Growers Ltd.) R. offered W. employment with their company, but before W. accepted he raised several concerns, including that because he was already 45 years old, and had worked for his previous employer for 25 years, he would require job security, fair treatment and reasonable remuneration. R. agreed to W.'s conditions and implied that if he performed well he would be guaranteed employment until retirement. W. went to work for R. and enjoyed many years of success within the company, including being its top salesperson for all 14 years in their employ. In 1986, W. was dismissed without notice, and R. maintained that the dismissal was for cause. W. was unable to find alternative employment, suffered depression for which he needed psychiatric treatment and went bankrupt. He sued R. for breach of contract and wrongful dismissal. At trial, W. was awarded 24 months' notice as damages for his wrongful dismissal and $15,000 in aggravated damages resulting from mental distress in both contract and tort. R. appealed. At the Court of Appeal, damages were reduced to a 15-month notice period, and no aggravated damages were awarded. W. appealed to the Supreme Court of Canada.

EXTRACT

[IACOBUCCI J.:]

. . . .

4. ISSUES

The cross-appeal raises one issue: can an undischarged bankrupt bring an action for wrongful dismissal?

The appeal raises five issues:

(a) Was there a fixed-term contract?
(b) Did the Court of Appeal err in overturning the trial judge's award for aggravated damages resulting from mental distress?
(c) Can the appellant sue in either contract or tort for "bad faith discharge"?
(d) Is the appellant entitled to punitive damages?
(e) Did the Court of Appeal err in reducing the appellant's reasonable notice damages from 24 to 15 months?

. . . .

5. ANALYSIS

. . . .

B. Fixed-Term Contract

The appellant submitted that the courts below erred in rejecting his claim that he had a fixed-term contract for employment until retirement. The

---

† [1997] 3 S.C.R. 701.

learned trial judge exhaustively reviewed all of the circumstances surrounding Wallace's hiring and concluded that there was insufficient evidence to support this claim. The Court of Appeal accepted the facts as they were found by the trial judge and agreed with his conclusion. In light of these concurrent findings of fact, I see no palpable error or other reason to interfere with the conclusion of the courts below.

C. Damages for Mental Distress

Relying upon the principles enunciated in *Vorvis, supra*, the Court of Appeal held that any award of damages beyond compensation for breach of contract for failure to give reasonable notice of termination "must be founded on a separately actionable course of conduct" (p. 184). Although there has been criticism of *Vorvis* this is an accurate statement of the law. The Court of Appeal also noted that this requirement necessarily negates the trial judge's reliance on concepts of foreseeability and matters in the contemplation of the parties. An employment contract is not one in which peace of mind is the very matter contracted for (see e.g. *Jarvis v. Swans Tours Ltd.*) and so, absent an independently actionable wrong, the foreseeability of mental distress or the fact that the parties contemplated its occurrence is of no consequence, subject to what I say on employer conduct below.

The Court of Appeal concluded that there was insufficient evidence to support a finding that the actions of UGG constituted a separate actionable wrong either in tort or in contract. I agree with these findings and see no reason to disturb them. I note, however, that in circumstances where the manner of dismissal has caused mental distress but falls short of an independent actionable wrong, the employee is not without recourse. Rather, the trial judge has discretion in these circumstances to extend the period of reasonable notice to which an employee is entitled. Thus, although recovery for mental distress might not be available under a separate head of damages, the possibility of recovery still remains. I will be returning to this point in my discussion of reasonable notice below.

D. Bad Faith Discharge

The appellant urged this Court to find that he could sue UGG either in contract or in tort for "bad faith discharge". With respect to the action in contract, he submitted that the Court should imply into the employment contract a term that the employee would not be fired except for cause or legitimate business reasons. I cannot accede to this submission. The law has long recognized the mutual right of both employers and employees to terminate an employment contract at any time provided there are no express provisions to the contrary. In *Farber v. Royal Trust Co.*, Gonthier J., speaking for the Court, summarized the general contractual principles applicable to contracts of employment as follows:

> In the context of an indeterminate employment contract, one party can resiliate the contract unilaterally. The resiliation is considered a dismissal if it originates with the employer and a resignation if it originates with the employee. If an employer dismisses an employee without cause, the employer must give the employee reasonable notice that the contract is about to be terminated or compensation in lieu thereof.

A requirement of "good faith" reasons for dismissal would, in effect, contravene these principles and deprive employers of the ability to determine the composition of their workforce. In the context of the accepted theories on the employment relationship, such a law would, in my opinion, be overly intrusive and inconsistent with established principles of employment law, and more appropriately, should be left to legislative enactment rather than judicial pronouncement.

I must also reject the appellant's claim that he can sue in tort for breach of a good faith and fair dealing obligation with regard to dismissals. The Court of Appeal noted the absence of persuasive authority on this point and concluded that such a tort has not yet been recognized by Canadian courts. I agree with these findings. To create such a tort in this case would therefore constitute a radical shift in the law, again a step better left to be taken by the legislatures.

For these reasons I conclude that the appellant is unable to sue in either tort or contract for "bad faith discharge". However, I will be returning to the subject of good faith and fair dealing in my discussion of reasonable notice below.

E. Punitive Damages

Punitive damages are an exception to the general rule that damages are meant to compensate the plaintiff. The purpose of such an award is the punishment of the defendant: S. M. Waddams, *The*

Law of Damages. The appellant argued that the trial judge and the Court of Appeal erred in refusing to award punitive damages. I do not agree. Relying on *Vorvis, supra,* Lockwood J. found that UGG did not engage in sufficiently "harsh, vindictive, reprehensible and malicious" conduct to merit condemnation by such an award. He also noted the absence of an actionable wrong. The Court of Appeal concurred. Again, there is no reason to interfere with these findings. Consequently, I agree with the courts below that there is no foundation for an award of punitive damages.

F.   Reasonable Notice

The Court of Appeal upheld the trial judge's findings of fact and agreed that in the circumstances of this case damages for failure to give notice ought to be at the high end of the scale. However, the court found the trial judge's award of 24 months' salary in lieu of notice to be excessive and reflective of an element of aggravated damages having crept into his determination. It overturned his award and substituted the equivalent of 15 months' salary. For the reasons which follow, I would restore the trial judge's award of damages in the amount of 24 months' salary in lieu of notice.

.   .   .   .

The contract of employment has many characteristics that set it apart from the ordinary commercial contract. Some of the views on this subject that have already been approved of in previous decisions of this Court (see e.g. *Machtinger, supra*) bear repeating. As K. Swinton noted in "Contract Law and the Employment Relationship: The Proper Forum for Reform", in B. J. Reiter and J. Swan, eds., *Studies in Contract Law*:

> ... the terms of the employment contract rarely result from an exercise of free bargaining power in the way that the paradigm commercial exchange between two traders does. Individual employees on the whole lack both the bargaining power and the information necessary to achieve more favourable contract provisions than those offered by the employer, particularly with regard to tenure.

This power imbalance is not limited to the employment contract itself. Rather, it informs virtually all facets of the employment relationship. In *Slaight Communications Inc. v. Davidson*, Dickson C.J., writing for the majority of the Court, had

occasion to comment on the nature of this relationship. He quoted with approval from P. Davies and M. Freedland, *Kahn-Freund's Labour and the Law*:

> [T]he relation between an employer and an isolated employee or worker is typically a relation between a bearer of power and one who is not a bearer of power. In its inception it is an act of submission, in its operation it is a condition of subordination....

This unequal balance of power led the majority of the Court in *Slaight Communications, supra,* to describe employees as a vulnerable group in society. The vulnerability of employees is underscored by the level of importance which our society attaches to employment. As Dickson C.J. noted in *Reference Re Public Service Employee Relations Act*:

> Work is one of the most fundamental aspects in a person's life, providing the individual with a means of financial support and, as importantly, a contributory role in society. A person's employment is an essential component of his or her sense of identity, self-worth and emotional well-being.

Thus, for most people, work is one of the defining features of their lives. Accordingly, any change in a person's employment status is bound to have far-reaching repercussions. In "Aggravated Damages and the Employment Contract", *supra,* Schai noted that, "[w]hen this change is involuntary, the extent of our 'personal dislocation' is even greater."

The point at which the employment relationship ruptures is the time when the employee is most vulnerable and hence, most in need of protection. In recognition of this need, the law ought to encourage conduct that minimizes the damage and dislocation (both economic and personal) that result from dismissal. In *Machtinger, supra,* it was noted that the manner in which employment can be terminated is equally important to an individual's identity as the work itself. By way of expanding upon this statement, I note that the loss of one's job is always a traumatic event. However, when termination is accompanied by acts of bad faith in the manner of discharge, the results can be especially devastating. In my opinion, to ensure that employees receive adequate protection, employers ought to be held to an obligation of good faith and fair dealing in the manner of dismissal, the breach of which will be compensated for by adding to the length of the notice period.

This approach finds support in the words of my colleague, Gonthier J., in *Farber, supra.* Writing for a unanimous Court he stated at p. 859:

> ... for the employment contract to be resiliated, it is not necessary for the employer to have intended to force the employee to leave his or her employment or to have been acting in bad faith when making substantial changes to the contract's essential terms. However, if the employer was acting in bad faith, this would have an impact on the damages awarded to the employee.

I find further support for this approach in the decisions of several cases wherein the manner of dismissal was among the factors considered in determining the notice period....

.   .   .   .

It has long been accepted that a dismissed employee is not entitled to compensation for injuries flowing from the fact of the dismissal itself: see *e.g. Addis, supra.* Thus, although the loss of a job is very often the cause of injured feelings and emotional upset, the law does not recognize these as compensable losses. However, where an employee can establish that an employer engaged in bad faith conduct or unfair dealing in the course of dismissal, injuries such as humiliation, embarrassment and damage to one's sense of self-worth and self-esteem might all be worthy of compensation depending upon the circumstances of the case. In these situations, compensation does not flow from the fact of dismissal itself, but rather from the manner in which the dismissal was effected by the employer.

Often the intangible injuries caused by bad faith conduct or unfair dealing on dismissal will lead to difficulties in finding alternative employment, a tangible loss which the Court of Appeal rightly recognized as warranting an addition to the notice period. It is likely that the more unfair or in bad faith the manner of dismissal is the more this will have an effect on the ability of the dismissed employee to find new employment. However, in my view the intangible injuries are sufficient to merit compensation in and of themselves. I recognize that bad faith conduct which affects employment prospects may be worthy of considerably more compensation than that which does not, but in both cases damage has resulted that should be compensable.

The availability of compensation for these types of injuries has been recognized in other areas of the law. In *McCarey v. Associated Newspapers Ltd. (No. 2)*, Pearson L.J. examined the scope of recovery in an action for libel. He stated:

> Compensatory damages, in a case in which they are at large, may include several different kinds of compensation to the injured plaintiff. They may include not only actual pecuniary loss and anticipated pecuniary loss or any social disadvantages which result, or may be thought likely to result, from the wrong which has been done. They may also include the natural injury to his feelings — the natural grief and distress which he may have felt at having been spoken of in defamatory terms, and if there has been any kind of high-handed, oppressive, insulting or contumelious behaviour by the defendant which increases the mental pain and suffering caused by the defamation and may constitute injury to the plaintiff's pride and self-confidence, those are proper elements to be taken into account in a case where the damages are at large.

.   .   .   .

In my view, there is no valid reason why the scope of compensable injuries in defamation situations should not be equally recognized in the context of wrongful dismissal from employment. The law should be mindful of the acute vulnerability of terminated employees and ensure their protection by encouraging proper conduct and preventing all injurious losses which might flow from acts of bad faith or unfair dealing on dismissal, both tangible and intangible. I note that there may be those who would say that this approach imposes an onerous obligation on employers. I would respond simply by saying that I fail to see how it can be onerous to treat people fairly, reasonably, and decently at a time of trauma and despair. In my view, the reasonable person would expect such treatment. So should the law.

In the case before this Court, the trial judge documented several examples of bad faith conduct on the part of UGG. He noted the abrupt manner in which Wallace was dismissed despite having received compliments on his work from his superiors only days before. He found that UGG made a conscious decision to "play hardball" with Wallace and maintained unfounded allegations of cause until the day the trial began. Further, as a result of UGG's persistence in maintaining these allegations, "[w]ord got around, and it was rumoured in the trade that he had been involved in some wrongdoing". Finally, he found that the dismissal and subsequent events were largely responsible for causing Wallace's depression. Having considered the *Bardal* list of factors, he stated:

> Taking [these] factors into account, and particularly the fact that the peremptory dismissal and the subsequent actions of the defendant made other employment in his field virtually unavailable, I conclude that an award at the top of the scale in such cases is warranted.

I agree with the trial judge's conclusion that the actions of UGG seriously diminished Wallace's prospects of finding similar employment. In light of this fact, and the other circumstances of this case, I am not persuaded that the trial judge erred in awarding the equivalent of 24 months' salary in lieu of notice. It may be that such an award is at the high end of the scale; however, taking into account all of the relevant factors, this award is not unreasonable and accordingly, I can see no reason to interfere. Therefore, for the reasons above, I would restore the order of the trial judge with respect to the appropriate period of reasonable notice and allow the appeal on this ground.

6. CONCLUSIONS AND DISPOSITION

I would dismiss the cross-appeal with costs and allow the appeal in part with costs here and in the courts below. I would set aside the judgment of the Manitoba Court of Appeal and restore the trial judge's award of 24 months' salary in lieu of notice. As explained above, the other aspects of the appellant's claim are rejected.

[McLACHLIN J. (dissenting in part):]

I have read the reasons of Justice Iacobucci. While I agree with much of his reasons, my view of the law leads me to differ both in method and in result.

. . . .

THE LAW

. . . .

Availability of Other Remedies

It is argued that employer misconduct in the manner of dismissal not affecting prospects of re-employment must be taken into account in calculating the notice period in order to avoid injustice and provide an adequate remedy to the employee in a case such as this. The answer to this argument is that the law affords other remedies for employer misconduct in these circumstances.

The law of tort and contract recognizes a number of independent causes of action for misconduct in dismissing an employee. If the employer defames the employee or wilfully inflicts mental distress, the employee can sue in tort. If the employer has lured the employee from a secure position with promises of better terms, the employee may be able to sue in tort for negligent misrepresentation or for breach of an express contractual term. Finally, unfair treatment at the time of dismissal may give rise to an action for breach of an implied term in the contract of employment.

The law has now developed to the point that to these traditional actions may now be added another: breach of an implied contractual term to act in good faith in dismissing an employee. I agree with Iacobucci J. that an employer must act in good faith and in fair dealing when dismissing employees, and more particularly that "employers ought to be candid, reasonable, honest and forthright with their employees and should refrain from engaging in conduct that is unfair or is in bad faith by being, for example, untruthful, misleading or unduly insensitive". I also agree that this obligation does not extend to prohibiting employers from dismissing employees without "good faith" reasons; such an extension of employment law would be "overly intrusive and inconsistent with established principles of employment law". Both employer and employee remain free to terminate the contract of employment without cause. This is not inconsistent with the duty of good faith. While some courts have recognized employer obligations of good faith outside of the dismissal context, this case does not require us to go beyond the context of dismissal.

I differ from my colleague, however, in that I see no reason why the expectation of good faith in dismissing employees that he accepts should not be viewed as an implied term of the contract of employment. To assert the duty of good faith in dismissing employees as a proposition of law, as does my colleague, is tantamount to saying that it is an obligation implied by law into the contractual relationship between employer and employee. In other words, it is an implied term of the contract.

. . . .

This is the type of implication that is involved in the proposed obligation of good faith. As Iacobucci J. points out, employment contracts have characteristics quite distinct from other types of contracts as a result of the often unequal bargaining power typically involved in the relationship. This results in employee vulnerability — a vulnerability that is especially acute at the time of dismissal. The nature of the relationship thereby necessitates some measure of protection for the vulnerable party. Requiring employers to treat their employees with good faith at the time of dismissal provides this special measure of protection. It fol-

lows that an implied term is necessary in the sense required to justify implication of a contractual term by law.

. . . .

APPLICATION OF THE LAW

. . . .

I would dismiss the cross-appeal and allow the appeal with costs here and in the courts below and restore the trial judge's award of 24 months' salary representing damages for wrongful dismissal and $15,000 representing compensation for mental distress and loss of reputation.

(e) *Lumley v. Wagner*†

HEADNOTE

. . . .

The agreement provided:

"The undersigned Mr Benjamin Lumley, possessor of Her Majesty's Theatre at London, and of the Italian Opera at Paris, of the one part, and Mademoiselle Johanna Wagner, cantatrice of the court of His Majesty the King of Prussia, with the consent of her father, Mr A Wagner, residing at Berlin, of the other part, have concerted and concluded the following contract. — First, Mademoiselle Johanna Wagner binds herself to sing for three months at the theatre of Mr Lumley, Her Majesty's, London, to date from April 1, 1852 (the time necessary for the journey comprised therein) and to give the parts following, 1st, Romeo, montecchi; 2nd, Fides, Prophets; 3rd, Valentine, Huguenots; 4th, Anna, Don Juan; 5th, Alice, Robert le Diable; 6th, an opera chosen

by common accord. Second, the three first parts must necessarily be, 1st, Romeo, 2nd, Fides, 3rd, Valentine; these parts once sung, and then only she will appear, if Mr Lumley desires it, in the three other operas mentioned aforesaid. Third, these six parts belong exclusively to Mademoiselle Wagner, and any other [cantatrice] shall not presume to sing them during the three months of her engagement. If Mr Lumley happens to be prevented, by any cause soever, from giving these operas, he is nevertheless held to pay Mademoiselle Johanna Wagner the salary stipulated lower down for the number of her parts as if she had sung them. Fourth, in the case where Mademoiselle Wagner should be prevented by reason of illness from singing in the course of a month as often as it has been stipulated, Mr Lumley is bound to pay the salary only for the parts sung. Fifth, Mademoiselle Johanna Wagner binds herself to sing twice a week during the run of the three months; however, if she herself was hindered from singing twice in any

† [1843–1860] All ER Rep 368. Reproduced by permission of Reed Elsevier (UK) Limited, trading as LexisNexis Butterworths.

week whatever, she will have the right to give at a later period the omitted representation. Sixth, if Mademoiselle Wagner, fulfilling the wishes of the direction, consent to sing more than twice a week in the course of three months, this last will give to Mademoiselle Wagner 50 pounds sterling for each representation extra. Seventh, Mr Lumley engages to pay Mademoiselle Wagner a salary of 400 pounds sterling per month, and payment will take place in such manner that she will receive 100 pounds sterling each week. Eighth, Mr Lumley will pay by letters of exchange to Mademoiselle Wagner at Berlin, Mar 15, 1852, the sum of 800 pounds sterling, a sum which will be deducted from her engagement in his retaining 100 pounds each month. Ninth, in all cases, except that where a verified illness would place upon her a hindrance, if Mademoiselle Wagner shall not arrive in London eight days after that from whence dates her engagement, Mr Lumley will have the right to regard the non-appearance as a rupture of the contract, and will be able to demand an indemnification. Tenth, in the case where Mr Lumley should cede his enterprise to another, he has the right to transfer this contract to his successor, and in that case Mademoiselle Wagner has the same obligations and the same rights towards the last as towards Mr Lumley. (Signed) JOHANNA WAGNER, ALBERT WAGNER."

The bill stated, that in November 1851, Joseph Becher met the plaintiff in Paris, when the plaintiff objected to the agreement as not containing a usual and necessary clause preventing the defendant Johanna Wagner from exercising her professional abilities in England without the consent of the plaintiff, whereupon Joseph Becher, as the agent of the defendants Johanna Wagner and Albert Wagner, and being fully authorised by them for the purpose, added an article in writing which was as follows:

"Mademoiselle Wagner engages herself not to use her talents at any other theatre, nor in any concert or re-union, public or private, without the written authorisation of Mr Lumley."

. . . . .

JUDGMENT

[LORD ST LEONARDS, L.C.:]

The question which I have to decide in the present case arises out of a very simple contract, the effect

of which is, that the defendant Johanna Warner should sing at Her Majesty's Theatre for a certain number of nights, and that she should not sing elsewhere (for that is the true construction) during that period. As I understand the points taken by the defendants' counsel in support of this appeal they in effect come to this, namely, that a court of equity ought not to grant an injunction except in cases connected with specific performance, or where the injunction, being to compel a party to forbear from committing an act (and not to perform an act) that injunction will complete the whole of the agreement remaining unexecuted.

. . . . .

The present is a mixed case, consisting not of two correlative acts to be done, one by the plaintiff and the other by the defendants, which state of facts may have and in some cases has introduced a very important difference, but of an act to be done by Johanna Wagner alone, to which is superadded a negative stipulation on her part to abstain from the commission of any act which will break in upon her affirmative covenant — the one being ancillary to, and concurrent and operating together with the other. The agreement to sing for the plaintiff during three months at his theatre, and during that time not to sing for anybody else, is not a correlative contract. It is, in effect, one contract, and though beyond all doubt this court could not interfere to enforce the specific performance of the whole of this contract, yet in all sound construction and according to the true spirit of the agreement, the engagement to perform for three months at one theatre must necessarily exclude the right to perform at the same time at another theatre. It was clearly intended that Johanna Wagner was to exert her vocal abilities to the utmost to aid the theatre to which she agreed to attach herself. I am of opinion that if she had attempted, even in the absence of any negative stipulation, to perform at another theatre, she would have broken the spirit and true meaning of the contract as much as she would now do with reference to the contract into which she has actually entered. Wherever this court has not proper jurisdiction to enforce specific performance, it operates to bind men's consciences, as far as they can be bound, to a true and literal performance of their agreements, and it will not suffer them to depart from their contracts at their pleasure, leaving the party with whom they have contracted to the mere chance of any damages which a jury may give. The exercise of this jurisdiction has, I believe, had a wholesome tendency towards the maintenance of that good faith which exists in this country to a much greater degree perhaps than in any other, and, although the jurisdiction is not to be extended, yet a judge would desert his duty who did not act up to what his predecessors have handed down as the rule for his guidance in the administration of such an equity.

It was objected that the operation of the injunction in the present case was mischievous, excluding the defendant Johanna Wagner from performing at any other theatre while this court had no power to compel her to perform at Her Majesty's Theatre. It is true that I have not the means of compelling her to sing, but she has no cause of complaint if I compel her to abstain from the commission of an act which she has bound herself not to do, and thus possibly cause her to fulfil her engagement. The jurisdiction which I now exercise is wholly within the power of the court, and, being of opinion that it is a proper case for interfering, I shall leave nothing unsatisfied by the judgment I pronounce. The effect, too, of the injunction, in restraining Johanna Wagner from singing elsewhere may, in the event of an action being brought against her by the plaintiff, prevent any such amount of vindictive damages being given against her as a jury might probably be inclined to give if she had carried her talents and exercised them at the rival theatre. The injunction may also, as I have said, tend to the fulfilment of her engagement, though, in continuing the injunction, I disclaim doing indirectly what I cannot do directly.

4 The Nature of Tort Law

(a) The Functions of Tort Law†

Allen M. Linden

The law of torts hovers over virtually every activity of modern society. The driver of every automobile on our highways, the pilot of every aeroplane in the sky, and the captain of every ship plying our waters must abide by the standards of tort law. The producers, distributors and repairers of every product, from bread to computers, must conform to tort law's counsel of caution. No profession is beyond its reach: a doctor cannot raise a scalpel, a lawyer cannot advise a client, nor can an architect design a building without being subject to potential tort liability. In the same way, teachers, government officials, police, and even jailers may be required to pay damages if someone is hurt as a result of their conduct. Those who engage in sports, such as golfers, hockey-players, and snowmobilers, may end up as parties to a tort action. The territory of tort law encompasses losses resulting from fires, floods, explosions, electricity, gas, and many other catastrophes that may occur in this increasingly complex world. A person who punches another person on the nose may have to answer for it not only in a tort case but also in the criminal courts. A person who says nasty things about another may be sued for defamation. Hence, any one of us may become a plaintiff or a defendant in a tort action at any moment. Tort law, therefore, is a subject of abiding concern not only to the judges and lawyers who must administer it but also to the public at large, whose every move is regulated by it.

Although it is relatively easy to point to the activities within the compass of tort law, it is not so simple to offer a satisfactory definition of a tort. The term itself is a derivation of the Latin word, *tortus*, which means twisted or crooked. The expression found its way into the early English language as a synonym for the word "wrong". It is no longer used in everyday language, but it has survived as a technical legal term to this day.

Many authors have striven to define tort law and to mark it off from criminal law, contract law and quasi-contract law, but none of them has been entirely successful. Perhaps the best working definition so far produced is "A tort is a civil wrong, other than a breach of contract, which the law will redress by an award of damages." But even this formulation does not tell us very much. It merely asserts that a tort consists of conduct for which the courts will order compensation, which is almost as circular as saying that a tort is a tort. Nevertheless, it is true that "A 'tort' is a legal construct ..., [which] only exists where the law says it exists."

A more promising description of tort law can be obtained by focussing on function. In tort litigation, the courts must decide whether to shift the loss suffered by one person, the plaintiff, to the shoulders of another person, the defendant. The principles and rules of the law of torts, which have been developed over the centuries, assist the courts in this task. No definition could possibly depict the

† From Allen M. Linden, *Canadian Tort Law*, 7th ed. (Toronto: Butterworths, 2001) at. 1–22. [Notes and/or References omitted.] Reproduced by permission of LexisNexis Canada Inc.

richness and variety of the subject matter of tort law. In order to know what tort law is, it is necessary to study in some detail what it aims to do and what it does in fact, as well as the basic principles incorporated within it. Only at the end of this book will the reader possess an accurate picture of the terrain of tort law.

Tort law is not one-dimensional; it serves several functions. It is "pluralistic". The purpose of this chapter is to identify in a preliminary and tentative way the main aims of modern tort law. Not all of its goals are harmonious, indeed some may be in conflict with others. Not all the purposes of tort law are expressed openly in the case law. On the contrary, some of them are unrecognized or dimly perceived, or even vehemently denied. Some are achieved only indirectly and some not at all. Thus tort law serves a potpourri of objectives, some conscious and some unconscious.

Some reject the idea that tort law serves any particular instrumental function. Professor Ernest Weinrib, for example, has argued that "goals have nothing to do with tort law". Those instrumentalists who believe the contrary, he contends, are not advancing a theory of tort law but rather a "theory of social goals" into which tort law may or may not fit. Professor Weinrib charmingly opines that tort law, like love, has no ulterior ends:

> Explaining love in terms of ulterior ends is necessarily a mistake, because a loving relationship has no ulterior end. Love is its own end. In that respect, tort law is just like love.

Professor Weinrib asserts that it is as unfair to criticize tort law for not achieving certain social goals as it is to "criticize a turtle for failing to fly". Tort law is non-instrumentalist, he insists, being concerned merely with the "propriety of activity".

It is true that tort law, like love, is valuable for its own sake, but there are many aspects of love and many facets of tort law. Professor Weinrib, by maintaining that there are no pragmatic ends of love and of torts, undervalues them both. There is more to love and to torts [than] just their intrinsic unpolluted merit, however splendid that may be. Neither should be sold short. True, the greatest thing about love is love itself, but love also inspires song, animates poetry, builds new families, encourages new enterprises, etc. Love can take credit for some of the good things that happen in our world, even though lovers may not start out with these effects in mind. Similarly, tort law may achieve beneficial effects, without necessarily setting out to do so, things like compensation, deterrence and education. Thus, whether by design or not, tort law, like love, is valuable not only intrinsically but also for its other contributions to a better world.

Like so many social institutions, tort law is being re-evaluated in the context of our times. It is often assailed as a relic of a bygone age which has no purpose in contemporary society. If it is true that tort law no longer serves us, it should be buried along with the other fossils of the legal system. Reports of the death of torts have been greatly exaggerated, however. The mere assertion that tort law is useless does not establish the truth of that indictment. There is a disturbing paucity of data relevant to the aims and efficacy of tort law. We are debating in the dark. What is more disconcerting is that we do not possess reliable techniques of measurement upon which to base valid conclusions. Unsubstantiated claims and counterclaims are no basis for rational choice. It may be that our society will ultimately choose to jettison tort law, but it should not be done until we have evaluated *all* of its benefits and *all* of its costs. It is too early for such a decision to be taken because our information is still fragmentary. We have barely begun to analyze the aims and functions of tort law. Empirical studies should be undertaken to measure the efficacy of tort law in achieving its goals. Only after these studies are concluded will we be able to make an informed decision about the destiny of tort law.

A. COMPENSATION

First and foremost, tort law is a compensator. A successful action puts money into the pocket of the claimant. This payment is supposed to reimburse the claimant for the economic and psychic damages suffered at the hands of the defendant.

The reparation function of modern tort law is so fundamental that some commentators have asserted that it is tort law's *only* legitimate task. The late Dean C.A. Wright, for example, contended simply that the "purpose of the law of torts is to adjust [the] losses [arising out of modern living] and to afford compensation for injuries sustained by one person as the result of the conduct of another". Another scholar has argued that justice requires, most of all, the reparation of wrongs. Indeed, he thought that penal sanctions might well be replaced by civil ones, once the latter "acquired a sufficient efficacy".

This view is inaccurate. If the sole role of tort law were universal compensation, it would have become extinct long ago. The truth is that only certain victims, "the deserving", win damages in tort. The "undeserving" are denied recovery. In other words, only those who are able to prove that they were injured through another's fault or negligence receive reparation, and those who cannot go without. "A loss must lie where it falls", asserted Oliver Wendell Holmes, unless there is a good reason to shift it. That good reason was fault. Holmes argued that the state's "cumbrous and expensive machinery ought not to be set in motion unless some clear benefit is to be derived from disturbing the status quo. State interference is an evil, where it cannot be shown to be a good." Such a benefit was derived when a loss was shifted from an innocent plaintiff to a wrong-doing defendant.

This theory had its heyday prior to the advent of the welfare state and widespread liability insurance. The interaction of these two factors changed the face of tort law. Increased social awareness coupled with liability insurance led to an increase in the incidence of tort liability. Devices such as *res ipsa loquitur*, negligence *per se*, and contributory negligence legislation were employed to compensate more and more claimants. Eventually, in opposition to Holmes, scholars began to contend that "worthwhile 'social gain' *is* achieved by shifting losses from innocent victims".

A new rationale for tort law — loss distribution — was devised to reflect these developments and to spur further growth along these lines. According to this theory, accident losses are no longer shifted from one individual to another. Rather, the costs are transferred to industrial enterprises and insured activities which generate most accidents. These activities do not bear these costs themselves but spread them throughout the community *via* price increases or insurance premiums. Thus, the expense is borne by the segment of society participating in the activity. Consequently, a massive loss that might bankrupt a defendant, if shifted to that individual, can be divided into infinitesimal portions to be exacted from many people without undue hardship to any of them. Pursuant to this reasoning, if tort law fails to compensate everyone, it is not performing its loss distribution task adequately. It is somewhat unsporting, however, to criticize tort law for not doing something it was never designed to do: the new criterion of loss-spreading was never taken into account by the architects of tort law.

When one begins to advocate that *all* accidental losses should be recompensed, one departs from the territory of tort law and enters the regime of social welfare. The logical extension of loss-distribution is social security. It is a mere "palliative," a temporary stopping-place on the way to a complete social insurance system. For tort law could not perform the role of social welfare adequately, even if its basis were strict liability rather than fault. Tort recovery certainly helps to cushion the financial blow of accidental injury. It is welcome enough if there is nothing else available, but if full and swift compensation is the only task of tort law, it should be replaced by something else less costly and less dilatory.

The loss-distribution theory was an admirable attempt by tort scholars to expand the incidence of tort reparation. It was a disguised movement toward increased social welfare by sincere reformers who were impatient with the sluggish advance of progressive legislation. Through this humane theory a few more accident victims may have won compensation, but it was still limited to those "lucky" enough to be hurt by activities in which the tort remedy and liability insurance operated. Its main contribution was that a private type of social welfare could be supplied to some of those who needed it, without any necessity for a dramatic break from the free enterprise system.

There is less need for loss-distribution in tort law today. Modern societies have begun to recognize an obligation toward their sick, their aged, and their poor. Hospital and medical care plans have been enacted. Workers' compensation, unemployment insurance, sick pay, disability, old age, and survivorship payments are becoming increasingly common. These benefits are available to individuals injured by tortious conduct as well as to those who are unable to establish any tort liability. One study has revealed that 40 per cent of all the money received by automobile accident victims came from non-tort sources such as these, and the proportion of this type of aid is steadily rising. As a consequence of these developments, a denial of tort recovery is no longer the tragedy it used to be.

We have erected a complex three-level system to furnish compensation for injured Canadians. At the bottom level are social insurance measures which provide hospital and medical care and some income replacement to all, regardless of the cause of injury or illness. On top of this are several schemes which provide fuller compensation on a no-fault basis for special groups in society such as workers and crime and auto accident victims. At the pinnacle is tort law, which provides more complete reparation for those who are able to prove that they were hurt through the fault of another person.

It has been urged that this complex structure should be unified and forged into a single enriched social welfare scheme which would treat all the sick and injured alike. This debate, however, cannot be divorced from a more general discussion about the guaranteed annual income and other anti-poverty measures. No one denies that both tort law and the present patchwork of welfare schemes need better co-ordination. The disagreement is over whether tort law should survive as an "additional or supplemental remedy," over and above the floor of social insurance. The key issue is whether the resources used to run the tort system would be more wisely spent if they were distributed through the social welfare system. Before attempting any conclusion on this position, the other functions of tort law have to be considered.

B. DETERRENCE

The second historic function of tort law is deterrence or the prevention of accidents. Such legal luminaries as Bentham, Austin, and Salmond believed that the purpose of tort law was not much different from that of the criminal law. Lord Mansfield once wrote that damages acted "as a punishment to the guilty, to deter from any such proceedings in the future...". This should surprise no one in view of the common roots of tort and criminal law.

Judges often express their desire to deter future torts in holding defendants liable, especially when an award of punitive damages is involved. For example, Mr. Justice La Forest, in awarding punitive damages in *Norberg v. Wynrib* declared that "the exchange of drugs for sex by a doctor in a position of power is conduct that cries out for deterrence". Mr. Justice Major in *Stewart v. Pettie*, recently articulated the deterrent role of negligence law as follows:

> One of the primary purposes of negligence law is to enforce reasonable standards of conduct so as to prevent the creation of reasonably foreseeable risks. In this way, tort law serves as a disincentive to risk-creating behaviour.

In *Galaske v. O'Donnell*, a case in which a driver was held liable for failing to buckle in a child passenger, Mr. Justice Cory indicated his desire to foster safety when he explained:

> If the fixing of responsibility on a driver to ensure that young passengers wear seat belts saves one child from death or devastating injury then all society will have benefited.

So, too, Mr. Justice La Forest has indicated in *Winnipeg Condominium Corporation No. 36 v. Bird Construction Co.*, a negligence case, that:

> Allowing recovery against contractors in tort for the cost of repair of dangerous defects thus serves an important preventative function by encouraging socially responsible behaviour ... tort law serves to encourage the repair of dangerous defects and thereby to protect the bodily integrity of inhabitants of buildings.

It may be said, therefore, that judges view tort law as a "whip that makes industry safer and saner".

The admonitory function of tort law operates in two ways. Firstly, individuals who are required to pay damages for losses caused by their substandard conduct will try to avoid a recurrence. Secondly, tort judgments against transgressors are meant to warn others. The threat of tort liability is supposed to deter wrongful conduct and to stimulate caution on the part of those who wish to avoid civil liability for their conduct. In other words, the lesson being taught to society is that tort, like crime, does not pay.

Deterrence has been one of the fundamental assumptions of tort law, but assumptions do not necessarily correspond with reality. On the empirical evidence so far collected, it is hard to tell whether the civil sanction has any sting left in it. Some scholars contend that tort law's deterrent role is a myth, while more charitable authors suggest that the possibility of deterrence is "of a low order".

Certainly, there are impediments in the way of successful deterrence through tort law. Firstly, some individuals are unwilling to conform to the behaviour patterns prescribed by tort law. Some motorists, for example, persist in driving too fast or with their ability impaired, in spite of legal prohibitions. This is not unique to tort law. There are many citizens in our society who knowingly violate the criminal law. Other branches of the law are similarly flouted by some members of our society. All that can be done with these wilful offenders is to impose whatever legal sanction is appropriate and hope that this attitude does not spread throughout society. Tort law and the other legal norms can have little influence on these people.

Secondly, certain persons may be willing to conform to the standard of care expected of them, but they may be unable to live up to it. The awkward, the accident-prone, and those of limited intelligence are sometimes incapable of performing reasonably, however hard they may try. Fortunately, most people are not inadequate to the demands of modern living and will act cautiously in order to avoid mishaps.

Thirdly, someone willing and able to live up to the standards of tort law may be totally ignorant of them. People cannot change their conduct to comply with directions of which they are not apprised. Fortunately, most everyday activities can be performed in a right way or in a wrong way. In most instances one can tell the difference between responsible and risky conduct. Juries have had to pass judgment upon these acts for centuries and they have not met with any major difficulties. In any event, the rules of the road are in statutory form and are known to drivers. Speed limits must be posted. Professional people and entrepreneurs learn the customs of their trades, which are relied upon as important indicators of due care. Of course there are borderline cases, but those individuals should realize that their conduct is at least questionable in these circumstances. People may sometimes investigate the risks inherent in a particular course of conduct and may even hire experts to advise them how to proceed. Another point to consider is that there are a substantial number of people who know more about tort law than the average person. Because of this, the behaviour of certain people, such as doctors, lawyers, law students, police officers, insurance people, adjusters, court officials, and service station employees may be affected more by tort law than that of the general public. In addition, there are many citizens who have been involved in tort litigation as parties, witnesses or jurors and have learned something about the operation of tort law.

Fourthly, an even graver deficiency plagues tort law. The advent of liability insurance has removed some of its prophylactic power because the civil sanction is rarely applied against the tortfeasors themselves. When a judgment against an individual is paid by the individual's insurer, whatever preventive force tort law retains is further enfeebled. Some scholars have argued, therefore, that there is no sting left in tort law in the motor vehicle accident area because liability insurance coverage for motorists is almost universal. This position is too simplistic. Despite compulsory insurance laws, a tiny percentage of Canadian motorists are still uninsured. These individuals remain subject to the full deterrent lash of tort law, since they have to pay personally for the consequences of their negligence. Of course, many of the uninsured drivers are judgment-proof and cannot pay damages awarded against them. However, when judgments are rendered against uninsured motorists they may lose their licences and be taken off the road altogether, if an unsatisfied judgment fund is forced to pay the awards on their behalf. Removal of such drivers from the highways is the most stringent deterrent of them all, and occurs as an indirect result of tort liability. There are, moreover, many motorists who carry only the minimum limits of liability insurance required by law. These people are personally responsible if a damage award against them exceeds this figure. Furthermore, the loss in question may not be covered by the terms of the insurance policy at all. For example, the person injured by the driver may be some person excluded by the provisions of the policy. Another possibility is that the motorist may have forfeited the right to be indemnified by violating one of the conditions of the policy. For instance, if the motorist drives while drunk, he or she is not covered by the policy, even though the insurer is initially responsible by statute to any third person who has suffered loss. Lastly, even if the insurer stands behind the motorist, the motorist must still undergo the inconvenience of being involved in a civil suit, something no one enjoys. Despite all these potentially unpleasant repercussions, one survey revealed that 58 per cent of the respondents felt that civil liability did not affect careful driving, whereas only 14 per cent thought that it did. It is hard to assess the reliability of this study, but it does seem to reveal the public's perception of the problem.

In addition to imposing civil liability for negligence, the common law courts withhold or reduce the recovery of anyone who is contributorily negligent with regard to their own safety. Contributory negligence is still being used to encourage care by plaintiffs. The knowledge that one will be denied compensation in whole or in part as a result of one's own negligence should spur one to use caution. This rule may be doubly influential, because the negligence of a driver may be imputed to passengers and to family. Thus, not only is the contributorily negligent actor waiving the right to recover but may also impede friends and relatives from receiving full damages for their injuries. The application of the seat belt defence is an example of the use of contributory negligence law as a deterrent to dangerous conduct.

1. Insurance Company Influence

Whereas liability insurance dulls the financial incentive of *drivers* to use care, it sharpens the motivation of insurance *companies* to prevent accidents. The more mishaps occur during an activity, the less profit is earned and the higher the cost of insurance coverage for those who engage in it. Whenever insurance premiums rise, dissatisfaction with the insurance industry intensifies. This [in] turn stimulates pressure for the state to nationalize the business. Since insurance companies want to avert this fate and to maximize profits, they try to reduce accidents.

One technique employed by insurance companies is the linking of each individual's premium to his or her accident record. A claim-free driver pays less than one who has been responsible for an accident. That cannot help but remind some motorists of their duty to exercise care. Indeed, Professor Fleming has indicated that an increase in premiums could be an even more effective deterrent than personal liability, since the former has to be paid if the motorist wishes to continue driving whereas a tort judgment probably could not be paid at all. A recent survey in the United States has shown that only 21 per cent of the respondents thought that their insurance premiums would be raised if they were involved in an accident. This figure certainly casts doubt on the efficacy of such a sanction. Nevertheless, if 21 per cent are deterred by this threat, *some* benefit may be derived from it. If the public were better informed about their rights and duties in relation to insurance coverage, this sanction might become more influential.

Another tool at the disposal of an insurer is the cancellation of a policy or refusal to provide coverage. In Canada, this is not as disastrous as it is elsewhere, because of the existence of a pooling mechanism which guarantees that insurance is available to all, regardless of how bad a risk they are. Strangely, an American study disclosed that only 2 per cent of the people interviewed expected the cancellation of their policy after an accident. Since an "unperceived penalty cannot deter future deviant conduct," the force of this sanction is minimal.

Insurers can stimulate their insureds to institute safer practices. One product liability insurance company was suddenly confronted by a series of claims against its insured arising from breaking ketchup bottles. Upon investigation, the company discovered that its insured had recently changed the design of its bottles. When the insurer suggested that this new type of container be abandoned, the insured complied. Another insurance company provided coverage for a well-known music composer, who had the dangerous habit of writing music at the same time that he was driving his automobile. As a result, he was frequently involved in accidents because of his inattention. His premium rates soared. Eventually, his insurance company informed him that his policy would have to be cancelled if he did not terminate this practice. Instead of giving up his music-writing while travelling, the composer hired a chauffeur to operate his car for him.

The insurance industry has also undertaken driver education campaigns, supported safety organizations, advocated defensive driving, combatted drunken driving, urged the use of seat belts and other worthwhile endeavours. More recently, these efforts have been stepped up, but there is still much more that can be done. Pressure from insurers for such measures as crashworthy vehicles, safer highways, tougher licensing laws, and stricter enforcement of traffic laws will accelerate their introduction.

To be sure, these efforts aimed at accident reduction are indirect and hardly of major significance. Direct government intervention would be far more effective. Unhappily though, most governments lack the courage to do the things necessary to cut accidents appreciably. The minimal efforts of the insurance industry are better than nothing.

2. Partnership with Criminal Law

Tort law may act as a partner of the criminal law. The civil sanction may reinforce the efforts of penal enforcement authorities, which are occasionally ineffectual. Criminal penalties are often so insignificant that they do not deter anyone. A highway traffic offence, for instance, may produce a fine of only $50, an amount that frightens no one. Demerit point schemes provide the additional threat of licence suspension, but most infractions cost only one or two points out of the 12 or 15 needed to revoke a driver's permit. A serious violation like drunk driving may lead to the loss of a licence, but such offences are less com-

91

mon than the minor ones that often precede collisions. Another reason for the inefficacy of the criminal law is that its enforcement is sporadic. Millions of highway infractions are reported each year but a far greater number are never detected. Every motorist has contravened some traffic law without having been prosecuted for it.

Tort law can assist penal law in this area. Evidence of the violation of a criminal statute may be relied upon by a civil court in a suit by a person injured thereby. There are, of course, limitations on civil enforcement. Some harm to an individual is necessary for an action to lie. Moreover, private citizens rather than the police are left to administer the sanction. Normally this would hamper its effectiveness, but because plaintiffs prosecuting their own claims have a financial incentive to succeed, they may well do a more thorough job than a prosecutor. Tort law adds to the list of potential law enforcement officers an entire army of zealous assistants. This additional sanction renders the criminal law "more effective". Lord Justice Goddard once concluded that "the real incentive for the observance by employers of their statutory duties under [certain statutes] is not their liability to substantial fines, but the possibility of heavy claims for damages". In addition, punitive damages are available in certain extreme cases, providing extra force to the civil sanction.

The decision of *Menow v. Honsberger and Jordan House Ltd.* is a good example of a tort action assisting in criminal law enforcement. The plaintiff was served alcoholic beverages by the employees of the defendant hotel after he had become intoxicated, in violation of the Liquor Control Act of Ontario. He was then ejected from the hotel into a situation of danger near a busy highway. Shortly thereafter, as he was staggering along the road, he was struck by a negligently driven vehicle. At trial, Mr. Justice Haines stated that "by committing this unlawful act, the corporate defendant has not only committed an offence under the relevant liquor statutes, but it has also breached a common law duty to the plaintiff not to serve him liquor when he was visibly intoxicated". This decision should put some teeth into the penal legislation, which is woefully under-enforced. Despite frequent arrests of drunken drivers who have visited bars, one rarely hears of prosecutions or cancelled tavern licences because of the violation of this statute. Mr. Justice Haines did not allude to this difficulty in his reasons, but this case cannot help but alert innkeepers to the risks they run not only from penal enforcement but also from civil proceedings

against them. Mr. Justice Haines pointed out that he did not want every tavern owner "to act as a watch dog for all patrons who enter his place of business and drink to excess", but he was prepared to countenance it in certain circumstances. Even a caution such as this should foster increased discretion by tavern owners.

There are, of course, numerous other statutes, the violation of which may yield tort liability. Violators of food and drug laws may be subjected to tort liability as well as penal fines. Anyone who fails to install or inspect a gas furnace according to the legislative requirements risks not only a penal prosecution but also civil liability. The availability of the tort remedy may act as a prod where the criminal law has become a dead letter.

One recurrent complaint about our society is that whenever we want to eradicate some nasty activity, we pass a law making it a crime. Consequently, we may have overloaded our police forces and oppressed some of our citizenry. As a result, the Law Reform Commission of Canada has called for restraint in the use of the criminal law. The sanction of tort law may be more attractive in combatting some of this anti-social conduct because it operates *only* at the behest of a victim. The increasing use of tort actions by rape and child abuse victims can never replace criminal law remedies, but it has some advantages, for example, discovery is available, it is more private, the claimant is more in control of the process and the burden of proof is less onerous. Although the stigma is not as powerful as that of criminal law, it does nevertheless express some public disapproval of the wrongful activity, it may supply a modicum of social control, and it allows for awards for damages for the victims, something that is more useful to them than a fine or jail sentence.

C.   EDUCATION

Tort law is an educator. Along with criminal prosecutions, coroners' inquests, royal commissions and the like, a tort trial is a teacher. It educates the public, not just potential tortfeasors but all of us. Indeed, Glanville Williams has suggested that making someone pay compensation may be "educationally superior to a fine" in that "it teaches a moral lesson". The communications explosion has magnified the importance of this didactic role of tort law. Malpractice, libel, and product liability cases in particular attract the attention of the press. Doctors, journalists, and manufacturers closely observe the outcomes of these disputes, which concern them so vitally. Their trade journals often report the results of litigation involving fellow professionals. Each annual report of the Canadian Medical Protective Association, for example, contains a summary of the medical malpractice suits that go to trial each year in Canada. Advice may be given. Conferences may be convened to discuss the problems dealt with in the litigation. Members of the public may become more alert in their dealings with these professionals. They may become less trusting and ask more questions. To be sure, this is not the most efficient way of curtailing substandard practices; other forms of regulations would undoubtedly be preferable. The sad fact is, however, that professional groups are reluctant to police their own professions strenuously, and manufacturers are often largely immune from government supervision. Until our society is prepared to use more effective weapons, the educational force of tort law may be all there is.

Tort law is also a reinforcer of values. Like the criminal law, tort law enshrines many of the traditional moral principles of Anglo-American society. This is a mixed blessing for many of these values are in need of reassessment. Tort law may well impede the birth of new moral principles through its conservation of the older values. If, however, any new moral ideals catch hold, they will infiltrate the principles of tort law. At worst, tort law slows down their acceptance and permits some sober second thoughts.

By dramatizing in open court certain acts of "wrong-doing", tort law may condemn "anti-social elements" and at the same time "exalt the good". Slipshod manufacturers, inadequate drivers, and careless doctors are subject to judicial disapproval in open court. Even if a defendant is insured, could not care less about the outcome, or refuses to alter future conduct, the law publicly marks the defendant as a "wrong-doer" and vindicates the plaintiff's complaint. In this way tort law, like criminal law, furnishes an opportunity to foster community feeling about common moral values. Obviously, failure to conform to the standards of tort law is not as morally reprehensible as murder, rape, robbery or arson. Nevertheless, all of these acts are torts as well as crimes. Under either legal categorization, such conduct is unacceptable to right-thinking individuals. Under either description, it should be, and is, publicly denounced.

Tort law may occasionally be *more* effective than criminal law for this purpose. A victim of a criminal assault might prefer to sue the attacker in tort rather than call the police, because the former course may provide some monetary gain while the latter will not. Further, such aggrieved persons may wish to take some action against their aggressors, but may not want them to end up in jail. Another benefit of tort proceedings is that they may be easily settled when the claimant's ardour cools, whereas criminal cases do not lend themselves to such efficient disposal. Some offensive conduct deserves public disapproval, but at the same time is too trivial for the criminal sanction. For example, such distasteful conduct as spitting in someone's eye can lead to official condemnation if the victim launches a tort suit. It is a costly and time-consuming avenue of redress, but it is available to those who feel outraged by such conduct. Such actions are permitted even though they may yield the winner only nominal damages.

One value at the heart of tort law is the notion of individual responsibility, something that is central to Western civilization. If people act responsibly, they should be rewarded; if they act irresponsibly, they should be punished. There is no need to disguise the fact that this is the underlying morality of the fault system. No one denies that the fault system is riddled with imperfections; it is costly, difficult to administer, denies compensation to many injured people, and is replete with delays. Nevertheless, it is also a mark of nobility when a society directs its members to conduct themselves reasonably in their relations with their fellow citizens, or pay for the consequences. A concomitant of this is that people must also look after themselves, or be denied compensation if they are hurt. There are some exceptions made for children and the mentally disabled, but none for the dull-witted or the awkward. Many people seem to feel that it is "just and fair" to make the "guilty" pay, not the "innocent", and that the "innocent" *should* receive compensation, but not the "guilty". Philosophers call this corrective justice. The philosophy of the age of reason, not determinism, still permeates tort law. The fundamental goal is individual restraint and respect for one's fellow creatures, something which is required more than ever in mass urban societies.

Tort law also demonstrates abiding respect for the dignity of the individual. It treats every claimant as unique, special, and different to everyone else in the world. In assessing damages under tort theory, each person is supposed to recover what each *personally* has lost. Not only does the person with a large salary or heavy medical costs receive full compensation, but the non-pecuniary or psychic losses are also recompensed. Pain and suffering is assessed. The music-lover, if deprived of hearing, receives more than one who is not interested in music. The golfer who is incapacitated gets more than a sedentary individual. Tort trials go to great lengths to calculate these individuals' losses. This is certainly one of the reasons why the tort system is so expensive and dilatory. There is also considerable doubt about how accurate this exercise is. Certainly lawyers and judges frequently encounter difficulty deciding what a case is "worth". Judges and juries may differ. Awards may vary from place to place and from time to time. Despite these demerits, however, a system that endeavours to achieve these aims manifests a rare concern for human beings, an attitude that deserves nourishment. In one way, those who argue that everyone should receive compensation for injuries are being more humane, because everyone is to be looked after, but they are also being less humane, because the special qualities and unique losses of each individual are ignored. Only tort law is tailored to deal with each person as an individual entity. This is unquestionably one of its weaknesses, but it is also one of its greatest strengths.

Tort law is, therefore, performing some of the functions of the school and, to an extent, the church. The moral principles upon which tort law is based are constantly being reiterated for the benefit of those who are involved and those who observe. This is a healthy thing, for these principles are useful guidelines for individuals to follow in ordering their relations with their fellow human beings.

D. PSYCHOLOGICAL FUNCTION

Tort law may perform certain psychological functions. For example, the tort action, like the criminal law, may provide some appeasement to those injured by wrongful conduct. Lord Diplock has contended that no one would suggest using tort law for the purpose of vengeance. Nevertheless, though it is distasteful to most of us, this has always been one of the unexpressed uses of tort law and criminal law. Too many human beings still seem to have need of such an outlet for their desire for revenge. The sad fact is that there is in many of us something primitive which tort law may satisfy.

This questionable service that tort law performs can be put in a more positive and acceptable form. It gives some psychological comfort to the injured. It can be said that tort law helps to keep the peace by providing a legal method of quenching the thirst for revenge. It will be recalled that this was the historical rationale for the creation of tort law. Money damages were paid to the victims of tortious conduct in the hope of curtailing blood feuds. If these legal avenues to revenge were closed today, some victims of wrongful conduct might once again take up clubs and axes to "get even" with their aggressors. It is better to pursue a wrongdoer with a writ than with a rifle.

There is some support for this view in the experience of the Soviet Union. Shortly after the revolution the tort action was abolished, but it soon had to be resurrected. Even Communists, purified as they were supposed to be from economic avarice, apparently obtained some psychological satisfaction from tort suits. It should also be pointed out that liability insurance was not permitted in the U.S.S.R. so that the tort sanction operated directly on the tortfeasors and their pocketbooks. Another clue to the personal revenge element in tort law is our insistence on defendants being sued personally, even though there is insurance against the loss. True, we say that we are playing this cat-and-mouse game to avoid distorting the deliberations of the jury, but in reality we may be doing it to permit victims to obtain a semblance of personal retribution.

Tort law may counteract the feeling of alienation and despair which pervades our society. Governments, corporations, unions, and universities have grown too large and impersonal. A feeling of helplessness and personal insignificance grips too many of our people. Many individuals feel that they have lost control over their lives. No one seems to care about them anymore. A protest march, a sit-in or some other dramatic act can change all this. For a time, people *do* seem to care about the protestors. The media takes notice of them. They seem to matter more. They become "relevant". There seems to be a psychological need for personal recognition, which may contribute something to the popularity of this type of activity. A tort suit may likewise provide some psychological satisfaction. Instead of rebelling or demonstrating with a picket sign, an aggrieved individual may begin a law suit. The tort trial is an institution that displays great concern for the individual, especially if there is a jury. The parties have the undivided attention of everyone in the court — judge, jury, counsel, witnesses, spectators and occasionally, the press and the public. The award of damages for pain and suffering clearly manifests "fellow feelings". As much time as is necessary to conclude the case is allocated to it, whether it be a day, a week, a month or a year. Without doubt this is a lavish process, but each accident victim is entitled to demand such an exhaustive hearing.

Of course, a litigant must be able to afford the elaborate psychiatric treatment. It is not provided to everyone as a matter of right. Moreover, there must be some legitimate grievance recognized by tort law, or the action can be snuffed out at an early stage. In addition, the promiscuous use of litigation is discouraged by the offer to settle technique. If someone wants the psychological satisfaction of dragging the defendant into court, even after an admission of liability and an offer to pay, this may be done, but the defendant's subsequent costs must be paid if the trial award is less than was offered in settlement by the defendant. Fortunately, not everyone demands a full-scale trial of his or her case. Most tort suits are settled. Nevertheless, the thought that this *is available*, if needed, should give some comfort to the alienated.

Tort trials enrich our society with ritual and symbolism. The solemnity, the formality, and the language of tort litigation contribute to a sense of mystery. This is something all societies seem to require. As agnosticism supplants religion in the modern world, rituals such as court proceedings are gaining in importance. More and more of us, suffering from "future shock", are searching for bridges with the past, points of stability, to comfort us as the world races by. The traditions of litigation may supply some medicine for this ailment.

Our society will never rid itself of disputes and quarrels. Indeed, it may not be wise to eliminate them even if we could. It is natural to seek a human resolution to these omnipresent human disagreements. Tort law, despite its manifold inadequacies, provides a forum for this symbolic quest for human justice. We do not know very much about the psychological reasons for the mystique surrounding the dispensation of human justice according to law. We do know, however, that for most people the process exudes an aura of dignity, humanity and impartiality. There is little danger that it will ever be replaced by computers providing mathematical answers to our problems.

E. MARKET DETERRENCE

The law of tort may reduce accidents through market deterrence. This must be distinguished from the type of deterrence discussed above, whereby tort law directly attacks the specific occasions of danger. Market or general deterrence functions *indirectly*. It lowers accident costs by making those activities that are accident-prone more expensive by requiring them to bear the full costs of the mishaps they produce. This renders safer substitutes more attractive, because they cost less.

There are certainly more effective ways of reducing accidents. The criminal law and administrative regulation are widely used to cut accidents. We prohibit certain activities altogether if they are too dangerous, even if they could pay their way in the market. For example, we forbid dynamite blasting or the firing of guns in the centre of the city. Further, we regulate the way in which certain activities are conducted. Automobiles, although they are allowed on the highways, may not be driven in excess of the speed limit and drivers must comply with the rules of the road.

There are, however, many types of activities we do not wish to prohibit altogether nor to supervise too closely. Market deterrence can function here as a useful adjunct to criminal and administrative law. We permit these activities to be carried on with only the minimum of control — tort law's general guideline of reasonable care. Thus businesspeople may carry on business as long as they do not negligently injure anyone. If they do hurt someone, they are required to pay the costs incurred by the victim. As the total of damage costs rises, the price of products or activities will increase accordingly. Eventually, businesspeople would have to institute safer practices or be driven out of business as their customers switch to less costly substitutes. This is accomplished automatically through the ordinary forces of the market, without any help from politicians and bureaucrats.

Only a fool would be content with market deterrence as the *only* tool for keeping accidents in check. Nevertheless, as a *subsidiary* technique the idea has some allure because it is founded on respect for individual choice in a free market economy. It permits people to decide whether they will engage in any activity and pay its full costs including the accident expenses, or whether they will engage in safer alternative activities which are less costly.

The foundation of this doctrine is simply economics, the theory that individuals know what is best for themselves. Because of this, we should permit them to make their own decisions about how to spend their money. In other words, the way a society allocates its resources should be a reflection of the individual choices made by all its members. If people want automobiles rather than schools, they should have automobiles rather than schools. As long as the prices of the various goods and services available reflect the full costs of providing them, the buyers will be able to make informed decisions.

If the full costs of accidents are not borne by the activity that produced them, the market process will be distorted. More individuals will choose a particular activity than should do so, because it is subsidized to the extent that it is relieved from any portion of its accident costs. The result would resemble the government paying part of the cost of the steel that goes into automobiles. Such a subsidy reduces the cost of and increases the demand for the product, which generates more accidents. Consequently market deterrence works best when the entire price of all accidents is loaded onto the activities generating it. It operates more effectively under an absolute liability system than it does under a fault-based regime. Nevertheless, it can function to a degree within a negligence system. The theory can also be utilized by government-operated social insurance schemes and even by loss insurance measures.

This market or general deterrence approach reduces accident costs in two ways. Firstly, it creates a financial incentive for people who are engaged in dangerous activities to switch to safer activities. If the participants in a risky activity have to pay for its full cost, some of them may transfer to a safer activity which is cheaper. Whenever someone decides to substitute a less hazardous activity for a more dangerous one, society benefits. Of course, any such decision would take into account not only the cost differential but also the quality of the substitute activity.

An example will illustrate the way this theory works. Let us say that someone is considering the purchase of a new automobile. Assume further that the expense of owning a car is $1,000 per year, which includes $200 for insurance. Without a car, annual transportation costs on bus, taxi and train would be $500. This $500 annual cost differential may help one to decide that it is not worth it to buy the car. This is good, because the fewer cars on the road, the fewer automobile collisions will

result. If one were not required to pay the $200 for insurance, as would be the case if the accident costs were borne by some government scheme financed out of general revenue, the smaller cost differential of $300 might make vehicle ownership more attractive, and one might buy the car. Consequently, market deterrence can foster the use of public transportation, which is less accident-prone than private motor-car traffic.

Market deterrence may also curtail the number of accidents in which youthful drivers are involved. It is established that younger drivers are far more accident-prone [than] older ones. Insurance costs, which reflect this propensity, are therefore higher for young people. Many youths who could afford to buy an old jalopy cannot pay the high insurance premiums exacted from them. Thus there may be fewer teenagers in old jalopies on the highways than there would be if the costs of accidents were paid out of government funds.

The second way in which general deterrence diminishes the expenses of accidents is to encourage people to alter the *way* in which they conduct their activities, rather than changing the *type* of activities altogether. Perhaps another example will be of assistance. Let us assume that a motorist spends an average amount of $200 per year on accident costs. Further, suppose that the motorist were to adopt a different kind of braking system on the car, the accident expenses would total only $100. The safer brakes are available at a cost of $50. The motorist might well decide to spend the $50 for the new brakes, cut the accident costs to $100, and thereby save $50 annually in accident costs. If the $200 accident costs were paid by the state, there would be no cost incentive to switch to the new brakes.

The market deterrence theory has not yet been empirically tested. We do not know how efficiently it operates, or indeed if it functions at all. It may work only with some activities, but not with others. Its effectiveness will partially depend upon the elasticity of the demand for the product or activity. It will also hinge on the proportion of the price made up by accident costs. In many activities the proportion of accident costs compared with labour and material costs will be so infinitesimal that the additional burden placed upon the activity by tort liability tends to keep these costs down. Market or general deterrence would tend to have more bite if *all* the costs of accidents — fault-caused as well as non-fault-caused — were included in the price of the activity. Even if this were the case there might not be sufficient price incentive to foster changes in the way activities are conducted. In any event, little harm is done by shifting the loss to the enterprise, because this course can also be supported on the ground that it is "just and fair" that accident costs be borne by those who engage in certain activities. It can also be justified by the theory of loss-distribution.

Another serious shortcoming of the market deterrence approach is that it discriminates heavily against the poor. By placing the full costs of accidents on the activities which generate them, we are permitting the rich to engage in dangerous activities which the poor cannot afford. In short, this "works like a regressive tax". This argument would have more force if market deterrence were used exclusively to curtail accidents. The fact is, however, that most really dangerous activities are prohibited for rich and poor alike by the criminal law. Furthermore, it is only in the marginally

risky situations that market deterrence operates. It must be admitted that if the market is going to be used at all, it must *necessarily* discriminate against the less affluent members of our society. This is what the market system is all about. But this should not discourage us unduly. The overwhelming majority of Canadians earn salaries which are relatively similar. There are only a few lucky ones at the top and a few unlucky ones at the bottom. For most people each expenditure involves a question of their priorities and how they wish to spend their limited resources.

In conclusion, tort law would probably never survive if market deterrence were its *only* aim. However, market deterrence may be achieved *in addition* to the other objectives of tort law, as a kind of bonus. In this context it is merely another factor to consider in deciding whether tort law deserves continued life.

(b)   Some Recent Obituaries of Tort Law[†]

Arthur Ripstein

Patrick Atiyah has long been a critic of tort law as an approach to accidents. His 1970 *Accidents, Compensation, and the Law* offered a six-count 'indictment' of the fault system. It featured unfavourable contrasts between tort liability and other means of dealing with accidental injuries and losses. That book is now in its fifth edition, and Peter Cane has replaced Atiyah as its author. Nonetheless, the general thrust of the book remains unchanged. Atiyah's most recent book, *The Damages Lottery*, expands those arguments for a broader audience. It opens with a striking pair of examples: a young girl loses her leg as a result of meningitis, but receives no compensation; a man slips on an over-polished dance floor, breaking his leg, and recovers a substantial sum from the local authority that operates the dance hall. The basic argument is already contained in the examples. Those who are injured as a result of the negligence of others col-

lect huge damage awards, which seek to provide full compensation, while those who fall ill or are injured in almost any other way — by non-negligent behaviour, by natural forces, or through the negligence of people who lack liability insurance — at most recover a fraction of their losses from some specialized social insurance scheme. This result is utterly arbitrary, because it shows an unfair preference for those who are injured in certain ways. This is unjust, since it is manifest that a person's need for compensation does not depend on the source of his or her injury. The situation is made worse by the fact that damages are paid either by insurance or (if the injurer is a public authority) by taxpayers. Either way, the costs are passed on to the public, in the form of higher prices of goods and services, and higher taxes both directly through the costs of awards, and indirectly because insurance premiums are deducted by businesses. As a

---

† (1998) 40 U.T.L.J. 561 at 561–67. Reproduced by permission of University of Toronto Press Incorporated (www.utpjournals.com).

result, the award of damages has no real impact on the injurer. Thus the prospect of liability will not deter carelessness. Since most cases are settled out of court, the system does not even provide an occasion for public accountability. Nonetheless, huge sums that might go to those in need are spent instead on determining liability. Thus, Atiyah concludes, it is an unjust and inefficient system.

While Atiyah's objections to the tort system have not changed, his view of the alternatives certainly have. In the first edition of *Accidents, Compensation, and the Law*, he found it 'difficult to resist the conclusion that the right path for reform is to abolish the tort system so far as personal injuries are concerned, and to use the money at present being poured into the tort system to improve the social security benefits, and the social services more generally.' His support for such programs was avowedly egalitarian, and rested on the idea that a person's life prospects ought not to depend on chance. Atiyah now regards such programs as bureaucratic and paternalistic. He even speculates that the rise in British tort claims may be the result of a sort of generalized dependency borne of compensation programs and the welfare state. Such programs, he now opines, leave people unwilling to take responsibility for protecting themselves against misfortune. Worse, they lead people to look for someone to blame every time something goes wrong.

Despite his new-found misgivings about social security programs, Atiyah still advocates abolishing the tort system for personal injuries. His opening examples suggest that he still supposes that misfortunes should be addressed on the basis of their urgency. He turns out to suppose no such thing. Instead, he advocates a mandatory no-fault system for road accidents, and a free market in private, first-party insurance. Universal coverage providing full compensation for everyone would be too expensive. Allowing people to choose the degree of protection they want for their own persons, income, and property is the obvious alternative. It will ensure that each person will receive the amount of compensation he or she is willing to pay for. (The one exception is motorists, who Atiyah thinks should be required to carry a mandatory minimum for their own good.) The government will be left only with a fall-back role for those unable to afford insurance. Although he sometimes talks as though he advocates taking the money that goes to compensating 'pop singers and tennis stars' and giving it to those who are in need, as it turns out, Atiyah objects only to high earners receiving large

tort awards. He offers no objection to their large incomes as such, and would allow them to insure those incomes.

The changes in Atiyah's proposed alternatives to tort reflect the temper of the times, coming as they do on the heels of the erosion of the welfare state. He presents the tort system as a wasteful government program that should be cut. But where his earlier alternatives were at least consonant with the moral impetus of his critiques, the adoption of his more recent proposals would exacerbate many of the problems for which he faults the tort system. Other advocates of private insurance argue on economic grounds that the tort system in general, and products liability law in particular, forces consumers to effectively purchase insurance against certain injuries. Since consumers pay for the insurance anyway, it is best left to consumers to choose the precise coverage they want. Atiyah's argument, by contrast, is supposed to derive from concerns about the fact that some people get huge damage awards while others receive nothing. His proposed alternative does nothing to remedy *that* problem. In a first-party system, the amount of compensation one receives is proportional to the insurance one buys. Although this may appear to be a principle that makes compensation proportional to prudence, in practice it would be compensation in proportion to wealth. Consider some examples of first-party insurance. High-income earners typically carry high levels of long-term disability insurance; low-income earners do not. The reason is not that people with high incomes are prudent ants, and those with small incomes feckless grasshoppers. It is that those with large incomes are better able to afford the costs of insuring. Again, Atiyah points to homeowner's insurance as an example of a successful first-party system that has pretty much displaced the tort system for property damage. Homeowner's policies cover falling trees no less than careless neighbours. Yet a system of homeowner's insurance is vulnerable to Atiyah's stated objection to the tort system. Opulent fixtures that suffer water damage are replaced at their full value, as are stolen furs and jewellery. But if a homeless person loses all of his or her possessions, the system of private homeowner's insurance does nothing. Even among those who purchase it, first-party insurance often magnifies distributive inequalities. Insurers, who are in business to make money, typically offer preferred rates to the least vulnerable, so that it costs almost as much to insure the contents of a small apartment as those of a large house. The point of these examples is not to malign those who sell or purchase first-part insurance. Any system that seeks to make up losses as they occur will leave existing distributive inequities in place, and sometimes magnify them. If those inequities trouble us — as they should — replacing tort law with first-party insurance does nothing to address them.

In the end, the main benefit Atiyah's alternative offers to the needy is reduced prices for goods and services, and perhaps reduced taxes, because manufacturers will not need to buy liability insurance. No numbers are offered, but even this promised side benefit sits uneasily with his other arguments. He is attuned to the ability of companies to pass the costs of liability insurance on to their customers. In contrast, he does not consider the ability of those with market power to pass the costs of their own first-party coverage on to their customers. Nor does he mention that under his proposed system, people would need to pay for their own first-party insurance, including insurance against the carelessness of others.

The failure of Atiyah's proposal to address the problem that motivates his criticism reflects a deeper tension in his views. His criticisms of the tort system presuppose more general objections to the distributional effects of schemes of private ordering. Tort law is a form of private ordering, inasmuch as it shifts burdens from one private citizen to another, without looking to the needs of either those involved, or third parties. Although Atiyah makes heavy weather of the role of legal institutions in leading to the outcomes he bemoans, other forms of legally sustained private ordering — most notably markets — have parallel effects. It is a pervasive feature of market society that vast disparities in wealth and well-being result from the relative scarcity of various assets and abilities. Like the tort system, markets are not primarily responsive to needs. In itself, this is not necessarily a bad thing. According to standard defences of market allocations, the mere fact that some people end up with more resources than others is not objectionable, provided that shifts in resources from one person to another come about in acceptable ways. Of course, which ways of changing holdings are acceptable is a matter of controversy, as is the appropriate range within which markets should operate. But almost everyone accepts that markets have a significant place in determining who does what and who owns what. In the same way, almost everyone accepts that some ways of changing holdings, such as gifts and voluntary exchanges, are acceptable, while others, such as

force and fraud, are not. Almost everyone also accepts that at least some losses appropriately lie where they fall.

Negligence law is best understood against the broader background of private ordering. If the results of private interactions are to be acceptable, changes in holdings that come about in the wrong ways need to be made up. A system of private ordering requires that one person not be able to displace the costs of his activities onto others. Those who take or damage the property of others in the course of pursuing their own ends need to repair what they have done. The same point applies to personal injuries: if one person carelessly injures another in the course of carrying out his purposes, it is appropriate that the injurer bear the costs of the injuries. That is why the fault system supposes that those who are wrongfully injured must be 'made whole' by their injurers, even if that means restoring a large income. Tort law thus gives expression to a familiar idea of responsibility, according to which the person who makes a mess must clean it up. The standard of care serves to determine who has made which mess in light of the amount of risk it is acceptable to impose on others. Those who exercise appropriate care are not responsible for injuries that result from their actions. From the point of view of the fault system, such accidents are matters of luck rather than responsibility. Those who fail to exercise appropriate care take risks with the safety of others. As a result, they must bear the costs if those risks ripen into injuries. In this sense, negligence liability is a basic element of a culture of responsibility.

Atiyah's rhetoric obscures the role of responsibility in tort law. To say that someone should 'take responsibility' for safety is ambiguous. Sometimes it means that someone should take precautions to avoid injuring others. Other times it means that someone should take precautions to avoid injuring herself. Still other times it means that people who choose to take risks ought to insure themselves, rather than becoming burdens to the public purse. Atiyah trades on this ambiguity by putting forward a litany of examples in which the law has been 'stretched' by plaintiffs seeking compensation from defendants whose responsibility is dubious. As he describes the cases, the defendants typically appear blameless. In some of them, we are left with the impression that if anyone ought to have been more careful, it was the plaintiff. Reflection on these examples is supposed to lead us to conclude that people should insure against their own carelessness, and perhaps also against their own bad luck. They should bear the costs of their choices, rather than trying to displace those costs onto others. Because they are examples in which we are not inclined to think that the defendant is not responsible for the plaintiff's injury, though, they distract us from the cases that are the central concern of the tort system, namely those in which the defendant *is* responsible. In those cases, the sort of reasoning that Atiyah invokes — don't try to find someone else to pin your problems on — leads to the conclusion that injurers should pay. If cases in which people with 'deep pockets' act at their peril involve troubling evasions of responsibility, so too does his system in which the security of accident victims is simply their problem.

Consider Atiyah's example of homeowner's insurance in this light. Homeowner's policies protect against deliberate wrongdoing, as well as against accidents and natural disasters. The person who does not carry adequate insurance against burglary may be foolish, even irresponsible. But that does not change the fact that the burglar is primarily responsible for the loss, and that a kind of justice is done if the stolen goods are recovered. The reason that damages for negligence seem compelling is the same. People do not have a responsibility to bear the costs of other people's wrongdoing. Justice requires that those who wrongfully injure others through their negligence must bear the costs their wrongdoing creates.

Of course, Atiyah is right to point out that as things stand, injured people typically recover their losses only if their injurers are adequately insured. But he overplays the importance of that fact. It is simply a reflection of the idea that people should take responsibility for their own affairs, both by taking precautions against injuring others and by making sure they have the resources to make up any losses they bring about. He also complains bitterly about the fact that taxpayers often bear the costs of liability judgments against public officials. Here too, he fails to take his own admonishments

about responsibility seriously. Just as individuals must not pursue their own ends at the cost of the safety of others, so too, when society sets itself a goal through its elected officials, it must not do so at the expense of the safety of particular citizens. Where public officials carelessly injure private citizens, the public, in whose interest those officials were acting, must bear the costs. The fact that some people are too ready to look for someone with 'deep pockets' to blame for their injuries does not change the fact that people sometimes have legitimate grievances against their injurers.

Atiyah's position thus seems to be in tension with itself. He is willing to accept the distributive effects of markets, but objects to restoring them so as to cancel the effects of wrongdoing. He is keen on responsibility, but unwilling to follow his commitments through to cases of responsibility to others. For Atiyah, the difference is that the tort system is a publicly funded compensation system, whereas the market, including the private-insurance market, is a matter of individual choice and responsibility. He tells us that '[i]t is time that the public understood that they themselves are paying for these damages awards.' A few pages later, he parlays this into a more general claim: 'Nobody would set up a social security or welfare program which only compensated those injured through the fault of others. Once it is grasped that the public is paying to the whole system, the basic structure of the system — the fault principle — becomes an absurdity.' But the only argument offered to show that the tort system is publicly funded rests on the claim that compensation costs are passed on to consumers in the form of higher prices. The same argument could be used to show that all incomes in a market society are always reflected in the prices of goods and services, and so they too are publicly funded. So understood, the idea of public funding loses all of its content. As a result, the contrast between the acceptable inequalities of the insurance market and the unacceptable inequalities of the tort system collapses.

(c) The Future of Tort Law: Mapping the Contours of the Debate†

Michael J. Trebilcock

1. EVALUATING TORT LAW

The recent crisis in the availability, affordability, and adequacy of liability insurance in the United States and to a lesser extent in Canada, and widespread public attention that has been generated in the United States in a number of huge mass tort claims, such as the asbestos, DES, and Agent Orange litigation, have precipitated much anguished political, judicial and academic soul-searching as to the goals and future of the tort system.

In evaluating the performance of the present tort system, it is obviously necessary to be clear on the criteria against which it is to be evaluated. Unfortunately, controversy begins with this very threshold question. First, there is a fundamental disagreement as to what goals the tort system is designed or can be made to serve. Second, even where there is agreement on objectives, there is often controversy or at least profound certainty as to what the empirical evidence proves as to how well the tort system achieves those objectives or how much better or worse alternative systems are likely to do in promoting those same objectives.

Law and economics scholars, drawing on concepts of economic efficiency, tend to stress the *deterrent* objectives of the tort system and to evaluate existing legal doctrine or proposed reforms to it in terms of whether appropriate incentives are created for the various causative contributors to a given negative outcome (such as personal injury) to minimize the sum of accident and avoidance costs by taking cost-justified precautions to reduce the likelihood and severity of that outcome.

Scholars who adopt a less individualistic, more communitarian perspective on tort law (such as many Critical Legal Studies scholars) tend to view most accidents as the inevitable by-product of the activities (e.g., motoring, manufacturing) which industrialized, interdependent society has collectively decided to embrace and are sceptical that economic incentives, such as internalization of accident costs through the tort system to least-cost avoiders of them, are likely to have a significant impact on accident-causing behaviour. Instead, drawing on notions of distributive justice, they stress that accident costs should be collectively, not individually, borne and that the tort system should be evaluated against its capacity to spread risk and provide meaningful *compensation* or insurance expeditiously and at low cost to the victims of these activities.

More classical tort scholars, drawing on Aristotelian and Kantian theories of corrective justice, stress notions of individual responsibility, like law and economics scholars. However, they see the purpose of tort law not as the deterrence of prospective wrong-doers but rather as imposing on a person whose morally culpable behaviour (intentional or negligent wrong-doing) has violated the equal individual *autonomy* of another an obligation to restore the latter as nearly as possible to his or her pre-interaction status.

While this description of the three major normative perspectives on the goals of tort law obscures important differences of viewpoint among scholars and judges who espouse one or the other of these general perspectives, and thus risks misstating the implications of each perspective, the general lines of current controversies about the future of tort law can be at least traced.

The *deterrence theorists* are not concerned with compensation of victims as a primary goal of the tort system (a backward-looking perspective), but view compensation rather as the tool by which accident costs are internalized to injurers in cases where cost-justified accident avoidance precautions were not taken. By confronting prospective injurers with the threat of damage awards, forward-looking incentives to take proper levels of care and avoid excessively risky activities are created.

† (1989) 15 Can. Bus. L.J. 471 at 471–81, 487–88. Reproduced with permission of the author and The Canadian Business Law Journal.

Having said this, there is less agreement among deterrence theorists as to what form a tort regime should take to promote efficiency objectives. Most deterrence theorists would stress that one cannot target only the conduct or activities of injurers; victims also often engage in conduct that contributes to the likelihood or severity of their injuries. Thus, compensating fully all victims of accidents would mute incentives on the victims' side of the accident equation to take cost-justified avoidance precautions. Thus, on this perspective, much attention is paid to the appropriate scope of defences such as voluntary assumption of risk or contributory or comparative negligence. On the injurers' side of the accident equation, attention focuses on how to define the appropriate standard of care under a negligence regime so as to generate efficient incentives, and on the larger question of whether, in some contexts, principally products liability, strict liability might be a more preferable legal regime than the traditional negligence regime. Under strict liability, a victim need only prove that a product defect caused his or her injury but not that the defect was itself caused by negligent conduct on the part of the manufacturer. Some deterrence theorists argue for strict liability, subject to appropriate defences such as voluntary assumption of risk and contributory negligence. They rely principally on four grounds.

First, it is argued that while strict liability may not influence levels of care to any greater extent than a negligence regime (i.e., it will be cheaper to pay damages than take more costly precautions), it will influence levels of activity of injurers and thus induce them to reduce inherently risky activities which do not *per se* attract liability under a negligence regime. The difficulty with this argument is that it is often unclear whose activities it is most important to attempt to influence in order to reduce the incidence of accidents. For example, suppose A, a drunken driver, swerves and collides with another car, causing B, the other driver, in turn to careen into a lamp-post. Assuming that A cannot be reached in a tort action (he is dead or judgment-proof), should the accident costs be internalized to the manufacturer or retailer of A's car, the manufacturer or retailer of the alcohol, the manufacturer or retailer of B's car, or the manufacturer or seller or owner of the lamp-post, or B? If any of these parties' activities were reduced, there would be fewer accidents of this kind, but given that it is impossible through tort law simultaneously to internalize accident costs to all activities contributing to an accident, how should a court go about

deciding whose activities should attract strict liability for the accident costs?

Second, it is sometimes argued that strict liability may be a more efficient regime than negligence, at least with respect to defective products, because the courts often will be unable to determine with accuracy whether a given defendant could have avoided an accident through precautions at a lower cost than expected accident costs (an economic definition of negligence). Therefore, by imposing strict liability on the manufacturer of the product, the burden of weighing accident costs against avoidance costs will be imposed on the best-placed decider — the party with superior information on avoidance and accident costs relative both to the plaintiff and the court. The defendant will then decide whether it is more efficient to modify or withdraw the product or pay the damage awards.

While this argument, which revolves around relative decision and error costs, has some force to it, it suffers from substantial indeterminacy. In replacing the least-cost avoider rule (the negligence rule) with the best-placed decider rule (strict liability), it is not clear where the line might be drawn in any principled way. For example, why not make all physicians strictly liable for medical procedures that turn out negatively, on the grounds that a court is not as well-placed as the physician to determine whether the procedure should have been handled differently or an alternative procedure, in retrospect, would have been more appropriate? Thus, a surgeon undertaking high-risk brain surgery that does not turn out as hoped would be strictly liable. The same reasoning could be extended to lawyers, engineers, architects, accountants, truck, bus or taxi operators or indeed almost any kind of professional or business defendant with any claim to specialized expertise. All of these are domains that have traditionally been governed by the negligence regime.

Third, it is sometimes argued that strict liability may conserve on adjudication costs because it avoids judicial determinations as to fault. This argument is also contested, with counter-arguments, stressing the expanded number of suits that will have to be processed by the courts under a strict liability regime, and difficult issues of adjudication that remain with respect to the definition of a product "defect" and proof of causative links between a defect, once defined, and the injury alleged to be attributable to the defect. Both issues are highly problematic in many contexts. The notion of a product defect is not self-defining and indeed will often involve inquiries not dissimilar from negligence inquiries. Causation issues, especially in the toxic tort context where there are often very long lags between initial exposure and ultimate manifestation and many intervening and confounding factors, often involve extremely complex factual and scientific inquiries.

Fourth, it is sometimes argued that strict liability increases incentives to innovate by maintaining consent pressure on manufacturers to investigate potential health hazards associated with their products and to explore alternative product designs or composition. Again, this argument has some force, although in some contexts it is not obviously efficient to have every manufacturer of, e.g., a particular chemical or drug, conducting basic research into its health properties rather than promoting more co-ordinated research efforts in other forums.

Apart from these theoretical difficulties that confront the formulation of an efficient liability regime, the empirical evidence on the deterrent properties of tort law in general or alternative formulations of liability rules and defences in particular is woefully inconclusive. Studies of the effects on accident rates of the adoption of partial no-fault auto insurance schemes in many U.S. states have reached divergent findings, although the most recent U.S. studies suggest minimal effects. On the other hand, one study of the effect on accident rates in Quebec, following the adoption of a comprehensive no-fault auto insurance scheme that prohibits all tort claims for personal injuries arising out of auto accidents, finds that fatalities on Quebec roads have increased by about 100 a year since the adoption of the scheme. Another recent study puts the increase in fatalities at over 150 a year.

In the medical malpractice area, the empirical evidence on the behavioural effects of the tort system is similarly inconclusive. Some argue that the dramatic increase in frequency and size of claims and correlative insurance premium increases have induced wasteful forms of defensive medicine and have led to socially detrimental withdrawal from or avoidance of certain high-risk specialities (e.g., obstetrics) by many physicians. Others argue that only a tiny fraction of *prima facie* cases of medical negligence generate legal claims and in turn only a trivial portion of cases involving even paid claims attract the attention of the disciplinary mechanisms of the medical profession. Thus, given the ineffectiveness of alternative quality control mechanisms, it is argued that there are too few tort claims to achieve optimal levels of care.

The compensation theorists point to the theoretical difficulties and controversies over the formulation of efficient liability regimes that focus on accident-avoidance incentives, and to the fragmentary and inconclusive empirical evidence as to what the tort system is actually achieving in this respect. They argue that deterrence objectives are best assigned to criminal law and regulatory regimes (e.g., in the United States, the Occupational Health and Safety Administration, the Consumer Product Safety Commission, the Food and Drug Administration, the Environmental Protection Agency, and like agencies in Canada). Thus, they would assign a minor role, if any, to deterrence as a goal of the tort system. In focussing instead on compensation as the primary goal, they point to empirical studies in the United States and elsewhere that show that only a small percentage of victims of accidents, let alone disabilities more generally, recover any or adequate compensation through the tort system, that the transaction costs entailed in the administration of the system (e.g., lawyers fees) mean that plaintiffs receive only about 40% of the money entering the system compared to much higher percentages under first-party and social insurance schemes, and that lengthy delays in payment of damages and the etiological-adversarial nature of the system are unconducive to the rehabilitation of victims. They argue that financial necessity is financial necessity, whatever the nature or cause of the misfortune that produces this state, and that requirements of horizontal equity require that all persons similarly financially impacted should be similarly treated. Some compensation theorists accordingly welcome the expansion of notions of strict liability, joint and several liability, and other doctrinal innovations such as market share liability because of the expanded prospect of victim recovery likely to be entailed. They would view the tort system as a form of social insurance, and justify strict liability as a risk-spreading device or more radically as a form of redistribution of wealth with presumptive "deep pockets" (e.g., corporations) held liable to victims of their activities, regardless of fault. As to what measures of compensation should be payable on this social insurance rationale for tort law, some compensation theorists would favour full compensation for pecuniary and non-pecuniary losses. Others would argue that compensating for non-pecuniary losses such as pain and suffering commodifies and monetizes what are inherently non-economic values and thus demeans them. Some law and economics scholars would reach a similar result, but by rea-

4. The Nature of Tort Law

soning that in explicit first-party insurance markets, one rarely observes individuals prepared to forgo income now in the form of insurance premiums in order to secure coverage against the subsequent risk of non-pecuniary losses, because by definition these are not losses which money can assuage. For example, it is argued that parents rarely insure against the death of a child, because money is unlikely to be able to replace or mitigate the loss entailed.

The major conceptual difficulty with strict liability, justified in social insurance terms, is that superior risk-spreading ability is what triggers liability. However, the internal structure of the superior risk-spreader rationale for liability makes it unclear whether either the presence of fault *or a defect* is logically required to ground liability. On risk-spreading rationales, why shouldn't a person who trips over a kitchen chair or cuts himself on a carving knife be able to sue the manufacturer? At this point, strict liability collapses into absolute liability, with an arbitrary designation of an insurer as the party liable. Indeed, why not allow the victim to sue anyone who ostensibly is a superior risk-bearer to him or to the chairmaker, for example, the latter's banker, law firm, accounting firm, securities underwriter, timber supplier, trucking operator, or indeed a large, well-endowed, well-insured, or well-diversified enterprise totally unconnected to either party?

At the limit, it is not clear why, if the courts are committed to spreading accident costs as thinly as possible, there is any logical stopping point short of rendering the state liable for all accident costs (whether or not this is an efficient form of insurance in other respects). Even short of this stopping point, the courts in pursuing a superior risk-bearer inquiry would seem required to give primacy to whether one party is insured or not; or, if neither party is insured, whether one is better diversified than the other; or, if neither is well-diversified but the adjudicator believes in the declining marginal utility of money and the interpersonal comparability of utility functions, the relative wealth of the parties. By long historical tradition in common law civil disputes, the courts are supposed to sedulously eschew these considerations. To now make these considerations determinative of liability would cast them in a radically new role.

Partly in the light of these implications, many compensation theorists would view the tort system, however designed, as incapable of meeting their distributive justice goals. Even under strict liability, delays, costs, and the etiological-adversarial charac-

ter of the system would be viewed as inconsistent with a humane and efficient compensation system. Moreover, many accidents and disabilities are unlikely to attract compensation under the tort system, however designed. Thus, reforms to the tort system would be a distant second-best to the adoption of social insurance systems in which entitlements to compensation are not contingent on proof of the fault or conduct of another. These theorists would see virtues in building on the experience with workers compensation systems, no-fault auto insurance systems, and more comprehensive accident compensation systems, such as the New Zealand Accident Compensation Scheme which provides a common set of publicly administered earnings-related benefits for victims of accidents or disease in the workplace; accidents on the highways, at home or elsewhere; and of medical misadventure. Some compensation theorists argue that even the New Zealand scheme perpetuates problems of horizontal equity in that victims of most illnesses or other forms of disability are unfairly excluded from the scheme and are relegated to much more modest social welfare benefits.

Autonomy theorists argue that the only coherent role that can be ascribed to the tort system is the rectification of the adverse consequences to one person of the morally culpable conduct of another. At least some such theorists would reject notions of strict liability as incompatible with a tort system designed to serve corrective justice ends. Corrective justice requires that each individual respect the equal individual autonomy of others by avoiding wrongful invasions of that autonomy, but would not countenance the imposition of liability on persons in the service of instrumental goals of general deterrence of others, risk-spreading, or wealth redistribution. Corrective justice seeks to correct past injustices, not to deter future behaviour of other potential wrongdoers or to compensate victims of misfortune whose misfortune is not directly caused by the morally culpable conduct of another. Where such conduct is the cause of another's misfortune, corrective justice would seem to require that all losses suffered as a result of that conduct be redressed in so far as money is able to do this.

Corrective justice (or autonomy) theorists emphasize that the form of tort law is inconsistent with general deterrence or redistributive justice objectives. Tort law typically involves a suit by a victim against an injurer where the nature of the interaction between the two has produced a negative impact on the plaintiff. If deterrence objectives were the central focus of tort law, it may be the case that there are any number of other causal agents of the outcome whose suppression may more fully advance deterrence objectives (e.g., in the case of a highway accident, the failure of highway designers to install a low-cost protective device), but the form of the action precludes an investigation of whether penalizing the injurer or addressing these other causal agents is likely to yield the highest deterrence returns. Moreover, the form of a tort action for personal injury requires that an injury to one person has actually occurred as the result of the conduct of another. If general deterrence objectives were the central focus of tort law, why wait for a dead or maimed body before attempting to deter accident-prone behaviour? For example, more clearly deterrence-driven legal regimes such as criminal sanctions for speeding or drunk driving attempt to interdict accident-prone behaviour before it causes accidents.

Similarly, corrective justice theorists argue that the form of a tort action is inconsistent with redistributive justice objectives. Why single out the party most immediately interacting with the plaintiff for liability, regardless of the quality of his conduct, on the grounds that he is a better risk-spreader or has a deeper pocket than the victim, when countless other people or institutions who are not parties to the action may be even better risk-spreaders or have even deeper pockets than the defendant? In other words, tort law is inherently incapable of promoting any patterned or coherent principle of distributive justice and should not be assigned this goal.

The logic of the corrective justice rationale for tort law is such that its force does not depend on empirical evidence as to how well or badly the tort system performs in deterring accidents or compensating victims generally, as both deterrence and general compensation goals are rejected as primary goals of the tort system. To the extent that society wishes to espouse these goals, autonomy theorists would argue that it should do so through instruments other than the tort system (although typically not concerning themselves with how to evaluate these alternatives).

Criticisms of autonomy theories of tort law stress the barrenness of non-instrumental rationales for tort law that ignore the relevance of the goals of both accident reduction and accident compensation, which are the only two concerns that are likely to matter to most members of the community contemplating the likely impact of an accident on their lives. To claim that tort law is inherently

incapable of serving these objectives, which must be advanced through other policy instruments, is to avoid joining the debate over whether tort law is, in that event, worth preserving. Moreover, it is argued that in tort law, even as classically conceived, the degree of moral culpability is not closely correlated with its legal consequences. A grossly delinquent wrong-doer may be lucky and only mildly injure someone. A mildly inadvertent wrong-doer may be unlucky and gravely injure a very high income-earner or class of victims and be exposed to enormous damages.

. . . .

THROUGH A GLASS DARKLY

I have sought to show in this essay the fundamental philosophic differences reflected in the major normative perspectives on the goals of the tort system and how these also translate into profoundly different agendas for reforming tort law or for replacing it. In attempting to discern the future through this philosophical haze, my best guess is that tort law, at least in the case of personal injuries, will play a diminishing role. All Canadian provinces and U.S. states deal with industrial accidents and disease largely through workers compensation schemes. Almost half the states in the United States have adopted partial no-fault first-party auto insurance schemes. Most Canadian provinces have also adopted partial no-fault schemes and Quebec a complete no-fault scheme. In the United States, a variety of special compensation schemes have been adopted for nuclear accident victims, lung-damaged coal miners, and victims of vaccine-related injuries. The increasing prominence of mass tort claims, especially in the United States, with increasingly non-individuated determinations of liability and of entitlements, has attenuated classical corrective justice and deterrence rationales for tort law, and placed an enormous administrative burden on the courts which they are ill-equipped to bear. All of these developments suggest the likelihood of an enlarged role for the state in the future in implementing and often administering *ad hoc* or more generally cast compensation schemes.

But as we begin to turn our minds to how these schemes might be designed, we will quickly be driven to a realization that the compensation and deterrence goals often ascribed to the tort system cannot be separated and will require reconciliation in any compensation scheme. In attempting this reconciliation, may of the problems that currently afflict the tort system will have to be confronted in new legal or institutional contexts. It may well be possible that we can achieve a better set of trade-offs than the tort system has achieved or is ever likely to achieve. But pretending that the trade-offs do not exist, or that safety issues can be confidently remitted elsewhere in the legal system when the evidence does not warrant such confidence, is to espouse the untenable proposition that compensating for accidents is better than preventing them.

(d) Mass Torts†

Jamie Cassels

In December 1984, a massive explosion and discharge of lethal gas from the Union Carbide factory in Bhopal, India, killed more than 2,500 people. In the intervening years hundreds more have died, and many thousands remain injured or affected. With the possible exception of the Chernobyl nuclear explosion (the long-term effects of which are still unknown) the Bhopal disaster was the worst single-incident industrial catastrophe in history.

. . . .

TOXIC TORTS: A NEW ACCIDENT PARADIGM?

While the law of tort has been substantially adapted to meet the conditions of life in the twentieth century, it remains fundamentally rooted in earlier social values and conceptions of human interaction. As many legal scholars have argued, the increasing prevalence of mass disasters, toxic injuries, and environmental damage not only throw up problems that the law is ill-suited to address, but, in fact, call into question the vary presuppositions about social life upon which traditional tort law is built.

Traditional tort law is *individualistic* and *mechanical*. It imagines a world that is populated by rational individuals pursuing their own self-interest. Occasionally such individuals may collide, in which case the task of law is to repair any damage done and to restore the boundaries between them by rearticulating the rights and duties that define their interactions. The paradigm of the traditional tort is a *traumatic* interaction between two *intentionalistic* agents. One person lights a fire that burns his neighbour's property; one person strikes another with her automobile. In such cases it is possible to say how the injury occurred and to assign liability for it upon the basis of individual responsibility. The dispute is bipolar and the goal is to achieve corrective justice between individuals rather than distributive justice between groups in society. The wider community is not involved or implicated in the problem except to the extent that it supposedly provides the social norms that make up the concept of 'reasonable care'. Causation in such cases is specific and mechanical. It is easy to trace the victim's injury to the acts or omissions of the defendant and to exclude other possible causes. There is a clean line between 'inevitable' and 'avoidable' injuries; between the 'natural' misfortunes of life and those for which another person should be held accountable.

Legal scholars are beginning to explore how this picture of the way in which people are hurt, and the way society attributes responsibility for those hurts, is vastly inadequate to portray the reality of harm in modern society. They argue that the earlier model of accidents as traumatic collisions between individuals maintains its hold on the legal imagination and diverts attention from the far

---

† From *The Uncertain Promise of Law: Lessons from Bhopal* (Toronto: University of Toronto Press, 1993) at ix, 76–83. Reproduced with permission of the author.

more serious problem of 'environmental' injury and illness. The trauma model accounts for only a very small fraction of human harm and ignores the 'social' or human-made source of most forms of disability.

The modern epidemiological understanding of the concepts of 'risks' and 'harm' has exposed the inadequacy of an atomistic understanding of human interaction, an individualistic understanding of responsibility, a traumatic view of injury, and a mechanical view of causation. Social and technological complexity reveal the degree to which society is interdependent and how intricate systems are implicated in the production of accidents and sickness. The development of epidemiological and statistical knowledge about disease has undermined our ability to draw a bright line between 'natural' and 'unnatural' forms of disability. When dealing with toxic injuries, poisoning, cancer, and other forms of environmental and industrial harm, the paradigm of mechanical causation is replaced by a paradigm of 'statistical correlation,' and even the concept of injury gives way to one of 'risk.' The disparities in economic and social power between large corporate concerns and the victims of injury have exposed the inadequacy of the narrow model of corrective justice to address the more pervasive problem of distributive injustice.

THE COMPENSATION PROMISE

Identifying the Defendant: Proof of Causation and Fault

Many argue that the function of tort law is to provide 'corrective justice.' This means that the law seeks, as best it can, to 'right the balance' between a victim and the agent who caused the victim's injury. What it is important to note about the corrective-justice model is that the law intervenes only when there has been a 'wrong' done by one person to another. According to the traditional view, one person is not responsible for the welfare of another unless the victim, who has the onus of proof, can establish that the defendant had a duty of care, breached that duty of care, and thus caused the victim's injuries.

These legal requirements reflect the values of due process and individualism. A person is 'innocent until proven guilty' and does not have any general responsibility for the welfare of others. While these values are widely shared, they ultimately reflect a general presumption that individual

victims must bear their own injuries *unless* they are able to overcome substantial evidentiary challenges and shift that loss to another party.

Mass-exposure problems are especially problematic in this regard. In the first place, they typically involve complex technology, dangerous processes, and toxic materials. The factual matrix is thus enormously complicated. Difficult scientific, technological, and medical questions may be involved. The collection of data and proof of technical and medical theories is time-consuming, controversial, and expensive.

In cases involving complex technology, such as Bhopal, even the apparently simple issues of mechanical causation and fault often prove to be enormously difficult. Ordinarily, a plaintiff must demonstrate that the incident was the result of carelessness; that, 'but for' the actions of the defendant, the accident would not have occurred. While little more than a straightforward factual investigation seems to be required, the matter is much more complicated. In the first place, as was the case in Bhopal, it may simply be unclear how the accident occurred at all. The 'facts' that must be investigated are all in the past. Indeed, they no longer exist. The incident must be reconstructed from physical evidence, much of which was destroyed or altered in the explosion; company records, which may be incomplete or misleading; expert testimony, which may be speculative or biased; and the recollection of witnesses, which is bound to be limited and contradictory, given the total chaos that reigned on the night of the disaster and the long period of time between it and a final trial. Given that burden of proof is generally left to the plaintiff, who has little information about the hazardous substance, the nature of the technology, or the workings of the process, proof of mechanical causation is enormously difficult, if not impossible.

Even when it is clear how the accident occurred, the questions of fault and causation can never be straightforward, for the court must still make normative judgments and factual inferences. The normative judgment is whether the conduct of the defendant fell below a reasonable standard of care. The factual inference is whether, through the exercise of reasonable care, the accident could have been prevented. This latter question is essentially hypothetical, often requiring that the court make a guess at determining the unknowable.

In the case of Bhopal, there was not only very little physical evidence concerning the cause of the disaster, but almost none on how it might have been prevented. While both sides agreed that the explosion was caused by the introduction of water into the MIC tank, Indian authorities theorized that this was a result of employee carelessness or a design flaw, while UCC stood by its sabotage theory. The normative issue of whether Union Carbide had been negligent would raise intensely political issues. The victims would focus on the double standard of safety that emerged from a comparison of the company's operations in different parts of the world, while Union Carbide would emphasize that, by 'local standards' and regulations, it had taken all reasonable precautions. The tension between these positions is found frequently in toxic cases, especially those involving 'socially beneficial' activities. While courts may sometimes set the standard of care high in order to ensure safety and compensation, there is a competing concern to avoid unduly impeding the development of new technologies and products. The victims may thus face the utilitarian sentiment that, in the name of 'social progress,' they must privately bear their injuries.

Even in situations where the defendant was clearly negligent, the victims must still demonstrate that the negligence was the effective cause of their injuries. The fact that they carry this burden of proof will often be fatal to their claim. The victims of Bhopal would argue that the disaster could have been avoided or mitigated by the storage of smaller quantities of the chemical and by a better cooling system; Union Carbide would assert that such a view was entirely hypothetical and unproven. While it was clear that the existing safety precautions at the plant were inadequate to prevent the disaster, little evidence was available to indicate what further precautions would have insured prevention. And while none of the warning systems and emergency devices at the plant were capable of minimizing the damage, it was by no means clear what specific steps would have been required to eliminate the danger.

Courts are not entirely insensitive to the problems encountered in attempting to prove causation and fault and, in some circumstances, will make inferences in the plaintiff's favour. Where, for example, substandard precautions may have 'materially contributed' to the risk, the court may shift the onus of proof to the defendant. Similarly, the principle of res ipsa loquitor (the thing speaks for itself) will sometimes be used to shift the burden of proof in situations where the plaintiff is unable to establish exactly how the accident occurred but is able to satisfy the court that the

accident probably would not have happened but for the defendant's negligence. In a technologically complex case like Bhopal's, where the disaster could have been caused by a number of factors, these principles are unlikely to prevail. The only meaningful way in which the burden of proof could be lowered is if the courts were willing to apply a standard of strict liability.

Multiple Defendants and Systems Accidents

The issue of factual causation in Bhopal and other mass-tort scenarios is further complicated by the large number of parties involved in complex industrial undertakings and the peculiar characteristics of toxic harms. Under the tort system, claimants must be able to trace their injuries back to the actions or omissions of a responsible party. But this individualistic orientation is ill-suited to disasters and toxic torts, which typically involve multiple actors interrelating through intricate chains of command and decision. It may simply be impossible to attribute responsibility to isolated individuals or firms. Thus, while the victims alleged that UCC was responsible for the disaster, the company in turn sought to remove itself from the sphere of responsibility, first by suggesting sabotage, second by distancing itself from the Indian operation, and third by reflecting blame back upon the government itself for failing to implement proper safety standards and for allowing a large population to settle so near to the plant. One of the parent company's most potent arguments would be that it was a virtual 'stranger' to the Indian operation; that it was merely a passive investor in the Indian-operated enterprise, having no control over its day-to-day operations and therefore no responsibility for its safety practices.

The problem of identifying a responsible party is a result of the structure of mass industrialization, the complex organization of modern business enterprises, and the peculiar characteristics of toxic harm. Numerous parties are involved in the design and operation of complicated technological processes that no one individual understands or controls. Intricate systems of production, control, and distribution make the lines of causation like the strands of a spider's web rather than the linear chain envisioned by tort law.

Several of these problems were confronted in the U.S. case of *Sindell v. Abbott Laboratories*, which involved the drug DES. This drug, which was taken by millions of pregnant women, was shown to have increased the risk of cancer in the children of the women who used it. Dozens of firms manufactured and marketed the product, and hundreds of young women are now suing for their resulting injuries. A major stumbling-block is the fact that the victims were often unable to say which brand of the drug their mothers used during pregnancy, and were therefore unable to trace liability to a particular manufacturer.

In the *Sindell* case the plaintiff established that she suffered from a malignant bladder tumour caused by DES, which her mother had taken during pregnancy. She could not, however, demonstrate which of a number of manufacturers of the drug was responsible for producing the drug that her mother actually took. She launched a class action on behalf of herself and other women in a similar position against five manufacturers. In its landmark decision, the California Supreme Court allowed the action against all of the manufacturers. The court reasoned that the law had to evolve to meet new technologies and new market conditions and that the defendants, as manufacturers of a dangerous product, were in a better position to discover and guard and warn against the hazards associated with their drug. In a case involving numerous producers and mass marketing, the traditional rule requiring the plaintiff to prove the identity of the particular manufacturer would effectively bar any recovery. Instead, the court held all of the manufacturers liable to the victims in proportion to their market share. The court held that the approach should be to 'measure the likelihood that any of the defendants supplied the product ... by the percentage which the DES sold by each of them bears to the entire production of the drug sold by all ... Each defendant would be liable for that share unless it could demonstrate that it did not make the product which caused the plaintiff's injuries.'

This theory, which has come to be known as 'market share' liability, is one of a variety of principles that shift the onus of proof in cases of multiple wrongdoers (other theories include alternative liability, concerted action, and enterprise liability). Yet the relaxation of causal requirements has by no means been unequivocally accepted by the courts. In a vigorous dissent in *Sindell*, Richardson J stated that the decision was offensive to the basic principles of tort law and involved a 'drastic expansion in liability' that would threaten basic medical research. He felt that the court had overreacted in order to achieve a 'socially satisfying result.'

The decision certainly did go against traditional notions of individual responsibility. While it is likely that only one of the manufacturers made the drug that caused the plaintiff's injuries, all of the manufacturers were held responsible to her. From an individualistic perspective it may seem 'unfair' to hold a company responsible for injuries that it probably did not directly 'cause.' Nevertheless, the court's decision was probably made easier because it was a class action involving many of the women who had been injured by the drug. Thus, there was a good chance that all of the manufacturers had, in fact, 'caused' a portion of the total harm suffered by the class.

In the case of Bhopal, the problem is somewhat different. In *Sindell* the difficulty was to find the *one* actor responsible for the injury in a situation where *all* of the defendants were negligent. But, in Bhopal, there may simply be no single responsible actor, and all the parties involved would argue that they had not been (equally) negligent. Instead, a large number of actors — designers, workers, managers, and company and government officials — may each have contributed in some way to the disaster. Traditionally, the law attempts to allocate responsibility in such a case according to the notion of contributory negligence. Liability is traced to individual agents and assessed against each actor according to comparative fault. But, in the case of a major industrial disaster, this attempt to simplify reality may be futile. In the first place, in complex business organizations, which include numerous individuals, interlocking departments, and linked companies, it will be extremely difficult to attribute responsibility to particular individuals or units, or to assess their relative contribution to the harm. As one analyst of corporate responsibility points out, the irony is that, 'at the same time that these organizations serve to amplify human power, they also divide and diffuse the accountability of the humans who labor within them.' Moreover, Bhopal is an example of what organizational analyst Charles Perrow, in his study of the Three Mile Island nuclear accident, calls a 'systems accident.' Systems, he explains, are complex organizations of people and technology with special characteristics that make the assignment of 'blame' for an accident almost meaningless. Systems are characterized by their 'interactive complexity', which makes the entire system incomprehensible to any one individual. Indeed, the increasing specialization and expertise prompted by the technical division of labour may make systems even more unstable by limiting the scope of each person's knowledge. Any one part of a system can fail in a trivial and unanticipated way and, in conjunction with other components of the system, such failure can lead to catastrophic results.

The narrow causal focus of both the government and Union Carbide — the former upon design defects and employee carelessness, the latter upon sabotage — were a natural, almost reflexive effort, to squeeze the facts of Bhopal into the traditional individualistic framework of tort responsibility. But individualistic conceptions of legal responsibility and causation do not fit well when the incident is the result of a complex combination of individual, corporate, and government decisions, actions, and omissions. It will often be impossible to isolate responsibility by focusing on the individual actions or omissions of only a few actors, and blame can easily be shifted from shoulder to shoulder *ad infinitum*.

(a)   *Buchan v. Ortho Pharmaceutical (Canada) Ltd.*[†]

[ROBINS J.A.:]

This appeal raises important questions concerning the scope of a drug manufacturer's duty to warn of dangers inherent in the use of oral contraceptives.

I

In December, 1974, the plaintiff, Pauline Jane Buchan, instituted these proceedings against the defendant, Ortho Pharmaceutical (Canada) Limited ("Ortho"), to recover damages for a stroke suffered by her in September, 1971, allegedly as a result of taking "Ortho-Novum 1/50"[,] a contraceptive pill manufactured and distributed by Ortho.... [At] trial Mr. J. Holland ... found Ortho liable for the plaintiff's injuries and awarded her damages totalling $606,795.31. Ortho now appeals to this Court from that judgment.

The first ground of appeal concerns the causal connection between the plaintiff's stroke and Ortho-Novum 1/50. Ortho argues that the trial judge erred in concluding "that Mrs. Buchan's use of oral contraceptives probably caused or, at the very least, materially contributed to her stroke". In Ortho's submission, the evidence accepted by the trial judge "does not go beyond showing a statistical relationship between oral contraceptives and stroke which cannot be treated as cause in an individual case" and, further, there was evidence which the trial judge ought to have accepted that

established the existence of other potential causes more likely to have caused the stroke than the contraceptive pill.

This ground of appeal raises the essentially factual question of whether the relation between the defendant's contraceptive pill and the plaintiff's injury is one of cause and effect in accordance with medical or scientific notions of physical sequence. If such a causal relation does not exist, that puts an end to the plaintiff's case, because, obviously, liability cannot be imposed for a loss to which the defendant's product has not contributed. ...

In July, 1971, the plaintiff was a 23-year-old, non-smoking, married woman in excellent health. She had been on a birth control programme for many years. In the summer of 1966, following the birth of her son, she took birth control pills at the suggestion of her family doctor for about six months. In January, 1967, a gynaecologist started her on long-lasting birth control injections of an experimental drug, Depo-Provera. She took these injections every three months until August, 1970, when she was advised that the experimental programme had been discontinued. For a while thereafter, she used other methods of birth control. On June 30, 1971, she visited a doctor to obtain a prescription for birth control pills. He prescribed Ortho-Novum 1/50. In September, 1971, after having taken this pill for slightly less than six weeks, she suffered a stroke or cerebrovascular accident. This has left her permanently disabled; she has

---

[†]   [1986] 25 D.L.R. (4th) 658 at 662–89.

some brain damage and her left arm and left leg are substantially paralyzed.

In 1971, the plaintiff had no diagnosed or known risks or predisposition to stroke. However, from a diagnosis made in 1982, it appears that she probably had a mitral valve prolapse ("MVP") in 1971, and the trial judge so found. This is a heart valve anomaly, fairly common in women, which can increase the possibility of stroke by slowing the circulation of the blood in the area of the mitral valve thus increasing the blood's tendency to clot. The trial judge had evidence before him that abnormal blood clotting is a known side-effect of birth control pills; that the estrogen component of the pill increases the tendency of blood to clot; that there is a significant statistical association between the pill and stroke, and that a combination of MVP and the pill could have the effect of multiplying the risk of stroke. He also had evidence to the effect that Depo-Provera does not contain estrogen and would not affect blood coagulation; that this drug would, in any event, have cleared the plaintiff's system before September, 1971; that the plaintiff had suffered no blood vessel abnormalities or arterial disease, and that she had experienced no clotting problems or thrombotic incidents since the stroke in question.

The trial judge, moreover, had the opinions of highly-qualified expert witnesses called on behalf of both the plaintiff and defendant who, among other things, discussed the numerous reports, studies and documents that were admitted into evidence. These opinions included one from a haematologist who said that "in the absence of the oral contraceptive pill that she received, the Ortho-Novum, it would have been very, very unlikely that Mrs. Buchan would have experienced the stroke"; another from an epidemiologist who said that there is "very solid evidence that the oral contraceptive pill is a cause of cerebral thromboembolism" and on "the balance of probabilities, Mrs. Buchan's stroke was caused by the oral contraceptive pill", and another from a neurologist who said that it is "most probable that the cause of Mrs. Buchan's stroke was a combination of taking the pill and having a condition [MVP] that would make it more likely that a clot would form".

[The trial judge held that the causal link was established. The Court of Appeal agreed.]

.   .   .   .   .

II

The gravamen of the plaintiff's case is that Ortho failed to warn of the danger of stroke inherent in the use of the oral contraceptive and that that failure caused or materially contributed to her injuries. There is no question of any defect or impropriety in the manufacture of the oral contraceptive, nor of its efficacy when taken as prescribed.

In holding Ortho liable in negligence for breach of a duty to warn, the trial judge made a number of specific findings, including:

1. that Ortho knew of the association between oral contraceptive use and thromboembolism or stroke;
2. that Ortho was under a common law duty to warn consumers of the dangerous side-effects of the drug both directly (by including a warning on the pill package) and indirectly (by warning physicians of the risk);
3. that Ortho's duty to warn was not discharged merely by warning physicians;
4. that Ortho's compliance with the labelling requirements laid down in the *Food and Drugs Act*, R.S.C. 1970, c. F-27, and regulations passed thereunder, did not relieve it of the duty to warn consumers and physicians of material risks of which it knew or should have known;
5. that the warning given by Ortho to both consumers and physicians was inadequate;
6. that Ortho's breach of the duty to warn consumers was causative of the plaintiff's injuries.

While Ortho acknowledges that manufacturers of prescription drugs are subject to a common law duty to warn prescribing physicians of the material risks involved in using their drugs of which they know or should know, it denies any duty to warn consumers directly. In the alternative, Ortho argues that its compliance with the statutory standard of disclosure established under the *Food and Drugs Act* satisfies any duty to consumers, and it is under no obligation to provide consumers with supplementary information to issue additional warnings. With respect to physicians, Ortho contends that the plaintiff's physician was aware of the then current medical information on the relationship between oral contraceptives and stroke when he prescribed the pill for the plaintiff, and any further warning by Ortho would have been redundant. In any event, Ortho says, in the circumstances any lack of warning on its part to prescribing physicians was not the proximate cause of the plaintiff's injuries. Furthermore, Ortho argues, a reasonable person in the plaintiff's position would have accepted her doctor's advice and taken the pill even if properly warned. Therefore, the argument concludes, the trial judge erred in finding the necessary causal link between Ortho's alleged breach of the duty to warn and the plaintiff's use of the pill.

III

Before considering the issues raised by Ortho it may perhaps be helpful to review briefly some general principles applicable in products liability cases involving a manufacturer's duty to warn consumers of dangers inherent in the use of a product.

As a matter of common law, it is well settled that a manufacturer of a product has a duty to warn consumers of dangers inherent in the use of its product of which it knows or has reason to know. The guiding principle of liability underlying the present law of products liability in this country was formulated by Lord Atkin in his classic statement in *M'Alister (or Donoghue) v. Stevenson*, [1932] A.C. 562 at p. 599 (H.L.):

> ...a manufacturer of products, which he sells in such a form as to show that he intends them to reach the ultimate consumer in the form in which they left him with no reasonable possibility of intermediate examination, and with the knowledge that the absence of reasonable care in the preparation or putting up of the products will result in an injury to the consumer's life or property, owes a duty to the consumer to take that reasonable care.

This statement has been the source of subsequent developments in products liability law based on negligence. The *rationale* is that one who brings himself into a relation with others through an activity which foreseeably exposes them to danger if proper care is not observed must exercise reasonable care to safeguard them from that danger. It can now be taken as a legal truism that the duty of reasonable care which lies at the foundation of the law of negligence commonly comprehends a duty to warn of danger, the breach of which will, when it is the cause of injury, give rise to liability: see, generally, Fleming, *The Law of Torts*, 6th ed., (1983), at p. 459 *ff.*, and Linden, *Canadian Tort Law*, 3rd ed., (1982), at p. 563 *ff.*

Once a duty to warn is recognized, it is manifest that the warning must be adequate. It should be communicated clearly and understandably in a manner calculated to inform the user of the nature of the risk and the extent of the danger; it should be in terms commensurate with the gravity of the potential hazard, and it should not be neutralized or negated by collateral efforts on the part of the manufacturer. The nature and extent of any given warning will depend on what is reasonable having regard to all the facts and circumstances relevant to the product in question.

The general principle to be applied in determining the degree of explicitness required in a warning was enunciated by the Supreme Court of Canada, speaking through Laskin J., in *Lambert et al. v. Lastoplex Chemicals Co. Ltd. et al.*, [1972] S.C.R. 569 at pp. 574–75, 25 D.L.R. (3d) 121 at p. 125, as follows:

> Where manufactured products are put on the market for ultimate purchase and use by the general public and carry danger (in this case, by reason of high inflammability), although put to the use for which they are intended, *the manufacturer, knowing of their hazardous nature, has a duty to specify the attendant dangers, which it must be taken to appreciate in a detail not known to the ordinary consumer or user.* A general warning, as for example, that the product is inflammable, will not suffice where the likelihood of fire may be increased according to the surroundings in which it may reasonably be expected that the product will be used. *The required explicitness of the warning will, of course, vary with the danger likely to be encountered in the ordinary use of the product.* (Emphasis added.)

The duty is a continuous one requiring that the manufacturer warn, not only of dangers known at the time of sale, but also of dangers discovered after the product has been sold and delivered. In the words of Ritchie J., speaking for the majority of the Supreme Court of Canada in *Rivtow Marine Ltd. v. Washington Iron Works et al.*, [1974] S.C.R. 1189 at p. 1200, 40 D.L.R. (3d) 530 at p. 536, [1973] 6 W.W.R. 692:

> ...the knowledge of the danger involved in the continued use of these cranes for the purpose for which they were designed carried with it a duty to warn those to whom the cranes had been supplied, and this duty arose at the moment when the respondents or either of them became seized with the knowledge.

Ordinarily, the warning must be addressed directly to the person likely to be injured. It is not, however, necessary that that be done in every case. Where, for example, the product is a highly technical one that is intended or expected to be used only under the supervision of experts, a warning to the experts will suffice: *Murphy v. St. Catharines General Hospital et al.*, [1964] 1 O.R. 239, 41 D.L.R. (2d) 697 (H.C.J.). Similarly, a warning to the ultimate user may not be necessary where intermediate examination is anticipated or the intervention of a learned intermediary is understood. ...

. . . .

In the present state of human knowledge, many drugs are clearly incapable of being made totally safe for their intended or ordinary use, even though they have been properly manufactured and are not impure or defective. Notwithstanding a medically recognizable risk, their marketing may be justified by their utility. Apart from any regulatory scheme under the *Food and Drugs Act*, the general rule at common law is that the manufacturer of such drugs, like the manufacturer of other products, has a duty to provide consumers with adequate warning of the potentially harmful side-effects that the manufacturer knows or has reason to know may be produced by the drug. There is, however, an important exception to that general rule. In the case of prescription drugs, the duty of manufacturers to warn consumers is discharged if the manufacturer provides prescribing physicians, rather than consumers, with adequate warning of the potential danger.

. . . .

There are no decisions dealing specifically with oral contraceptives in this country or in England. In most of the jurisdictions in the United States in which the question has been considered, the learned intermediary rule has been adhered to, and manufacturers of oral contraceptives have accordingly been held under a duty to warn only prescribing physicians of the risks associated with their product. Very recently, however, several state courts have concluded that oral contraceptives bear characteristics which render them vastly different from other prescription drugs and which demand that manufacturers be required to warn users directly of risks associated with their use. The reasoning which prompted these courts to hold the learned intermediary rule inapplicable to birth control pills is clearly articulated in the decision of the

Supreme Judicial Court of Massachusetts in *MacDonald v. Ortho Pharmaceutical Corp.* (1985), 475 N.E. 2d 65 (Mass.); *certiorari* denied 106 S.Ct. 250.

In that case, which, like this one, involved a stroke found to have been caused by the ingestion of Ortho-Novum, the majority (4:1) of the court, *per* Abrams J., said at p. 70:

> The oral contraceptive thus stands apart from other prescription drugs in light of the heightened participation of patients in decisions relating to use of "the pill"; the substantial risks affiliated with the product's use; the feasibility of direct warnings by the manufacturer to the user; the limited participation of the physician (annual prescriptions); and the possibility that oral communications between physicians and consumers may be insufficient or too scanty standing alone fully to apprise consumers of the product's dangers at the time the initial selection of a contraceptive method is made as well as at subsequent points when alternative methods may be considered. *We conclude that the manufacturer of oral contraceptives is not justified in relying on warnings to the medical profession to satisfy its common law duty to warn, and that the manufacturer's obligation encompasses a duty to warn the ultimate user.* Thus, the manufacturer's duty is to provide to the consumer written warnings conveying reasonable notice of the nature, gravity, and likelihood of known or knowable side effects, and advising the consumer to seek fuller explanation from the prescribing physician or other doctor of any such information of concern to the consumer. (Emphasis added.)

. . . .

V

Taking Ortho's most favourable position, it was obliged to warn only prescribing physicians and not consumers. What warnings then did Ortho in fact give physicians? Liability in this case, it is to be remembered, must be determined within a 1971 framework; changes which have since occurred in either the state of medical knowledge or the form of warnings provided consumers or physicians are not the concern of this lawsuit.

Like other drug manufacturers, Ortho uses a number of methods of communicating information to doctors about its birth control products including pamphlets, package inserts, advertisements, "Dear Doctor" letters and oral information by sales representatives. However, none of the Ortho information intended for doctors contained any warning or made any mention of the risk of stroke associated with the use of oral contraceptives. I shall reproduce by way of example some of the warnings given by Ortho in the information and promotional material disseminated by it to the medical profession in Canada.

... Ortho's statement concerning its product in the 1971 CPS, headed "Ortho-Novum Preparations", omits any mention of cerebral thrombosis or stroke when dealing with "Adverse Effects". Instead, the following appears:

> *Adverse Effects*: The following adverse effects have been observed with varying incidence in patients receiving oral contraceptives: ... Thrombophlebitis, pulmonary embolism and neuro-ocular lesions have been observed in users of oral contraceptives, although a cause and effect relationship has neither been established nor disproved.

This warning is to be compared with that issued to physicians in the United States by Ortho's sister company, Ortho Pharmaceutical Corporation ("Ortho U.S.") in the Physicians' Desk Reference, the American equivalent to the CPS. There, Ortho U.S. specifically warned doctors of the "statistically significant association between cerebral thrombosis and embolism and the use of oral contraceptives" revealed by studies in the United States and Great Britain. The warning reads:

> *Warnings*:
>
> 1. The physician should be alert to the earliest manifestations of thrombotic disorders (thrombophlebitis, cerebrovascular disorders, pulmonary embolism, and retinal thrombosis). Should any of these occur or be suspected the drug should be discontinued immediately.
>
> Retrospective studies of morbidity and mortality in Great Britain and studies of morbidity in the United States have shown a statistically significant association between thrombophlebitis, pulmonary embolism, and cerebral thrombosis and embolism and the use of oral contraceptives. There have been three principle studies in Great Britain leading to this conclusion, and one in this country. The estimate of the relative risk of thromboembolism in the study by Vessey and Doll was about sevenfold, while Sartwell and associates in the United States found a relative risk of 4.4, meaning that the users are several times as likely to undergo thromboembolic disease without evident cause as non-users. The American study also indicated that the risk did not persist after discon-

tinuation of administration, and that it was not enhanced by long continued administration. The American study was not designed to evaluate a difference between products. However, the study suggested that there might be an increased risk of thromboembolic disease in users of sequential products. This risk cannot be [quantified], and further studies to confirm this finding are desirable.

It is to be noted that Ortho and Ortho U.S. are wholly-owned subsidiaries of Johnson & Johnson, the giant American manufacturer of pharmaceutical products ... [i]t can properly be assumed that Ortho was aware of or had available to it all of the information possessed by Ortho U.S. with respect to their mutual products including adverse reaction reports, medical and scientific studies on birth control pills and, in particular, the information which led to the warning given to prescribing physicians in the United States. Indeed, I do not understand Ortho to suggest that it had any less knowledge than Ortho U.S. about the drugs which they each manufactured and promoted in their respective countries.

Ortho also provided physicians with "file cards" describing Ortho-Novum products. File cards are also recognized as an important and convenient source of information for doctors about a drug's properties. The file card on Ortho-Novum read, in part, as follows:

> This new low-dosage form of ORTHO-NOVUM Tablets [1/50] has proven virtually 100 per cent effective in conception control. Clinical experience involved 4,977 patients who completed a total of 51,544 menstrual cycles. Minor side effects were experienced by a relatively small percentage of patients, and these tended to disappear spontaneously after the early cycles of use.

The only warning was as follows:

> Since it has been suggested that there may be a causal relationship between the use of progestin-estrogen compounds and the development of thrombophlebitis, physicians should be cautious in prescribing ORTHO-NOVUM for patients with thromboembolic disease or a history of thrombophlebitis.
>
> Patients with pre-existing fibroids, epilepsy, migraine, asthma or a history of psychic depression, should be carefully observed.

Significantly, as early as 1968, Ortho U.S. revised its file card to reflect the then available data concerning thromboembolic complications in oral contraceptive users and their increased mortality and morbidity rates. There, doctors were warned, in part, as follows:

> The physician should be alert to the earliest manifestations of thrombolic disorders (thrombophlebitis, cerebrovascular disorders, pulmonary embolism and retinal thrombosis). Should any of these occur or be suspected, the drug should be discontinued immediately. Studies conducted in Great Britain and reported in April 1968 estimate there is a seven to tenfold increase in mortality and morbidity due to thromboembolic diseases in women taking oral contraceptives. In these controlled retrospective studies, involving 36 reported deaths and 58 hospitalizations due to "idiopathic" thromboembolism, statistical evaluation indicated that the differences observed between users and non-users were highly significant.

. . . .

VI

. . . .

Whether a particular warning is adequate will depend on what is reasonable in the circumstances. But the fact that a drug is ordinarily safe and effective and the danger may be rare or involve only a small percentage of users does not necessarily relieve the manufacturer of the duty to warn. While a low probability of injury or a small class of endangered users are factors to be taken into account in determining what is reasonable, these factors must be balanced against such considerations as the nature of the drug, the necessity for taking it, and the magnitude of the increased danger to the individual consumers. Similarly, where medical evidence exists which tends to show a serious danger inherent in the use of a drug, the manufacturer is not entitled to ignore or discount that information in its warning solely because it finds it to be unconvincing; the manufacturer is obliged to be forthright and to tell the whole story. The extent of the warning and the steps to be taken to bring the warning home to physicians should be commensurate with the potential danger — the graver the dangers, the higher the duty.

A reading of Ortho U.S.'s warnings to physicians makes it manifest that Ortho was aware or should have been aware of the association between oral contraceptive use and stroke.... I think it evi-

dent that Ortho failed to give the medical profession warnings commensurate with its knowledge of the dangers inherent in the use of Ortho-Novum; more specifically, it breached its duty to warn of the risk of stroke associated with the use of Ortho-Novum.

. . . .

IX

. . . .

The suggestion that the determination of this causation issue other than by way of an objective test would place an undue burden on drug manufacturers is answered by noting that drug manufacturers are in a position to escape all liability by the simple expedient of providing a clear and forthright warning of the dangers inherent in the use of their products of which they know or ought to know. In my opinion, it is sound in principle and in policy to adopt an approach which facilitates meaningful consumer choice and promotes market-place honesty by encouraging full disclosure. This is preferable to invoking evidentiary burdens that serve to exonerate negligent manufacturers as well as manufacturers who would rather risk liability than provide information which might prejudicially affect their volume of sales.

. . . .

XI

Before leaving this case, I would return to the question of whether a manufacturer of oral contraceptives is under a duty at common law to warn consumers directly. In doing so, I am not unmindful of the fact that anything I may say at this stage is not necessary to my decision. In deference, however, to the thorough arguments presented on the issue, I make these brief comments.

I do not quarrel with the general proposition advanced by the defendant that where prescription drugs are concerned, the manufacturer's duty to warn is limited to an obligation to warn prescribing physicians of potential dangers that may result from the drug's use. This special standard represents an understandable and sensible exception to the well-recognized common law principle of tort liability that the manufacturer of a product has a duty to warn users of dangers inherent in the use of the product. The question here comes down to whether the *rationale* which is relied on to support this exception with respect to prescription drugs generally can be justified in the case of oral contraceptives.

There can be little doubt that oral contraceptives have presented society with problems unique in the history of human therapeutics. At no time have so many people taken such potent drugs voluntarily over such a protracted time for an objective other than the control of disease. This has introduced a novel element in the doctor-patient relationship. As the advisory committee pointed out, "in prescribing these drugs, the doctor is usually acting neither to treat nor to prevent a disease. He is prescribing for socioeconomic reasons". Furthermore, unlike the selection of an appropriate drug for the treatment of illness or injury where patient involvement is typically minimal or nonexistent, consumer demand for oral contraceptives prompts their use more often than doctors' advice. The decision to use the pill is one in which consumers are actively involved; more frequently than not, they have made the decision before visiting a doctor to obtain a prescription.

For these reasons, as well as those stated in *MacDonald v. Ortho Pharmaceutical Corp.* (1985), 475 N.E. 2d 65, which I quoted earlier, I am

of the view that oral contraceptives bear characteristics distinguishing them from most therapeutic, diagnostic and curative prescription drugs. The *rationale* underlying the learned intermediary rule, in my opinion, does not hold up in the case of oral contraceptives. Manufacturers of this drug should be obliged to satisfy the general common law duty to warn the ultimate consumer as well as prescribing physicians. To require this would not be to impose any real burden on drug manufacturers or to unduly interfere with the doctor-patient relationship as it exists with regard to the prescription of this drug. What is more, appropriate warnings conveying reasonable notice of the nature, gravity and likelihood of known or knowable side-effects and advising the consumer to seek further explanation from her doctor of any information of concern to her, would promote the desirable objective of ensuring that women are fully apprised of the information needed to balance the benefits and risks of this form of birth control and to make informed and intelligent decisions in consultation with their doctors on whether to use or continue to use oral contraceptives.

. . . .

Appeal dismissed.

(b) *Pittman Estate v. Bain, Toronto Hospital and Canadian Red Cross Society*†

[LANG J.:]

INTRODUCTION

In late 1984, Kenneth Pittman had cardiac surgery at the Toronto General Hospital (the Hospital). He was transfused with cryoprecipitate, a blood component intended to stop his bleeding. It succeeded in stopping the bleeding but, unbeknownst to all, it was contaminated with the human immunodeficiency virus (HIV). A glossary of technical terms

that occur in this judgment is provided in Appendix A [of the original]. The "gift of life" proved fatal to Kenneth Pittman, who died of an HIV-related pneumonia in 1990.

The Canadian Red Cross Society (CRCS) had collected that blood from an unwitting Mr. L. in November, 1994. (A list of acronyms of health organizations mentioned in this judgment is provided in Appendix B [of the original].) In November, 1985, Mr. L. returned to give blood a second time. The CRCS was then able to test blood for

---

† (1994), 112 D.L.R. (4th) 257 at 265–68, 275–80, 310–13, 376–78, 383, 386–87, 412, 456–58.

HIV. They learned that Mr. L.'s blood was tainted with HIV and so advised him.

In June, 1987, the CRCS traced Mr. L.'s potentially tainted 1984 donation to the Hospital, and so advised the Hospital.

It was not until February, 1989, that the Hospital traced the blood to the 1984 transfusion to Mr. Pittman. In April, 1989, the head of the Hospital blood bank telephoned Mr. Pittman's family doctor, Dr. Bain, and advised him.

Dr. Bain, concerned about the client's cardiac condition and mental health and, operating on the assumption that Mr. Pittman was not having sexual intercourse with Mrs. Pittman, did not advise Mr. Pittman of his possible infection.

Mr. Pittman died from pneumonia-related causes in March 1990. In April, Dr. Bain learned that Mr. Pittman had been HIV positive (HIV+). In September, 1990, Mrs. Pittman learned that she is HIV+.

The Pittman family sues the CRCS, the Hospital and Dr. Bain for the harm that they have suffered.

ISSUES

(a) Red Cross Liability

The Pittman family sues the CRCS, alleging that it fell below the appropriate standard of care in failing to adequately screen blood donors, and in failing to test donated blood to reduce the risk of infection to the recipient. The Pittmans further allege that the CRCS was negligent in failing to implement, in a timely manner, a program to search for the recipients of potentially tainted blood and for those consequently at risk (lookback program).

(b) Hospital Liability

The Pittmans sue the Hospital on an implied contractual warranty basis for the provision of the tainted blood that was transfused into Mr. Pittman. The tainted blood led ultimately to the transmission of the virus to Rochelle Pittman. The Pittmans also sue the Hospital in negligence for its delay in, and manner of, implementing a lookback program.

(c) Dr. Bain Liability

The Pittman family seeks damages from Dr. Stanley Bain, alleging that he fell below the appropriate standard of care when he decided to withhold information of the potentially tainted transfusion from Mr. and Mrs. Pittman.

The plaintiffs seek approximately $1,500,000 in damages. The defendants have various cross-claims against each other.

Fact Specific

As this is the first decision in Ontario concerning transfusion-related AIDS, it is important to note that the findings are based upon the particular facts of this case.

This case deals with the transfusion of cryoprecipitate, a component made from the donations of many donors. This case does not deal with fractionated blood products that were routinely used by hemophiliacs, such as Factor VIII and Factor IX.

Further, this case is about a 1984 transfusion and is not concerned in any way with any alleged delay by the CRCS in implementing HIV testing. Nor is there an issue in this case about the 1984 surgery itself or the transfusion; it is conceded by the plaintiffs that the surgery was necessary, and the transfusion essential.

The result in this case, for reasons that will become apparent, is particular to its unique facts. Unfortunately, notwithstanding the length and expense of this trial, its conclusion cannot be taken to be of general application to other cases of transfusion-related AIDS.

A further cautionary note is needed. As the AIDS epidemic unfolded in the 1980s, our society took good health for granted, and presumed that its blood supply was safe. That was so even though national blood collection and distribution was then only 35 years of age in Canada. As the first cases of an apparently fatal illness from an immunodeficiency were identified in the United States, research began and controversy abounded. That controversy culminated in the eventual acceptance that this disease was caused by a virus, and that it was transmissible by blood. While much more is known today about AIDS, controversy continues in many areas, including treatment. It is crucial that the defendants' actions in the 1980s not be judged with the benefit of 1993 information, knowledge and by hindsight. To do so might comfort some by providing scapegoats to blame for the appalling suffering caused by this disease. But this would not be just.

. . . .

BACKGROUND

. . . .

AIDS As We Now Understand It

I now canvass the current state of knowledge about HIV and AIDS, conscious of the obligation not to use today's knowledge as a measure of earlier conduct. None the less, it assists to approach the problem with an understanding of the cause of the disease and its progression.

In addition, this information will be necessary to decide whether Mr. Pittman died of an AIDS-related illness, when Mrs. Pittman was infected, and what the progression of her illness and her life expectancy will be.

The name of the disease, the Acquired Immune Deficiency Syndrome (AIDS), is descriptive of its effect. In this disease, the immune system is increasingly unable to produce the antibodies necessary to fight infection. As the immune system becomes increasingly compromised, the patient becomes more and more susceptible to the onset of infection. HIV is now generally accepted as the causal agent of AIDS. Experts now accept that one will not progress to AIDS unless they are HIV+, but there remains some question as to whether a second trigger is also necessary to take an asymptomatic carrier to clinical AIDS.

Knowledge about the disease continued to develop even as this trial progressed. What follows is a very simplistic explanation of a complex process based on the evidence that was before this court in 1993.

HIV affects a particular group of white blood cells, namely, T-4 cells, or T-helper lymphocytes. Those cells are of great significance to the body's immune infrastructure as the co-ordinate cell-mediated immunity, and activate a set of antibody-producing cells to fight invading infection. If the T-helper lymphocyte cells are damaged, compromised or prejudiced, the immune system becomes deficient, and becomes progressively more vulnerable to opportunistic infection.

When the HIV enters the system, the virus binds to and enters the CD4 receptor, a surface marker on T-helper lymphocytes. From there, over varying periods of time, it invades the T-helper cell itself and remains there. When the T-helper cell is called into action to fight infection, it starts to multiply, and its nucleus divides. That division and multiplication of the nuclear material of the T-

helper lymphocyte leads to the activation of the HIV virus, and the creation of several thousand individual virus molecules inside the infected T-4 lymphocytes. The cell blows up like a balloon, dies and releases viral particles, each one of which will infect a new CD4 cell and, through it, new T-4 lymphocytes. As the T-helpers are invaded by and eventually destroyed by HIV, the immune system is progressively less capable of fighting such invaders as fungi, viruses, parasites and certain bacteria including certain types of pneumonia.

This progression of HIV to AIDS is often described as various stages. To assist in understanding those stages of progression from infection to death, annexed as Appendix D [of the original] is a chart produced by Dr. Lange showing the changes in the sufferer's viral load (pattern of HIV, ex. 21, Appendix D). While one may take issue with some of the information contained in the chart, it does provide a useful guide to understanding the progression of the disease.

In the first phase, which occurs in the few weeks following entry of the virus into a person, the viral count in the body is high. In this phase, a percentage of people experience a primary infection as their body seroconverts, that is, when their bodies begin to produce antibodies to the HIV. Within two to six months of infection, 95% of HIV recipients seroconvert. In the case of Mrs. Pittman, the possibility of a primary infection is important because she was not tested for HIV until after her husband's death. If, as is argued, she experienced such a primary mononucleosis type infection in 1988, that might assist in determining when she likely was infected by her husband.

The disease then progresses to a second stage where the viral count in the blood is well below the earlier levels, but where the virus remains active within the lymph system. This asymptomatic stage usually lasts from two to ten years during which time the infected person appears well and the infection remains latent, although the virus continues to multiply and destroy T-helper lymphocytes. The destruction of the T-helper lymphocytes can be seen in the infected person's gradually diminishing CD4 count which, with some fluctuations, will fall from an initial high in a range of 500 to 1,500 per microlitre of blood, to a level below 200.

The progression of the disease during this second and latent phase is unpredictable in the individual sufferer. As the CD4 count diminishes to and falls below the 200 range, the patient becomes more susceptible to opportunistic infections, and usually but not always progresses to the final stage of AIDS. This stage is referred to as "disease AIDS" or often simply as AIDS.

While about 50% of people develop AIDS within eight to ten years from the initial exposure, some do so within as short a time frame as six months, with no early warning clinical symptoms. On the other hand, some people do not develop AIDS even after 15 years. Only time will tell if there are some HIV+ carriers who never will develop AIDS. At the moment there is no recognized factor or factors that determine the progression or rate of the pathogenic progress from HIV to clinical AIDS.

During the asymptomatic period, it is important to monitor the person for treatment purposes. The CD4 count, or the ratio of the CD4 cells to the CD8s, or the p24 antigen count are monitored. If those tests indicate that the patient is becoming progressively more immunocompromised, the physician and patient will consider prophylactic antibiotics and vaccines, and whether the drug known as Zidovudine (AZT) should be prescribed. Treatment then concentrates on slowing down the decline of the immune system, since there is no way to restore it.

At one point, physicians and researchers used the term ARC (AIDS-related complex). Experts no longer use this term as it was ill-defined and really just referred to mild AIDS. None the less, it is helpful to explain its earlier application as the term is frequently used in the literature. AIDS-related complex, or ARC, applied to those persons whose CD4 counts had dropped to the 200 to 300 range, and who displayed such symptoms as malaise, fatigue, an inability to function normally, greater than 10% weight loss, diarrhoea, skin rashes, persistent low grade fever, or swollen lymph glands or oral thrush. This stage is really, though, a part of the continuum as the sufferer progresses from asymptomatic to full-blown AIDS.

When the infected person comes to the third phase of disease AIDS, the viral load again increases in the blood, and, presumably in the semen, so that a sexual partner becomes increasingly vulnerable to the transmission of HIV. Once AIDS develops, it almost inevitably leads to the death of the patient over varying periods of time, but often within a two-year period.

. . . .

While the above review attempts to simplify the present learning on the pathological process of AIDS, it must be remembered that the issue was replete with controversy in the early 1980s, and, in some aspects, remains so today. Dr. Lange and Dr. Francis, both American experts for the plaintiffs, were at the forefront at the time AIDS was first recognized. Indeed, they acknowledged that their views were at the cutting edge of scientific opinion, and that generally it takes one or two years before cutting edge views are disseminated through the scientific community and achieve recognition. This was certainly the case with respect to identification of the etiological agent for AIDS. While it was first isolated by the Pasteur Institute in France in 1983, it required a further study and a second announcement by Gallo in the U.S. before HIV was generally accepted in April, 1984. None the less even today controversy remains about HIV, its responsibility for CD4 depletion, its effects in different individuals, the duration of the latent period and other issues.

None the less, even in 1984, there was clearly cause for concern in the U.S. because the incidence of AIDS cases was doubling every six months, and AIDS was appearing in hemophiliacs. As transmissibility by blood changed from mere speculation to a possibility, and from a possibility to a probability, U.S. regulators and blood banks had to make decisions about how to protect their blood supplies. Canada lagged several months behind the incidence of the disease in the U.S., and also approached more cautiously the issues of ensuring the safety of the blood supply.

. . . .

RED CROSS BLOOD COLLECTION

. . . .

Standard of Care

There are no Canadian cases that set the standard of care to be applied to blood collectors and distributors. Therefore, this is a new issue in Canada. The court must decide the nature and scope of the CRCS's duty to Mr. Pittman and to Mrs. Pittman, as well as the appropriate standard of care against which to measure the CRCS's 1984 conduct to determine whether it was negligent.

There are two separate allegations of failure to meet the appropriate standard of care that have been made against the CRCS. The first relates to the alleged failure in screening out high risk blood donors in November, 1984, when the HIV-infected blood was donated. The second relates to the length of time it took the CRCS to trace the possibly infected 1984 donation after it was discovered that the donor of the blood had tested HIV+ following a subsequent donation. Was the CRCS lookback program adequate?

If there was a breach of the standard of care by the CRCS in either blood collection or lookback, the court will then have to consider whether that breach caused any damage to the plaintiffs.

In order to determine the applicable standard of care, it is helpful to first delineate the duties of the CRCS. Its mandate as set out in its letters patent includes the following worthy aims:

> ... to prevent and alleviate human suffering, and to work for the improvement of health and prevention of disease anywhere in the world ...

... Applying these broad objectives to its blood collection role, the CRCS assumed the dual obligations of protecting both the safety and the sufficiency of the Canadian blood supply.

By accepting that duty of protecting the blood supply, the plaintiffs argue, the CRCS should be held to a standard of care approaching strict or absolute liability for its blood components. While acknowledging that the American concept of strict tort liability has no place in Canadian law, the plaintiffs argue that the CRCS obligation is akin to the obligation placed on manufacturers of food or pharmaceuticals, an obligation that will be discussed shortly.

The CRCS replies that blood, as a biologic, is inherently unsafe, and that to set its obligation at such a high level, would jeopardize its other obligation: to ensure the sufficiency of the essential blood supply to Canadians.

In 1936 the Ontario Court of Appeal in *Shandloff v. City Dairy Ltd. and Moscoe*, [1936] 4 D.L.R. 712, considered a tort claim against a milk manufacturer. The plaintiff, who had found pieces of glass in her milk bottle, could not establish where in the chain of production negligence had occurred. None the less, the trial judge inferred negligence on the part of the manufacturer from the presence of the glass in the bottle. Indeed this finding was made in the face of another finding that the manufacturer had taken every reasonable

precaution to ensure that this type of problem did not occur.

The court spoke of the duty of care owed by the manufacturer of such products to the consumer that had begun with *Donoghue v. Stevenson*, [1932] A.C. 562 (H.L.).

A similar Canadian case is that of *Heimler v. Calvert Caterers Ltd.* (1975), 56 D.L.R. (3d) 643, (C.A.), where a guest at a wedding reception contracted typhoid fever from the food. Contamination had occurred because the preparer of the food, an employee of the caterer, who did not realize that she was a typhoid carrier, had neglected to properly clean her hands of fecal matter after using the toilet. Although the caterer had taken all reasonable precautions, it was held liable in tort trial. On appeal, the court, observed as follow (at p. 644):

> The standard of care demanded from those engaged in the food-handling business, is an extremely high standard and as Middleton J.A., observed in *Shandloff v. City Diary Ltd. and Moscoe*, [1936] O.R. 579, [1936] 4 D.L.R. 712, the lack of care essential to the establishment of such a claim increases according to the danger to the ultimate consumer, and where the thing is in itself dangerous, the care necessary approximates to and almost becomes an absolute liability.

In my view, these two cases do more than draw reasonable inferences from the facts before the respective courts. The court was able to infer negligence on the common sense principles recently affirmed by the Supreme Court of Canada in *Snell v. Farrell*, [1990] 2 S.C.R. 311, without the need to invoke the concept of strict liability. Even accepting the wisdom of the strict liability cases, their facts differ from those before me.

In this case, the blood was not contaminated by the CRCS, or one of its employees, but rather came to it in a contaminated condition. The issue is not whether the CRCS "manufactured" the product negligently, but rather whether it was negligent in the exercise of skill in its collection and distribution of an already contaminated product.

The issue of strict liability in tort, while widely accepted in the U.S., has not been embraced in this jurisdiction. Strict liability in tort would be especially inappropriate in situations where the defective product was not produced by the defendant, but was manufactured by another and merely distributed by the defendant. Such a situation is discussed in Waddams, *Products Liability*, 3rd ed. (1993):

... there is the case of a product that is defective because it incorporates a defective part manufactured by some other person for whom the defendant is not responsible. Some American cases have held that the manufacturer of the completed product is liable in such circumstances, but it seems doubtful that a similar result would be reached where the plaintiff is required to prove negligence, if the manufacturer has taken all reasonable care in the selection and supervision of the supplier.

In an argument similar to that advanced in support of strict liability, the plaintiffs maintain that, with the risk of transmission through blood of a fatal disease such as AIDS, the CRCS was under a higher standard of care than it would have been had the risk been of a less dangerous infection. The dangerous nature of a product might indicate that a higher standard of care is required in dealing with it, or that the consumer should be adequately warned of the risks. Certainly, the plaintiffs can find support for these propositions in the case law: see *Rae v. T. Eaton Co. (Maritimes) Ltd.* (1961), 28 D.L.R. (2d) 522 at p. 535 (N.S.S.C.) (artificial snow can exploding). However, the collection and distribution of blood cannot be likened to the manufacture of artificial snow, or other commercial products that bring with them an element of danger.

In cases involving commercial products, there are policy considerations in support of liability that are not applicable to a blood bank. While the fact that the CRCS is a non-profit organization does not exculpate it from responsibility for negligence, it should not be held to the standard of care imposed on commercial manufacturers who are in the business for a profit and who pass on to their consumers the expense of their liability. Furthermore, the responsibility for regulating the CRCS is that of the public health authorities, and should not be left to consumer litigation.

In the case of blood, the societal need for the component produces different considerations. This is not a product that should be removed from the market if inherently dangerous. Blood is an essential source of life to many. Although it is a biologic, and, therefore, dangerous, the need for the product outweighs the risk. This does not relieve the collector of the blood from the duty to exercise reasonable care, but it perhaps dictates that the collector who does exercise reasonable care, should not be held liable, in the absence of fault on its part, for something that it could not reasonably prevent.

. . . .

At least by December, 1986, it was clear to the CRCS that lookback required priority. It was that month that NACAIDS wrote that the CRCS should follow up recipients at risk, and offer them the opportunity for testing and counselling.

In not responding promptly to the serious risks to the recipients of potentially tainted blood, the CRCS did not meet the standard of care expected of the organization charged with protecting Canada's blood supply. The CRCS should reasonably have completed its lookback program some months before it did so in June, 1987.

The CRCS was also negligent in waiting until June of 1987 before requiring the hospitals to maintain transfusion records by unit number. Such a requirement should reasonably have been made in June, 1986, when the CRCS first appreciated the importance of such a program, and appreciated that tracing would be difficult in many Toronto hospitals where records were often kept alphabetically by patient name. There was little point in completing its own lookback expeditiously when the CRCS knew that the TGH would be unable to perform its part of the program.

Even when it did ask the Hospital to begin its lookback, the CRCS did not bring home to the Hospital the urgency of the program and the potential risk to the recipients. The CRCS takes the position that its responsibilities ended when it notified the Hospital of Mr. L.'s potentially tainted transfusion. I cannot agree. The CRCS had an ongoing obligation to monitor the Hospital's progress and the eventual outcome of the warning to be given to the recipient.

Instead of monitoring the Hospital to ensure it could and would promptly respond to the demands of the situation, the CRCS appears to have done nothing. It was not until November, 1988, that it followed up only to learn that the Hospital was "attempting to computerize their past records".

Given the importance of this issue and the threat to those at risk, the CRCS had a duty to carefully monitor the Hospital's progress, a duty that it breached. If it had monitored the Hospital's progress, it would have realized that the delay caused by including lookback with a computerization of all its blood bank records was an unacceptable one. If it had known that the delay would be a further 22 months, the CRCS, with the Hospital, should have considered alternative methods of notifying those potentially at risk.

While the CRCS feared public announcements would provoke panic in the community, in the absence of reasonable alternatives, the CRCS was under an overriding duty to inform those recipients of the risk of transfusion-associated AIDS. Further, other possible means were at hand. The CRCS or the Hospital could have written family doctors, cardiologists or other specialists, or hospital cardiac patients to give them information about the risks of transfusion-associated AIDS and counselling about the ramifications. The CRCS did not give any such proposal reasonable consideration, choosing instead to abdicate responsibility to the Hospital for follow-up. In doing so, the CRCS acted negligently.

In addition, while it was proper for the lookback to contemplate the warning to the recipient to be done by his family physician, it was under an obligation of ensuring that the family doctor was properly informed for the purpose. At the very least, the CRCS should have required that the Hospital provide the doctor with a copy of the lookback form, and that it follow up with the doctor after the notification. The CRCS did not impose even these minimal requirements, let alone ensuring that the family physician had up-to-date information or resources from which to ascertain the risk to the patient, the advantages and disadvantages of testing, and the possibilities of treatment.

In failing to expeditiously implement its own lookback; in failing, in a timely manner, to require hospitals to keep records by unit number, in failing to monitor the Hospital's lookback program, and in failing to follow up on its notification program, the CRCS fell below the standard of care expected of a blood banker charged with using its best efforts to protect transfusion recipients.

. . . .

DR. STANLEY BAIN

In April, 1989, the Hospital told Dr. Bain that Mr. Pittman had been transfused in 1984 with potentially HIV-contaminated blood components. As Mr. Pittman's family doctor, and based upon his view of his patient's best interests, Dr. Stanley Bain decided to withhold information that Mr. Pittman might have been transfused with HIV-tainted blood.

The court must determine whether Dr. Bain's decision was a negligent one, in the sense that it fell below the standard of care expected of a reasonable, prudent family physician of similar experience.

. . . .

It was Dr. Bain's position that he carefully considered whether to tell Mr. Pittman about his receipt of potentially tainted 1984 transfusion from a donor who tested HIV+ in 1985. He says that his careful consideration included a review of Mr. Pittman's medical chart that indicated his depression, and sexual abstinence as well as a review of relevant literature, and consultations with colleagues. Each of these aspects of Dr. Bain's analysis[] requires review.

Review of Chart and Literature

At the end of his telephone conversation with Dr. Francombe, Dr. Bain's first step was to review Mr. Pittman's chart. This review confirmed his initial recollection about Mr. Pittman's emotional difficulties, as well as his cardiac condition.

A year earlier, Dr. Bain had attended a meeting of the Canadian College of Family Physicians in Montreal, where an overview of HIV/AIDS was given by Dr. Mark Steben. He remembered information from that conference, although he did not have a copy of Dr. Steben's paper. Dr. Bain also reviewed a March, 1988 article from the Journal of the Medical Association of Georgia that he got through the NYGH library as one of the few articles in which there was a statistical assessment of the lookback program. The authors reported as follows:

> In this programme, recipients of untested blood from donors later found to be anti-HIV positive[] are notified and tested. In our experience, of those recipients whose results we were able to obtain, 37% were positive.

Mindful that his patient had a 37% likelihood of being HIV+, Dr. Bain reviewed Mr. Pittman's chart for symptoms of infection. He says that he found none.

It was now more than four years since the suspect transfusion, and it was Dr. Bain's understanding that clinical signs of AIDS usually occurred at a median time of about 27 months from the date of infection.

Dr. Bain saw Mr. Pittman on May 23rd, and testified that after looking at his history, and physically examining him, he thought it likely that Mr.

Pittman was in the 63% of the population who did not become HIV+ after receiving a potentially tainted transfusion.

Risk of Transmission to Mrs. Pittman

None the less, in case of error, Dr. Bain knew that it was important to rule out any risk of infectivity to others. He knew Mr. Pittman to be a devoted family man. Therefore, his concern about Mr. Pittman infecting others was limited to a risk of Mrs. Pittman if she and her husband had an ongoing sexual relationship. Dr. Bain concluded that the couple no longer had such a relationship, and hence that there was no ongoing risk to Mrs. Pittman.

. . . .

While by no means certain, it is probable, particularly given my finding that Mr. Pittman died from his AIDS-defining illness in 1990, and given the evidence of increasing viral load with progression of the virus, that Mrs. Pittman contracted HIV in the year immediately preceding her husband's death.

Summary

Dr. Bain was negligent in withholding the information from Mr. Pittman that his 1984 transfusion was potentially tainted with HIV. Had Mr. Pittman been given this information, it is likely that he would have sought treatment, and that his life could have been prolonged by approximately two years.

Further, had Mr. Pittman been told, he would have told Mrs. Pittman. Mrs Pittman probably contracted HIV from her husband during the last year of his life. Had Mr. and Mrs. Pittman known of the risks, they likely would have taken steps to protect Mrs. Pittman.

. . . .

CONCLUSION

On the facts of this case, the CRCS was not negligent in collecting blood from Mr. L. on November 13, 1984, in Ajax, Ontario. Nor were they negligent in distributing the component of that blood, cryoprecipitate, to the Hospital for transfusion.

All parties agreed that Mr. Pittman's cardiac surgery was urgent, and that his transfusion with cryoprecipitate was reasonable. There was, therefore, no claim in this case that the CRCS or the Hospital should have warned Mr. Pittman of the risks of transfusion-related AIDS. Such a warning would not have changed the result.

The Hospital cannot and should not be held strictly liable on an implied contractual warranty that the cryoprecipitate was fit for its purpose. In the admitted absence of negligence on the part of the Hospital for the transfusion of cryoprecipitate, the Hospital should not be held contractually responsible for the tainted blood.

In 1986, after the CRCS became aware that Mr. L's 1984 donation was potentially tainted, it had a duty to notify the recipients of that donation of the serious threat to their health, and to the health of their sexual partners. In 1987, after the Hospital learned of the potentially tainted transfusion, it had a similar obligation to notify its former patient of the serious consequences of the 1984 blood transfusion. In 1989, when Dr. Bain was told of the potentially tainted transfusion, he had a duty, in the circumstances, to give that information to Mr. Pittman. Each of the CRCS, the Hospital, and Dr. Bain was negligent in this regard. Each failed to notify Mr. Pittman in a manner that would have brought to his immediate attention the serious threat to his health, and that of Mrs. Pittman, posed by the potentially tainted blood.

That negligence prevented Mr. Pittman from seeking medical treatment and management of his health for HIV infection. As a result, Mr. Pittman died in March, 1990, of an HIV-related pneumonia. Had he been told of his possible infection, Mr. Pittman could likely have extended his own life by approximately two years.

Had Mr. Pittman been told of his possible infection, he would have disclosed that to Mrs. Pittman. Together, they would have taken precautions that would have prevented the transmission of HIV to Mrs. Pittman, a transmission that probably occurred in the last year of Mr. Pittman's life.

In the result, Mr. Pittman's estate, Mrs. Pittman and the Pittman children have suffered a compensable loss. I have found that the loss was caused by the negligence of Dr. Bain, but that the failure of the CRCS and the Hospital to conduct an expeditious lookback program contributed to that loss. Accordingly, I have allocated responsibility for the loss at 40% to Dr. Bain, 30% to the CRCS and 30% to the Hospital. Counsel have yet to provide me with the information needed to complete the value of Mrs. Pittman's loss of income and future care costs. Subject to adjustment of the damages after those further submissions by counsel, I assess total damages at $515,076.57. In addition, counsel will make submissions as to pre-judgment interest and costs.

Finally, I cannot leave this case without commenting on the tragedy that has befallen Mr. and Mrs. Pittman. It is a tragedy that has been compounded by the financial and emotional stress of a trial that began one year and one week ago today. Mrs Pittman has proven her claim. Unfortunately, because the result is fact-specific, it cannot be generally applied to other outstanding cases. It will compound the tragedy of transfusion-associated AIDS, if more cases must be decided by the litigation process. Litigation is a fault-driven process where each case must be decided on its own merits. It is ill-suited to an expeditious resolution of such tragic situations

I end with an apology for the errors of structure, syntax, punctuation, grammar and flow of this judgment, as well as the rudimentary index. It undoubtedly would have benefited from an opportunity to polish its presentation. None the less, as I had come to a decision on all issues between the parties, and the substance of that decision would not change with further deliberation, it seemed wrong to withhold the result for matter of form, given the March 15th deadline for acceptance of the government compensation package.

Judgment will go in favour of the estate of Mr. Pittman, and in favour of Mrs. Pittman and the Pittman children in accordance with this judgment with the amount of damages to be adjusted after final submissions by counsel on the outstanding matters.

Judgment for plaintiffs.

(c) *Jordan House Ltd. v. Menow*†

[LASKIN J.:]

This is a case of first instance. The principal issue is whether the operator of a hotel may be charged with a duty of care to a patron of the hotel beverage room who becomes intoxicated there, a duty to take reasonable care to safeguard him from the likely risk of personal injury if he is turned out of the hotel to make his way alone. If such a duty may be imposed, it falls to determine the nature or scope of the duty to the intoxicated patron. This determination must then be related to the present case by inquiring whether on its facts there has been a breach of the duty by the appellant hotel so as to engage its liability to the respondent plaintiff for personal injuries. I shall refer later in these reasons to another issue raised on behalf of the respondent Honsberger.

There are concurrent findings of fact in this case by the trial judge, Haines J., and by the Ontario Court of Appeal in favour of Menow, on the basis of which he was awarded damages against the appellant hotel and against the respondent Honsberger under an equal apportionment of fault among all three parties. Honsberger was the driver of a car which struck Menow as he was walking east near the centre line of Highway No. 8 after having been ejected from the hotel. Neither the quantum of damages nor the apportionment of fault is in issue in this appeal.

The hotel premises front on Highway No. 8, a much-travelled two-lane highway running east and west between Hamilton and Niagara Falls, Ontario. The road is asphalt, twenty-one feet wide, and, at the material time, January 18, 1968, the shoulders were icy, with snowbanks beyond them, and the pavement itself was wet although not slippery.

---

† [1974] S.C.R. 239 at 241–43, 247–51.

Menow was employed by a fruit farmer and lived alone on his employer's farm which was on a side road about two and one-half miles east of the hotel. The direct route to his abode was along the highway and then north along the side road.

Menow was a frequent patron of the hotel's beverage room, where beer was served, and was well known to the owner-operator of the hotel, one Fernick. He was often there in the company of his employer and the latter's foreman, also well known to Fernick. Menow had a tendency to drink to excess and then to act recklessly, although ordinarily he was courteous and mannerly. The hotel management and the beverage room employees knew of his propensities, and, indeed, about a year before the events out of which this case arose he had been barred from the hotel for a period of time because he annoyed other customers, and thereafter the hotel's employees were instructed not to serve him unless he was accompanied by a responsible person.

On January 18, 1968, Menow, his employer and the foreman arrived at the hotel at about 5.15 p.m. and drank beer. The employer and the foreman departed within a short time, leaving the plaintiff there alone. Fernick came on duty at about 7 p.m. and saw that the plaintiff was then sober. He was served with beer from time to time, and there is a finding that towards 10 p.m. Fernick was aware that Menow was drinking to excess and that he had become intoxicated, the hotel having sold beer to Menow past the point of visible or apparent intoxication. At about 10 p.m. or 10.15 p.m. Menow was seen wandering around to other tables in the beverage room and consequently was ejected from the hotel by employees thereof, Fernick then knowing that the plaintiff was unable to take care of himself by reason of intoxication and that he would have to go home, probably by foot, by way of a main highway.

No excessive force was used in turning Menow out of the hotel. The evidence shows that he was put out on a dark and rainy night and that he was wearing dark clothes not readily visible to motorists. It appears that Menow, when he was outside the hotel, was picked up by an unknown third person and taken part of the way home, being let out on Highway No. 8 at 13th Street. The ride had not been arranged by the hotel. It was while continuing in an easterly direction and, indeed, while walking beyond 11th Street, his turn-off point (because, according to his testimony, he was looking for a friend) that Menow was struck by the Honsberger vehicle. It is unnecessary to detail the circum-stances attending the accident because Honsberger does not challenge in this Court the finding of negligence and the apportionment of one-third fault against him. It is enough to say that the accident occurred within half an hour after Menow was ejected from the hotel, and that he was staggering near the centre of the highway when he was hit by the Honsberger vehicle which was travelling east.

. . . .

I return to the main issue. The common law assesses liability for negligence on the basis of breach of a duty of care arising from a foreseeable and unreasonable risk of harm to one person created by the act or omission of another. This is the generality which exhibits the flexibility of the common law; but since liability is predicated upon fault, the guiding principle assumes a nexus or relationship between the injured person and the injuring person which makes it reasonable to conclude that the latter owes a duty to the former not to expose him to an unreasonable risk of harm. Moreover, in considering whether the risk of injury to which a person may be exposed is one that he should not reasonably have to run, it is relevant to relate the probability and the gravity of injury to the burden that would be imposed upon the prospective defendant in taking avoiding measures. *Bolton v. Stone* [[1951] A.C. 850], in the House of Lords and *Lambert v. Lastoplex Chemicals Co. Ltd.* [[1972] S.C.R. 569], in this Court illustrate the relationship between the remoteness or likelihood of injury and the fixing of an obligation to take preventive measures according to the gravity thereof.

In the present case, it may be said from one point of view that Menow created a risk of injury to himself by excessive drinking on the night in question. If the hotel's only involvement was the supplying of the beer consumed by Menow, it would be difficult to support the imposition of common law liability upon it for injuries suffered by Menow after being shown the door of the hotel and after leaving the hotel. Other persons on the highway, seeing Menow in an intoxicated condition, would not, by reason of that fact alone, come under any legal duty to steer him to safety, although it might be expected that good Samaritan impulses would move them to offer help. They would, however, be under a legal duty, as motorists for example, to take reasonable care to avoid hitting him, a duty in which Honsberger failed in this case. The hotel, however, was not in the position of persons in general who see an intoxicated person who appears to be unable to control his steps. It was in an invitor-invitee relationship with Menow as one of its patrons, and it was aware, through its employees, of his intoxicated condition, a condition which, on the findings of the trial judge, it fed in violation of applicable liquor licence and liquor control legislation. There was a probable risk of personal injury to Menow if he was turned out of the hotel to proceed on foot on a much-travelled highway passing in front of the hotel.

There is, in my opinion, nothing unreasonable in calling upon the hotel in such circumstances to take care to see that Menow is not exposed to injury because of his intoxication. No inordinate burden would be placed upon it in obliging it to respond to Menow's need for protection. A call to the police or a call to his employer immediately come to mind as easily available preventive measures; or a taxi-cab could be summoned to take him home, or arrangements made to this end with another patron able and willing to do so. The evidence shows that the hotel had experience with or was sensitive to the occasional need to take care of intoxicated patrons. The operator had in other like instances provided rides. He also had spare rooms at the time into one of which Menow could have been put.

Given the relationship between Menow and the hotel, the hotel operator's knowledge of Menow's propensity to drink and his instruction to his employees not to serve him unless he was accompanied by a responsible person, the fact that Menow was served not only in breach of this instruction but as well in breach of statutory injunctions against serving a patron who was apparently in an intoxicated condition, and the fact that the hotel operator was aware that Menow was intoxicated, the proper conclusion is that the hotel came under a duty to Menow to see that he got home safely by taking him under its charge or putting him under the charge of a responsible person, or to see that he was not turned out alone until he was in a reasonably fit condition to look after himself. There was, in this case, a breach of this duty for which the hotel must respond according to the degree of fault found against it. The harm that ensued was that which was reasonably foreseeable by reason of what the hotel did (in turning Menow out) and failed to do (in not taking preventive measures).

The imposition of liability upon the hotel in the circumstances that I have recounted has roots in an earlier decision of this Court when related to the evolutionary principles stemming from *Donoghue v. Stevenson*, which have become part of this Court's course of decision. The affinity of *Dunn v. Dominion Atlantic Railway Co.* with the present case is sufficiently shown by the following three sentences from the reasons of Anglin J., who was one of the plurality of this Court which allowed the appeal of the administrator of the estate of a deceased passenger, killed by a passing train when put off at a closed and unlighted station in a drunken condition:

> The right of removal of a disorderly passenger which is conferred on the conductor (under a railway bylaw) is not absolute. It must be exercised reasonably. He cannot under it justify putting a passenger off the train under such circumstances that, as a direct consequence, he is exposed to danger of losing his life or of serious personal injury.

I do not regard the *Dunn* case as turning on the fact that the defendant was a common carrier, any more than I regard it as relevant here whether or not the defendant hotel was under innkeeper's liability in respect of the operation of its beverage room.

The risk of harm to which Menow was exposed by the hotel was not abated to its exoneration by reason of the fortuitous circumstance that Menow obtained a ride part of the way home. The short period of time that elapsed between the time that he was removed from the hotel and the time of the accident is telling in this respect, as is the fact that the risk was not increased or changed in kind when he was dropped off at 13th Street. Counsel for the appellant did not argue on causation, but did contend that any duty that the hotel might have had evaporated because of voluntary assumption of risk. The argument is untenable, whether put on the basis of Menow's self-intoxication or on the basis of the situation that faced him when he was put out of the hotel. In his condition, as found by the trial judge, it is impossible to say that he both appreciated the risk of injury and impliedly agreed to bear the legal consequences. However, the trial judge did find Menow contributorily negligent in becoming intoxicated, adverting in this connection to s.80(2) of *The Liquor Control Act* which enjoins any person against being in an intoxicated condition in a public place. This finding has not been attacked.

The result to which I would come here does not mean (to use the words of the trial judge) that

I would impose "a duty on every tavern-owner to act as a watch dog for all patrons who enter his place of business and drink to excess". A great deal turns on the knowledge of the operator (or his employees) of the patron and his condition

where the issue is liability in negligence for injuries suffered by the patron.

I would dismiss the appeal with costs.

(d) *Stewart v. Pettie*†

[MAJOR J.:]

On December 8, 1985, Gillian Stewart, her husband Keith Stewart, her brother Stuart Pettie, and his wife Shelley Pettie went to the Stage West, a dinner theatre in Edmonton for an evening of dinner and live theatre. Before the evening was finished tragedy had struck. After leaving Stage West at the conclusion of the evening a minor single vehicle accident left Gillian Stewart a quadriplegic. Among others, she sued Mayfield Investments Ltd. (Mayfield), the owner of Stage West claiming contribution for her injuries. This appeal is to decide whether on the facts of this case the principles of commercial host liability, first established by this Court in *Jordan House Ltd. v. Menow*, [1974] S.C.R. 239, apply to impose liability on Mayfield.

I. THE FACTS

Gillian Stewart and her sister-in-law, Shelley Pettie, were both employed by Dispensaries Limited. For its 1985 Christmas party, Dispensaries Limited paid the price of admission for its employees and their spouses and friends to attend a performance at Stage West, a dinner theatre operated in Edmonton by the appellant, Mayfield Investments Ltd., and located at the Mayfield Inn. The admission price included the dinner and performance, but did not include the cost of alcohol consumed.

The two sisters-in-law, with their husbands, went to the dinner theatre together in Stuart Pettie's car, with Stuart Pettie driving. They arrived at the dinner theatre around 6:00 p.m., and were

seated by a hostess at a table which they selected from a group of tables which had been set aside for the approximately 60 people in the Dispensaries Limited group.

The dinner theatre was organized with a full buffet dinner to be followed at 7:45 p.m. by a three-act play. In addition, cocktail waitresses provided table service of alcohol. The Stewart and Pettie table was served by the same waitress all evening, and she kept a running total of all alcohol ordered, which she then presented at the end of the evening for payment. Waitresses would take drink orders during dinner and before the play started, and would also take drink orders during the two intermissions. No orders were taken while the play was in progress.

Stuart Pettie and Keith Stewart each ordered several drinks over the course of the evening, ordering the first drinks before dinner, and, in addition, ordering drinks after dinner but before Act I, and then during each of the two intermissions. Their wives, on the other hand, had no alcohol during the entire evening. They were present at the table during the entire course of the evening, while the drinks were ordered, served, and consumed. Gillian Stewart's testimony was clear that she knew, at least in general terms, the amount that Stuart Pettie had to drink during the evening.

Stuart Pettie was drinking "double" rum and cokes throughout the evening. The trial judge found that he drank five to seven of these drinks, or 10 to 14 ounces of liquor. The trial judge also found that despite the amount that he had to drink, Stuart Pettie exhibited no signs of intoxica-

† [1995] 1 S.C.R. 131 at 135–38, 141–53.

tion. This appearance was deceiving, however, as he was intoxicated by the end of the evening.

The group left the dinner theatre around 11:00 p.m. Once out in the parking lot, they had a discussion amongst themselves about whether or not Stuart Pettie was fit to drive, given the fact that he had been drinking. Neither his wife, nor his sister (who acknowledged that she knew what her brother was like when he was drunk), had any concerns about letting Stuart Pettie drive. All four therefore got into the car and started home, with Stuart Pettie driving, Keith Stewart in the front passenger seat, and their spouses in the back seat.

That particular December night in Edmonton there was a frost which made the roads unusually slippery. The trial judge found that Pettie was driving slower than the speed limit (50 km/h in a 60 km/h zone), and also accepted the evidence of Gillian Stewart that he was driving properly, safely and cautiously in the circumstances. Despite his caution, Stuart Pettie suddenly lost momentary control of the vehicle. The car swerved to the right, hopped the curb, and struck a light pole and noise abatement wall which ran alongside the road. Three of the four persons in the vehicle suffered no serious injuries. Gillian Stewart, however, who was not wearing a seat belt, was thrown across the car, struck her head, and was rendered a quadriplegic.

The expert testimony at trial was that had she been wearing her seat belt (which was not required in Alberta in 1985) her injuries would have been prevented.

About an hour after the accident, Stuart Pettie registered blood alcohol readings of .190 and .200. The trial judge found that, while it is not clear what his blood alcohol reading would have been at the time of the accident, he was, without a doubt, intoxicated, and that his blood alcohol content would have been certainly over .1.

The Stewarts brought an action against Stuart Pettie, Mayfield, and the City of Edmonton. The action as against Stuart Pettie was settled, with Stuart Pettie admitting gross negligence (as was necessary under then-existing legislation covering gratuitous passengers). The action as against the City of Edmonton was settled prior to trial. The plaintiffs were unsuccessful at trial as against Mayfield Investments Ltd., but the trial judge awarded a provisional 10 percent against them in the event he was overturned on appeal. He also assessed 25 percent against Gillian Stewart for contributory negligence for failing to wear her seat belt. Finally, the trial judge found that Pettie's driving, while negligent, was not grossly negligent.

The Court of Appeal allowed the appeal and found that Mayfield was negligent. They did not, however, disturb the trial judge's apportionment, or his finding on the contributory negligence or gross negligence issues. Mayfield Investments Ltd. sought and was granted leave to appeal to this Court, and the Stewarts sought and were granted leave to cross-appeal the finding that Stuart Pettie was not grossly negligent in this driving.

. . . .

IV. ANALYSIS

1. Was Mayfield Investments Ltd. negligent in failing to take any steps to ensure that Stuart Pettie did not drive after leaving Stage West?

This Court has not previously considered a case involving the liability of a commercial host where the plaintiff was not the person who became inebriated in the defendant's establishment. In both *Jordan House Ltd. v. Menow, supra,* and *Crocker v. Sundance Northwest Resorts Ltd.,* it was the plaintiff who became drunk and as a consequence was unable to look after himself.

. . . .

The present appeal is one in which a third party is claiming against the commercial host. This raises the question of whether the establishment owed any duty of care to that third party. If a duty of care is found to exist, then it is necessary to consider what standard of care was necessary and whether that standard was met.

Another consideration is whether there was a causal connection between the defendant's allegedly negligent conduct and the damage suffered by the plaintiff.

A. Duty of Care

The "modern" approach to determining the existence of a duty of care is that established by the House of Lords in *Anns v. Merton London Borough Council,* and adopted by this Court in City of *Kamloops v. Nielsen.* This test, as established by Wilson J. in *Kamloops,* paraphrasing *Anns* is:

(1) is there a sufficiently close relationship between the parties ... so that, in the reasonable contemplation of the authority, carelessness on its part might cause damage to that person? If so,

(2) are there any considerations which ought to negative or limit (a) the scope of the duty and (b) the class of persons to whom it is owed or (c) the damages to which a breach of it may give rise?

This approach has been approved in *Just v. British Columbia*, and *Hall v. Hebert*. The basis of the test is the historic case of *Donoghue v. Stevenson*, which established the "neighbour principle": that actors owe a duty of care to those whom they ought reasonably [to] have in contemplation as being at risk when they act.

In *Jordan House Ltd. v. Menow, supra*, it was established that a duty of care exists between alcohol-serving establishments and their patrons who become intoxicated, with the result that they were unable to look after themselves. The plaintiff, who was a well-known patron of that bar, became intoxicated and began annoying customers. He was ejected from the bar, even though the waiters and employees of the bar knew that, in order to get home, he would have to walk along a busy highway. While doing so, he was struck by a car. Laskin J. (as he then was) said that the bar owed a duty of care to Menow not to place him in a situation where he was at risk of injury. He said (at pp. 247–48):

> If the hotel's only involvement was the supplying of the beer consumed by Menow, it would be difficult to support the imposition of common law liability upon it for injuries suffered by Menow after being shown the door of the hotel and after leaving the hotel.... The hotel, however, was not in the position of persons in general who see an intoxicated person who appears to be unable to control his steps. It was in an invitor-invitee relationship with Menow as one of its patrons, and it was aware, through its employees, of his intoxicated condition, a condition which, on the findings of the trial judge, it fed in violation of applicable liquor licence and liquor control legislation. There was a probable risk of personal injury to Menow if he was turned out of the hotel to proceed on foot on a much-travelled highway passing in front of the hotel.
>
> There is, in my opinion, nothing unreasonable in calling upon the hotel in such circumstances to take care to see that Menow is not exposed to injury because of his intoxication.

Laskin J. held that the hotel had breached the duty owed to Menow by turning him out of the hotel in circumstances in which they knew that he would have to walk along the highway. The risk to Menow that the hotel's actions created was foreseeable. The hotel was therefore found to be liable for one-third of Menow's injuries.

It is a logical step to move from finding that a duty of care is owed to patrons of the bar to finding that a duty is also owed to third parties who might reasonably be expected to come into contact with the patron, and to whom the patron may pose some risk. It is clear that a bar owes a duty of care to patrons, and as a result, may be required to prevent an intoxicated patron from driving where it is apparent that he intends to drive. Equally such a duty is owed, in that situation, to third parties who may be using the highways. In fact, it is the same problem which creates the risk to the third parties as creates the risk to the patron. If the patron drives while intoxicated and is involved in an accident, it is only chance which results in the patron being injured rather than a third party. The risk to third parties from the patron's intoxicated driving is real and foreseeable.

In this case, there was a sufficient degree of proximity between Mayfield Investments Ltd. and Gillian Stewart that a duty of care existed between them. The more difficult question is what was the standard of care and whether or not it was breached.

Before moving to the standard of care test, two points deserve comment. In so far as the existence of a duty of care is concerned it is irrelevant that Gillian Stewart was a passenger in the vehicle driven by the patron rather than the passenger or driver of another vehicle, other than for ancillary purposes such as contributory negligence. The duty of care arises because Gillian Stewart was a member of a class of persons who could be expected to be on the highway. It is this class of persons to whom the duty is owed.

On the second point, the respondents argue that Mayfield Investments Ltd. owed two duties of care to Gillian Stewart: first, not to serve Stuart Pettie past the point of intoxication, and second, having served him past the point of intoxication, to take positive steps to ensure that he did not drive a car. The respondents say that Mayfield breached both duties, and therefore should be liable to Gillian Stewart for her injuries.

I believe this argument confuses the existence of the duty of care with the standard of care required of Mayfield. The question of whether a duty of care exists is a question of the relationship between the parties, not a question of conduct. The question of what conduct is required to satisfy the duty is a question of the appropriate standard of care. The point is made by Fleming in his book *The Law of Torts* (8th ed. 1992), at pp. 105–6:

> The general standard of conduct required by law is a necessary complement of the legal concept of "duty". There is not only the question "Did the defendant owe a duty to be careful?" but also "What precisely was required of him to discharge it?" Indeed, it is not uncommon to encounter formulations of the standard of care in terms of "duty", as when it is asserted that a motorist is under a duty to keep a proper lookout or give a turn signal. But this method of expression is best avoided. In the first place, the duty issue is already sufficiently complex without fragmenting it further to cover an endless series of details of conduct. "Duty" is more appropriately reserved for the problem of whether the relation between the parties (like manufacturer and consumer or occupier and trespasser) warrants the imposition upon one of an obligation of care for the benefit of the other, and it is more convenient to deal with individual conduct in terms of the legal standard of what is required to meet that obligation. Secondly, it is apt to obscure the division of functions between judge and jury. It is for the court to determine the existence of a duty relationship and to lay down in general terms the standard of care by which to measure the defendant's conduct; it is for the jury to translate the general into a particular standard suitable for the case in hand and to decide whether that standard has been attained.

There is no question that commercial vendors of alcohol owe a general duty of care to persons who can be expected to use the highways. To paraphrase Wilson J. in *City of Kamloops v. Nielsen*, it clearly ought to be in the reasonable contemplation of such people that carelessness on their part might cause injury to such third parties. It remains to determine what standard of care is necessary to discharge the duty.

B. Standard of Care

Laskin J. said in *Jordan House Ltd. v. Menow*, *supra*, at p. 247, "The common law assesses liability for negligence on the basis of breach of a duty of care arising from a foreseeable and unreasonable risk of harm to one person created by the act or omission of another." The respondents argued, and the Court of Appeal agreed, that Mayfield was negligent because they (a) served Stuart Pettie past the point of intoxication, and (b) failed to take any steps to prevent harm from coming to himself or a third person once he was intoxicated.

I doubt that any liability can flow from the mere fact that Mayfield may have over-served Pettie. To hold that over-serving Pettie *per se* is negligent is to ignore the fact that injury to a class of persons must be foreseeable as a result of the impugned conduct. I fail to see how the mere fact that an individual is over-imbibing can lead, by itself, to <u>any</u> risk of harm to third parties. It is only if there is some foreseeable risk of harm to the patron or to a third party that Mayfield and others in their position will be required to take some action. This standard of care is the second "duty" identified by the respondents and the Court of Appeal.

It is true that applicable liquor control legislation in Alberta, and across the country, prohibits serving alcohol to persons who are apparently intoxicated. Counsel for the respondents pressed that point in argument. There are, however, two problems with this argument. The first is that it is not clear that there was any violation of liquor control legislation in this case, given the fact that Pettie was apparently not exhibiting any signs of intoxication. Moreover, even if it could be said that Mayfield was in violation of legislation, this fact alone does not ground liability: *The Queen in right of Canada v. Saskatchewan Wheat Pool*. Without a reasonably foreseeable risk of harm to him or a third party, the fact of over-serving Pettie is an innocuous act. Therefore, liability on the part of Mayfield, if it is to be found, must be in their failure to take any affirmative action to prevent the reasonably foreseeable risk to Gillian Stewart.

Historically, the courts have been reluctant to impose liability for a failure by an individual to take some positive action. This reluctance has been tempered in recent years where the relationship between the parties is such that the imposition of such an obligation has been warranted. In those cases, there has been some "special relationship" between the parties warranting the imposition of a positive duty. *Jordan House Ltd. v. Menow*, *supra*, was such a case.

A similar positive obligation was found to exist in *Crocker v. Sundance Northwest Resorts Ltd.*, *supra*. The plaintiff entered a "tubing" competition put on by the defendant ski-hill. Before the race, the plaintiff became drunk in the ski-hill's bar, and by the time he was to race, was visibly intoxicated. The organizers of the race suggested that he not compete, but permitted him to do so nevertheless. As a result, he was thrown from his tube, and rendered a quadriplegic.

In finding liability on the part of the owner Sundance, Wilson J. noted that courts have increasingly required a duty to act where there is a "special relationship" between the parties. Canadian courts have been willing to expand the kinds of relationships to which a positive duty to act attaches. Wilson J. reviewed cases where the courts will require a positive action on the part of the defendant, and said at p. 1197:

> The common thread running through these cases is that one is under a duty not to place another person in a position where it is foreseeable that the person could suffer injury.

Wilson J. said that, given the fact that the activity was under Sundance's full control and was promoted by it for commercial gain, Sundance was under a positive obligation as the promoter of a dangerous sport to take all reasonable steps to prevent a visibly incapacitated person from participating. She concluded that these precautions were not taken.

It is apparent from Wilson J.'s reasoning that there are two questions to be answered. The first is whether the defendant was required, in the circumstances, to take any positive steps at all. If this is answered in the affirmative, the next question is whether the steps taken by the defendants were sufficient to discharge the burden placed on them.

There is no dispute that neither the appellant nor anyone on its behalf took any steps to ensure that Stuart Pettie did not drive. Mayfield suggested that they remained "vigilant" and maintained "careful observation" of Stuart Pettie, and that this should be sufficient. However, remaining "vigilant" is not the same as taking positive steps, and it is common ground that none of Mayfield's employees made inquires about whether Stuart Pettie intended to drive or suggested any alternative. Therefore, if Mayfield is to avoid liability, it will have to be on the basis that, on the facts of this case, Mayfield had no obligation to take any positive steps to ensure that Stuart Pettie did not drive.

. . . .

There is little difficulty with the proposition, supported by the above cases, that the necessary "special relationship" exists between vendors of alcohol and the motoring public. This is no more than a restatement of the fact, already mentioned, that a general duty of care exists between establishments in Mayfield's position and persons using the highways.

I do, however, have difficulty accepting the proposition that the mere existence of this "special relationship", without more, permits the imposition of a positive obligation to act. Every person who enters a bar or restaurant is in an invitor-invitee relationship with the establishment, and is therefore in a "special relationship" with that establishment. However, it does not make sense to suggest that, simply as a result of this relationship, a commercial host cannot consider other relevant factors in determining whether in the circumstances positive steps are necessary.

The existence of this "special relationship" will frequently warrant the imposition of a positive obligation to act, but the sine qua non of tortious liability remains the foreseeability of the risk. Where no risk is foreseeable as a result of the circumstances, no action will be required, despite the existence of a special relationship. The respondents argue that Mayfield should have taken positive action, even though Mayfield knew that the driver was with three other people, two of whom were sober, and it was reasonable to infer from all of the circumstances that the group was travelling together.

One of the primary purposes of negligence law is to enforce reasonable standards of conduct so as to prevent the creation of reasonably foreseeable risks. In this way, tort law serves as a disincentive to risk-creating behaviour. To impose liability even where the risk which materialized was not reasonably foreseeable is to lay a portion of the loss at the feet of a party who has, in the circumstances, acted reasonably. Tort law does not require the wisdom of Solomon. All it requires is that people act reasonably in the circumstances. The "reasonable person" of negligence law was described by Laidlaw J.A. in this way in *Arland v. Taylor*:

> He is not an extraordinary or unusual creature; he is not superhuman; he is not required to display the highest skill of which anyone is capable; he is not a genius who can perform uncommon feats, nor is he possessed of unusual powers of foresight. He is a person of normal intelligence who makes prudence a guide to his conduct. He does nothing that a

prudent man would not do and does not omit to do anything a prudent man would do. He acts in accord with general and approved practice. His conduct is guided by considerations which ordinarily regulate the conduct of human affairs. His conduct is the standard "adopted in the community by persons of ordinary intelligence and prudence."

Obviously, the fact that tragedy has befallen Gillian Stewart cannot, in itself, lead to a finding of liability on the part of Mayfield. The question is whether, before 11:00 p.m. on December 8, 1985, the circumstances were such that a reasonably prudent establishment should have foreseen that Stuart Pettie would drive, and therefore should have taken steps to prevent this.

I agree with the Court of Appeal that Mayfield cannot escape liability simply because Stuart Pettie was apparently not exhibiting any visible signs of intoxication. The waitress kept a running tab, and knew that Pettie had consumed 10 to 14 ounces of alcohol over a five-hour period. On the basis of this knowledge alone, she either knew or should have known that Pettie was becoming intoxicated, and this is so whether or not he was exhibiting visible symptoms.

However, I disagree with the Court of Appeal that the presence of the two sober women at the table cannot act to relieve Mayfield of liability. Laskin J. in *Jordan House Ltd. v. Menow, supra*, made it clear that the hotel's duty to Menow in that case could have been discharged by making sure "that he got home safely by taking him under its charge or putting him under the charge of a responsible person ..." (p. 249, emphasis added). Had Pettie been alone and intoxicated, Mayfield could have discharged its duty as established in *Jordan House Ltd. v. Menow* by calling Pettie's wife or sister to take charge of him. How, then, can Mayfield be liable when Pettie was already in their charge, and they knew how much he had had to drink? While it is technically true that Stuart Pettie was not "put into" the care of his sober wife and sister, this is surely a matter of semantics. He was already in their care, and they knew how much he had to drink. It is not reasonable to suggest in these circumstances that Mayfield had to do more.

Mayfield would have known that the group arrived together, that they spent the evening together, and that they left together. In addition, they would have known that they were part of the Dispensaries Limited Company Christmas party, and that two sober adults were present at the table when the drinks were ordered and consumed. In the circumstances, it was reasonable for Mayfield to assume that the four people at the table were not travelling separately, and it was reasonable for Mayfield to assume that one of the two sober people who were at the table would either drive or find alternative transportation.

The trial judge was correct in concluding on these facts that it was not necessary for Mayfield to enquire who was driving or that it would have made any difference if they had. It was not reasonably foreseeable that Stuart Pettie would be driving when a sober wife and sister were present with full knowledge of the circumstances.

I agree that establishments which serve alcohol must either intervene in appropriate circumstances or risk liability, and that this liability cannot be avoided where the establishment has intentionally structured the environment in such a way as to make it impossible to know whether intervention is necessary. Such was the situation in *Canada Trust Co. v. Porter, supra*, where the alcohol was served from behind a bar and it was impossible for the establishment either to monitor the amount consumed or to determine whether intervention was necessary. A similar situation arose in *Gouge v. Three Top Investment Holdings Inc.*, where the plaintiff attended a company Christmas party which had a "cash bar", over-indulged, and then was involved in an accident. In such circumstances, it would not be open to the establishment to claim that they could not foresee the risk created when the inability to foresee the risk was the direct result of the way the serving environment was structured.

However that was not the situation here. Mayfield was aware of the circumstances in which Stuart Pettie was drinking. In the environment of the case at bar, it was not reasonable for them to intervene.

On the facts of this case I conclude that Mayfield Investments Ltd. did not breach the duty of care they owed to Gillian Stewart. On this basis I would allow the appeal.

(e) *Childs v. Desormeaux*†

[WEILER J.A.:]

In this appeal we are asked to decide whether homeowners owe a duty of care to a user of the road who is injured by the driving of an impaired guest after attending a Bring Your Own Booze party ("BYOB") at their home.

Over the past 30 years, the law respecting liability on commercial hosts for alcohol-related injuries has steadily evolved. The starting point was the decision of the Supreme Court of Canada in *Menow v. Jordan House Ltd.*, [1974] S.C.R. 239. The Supreme Court held that a hotel owed a duty of care to a visibly intoxicated patron whom it ejected, after serving him beer when he was visibly intoxicated in violation of applicable liquor licensing legislation, and in the knowledge that he would have to walk along a well-travelled highway at night in order to get home. More recently, in *Stewart v. Pettie*, [1995] 1 S.C.R. 131, the Supreme Court held that a commercial host also owes a duty of care to third parties who are users of the road to take reasonable steps to prevent a patron, whom the host should have known was intoxicated, from driving.

In this case, a user of the road, Zoë Childs, was seriously injured when the car in which she was riding was struck by another car driven by an impaired driver, Desmond Desormeaux. Prior to the collision, Desormeaux attended a BYOB party at the home of social hosts Julie Zimmerman and Dwight Courrier and became impaired. Childs sued Desormeaux, as well as Zimmerman and Courrier, alleging that their negligence contributed to her injuries. The trial judge held Desormeaux liable for the injuries caused to Childs. No appeal is taken from that decision.

In relation to Zimmerman and Courrier, the trial judge held that Childs was asking the court to impose liability for a new duty of care, rather than one falling within one of the recognized categories of duties in tort law. Before imposing liability for a new duty of care, the court must be satisfied: (1) that the relationship of the parties is suffi-

ciently close to give rise to a duty of care and (2) that there are no policy considerations that negative or limit the scope of the duty.

The trial judge held that the first requirement was satisfied. He held that the social hosts had a duty to monitor Desormeaux's drinking while at the party because he had a history of being a heavy drinker and had arrived at the party with two passengers who were intoxicated. The trial judge declined, however, to impose a duty of care on Zimmerman and Courrier for policy reasons. Accordingly, he dismissed the action. ...

I agree with the trial judge that the action should be dismissed but not for the reason that he gave. Unlike the trial judge, on the specific facts of this case, I would not hold that the social hosts owed a duty of care to users of the road. There are a number of factors that lead me to this conclusion.

First, the party hosted by the defendants, Courrier and Zimmerman, was a BYOB party. Thus, the social hosts did not provide, nor did they serve, the alcohol consumed by Desormeaux. Second, there was no evidence to suggest that the social hosts knew how much alcohol Desormeaux drank while at the party. Third, and most importantly, the trial judge did not find that the social hosts knew that Desormeaux was impaired when he drove away from the party.

To the extent the trial judge's reasons may be read as implicitly holding that Courrier and Zimmerman should have known that Desormeaux was intoxicated because, despite knowing Desormeaux's history as a heavy drinker, they did not monitor his drinking, the trial judge erred. A person's history of drinking is not the basis of a commercial host's duty to monitor a patron's drinking; still less should it form the basis for imposing any duty on a social host to monitor a guest's drinking at a BYOB party where alcohol is neither provided nor served by the social hosts. The trial judge's errors also undermined his finding that the social hosts were negligent because they did not stop Desormeaux from driving his car.

† 71 O.R. (3d) 195. © Law Society of Upper Canada. Reproduced with permission.

Because it is unnecessary for me to do so, I do not decide whether liability should be negated for policy reasons. Such a conclusion should not be reached in a vacuum, but in the context of an overall weighing of whether it is just and fair to impose liability. In order to determine whether the potential benefits of imposing a duty of care on social hosts towards users of the road outweigh the burden placed on social hosts in their interaction with their guests, the extent of the burden must first be determined. That determination is left for another day.

My conclusion that this appeal should be dismissed should not be interpreted to mean that social hosts are immune from liability to innocent third party users of the road for damages caused by impaired guests who drive a car. On the contrary, I do not foreclose social host liability, particularly when it is shown that a social host knew that an intoxicated guest was going to drive a car and did nothing to protect innocent third parties.

. . . .

Social host liability is not simply an extension of commercial host liability. In the following portions of this judgment, I point out that there are significant differences between the relationship of a commercial host and a social host. Commercial hosts serve alcohol for profit and, as a result, the relationship between the commercial host and the drinker is a contractual one giving each party certain legitimate expectations. The relationship between a social host and a guest, who is often a family member or a friend, is an informal one, and, as a result, the expectations they have of one another differ widely. Commercial hosts are closely regulated by statute and have a statutory duty not to serve alcohol to a visibly intoxicated person. To comply with their statutory duty, commercial hosts must monitor the alcohol consumption of their patrons and control the structure of the environment in which alcohol is served. Alcohol consumption is a prevalent feature in the ordinary, day-to-day social interaction between social hosts and their guests, but there are no statutory standards against which to judge the imposition of a duty at common law on social hosts. The supply and service of alcohol is unregulated and the environment in which it is served varies widely. At a **BYOB** party, social hosts do not assume control over the supply and service of alcohol; they merely provide the venue for the consumption of alcohol. Com-

mercial hosts carry liability insurance as part of the cost of doing business and can spread the cost of their premiums among their patrons. Social hosts often do not have insurance, or have limited insurance for this type of risk and have no means of passing on the costs of insurance premiums to others. Thus, social hosts do not fall neatly into the same category as commercial hosts. Rather, the differences between the situation of a commercial host and a social host require us to consider whether to impose a duty of care to this new category. I would therefore conclude that the trial judge did not err in holding that imposing liability on the social hosts to users of the road in the circumstances of this case involved the recognition of a new duty of care. ...

. . . .

If a person's history of drinking is not the basis of a commercial host's duty to monitor a patron's drinking; still less should it form the basis for imposing any duty on a social host to monitor a guest's drinking at a party where alcohol is neither provided nor served by the social hosts.

I would hold that the trial judge erred in imposing an obligation on the social hosts to users of the road based on the social hosts' knowledge of Desormeaux's drinking habits and dated convictions for impaired driving. Rather, the social hosts' knowledge of Desormeaux's propensity to drink is but one factor to consider in determining whether the social hosts knew that Desormeaux was intoxicated when he left the party and [was] about to drive.

. . . .

The atmosphere in which alcohol is consumed in commercial establishments is uniform because of the conformity imposed by statutory requirements. The consumption of alcohol in a social setting, on the other hand, has many variations and the same sweeping analysis cannot be made. It is therefore necessary to engage in an analysis of the specific features of this case as compared to the commercial host situation before dealing with broader policy considerations.

The relationship between a commercial host and a patron is a contractual one. One of the expectations implicit in that relationship is the expectation on the part of the patron that his or her safety will not be jeopardized as a result of the act of the commercial host in serving him or her alcohol or, having done so, in permitting him to engage in a dangerous activity. ...

Here, there was no contractual relationship between the social hosts and their guests, nor were the social hosts serving alcohol to Desormeaux thereby jeopardizing his safety and that of users of the road. Julie Zimmerman testified that only three-quarters of a bottle of champagne was poured out at midnight for all the guests in one and one-half ounce glasses. There appears to be no evidence as to whether Desormeaux had any. As it was the guests who brought their own alcohol and who decided how much to serve themselves, there was no reason for the social hosts to think that their guests were relying on them to control their alcohol consumption.

The statutory obligations on a commercial host require the commercial host to monitor the patron's consumption of alcohol thereby controlling the conduct of that person. If a party has the right to control the conduct of a person, a failure to exercise that control reasonably resulting in the very kind of damage likely to result from such failure may be actionable by the injured plaintiff....

. . . .

The commercial host's statutory obligation to monitor alcohol consumption is therefore a consideration that bears on the court's determination as to whether it is just and fair to impose liability on the host.

In order to be in a position to monitor consumption as required by statute, the commercial host must control the structure of the environment in which alcohol is served. While breach of a statutory obligation alone is not sufficient to ground liability at common law, the court may have regard to statutory standards as useful evidence of the standard required of the parties at common law....

. . . .

In the present case, the social hosts had no similar statutory duty requiring them to monitor the drinking conduct of their guests or to control the structure of the environment in which alcohol was served. In deciding that the social hosts owed Desormeaux a duty of care, the trial judge did not discuss the fact this was a BYOB party and that the expectations of the guests would have been different from those of a patron in a commercial establishment. Instead, he held the social hosts to the same duty of care as a commercial establishment and indeed held that the fact this was a BYOB party required a higher duty of care.

Nor was there any de facto assumption of control on the part of Courrier and Zimmerman over their guests' drinking. A distinguishing feature of this case is that Courrier and Zimmerman did not supply or serve alcohol to their guests. In serving a person alcohol to the point of intoxication while knowing that the person is likely to drive afterwards, the host contributes to the risk of the guest committing a tort against the plaintiff. The host places the guest and users of the highway in a potentially hazardous position and is an active participant in creating the danger of an accident due to intoxication.... A person who undertakes to do an act has an obligation not to act carelessly.... Here, the social hosts were not in this sense active participants in creating the danger to users of the highway.

To summarize, in the absence of some assumption of control by a person or justified reliance on that person by another, arising out of the circumstances or as a result of the imposition of a statutory duty, the common law does not make one person liable for the conduct of a second person simply because the second person occasions damage to a third party that is reasonably foreseeable. The person sought to be held liable must be implicated in the creation of the risk. In this case, the social hosts did not assume control over the supply or service of alcohol, nor did they serve alcohol to Desormeaux when he was visibly impaired. The social hosts had no statutory duty to monitor the consumption of alcohol or to control the structure of the atmosphere in which alcohol was served. There is no evidence that anyone relied on them to do so. The social hosts had no reason to monitor Desormeaux's consumption of alcohol because he could have stayed over if he wished to do so. I cannot accept the proposition that by merely supplying the venue of a BYOB party, a host assumes legal responsibility to third party users of the road for monitoring the alcohol consumed by guests, even when the guest includes a known drinker. As I have indicated, the hosts' knowledge of Desormeaux's drinking history is a factor in determining the social hosts' knowledge of his intoxication. The trial judge did not find that the social hosts knew Desormeaux was intoxicated at the time he left the party. A person's drinking history is not, of itself, a sufficient basis on which to hold that a social host should know a person is intoxicated. To the extent the trial judge implicitly concluded that the social hosts should have known Desormeaux was impaired because of his drinking history and because they did not monitor his drinking, he erred. The trial judge's errors taint his holding that the social hosts were also negligent because they did not stop Desormeaux from driving. Counsel for the appellant did not point to other evidence to support that finding. It would not be just and fair in the circumstances to impose a duty of care.

(f)   *Dobson (Litigation Guardian of) v. Dobson*†

[CORY J.:]

. . . .

II.   FACTS

On March 14, 1993, the appellant was in the 27th week of her pregnancy. On that day, she was driving towards Moncton in a snowstorm. She lost control of her vehicle on a patch of slush and struck an oncoming vehicle. It is alleged that the accident was caused by her negligent driving. The infant respondent, Ryan Dobson, was allegedly injured while *in utero*, and was delivered prematurely by Caesarean section later that same day. He suffers from permanent mental and physical impairment, including cerebral palsy.

The infant respondent, by his grandfather and litigation guardian, launched a tort claim against, *inter alia*, the appellant for the damages he sustained. The respondent's father was the owner of the vehicle driven by the appellant. As required by provincial law, he was insured against damages caused by the negligence of drivers of his motor vehicle.

The issues of liability and quantum of damages were severed by a consent order dated June 25, 1996. Thus, the only question to be determined is whether Ryan Dobson has the legal capacity to bring a tort action against his mother for her allegedly negligent act which occurred while he was in utero. Miller J., on an application for determination of this question of law, found that the infant respondent had the legal capacity to sue for injuries caused by the appellant's prenatal negligence. The Court of Appeal dismissed the appeal from that decision.

. . . .

V.   ANALYSIS

. . . .

B.   Imposing a Duty of Care in This Situation

The test set out in *Kamloops*, *supra*, must be considered and applied in determining whether the appellant mother should be held liable to her child in the present case. This analysis is particularly important in light of the significant policy consequences raised by this appeal. In *Kamloops*, it was held that before imposing a duty of care, the court must be satisfied: (1) that there is a sufficiently close relationship between the parties to give rise to the duty of care; and (2) that there are no public policy considerations which ought to negative or limit the scope of the duty, the class of persons to whom it is owed, or the damages to which a breach of it may give rise.

The first criterion may be satisfied if it is assumed that a pregnant woman and her foetus can be treated as distinct legal entities. It should be noted that this assumption might be seen as

---

† [1999] 2 S.C.R. 753.

being contrary to the holding of McLachlin J. in *Winnipeg, supra,* at p. 945 that "the law has always treated the mother and unborn child as one". Nonetheless, it is appropriate in the present case to assume, without deciding, that a pregnant woman and her foetus can be treated as separate legal entities. Based on this assumption, a pregnant woman and her foetus are within the closest possible physical proximity that two "legal persons" could be. With regard to foreseeability, it is clear that almost any careless act or omission by a pregnant woman could be expected to have a detrimental impact on foetal development. Indeed, the very existence of the foetus depends upon the pregnant woman. Thus, on the basis of the assumption of separate legal identities, it is possible to proceed to the more relevant analysis for the purposes of the present appeal, the second stage of the *Kamloops* test.

However, even if it is assumed that the first stage of the *Kamloops* test is satisfied, the public policy considerations in this case clearly indicate that a legal duty of care should not be imposed upon a pregnant woman towards her foetus or subsequently born child. The second branch of the *Kamloops* test requires a consideration of those public policy consequences which may negate or limit the imposition of such a duty of care upon mothers-to-be. Although increased medical knowledge makes the consequences of certain behaviour more foreseeable, and facilitates the establishment of a causative link in negligence suits, public policy must also be considered. Significant policy concerns militate against the imposition of maternal tort liability for prenatal negligence. These relate primarily to (1) the privacy and autonomy rights of women and (2) the difficulties inherent in articulating a judicial standard of conduct for pregnant women.

. . . .

1. Privacy and Autonomy Rights of Women

First and foremost, for reasons of public policy, the Court should not impose a duty of care upon a pregnant woman towards her foetus or subsequently born child. To do so would result in very extensive and unacceptable intrusions into the bodily integrity, privacy and autonomy rights of women. It is true that Canadian tort law presently allows a child born alive and viable to sue a third-party for injuries which were negligently inflicted while *in utero*: *Montreal Tramways, supra*. However,

of fundamental importance to the public policy analysis is the particularly unique relationship that exists between a pregnant woman and the foetus she carries.

(A) OVERVIEW

Pregnancy represents not only the hope of future generations but also the continuation of the species. It is difficult to imagine a human condition that is more important to society. From the dawn of history, the pregnant woman has represented fertility and hope. Biology decrees that it is only women who can bear children. Usually, a pregnant woman does all that is possible to protect the health and well-being of her foetus. On occasion, she may sacrifice her own health and well-being for the benefit of the foetus she carries. Yet it should not be forgotten that the pregnant woman — in addition to being the carrier of the foetus within her — is also an individual whose bodily integrity, privacy and autonomy rights must be protected.

The unique and special relationship between a mother-to-be and her foetus determines the outcome of this appeal. There is no other relationship in the realm of human existence which can serve as a basis for comparison. It is for this reason that there can be no analogy between a child's action for prenatal negligence brought against some third-party tortfeasor, on the one hand, and against his or her mother, on the other. The inseparable unity between an expectant woman and her foetus distinguishes the situation of the mother-to-be from that of a negligent third-party. The biological reality is that a pregnant woman and her foetus are bonded in a union. This was recognized in the majority reasons of McLachlin J. in *Winnipeg, supra*, at pp. 944–45:

> Before birth the mother and unborn child are one in the sense that "[t]he 'life' of the foetus is intimately connected with, and cannot be regarded in isolation from, the life of the pregnant woman": *Paton v. United Kingdom* ..., applied in *Re F (in utero)*.... It is only after birth that the fetus assumes a separate personality. Accordingly, the law has always treated the mother and unborn child as one. To sue a pregnant woman on behalf of her unborn fetus therefore posits the anomaly of one part of a legal and physical entity suing itself.

It was recognized in both *Montreal Tramways, supra*, and *Duval, supra*, that the strongest argument for imposing a duty of care upon third parties towards unborn children is that tort law is designed to provide compensation for harm caused by negligence and, to a lesser extent, to deter tort-feasors. It was submitted that to deny recognition to the type of action at issue in this appeal could leave an infant plaintiff without the protection and compensation provided by tort law, solely because the defendant is his or her mother. Accordingly, it was argued that the compensatory principle should be the basis for the imposition of a similar duty of care upon expectant women.

Yet, this argument fails to take into account the fundamental difference between a mother-to-be and a third-party defendant. The unique relationship between a pregnant woman and her foetus is so very different from the relationship with third parties. Everything the pregnant woman does or fails to do may have a potentially detrimental impact on her foetus. Everything the pregnant woman eats or drinks, and every physical action she takes, may affect the foetus. Indeed, the foetus is entirely dependent upon its mother-to-be. Although the imposition of tort liability on a third party for prenatal negligence advances the interests of both mother and child, it does not significantly impair the right of third parties to control their own lives. In contrast to the third-party defendant, a pregnant woman's every waking and sleeping moment, in essence, her entire existence, is connected to the foetus she may potentially harm. If a mother were to be held liable for prenatal negligence, this could render the most mundane decision taken in the course of her daily life as a pregnant woman subject to the scrutiny of the courts.

Is she to be liable in tort for failing to regulate her diet to provide the best nutrients for the foetus? Is she to be required to abstain from smoking and all alcoholic beverages? Should she be found liable for failing to abstain from strenuous exercise or unprotected sexual activity to protect her foetus? Must she undertake frequent safety checks of her premises in order to avoid falling and causing injury to the foetus? There is no rational and principled limit to the types of claims which may be brought if such a tortious duty of care were imposed upon pregnant women.

Whether it be considered a life-giving miracle or a matter of harsh reality, it is the biology of the human race which decrees that a pregnant woman must stand in a uniquely different situation to her foetus than any third-party. The relationship between a pregnant woman and her foetus is of fundamental importance to the future mother and her born alive child, to their immediate family and

to our society. So far as the foetus is concerned, this relationship is one of complete dependence. As to the pregnant woman, in most circumstances, the relationship is marked by her complete dedication to the well-being of her foetus. This dedication is profound and deep. It affects a pregnant woman physically, psychologically and emotionally. It is a very significant factor in this uniquely important relationship. The consequences of imposing tort liability on mothers for prenatal negligence raise vastly different considerations, and will have fundamentally different results, from the imposition of such liability on third parties.

In *Winnipeg, supra*, the majority rejected an argument which sought to extend tort principles in order to justify the forced confinement and treatment of a pregnant woman with a glue-sniffing addiction, as a means of protecting her foetus. McLachlin J. observed that difficult legal and social issues arise in examining the policy considerations under the second branch of the *Kamloops* test. First, the recognition of a duty of care owed by a pregnant woman to her foetus has a very real potential to intrude upon that woman's fundamental rights. Any intervention may create a conflict between a pregnant woman as an autonomous decision-maker and the foetus she carries. Second, the judicial definition of an appropriate standard of care is fraught with insoluble problems due to the difficulty of distinguishing tortious and non-tortious behaviour in the daily life of an expectant woman. Third, certain so-called lifestyle "choices" such as alcoholism and drug addiction may be beyond the control of the pregnant woman, and hence the deterrent value of the imposition of a duty of care may be non-existent. Lastly, the imposition of a duty of care upon a pregnant woman towards her foetus could increase, to an unwarranted degree, the level of external scrutiny focussed upon her. In *Winnipeg, supra*, it was held that the lifestyle choices of a pregnant woman should not be regulated because to do so would result in an unacceptably high degree of intrusion into her privacy and autonomy rights. If that is so, then it follows that negligent acts resulting from unreasonable lapses of attention, which may so often occur in the course of a pregnant woman's daily life, should not form the basis for the imposition of tort liability on mothers.

On behalf of the infant respondent, it was argued that the reasoning in *Winnipeg* is not determinative because it dealt with the standing of the foetus to sue while still *in utero*. In *Winnipeg*, the foetus which sought the detention of its mother-to-be was not a legal person and possessed no legal rights. By contrast, the present action is brought on behalf of an infant born alive whose legal rights and interests vested at the moment of birth. In other words, the sole issue in this appeal is whether a child born alive — as opposed to a foetus — should be able to recover damages for prenatal negligence from every person except his or her mother. Despite the important legal distinction between a foetus and a child born alive, as a matter of social policy and pragmatic reality, both situations involve the imposition of a duty of care upon a pregnant woman towards either her foetus or her subsequently born child. To impose either duty of care would require judicial scrutiny into every aspect of that woman's behaviour during pregnancy. Irrespective of whether the duty of care is imposed upon a pregnant woman towards her foetus or her subsequently born child, both would involve severe intrusions into the bodily integrity, privacy and autonomous decision-making of that woman. Accordingly, the policy concerns raised by McLachlin J. in *Winnipeg* are equally pertinent to this appeal.

. . . .

At trial, Miller J. observed that the existing jurisprudence permits recovery from third parties, and permits a child to sue his or her parents for postnatal negligence. He held that to permit an action by a child against his mother for prenatal negligence is a "reasonable progression" in tort jurisprudence. With respect, I believe that the imposition of a duty of care upon pregnant women in these circumstances cannot be characterized as a reasonable progression. Rather, in my view, it constitutes a severe intrusion into the lives of pregnant women, with attendant and potentially damaging effects on the family unit. This case raises social policy concerns of a very real significance. Indeed, they are of such magnitude that they are more properly the subject of study, debate and action by the legislature.

. . . .

(C) AMERICAN CASE LAW

. . . .

The willingness of the trial judge and the New Brunswick Court of Appeal to impose tort liability on mothers for prenatal negligence appears to be based in large part on principles of tort law which, to date, have been applied solely to negligent third parties. The infant respondent argues that these general principles, which may result in third-party liability, may equally result in maternal prenatal liability. Yet, I agree with the position put forward by the dissent in *Bonte*, which was expressed as follows: "[W]hether to subject the day-to-day decisions and acts of a woman concerning her pregnancy to judicial scrutiny is not properly a question to be decided by a mechanical application of logic" (p. 467).

Rather, it is the policy concerns, so central to this issue, which should determine whether tort liability should be imposed on mothers for prenatal negligence. With the greatest respect, I am of the view that the judgments below failed to appreciate fully the extensive intrusion into the privacy and autonomy rights of women that would be required by the imposition of tort liability on mothers for prenatal negligence. Such a rule of law would have profound implications and consequences for all Canadian women who are or may become pregnant.

. . . .

(D) CONSEQUENCES OF RECOGNIZING THIS CAUSE OF ACTION

. . . .

The primary purposes of tort law are to provide compensation to the injured and deterrence to the tortfeasor. In the ordinary course of events, the imposition of tort liability on a mother for prenatal negligence would provide neither compensation nor deterrence. The pressing societal issue at the heart of this appeal is the lack of financial support currently available for the care of children with special needs. The imposition of a legal duty of care on a pregnant woman towards her foetus or subsequently born child will not solve this problem. If anything, attempting to address this social problem in a litigious setting would merely exacerbate the pain and trauma of a tragic situation. It may well be that carefully considered legislation could create a fund to compensate children with prenatally inflicted injuries. Alternatively, amendments to the motor vehicle insurance laws could achieve the same result in a more limited context. If, as a society, Canadians believe that children who sustain damages as a result of maternal prenatal negligence should be financially compensated, then the solution should be formulated, after careful study and debate, by the legislature.

2. *Difficulties of Articulating a Judicial Standard of Conduct for Pregnant Women*

The infant respondent and certain interveners argued that a legal duty of care should be imposed upon a pregnant woman towards her foetus or born alive child. If such a duty of care is imposed upon pregnant women, then a judicially defined standard of conduct would have to be met. One intervener argued that tort liability should be imposed where a woman's conduct fails to conform to a "reasonable pregnant woman" standard, which would apply to all aspects of her behaviour while pregnant. By contrast, the infant respondent argued in favour of the test put forward by the Court of Appeal in this case. This test draws a distinction between those situations in which a pregnant woman owes a "general duty of care" and those which relate to "lifestyle choices peculiar to parenthood". In the latter cases, a mother would be immune from tort liability for prenatal negligence. Another strand in the respondent's argument is that, at the very least, a mother should be held liable for all damages suffered by her born alive child as a result of prenatal injuries caused by her allegedly negligent driving. It was argued that the existence of a mandatory insurance regime for motor vehicle negligence entitles the born alive child to compensation in such cases.

I believe that the courts cannot, and should not, articulate a standard of conduct for pregnant women. To do so raises all of the troubling questions posed by Cunningham J. in *Stallman, supra* (at p. 360):

> It must be asked. By what judicially defined standard would a mother have her every act or omission while pregnant subjected to State scrutiny? By what objective standard could a jury be guided in determining whether a pregnant woman did all that was necessary in order not to breach a legal duty to not interfere with her fetus' separate and independent right to be born whole? In what way would prejudicial and stereotypical beliefs about the reproductive abilities of women be kept from interfering with a jury's determination of whether a particular woman was negligent at any point during her pregnancy?

For the reasons set out later, I am of the view that the various approaches advocated by the infant respondent and the interveners fail to avoid the pitfalls of a judicially defined standard of care for pregnant women. To adopt the "reasonable pregnant woman" standard involves far-reaching implications and extensive intrusions into the rights of bodily integrity, privacy and autonomy of pregnant women. The test articulated by the Court of Appeal is, I believe, inconsistent with general principles of tort law and unworkable in practice. Finally, if the existence of motor vehicle insurance is to be relied upon as the basis for imposing a legal duty of care upon pregnant women, then this solution should be enacted by the legislature. A specific and insurance-dependent rule of tort liability cannot, and should not, be created by the courts.

(A) REASONABLE PREGNANT WOMAN STANDARD

Linked to the unpredictable impact on the privacy and autonomy rights of women[] lies the difficult, perhaps impossible, task of judicially defining a standard of conduct for pregnant women. An intervener argued that a mother-to-be should be held liable for all negligent behaviour causing damages to her foetus, which would be determined in accordance with a "reasonable pregnant woman" standard. An intervener submitted that, once aware of the pregnancy, a woman should be required to conform to the standard of behaviour of a "reasonably prudent expectant mother conducting herself under similar circumstances": D. Santello, "Maternal Tort Liability for Prenatal Injuries" (1988), 22 *Suffolk U. L. Rev.* 747, at p. 775. This would involve an analysis of the risks associated with a given activity, the gravity of the possible injury, and the likelihood of that injury occurring. The standard of care would be reasonable rather than absolute, and thus a pregnant woman would not be expected to act as the insurer for the health of her subsequently born child.

In my view, this standard is inappropriate. It raises the spectre of judicial scrutiny and potential liability imposed for "lifestyle choices". Thus, it brings into play all of the policy concerns articulated in *Winnipeg, supra*. For instance, it would be open to the trier of fact to determine that a "reasonable pregnant woman", who knows or has reason to know of her condition, should not smoke cigarettes or drink alcohol. Decisions involving the standard of care in tort law focus upon generally accepted norms, rather than on the individual woman. This objective standard would permit triers of fact to dictate, according to their own notions of

141

proper conduct, the manner in which an expectant woman should behave throughout her pregnancy. Accordingly, a pregnant woman whose lifestyle conduct was under judicial scrutiny would not benefit from a truly individual standard, which takes into account her personal situation and acknowledges her autonomy.

The importance of an individual standard of assessment is emphasized by the great disparities which exist in the financial situations, education, access to health services and ethnic backgrounds of pregnant women. These disparities would inevitably lead to an unfair application of a uniform legal standard concerned with the reasonable pregnant woman. In this regard, Cunningham J. noted in *Stallman, supra*, at p. 360:

> Pregnancy does not come only to those women who have within their means all that is necessary to effectuate the best possible prenatal environment: any female of child-bearing age may become pregnant. Within this pool of potential defendants are representatives of all socio-economic backgrounds: the well-educated and the ignorant; the rich and the poor; those women who have access to good health care and good prenatal care and those who, for an infinite number of reasons, have not had access to any health care services.

Tort law is concerned with the application of objective standards of reasonable behaviour to impugned conduct. It cannot adequately address the profound public policy implications raised by this appeal. Brock C.J. and Batchelder J., in dissent, expressed serious doubts as to whether it is "possible to subject a woman's judgment, action, and behavior as they relate to the well-being of her fetus to a judicial determination of reasonableness in a manner that is consistent and free from arbitrary results": *Bonte, supra*, at p. 468. I share those reservations.

(B) LIFESTYLE CHOICES PECULIAR TO PARENTHOOD

. . . .

The Court of Appeal also referred to a "general duty of care" in articulating its test for maternal tort liability. With respect, there can be no such duty owed to the public at large. As a matter of tort law, a duty of care must always be owed by one person to another. Negligence cannot exist in the abstract. There must be a specific duty owed to a foreseeable plaintiff, which is breached, in order

for negligence to arise. A "general duty of care" does not exist. Accordingly, it cannot be used as a legal test for the imposition of tort liability in cases of prenatal negligence. Even if it were possible to identify readily those activities in which a woman owes a "general duty of care", this would not limit the extent of external scrutiny and control over a pregnant woman's daily life. To rely on the "general duty of care" distinction, in order to hold that this appeal does not raise important issues of social policy, is bound to introduce a significant element of uncertainty into tort law.

Moreover, it is clear that the duty of care imposed by the Court of Appeal is by no means narrow. It would impose tort liability on mothers for prenatal negligence in all situations in which a "general duty of care" is owed to third parties. The distinction between lifestyle choices and a so-called "general duty of care" involves a standard which can be readily applied to many areas of a pregnant woman's behaviour, most of which are not protected by insurance. The potential breadth of maternal tort liability under this test was recognized by Professor Ian R. Kerr in "Pre-Natal Fictions and Post-Partum Actions" (1998):

> [E]mploying the distinction between duties owed to the general public and those peculiar to parenthood does not assist the Court in narrowing the issue in *Dobson*. In fact, it has the very opposite effect. The rule that the Court of Appeal has derived from Fleming's distinction is that *duties owed by a pregnant woman to the general public are owed to her unborn child as well*. The consequence of this rule, which seems to have gone completely unnoticed by the Court, is that it will allow a child's litigation guardian to commence actions for prenatal injuries resulting from innumerable sorts of lifestyle choices that a pregnant woman might embrace. These would include activities such as rollerblading, shopping in a crowded mall, spraying weedkiller on her crops, sailing, lighting fireworks for her children on Canada day, or any other activity where there is risk of harm to the general public. There is nothing unique or narrow about the act of driving a car. It is just as much a lifestyle choice as any of the other activities just mentioned....
>
> Ironically, in its attempt to shield women from inquisitions into alleged parental indiscretions such as smoking and drinking, the Court of Appeal has expanded the liability of pregnant women. [Emphasis in original.]

In essence, a rule of tort law attempting to distinguish between acts of a mother-to-be involving privacy interests and those constituting common torts would of necessity result in arbitrary line-drawing and inconsistent verdicts. Simply to state that a "general duty of care" will not apply to "lifestyle choices" is to leave open the possibility that many actions taken by pregnant women will not be considered lifestyle choices for the purposes of litigation. Is drug use, if prescribed by a physician, a lifestyle choice? Is a hazardous work environment a lifestyle choice? Indeed, is it not arguable that driving while pregnant, for the benefit and welfare of the family, constitutes a lifestyle choice?

In *Winnipeg, supra*, it was argued that the potential state intrusions on behalf of the foetus would be minimal because the duty of care could be defined narrowly. It was submitted that the standard should be "to refrain from activities that have no substantial value to a pregnant woman's well-being or right of self-determination". In rejecting this test as too vague and broad, McLachlin J. observed that the proposed standard raised the following intractable questions:

> What does substantial value to a woman's well-being mean? What does a woman's well-being include? What is involved in a woman's right of self-determination — all her choices, or merely some of them? And if some only, what is the criterion of distinction? Although it may be easy to determine that abusing solvents does not add substantial value to a pregnant woman's well-being and may not be the type of self-determination that deserves protection, other behaviours are not as easily classified.

Similarly the test proposed by the Court of Appeal fails to articulate a workable judicial standard for distinguishing between tortious and non-tortious conduct. Just as McLachlin J. could not identify a bright line to ground liability on the basis of conduct which fails to add "substantial value to a pregnant woman's well-being", a similar difficulty is presented by a liability rule defined by behaviour involving "lifestyle choices" or conduct "peculiar to parenthood". The determination of whether a duty of care should be imposed must be made by considering the effects of tort liability on the privacy and autonomy interests of women, and upon their families, rather than by reference to a formalistic characterisation of the conduct in question.

. . . .

VI. SUMMARY

Perhaps a very brief summary of some of the more significant conclusions reached in these reasons may be of assistance. This is the first case in which Canadian courts have had to examine the theory of maternal tort liability for prenatal negligence. The judicial recognition of a legal duty of care owed by a pregnant woman towards her foetus or subsequently born child requires that the two-step test articulated in *Kamloops, supra*, be satisfied. The conclusion reached with respect to the second branch of that test determines the outcome of this appeal. The public policy concerns raised in this case are of such a nature and magnitude that they clearly indicate that a legal duty of care cannot, and should not, be imposed by the courts upon a pregnant woman towards her foetus or subsequently born child. However, unlike the courts, the legislature may, as did the Parliament of the United Kingdom, enact legislation in this field, subject to the limits imposed by the *Canadian Charter of Rights and Freedoms*.

Biology dictates that only women can become pregnant and bear children. In light of this very demanding biological reality, the courts should be hesitant to impose additional burdens upon pregnant women. In addition, the relationship between an expectant woman and her foetus is truly unique. Accordingly, there can be no meaningful analogy between a child's action for prenatal negligence against a third-party tortfeasor, on the one hand, and against his or her mother, on the other.

The actions of a pregnant woman, including driving, are inextricably linked to her familial role, her working life, and her rights of privacy, bodily integrity and autonomous decision-making. Moreover, the judicial recognition of this cause of action would involve severe psychological consequences for the relationship between mother and child, as well as the family unit as a whole. It is apparent that the imposition of tort liability in this context would have profound effects upon every pregnant woman and upon Canadian society in general. Therefore, I must agree with the conclusion reached by Brock C.J. and Batchelder J., dissenting in *Bonte, supra* (at p. 468):

> Such after-the-fact judicial scrutiny of the subtle and complicated factors affecting a woman's pregnancy may make life for women who are pregnant or who are merely contemplating pregnancy intolerable. For these reasons, we are convinced that the best course is to allow

the duty of a mother to her fetus to remain a moral obligation which, for the vast majority of women, is already freely recognized and respected without compulsion by law.

There is as well a need for judicial restraint in the development of tort law as it pertains to sensitive and far-reaching issues of public policy. The imposition of a legal duty of care upon a pregnant woman towards her foetus or subsequently born child cannot be characterized as the simple application of existing tort rules to meet the requirements of a specific case. Rather, it constitutes a severe intrusion into the lives of pregnant women, with potentially damaging effects on the family unit.

Moreover, there can be no satisfactory judicial articulation of a standard of conduct for pregnant women. A rule based on a "reasonable pregnant woman" standard raises the spectre of tort liability for lifestyle choices, and undermines the privacy and autonomy rights of women. A compromise judicial solution, based on the murky distinction between "lifestyle choices peculiar to parenthood" and a "general duty of care" owed to third parties, is simply too vague to be manageable, and will inevitably lead to inequitable and uncertain results.

Finally, a rule based on a strictly defined motor vehicle exception to delineate the scope of maternal tort liability should not be created by the judiciary. To do so would be to sanction a legal solution based solely on access to insurance. If this approach were to be adopted, the provincial legislatures would be required to amend their legislative compensation regimes for motor vehicle accidents. Any such amendment might well be required to specify that it constituted an exception to the general rule of maternal tort immunity for prenatal negligence, and that the injured child could not recover damages above the limit established by the insurance scheme. A carefully tailored solution could benefit both the injured child and his or her family, without unduly restricting the privacy and autonomy rights of Canadian women.

. . . .

[MAJOR J. (dissenting):]

. . . .

THE FIRST BRANCH OF THE *KAMLOOPS* TEST

These two objections correspond to the two-step test in *Anns v. Merton London Borough Council*, which was adopted by this Court in City of *Kamloops v. Nielsen*. The test was stated by Wilson J. at pp. 10–11:

> (1) is there a sufficiently close relationship between the parties (the [defendant] and the person who has suffered the damage) so that, in the reasonable contemplation of the [defendant], carelessness on its part might cause damage to that person? If so,
>
> (2) are there any considerations which ought to negative or limit (a) the scope of the duty and (b) the class of persons to whom it is owed or (c) the damages to which a breach of it may give rise?

The parties to the present action are a mother and her born alive child, not a pregnant woman and her foetus. The parties are separate legal entities. This distinguishes the appeal from cases dealing with abortion (see *R. v. Morgentaler*; *Tremblay v. Daigle*) and the autonomy rights of pregnant women (see *Winnipeg*, *supra*).

The well-settled rule that a born alive child has a right to sue third parties for injuries prenatally sustained (*i.e.*, the "born alive rule") does not entail an assertion of foetal rights. If the rule is applied in the present case, the duty of care at issue would not be owed by the pregnant woman to her foetus. It would be owed to her born alive child.

The foetus has no cause of action. There is no doubt that a foetus can be injured in a car accident. But this physical injury is not an actionable harm. It is not a legal fact. It is legally meaningless until it arises as the suffering of a legal person — the born alive child. Had there been no birth, no legally recognized injury would have taken place. Birth transforms the physical injury sustained by the foetus into an actionable harm. Not the injury to the foetus but the injury to the born alive child's mental and physical functioning is actionable.

As Lamont J. put it in *Montreal Tramways*, *supra*, at p. 463, "[t]he wrongful act of the Company <u>produced its damage on the birth of the child</u> and the right of action was then complete" (emphasis added). There was no legal damage, though there was physical injury, before the birth of the child. The actionable damage did not antecede the birth. What is actionable in this appeal is not whatever it was that happened to the respondent as a foetus. What is actionable in this appeal is what is now happening to the respondent as a child. It is the child's cerebral palsy and related injuries that are actionable.

There is no such thing as "liability for prenatal injuries". Under existing Canadian law the foetus does not exist for purposes of state protection or civil action: see *Winnipeg, supra*. The pregnant woman has no responsibility for damages or otherwise to the foetus and that is so whether the harm is accidental, negligent or deliberate. While most pregnant women take special care to ensure a healthy foetus, there is no legal requirement that they do so. Only damages to a legal person are actionable.

The law of tort views a born alive child as a person capable of suing third parties for damages resulting from injuries inflicted on her as a foetus. Absent the born alive child, however, foetal injuries are legally irrelevant. Thus, while there is no liability for prenatal injuries, there is liability for postnatal injuries resulting from prenatal events caused by a third party's negligence.

The ability of the child to sue depends on his legal existence. In this appeal, the physical injury sustained *in utero* is irrelevant to the question of standing. It has relevance only as a matter of causation. The plaintiff must prove, on the balance of probabilities, that his damages were in fact caused by the defendant's negligence. Ryan Dobson must prove that his damages result from the negligent driving of his mother.

A pregnant woman cannot owe a duty of care to her foetus any more than she can owe a duty of care to herself. The duty of care is owed to the born alive child. Whatever may be said as a matter of policy, the trial judge's "reasonable progression" is not inconsistent with the legal unity of pregnant woman and foetus. It has nothing to do with that unity.

In Canada, a pregnant woman has an unrestricted legal right to an abortion from conception to the time of birth, but once the child is born alive he is a legal person with all the rights that accompany that status. The right of the pregnant woman to terminate her pregnancy is unrelated to her possible responsibility to her child once born alive. An application of the first branch of the *Kamloops* test to the present case would unquestionably find that the appellant mother while driving her car owed a duty of care to other users of the highway and to passengers in her car. In

my opinion, the duty of care owed by the mother to her born alive child is obvious, providing she knows or ought to know that she is pregnant at the time of the act.

THE SECOND BRANCH OF THE *KAMLOOPS* TEST

The next question is whether policy reasons as contemplated in *Kamloops* deprive the born alive plaintiff Ryan Dobson of his cause of action.

In para. 31 of his reasons, Cory J. postulates that such policy considerations do exist. He states:

> On behalf of the infant respondent, it was argued that the reasoning in *Winnipeg* is not determinative because it dealt with the standing of the foetus to sue while still *in utero*. In *Winnipeg* the foetus which sought the detention of its mother-to-be was not a legal person and possessed no legal rights. By contrast, the present action is brought on behalf of an infant born alive whose legal rights and interests vested at the moment of birth. In other words, the sole issue in this appeal is whether a child born alive — as opposed to a foetus — should be able to recover damages for prenatal negligence from every person except his or her mother. Despite the important legal distinction between a foetus and a child born alive, as a matter of social policy and pragmatic reality, both situations involve the imposition of a duty of care upon a pregnant woman towards either her foetus or her subsequently born child. To impose either duty of care would require judicial scrutiny into every aspect of that woman's behaviour during pregnancy. Irrespective of whether the duty of care is imposed upon a pregnant woman towards her foetus or her subsequently born child, both would involve severe intrusions into the bodily integrity, privacy and autonomous decision-making of that woman. Accordingly, the policy concerns raised by McLachlin J. in Winnipeg are equally pertinent to this appeal.

In my opinion, the policy concerns raised in *Winnipeg, supra*, relative to the pregnant woman and her foetus do not apply to the mother and her born alive child. This action was brought on behalf of a legal person, not a foetus. Cory J. suggests that, from the perspective of a pregnant woman, the important legal distinction between her foetus and her born alive child might not appear relevant. In his view, a pregnant woman might conclude that the behavioural restrictions to which she would be subjected in either case are identical. But the compelling point of departure is that, in contrast to *Winnipeg, supra,* in this appeal the pregnant woman's perspective is not the only legally recognized perspective. It competes with the recognized perspective of her born alive child.

The issue here is twofold. First, would a finding that Cynthia Dobson owes the respondent a duty of care result in additional behavioural restrictions on her while she was pregnant? If so, are those restrictions of a nature that would justify a finding that the respondent's right to commence a tort action against his mother for prenatal injuries allegedly sustained as a result of her negligent driving should give way to Cynthia Dobson's autonomy rights on policy grounds?

I respectfully disagree with Cory J. that sufficient policy concerns have been raised on the facts of this case to negative the child's right to sue in tort. The appellant Cynthia Dobson was already under a legal obligation to drive carefully. She owed a duty of care to passengers in her car and to other users of the highway, such as John Carter, the other motorist involved in the collision. If her negligent driving caused the collision, she will be liable to John Carter.

In these circumstances, it would be unjustified to hold that the appellant should not be liable to her born alive child on the grounds that such liability would restrict her freedom of action. Her freedom of action in respect of her driving was already restricted by her duty of care to users of the highway. Hence, to acknowledge that the suffering of her born alive child, Ryan Dobson, was within the reasonably foreseeable ambit of the risk created by her negligent driving is hardly a limitation of her freedom of action. The appellant mother would not have had to take any further precautions, additional to those she was already legally obliged to take, in order to avoid liability to her born alive child.

The appellant's autonomy interests are not in issue. She was not legally free to operate a motor vehicle without due care. She did not have the freedom to drive carelessly. Therefore, it cannot be said that the imposition of a duty of care to her born alive child would restrict her freedom to drive. The respondent child cannot take away from his mother a freedom she did not have.

I respectfully disagree with McLachlin J. that the liberty and equality interests of pregnant women are in issue in this appeal. The values enshrined in the *Canadian Charter of Rights and Freedoms* do not grant pregnant women interests of any kind in negligent driving.

On the facts of this case, Ryan Dobson's *prima facie* right to sue in tort arises only on the same grounds and in the same way as that of the driver of the other car. In these circumstances, the appellant's freedom of action is not in issue, and the suggestion that her son's rights ought to be negatived so as to protect her freedom of action is misplaced.

Where a pregnant woman already owes a duty of care to a third party in respect of the same behaviour for which her born alive child seeks to find her liable, policy considerations pertinent to the pregnant woman's freedom of action cannot operate so as to negative the child's *prima facie* right to sue. The duty of care imposed on the pregnant woman is not more onerous because of her potential liability to her born alive child.

The presence of a duty of care owed to a third party in respect of the same behaviour for which her born alive child seeks to find her liable precludes a pregnant woman from arguing successfully that her freedom of action would be restricted by the imposition of a duty of care to her born alive child. A grant of immunity from tort liability rooted in policy considerations pertinent to a pregnant woman's freedom of action must necessarily rest on a showing that such freedom of action would be restricted by the imposition of a duty of care to the born alive child. No such showing seems possible where the pregnant woman's freedom of action is already restricted in the very same respect by a duty of care owed to a third party.

I disagree with McLachlin J. that this view of the matter violates the principle that the duty of care in tort must be founded on the relationship between the actual parties to the dispute before the court. The point is not that the child's *prima facie* right to sue arising from the first branch of *Kamloops* is conditional on the "serendipitous coincidence" that a third party is owed a duty of care. The point is that, where a duty of care is owed to a third party, the child's *prima facie* right to sue cannot be negatived under the second branch of *Kamloops* on policy grounds flowing from the pregnant woman's freedom of action. The point is precisely that where, as here, a pregnant woman's freedom of action is not in issue, nothing in the relationship between the actual parties to the dispute can possibly support the proposition that the imposition of liability to her born alive child would infringe her freedom of action.

But matters are different where the pregnant woman does not owe a third party a duty of care in respect of the behaviour, as, for instance, in her lifestyle choices such as smoking, drinking, and dietary and health-care decisions. That is also true of various other activities that may place the pregnant woman in harm's way. The examples range from an unhealthy work or home environment to activities as extreme as bungy jumping. In such cases, the second branch of the *Kamloops* test may prevent the imposition of a duty of care because her freedom of action is in issue and policy reasons for immunity can be adduced. The distinction is plain and is obscured only by slippery slope and flood-gate types of argument founded in an understandably emotional response to the question.

Assume, for example, that another pregnant woman was a passenger in Cynthia Dobson's car. If, as a result of negligent driving, the other pregnant woman gave birth to an injured child, there is absolutely no doubt that that born alive child would have a right to sue Cynthia Dobson: see *Tramways*, *supra*, and *Duval*, *supra*. In those circumstances, policy reasons flowing from Cynthia Dobson's freedom of action capable of negativing Ryan Dobson's right to sue seem impossible to formulate. His mother's freedom of action in respect of her driving was already restricted by the duty of care she owed to, *inter alia*, another born alive child.

The example confirms that no intrusion into a pregnant woman's freedom of action can be demonstrated in cases where a duty of care owed to a third party in respect of the same behaviour forms part of the factual situation. In such cases, the pregnant woman's freedom of action is not in issue.

(g) Helen Palsgraf v. The Long Island Railroad Company†

[CARDOZO Ch. J.:]

Plaintiff was standing on a platform of defendant's railroad after buying a ticket to go to Rockaway Beach. A train stopped at the station, bound for another place. Two men ran forward to catch it. One of the men reached the platform of the car without mishap, though the train was already moving. The other man, carrying a package, jumped aboard the car, but seemed unsteady as if about to fall. A guard on the car, who had held the door open, reached forward to help him in, and another guard on the platform pushed him from behind. In this act, the package was dislodged, and fell upon the rails. It was a package of small size, about fifteen inches long, and was covered by a newspaper. In fact it contained fireworks, but there was nothing in its appearance to give notice of its contents. The fireworks when they fell exploded. The shock of the explosion threw down some scales at the other end of the platform, many feet away. The scales struck the plaintiff, causing injuries for which she sues.

The conduct of the defendant's guard, if a wrong in its relation to the holder of the package, was not a wrong in its relation to the plaintiff, standing far away. Relatively to her it was not negligence at all. Nothing in the situation gave notice that the falling package had in it the potency of peril to persons thus removed. Negligence is not actionable unless it involves the invasion of a legally protected interest, the violation of a right. "Proof of negligence in the air, so to speak, will not do"....

. . . .

A different conclusion will involve us, and swiftly too, in a maze of contradictions. A guard stumbles over a package which has been left upon

---

† (1928), 248 N.Y. 339.

a platform. It seems to be a bundle of newspapers. It turns out to be a can of dynamite. To the eye of ordinary vigilance, the bundle is abandoned waste, which may be kicked or trod on with impunity. Is a passenger at the other end of the platform protected by the law against the unsuspected hazard concealed beneath the waste? If not, is the result to be any different, so far as the distant passenger is concerned, when the guard stumbles over a valise which a truckman or a porter has left upon the walk? ... The diversity of interests emphasizes the futility of the effort to build the plaintiff's right upon the basis of a wrong to some one else. The gain is one of emphasis, for a like result would follow if the interests were the same. Even then, the orbit of the danger as disclosed to the eye of reasonable vigilance would be the orbit of the duty. One who jostles one's neighbor in a crowd does not invade the rights of others standing at the outer fringe when the unintended contact casts a bomb upon the ground. The wrongdoer as to them is the man who carries the bomb, not the one who explodes it without suspicion of the danger. Life will have to be made over, and human nature transformed, before prevision so extravagant can be accepted as the norm of conduct, the customary standard to which behavior must conform.

. . . .

Negligence, like risk, is thus a term of relation. Negligence in the abstract, apart from things related, is surely not a tort, if indeed it is understandable at all.... Negligence is not a tort unless it results in the commission of a wrong, and the commission of a wrong imports the violation of a right, in this case, we are told, the right to be protected against interference with one's bodily security. But bodily security is protected, not against all forms of interference or aggression, but only against some. One who seeks redress at law does not make out a cause of action by showing without more that there has been damage to his person. If the harm was not willful, he must show that the act as to him had possibilities of danger so many and apparent as to entitle him to be protected against the doing of it though the harm was unintended. ...

[ANDREWS J. (dissenting):]

Assisting a passenger to board a train, the defendant's servant negligently knocked a package from his arms. It fell between the platform and the cars. Of its contents the servant knew and could know nothing. A violent explosion followed. The concussion broke some scales standing a considerable distance away. In falling they injured the plaintiff, an intending passenger.

Upon these facts may she recover the damages she has suffered in an action brought against the master? The result we shall reach depends upon our theory as to the nature of negligence. Is it a relative concept — the breach of some duty owing to a particular person or to particular persons? Or where there is an act which unreasonably threatens the safety of others, is the doer liable for all its proximate consequences, even where they result in injury to one who would generally be thought to be outside the radius of danger? This is not a mere dispute as to words. We might not believe that to the average mind the dropping of the bundle would seem to involve the probability of harm to the plaintiff standing many feet away whatever might be the case as to the owner or to one so near as to be likely to be struck by its fall. If, however, we adopt the second hypothesis we have to inquire only as to the relation between cause and effect. We deal in terms of proximate cause, not of negligence.

. . . .

It may well be that there is no such thing as negligence in the abstract. "Proof of negligence in the air, so to speak, will not do." In an empty world negligence would not exist. It does involve a relationship between man and his fellows. But not merely a relationship between man and those whom he might reasonably expect his act would injure. Rather, a relationship between him and those whom he does in fact injure. If his act has a tendency to harm some one, it harms him a mile away as surely as it does those on the scene. We now permit children to recover for the negligent killing of the father. It was never prevented on the theory that no duty was owing to them. A husband may be compensated for the loss of his wife's services. To say that the wrongdoer was negligent as to the husband as well as to the wife is merely an attempt to fit facts to theory. An insurance company paying a fire loss recovers its payment of the negligent incendiary. We speak of subrogation — of suing in the right of the insured. Behind the cloud of words is the fact they hide, that the act, wrongful as to the insured, has also injured the company.

Even if it be true that the fault of father, wife or insured will prevent recovery, it is because we consider the original negligence not the proximate cause of the injury. (Pollock, Torts [12th ed.], 463.)

. . . .

The proposition is this. Every one owes to the world at large the duty of refraining from those acts that may unreasonably threaten the safety of others. Such an act occurs. Not only is he wronged to whom harm might reasonably be expected to result, but he also who is in fact injured, even if he be outside what would generally be thought the danger zone. There needs be duty due the one complaining but this is not a duty to a particular individual because as to him harm might be expected. Harm to some one being the natural result of the act, not only that one alone, but all those in fact injured may complain. We have never, I think, held otherwise. Indeed in the Di Caprio case we said that a breach of a general ordinance defining the degree of care to be exercised in one's calling is evidence of negligence as to every one. We did not limit this statement to those who might be expected to be exposed to danger. Unreasonable risk being taken, its consequences are not confined to those who might probably be hurt.

. . . .

Take the illustration given in an unpublished manuscript by a distinguished and helpful writer on the law of torts. A chauffeur negligently collides with another car which is filled with dynamite, although he could not know it. An explosion follows. A, walking on the sidewalk nearby, is killed. B, sitting in a window of a building opposite, is cut by flying glass. C, likewise sitting in a window a block away, is similarly injured. And a further illustration. A nursemaid, ten blocks away, startled by the noise, involuntarily drops a baby from her arms to the walk. We are told that C may not recover while A may. As to B it is a question for court or jury. We will all agree that the baby might not. Because, we are again told, the chauffeur had no reason to believe his conduct involved any risk of injuring either C or the baby. As to them he was not negligent.

But the chauffeur, being negligent in risking the collision, his belief that the scope of the harm he might do would be limited is immaterial. His act unreasonably jeopardized the safety of any one who might be affected by it. C's injury and that of the baby were directly traceable to the collision. Without that, the injury would not have happened. C had the right to sit in his office, secure from such dangers. The baby was entitled to use the sidewalk with reasonable safety.

The true theory is, it seems to me, that the injury to C, if in truth he is to be denied recovery, and the injury to the baby is that their several injuries were not the proximate result of the negligence. And here not what the chauffeur had reason to believe would be the result of his conduct, but what the prudent would foresee, may have a bearing. May have some bearing, for the problem of proximate cause is not to be solved by any one consideration.

. . . .

This last suggestion is the factor which must determine the case before us. The act upon which defendant's liability rests is knocking an apparently harmless package onto the platform. The act was negligent. For its proximate consequences the defendant is liable. If its contents were broken, to the owner; if it fell upon and crushed a passenger's foot, then to him. If it exploded and injured one in the immediate vicinity, to him also as to A in the illustration. Mrs. Palsgraf was standing some distance away. How far cannot be told from the record — apparently twenty-five or thirty feet. Perhaps less. Except for the explosion, she would not have been injured. We are told by the appellant in his brief "it cannot be denied that the explosion was the direct cause of the plaintiff's injuries." So it was a substantial factor in producing the result — there was here a natural and continuous sequence — direct connection. The only intervening cause was that instead of blowing her to the ground the concussion smashed the weighing machine which in turn fell upon her. There was no remoteness in time, little in space. And surely, given such an explosion as here it needed no great foresight to predict that the natural result would be to injure one on the platform at no greater distance from its scene than was the plaintiff. Just how no one might be able to predict. Whether by flying fragments, by broken glass, by wreckage of machines or structures no one could say. But injury in some form was most probable.

149

(h) *Palsgraf* Revisited†

William L. Prosser

Perhaps the most celebrated of all tort cases is *Palsgraf v. Long Island Railroad Company*. Certainly it is one of the most controversial. Thirteen judges in all passed upon the case, and seven of them were for the plaintiff, at least in the sense that they considered that the issue was one to be left to the jury. Four of the remaining six, sitting on the Court of Appeals of New York, had the final word, and they set aside the verdict, dismissed the complaint, and ordered judgment for the defendant. The Advisers of the *Restatement of Torts* debated the question long and vigorously and approved the case by a narrowly divided vote. Subsequent decisions, even when they cite *Palsgraf*, have remained in a state of disagreement and confusion, and the problem presented cannot be said by any means to be settled and disposed of. The legal writers have galloped off in all directions, in a tangle of duty, negligence, foresight, hindsight, direct and intervening causes, the division and classification of interests and injuries, liability without fault or in excess of fault, social policy, the balancing of various claims to protection or immunity, and everything else that inevitably becomes involved in any discussion of "proximate cause."

It may be worse than useless to add another article to the spate. The excuse must be the fascination which the case has for both teachers and students of torts, the never-ending new facets which it offers year after year in the classroom, and the fact that, if one may judge by what has appeared in print, the writer is the one man alive who is not absolutely and altogether sure of the answer. An expression of difficulties, uncertainties and doubts, arriving at no very definite conclusion, may at least be something of a novelty.

Helen Palsgraf "was standing on a platform of defendant's railroad after buying a ticket to go to Rockaway Beach. A train stopped at the station, bound for another place. Two men ran forward to catch it. One of the men reached the platform of the car without mishap, though the train was already moving. The other man, carrying a pack-age, jumped aboard the car, but seemed unsteady as if about to fall. A guard on the car, who had held the door open, reached forward to help him in, and another guard on the platform pushed him from behind. In this act, the package was dislodged, and fell upon the rails. It was a package of small size, about fifteen inches long, and covered by a newspaper. In fact it contained fireworks, but there was nothing in its appearance to give notice of its contents. The fireworks when they fell exploded. The shock of the explosion threw down some scales at the other end of the platform, many feet away. The scales struck the plaintiff, causing injuries for which she sues." The date was not July 4, but August 24, 1924, and no one in the station except the man with the package and his companion had any reason whatever to suppose that he was carrying anything explosive.

The defendant offered no evidence and moved to dismiss the case. The trial court denied the motion, and instructed the jury that if the defendant's guards were careless and negligent in the way they handled the passenger boarding the train, the plaintiff was entitled to recover. The jury returned a verdict for the plaintiff in the sum of $6,000. Defendant's motion for a new trial was denied, and judgment was entered on the verdict.

On the first appeal the judges of the appellate division saw nothing in the case but "proximate cause." Three of them, in a short opinion, said that the causal connection was similar to that in the *Squib Case*, and that the fact the guards did not know that the bundle contained an explosive was no defense. Two others, in even fewer words, said that the explosion was not a likely or natural result of the conduct of the guards, and that the negligence of the passenger carrying the explosive was an "independent intervening cause." The judgment for the plaintiff was affirmed. No one seemed to consider the case at all important.

It might never have been important if there had not occurred, at this point, one of those accidents which shape the course of the law. The opin-

† (November 1953) 52:1 Mich. L. Rev. 1 at 1–8, 16–19. [Notes and/or References omitted.] Reproduced with permission of the publisher.

ion of the appellate division fell into the hands of Professor Francis H. Bohlen of Pennsylvania, who was at that time the Reporter of the American Law Institute for the *Restatement of the Law of Torts*. Bohlen was even then struggling with the problem of duty in negligence cases, and particularly with duty to the unforeseeable plaintiff. He was well aware of the confusion in the cases of "proximate cause," and he was disposed to accept the position, already advanced by Bingham and Green, that in such cases as this the question is essentially one of duty, and that unless the defendant's conduct involves some foreseeable risk to the plaintiff, the defendant is under no duty to him at all, whatever his duty may be toward anyone else. He had prepared, for submission to his advisers, a draft of a section which stated this view. *Palsgraf* provided a perfect illustration, and Bohlen added a statement of the facts to his explanatory notes.

Among the advisers who met to consider this draft was Chief Judge Cardozo of the New York Court of Appeals, who found himself suddenly and unexpectedly confronted with a discussion, by an eminent and entirely impartial group, of a lower New York decision which might very possibly be appealed to his court. He concluded that there would be no impropriety in his presence at the meeting, although he took no part in the discussion, and did not vote. He sat therefore as audience, to a long and lively debate, ranging over nearly all of the questions which since have surrounded *Palsgraf*, and going far beyond the scope of the arguments of counsel in the case, who were still foundering in the morass of proximate cause. The decision, by a narrow margin which may have consisted of a single vote, upheld the Reporter and approved his section.

Cardozo was convinced by the majority. When the appeal came on his return to Albany, he adopted their view, with the concurrence of three other judges of the court of appeals, as the law of the case. There was no liability, he said, because there was no negligence toward the plaintiff. Negligence must be a matter of some relation between the parties, some duty, which could be founded only on the foreseeability of some harm to the plaintiff in fact injured. "Negligence in the air, so to speak, will not do." The defendant's conduct did not become a wrong to Mrs. Palsgraf merely because it threatened injury to someone else. She must sue "in her own right for a wrong personal to her, and not as the vicarious beneficiary of a breach of duty to another." Assuming, without

deciding, that negligence toward the plaintiff would entail liability for any and all consequences, however novel or extraordinary, there was no such negligence here. The conduct of the guards toward the passenger involved no foreseeable risk that the plaintiff might be injured; it was therefore no tort as to her, and as a matter of law she could not recover. Cardozo added: "There is room for argument that a distinction is to be drawn according to the diversity of interests invaded by the act, as where conduct negligent in that it threatens an insignificant invasion of an interest in property results in an unforeseeable invasion of an interest of another order, as e.g., one of bodily security. Perhaps other distinctions may be necessary. We do not go into the questions now."

Judge Andrews, dissenting, met the issue head on. Negligence, he said, does not depend upon a relation between the defendant and the plaintiff; it is a wrong toward anyone in fact injured by the negligent act. There is a duty toward the world at large not to be negligent toward any person; and when an injury to the plaintiff results from a breach of this duty, she may have a cause of action. There are limitations upon this liability, but they are limitations of "proximate cause," and the remoteness of the damage. On this what the prudent might foresee may have a bearing, but it is only "some bearing, for the problem of proximate cause is not to be solved by any one consideration." It is not a question of logic, but of practical politics; and the courts do the best they can to draw an uncertain and wavering line, which will be practical and in keeping with the general understanding of mankind. The injury here was direct and immediate; the distance was short; there was no remoteness in time, little in space. It cannot be said as a matter of law that the plaintiff's injuries were not the proximate result of the negligence.

So ended the *Palsgraf* case. Before leaving the opinions, the comment may be ventured that, with due respect to the superlative style in which both are written, neither of them wears well on long acquaintance. Both of them beg the question shamelessly, stating dogmatic propositions without reason or explanation. If there is or is not a duty to the plaintiff not to injure her in this way, nothing else remains to be said. Both of them assume that there was no relation whatever between the defendant and the plaintiff on which a duty might be founded; both utterly ignore the fact, on which the appellate division laid stress, that Mrs. Palsgraf was a passenger. From the moment that she bought her ticket the defendant did in fact owe her a duty of the highest care, one of the most stringent known to the law. The question was not one of injury to some stranger across the street, but of whether the duty to a passenger extended to the consequences of negligence threatening another passenger — which may very well be a different thing altogether.

There is, furthermore, the question left unanswered by Cardozo: what would have been the result if the explosion had injured the owner of the package, or had damaged his suitcase on a baggage truck? There is also the troublesome matter of the scale. It is difficult to escape the conclusion that anything on a railroad platform so easily knocked over, whether by a paltry explosion of fireworks which damaged nothing else, or by a jostling and panicky crowd, had no business being there; and if there was negligence in having the scale, it was certainly negligence toward the plaintiff herself, who was standing beside it. There is no mention of this at all, undoubtedly because the idea never occurred to counsel; but it occurs every year to some one of my law school freshmen, who then concludes that he is brighter than the New York Court of Appeals.

. . . .

FORESEEABILITY AND RISK

We come next to the effect on this nebulous "duty" of the fact that the damage was, or was not, reasonably to be foreseen by a reasonable man in the position of the defendant. It needs no argument to show that duty does not always coincide with the foreseeable risk. The expert swimmer, with a boat at hand, who sees another drowning before his eyes, may sit on the dock, smoke his pipe, and watch him drown. But it is still possible, as Cardozo contended, that the risk may be an outer boundary beyond which duty cannot extend, and that there is never any duty as to the unforeseeable plaintiff or the unforeseeable damage.

Over this there is an ancient controversy which goes back to Baron Pollock in 1850. One position, of which Professor Seavey is the modern protagonist, is that the risk which determines the existence of negligence in the first instance limits the recovery for it, and that the same factors which characterize the conduct as wrongful define the scope of liability for its consequences. The other is that what the defendant might foresee is important in determining whether he was at fault at all but is

not decisive as to the extent of the consequences for which, once negligent, he will be liable. The courts have fluctuated and vacillated between the two positions, and neither has been adopted with entire consistency or carried to all of its logical conclusions. In support of the limitation of liability to the foreseeable risk, it has been contended that it is more just, since the damages are consistent with the fault, and negligence may be only a slight deviation from the social standard, while its consequences may be out of all proportion to it. It is certainly more just from the point of view of the defendant, but it may be doubted that the plaintiff will appreciate the justice. The plaintiff has been hurt and some one must bear the loss. Essentially the choice is between an innocent plaintiff and a defendant who is admittedly at fault. If the loss is out of all proportion to the defendant's fault, it can be no less out of proportion to the plaintiff's innocence. If it is unjust to the defendant to make him bear the loss which he could not have foreseen, it is no less unjust to the plaintiff to make him bear a loss which he too could not have foreseen and which is not even due to his own negligence but to that of another. In these cases there is no justice to be had.

It has been said that the limitation is more rational, since it is more consistent with the "underlying theory" of negligence. This is true if we postulate an underlying theory of negligence in the abstract without its consequences; but there is no such thing. A cause of action for negligence must include damages as well as fault; and when we come to state a theory as to whether the plaintiff's damage is included as compensable, we are once more begging the question. Once again the dog chases its tail.

It has been said finally that the limitation is easier to administer, since it fixes the nearest thing to a definite boundary that is possible and gives us a degree of predictable certainty in the law. Predictable certainty and facility of administration are very desirable things if they are not purchased at too great a price. What degree of certainty does the limitation of foreseeable risk bring to these cases?

It is relatively easy to say that the total risk, made up of the aggregate of all the possibilities of harm, large or small, probable or fantastic, is so great that the reasonable man of ordinary prudence would not drive at an excessive speed. It is quite another matter to say that any one fragment of that risk, consisting of the particular consequences that have in fact occurred, would have been sufficient in itself for the reasonable man to have it in mind and be deterred, or that it is so significant a part of the whole that liability should attach to it. Herein lies the distinction between the original fault and its results.

It is clearly foreseeable that the speeding driver may hit another car and kill a man. But what of the possibility that he may only bruise a shin, and cancer may develop from the bruise? Or that the car with which he collides may be thrown out of control and hit a third car, or even a fourth? Or that he will hit a man, whose body will be thrown several feet through the air and injure a person on the sidewalk? Or that he will narrowly miss a pregnant woman, who will be frightened into a miscarriage; or that he will injure her unborn child? or that he will endanger a child in the street, and its rescuer will sustain a broken arm? Or that the person he injures may be left helpless in the street and be run over by another car? Or that he will hit a power line pole, mix up electric wires and start a fire, or kill a workman operating a machine two miles away? Or that he will hit a man carrying a shotgun, and the gun will be discharged, and a bystander be shot in the leg? There is a mathematical chance of all of these possibilities. All of them have occurred, and can occur again; and all of them have been held "proximate" by some court. But which of them are "foreseeable" in the sense of being a significant part of the risk recognizable in advance?

Such piecemeal foresight is a rope of sand, and offers neither certainty nor convenience, as the floundering in the cases seems to show. Here is Learned Hand, a great judge, blandly assuring us that it is beyond reasonable anticipation that a barge with which the defendant collides will sink, and will be carrying insurance. Here is Pennsylva-nia, twice asserting that no reasonable man could foresee that any object struck by a speeding train or bus would fly off at an angle and hit a person not directly in its path. Here is Wisconsin, affirming that when a child is run down in the street there is no recognizable risk that its mother, in the vicinity, may suffer mental shock. Here is New York, solemnly declaring that the foreseeability of the spread of fire ends at the first adjoining house. I do not believe these things. I think they are rubbish. At the other extreme is another New York case, finding it all foreseeable when a collision forced a taxicab over a sidewalk and into a building, and loosened a stone, which fell upon a bystander and killed her, while the taxicab was being removed twenty minutes later by a wrecking car. There is also Texas, which had no difficulty at all in foreseeing that a mudhole left by a defendant in a highway would stall a car, that a rescuer attempting to tow it out would get his wooden leg stuck in the mud, and that a loop in the tow rope would lasso his good leg and break it. Illustrations might be multiplied, as every negligence lawyer knows, but surely these are enough.

Foreseeability of risk, in short, carries only an illusion of certainty in defining the consequences for which the defendant will be liable. The attempt to broaden it by talking instead of consequences which are "normal" to the risk, or reasonably attachable to it, or "not highly extraordinary" in the light of it, seems in part at least to abandon the original reasoning and adds nothing in the way of definiteness. One of my students told me once that all this meant to him was that what happened should not be "too cockeyed and far-fetched." If that is true, why not look to the cockeyed consequences themselves rather than to the original fault?

(i) *Alcock v. Chief Constable of South Yorkshire*†

[LORD KEITH OF KINKEL:]

My Lords, the litigation with which these appeals are concerned arose out of the disaster at Hillsborough Stadium, Sheffield, which occurred on 15 April 1989. On that day a football match was arranged to be played at the stadium between the Liverpool and the Nottingham Forest football

---

† [1991] 4 All E.R. 907 at 910–15.

clubs. It was a semi-final of the FA Cup. The South Yorkshire police force, which was responsible for crowd control at the match, allowed an excessively large number of intending spectators to enter the ground at the Leppings Lane end, an area reserved for Liverpool supporters. They crammed into pens 3 and 4, below the West Stand, and in the resulting crush 95 people were killed and over 400 physically injured. Scenes from the ground were broadcast live on television from time to time during the course of the disaster, and recordings were broadcast later. The Chief Constable of South Yorkshire has admitted liability in negligence in respect of the deaths and physical injuries. Sixteen separate actions were brought against him by persons none of whom was present in the area where the disaster occurred, although four of them were elsewhere in the ground. All of them were connected in various ways with persons who were in that area, being related to such persons or, in one case, being a fiancé. In most cases the person with whom the plaintiff was concerned was killed, in other cases that person was injured, and in one case turned out to be uninjured. All the plaintiffs claim damages for nervous shock resulting in psychiatric illness which they allege was caused by the experiences inflicted on them by the disaster.

The actions came on for trial before Hidden J. on 19 June 1990, and he gave the judgment on 31 July 1990. That judgment was concerned with the question whether the defendant owed a duty of care in relation to nervous shock to any, and if so to which, of the plaintiffs. The defendant admitted that if he owed such a duty to any plaintiff, and if that plaintiff could show causation, then the defendant was in breach of duty and liable in damages to that plaintiff. For the purposes of this judgment Hidden J. assumed in the case of each plaintiff that causation was established, leaving that matter to be dealt with, if necessary, in further proceedings. In the result, he found in favour of ten out of the sixteen plaintiffs before him and against six of them. The defendant appealed to the Court of Appeal in the cases of nine out of the ten successful plaintiffs, and the six unsuccessful plaintiffs also appealed to that court. On 3 May 1991 the Court of Appeal (Parker, Stocker and Nolan L.JJ.) gave judgment allowing the defendant's appeals in the cases of the nine formerly successful plaintiffs and rejecting the appeals of the six unsuccessful ones. Ten only of these fifteen plaintiffs now appeal to your Lordships' House, with leave granted in the Court of Appeal.

The circumstances affecting each of the ten appellants were thus summarised in the judgment of Parker L.J.:

... Brian Harrison was at the ground. He was in the West Stand. He knew both of his brothers would be in the pens behind the goal. He saw the horrifying scene as it developed and realised that people in the two pens had been either killed or injured. When, six minutes after the start, the match was abandoned he tried to find his brothers. He failed to do so. He stopped up all night waiting for the news. At 6 am he learnt that his family were setting off to Sheffield. At 11 am he was informed by telephone that both his brothers were dead....

Mr. and Mrs. Copoc lost their son. They saw the scenes on live television. Mrs. Copoc was up all night. She was informed by police officers at 6 am that her son was dead. Mr. Copoc went to Sheffield at 4 am with his nephew. He was informed at 6.10 am of his son's death and later identified the body....

Brenda Hennessey lost her brother. She watched television from about 3.30 pm and, although she then realised there had been deaths and injuries in the pens, she was not worried because she believed her brother to be in a stand seat. However, at about 5 pm she learnt from her brother's wife that he had a ticket in the Leppings Lane terrace. At 6 pm she learnt from members of the family who had gone to Sheffield that her brother was dead.

Denise Hough lost her brother. She was 11 years older than her brother and had fostered him for several years although he no longer lived with her. She knew he had a ticket at the Leppings Lane end and would be behind the goal. She was told by a friend that there was trouble at the game. She watched television. At 4.40 am she was informed by her mother that her brother was dead. Two days later, on 17 April, she went with her mother to Sheffield and confirmed an earlier identification of the body. His face was bruised and swollen.

Stephen Jones lost his brother. He knew that his brother was at the match. He watched television and saw bodies and believed them to be dead. He did not know his brother was dead until 2.45 am when, having gone to the temporary mortuary at Hillsborough, he found his parents there in tears....

Robert Alcock lost his brother-in-law. He was in the West Stand, with his nephew (the brother-in-law's-son). He witnessed the scenes from the West Stand and was sickened by what he saw but was not then concerned for his brother-in-law whom he believed to be in the stand because, on the way to the match, he had swapped a terrace ticket which he held for a stand ticket. Tragically, however, the brother-in-law had, unknown to the plaintiff, returned to the terrace. After the match the plaintiff left the ground for a rendezvous with the brother-in-law, who did not arrive. He and his nephew became worried and searched without success. At about midnight they went to the mortuary, where the plaintiff identified the body, which was blue with bruising and the chest of which was red. The sight appalled him....

Catherine Jones lost a brother. She knew he was at the match and would normally be behind the goal. At 3.30 pm whilst shopping she heard that there was trouble at the match and at 4.30 pm that there were deaths. At 5.15 pm she went home and heard on the radio that the death toll was mounting. At 7 pm a friend telephone from Sheffield to say that people at the hospital were describing someone who might be her brother. At 9 pm her parents set off for Sheffield. At 10 pm she watched recorded television in the hope of seeing her brother alive. She thought mistakenly, she saw him collapsed on the pitch. At 5 am her father returned from Sheffield and told her that her brother was dead.

Joseph Kehoe lost a 14-year-old grandson, the son of his daughter and her divorced husband. Unknown to the grandfather the boy had gone to the match with his father. In the afternoon the plaintiff heard on the radio that there had been deaths at Hillsborough. He later saw scenes of the disaster on recorded television. He later learnt that his grandson was at the match. He became worried. At 3 am he was telephoned by another daughter to say that both the boy and his father were dead....

Alexandra Penk lost her fiancé, Carl Rimmer. They had known each other for four years and recently became engaged. They planned to marry in late 1989 or at the latest early in 1990. She knew he was at the match and would be in the Leppings Lane terraces. She saw television in her sister's house and knew instinctively that her fiancé was in trouble. She continued to watch in the hope of seeing him but did not do so. She was told at about 11 pm that he was dead.

The question of liability in negligence for what is commonly, if inaccurately, described as "nervous shock" has only twice been considered by this House, in *Hay (or Bourhill) v. Young*, and in *McLoughlin v. O'Brian*. In the latter case the plaintiff, after learning of the motor accident involving her husband and three of her children about two hours after it had happened, went to the hospital where they had been taken. There she was told that one of the children had been killed, and saw her husband and the other two in a distressed condition and bearing on their persons the immediate effects of the accident. She claimed to have suffered psychiatric illness as a result of her experience, and at the trial of her action of damages against those responsible for the accident this was assumed to be the fact. This House, reversing the Court of Appeal, held that she was entitled to recover damages. The leading speech was delivered by Lord Wilberforce. Having set out the position so far reached in the decided cases on nervous shock, he expressed the opinion that foreseeability did not of itself and automatically give rise to a duty of care owed to a person or class of persons and that considerations of policy entered into the conclusion that such a duty existed. He then considered the arguments on policy which had led the Court of Appeal to reject the plaintiff's claim, and concluded that they were not of great force. He continued:

> But these discounts accepted, there remains, in my opinion, just because "shock" in its nature is capable of affecting so wide a range of people, a real need for the law to place some limitation on the extent of admissible claims. It is necessary to consider three elements inherent in any claim: the class of persons whose claims should be recognised; the proximity of such persons to the accident; and the means by which the shock is caused. As regards the class of persons, the possible range is between the closet of family ties, of parent and child, or husband and wife, and the ordinary bystander. Existing law recognises the claims of the first; it denies that of the second, either on the basis that such persons must be assumed to be possessed of fortitude sufficient to enable them to endure the calamities of modern life or that defendants cannot be expected to compensate the world at large. In my opinion, these positions are justifiable, and since the present case falls within the first class it is strictly unnecessary to say more. I think, however, that it should follow that other cases involving less close relationships must be very carefully scrutinised. I cannot say that they should never be admitted. The closer the tie (not merely in relationship, but in care) the greater the claim for consideration. The claim, in any case, has to be judged in the light of the other factors, such as proximity to the scene and place, and the nature of the accident. As regards proxim-

ity to the accident, it is obvious that this must be close in both time and space. It is after all, the fact and consequence of the defendant's negligence that must be proved to have caused the "nervous shock". Experience has shown that to insist on direct and immediate sight or hearing would be impractical and unjust and that under what may be called the "aftermath" doctrine, one who, from close proximity comes very soon on the scene, should not be excluded.... Finally, and by way of reinforcement of "aftermath" cases, I would accept, by analogy with "rescue" situations, that a person of whom it could be said that one could expect nothing else than that he or she would come immediately to the scene (normally a parent or a spouse) could be regarded as being within the scope of foresight and duty. Where there is not immediate presence, account must be taken of the possibility of alterations in the circumstances, for which the defendant should not be responsible. Subject only to these qualifications, I think that a strict test of proximity by sight or hearing should be applied by the courts. Lastly, as regards communication, there is no case in which the law has compensated shock brought about by communication by a third party. In *Hambrook v. Stokes Bros.*, indeed, it was said that liability would not arise in such a case, and this is surely right. It was so decided in *Abramzik v. Brenner*. The shock must come through sight or hearing of the event or of its immediate aftermath. Whether some equivalent of sight or hearing, e.g., through simultaneous television, would suffice may have to be considered.

Lord Bridge of Harwich, with whom Lord Scarman agreed, appears to have rested his finding of liability simply on the test of reasonable foreseeability of psychiatric illness affecting the plaintiff as a result of the consequences of the road accident. Lord Edmund-Davies and Lord Russell of Killowen both considered the policy arguments which had led the Court of Appeal to dismiss the plaintiff's claim to be unsound. Neither speech contained anything inconsistent with that of Lord Wilberforce.

It was argued for the appellants in the present case that reasonable foreseeability of the risk of injury to them in the particular form of psychiatric illness was all that was required to bring home liability to the respondent. In the ordinary case of direct physical injury suffered in an accident at work or elsewhere, reasonable foreseeability of the risk is indeed the only test that need be applied to determine liability. But injury by psychiatric illness is more subtle, as Lord Macmillan observed in

Bourhill v. Young. In the present type of case it is a secondary sort of injury brought about by the infliction of physical injury, or the risk of physical injury, upon another person. That can affect those closely connected with that person in various ways. One way is by subjecting a close relative to the stress and strain of caring for the injured person over a prolonged period, but psychiatric illness due to such stress and strain has not so far been treated as founding a claim in damages. So I am of the opinion that in addition to reasonable foreseeability liability for injury in the particular form of psychiatric illness must depend in addition upon a requisite relationship of proximity between the claimant and the party said to owe the duty. Lord Atkin in *M'Alister (or Donoghue) v. Stevenson* described those to whom a duty of care is owed as being —

> persons who are so closely and directly affected by my act that I ought reasonably to have them in contemplation as being so affected when I am directing my mind to the acts or omissions which are called in question.

The concept of a person being closely and directly affected has been conveniently labelled "proximity", and this concept has been applied in certain categories of cases, particularly those concerned with pure economic loss, to limit and control the consequences as regards liability which would follow if reasonable foreseeability were the sole criterion.

As regards the class of persons to whom a duty may be owed to take reasonable care to avoid inflicting psychiatric illness through nervous shock sustained by reason of physical injury or peril to another, I think it sufficient that reasonable foreseeability should be the guide. I would not seek to limit the class by reference to particular relationships such as husband and wife or parent and child. The kinds of relationship which may involve close ties of love and affection are numerous, and it is the existence of such ties which leads to mental disturbance when the loved one suffers a catastrophe. They may be present in family relationships or those of close friendship, and may be stronger in the case of engaged couples than in that of persons who have been married to each other for many years. It is common knowledge that such ties exist, and reasonably foreseeable that those bound by them may in certain circumstances be at real risk of psychiatric illness if the loved one is injured or put in peril. The closeness of the tie would, however, require to be proved by a plaintiff, though no doubt being capable of being presumed in appropriate cases. The case of a bystander unconnected with the victims of an accident is difficult. Psychiatric injury to him would not ordinarily, in my view, be within the range of reasonable foreseeability, but could not perhaps be entirely excluded from it if the circumstances of a catastrophe occurring very close to him were particularly horrific.

In the case of those within the sphere of reasonable foreseeability the proximity factors mentioned by Lord Wilberforce in *McLoughlin v. O'Brian*, must, however, be taken into account in judging whether a duty of care exists. The first of these is proximity of the plaintiff to the accident in time and space. For this purpose the accident is to be taken to include its immediate aftermath, which in *McLoughlin*'s case was held to cover the scene at the hospital which was experienced by the plaintiff some two hours after the accident. In *Jaensch v. Coffey* the plaintiff saw her injured husband at the hospital to which he had been taken in severe pain before and between his undergoing a series of emergency operations, and the next day stayed with him in the intensive care unit and thought he was going to die. She was held entitled to recover damages for the psychiatric illness she suffered as a result. Deane J. said:

> ... the aftermath of the accident extended to the hospital to which the injured person was taken and persisted for so long as he remained in the state produced by the accident up to and including immediate post-accident treatment.... Her psychiatric injuries were the result of the impact upon her of the facts of the accident itself and its aftermath while she was present at the aftermath of the accident at the hospital.

As regards the means by which the shock is suffered, Lord Wilberforce said in *McLoughlin*'s case that it must come through sight or hearing of the event or of its immediate aftermath. He also said that it was surely right that the law should not compensate shock brought about by communication by a third party. On that basis it is open to serious doubt whether *Hevican v. Ruane*, and *Ravenscroft v. Rederiaktiebølaget Transatlantic*, were correctly decided, since in both of these cases the effective cause of the psychiatric illness would

appear to have been the fact of a son's death and the news of it.

Of the present appellants two, Brian Harrison and Robert Alcock, were present at the Hillsborough ground, both of them in the West Stand, from which they witnessed the scenes in pens 3 and 4. Brian Harrison lost two brothers, while Robert Alcock lost a brother-in-law and identified the body at the mortuary at midnight. In neither of these cases was there any evidence of particularly close ties of love or affection with the brothers or brother-in-law. In my opinion the mere fact of the particular relationship was insufficient to place the plaintiff within the class of persons to whom a duty of care could be owed by the defendant as being foreseeably at risk of psychiatric illness by reason of injury or peril to the individuals concerned. The same is true of other plaintiffs who were not present at the ground and who lost brothers, or in one case a grandson. I would, however, place in the category of members to which risk of psychiatric illness was reasonably foreseeable Mr. and Mrs. Copoc, whose son was killed, and Alexandra Penk, who lost her fiancé. In each of these cases the closest ties of love and affection fall to be presumed from the fact of the particular relationship, and there is no suggestion of anything which might tend to rebut that presumption. These three all watched scenes in Hillsborough on television, but none of these depicted suffering of recognisable individuals, such being excluded by the broadcasting code of ethics, a position known to the defendant. In my opinion the viewing of these scenes cannot be equiparated with the viewer being within "sight or hearing of the event or of its immediate aftermath", to use the words of Lord Wilberforce in *McLoughlin v. O'Brian*, nor can the scenes reasonably be regarded as giving rise to shock, in the sense of a sudden assault on the nervous system. They were capable of giving rise to anxiety for the safety of relatives known or believed to be present in the area affected by the crush, and undoubtedly did so, but that is very different from seeing the fate of the relative or his condition shortly after the event. The viewing of the television scenes did not create the necessary degree of proximity.

My Lords, for these reasons I would dismiss each of these appeals.

(j) *Corothers v. Slobodian*†

[RITCHIE J.:]

This is an appeal from a judgment of the Court of Appeal of Saskatchewan affirming the judgment rendered at trial by Mr. Justice C.S. Davis whereby he had dismissed the appellants' claim against all the respondents for damages sustained by Mrs. Corothers when she was struck by a semi-trailer truck operated by the respondent Slobodian and owned by J. Kearns Transport Ltd., while running along the side of the highway to seek aid for a man and his wife who had been seriously injured in a head-on collision between the Monarch car in which they were driving and a Volvo owned by the respondent Thomas Russell Poupard and driven by his son, who was unfortunately killed in the accident.

I have had the benefit of reading the reasons for judgment prepared for delivery by my brother Pigeon and I am, generally speaking, in accord with his careful analysis of the facts giving rise to the action which is the subject-matter of this appeal.

There does not appear to be any dispute about the fact that Neil Francis Poupard, who was driving his father's Volvo car in an easterly direction, was on his wrong side of the highway when he collided head-on with a Monarch driven by Anton Hammerschmid, and that his negligence was the sole cause of that collision.

The immediate results of the collision between the two vehicles are, as I have indicated, fully and accurately described in the reasons for judgment of my brother Pigeon and disclose that when Mrs. Corothers came upon the scene immediately after the impact she was faced with a situation of the utmost gravity, dead bodies were strewn over the highway which was also blocked by debris and the remains of the two vehicles. She turned her attention at once to the condition of the driver of the Monarch and his wife; the driver was unable to get to his feet, his face was covered with blood coming from his nose and eyes, he had difficulty in breathing and his leg was also bleeding profusely. His wife was lying partially on the floor of the car unconscious and making no sound except a low moan. The appellant's action in running up the highway to seek help as she did was, in my opinion, more than justified by the imminent peril in which she found the Hammerschmids. It was indeed a question of life and death as the subsequent death of Mrs. Hammerschmid [unhappily] demonstrated, and it was a situation for which the driver of the Volvo was solely responsible.

Mrs. Corothers was, in my opinion, a true "rescuer" as that role was described by Cardozo J. in *Wagner v. International R. Co. (N.Y.)*, where he said:

> Danger invites rescue. The cry of distress is the summons to relief. The law does not ignore these reactions of the mind in tracing conduct to its consequences. It recognises them as normal. It places their effects within the range of the natural and probable. The wrong that imperils life is a wrong to the imperilled victim; it is a wrong also to his rescuer ... The risk of rescue, if only it be not wanton, is born of the occasion. The emergency begets the man. The wrongdoer may not have foreseen the coming of a deliverer. He is accountable as if he had.

This language was expressly adopted by Willmer L.J. in *Baker v. T.E. Hopkins & Son Ltd.*

The duty of a wrongdoer to the rescuer of his victim was developed in the United States of America some time before it received authoritative approval in England where it had sometimes been held that the doctrine of voluntary assumption of risk could be invoked as a defence to the rescuer's claim, but in the case of *Haynes v. Harwood*, Greer L.J. accepted the American rule as stated by Professor Goodhart in the Cambridge Law Journal, vol. v., at p. 192, in the following terms:

> In accurately summing up the American authorities ... the learned author says this (p. 196): "The American rule is that the doctrine of the assumption of risk does not

---

† [1975] 2 S.C.R. 633 at 637–43.

apply where the plaintiff has, under an exigency caused by the defendant's wrongful misconduct, consciously and deliberately faced a risk, even of death, to rescue another from imminent danger of personal injury or death, whether the person endangered is one to whom he owes a duty of protection, as a member of his family, or is a mere stranger to whom he owes no such special duty." In my judgment that passage not only represents the law of the United States, but I think it also accurately represents the law of this country.

In commenting on the difficulties raised by some of the earlier authorities in defining the scope of the wrongdoer's duty in cases where the plaintiff has sustained injury in rescuing or attempting to rescue a victim from the consequences of the wrongdoing, Fleming in the 4th edition of his *Law of Torts* at p. 158 has this to say:

> These various difficulties are therefore best overcome by basing the rescuer's cause of action on the defendant's negligence, not in its tendency to imperil the person rescued, but in its tendency to induce the rescuer to encounter the danger. Thus viewed, the duty to the rescuer is clearly independent rather than derivative, and it becomes immaterial that the person to be rescued and the defendant are one and the same.

And the same learned author further states, at p. 159:

> Much like voluntary assumption of risk, so the plea of contributory negligence has also fallen into disfavour. Today, it stands no real chance of success unless the rescue attempt was utterly foolhardy.

This latter statement is supported also in the reasons for judgment of Willmer L.J. in *Baker v. T.E. Hopkins & Son Ltd.*, *supra*, at p. 981 where he says:

> Assuming the rescuer not to have acted unreasonably, therefore, it seems to me that he must normally belong to the class of persons who ought to be within the contemplation of the wrongdoer as being closely and directly affected by the latter's act.

The same thought was more fully expressed in a passage from the reasons for judgment of Lord Denning in *Videan v. British Transport Commission* [[1963] 2 Q.B. 650], at p. 669, which was expressly adopted in this Court in *Horsley v. MacLaren* [[1972] S.C.R. 441], at p. 444, and reads as follows:

> It seems to me that, if a person *by his fault* creates a situation of peril, he must answer for it to any person who attempts to rescue the person who is in danger. He owes a duty to such a person above all others. The rescuer may act instinctively out of humanity or deliberately out of courage. But whichever it is, so long as it is not wanton interference, if the rescuer is killed or injured in the attempt, he can recover damages *from the one whose fault has been the cause of it*.

In my opinion there was nothing wanton in Mrs. Corothers' behaviour in face of the peril to the Hammerschmids. The fact that she parked her car on the far left side of the highway is explained by the state of the highway at the scene after the collision and her action in going for help as she did and in attempting to flag down the approaching traffic, were, in my view, perfectly normal reactions to the cry of distress from the injured man and the situation which I have described.

In the course of his reasons for judgment in the Court of Appeal, Mr. Justice Woods had this to say:

> It is to be noted that the female plaintiff had completed all that she was going to do at the scene of the collision before the arrival of the truck driven by Slobodian. She had left the scene of the accident and her activities had reached a new stage. The situation of peril created by Poupard had ended. The plaintiff was not then acting in danger nor anticipating any danger created by the acts of Poupard. The injury suffered arose from a new act or circumstance, which was not one that ought reasonably to have been foreseeable by Poupard.

With the greatest respect for the views thus expressed I am unable to agree that "the situation of peril ... had ended" so long as Mr. Hammerschmid was seriously injured and apparently helpless and his wife near to death on the floor of the car due to Poupard's negligence. Mr. Justice Woods' approach appears to me to amount to a finding that Mrs. Corothers' actions constituted a *novus actus interveniens* breaking the chain of causation activated by the negligence of Poupard and it seems to me that this reasoning runs contrary to the principle now accepted in this country establishing the duty owing by a wrong-doer to the rescuer of a victim of his negligence and that Mrs.

Corothers, having been injured in an attempt to rescue such a victim "can recover damages from the one whose fault has been the cause of it."

The negligence in the driving of the Volvo gave rise to an independent and direct obligation to Mrs. Corothers which continued so long as she was engaged in her attempt at rescue, and unless it be accepted that this obligation did not extend beyond the time when she left the actual scene of the collision and that her injury was solely attributable to an intervening act of negligence by Slobodian, it must be concluded that, if Poupard's negligence was not the sole cause of the second accident, it was assuredly a cause which contributed to it in substantial degree. It should be observed that even if there was something wrongful about the conduct of Slobodian when faced with the gesticulating figure of Mrs. Corothers approaching on the edge of his right side of the highway, his actions were in any event such as to be a reasonably foreseeable consequence of the prior negligence of Poupard. In this regard some assistance is to be derived from the judgment of the High Court of Australia in *Chapman v. Hearse* [(1961), 106 C.L.R. 112], where a negligent driver (Chapman) had caused a motor vehicle collision in which he was thrown on to the highway and seriously injured and a passing motorist who happened to be a doctor, stopped to give him assistance when he was struck and killed by an approaching vehicle whose driver (Hearse) was also found to be negligent. The doctor's executors sued Hearse who claimed indemnity or contribution from Chapman, and whose claim was allowed to the extent of one-fourth of his damages both at trial and in the Supreme Court of South Australia. In dismissing the appeal, the High Court observed, at p. 125:

> There can, we think, be no doubt that Dr. Cherry's presence in the roadway was, immediately, the result of Chapman's negligent driving and if any support for this conclusion should be thought to be necessary ample can be found in the analogous so-called "rescue cases". The degree of risk which his presence in the roadway entailed depended, of course, on the circumstances as they in fact existed and the circumstances were, in fact, such that the risk of injury from passing traffic was real and substantial and not, as would have been the case if the accident had happened in broad daylight, remote and fanciful. Perhaps, some confirmation for the proposition that the risk was substantial may be found in the fact that within a minute or two, or even less, Dr. Cherry was run down by a driver whose vision of the roadway must have been impeded to a great extent by the prevailing conditions. In these circumstances, we have no doubt that Chapman's negligence must be regarded as a cause of Dr. Cherry's death and since, for the reasons which we have given, some casualty of that character was within the realm of reasonable foreseeability the judgment against Chapman should stand.

As I have indicated, the potential danger to which Mrs. Corothers was exposed by reason of her presence on the south shoulder of the highway was a reasonably foreseeable consequence of Poupard's negligence which in my view was a cause, if not the only cause, of Mrs. Corothers' injury.

(k) *Clarke v. Canada (TD)*†

NOTE

The plaintiff was an R.C.M.P. officer who resigned from the force in 1987, claiming that she was driven to do so as a result of stress and depression, which was triggered by sexual and other forms of harassment engaged in by her male colleagues and supervisors. Her first claim in the case was for wrongful dismissal, in effect arguing that her resignation constituted a constructive dismissal. The Court held that as an R.C.M.P. officer she did not have the status to sue on

---

† (1994), 3 C.C.E.L. (2d) 172 (Fed. Ct., T.D.).

an employment contract. Her second claim was based in tort, alleging both negligence and intentional infliction of nervous shock. The extracts below focus on the tort claims.

EXTRACT

[DUBÉ J.:]

. . . .

The plaintiff testified that she experienced problems in the traffic section under Corporal Warren McDonald's supervision, and that he showed favouritism to male members, and was unjustly critical of her performance. She also began to be subjected to unwelcome comments by male members on the general duty shift alongside which she frequently worked. She was told by the sergeant supervising this shift, in the presence of other members, that she wasn't a real woman until she had a child, that she should go home and start a family. Other members referred to her as a "butch" and a "metermaid." Such comments continued despite the plaintiff's objections.

On one occasion she was grabbed and kissed by a member who told her to call him when her husband was away if she wanted a real man. One night shift, a Corporal T.C. Steeves began viewing a pornographic movie in the same work area occupied by the plaintiff. She complained, and was told to "hit the road" if she didn't like it. The members on general duty told her bluntly they did not want her assistance on complaints called in, to mind her own business and stick to traffic work. The plaintiff found that the members responsible for the above actions were hostile toward her and other female members. She felt that she could not rely on them for assistance when needed and that she was not welcome on their shift.

In March 1984 the plaintiff was transferred back to general duties on Corporal Bruce Bishop's shift, under Sergeant Robert Williams' supervision. In September 1984, Corporal Fred Mazur replaced Cpl. Bishop as the plaintiff's supervisor. She remained on his shift until February 1987 and felt ostracized throughout that period. Harassing incidents continued. On one occasion, she arrived at her work station to find a pair of plastic breasts taped to her work station with her regimental number and "RCMP GIRL" written on them. Several male members present were laughing. The plaintiff complained to Cpl. Mazur who took no steps to discipline the constables. Cpl. Mazur testified that he could not say whether the breasts might be called offensive because he had not seen them.

On another occasion, members of the Force were displaying the centerfold of a *Playboy* magazine. When she objected to Cpl. Mazur, he told her they would appreciate it for her. There were also other incidents of pornographic movies being shown during night shifts. The plaintiff testified that sometimes Cpl. Mazur attended. A further gross experience occurred when a suit of soft body-armor she had ordered was placed in her basket in an open area of the detachment with "Your playtex cross your heart soft-armor bra" written on the packaging.

Many of these allegations were confirmed by the evidence of Linda Ley, a secretary at the detachment at the time, who said the plaintiff would come into her office crying and appeared to be depressed. According to Ms. Ley, some members were "cruel" to the plaintiff, and "there was almost an attempt made to isolate her, to not let her be part of the office, to exclude her." None of the male constables named by the plaintiff at the trial was called as a witness by the defendant. The plaintiff's superiors who were called to testify did not specifically deny any of these offensive incidents. Some of them criticized the plaintiff's own performance.

The plaintiff stated that the work environment caused her unhappiness and began to affect her health. In particular, she noticed a worsening of an exertion-related asthma condition which had developed in the Red Deer climate and for which she had been treated with medication since 1982 by Dr. R.C. Cooper. She no longer looked forward to going to work. She felt "like a piece of dirt."

. . . .

From 1985 to 1986, the work environment affected the plaintiff's performance. She became tentative, hesitant to handle complaints and investigations, and even found it difficult just to go to the office. At that stage, the plaintiff sensed there was no point in making a formal grievance as she would obtain no support from her superiors.

In addition, in June 1986 her first annual performance evaluation after the meeting with Insp. Pearson went down. Cpl. Mazur wrote that the plaintiff was a poor investigator; his concerns were concurred in by Sgt. Williams. However, in February 1985, the plaintiff had attended an investigator course run by experienced criminal investigators and was assessed as having better than average ability.

Cpl. Mazur, endorsed by Sgt. Williams, strongly recommended that the plaintiff be transferred to traffic or administration, where "she could do a good job." Insp. Pearson opposed the plaintiff's transfer, although Cpl. Mazur's recommendation would normally have been an important factor, because he "wasn't about to transfer a member with poor performance" to another detachment. If he had recommended the plaintiff's transfer to traffic section, it would have gone through, whereas without his recommendation, the chances of transfer were minimal.

On August 29, 1986, the plaintiff herself requested a transfer, citing asthma as the motivating factor, and met with Sgt. Williams at his request that same day. According to the plaintiff, he advised her that she could either quit, accept a medical discharge, or that he would see her fired by the end of the year. When asked how she remembered Sgt. Williams' options so clearly, the plaintiff stated that the final option he had presented shocked her so much that "it just burned in" her memory.

Sgt. Williams testified that he never uttered such threats but merely mentioned that the RCMP was not happy with her performance and that it was time for her to move on. It is significant that Sgt. Williams testified that he had kept notes of the meeting, but did not know where they were or if they had been destroyed.

At that time, many written comments and reprimands were being placed in her file. On her second working day following the meeting with Sgt. Williams, Cpl. Mazur issued three negative 1004s (unfavourable comments from her superiors as to her performance). In the ensuing period, she was inundated with negative 1004s.

Both the plaintiff and her husband testified to a deterioration in her condition from August 29, 1986. The latter stated that in the ensuing period he would arrive home from night shift to find the plaintiff had been sitting up in the dark all night crying. The plaintiff testified that her sleeping and eating were affected, she began to withdraw and couldn't stop crying.

. . . .

As a result [of a doctor's recommendation], on February 26, 1987 the plaintiff was posted temporarily to the Innisfail Freeway Patrol, where she performed "most satisfactorily." On April 22, 1987, she was transferred to the Beaverlodge Detachment. There, too, her supervisors found her work satisfactory in all respects. She was not subjected to any harassment at these two posts.

In May 1987, the plaintiff learned she was under investigation to determine whether criminal assault charges would be laid for incidents with prisoners occurring in 1982, 1983 and August 1986. Her uncontradicted testimony was that each one of these had been known to her superiors at the time of its occurrence. For example, the incident of August 1986 had been witnessed by other members, including Sgt. Williams, who stated that in his opinion as an experienced criminal investigator, the incident had not warranted the laying of criminal charges.

The plaintiff's husband testified that her condition, which had improved following her transfer away from Red Deer City, deteriorated markedly with news of the criminal investigation. The plaintiff stated that the investigation, coming at a time when she was doing well at Beaverlodge, away from the discrimination and stress of Red Deer, pushed her to the limit and left her no alternative but to resign. She felt the RCMP would "keep hounding after me and hounding after me until I finally leave." In July 1987 she resigned from the RCMP, giving asthma as the reason. When asked why she had done so, she stated "I just wanted to go. I didn't want to go into details any more. I just wanted some peace."

The plaintiff believed that if she quit, the criminal investigation would be dropped. However, in November 1987, she was charged with assault in relation to the 1982 and 1986 incidents. Again her condition deteriorated. In September 1988 the plaintiff underwent a jury trial and was found not guilty on both counts. None of the plaintiff's superiors testifying seems to know who laid these charges against her. Chief Superintendent R.K. Leatherdale speculated that the member named to conduct the internal criminal investigation was responsible.

My assessment of the evidence is that the plaintiff was in fact harassed by male constables and that her RCMP superiors failed to come to her assistance. I also find that the harassment was the major cause for her resignation. She did suffer from asthma and did indicate the condition was the reason for her transfer request. She also informed some people that she had resigned because of her sickness, but the real cause for her resignation was stress, depression and anxiety caused by harassment on the part of male members of the RCMP and failure to intervene by her superiors. I found her to be a credible witness.

Her own physician, Dr. Cooper, testified that her asthma could be aggravated by stress and that she was suffering from depression. He followed her from 1982 to 1987 and saw her situation worsen. This was confirmed by the report of the divisional Health Services officer, Dr. Shih, who described her condition in February 1987 as a "mental crisis."

. . . .

4.   LIABILITY IN TORT

. . . .

It is trite law that in order to engage the vicarious liability of the Crown, the plaintiff must establish, first, that a tort has been committed by a servant of the Crown, and second, that the tort was committed in the course of the servant's employment. In the instant case the plaintiff bases her claim on both intentional infliction of nervous shock and negligence. I will deal with each issue separately.

(i)   Intentional Infliction of Nervous Shock

As noted by Noël J. in the *Boothman* case, judicial recognition of this cause of action in tort originates with the *Wilkinson v. Downton* case, in which a practical joker informed a woman her husband had been seriously injured, thereby inducing a state of nervous shock and prolonged mental and physical suffering. In finding the defendant liable, Wright J. stated:

> The defendant has ... wilfully done an act calculated to cause physical harm to the plaintiff — that is, to infringe her legal right to personal safety, and has in fact thereby caused physical harm to her. That proposition, without more, appears to me to state a good cause of action, there being no justification alleged for the act. This wilful *injuria* is in law malicious, although no malicious purpose to cause the harm which was caused nor any motive of spite is imputed to the defendant.
>
> It is difficult to imagine that such a statement, made suddenly and with apparent seriousness, could fail to produce grave effects under the circumstances upon but an excep-

tionally indifferent person, and therefore an intention to produce such effect must be imputed, and it is no answer in law to say that more harm was done than was anticipated, for that is commonly the case with all wrongs. [Emphasis added.]

The *Wilkinson* principle was adopted and applied in a number of Canadian cases. In *Purdy*, the court found that an intention to cause the plaintiff nervous shock ought to be imputed to the defendant. In *Abramzik*, Culliton C.J.S. noted "there can be no doubt but that an action will lie for the wilful infliction of shock, or a reckless disregard as to whether or not shock will ensue from the act committed." In *Rahemtulla*, McLachlin J., as she then was, applied three criteria gleaned from prior cases: first, outrageous or flagrant and extreme conduct; second, conduct calculated "to produce some effect of the kind which was produced"; third, conduct producing actual harm, *i.e.*, a visible and provable illness. In *Timmermans*, Catzman J. found the defendant's limited intention and motivation did not relieve him from liability, particularly in light of his knowledge of the plaintiff's fragile emotional state.

The above cases involved single precipitating events. However, the recent *Boothman* decision on which the plaintiff relies concerned a course of harassing and intimidating conduct over a seven month period which caused a severe mental breakdown that was ongoing at the time of the trial seven years later. Noël J. found the defendant, who supervised the plaintiff and who was her sole co-worker, had hired the plaintiff because of her emotional vulnerability, exploited it in order to dominate her and, when that failed, drove her to breakdown and quit. He concluded that the supervisor's authority had been exercised wrongfully to inflict mental pain and suffering, to harass, humiliate, interfere with and assault the plaintiff. He found wilful *injuria* of the *Wilkinson* type, combined with malicious purpose owing to knowledge of the plaintiff's psychological fragility, and awarded damages for assault and intentional infliction of nervous shock, in addition to exemplary damages.

Doctrinal authorities have summarized principles arising from the case law as follows. Fridman states that:

> ... [T]he defendant may bring about such [emotional or mental] harm without any physical touching of the plaintiff, the absence of any threat to the plaintiff's physical safety, and without in any way infringing the plaintiff's

freedom of movement. It is essential that the defendant cause the harm by his own direct act.

Both extreme conduct and "objective and substantially harmful physical or psychopathological consequences," rather than "mere anguish or fright," are required in order for a cause of action to arise. As to the former, Linden notes that:

> ... The quality of outrageousness might ... be based on the special position of authority of the defendant. If a landlord, a police officer, or a school principal uttered insults or threats to someone over whose future well-being they had some control, these acts might be considered beyond the bounds of decency, and therefore actionable.

Prosser adds that:

> Another basis on which extreme outrage may be found lies in the defendant's knowledge that the plaintiff is especially sensitive, susceptible and vulnerable to injury through mental distress at the particular conduct....
>
> The gist of the outrage is the defendant's knowledge of the plaintiff's vulnerability, and where there is no such knowledge, conduct which is otherwise sufficiently extreme leads to no liability, even though the plaintiff may in fact suffer serious injury because of it.

Fleming comments on the international elements as follows:

> Cases will be rare where nervous shock involving physical injury was fully intended. More frequently, the defendant's aim would have been merely to frighten, terrify or alarm his victim. But this is quite sufficient, provided his conduct was of a kind reasonably capable of terrifying a normal person, or was known or ought to have been known to the defendant to be likely to terrify the plaintiff for reasons special to him. Such conduct could be described as reckless.
>
> ...
>
> "Calculated" to cause harm has not been narrowly interpreted.

Irvine suggests that the interpretation of the term "calculated" that accords best with its own use in Wilkinson and the subsequent case law is:

> ... that nervous shock or such like harm was not even reasonably foreseeable, given the defendant's limited knowledge of his victim's frailties; still less intended: but that some unwelcome, uncomfortable or unpleasant emotional apprehension or sensation ... was foreseen and intended, even though that apprehension or emotional discomfort so foreseen fell far short of the traumatic nervous shock in fact caused.

Irvine also cites case law to the effect that limitation of liability based on remoteness and lack of foreseeability is inapplicable in the field of intentional torts.

The case at hand involves a situation unlike those occurring in any of the decisions reviewed. First, several of the plaintiff's fellow members and superiors are involved, as opposed to a single individual. A further distinction is that here the impugned behaviour involves both a course of conduct on the part of a number of those individuals, as well as discrete acts or omissions on the part of the same or other individuals, over a four year period. Given this unique set of circumstances, I am nevertheless satisfied that the above authorities support the plaintiff's claim for intentional infliction of nervous shock, for reasons already given.

I am satisfied that the evidence reviewed above establishes that the conduct directed toward the plaintiff was extreme, and calculated "to produce some effect of the kind which was produced." I have also concluded that the plaintiff's mental and physical deterioration until her reassignment in February 1987 meets the third criterion outlined in *Rahemtulla*, *i.e.*, actual harm in the form of illness. In my view the plaintiff's condition, attested to by both Drs. Cooper and Shih, was analogous to those for which damages were awarded in that case and in the *Timmermans* case.

Further, the uncontradicted evidence concerning the plaintiff's condition in response to learning of the criminal investigation establishes that it, too, was more than "mere anguish and fright." That evidence is that the plaintiff's depression in Red Deer in 1986 was nothing compared to her depression when the investigation began. I note that in *Rahemtulla*, McLachlin J. found the plaintiff's response to the defendant's tortious conduct met the third criterion of actual harm despite the absence of expert medical evidence. Noël J. noted in *Boothman*, that the requirement that recognizable psychiatric illness be proven appears to be most stringently observed in claims for negligent infliction of nervous shock, which typically involve reactions to witnessing accidents or their victims, and in which the ordinary rules of negligence apply.

Having concluded the plaintiff was subjected to the intentional infliction of nervous shock by servants of the Crown, I must consider whether the tortious conduct occurred during the course of their employment. In my view, there can be no question that those acting in a supervisory capacity or in a position of authority with respect to the plaintiff were acting in the course of their employment. I concur with Noël J. in *Boothman* that there is

> ... no difference in law between the case of a servant who, entrusted with the supervision of personnel, abuses that authority in the manner described in these reasons, and that of a servant entrusted with the care of goods who converts those goods for his or her own use. In both cases, the wrong is directly attributable and connected to the duty or responsibility conferred on the servant.

With respect to the plaintiff's fellow members or peers, the question is:

> ... whether the activity was reasonably incidental to the performance of [their] authorized duties, or involved so substantial a departure that the servant must be regarded as a stranger *vis-à-vis* his master.

In my view, the impugned conduct toward the plaintiff occurred strictly within the confines of the working relationship and was occasioned by it. I find that the servants of the Crown were acting during the course of employment.

(ii) Negligence

. . . .

... In my view there is no doubt that as the plaintiff's immediate supervisor, Cpl. Mazur owed the plaintiff a duty of care and breached that duty consistently. I find that over a lengthy period, he deliberately refused to exercise his authority to put an end to the conduct of harassment of which he was well aware and which he in fact participated in on occasion, thus condoning that behaviour. He further neglected utterly to respond to the plaintiff's distress signals as his position of responsibility required him to do. And, as mentioned earlier, superior RCMP officers failed to come to the plaintiff's assistance.

In my view, the circumstances of this case present no issue of remoteness or foreseeability. Cpl. Mazur was not an unconcerned bystander without authority to exert control over the behav-

iour of his subordinates; his negligence played a direct causative role in the damage suffered by the plaintiff, and he was clearly acting in the course of his employment.

. . . .

6. DAMAGES

. . . .

Based on the plaintiff's figures, I have concluded $88,000 is suitable award for lost earnings from September 1987 to September 1990. I have arrived at this figure on the basis that no award should be made for 1987, the final months of which the plaintiff testified she simply "took off."

. . . .

In the determining an appropriate award for pain and suffering in the present case, I have taken into account evidence of the plaintiff's condition during her final year on the force and her efforts to attenuate her difficulties with professional assistance provided by, or on referral by, RCMP services. I have also considered the plaintiff's testimony that she did not recover from her experiences on the force for three years, but that over that period she did not seek any professional assistance to relieve her problems or to assist her in speeding up the recovery process. In my view the fact that she did not actively seek out psychological or psychiatric help does not represent a failure to mitigate analogous to actual refusal of offers of professional help, but is still a factor to be weighed.

As Noël J., noted in *Boothman*, precise measurement of non-pecuniary damages is always difficult. However, taking into account previous awards for intentional infliction of nervous shock, I am of the view that, as in those cases, $5,000 will provide the plaintiff "a reasonable measure of consolation" for her injured dignity arising from that tortious conduct.

CONCLUSION

Judgment is awarded to the plaintiff in the amount of $93,000, being $88,000 for special damages for lost earnings, and $5,000 for general damages. She will also receive interest calculated pursuant to the provisions of the *Alberta Judgment Interest Act*.

(I) *Bazley v. Curry*†

[McLACHLIN J.:]

I. INTRODUCTION

It is tragic but true that people working with the vulnerable sometimes abuse their positions and commit wrongs against the very people they are engaged to help. The abused person may later seek to recover damages for the wrong. But judgment against the wrongdoer may prove a hollow remedy. This raises the question of whether the organization that employed the offender should be held liable for the wrong. The law refers to such liability as "vicarious" liability. It is also known as "strict" or "no-fault" liability, because it is imposed in the absence of fault of the employer. The issue in this case is whether such liability lies for an employee's sexual abuse of children in his care.

II. FACTS

The appellant, the Children's Foundation, is a non-profit organization. It operated two residential care facilities for the treatment of emotionally troubled children between the ages of six and twelve. As substitute parent, it practised "total intervention" in all aspects of the lives of the children it cared for. The Foundation authorized its employees to act as parent figures for the children. It charged them to care for the children physically, mentally and emotionally. The employees were to do everything a parent would do, from general supervision to intimate duties like bathing and tucking in at bedtime.

The Foundation hired Mr. Curry, a paedophile, to work in its Vancouver home. The Foundation did not know he was a paedophile. It checked and was told he was a suitable employee. Into this environment, too, came the child Patrick Bazley, young and emotionally vulnerable. Curry began a seduction. Over the months, step by subtle step, bathing became sexual exploration; tucking in in a darkened room became sexual abuse.

Someone complained about Curry. The Foundation inquired and upon verifying that Curry had abused a child in one of its homes, immediately discharged him. In 1992, Curry was convicted of 19 counts of sexual abuse, two of which related to Bazley. Curry has since died.

Bazley sued the Foundation for compensation for the injury he suffered while in its care. The Foundation took the position that since it had committed no fault in hiring or supervising Curry, it was not legally responsible for what he had done. The parties stated a case to determine whether (assuming the appellant was not, in fact, negligent) the appellant was nonetheless vicariously liable for its employee's tortious conduct. The chambers judge found that it was and the Court of Appeal dismissed the appeal.

. . . . .

V. ANALYSIS

A. May Employers Be Held Vicariously Liable for Their Employees' Sexual Assaults on Clients or Persons Within Their Care?

Both parties agree that the answer to this question is governed by the "Salmond" test, which posits that employers are vicariously liable for (1) employee acts authorized by the employer; or (2) unauthorized acts so connected with authorized acts that they may be regarded as modes (albeit improper modes) of doing an authorized act. Both parties also agree that we are here concerned with the second branch of the test. They diverge, however, on what the second branch of the test means. The Foundation says that its employee's sexual assaults of Bazley were not "modes" of doing an authorized act. Bazley, on the other hand, submits that the assaults were a mode of performing authorized tasks, and that courts have often found employers vicariously liable for intentional wrongs of employees comparable to sexual assault.

---

† (June 17, 1999) File No. 26013 (S.C.C.).

1 Previous Cases

. . . .

Looking at these three general classes of cases in which employers have been held vicariously liable for employees' unauthorized torts, one sees a progression from accidents, to accident-like intentional torts, to torts that bear no relationship to either agency-like conduct or accident. In search of a unifying principle, one asks what the three classes of cases have in common. At first glance, it may seem little. Yet with the benefit of hindsight it is possible to posit one common feature: in each case it can be said that the employer's enterprise had created the risk that produced the tortious act. The language of "furtherance of the employer's aims" and the employer's creation of "a situation of friction" may be seen as limited formulations of the concept of enterprise risk that underlies the dishonest employee cases. The common theme resides in the idea that where the employee's conduct is closely tied to a risk that the employer's enterprise has placed in the community, the employer may justly be held vicariously liable for the employee's wrong.

If employers are vicariously liable for acts like employee theft, why not for sexual abuse? That was the question before the English Court of Appeal in *S.T. v. North Yorkshire County Council*, where the court applied the Salmond test to reverse a finding of vicarious liability against a school council for a teacher who sexually accosted a mentally handicapped student during a school field trip to the continent. It held that the sexual tort was not an unauthorized mode of performing an authorized act; it was an independent act, outside the scope of the teacher's authority. The court recognized the difficulty of saying that some intentional acts, like a store clerk's assault, do not attract vicarious liability, while other intentional acts, like theft, do. In the end, however, it did not confront the underlying policy of vicarious liability, preferring to reason that sexual abuse was closer to the store clerk's assault than to a solicitor's clerk's theft. It interpreted the stolen property cases of *Levy Brothers* and *Lloyd*, thought by many to be developing law, as a minor off-shoot of a line of cases concerning entrustment of goods — a departure from the "general" rule.

The *S.T.* decision thus fails to successfully integrate the dishonest employee cases. It also rests on the questionable conclusion that sexual torts by caretakers against children are closer to a shop assault than a bank employee's conversion. (While a molestation is a physical attack, it is equally arguable that the trust-abusing character of child abuse fits more in the dishonesty genre.) Furthermore, the opinion's reasoning depends on the level of generality with which the sexual act is described. Instead of describing the act in terms of the employee's duties of supervising and caring for vulnerable students during a study trip abroad, the Court of Appeal cast it in terms unrelated to those duties. Important legal decisions should not turn on such semantics. As Atiyah points out: "conduct can be correctly described at varying levels of generality, and no one description of the 'act' on which the servant was engaged is necessarily more correct than any other". Finally, the reasoning in *S.T.* leads to anomalies. Lowry J.'s question in the chambers decision appealed from (at p. 223) remains unanswered: "If a postal clerk's theft and a solicitor's clerk's fraud can be said to have been committed in the course of their employment, I can see no sound basis in principle on which it can be concluded that Curry's criminal conduct should not attract vicarious liability". Or, as Wilkinson J. expressed more bluntly in the companion appeal (*G.J. v. Griffiths*, "[s]urely a distinction is not to be drawn attributing a higher standard to the way society looks after its jewellery than its children."

To return to the approach suggested earlier, precedent does not resolve the issue before us. We must therefore proceed to the second stage of the inquiry — a consideration of the policy reasons for vicarious liability, in the hope of discerning a principle to guide courts in future cases.

2 Policy Considerations

Vicarious liability has always been concerned with policy. The view of early English law that a master was responsible for all the wrongs of his servants (as well as his wife's and his children's) represented a policy choice, however inarticulate, as to who should bear the loss of wrongdoing and how best to deter it. The narrowing of vicarious responsibility with the expansion of commerce and trade and the rise of industrialism also represented a policy choice. Indeed, it represented a compromise between two policies — the social interest in furnishing an innocent tort victim with recourse against a financially responsible defendant, and a concern not to foist undue burdens on business enterprises. The expansion of vicarious liability in the 20th century from authorization-based liability to broader classes of ascription is doubtless driven by yet other policy concerns. "[V]icarious liability cannot parade as a deduction from legalistic premises, but should be frankly recognized as having its basis in a combination of policy considerations".

A focus on policy is not to diminish the importance of legal principle. It is vital that the courts attempt to articulate general legal principles to lend certainty to the law and guide future applications. However, in areas of jurisprudence where changes have been occurring in response to policy considerations, the best route to enduring principle may well lie through policy. The law of vicarious liability is just such a domain.

Recognizing the policy-driven perspective of the law of vicarious liability, La Forest J. in *London Drugs, supra*, opined that vicarious liability was traditionally considered to rest on one of two logical bases: (1) that the employee's acts are regarded in law as being authorized by the employer and hence as being the employer's acts (the "master's tort theory" or "direct liability theory"); or (2) that the employer was the employee's superior in charge or command of the employee (the "servant's tort theory"). La Forest J., quoting Fridman, went on to note, however, that "neither of the logical bases for vicarious liability succeeds completely in explaining the operation of the doctrine ... express[ing] 'not so much the true rationale of vicarious liability but an attempt by the law to give some formal, technical explanation of why the law imposes vicarious liability'" (p. 336). Faced with the absence in the existing law of a coherent principle to explain vicarious liability, La Forest J. found its basis in policy: "[T]he vicarious liability regime is best seen as a response to a number of policy concerns. In its traditional domain, these are primarily linked to compensation, deterrence and loss internalization."

Fleming has identified similar policies lying at the heart of vicarious liability. In his view, two fundamental concerns underlie the imposition of vicarious liability: (1) provision of a just and practical remedy for the harm; and (2) deterrence of future harm. While different formulations of the policy interests at stake may be made (for example, loss internalization is a hybrid of the two), I believe that these two ideas usefully embrace the main policy considerations that have been advanced.

First and foremost is the concern to provide a just and practical remedy to people who suffer as a consequence of wrongs perpetrated by an employee. Fleming expresses this succinctly: "a person who employs others to advance his own economic interest should in fairness be placed under a corresponding liability for losses incurred in the course of the enterprise". The idea that the person who introduces a risk incurs a duty to those who may be injured lies at the heart of tort law. As Cardozo C.J. stated in *Palsgraf v. Long Island R. Co.*, "[t]he risk reasonably to be perceived defines the duty to be obeyed, and risk imports relation; it is risk to another or to others within the range of apprehension." This principle of fairness applies to the employment enterprise and hence to the issue of vicarious liability. While charitable enterprises may not employ people to advance their economic interests, other factors, discussed below, make it fair that they should bear the burden of providing a just and practical remedy for wrongs perpetrated by their employees. This policy interest embraces a number of subsidiary goals. The first is the goal of effective compensation. "One of the most important social goals served by vicarious liability is victim compensation. Vicarious liability improves the chances that the victim can recover the judgment from a solvent defendant." Or to quote Fleming, the master is "a more promising source of recompense than his servant who is apt to be a man of straw".

. . . .

The second major policy consideration underlying vicarious liability is deterrence of future harm. Fixing the employer with responsibility for the employee's wrongful act, even where the employer is not negligent, may have a deterrent effect. Employers are often in a position to reduce accidents and intentional wrongs by efficient organization and supervision. Failure to take such measures may not suffice to establish a case of tortious negligence directly against the employer. Perhaps the harm cannot be shown to have been foreseeable under negligence law. Perhaps the employer can avail itself of the defence of compliance with the industry standard. Or perhaps the employer, while complying with the standard of reasonable care, was not as scrupulously diligent as it might feasibly have been. As Wilkinson J. explained in the companion appeal's trial judgment:

> If the scourge of sexual predation is to be
> stamped out, or at least controlled, there must
> be powerful motivation acting upon those who
> control institutions engaged in the care, protec-
> tion and nurturing of children. That motivation
> will not in my view be sufficiently supplied by

the likelihood of liability in negligence. In many cases evidence will be lacking or have long since disappeared. The proof of appropriate standards is a difficult and uneven matter.

I agree. Beyond the narrow band of employer conduct that attracts direct liability in negligence lies a vast area where imaginative and efficient administration and supervision can reduce the risk that the employer has introduced into the community. Holding the employer vicariously liable for the wrongs of its employee may encourage the employer to take such steps, and hence, reduce the risk of future harm. A related consideration raised by Fleming is that by holding the employer liable, "the law furnishes an incentive to discipline servants guilty of wrongdoing" (p. 410).

The policy grounds supporting the imposition of vicarious liability — fair compensation and deterrence — are related. The policy consideration of deterrence is linked to the policy consideration of fair compensation based on the employer's introduction or enhancement of a risk. The introduction of the enterprise into the community with its attendant risk, in turn, implies the possibility of managing the risk to minimize the costs of the harm that may flow from it.

Policy considerations relating to the fair allocation of loss to risk-creating enterprises and the deterrence of harms tend to support the imposition of vicarious liability on employers. But, as Fleming notes, there often exists a countervailing concern. At one time the law held masters responsible for *all* wrongs committed by servants. Later, that policy was abandoned as too harsh in a complex commercial society where masters might not be in a position to supervise their servants closely. Servants may commit acts, even on working premises and during working hours, which are so unconnected with the employment that it would seem unreasonable to fix an employer with responsibility for them. For example, if a man assaults his wife's lover (who coincidentally happens to be a co-worker) in the employees' lounge at work, few would argue that the employer should be held responsible. Similarly, an employer would not be liable for the harm caused by a security guard who decides to commit arson for his or her own amusement: see, e.g., *Plains Engineering Ltd. v. Barnes Security Services Ltd.* (1987), 43 C.C.L.T. 129 (Alta. Q.B.).

On further analysis, however, this apparently negative policy consideration of when liability would be appropriate is revealed as nothing more than the absence of the twin policies of fair compensation and deterrence that justify vicarious liability. A wrong that is only coincidentally linked to the activity of the employer and duties of the employee cannot justify the imposition of vicarious liability on the employer. To impose vicarious liability on the employer for such a wrong does not respond to common sense notions of fairness. Nor does it serve to deter future harms. Because the wrong is essentially independent of the employment situation, there is little the employer could have done to prevent it. Where vicarious liability is not closely and materially related to a risk introduced or enhanced by the employer, it serves no deterrent purpose, and relegates the employer to the status of an involuntary insurer. I conclude that a meaningful articulation of when vicarious liability should follow in new situations ought to be animated by the twin policy goals of fair compensation and deterrence that underlie the doctrine, rather than by artificial or semantic distinctions.

3   From Precedent and Policy to Principle

.   .   .   .

Reviewing the jurisprudence, and considering the policy issues involved, I conclude that in determining whether an employer is vicariously liable for an employee's unauthorized, intentional wrong in cases where precedent is inconclusive, courts should be guided by the following principles:

(1) They should openly confront the question of whether liability should lie against the employer, rather than obscuring the decision beneath semantic discussions of "scope of employment" and "mode of conduct".

(2) The fundamental question is whether the wrongful act is *sufficiently related* to conduct authorized by the employer to justify the imposition of vicarious liability. Vicarious liability is generally appropriate where there is a significant connection between the *creation or enhancement of a risk* and the wrong that accrues therefrom, even if unrelated to the employer's desires. Where this is so, vicarious liability will serve the policy considerations of provision of an adequate and just remedy and deterrence. Incidental connections to the employment enterprise, like time and place (without more), will not suffice. Once engaged in a particular business, it is

169

fair that an employer be made to pay the generally foreseeable costs of that business. In contrast, to impose liability for costs unrelated to the risk would effectively make the employer an involuntary insurer.

(3) In determining the sufficiency of the connection between the *employer's creation or enhancement of the risk* and the wrong complained of, subsidiary factors may be considered. These may vary with the nature of the case. When related to intentional torts, the relevant factors may include, but are not limited to, the following:

   (a) the opportunity that the enterprise afforded the employee to abuse his or her power;

   (b) the extent to which the wrongful act may have furthered the employer's aims (and hence be more likely to have been committed by the employee);

   (c) the extent to which the wrongful act was related to friction, confrontation or intimacy inherent in the employer's enterprise;

   (d) the extent of power conferred on the employee in relation to the victim;

   (e) the vulnerability of potential victims to wrongful exercise of the employee's power.

Applying these general considerations to sexual abuse by employees, there must be a strong connection between what the employer was asking the employee to do (the risk created by the employer's enterprise) and the wrongful act. It must be possible to say that the employer *significantly* increased the risk of the harm by putting the employee in his or her position and requiring him to perform the assigned tasks. The policy considerations that justify imposition of vicarious liability for an employee's sexual misconduct are unlikely to be satisfied by incidental considerations of time and place. For example, an incidental or random attack by an employee that merely happens to take place on the employer's premises during working hours will scarcely justify holding the employer liable. Such an attack is unlikely to be related to the business the employer is conducting or what the employee was asked to do and, hence, to any risk that was created. Nor is the imposition of liability likely to have a significant deterrent effect; short of closing the premises or discharging all employees, little can be done to avoid the random wrong. Nor is foreseeability of harm used in negligence law the

test. What is required is a material increase in the risk as a consequence of the employer's enterprise and the duties he entrusted to the employee, mindful of the policies behind vicarious liability.

What factors are relevant to whether an employer's enterprise has introduced or significantly exacerbated a risk of sexual abuse by an employee? (Again, I speak generally, supplementing the factors suggested above.) It is obvious that the risk of an employee sexually abusing a child may be materially enhanced by giving the employee an opportunity to commit the abuse. There are many kinds of opportunity and the nature of the opportunity in a particular case must be carefully evaluated in determining whether it has, in fact, materially increased the risk of the harm that ensued. If an employee is permitted or required to be with children for brief periods of time, there may be a small risk of such harm — perhaps not much greater than if the employee were a stranger. If an employee is permitted or required to be alone with a child for extended periods of time, the opportunity for abuse may be greater. If in addition to being permitted to be alone with a child for extended periods, the employee is expected to supervise the child in intimate activities like bathing or toiletting, the opportunity for abuse becomes greater still. As the opportunity for abuse becomes greater, so the risk of harm increases.

The risk of harm may also be enhanced by the nature of the relationship the employment establishes between the employee and the child. Employment that puts the employee in a position of intimacy and power over the child (i.e., a parent-like, role-model relationship) may enhance the risk of the employee feeling that he or she is able to take advantage of the child and the child submitting without effective complaint. The more the employer encourages the employee to stand in a position of respect and suggests that the child should emulate and obey the employee, the more the risk may be enhanced. In other words, the more an enterprise requires the exercise of power or authority for its successful operation, the more materially likely it is that an abuse of that power relationship can be fairly ascribed to the employer. See *Boothman v. Canada, supra*.

Other factors may be important too, depending on the nature of the case. To require or permit an employee to touch the client in intimate body zones may enhance the risk of sexual touching, just as permitting an employee to handle large sums of money may enhance the risk of embezzlement or conversion. This is the common sense core of the "mode of conduct" argument accepted by the trial judge in this case. (The same factor might of course be analyzed in terms of enhanced opportunity.) Time and place arguments may also be relevant in particular cases. The mere fact that the wrong occurred during working hours or on the jobsite may not, standing alone, be of much importance; the assessment of material increase in risk cannot be resolved by the mechanical application of spatial and temporal factors. This said, spatial and temporal factors may tend to *negate* the suggestion of materially enhanced risk of harm, insofar as they suggest that the conduct was essentially unrelated to the employment and any enhanced risk it may have created (for example, the employee's tort occurred offsite and after hours). The policy considerations of fair compensation and deterrence upon which vicarious liability is premised may be attenuated or completely eliminated in such circumstances.

In summary, the test for vicarious liability for an employee's sexual abuse of a client should focus on whether the employer's enterprise and empowerment of the employee materially increased the risk of the sexual assault and hence the harm. The test must not be applied mechanically, but with a sensitive view to the policy considerations that justify the imposition of vicarious liability — fair and efficient compensation for wrong and deterrence. This requires trial judges to investigate the employee's specific duties and determine whether they gave rise to special opportunities for wrongdoing. Because of the peculiar exercises of power and trust that pervade cases such as child abuse, special attention should be paid to the existence of a power or dependency relationship, which on its own often creates a considerable risk of wrongdoing.

(a) *Andrews v. Grand & Toy Alberta Ltd.*[†]

[DICKSON J.:]

This is a negligence action for personal injury involving a young man rendered a quadriplegic in a traffic accident for which the respondent Anderson and his employer, Grand & Toy Alberta Ltd., have been found partially liable. Leave to appeal to this Court was granted on the question of whether the Appellate Division of the Supreme Court of Alberta erred in law in the assessment of damages. At trial Mr. Justice Kirby awarded $1,022,477.48; the Appellate Division reduced the sum to $516,544.48.

. . . .

The method of assessing general damages in separate amounts, as has been done in this case, in my opinion, is a sound one. It is the only way in which any meaningful review of the award is possible on appeal and the only way of affording reasonable guidance in future cases. Equally important, it discloses to the litigants and their advisers the components of the overall award, assuring them thereby that each of the various heads of damage going to make up the claim has been given thoughtful consideration.

The subject of damages for personal injury is an area of the law which cries out for legislative reform. The expenditure of time and money in the determination of fault and of damage is prodigal.

The disparity resulting from lack of provision for victims who cannot establish fault must be disturbing. When it is determined that compensation is to be made, it is highly irrational to be tied to a lump-sum system and a once-and-for-all award.

The lump-sum award presents problems of great importance. It is subject to inflation, it is subject to fluctuation on investment, income from it is subject to tax. After judgement, new needs of the plaintiff arise and present needs are extinguished; yet, our law of damages knows nothing of periodic payment. The difficulties are greatest where there is a continuing need for intensive and expensive care and a long-term loss of earning capacity. It should be possible to devise some system whereby payments would be subject to periodic review and variation in the light of the continuing needs of the injured person and the cost of meeting those needs. In making this comment I am not unaware of the negative recommendation of the British Law Commission (Law Com. 56 — *Report on Personal Injury Litigation — Assessment of Damages*) following strong opposition from insurance interests and the plaintiffs' bar.

The apparent reliability of assessments provided by modern actuarial practice is largely illusionary, for actuarial science deals with probabilities, not actualities. This is in no way to denigrate a respected profession, but it is obvious that the validity of the answers given by the actuarial witness, as with a computer, depends upon the soundness of the postulates from which he proceeds.

---

† (1978), 83 D.L.R. (3d) 452 at 456–59, 475–78.

Although a useful aid, and a sharper tool than the "multiplier-multiplicand" approach favoured in some jurisdictions, actuarial evidence speaks in terms of group experience. It cannot, and does not purport to, speak as to the individual sufferer. So long as we are tied to lump-sum awards, however, we are tied also to actuarial calculations as the best available means of determining amount.

In spite of these severe difficulties with the present law of personal injury compensation, the positive administrative machinery required for a system of reviewable periodic payments, and the need to hear all interested parties in order to fashion a more enlightened system, both dictate that the appropriate body to act must be the Legislature, rather than the Courts. Until such time as the Legislature acts, the Courts must proceed on established principles to award damages which compensate accident victims with justice and humanity for the losses they may suffer.

. . . .

NON-PECUNIARY LOSSES

Andrews used to be a healthy young man, athletically active and socially congenial. Now he is a cripple, deprived of many of life's pleasures and subjected to pain and disability. For this, he is entitled to compensation. But the problem here is qualitatively different from that of pecuniary losses. There is no medium of exchange for happiness. There is no market for expectation of life. The monetary evaluation of non-pecuniary losses is a philosophical and policy exercise more than a legal or logical one. The award must be fair and reasonable, fairness being gauged by earlier decisions; but the award must also of necessity be arbitrary or conventional. No money can provide true restitution. Money can provide for proper care: this is the reason that I think the paramount concern of the Courts when awarding damages for personal injuries should be to assure that there will be adequate future care.

However, if the principle of paramountcy of care is accepted, then it follows that there is more room for the consideration of other policy factors in the assessment of damages for non-pecuniary losses. In particular, this is the area where the social burden of the large awards deserves considerable weight. The sheer fact is that there is no objective yardstick for translating non-pecuniary losses, such as pain and suffering and loss of amenities, into monetary terms. This area is open to widely extravagant claims. It is in this area that awards in the United States have soared to dramatically high levels in recent years. Statistically, it is the area where the danger of excessive burden of expense is greatest.

It is also the area where there is the clearest justification for moderation. As one English commentator has suggested, there are three theoretical approaches to the problem of non-pecuniary loss. The first, the "conceptual" approach, treats each faculty as a proprietary asset with an objective value, independent of the individual's own use or enjoyment of it. This was the ancient "bot", or tariff system, which prevailed in the days of King Alfred, when a thumb was worth 30 shillings. Our law has long since thought such a solution unsubtle. The second, the "personal" approach, values the injury in terms of the loss of human happiness by the particular victim. The third, or "functional" approach, accepts the personal premise of the second, but rather than attempting to set a value on lost happiness, it attempts to assess the compensation required to provide the injured person "with reasonable solace for his misfortune". "Solace" in this sense is taken to mean physical arrangements which can make his life more endurable rather than "solace" in the sense of sympathy. To my mind, this last approach has much to commend it, as it provides a rationale as to why money is considered compensation for non-pecuniary losses such as loss of amenities, pain and suffering, and loss of expectation of life. Money is awarded because it will serve a useful function in making up for what has been lost in the only way possible, accepting that what has been lost is incapable of being replaced in any direct way. As Windeyer, J., said in *Skelton v. Collins, supra,* at p. 495:

> ... he is, I do not doubt, entitled to compensation for what he suffers. Money may be compensation for him if having it can give him pleasure or satisfaction.... But the money is not then a recompense for a loss of something having a money value. It is given as some consolation or solace for the distress that is the consequence of a loss on which no monetary value can be put.

If damages for non-pecuniary loss are viewed from a functional perspective, it is reasonable that large amounts should not be awarded once a person is properly provided for in terms of future care for his injuries and disabilities. The money for future care is to provide physical arrangements for assistance, equipment and facilities directly related to the injuries. Additional money to make life more endurable should then be seen as providing more general physical arrangements above and beyond those relating directly to the injuries. The result is a coordinated and interlocking basis for compensation, and a more rational justification for non-pecuniary loss compensation.

However one may view such awards in a theoretical perspective, the amounts are still largely arbitrary or conventional. As Lord Denning, M.R., said in *Ward v. James*, [1965] 1 All E.R. 563, there is a great need in this area for assessability, uniformity and predictability. In my opinion, this does not mean that the courts should not have regard to the individual situation of the victim. On the contrary, they must do so to determine what has been lost. For example, the loss of a finger would be a greater loss of amenities for an amateur pianist than for a person not engaged in such an activity. Greater compensation would be required to provide things and activities which would function to make up for this loss. But there should be guidelines for the translation into monetary terms of what has been lost. There must be an exchange rate, albeit conventional. In *Warren v. King, supra*, at p. 528 the following dictum of Harman, L.J., appears, which I would adopt, in respect of the assessment of non-pecuniary loss for a living plaintiff:

> It seems to me that the first element in assessing such compensation is not to add up items as loss of pleasures, of earnings, of marriage prospects, of children and so on, but to consider the matter from the other side, what can be done to alleviate the disaster to the victim, what will it cost to enable her to live as tolerably as may be in the circumstances.

Cases like the present enable the Court to establish a rough upper parameter on these awards. It is difficult to conceive of a person of his age losing more than Andrews has lost. Of course, the figures must be viewed flexibly in future cases in recognition of the inevitable differences in injuries, the situation of the victim, and changing economic conditions.

The amounts of such awards should not vary greatly from one part of the country to another. Everyone in Canada, wherever he may reside, is entitled to a more or less equal measure of compensation for similar non-pecuniary loss. Variation should be made for what a particular individual has lost in the way of amenities and enjoyment of life, and for what will function to make up for this loss, but variation should not be made merely for the Province in which he happens to live.

. . . .

There is an extensive review of authorities in the Court of Appeal judgement in this case as well as in the *Thornton* and *Teno* cases, *supra*, to which I have referred. I need not review these past authorities. What is important is the general picture. It is clear that until very recently damages for non-pecuniary losses, even from very serious injuries such as quadriplegia, were substantially below $100,000. Recently, though, the figures have increased markedly. In *Jackson v. Millar et al.* (1975), 59 D.L.R. (3d) 246, [1976] 1 S.C.R. 225, this Court affirmed a figure of $150,000 for non-pecuniary loss in an Ontario case of a paraplegic. However, this was done essentially on the principle of non-interference with awards allowed by provincial Courts of Appeal. The need for a general assessment with respect to damages for non-pecuniary loss, which is now apparent, was not as evident at that time. Even in Ontario, prior to these recent cases, general damages allocable for non-pecuniary loss, such as pain and suffering and loss of amenities, were well below $100,000.

In the present case, $150,000 was awarded at trial, but this amount was reduced to $100,000 by the Appellate Division. In *Thornton* and *Teno* $200,000 was awarded in each case, unchanged in the provincial Courts of Appeal.

I would adopt as the appropriate award in the case of a young adult quadriplegic like Andrews the amount of $100,000. Save in exceptional circumstances, this should be regarded as an upper limit of non-pecuniary loss in cases of this nature.

(b) A Critique of American Tort Law†

Richard L. Abel

TORT LAW AND CAPITALISM

Tort law is intimately related to the rise of capitalism as both cause and effect. Because capitalism separates those who produce from those who own the means of production workers lose control over their own safety. Because capitalists have to maximize profit in a competitive market they *must* sacrifice the health and safety of others — workers, consumers, those affected by environmental danger. Tort law has reflected this compulsion in many ways: the choice of negligence over strict liability, the fellow-servant rule and assumption of risk, exculpatory clauses, the lower standard of care for landowners and professionals. Capitalism fosters injury for another reason: it must constantly expand its markets and increase consumption; torts contribute to this end, just like planned obsolescence and warfare.

. . . .

CRITIQUE OF TORT LAW

Discriminating Against Class, Race, and Gender

Liberal legalism, the dominant political philosophy under capitalism, decries explicit, de jure discrimination. Therefore tort law gradually eliminates distinctions between patients who are injured in charitable and in profit-making hospitals, fee paying automobile passengers and gratuitous guests, business and social guests injured by landowner negligence, those injured by medical malpractice and other tort victims. But insistence on superficial equality hides the persistence of numerous invisible inequalities. First (and foremost) there is inequality in the incidence of injury and illness: capitalists, professionals, white, pink, and blue collar workers are exposed to vastly different hazards in the workplace; consumers (of household goods, foods, auto-

mobiles, medical care, etc.) suffer different risks of injury depending on the quality of the products and services they buy (necessarily a reflection of class); residential segregation by class determines the level of environmental pollution that members of a household will endure. For the same reasons, ethnic differences in employment, consumption, and residence will produce racial inequalities in incidence. Women are exposed to more dangers in the home than are men, but conversely may be "protected" from hazards at work by being excluded from dangerous jobs with higher pay and status.

Second, class, race, and gender will affect the extent to which and the way in which the experience of injury is transformed into a claim for legal redress: the sense of entitlement to physical, mental, and emotional well-being (women only recently began to resist abuse by their husbands; textile workers are just now coming to view chronic shortness of breath as unnatural) the feeling of competence to assert a claim and to withstand retaliation; the capacity to mobilize the legal process, which includes choosing and controlling a lawyer and preparing evidence; and financial and emotional resources, which will affect the quality of legal representation obtained and the ability of the claimant to overcome opposition and delay in order to pursue negotiation or litigation to a satisfactory conclusion.

Third, the law discriminates in the availability and generosity of the remedies it offers. The greatest difference is between tort damages and other compensation systems. An injured blue-collar worker is far more likely than someone from another occupational category to be relegated to workers' compensation, which pays only a fraction of tort damages and rejects some tortious injuries altogether. But other oppressed categories — the poor, the elderly, women, children, and ethnic minorities — are also excluded from tort recovery. Thus the victims of violent crimes, whose assailants

† (1981) 8:2 *British Journal of Law and Society* at 199, 201—204, 206, 209—10. [Notes and/or References omitted.] Reproduced with permission of British Journal of Law and Society, Cardiff Law School, Cardiff University and the author.

are unidentifiable or judgment proof, are relegated to state compensation schemes that reach very few victims and pay even them inadequate amounts. Women and children who are injured by intimates are left without any remedy. The poor and minorities, who either cannot evade the draft or enlist in the military as an alternative to structural unemployment, are dependent on niggardly veterans' benefits when injured in war. And when they are victims of governmental misconduct — police violence, abuse in prisons, schools, and mental institutions — they may be completely remediless[,] either because of sovereign immunity or because officials possess substantial tactical advantages in defending against such claims.

Another form of remedial discrimination is internal to the tort system: the quantum of damages preserves, and indeed amplifies, the present unequal distribution of wealth and income. Imagine a car crash between A, who is unemployed and drives a worthless jalopy, and B, who owns a Rolls-Royce and earns a high income. If A is negligent and B non-negligent, A will have to pay for the damage to the Rolls and to B's earning capacity. But if B is negligent and A non-negligent, B will have to pay virtually nothing. This inequality is exaggerated by the fact that damages for pain and suffering are often expressed as a multiple of the pecuniary damages (usually two-to-one). If we make the hypothetical more realistic by giving both parties liability insurance the inequality remains: A's insurance premium will have to reflect the possibility of injury to B, and be higher than would be necessary to protect A and others like him, whereas B's premium will reflect the possibility of an injury to A, and be lower than would be necessary to protect a world of Bs. A thus pays part of the cost of protecting the privileges of B.

Producing Illness and Injury

Capitalist tort law systematically encourages unsafety. The dynamic of capitalism — competitive pursuit of profit — impels the enterprise to endanger the workers it employs, the consumers of its products and services, and those who inhabit the environment it pollutes. The cost of safety almost always diminishes profits. The capitalist, therefore, *must* be as unsafe as he can get away with being. Tort law purports to curb these destructive consequences of capitalism. The legal-economic rationale that presently dominates and shapes tort principles is market deterrence, which argues that the most

efficient means to promote an optimum level of safety is to internalize accident costs by making those who negligently cause accidents legally liable for their consequences. But there are fundamental theoretical and empirical reasons why market deterrence does not and cannot work.... [A] court is required to decide whether a *particular* injury was negligently inflicted, but the economic conceptualization of negligence as sub-optimal safety (epitomized in Learned Hand's formula weighing the cost of accident avoidance against the cost of injury discounted by its probability) can only meaningfully be applied to an ongoing activity. The inevitable errors in determining negligence can only lead to inadequate safety.... [A] court is required to determine whether or not a particular actor *caused* a given injury or illness, a dichotomous decision. But we know that causation is probabilistic and that for any event there are a multiplicity of contributing causes. The imposition of liability on one party (or even several) necessarily fails to internalize the accident costs in other casual activities.

... [T]here is an inescapable tension between promoting safety through accident cost internalization and spreading these costs — another goal of tort law. The most important mechanism for spreading costs is liability insurance, which has become so widespread, and which discriminates so crudely among insured in setting premiums, that it alone virtually destroys the capacity of tort liability to optimize safety.

... [I]n order for liability costs to alter the behaviour of entrepreneurs the latter must be unable to pass these costs on to consumers; but this condition will not be satisfied if liability costs are an insignificant percentage of the price of the good or service (as they usually are), if demand is relatively price inelastic (the good or service is a necessity), or if the market is highly oligopolistic.... [M]arket deterrence assumes that all actors who "cause" accidents are economic maximizers and consequently argues that victims must be *denied* compensation (in whole or in part) in order to motivate them to protect themselves. This can only diminish the concern of capitalists for the safety of others.

... [A]nd most important, market deterrence assumes that the legal system fully internalizes *all* the costs of negligent accidents. Yet we have just seen in the previous section that capitalist tort law systematically denies compensation for injury and illness and does so in a highly discriminatory manner. Therefore, the theory of market deterrence logically compels the conclusion that capitalist tort law encourages unsafety and subjects the most oppressed sectors of the population to the greatest danger. It motivates the entrepreneur to reduce *liability* costs, not accident costs, to seek to evade the consequences of unsafety, not to enhance safety. Thus we have Ford producing a Pinto with a gasoline tank it knew to be explosive. Johns-Manville continuing to subject its workers to asbestos for decades after it learned they could suffer lung damage and cancer, American Airlines flying the DC-10 that crashed in Chicago when it knew of the faulty pylon, and drug companies selling thalidomide they knew to be dangerous. The capitalist response to the threat of tort liability is to strive to externalize accident costs by concealing information (denying workers access to their medical records), threatening retaliation against those who seek compensation, and using the enormous resources of the enterprise (and of its liability insurer) to coerce victims into accepting inadequate settlements, to overwhelm them in litigation, and to pass legislation that immunizes the enterprise from liability costs (as the nuclear energy industry has done with the Price-Anderson Act). We know from studies of the deterrent effect of criminal sanctions that certainty is more important than severity; because it is so unlikely that damages will ever be paid, tort liability is an empty threat, incapable of promoting safety.

. . . .

Reproducing Bourgeois Ideology

It would be a mistake to interpret legal phenomena solely in terms of their instrumental effect upon material conditions. Tort law is also significant in the reproduction of bourgeois ideology. The fault concept upon which that law was built reinforces a central element of bourgeois ideology — individualism. Predicating liability upon the defendant's fault and denying recovery because of the victim's fault perfectly express the bourgeois belief that each person controls his or her own fate. And indeed the bourgeoisie experience this control in their own lives — in their work, their consumption, and their environment — an experience epitomized in the contemporary "sauve qui peut" obsession with *personal* physical, mental, and emotional well-being. But the nineteenth-century concept of fault is too moralistic for today's tastes and too patently inconsistent with the reality — that collective consequences are caused by the confluence of multiple,

ongoing, collective activities. As a result of these tensions strict liability has progressively displaced negligence and the defenses of contributory negligence and assumption of risk have been eroded through doctrinal change and jury nullification. Yet individualism has been saved, if in a modified form. The triumph of economic analysis has redefined fault as the efficient allocation of resources, a concept that appears scientific and apolitical rather than mushy and moralistic. And economic efficiency sees everyone as potentially capable of avoiding accidents, thereby equating the car driver with the automobile manufacturer, the worker with the boss. Fault translated into the language of economics has once again infiltrated strict liability under cover of the requirement of a defect; fault has revived contributory negligence in the guise of doctrines of comparative negligence and unforeseeable use; and it has answered the problem of concurrent causation by comparing the fault of multiple tort-feasors. And individualism also survives in the rejection of affirmative duties, a rejection that asserts that *each* man is an island, sole unto himself.

. . . .

A SOCIALIST APPROACH TO INJURY AND ILLNESS

. . . .

The two requirements of a just approach to illness and injury — equalizing risk and restoring control to those who undergo danger — cannot be satisfied without radical change: in the division of labour (a reduction in specialization and perhaps rotation between hand work and head work, such as occurred during the Chinese cultural revolution and in many intentional communities); and in control over the means of production (which must be transferred from capitalists to workers). The first steps might be forms of cooperative enterprise and worker involvement in improving health and safety in the workplace — *not* nationalization of industry, which simply substitutes the state for capital. Since both reforms would threaten capitalist control vigorous resistance can be expected, and is already visible in the Reagan administration's decision to withdraw funding from the national cooperative bank and in its attacks on OSHA [Occupational Safety and Health Administration]. The strength

177

of capitalist opposition may also explain the timidity of unions. But for precisely these reasons, occupational health and safety is an excellent issue for rank and file activists and for organizing unorganized workers. It is harder to see how to equalize exposure to the risks posed by consumer goods and services and by residence (although economic equality and its political and social consequences would advance this goal) and how to empower those exposed to such risks to control their own safety (increased self-reliance may be necessary since consumers are a diffuse category, unlike those who share the same workplace or residential area).

... The paramount criterion for a just compensation system should be equality: it should respond to all victims if it responds to any, and the response to each should be equal. The first requirement mandates equality among victims whether or not their misfortunes were caused by fault (their own or that of others), or by human actors at all: those who suffer from tort, unavoidable accident, illness, and congenital disability should be treated alike. After all, that is how we respond to the misfortunes of those we love. The second requirement argues that inequalities of wealth and income should not be reproduced in the level of compensation, for this would maintain those inequalities materially and reaffirm them symbolically. Thus there should be *no* compensation for damage to either property or individual earning power: those who enjoy privileges of wealth or income should pay to protect them against loss.... We need, instead, to recreate a society that responds to misfortune with personal care rather than relegating the victim to the scrap heap of welfare and custodial institutions: nursing homes, hospitals, "special" schools, and ghettos for the aged and the mentally ill — the sanitized and less visible skid rows of our society.

(c) Hoovering as a Hobby and Other Stories: Gendered Assessments of Personal Injury Damages†

Regina Graycar

II. THE ASSESSMENT OF DAMAGES FOR LOSS OF EARNING CAPACITY: LOSS OF CAPACITY TO DO PAID WORK

When women are injured in an accident, assessment of their damages can be negatively affected by stereotypes and assumptions. This is sometimes done explicitly, for example by the use of depressed "female" wage figures or work life tables for women. But equally importantly, this sometimes occurs implicitly through the use of stereotypes and gendered assumptions about women's lack of attachment to the paid labour market. Most of my research has focused on the second category, which is the subject of this article. But first, I want to briefly mention the former category, which is represented by the use of explicitly gendered and sometimes race-specific actuarial tables to calculate loss of future earning capacity. While the trend of using gendered wage tables does not seem to have captured widespread currency in Australia, it is quite common in North America. One of the best known cases in this country is *Tucker v. Asleson*, a B.C. decision. In that case, the female plaintiff (note that I just used an adjective: a 1985 edition of a widely used Australian torts text refers to "plaintiffs" and "female plaintiffs") argued that her loss of future earning capacity should be assessed on the basis of tables of average earnings for a university-educated male — an amount of $947,000. The defendant argued that female tables should be

† (1997) 31:1 U.B.C. L. Rev. 17 at 20–31. [Notes and/or References omitted.] Reproduced by permission of the author and the publisher.

used, which, because of the history of sex discrimination in employment, would have amounted to only $302,000. In what is often described as a landmark decision, the trial judge accepted the plaintiff's argument and used the male wage figures, a decision that was not disturbed by the majority of the B.C.C.A. However, the choice of wage table is arguably nowhere near as important to the final outcome of the case as the trial judge's decision that 60–65% was the appropriate reduction for vicissitudes. Overall, a hollow victory for the plaintiff. This case clearly demonstrates that explicitly gendered rationales for reduction of damages are not so separate as they may superficially appear from the more implicit uses of gender stereotypes. The same factors that lead to women's average earnings being significantly less than those of men (such as the unequal distribution of work in the home and discriminatory assumptions about women's lack of attachment to paid work) are also relied on by courts to reduce awards for vicissitudes. So, it is arguable that the use of both female wage tables and a reduction for vicissitudes constitutes double discounting. Although I will not discuss the tables in any further detail, I would endorse the cautionary view of Mr. Justice Dickson (as he then was) in *Andrews v. Grand & Toy Alberta*:

> The apparent reliability of assessments provided by modern actuarial practice is largely illusionary, for actuarial science deals with probabilities, not actualities.... [A]ctuarial evidence speaks in terms of group experience. It cannot, and does not purport to, speak as to the individual sufferer.

Most of the research I have undertaken in Australia as part of a large research project has been focused on the implicit rationales: the "damaging stereotypes" used to reduce awards to women. This can be illustrated through a case that reached the High Court of Australia in 1995. Leonie Wynn was injured in a motor vehicle accident when she was 30 and a senior employee of American Express. She had been promoted several times, had a number of staff responsible to her, and worked long hours — often working at home until one or two in the morning. The extensive computer work aggravated her whiplash injury and she was forced to resign at age 32. The work she subsequently undertook was far less remunerative and only part-time. By the time the matter came to trial, she had married her long-term partner

(with whom she lived while employed by American Express) and had a child.

The main basis of the respondent's challenge to the trial judge's award was, as put by Handley J.A., that he "had failed to make proper allowance for vicissitudes. He held that it was not probable that but for injury, the plaintiff would simply have retired to the laudable but limited role of housewife and mother and abandoned her business career." The trial judge had assessed damages on the basis that Ms. Wynn would have worked for American Express until age 60 and, after considering all the factors raised (such as possible maternity leave), reduced her assessed damages by five percent for vicissitudes.

In the N.S.W. Court of Appeal, much was made of the stressful nature of her job, the onerous responsibility it carried and the very long working hours. With regard to child care, the Court said, "if the plaintiff ... continued her demanding business career after marriage and after the birth of her child or children, she and her husband would necessarily have been faced with the necessity of engaging a full-time nanny for the children and substantial household help during the week," and her damages were reduced to take this cost into account.

The Court of Appeal also expressed a number of reservations about the trial judge's finding that Ms. Wynn was likely to continue to exercise her earning capacity at a senior executive level. First, they did not accept that she would be further promoted because that would have required another overseas posting:

> It would have involved separation from her fiancé or husband, whose business interests would have kept him in Sydney, except during holidays, and likewise either separation from any children or a decision not to have any. The plaintiff was thirty-two when she resigned and her childbearing years were already limited....

The Court held that the trial judge had erred in allowing only five percent for vicissitudes. Not only was the possibility of "burn out" not taken into account, but the Court also stated that the judge's finding that it was "quite probable" that she would have been further promoted could not be supported, although there is no mention in the judgment of there having been any evidence to the contrary at trial. After adding "a fair allowance" for domestic help, a figure the Court expressly acknowledged was based on no direct evidence ("the Court must do the best it can"), the Court of Appeal summed up as follows:

> The allowance for vicissitudes in my opinion should include two years' absence from work to have two children (8% of the 23.75 years [the estimated period of working life]) together with an allowance for the prospect that the plaintiff would be unable or unwilling to remain in her job which placed such heavy demands on her time, energy and health and the love and patience of her husband. The plaintiff, of course, could have worked until sixty or later in a less demanding job but would then have earned substantially reduced salary and benefits.... A fair allowance for such vicissitudes in my opinion would be 20% and this with the 8% allowance for having two children gives a total deduction for vicissitudes of 28% which I would adopt.

Applying this reasoning, Ms. Wynn's damages for loss of future earning capacity were reduced from over $700,000 to $411,350. She appealed and during the special leave application, one member of the High Court, McHugh J., asked: "Well, supposing the applicant had been a male, could you imagine a judge making a finding like this?" Is it more likely that in that event, the court might instead have described the plaintiff as another court described a similar, though not chromosomally challenged, plaintiff, as "a young man with bright prospects, who has been deprived of the ability to choose to continue his career." Commenting on the *Wynn* decision, Professor Cooper-Stephenson suggested that if a rubric was needed for it, it should be "Don't Leave Work Without It" or perhaps simply, "Don't Leave Home."

The *Wynn* case resonates with many of the cases I have come across in my research: what they have in common is a tendency to treat women's paid work as marginal, as worthy of comment, and as requiring an explanation, rather than as something that adult, gender-neutral people just do. The judgments often provide an explanation for why a woman works, coupled with an underlying assumption that should the particular reason given for her employment disappear she would no longer engage in paid work. For example, a woman works because her husband left her and she's a single parent (or might become one); another works to escape her husband who is violent. Another works because her husband is unemployed and therefore cannot support her and the children; while another wants to help her daughter to attend university. One woman's religious beliefs were said by a judge

to lie behind her view that "her role was to provide financial support to her maximum capacity for her husband and children. A young South Australian woman had her damages reduced on appeal because it was held that she was unlikely to take over her mother's role in the management of a family business as she had three brothers and the business might have to support their families. Perhaps the best explanation comes from Lord Denning, then English Master of the Rolls, in 1974:

> Many a married woman seeks work. She does so when the children grow up and leave the home. She does it, not solely to earn money, helpful as it is: but to fill her time with useful occupation, rather than sit idly at home waiting for her husband to return. The devil tempts those who have nothing to do.

One particularly common assumption that appears in the Australian case law is that sole parents are more likely than women in two-parent households to be engaged in paid work. In fact, the opposite is true, both in Canada and in Australia, according to data from both the Australian Bureau of Statistics and Statistics Canada. I mention this to draw attention to a phenomenon that seems common in these cases: that is, basing fact finding and judicial decision making on completely erroneous assumptions, an issue I will return to later.

Paid work for women, particularly married women, is often seen to be in direct competition with other aspects of their lives — with other roles they fulfil or are expected to fulfil. In one Australian case, *Becin v. G.E.L. Australia & Ors.*, the court decided that a woman would not be successful running her own business because "she may have succumbed to competing family demands." Women's capacity to bear children is also used, in a number of different (and often contrasting) ways, to disadvantage women. For young women, damages are discounted because they may in the future take time out of the workforce to have children (irrespective of whether they indicated that they did not want to do so or planned to have no more children). In 1996, the B.C. Court of Appeal reduced a trial judge's award, deciding that the plaintiff would not have spent her working life at her pre-accident employment: "[s]he hopes to raise a family when her spouse is suitably employed." But an older woman might have her damages reduced when she no longer has children to care for or because she is considered unemployable after a history of time out of the paid workforce for family responsibilities, or because, in the words of one judge, she "may well have taken breaks from her employment, for example, when her children married and had families to visit and to assist them with their children...."

Just as in *Wynn*, a court may consider that the workplace might prove too demanding for a woman (who could not be expected to keep up such a pace), or, that a woman's husband might not want her to undertake full-time paid work because, as she and he "aged and became financially secure, her husband's attitude might have induced [her] to retire early or to reduce her working hours." And, while the New South Wales Court of Appeal treated difficulties that would confront Ms. Wynn in travelling overseas to secure her promotion as almost insurmountable, another female plaintiff's award was reduced since she "may well have taken breaks from her employment ... during any transfers in his work by her husband." For yet another woman, damages for future economic loss were reduced because of her husband's peripatetic employment since, according to the court, "there must also be taken into account ... the consequences of being married to a serviceman."

When the High Court reviewed the decision in *Wynn*, they allowed the appeal in part. The Court decided that a more appropriate reduction for vicissitudes was 12.5% and refused to discount the award to allow for the costs of child care. The Court pointed out that such costs may be incurred by men or women whether or not the child's mother is in the paid workforce. The Court also said that there was "nothing in the evidence to suggest that the appellant was any less able than any other career-oriented person, whether male or female, to successfully combine a demanding career and family responsibilities."

III. THE VALUATION OF A WOMAN'S LOSS OF CAPACITY TO WORK IN THE HOME

Because the law of torts values some losses of working capacity over others, injuries to women are often characterized as giving rise to non-economic loss, a characterization that has significant consequences in damages assessment. The failure to recognize the economic nature of women's work in the home is closely related to the common law's historical treatment of a woman's loss of domestic working capacity as a loss not to herself but to her husband through his action for loss of "consortium" and "servitium."

At common law, a loss of capacity to provide household services, although historically characterized as an economic loss, was actionable *only* by the woman's husband in an action for loss of consortium. Such an action included damages not only for loss of services, but also for loss of society and companionship, including sexual services. After it was held by the House of Lords in *Best v. Samuel Fox & Co. Ltd.* in 1952 that at common law, women did not have a corresponding right of action for loss of their husband's consortium, the action was extended by statute in some jurisdictions (*e.g.* South Australia and more recently Queensland), while in others it was abolished (*e.g.* New South Wales).

Neither approach addressed the real problem, as was so clearly shown in Ann Riseley's wonderfully titled, "Sex, Housework and the Law." The extension to women of the ability to sue for loss of their husband's consortium is a graphic illustration of how empty the formal equality or sameness model of equality can be for women. If the major element in a loss of consortium award is the loss of services, the "reform" is Pyrrhic: most women do not lose their husbands' household services when they are injured since they never had them in the first place. And, as for abolishing the action, which it may have rhetorical appeal, in practice there is a real loss which is then left to lie where it falls. The only satisfactory approach is to replace the secondary action for loss of consortium with a primary cause of action for loss of capacity to work in the home. This had been done by statute in the Australian Capital Territory and, in effect, by common law development in some Canadian provinces.

The old approach (a secondary action) allowed some tortuous conceptualizations of a woman's injury as partly hers and partly someone else's (and remember that only a *de jure* husband ever had a right to claim damages for that loss). In one case, a court described a woman's loss of capacity to work in the home as "a partial loss of capacity to carry out housework resulting in: (a) a loss to the family of part of her services ...; (b) a loss to herself by inability to fully satisfy her personal needs in daily life ...; and (c) a personal loss of the capacity to perform for others voluntarily."

The personal loss, the part claimed by the woman herself, has tended to be characterized as non-economic, rather than economic, as a loss of amenity or loss of enjoyment of life. This characterization mirrors what is effectively a false dichotomy between work (something done outside of the home for wages) and other non-remunerative activity. So, for example, the court in the case just referred to said: "the injured plaintiff has in such a case as this lost part of a capacity, the exercise of which can give to her pride and satisfaction and the receipt of gratitude, and the loss of which can lead to frustration and feelings of inadequacy." This approach, of characterizing a loss of capacity to work in the home as a loss of enjoyment of life and therefore non-economic (which has its B.C. counterpart in *Bourton v. England*), is the approach that I have characterized as "hoovering as a hobby."

A number of consequences flow from characterizing work in the home as non-economic: first, non-economic losses tend to be much lower than economic losses and secondly, non-economic losses are increasingly being abolished or limited by statutory modifications to common law damages. This is something that should be closely scrutinized in the current B.C. debate about no-fault: in all the jurisdictions (such as New Zealand) that made the change to no-fault in the 1970s and 1980s, little if any account was taken of the impact of such a change on the treatment of women's work in damages assessment.

Another related trend is to assume that since women now increasingly work outside the home, housework is shared. This assumption is, of course, unfounded, as a large body of recent empirical evidence clearly tells us that women's increased participation in the paid labour market has had little or no effect on the distribution of housework. Yet remarkably, for some reason, courts state this erroneous conclusion as if it were a matter of judicial notice.

I should stress that the assumption is not confined to damages law, as a well-known Australian custody case illustrates:

> [T]here has come a radical change in the division of responsibilities between parents and in the ability of the mother to devote the whole of her time and attention to the household and to the family. As frequently as not, the mother works, thereby reducing the time which she can devote to her children. A corresponding development has been that the father gives more of his time to the household and to the family.

The High Court did not cite any evidence for its conclusion: indeed, it would have been nigh on impossible to find any. There are numerous examples in both Canadian and Australian case law of similar reasoning, but my favourite quote is extracurial. A judge was on a panel talking about damages for loss of capacity to do housework and said:

> Those, incidentally, who care to dabble in jurimetrics might like to consider what is to be made of this: of the seven wives of the seven judges of the Court of Appeal, three are in full-time professions or occupations, two are in part-time professions or occupations, one was in full-time employment before marriage, and the remaining one in part-time employment before marriage. I would think therefore that all of us have experience of what might be regarded as a more modern way of life, in which household tasks are shared.

This misperception would not be of any particular significance were it not for the fact that it is used to reduce a woman's damages for loss of capacity to do housework. In a number of cases, both in Australia and in Canada, this same assumption — that housework is shared — has been used to reduce damages either where this loss is recognized as a primary loss, or in the older cases, where the loss is treated as a loss of consortium. In one of the latter cases, a New South Wales court decided that the loss to the husband of his wife's services was not so great: as the judge put it, "regard must be had to the public mores ... and where a husband [and] wife are both working ... the sharing of domestic burdens with the wife is expected of the husband, even where his wife is perfectly healthy." More recently, in B.C., a trial judge noted:

> This is a family of two spouses both of whom work outside the home. The plaintiff plans to continue her career. In that type of family as opposed to a traditional family where one spouse remains at home, it is reasonable to expect both spouses to contribute fairly equally to the domestic work.

It may be "reasonable" but it is certainly not empirically sound. According to a very recent Statistics Canada publication:

> Women, on average, spent 78% more time in 1992 on unpaid work than men did.... They also spent 11% less time on unpaid work in 1992 than in 1961, though their participation in the labour force had nearly doubled over the same period. In contrast, men spent 6% more time on unpaid work. Nonetheless, women still

did about two-thirds of the unpaid work in 1992.

These figures are almost identical to those I am familiar with from Australia. While we all might hope that housework is more fairly shared in households, particularly those where both members of a couple are in paid work, my concerns are that reducing damages on the basis of assumptions that bear no relationship either to the individual case or to the national statistical data will not adequately compensate individuals [] nor is it likely to lead the way to more equal sharing of work in the home.

Before I leave behind the issue of empirical evidence on work in the home, here is another of my favourites: a U.S. mail survey of housework in judges' home[s]:

Few judges — men or women — listed themselves as the primary person to do housework.... In women judges' families, however, over two-thirds of housework was done by hired help, compared to only 14 per cent of men's household's....

... Slightly over 82 per cent of men judges had spouses who took the major responsibility for running their household,... [while] only 9.3 per cent of women judges had spouses who carried the primary responsibility for the household. Nearly two-thirds of women judges took the primary household responsibility themselves, and another 12.5 per cent shared it equally with their husbands.

So after the final verdict has been handed down, the washing up is still in the sink and the bathroom does not bear close inspection.

(d) *Family Law Act*†

PART V
DEPENDANTS' CLAIM FOR DAMAGES

61.(1) If a person is injured or killed by the fault or neglect of another under circumstances where the person is entitled to recover damages, or would have been entitled if not killed, the spouse, as defined in Part III (Support Obligations), children, grandchildren, parents, grandparents, brothers and sisters of the person are entitled to recover their pecuniary loss resulting from the injury or death from the person from whom the person injured or killed is entitled to recover or would have been entitled if not killed, and to maintain an action for the purpose in a court of competent jurisdiction.

(2) The damages recoverable in a claim under subsection (1) may include,

(a) actual expenses reasonably incurred for the benefit of the person injured or killed;

(b) actual funeral expenses reasonably incurred;

(c) a reasonable allowance for travel expenses actually incurred in visiting the person during his or her treatment or recovery;

(d) where, as a result of the injury, the claimant provides nursing, housekeeping or other services for the person, a reasonable allowance for loss of income or the value of the services; and

(e) an amount to compensate for the loss of guidance, care and companionship that the claimant might reasonably have expected to receive from the person if the injury or death had not occurred.

(3) In an action under subsection (1), the right to damages is subject to any apportionment of damages due to contributory fault or neglect of the person who was injured or killed.

---

† R.S.O. 1990, c. F.3, as am. by S.O. 2005, c. 5, s. 27.

(e) The No-Fault Concept and Its History in Canada†

Craig Brown

THE FAULT SYSTEM AND THE GOAL OF COMPENSATION

Before examining the details of various schemes and the legal problems attendant upon them, it is appropriate to provide a brief account of the history of automobile insurance in Canada relevant to the development of the no-fault concept. As mentioned, the central idea of no-fault insurance is to make compensation available to the victims of automobile accidents, at least those who are innocent of serious misconduct, such as driving while intoxicated. But the implementation of no-fault insurance is only part, and a recent part at that, of a long story in which the automobile accident reparations system, originally based on pure tort principles, has gradually been modified by legislation so as to pursue more effectively the goal of compensating the victims of automobile accidents.

Most observers attribute a compensation goal to tort law in its "pure" form — that is, tort law unmodified by legislation. But that goal is only achieved when (a) the injured person is able to prove fault (mostly negligence) on the part of a defendant, and (b) the defendant has sufficient funds to pay for the damages. In the particular context of automobile accidents it has long been apparent that these conditions are not always easy to meet. Quite apart from concerns about the practical application of the notion of "fault" to the realities of driving, there is the problem of proving facts which might constitute fault whatever standard of conduct is applied. Crucial events often happen in fractions of a second and details have to be recalled months later by the claimant or other witnesses who may themselves have been injured at the time. Thus, it can be difficult to satisfy the burden of proof.

The first legislative incursion into the common law was designed to address this problem. In 1906 legislation was passed in Ontario reversing the burden of proof in cases of loss or damage suffered by reason of the operation of a motor vehicle. Whereas the common law required the plaintiff to prove fault, a motorist-defendant now had the onus of disproving it. Although this quite sensibly does not apply to collisions between two or more motor vehicles, it does represent a step along the spectrum from negligence to strict liability.

A form of strict liability has, in fact, been in place since the early 1930s. Under what is called either the Highway Traffic Act or the Motor Vehicles Act, the owner of an automobile is liable without any personal fault where another person, driving the vehicle with the owner's consent, negligently causes injury or damage to a third party. As one writer has observed,

> ... the immediate object of such legislation was undoubtedly to make available the assets of the owner to anyone harmed by reason of negligence in the operation of the vehicle.

This imposition of vicarious liability was accompanied by a legislative intervention relating to automobile liability insurance. In the Uniform Automobile Insurance Act, adopted as part of the Insurance Act in most provinces, certain features were imposed upon all automobile liability policies. In particular, insurers were required to agree to provide cover against liability imposed by law upon the insured named in the contract " ... and every other person who with his consent personally drives an automobile owned by the insured ... for loss or damage, arising from the ownership, use or operation" of the motor vehicle. This provision addressed the difficulty posed by the common law requirement of privity of contract which had caused the Privy Council to deny the claim for indemnity by the daughter of a named insured owner under a liability policy. More generally, it ensured that, where the owner did have liability insurance, its proceeds were available as compensation for a third party injured or otherwise caused loss through the negligent operation of the insured

---

† From *No-Fault Automobile Insurance in Canada* (Toronto: Carswell, 1988) at 4–12. [Notes and/or References omitted.] Reproduced by permission of Carswell, a division of Thomson Reuters Canada Limited.

vehicle. In other words, it made compensation more widely available.

A particularly significant statutory modification of common law contract rules was a provision giving an injured third party a direct right of action against the insurer of the person — usually the automobile owner — primarily liable. Unlike the direct action available with respect to non-automobile liability insurance, the right of action in automobile cases is not prejudiced by the insured's violation of the law or policy terms, or by the invalidity of the policy arising, for example, from a material non-disclosure. Although the insurer may, in certain circumstances, claim reimbursement from the insured, the clear purpose of this provision was, and is, to make money available to injured victims. To obtain this benefit victims must still have a tort claim against the insured, but any contractual impediments pertaining to the insured's rights against the insurer do not prevent recovery.

Another reform has been the abolition in several provinces of the "guest passenger" rule. Under that rule a non-paying passenger in a private automobile could not recover in tort against the driver unless there was proof of "gross negligence." Clearly, the removal of this rule has increased the number of claimants who may now recover in tort.

Each of these developments improved the chances that an innocent victim of an automobile accident would be compensated at least to some extent. But there still had to be a proof of fault and, in most cases, the defendant had to have liability insurance. To pursue further the compensation goal of tort law as it applied to automobile accidents, provinces instituted incentives to induce the owners of motor vehicles to buy liability insurance. These were the so-called "Financial Responsibility Laws" which required proof by any motorist responsible for an accident, that she could pay, by insurance or otherwise, any damages resulting. If proof was not forthcoming, penalties followed. In 1945, Manitoba supplemented this by creating an Unsatisfied Judgment Fund from which payments were made to victims whose losses and injuries had been caused by uninsured or unidentified motorists. This basic concept was copied by all of the other provinces. The funds were made up of contributions by those who, upon registering their vehicles, chose not to buy liability insurance. This was not a form of insurance for such people because, under threat of the loss of their driving privileges, they were required to reimburse the fund for any losses they caused.

Not content with financial responsibility laws as a means of encouraging the availability of insurance to pay judgments, all provinces have now resorted to regimes of compulsory automobile liability insurance. Accordingly, it is a criminal offence for an uninsured motor vehicle to be operated on public highways. Registrants of motor vehicles are required to provide details of insurance when obtaining licences or renewals of licences for their vehicles and police officers routinely demand proof of insurance when a motorist is stopped for whatever reason. Offenders are liable to pay heavy fines. Special arrangements are made to provide cover for high-risk applicants. All this is clearly designed to protect victims (rather than insured defendants). It is, in short, a form of compensation plan.

To fill remaining gaps — where injury is caused by an uninsured vehicle (being either operated contrary to the compulsory insurance law or from another jurisdiction) or one which cannot be identified — there is still the need for residual cover. In Ontario, the introduction of compulsory insurance was accompanied by the transfer of most of this function from the public fund to the private insurance industry. Uninsured and unidentified motorist cover was part of the package of insurance which became compulsory.

In addition to the problems of the defendant who has no insurance or who cannot be located, there is that of the defendant with some insurance, but not enough to cover the loss that occurs. To deal with this, many insurers now offer underinsured motorist cover, although they are not compelled to do so by legislation. To agreed limits, this cover, provided by the victim's own insurer, tops up damages when they are only partially met by the defendant's liability insurer.

Note the central point in these most recent developments. A system which relies solely on third-party fault as the determinant of eligibility of compensation necessarily relies upon the assets and/or insurance of third parties as the source of that compensation. Because, in advance of an accident, the potential victim cannot identify the potential tortfeasor, she, the victim, can have no control over the level of financial responsibility of that other person. To be completely sure that her losses will be met, a person has to make arrangements with her own insurer. Even under a fault system, first-party insurance is necessary to ensure that victims get adequately compensated.

But, as noted at the start of this section, the fault system also requires proof that some other person was negligent. Regardless of the innocence of the victim, this implication of a third party is vital. Without it, whatever devices exist to encourage the purchase of insurance, provide funds to cover the case of uninsured or unidentified motorists, or to top up inadequate sources of compensation, no payment is available at all. It is this fact that the concept of no-fault insurance addresses.

NO-FAULT IN CANADA

Saskatchewan

The first automobile no-fault scheme in Canada was introduced in Saskatchewan in 1946. On the recommendation of a special committee, the Saskatchewan legislature enacted the Automobile Insurance Act in that year. The committee had been heavily influenced by a report which had been presented 14 years earlier to the Council for Research in the Social Sciences at Columbia University. The Columbia Report had recommended a "completely new approach" and rejected the accepted bases for legal liability. It proposed a form of strict liability upon owners of motor vehicles for personal injury or death caused by the operation of their motor vehicles and that this be backed by compulsory insurance. The proposed benefits were generous: full medical care, a weekly indemnity based on two/thirds of the average weekly earnings and allowances for dismemberment and disfigurement as well as death benefits. The Saskatchewan committee concluded that:

> the fundamental principle of this plan more nearly solves the problem of the uncompensated victims of automobile accidents than does any other yet promulgated.... [T]he application of the rule of negligence in particular cases leaves much to be desired. The statutory attempts to solve the question of liability in motor vehicle cases is an indication that the legislatures themselves appreciate the inadequacy of the liability laws.

However, in setting up its plan, Saskatchewan did not simply adopt the Columbia plan:

> It is felt, for instance, that the motorist can not, having regard to the average income in this province, bear the full burden of a thorough-going compensation scheme. At the same time, it is considered necessary that the victims of automobile accidents and their families should be guaranteed a certain minimum of security, which will enable them to withstand

the economic shock consequent upon these accidents. The existence of a Government Insurance Corporation can be utilized to reduce the cost to the motorist. The legislation can be framed to provide for prompt payment. The existing judicial machinery may be used in place of the administrative board contemplated by the Columbia Committee and the cost of recovering can be reduced to a minimum.... The Committee has had nevertheless considerable assistance from the finding of the Columbia Committee.

In the result, the Committee proposed a limited application of no-fault principles, already operating in workers' compensation plans, to automobile accidents. The scheme, along with other aspects of automobile insurance, was to be operated by a government agency, the Saskatchewan Government Insurance Office. Except for the call for government administration, the recommendations provided a prototype for schemes which would later be adopted in most Canadian jurisdictions.

The recommended coverage was for bodily injury and death resulting from "driving, operating, riding in an open motor vehicle on the public highway" or "collision with, being struck, run down or run over by a motor vehicle on a public highway." Persons operating or passengers riding in a vehicle in respect of which no premium was payable were excluded, as were persons entitled to workers' compensation; persons injured as a consequence of a criminal act, gross and wanton negligence, or driving impeded by alcohol; persons injured as a result of attaching a toboggan, skis or bicycle to a moving vehicle; persons riding on a part of a vehicle not designed for the carriage of a load or assuming a position no reasonable person would consider ordinarily safe; and persons failing to comply with the registration laws or knowingly giving false information in order to escape paying a fair premium.

Income-replacement benefits were to be payable periodically up to a maximum of $25 per week. These benefits would continue for 12 months if the claimant could not perform any duty pertaining to her occupation because of her injuries. For payments to continue after that period, the claimant had to be unable to engage in any occupation, but even here there was a maximum total amount of $3,000. The unemployed were to be indemnified to the level of lost unemployment benefits to a maximum of $25 per week. A housewife would be able to get $12.50 per week for up to 12 consecutive weeks. There was also a minimum payment to ensure that the weekly income of a victim of an automobile accident did not fall below $10 even if the victim was earning less than that amount prior to the accident.

In addition to income-replacement benefits, an amount of up to $225 was to be made available for "pain and suffering and out-of-pocket expenses" with a further amount, calculated by reference to a schedule of payments ranging from $250 to $2,000 for dismemberment or disfigurement.

In the event of the death of an accident victim, a lump sum of $3,000 was to be payable to a "primary" dependant (usually the spouse) and $625 each to "secondary" dependants (usually children), up to a maximum of $5,000 total. Where there were no dependants, $1,000 was to be paid to the estate. In all death cases $125 was to be payable for funeral expenses.

The plan was compulsory, enforced by making the purchase of insurance a condition precedent to obtaining a certificate of registration of a vehicle or an operator's licence. Disputes were referable to the District Court, although, unlike other actions in that court, restrictions were imposed on appeals and awards for costs.

While the benefits referred to were payable without regard to the fault of a third party, the plan did not abolish tort rights against third parties. The injured victim was free to pursue a negligent third party for any damages in excess of the no-fault benefits to which the victim was entitled. In this sense, the scheme was an "add-on" one.

Further, the insurer, on paying the no-fault claim, was subrogated to any claims against third parties who were not participants in the scheme — visitors from other jurisdictions or Saskatchewan residents who had not paid premiums — or who were guilty of gross negligence, wilful or wanton misconduct or were hit and run drivers. It was thought appropriate that such a driver, and not the participants in the plan, should ultimately bear the cost of the accident.

"Fault" continued to be relevant in other ways as well. Any person injured "while pursuing some more than ordinary careless course of conduct" such as gross negligence, or driving while intoxicated, was to be excluded from receipt of benefits. Premium adjustments consequent upon traffic convictions or other evidence of carelessness were envisaged and the insurer was given authority to recommend suspension or cancellation of drivers' licences.

Over the years of its existence, the Saskatchewan plan's details — terms, conditions, limits and amounts — have undergone considerable changes. But the fundamental principle requiring the provision of basic benefits without regard to the fault of some third party has remained intact, and the Saskatchewan experience has served as a model for many other jurisdictions, not only in Canada. The administrative model — the use of a government body as the insurer — has also been copied elsewhere.

(f)   Multi-Provincial/Territorial Assistance Program Agreement†

This Agreement made between

HER MAJESTY THE QUEEN IN RIGHT OF THE PROVINCE OF ONTARIO (herein the "Province")

and

_____

(herein the "direct recipient")

WHEREAS the Province is aware that the direct recipient may have been infected with HIV through the blood supply (i.e., through the receipt of a blood transfusion or other blood product);

AND WHEREAS, without admitting any liability for such infection (which liability is specifically denied), the Province wishes to provide assistance to the direct recipient, the spouse and the dependants;

---

† Multi-Provincial/Territorial Assistance Program Agreement, Province of Ontario and direct recipient, March 15, 1994.

THEREFORE in consideration of the mutual provisions of this Agreement, the Parties thereto agree as follows:

1. DEFINITIONS

1.1 In this Agreement:

(a) "dependant" means a biological child of the direct recipient born before September 15, 1994 or a child which was legally adopted by the direct recipient before September 15, 1993 and who at the date of death of the direct recipient is:

   (i) *en ventre sa mere* or under the age of 18 years;

  (ii) between the ages of 18 and 25 years and in full time attendance at a secondary or post secondary educational institution; or,

 (iii) unable, by reason of mental or physical disability to reside in an unsupervised environment;

(b) "federal program" means the compensation program provided by the Government of Canada pursuant to the *HIV — Direct Recipients and Thalidomide Victims Assistance Order* (P.C. 1990 — 4/872);

(c) "HIV" means the Human Immunodeficiency Virus;

(d) "parent" means the biological or adoptive parent of the direct recipient providing such parental relationship has not been severed by a court order;

(e) "Releasing Parties" means the persons identified as Releasing Parties in Schedule "A" to this Agreement;

(f) "spouse" means a person who, as at September 15, 1993:

   (i) was a person legally married to the direct recipient; or,

  (ii) where there is no person legally married to the direct recipient, was a person who cohabited with the direct recipient in a continuous relationship of some permanence and commitment akin to marriage throughout the 12 month period immediately preceding September 15, 1993, and whether the person is the same or opposite sex of the direct recipient;

(g) "year" means the period from April 1 of one year to March 31 of the next.

2. DIRECT RECIPIENT ANNUAL PAYMENT

2.1 Provided the direct recipient meets the criteria specified in section 7.2(a) the Province will pay to the direct recipient the sum of twenty two thousand ($22,000) dollars on execution of this Agreement by all parties.

2.2 (a) Provided the direct recipient meets the criteria specified in section 7.2(a) and is living on April 1 of the year following:

   (i) the year in which the direct recipient receives the last payment for which he/she is eligible under the federal program, where the direct recipient is enroled to receive benefits under the federal program; or,

  (ii) the date of execution of this Agreement, where the direct recipient is not enroled to receive benefits under the federal program;

the Province will pay to the direct recipient the sum of thirty thousand ($30,000) dollars.

(b) For each succeeding year that the direct recipient is alive on April 1, the Province will pay to the direct recipient the sum of thirty thousand ($30,000) dollars.

3. SURVIVOR BENEFITS

3.1 (a) Upon the death of the direct recipient and provided the direct recipient has a surviving spouse, the Province will pay to the spouse the sum of twenty thousand ($20,000) dollars.

(b) the sum referred to in clause (a) above will be paid to the spouse on the date the Province is notified of the death of the direct recipient or April 1, 1994 whichever is later.

3.2 (a) Subject to section 3.3, in addition to the sum referred to in section 3.1 the Province will pay to the spouse the sum of twenty thousand ($20,000) dollars per year in accordance with clause (b) below.

(b) The payments referred to in clause (a) above will be paid for each year that the spouse is alive on April 1 of such year commencing on the later of:

   (i) April 1 of the year following the year in which the payment referred to in section 3.1 is made; or,

   (ii) April 1 of the year following the year that the last payment under the federal program for which the direct recipient or his/her estate is eligible is made on behalf of the direct recipient or his/her estate, where the direct recipient is enroled to receive benefits under the federal program;

and will continue until the date of death of the spouse or until the sum of all payments made to the spouse pursuant to this provision equals eighty thousand ($80,000) dollars, whichever is earlier.

3.3 Should the spouse die having received only a portion of the payments referred to in sections 3.1 and 3.2 and there are surviving dependants of the direct recipient, all remaining payments which would otherwise have been made to the spouse shall be paid to those dependants who are alive at the time such payments would have been made to the spouse, in equal shares.

3.4 Should there be no spouse at the date of death of the direct recipient but there are surviving dependants, the payments which would otherwise have been made to the spouse pursuant to sections 3.1 and 3.2 shall be paid to those dependants who are alive at the time such payments would have been made to the spouse, in equal shares.

3.5 (a) Upon the death of the direct recipient and provided there are surviving dependants, the Province will pay to each surviving dependant the sum of four thousand ($4,000) dollars.

(b) The sum referred to in clause (a) above will be paid to the dependents on the date the Province is notified of the death of the direct recipient or April 1, 1994, whichever is later.

3.6 (a) In addition to the sum referred to in section 3.5, the Province will pay to each surviving dependant the sum of four ($4,000) dollars per year in accordance with clause (b) below.

(b) The payments referred to in clause (a) above will be paid for each year that the dependant is alive on April 1 of such year commencing on the later of:

   (i) April 1 of the year following the year in which the payment referred to in section 3.5 is made; or,

   (ii) April 1 of the year following the year that the last payment under the federal program for which the direct recipient or his/her estate is eligible is made on behalf of the direct recipient or his/her estate, where the direct recipient is enroled to receive benefits under the federal program;

and will continue until the date of death of the dependant or until the sum of all payments made to the dependant pursuant to this provision equals sixteen thousand ($16,000) dollars, whichever is earlier.

4.   VERIFICATION

4.1 The obligation of the Province to make the payments provided for in this Agreement is subject to:

(a) delivery to the Province of such evidence as it may require to confirm the eligibility for payment of the direct recipient, spouse, and dependants as the case may be;

(b) receipt by the Province of a Release in the form annexed hereto as Schedule "A" executed in the manner that the Province may require by the direct recipient, spouse, dependants, and parents as the Province may direct;

(c) subject to (d) below, where any of the Releasing Parties have commenced an action against any of the Released Parties as defined in Schedule "A", the withdrawal or discontinuance of such action against all Released Parties before April 1, 1994; and,

(d) where an action referred to in clause (c) involves a person under the age of majority or under legal disability, the withdrawal or discontinuance shall be obtained as soon as practicable.

4.2 Notwithstanding clause 4.1(b), where a Releasing Party is either under the age of majority or unable to provide a Release due to legal disability, the payment referred to in section 2.1 may be made on receipt of an affidavit from any person that the Province may require. No other payments pursuant to this Agreement will be made without a valid and binding Release from such persons.

5. SUSPENSION OF PAYMENTS

5.1 Where:

(a) payments are made in accordance with subsections 2.2(a)(ii), 3.2(b)(i) or 3.6(b)(i) of this Agreement; and,

(b) prior to the completion of such payments the direct recipient or his/her estate enrolls to receive benefits under the federal program;

all payments remaining to be made pursuant to the applicable sections shall be suspended and shall recommence on April 1 of the year following the year that the last payment under the federal program for which the direct recipient or estate is eligible is made on behalf of the direct recipient.

6. TAX AND SOCIAL ASSISTANCE EXEMPTION

6.1 The Province agrees that it will take all reasonable steps so that the payments made under this Agreement will not be considered as income for the purposes of the *Income Tax Act*, R.S.O. 1990, c. 1.2.

6.2 The Province agrees that it will request the Government of Canada to provide a similar exemption as that referred to in section 6.1 for the purposes of the Federal *Income Tax Act*.

6.3 The Province agrees that it will take reasonable steps so that the payments made under this Agreement will not be considered as income for purposes of qualification, or calculation of benefits pursuant to the *Family Benefits Act*, R.S.O. 1990, c. F.2, or *The General Welfare Assistance Act*, R.S.O. 1990, c. G.6, as the case may be.

6.4 The direct recipient understands and recognises that the obligation of the Province pursuant to section 6.1 is subject to the passage

of any legislative or regulatory amendments which may be required.

7. REPRESENTATIONS AND WARRANTIES

7.1 For the purposes of this section 7, "direct recipient" means:

(a) the person identified as the "direct recipient" in the title portion of this Agreement, where that person is of the age of majority and under no legal disability;

(b) the parent or guardian of the person identified as the "direct recipient" in the title portion of this Agreement, where that person is not of the age of majority; or,

(c) the individual with legal authority to settle legal affairs of the person identified as the "direct recipient" in the title portion of this Agreement where that person is of the age of majority but under legal disability.

7.2 The direct recipient hereby represents and warrants to the Province: [check appropriate boxes where applicable]

(a) that he/she has received or would qualify for ex gratia payments from the Government of Canada on the basis of being an "HIV infected blood or blood product recipient" as defined in the *HIV — Direct Recipients and Thalidomide Victims Assistance Order* (P.C. 1990 — 4/872);

(b) that his/her date of birth is _____ ;

(c) [ ] (i) that _____ is his/her spouse as defined in this Agreement; or,

[ ] (ii) that he/she has no spouse as defined in this agreement;

(d) that as of the date of execution of this agreement, the following are his/her dependants as defined in this agreement: (if "none" state "none")

Name   Date of Birth

. . . .

7.3. The direct recipient hereby agrees to take all reasonable steps to ensure that the release required pursuant to section 4.1 of this Agreement is legally binding upon each of the Releasing parties.

7.4 The direct recipient hereby agrees that the Province or any agent thereof may seek any information which the Province may require to confirm eligibility for payments under this agreement from any person, agency, corporation or government which may possess such information and hereby expressly and irrevocably authorizes such person, agency, corporation or government to release such information to the Province or its agent.

7.5 The direct recipient acknowledges that the Province is relying upon the representations made in this Agreement. The direct recipient understands and agrees that if any misrepresentations are made by the direct recipient, whether innocent or otherwise, the Province may discontinue payments pursuant to this Agreement and require repayment of all payments previously paid under this Agreement.

8.   CURE FOR AIDS

8.1 In the event that a cure or control for HIV or AIDS is discovered while the direct recipient is still living which has the effect of permitting the direct recipient to continue living with a reasonable quality of life including the ability for employment, all payments payable under this Agreement will cease.

9.   CHOICE OF ALTERNATE ASSISTANCE BY ANOTHER GOVERNMENT

9.1 If another Province or Territory of Canada offers financial assistance ("assistance by another Government") to persons infected with HIV through the blood supply, and any of the Releasing Parties qualifies for that assistance by another Government, then such Releasing Party must choose between the assistance by another Government and payments pursuant to this agreement. If any of the Releasing Parties choose or receive assistance by another Government then such Releasing Party shall no longer be entitled to receive further payments under this Agreement and shall reimburse the Province for all payments made to such Releasing Party pursuant to his Agreement.

9.2 For the purposes of reimbursement pursuant to section 9.1 above, the direct recipient hereby:

(a) irrevocably assigns his or her right to receive assistance by another Government to the Province up to the amount of the payments paid to that direct recipient pursuant to this Agreement; and,

(b) expressly and irrevocably authorizes and directs the other Government to make payment of the amount of such benefits directly to the Province.

10.   GENERAL

10.1 This Agreement constitutes the whole Agreement between the parties. No representation, statement or agreement not expressly contained herein shall be binding upon any party.

10.2 This Agreement will be governed by and construed in accordance with the laws of the Province of Ontario.

10.3 The recitals and headings used in this Agreement are for convenience only and shall not be used in interpreting this Agreement or any part thereof.

10.4 If any provision of this Agreement is or becomes illegal or not enforceable, then such provision will be considered separate and severable from this Agreement and the remaining terms and conditions will remain in force and be binding on the parties as though such provision had never been included.

10.5 All payments required to be made by the Province pursuant to this Agreement shall be made within thirty days of the date specified for such payment in this Agreement.

10.6 All payments payable to persons who are under the age of majority at the date such payment is made or unable due to mental disability to manage such payments shall be paid into court.

SCHEDULE "A"
DIRECT RECIPIENT RELEASE FORM

In this Release:

"direct recipient" means _____(name)_____, and his/her heirs, assigns, executors and administrators;

"Released Parties" means, individually and collectively:

(a) the governments of the Provinces of Alberta, British Columbia, Manitoba, New Brunswick, Newfoundland, Nova Scotia, Ontario, Prince Edward Island, Quebec and Saskatchewan, the Yukon and Northwest Territories and each of their past or present ministers;

(b) the Canadian Blood Agency;

(c) the Canadian Blood Committee and its members;

(d) the Canadian Red Cross Society/la Société canadienne de la Croix-Rouge;

(e) Miles Canada Inc., Miles Inc., Bayer A.G., Armour Pharmaceutical Company, U.S.V. Canada Inc., Rorer Group Inc., Rhone-Poulenc Rorer Inc., Baxter Healthcare Corporation, Baxter Corporation, Baxter International Inc., Baxter World Trade Corporation, Connaught Laboratories Limited, Connaught Biologics Limited and their related corporations as defined in the *Income Tax Act* of Canada;

(f) Canadian Medical Protective Association, Commercial Union Assurance Company of Canada, The General Accident Insurance Company of Canada, The Guarantee Company of North America, Halifax Insurance Company, Manitoba Public Insurance Corporation, Royal Insurance Company of Canada, Quebec Assurance Company, Western Assurance Company, Saskatchewan Government Insurance, The Dominion of Canada General Insurance Company, The Dominion of Canada Group, The Casualty Company of Canada, The Canadian Indemnity Company, The Canadian General Insurance Company, Traders General Insurance Company, Scottish & York Insurance Company, Victoria Insurance Company, Toronto General Insurance Company;

(g) any operators of hospitals or health care facilities at which the direct recipient received blood, blood products, treatment or advice; and,

(h) any health caregiver who treated or provided advice or care to the direct recipient;

and includes their respective parent, subsidiary and affiliated corporations, past or present employees, agents, officers, directors, volunteers, representatives, executors, administrators and successors;

"Releasing Parties" means the parties who have executed this Release and their respective heirs, executors, administrators, successors and assigns.

For the sum of one dollar and other good and valuable consideration, the receipt and sufficiency of which is hereby acknowledged, the Releasing Parties hereby:

(i) release and forever discharge the Released Parties of and from all actions, causes of action, claims and demands of every nature or kind which the Releasing Parties have or may have against the Released parties with respect to the infection of the direct recipient with HIV and any of the consequences of such infection which have occurred or may in future occur to the direct recipient as a result of such infection, including the death of the direct recipient;

(ii) covenant and agree that the Releasing Parties will immediately discontinue any action, suit, or proceeding of any kind in any Court of law or equity brought directly or indirectly against the Released Parties and will not now or at any time hereafter institute, commence, maintain or assign any action, suit or proceeding of any kind in any Court of law or equity, nor cause, assist in acquiesce in or permit the Releasing Parties' names to be used in any legal action of any kind, directly or indirectly against the Released Parties on account of any and all actions, causes of action, claims, suits, debts, contracts, damages, demands, costs and expenses of every nature and kind whatsoever whether known or unknown, which the Releasing Parties had, may now have, or at any time hereafter may have with respect to any matter related to the infection of the direct recipient with HIV and any of the consequences of such infection which have occurred or may in future occur to the direct recipient as a result of such infection including the death of the direct recipient;

(iii) covenant and agree that this Agreement is a complete defence to any action or proceeding that may be brought, instituted or taken by the Releasing Parties, or on the Releasing Parties' behalf with respect to any matter related to the infection of the direct recipient with HIV and any of the consequences of such infection which have occurred or may in future occur to the direct recipient as a result of such infection including the death of the direct recipient, against the Released Parties, and will forever be a complete bar to the commencement or prosecution of any such action or proceeding whatsoever against the Released Parties, and agree to, and do hereby consent to the dismissal of any such action or proceeding;

(iv) covenant and agree not to make any claim, demand or to maintain any action or bring any proceeding with respect to any matter related to the infection of the direct recipient with HIV and any of the consequences of such infection which have occurred or may in future occur to the direct recipient as a result of such infection including the death of the direct recipient against any person, firm, government, corporation or other entity who/which might claim damages from the Released Parties and/or contribution and/or indemnity and/or other relief over under the provisions of the *Negligence Act*, R.S.O. 1990, c. N.1, the common law or any other statute of this or any other jurisdiction or otherwise from the Released Parties and will immediately discontinue any such action or proceeding which results in such a claim being made.

Nothing in this release shall be construed as affecting any claim, cause of action or demand of any nature and kind which is based upon a contract of insurance made between any of the Releasing Parties and a Released Party named in clause (f) of this release.

The Releasing Parties hereby acknowledge that this Release is made with a denial of liability by the Released Parties and nothing in it nor any action of the Released Parties shall be construed as an admission of liability by the Released Parties.

The Releasing Parties hereby represent and warrant that they have each read this Release in its entirety and obtained legal advice in connection with the terms and effect of this Release and acknowledge that they fully understand and accept each and every term and condition of this Release. A Certificate of Legal Advice is attached to and forms part of this Release.

This Release may be executed in counterparts and where so executed all the counterparts together shall constitute one Release.

IN WITNESS WHEREOF this RELEASE has been executed by each of the Releasing Parties, this _____ day of _____, 19___.

SIGNED SEALED AND DELIVERED
in the presence of:

_____

(g) Compensation Package Leaves Victims Bitter†

Sharon Kirkey

Andre and Carole Hotte are like many victims of Canada's tainted blood tragedy.

The Vanier couple is bitter about accepting a government compensation package and giving up the right to sue. But time is running out.

"I didn't have any choice. My doctor told me last week I might not see Christmas," said Andre, a hemophiliac who contracted the HIV virus linked to AIDS from blood products used to treat him.

† From *Ottawa Citizen* (March 16, 1994) A1. Material reproduced with the express permission of Ottawa Citizen Group, Inc., a CanWest Partnership.

Hotte is among the 91 per cent of HIV-infected Canadians who signed up for a compensation package by Tuesday's deadline. In accepting the package, these people have signed away their right to sue the Red Cross, the provinces, hospitals, drug companies and doctors for negligence.

By 5 p.m. Tuesday, 826 of the 910 eligible victims had sent in their waivers to the Canadian Blood Agency, which is administering the package.

Those who accepted the package will receive an initial payment of $22,000. The person who contracted HIV directly through the blood supply will receive $30,000 a year for life; surviving spouses will receive $20,000 annually for five years and their children $4,000 a year for the same period.

Although an inquiry into what went wrong with the blood system is far from over, Tuesday was the last day to accept the package.

More than 1,000 Canadians were infected with HIV from tainted blood products from 1978 to November, 1985, before a national screening program was in place.

Many victims who had hoped to sue dropped those plans Monday, after a test court case. In the first tainted-blood case to work its way through the courts, Ontario Justice Susan Lang ruled that the Red Cross and a Toronto hospital were not negligent in giving a man tainted blood. Instead, Lang found the hospital, the Red Cross and Dr. Stanley Bain negligent for not doing enough to notify

Rochelle Pittmann and husband Ken that he had received HIV-tainted blood during a heart operation in 1984. Ken Pittman died believing pneumonia and heart disease were killing him. His family was awarded $500,000 in damages.

Ottawa lawyer Richard Bosada, who represents eight local tainted-blood victims — all but one of whom had accepted the compensation package late Tuesday — said he was shocked that the Red Cross was found not to be negligent.

"This is a tragedy that is a day-to-day occurrence (for victims)."

Johanne Decarie, a 34-year-old Rockland woman who was infected with HIV-tainted blood and blood products after receiving a transfusion in 1985, has decided to drop her lawsuit against the Red Cross and the Ottawa General Hospital, site of the transfusion.

Unaware that she had the virus, Decarie infected her husband and bore a child with HIV.

"(Decarie) weighed the impact on her family of going through a very stressful court process and decided that the uncertainty was not worth the extra money that she might be able to get further down the line," said her lawyer, Peggy Malpass. "The package gives families some financial certainty now and a real break from the stress of court litigation."

Malpass said Decarie made her decision before Monday's ruling in the Pittman case.

FACTS

Who's eligible: People in all provinces and territories except Nova Scotia infected with HIV through the blood supply from 1978 to 1989. Nova Scotia offered a separate package last year.

Victims' benefits: Immediate payment of $22,000, plus $30,000 a year for life.

Survivors' benefits: Widows and widowers would get $20,000 annually for five years; children left without a parent would get $4,000 annually for five years.

The catch: Victims waive [their] rights to sue the parties putting up the money.

Who's paying: The provinces and territories, the Red Cross, four drug companies — Connaught Laboratories, Miles Laboratories, Baxter Travenol Laboratories and Armour Pharmaceutical — and a number of insurance companies.

7 Fiduciary Relationships

(a) Fiduciary Relationships†

Timothy G. Youdan

The paradigm fiduciary relationship is that of trustee and beneficiary. Until recently, the question whether a particular relationship should be characterized as fiduciary was answered mainly by a process of analogy so that over the course of time various legal relationships, in addition to that of trustee and beneficiary, became accepted as fiduciary relationships. The list of fiduciary relationships included such relationships as principal and agent, partners, director and company, and solicitor and client.

In *Laskin v. Bache & Co. Inc.*, the Ontario Court of Appeal stated that, "the category of cases in which fiduciary duties and obligations arise from the circumstances of the case and the relationship of the parties is no more 'closed' than the categories of negligence at common law". This principle was implicitly applied by the Supreme Court of Canada in *Canadian Aero Services Ltd. v. O'Malley* in holding that senior officers of a corporation, as well as directors, may be in a fiduciary relationship to the corporation. In *Guerin v. R.*, Dickson J., in a judgment concurred in by the majority of the court, held that the Crown was, in the circumstances of the case, in a fiduciary relationship to an Indian band and he stated:

> It is sometimes said that the nature of fiduciary relationships is both established and exhausted by the standard categories of agent, trustee, partner, director and the like. I do not

agree. It is the nature of the relationship, not the specific category of actor involved that gives rise to the fiduciary duty. The categories of fiduciary, like those of negligence, should not be considered closed.

Dickson J.'s statement, like the similar statement of the Ontario Court of Appeal in *Laskin v. Bache & Co.*, suggests two ways in which the range of fiduciary relationship may be expanded. First, it accepts the possibility of new particular types of relationships being admitted to the "standard categories" of fiduciary relationships. Second, it asserts that fiduciary relationships may be found on the facts of a particular case, even though the relationship between the parties does not come within the list of "standard categories".

The courts have not established any precise criteria for determining whether a given relationship shall be held to be fiduciary. The following statement by Wilson J. in her dissenting judgment in *Frame v. Smith* has been influential:

> Relationships in which a fiduciary obligation have [*sic*] been imposed seem to possess three general characteristics:
> (1) The fiduciary has scope for the exercise of some discretion or power.
> (2) The fiduciary can unilaterally exercise that power or discretion so as to affect the beneficiary's legal or practical interests.

---

† From "Liability for Breach of Fiduciary Obligation" (1997) Can. Bus. L.J. 1 at 1–5. [Notes and/or References omitted.] This was originally from 1996 Law Society of Upper Canada Special Lectures. Reproduced with permission of the author and Irwin Law.

(3) The beneficiary is peculiarly vulnerable to or at the mercy of the fiduciary holding the discretion or power.

As a test for determining whether a given relationship is fiduciary, these guidelines are over-inclusive. For example, in many contractual relationships, one party has power that can affect the interests of the other party and that other party may be "at the mercy" of the one with such power. Yet, without more, such contractual relationships are not fiduciary ones.

In the recent case of *Hodgkinson v. Simms* La Forest J. limited the applicability of Wilson J.'s test to the recognition of "standard categories" of fiduciary relationships. He stated:

> Wilson J.'s guidelines constitute *indicia* that help recognize a fiduciary relationship rather then ingredients that define it.
>
> ...
>
> In seeking to determine whether new classes of relationships are *per se* fiduciary, Wilson J.'s three-step analysis is a useful guide.
>
> ...
>
> [T]he three-step analysis proposed by Wilson J. encounters difficulties in identifying relationships described by a slightly different use of the term "fiduciary", *viz.*, situations in which fiduciary obligations, though not innate to a given relationship, arise as a matter of fact out of the specific circumstances of that particular relationship ...

Although the position of La Forest J. is not completely clear, it appears that, for him, the essential element in finding that a fiduciary relationship outside of the established categories is "evidence of a mutual understanding that one party has relinquished its own self-interest and agreed to act solely on behalf of the other party".

I would make three comments on the attempt by the Supreme Court in *Hodgkinson v. Simms* to clarify the process of determining the existence of a fiduciary relationship.

(1) Although La Forest J., in the passage quoted above, refers to a "mutual understanding" and whether one party has relinquished its own self-interest, in other parts of his judgment he suggests that a fiduciary relationship may be created on the basis of reasonable expectations:

> The existence of a fiduciary duty in a given case will depend upon the reasonable expectations of the parties, and these in turn depend on factors such as trust, confidence, complexity of subject matter, and community or industry standards.

This may be interpreted to mean that a fiduciary relationship may be found to exist, even outside of the standard categories, in the absence of a mutual understanding that the fiduciary will relinquish his or her self-interest and act solely on behalf of the other party. In view of La Forest J.'s earlier comment emphasizing the necessity for such an understanding, I do not think this is the correct interpretation of his position. It is possible that such an understanding may not be required in some circumstances in the standard categories (although ordinarily, it will be possible to infer the understanding from the act of entering into the particular relationship). Outside of the standard categories, I suggest that references by La Forest J. to reasonable expectations merely indicate that the required mutual understanding will be determined objectively so that, as in contract law, the understanding may be held to exist even where it is not proved that the alleged fiduciary subjectively recognized his fiduciary position.

(2) The requirement that one party act solely in the interest of another party does not wholly capture the requirements for a fiduciary relationship. Not all persons who have so agreed to act on behalf of another will be fiduciaries. For example, a broker whose terms of engagement require that he merely act on the directions of his principal — a mere "order-taker" — should not be held to be a fiduciary even though in carrying out this engagement he acts solely in the interests of his principal. Having rejected Wilson J.'s guidelines as a useful test for finding a fiduciary relationship, La Forest J. needed to find some other basis for distinguishing fiduciary relationships from others in which one party may act on behalf of another party. He did this, apparently, by reference to general notions of "trust" and "confidence" and reliance on skill, knowledge and advice.

(3) The chief difference between the position of La Forest J. and that of Sopinka and McLachlin JJ. appears to relate to the relevance of vulnerability. Sopinka and McLachlin JJ. considered that *LAC Minerals Ltd. v. International Corona Resources Ltd.* was indistinguishable and that the judgment

of Sopinka J., writing for a majority of the court on the existence of a fiduciary relationship, made vulnerability an indispensable requirement for a finding of a fiduciary relationship. However, the difference between the position of La Forest J. and that of Sopinka and McLachlin JJ. does not seem to be based on fundamental disagreement about the applicable principles. The explanation for their different conclusions appears to lie in their different treatment of the facts. Sopinka and McLachlin JJ. recognized that vulnerability need not pre-exist the creation of the relationship in question; the vulnerability may be created by the relationship. Obviously, in the case of the standard categories of fiduciary relationships there often will be no pre-existing vulnerability. For example, the fact that the beneficiary of a trust is rich, powerful and sophisticated and that the trustee is poor, weak and inexperienced does not prevent the relationship being one in which the trustee owes fiduciary obligations to the beneficiary. Even outside of the standard categories, there may similarly be no pre-existing vulnerability. A person who is quite capable of looking after himself with respect to a particular activity may nevertheless choose to enter into a relationship in which he can rely on another person to act on his behalf with respect to that activity, and the relationship may thus be a fiduciary one.

(b) *Norberg v. Wynrib*†

[La FOREST J.:]

This case concerns the civil liability of a doctor who gave drugs to a chemically dependent woman patient in exchange for sexual contact. The central issue is whether the defence of consent can be raised against the intentional tort of battery in such circumstances. The case also raises the issue [of] whether the action is barred by reason of illegality or immorality.

FACTS

In 1978, the appellant, then a modestly educated young woman in her late teens, began to experience severe headaches and pains in her jaw. She went to doctors and dentists but none of them could diagnose the cause of her excruciating pain. They prescribed various types of painkillers. However, the medication provided no relief. The headaches became worse. More and more medication was prescribed in increasing amounts and dosages. In addition to this medication, her sister, a drug addict, gave her Fiorinal, a painkiller drug. Finally, in December 1978, a dentist diagnosed her difficulty as being related to an abscessed tooth. It was extracted and at last her pain was relived.

But now the appellant had a new problem. She had a craving for painkillers. Her sister gave her more Fiorinal. In 1981, when she broke her ankle, she found a doctor who was willing to prescribe Fiorinal for her. She continued to obtain prescriptions from him until he retired. However, his replacement refused to give her more pills. She discussed the situation with her sister and in March 1982 she commenced to see Dr. Wynrib, an elderly medical practitioner in his seventies. She told him she was experiencing pain in the ankle she had broken in 1981 and asked for Fiorinal. He gave her the prescription. She kept going back to him using that ankle injury and other illnesses as a pretext for obtaining prescriptions. Her dependence on Fiorinal continued to increase as did her depend-

---

† [1992] 2 S.C.R. 226 at 237–41, 247–50, 256–59, 261, 268–75, 289–91, 298-301.

ence on Dr. Wynrib. But the pretext could not continue. Later in 1982, Dr. Wynrib confronted the appellant. The appellant described this confrontation as follows:

> I had gone into his office one day and I asked him — I asked him for a prescription of Fiorinal, and I remember that he sat back in his chair and he pulled out like the medical file and he looked at me and he asked me come on, Laura, why is the real reason you're taking the Fiorinal. I told him because it's for my back or my ankle, whatever it was that I had been asking him for, and he said — no he said. And he looked again over my file. He said you can't be taking them for this long and not be addicted to them. Why is the real reason. And I denied it again. I said it's for the pain. And he told me that if I didn't admit to him that I was addicted to the Fiorinal that he wouldn't give me any more prescriptions. And I remember that I had started crying and I had denied [sic] to him, and he had told me to leave the office. And I wouldn't leave the office and finally I admitted to him that I was addicted to the Fiorinal.

Dr. Wynrib responded by giving the appellant another prescription.

After the appellant admitted to Dr. Wynrib that she was addicted to Fiorinal, she testified that he told her that "if I was good to him he would be good to me" and he made suggestions by pointing upstairs where he lived above his office. The appellant recognized this for what it was and sought her drugs elsewhere. She managed to secure Fiorinal through other doctors and by buying [it] off the street. Her tolerance and dependence grew. Eventually the other doctors reduced her supply. She was, as she put it, desperate. Near the end of 1983 she went back to Dr. Wynrib because she knew he would give her Fiorinal. She gave in to his demands.

Initially the sexual encounters took place in the back examination room of his office. He kissed her and fondled her breasts. In time, he required her to meet him upstairs in his bedroom where he kept a bottle of Fiorinal in his dresser drawer beside the bed. She managed to stall him for awhile by asking for the Fiorinal first and then leaving after she obtained it. But this device did not work long. Dr. Wynrib told her that he would not give her the Fiorinal until she complied with his demands. The pattern was that he would tell her to undress and put the bottle of Fiorinal by his bed for her to see. Both parties would lie on the

bed. Dr. Wynrib would kiss the appellant, touch her and then get on top of her. He would go through the motions of intercourse. There was no penetrating, however, because he could not sustain an erection. On at least one occasion, however he penetrated her with his fingers. He would give her pills each time she visited him in his apartment. She then would go back to his office the next day and he would write out a prescription. When the encounters began, the appellant did not want to believe what was happening. She thought he would do it once and then stop. However, the appellant testified that these incidences of simulated intercourse occurred 10 or 12 times, up to the early part of 1985.

. . . .

At trial, the respondent did not testify. However, the appellant admitted that Dr. Wynrib did not at any time use physical force. She also testified that he did things for her such as giving her money as well as coffee and cookies. She agreed that she "played" on the fact that he liked her and that she knew throughout the relationship that he was lonely.

The appellant continues to attend Narcotics Anonymous and other similar programs. She has done volunteer work at the crisis and counselling centre in the area where she lives and has completed credits towards a social worker program. Her hope is to work in the area of drug rehabilitation. She daily thinks with shame and remorse about what happened with Dr. Wynrib. She returned to the rehabilitation centre for more treatment after her first child was born. She felt that she did not deserve to have a child because of what she had done with Dr. Wynrib. Her craving for drugs continues but she has learned to live without them.

. . . .

... At trial and in the Court of Appeal, the appellant sought recovery on a number of grounds: sexual assault, negligence, breach of fiduciary duty, and breach of contract. In this Court, however, counsel particularly stressed the assault claim and I am content to dispose of the case on this basis. The other claims would appear to give rise to difficulties that would not arise in the ordinary doctor-client case. In particular, the appellant here did not come to the doctor for treatment. Rather she intended to use him to obtain drugs. Given the manner in which I propose to deal with the case, however it is unnecessary for me to explore these matters.

ASSAULT — THE NATURE OF CONSENT

The alleged sexual assault in this case falls under the tort of battery. A battery is the intentional infliction of unlawful force on another person. Consent, express or implied, is a defence to battery. Failure to resist or protest is an indication of consent "if a reasonable person who is aware of the consequences and capable of protest or resistance would voice his objection": see Fleming, *The Law of Torts* (7th ed. 1987), at pp. 72–73. However, the consent must be genuine; it must not be obtained by force or threat of force or be given under the influence of drugs. Consent may also be vitiated by fraud or deceit as to the nature of the defendant's conduct. The courts below considered these to be the only factors that would vitiate consent.

In my view, this approach to consent in this kind of case is too limited. As Heuston and Buckley, *Salmond and Heuston on the Law of Torts* (19th ed. 1987), at pp. 564–65, put it: "A man cannot be said to be 'willing' unless he is in a position to choose freely; and freedom of choice predicates the absence from his mind of any feeling of constraint interfering with the freedom of his will". A "feeling of constraint" so as to "interfere with the freedom of a person's will" can arise in a number of situations not involving force, threats of force, fraud or incapacity. The concept of consent as it operates in tort law is based on a presumption of individual autonomy and free will. It is presumed that the individual has freedom to consent or not to consent. This presumption, however, is untenable in certain circumstances. A position of relative weakness can, in some circumstances, interfere with the freedom of a person's will. Our notion of consent must, therefore, be modified to appreciate the power relationship between the parties.

An assumption of individual autonomy and free will is not confined to tort law. It is also the underlying premise of contract law. The supposition of contract law is that two parties agree or consent to a particular course of action. However, contract law has evolved in such a way that it recognizes that contracting parties do not always have equality in their bargaining strength. The doctrines of duress, undue influence, and unconscionability have arisen to protect the vulnerable when they are in a relationship of unequal power. For reasons of public policy, the law will not always hold weaker parties to the bargains they make. Professor Klippert in his book *Unjust Enrichment* refers to the doctrines of duress, undue influence, and unconscionability as "justice factors". He lumps these together under the general term "coercion" and states, at p. 156, that "[i]n essence the common thread is an illegitimate use of power or unlawful pressure which vitiates a person's freedom of choice". In a situation where a plaintiff is induced to enter into an unconscionable transaction because of an inequitable disparity in bargaining strength, it cannot be said that the plaintiff's act is voluntary: see Klippert, *supra*, at p. 170.

If the "justice factor" of unconscionability is used to address the issue of voluntariness in the law of contract, it seems reasonable that it be examined to address the issue of voluntariness in the law of tort. This provides insight into the issue of consent: for consent to be genuine, it must be voluntary. The factual context of each case must, of course, be evaluated to determine if there has been genuine consent. However, the principles that have been developed in the area of unconscionable transactions to negate the legal effectiveness of certain contracts provide a useful framework for this evaluation.

An unconscionable transaction arises in contract law where there is an overwhelming imbalance in the power relationship between the parties. In *Morrison v. Coast Finance Ltd.* Davey J.A. outlined the factors to be considered in a claim of unconscionability:

> ... a plea that a bargain is unconscionable invokes relief against an unfair advantage gained by an unconscientious use of power by a stronger party against a weaker. On such a claim the material ingredients are proof of inequality in the position of the parties arising out of the ignorance, need or distress of the weaker, which left him in the power of the stronger, and proof of substantial unfairness of the bargain obtained by the stronger. On proof of those circumstances, it creates a presumption of fraud which the stronger must repel by proving that the bargain was fair, just and reasonable....

In *Lloyds Bank Ltd. v. Bundy*, Lord Denning M.R. took a wider approach and developed the general principle of "inequality of bargaining power":

. . . .

An inequality of bargaining power may arise in a number of ways. As Boyle and Percy, *Contracts: Cases and Commentaries* (4th ed. 1989), note, at pp. 637–38:

> [A person] may be intellectually weaker by reason of a disease of the mind, economically weaker or simply situationally weaker because of temporary circumstances. Alternatively, the "weakness" may arise out of a special relationship in which trust and confidence has been reposed in the other party. The comparative weakness or special relationship is, in every case, a fact to be proven.

As the last sentence of this passage suggests, the circumstances of each case must be examined to determine if there is an overwhelming imbalance of power in the relationship between the parties.

It may be argued that an unconscionable transaction does not, in fact, vitiate consent: the weaker party retains the power to give real consent but the law nevertheless provides relief on the basis of social policy. This may be more in line with Lord Denning's formulation of "inequality of bargaining power" in *Lloyds Bank Ltd. v. Bundy, supra*, when one takes into account his statement that it is not necessary to establish that the will of the weaker party was "dominated" or "overcome" by the other party. But whichever way one approaches the problem, the result is the same: on grounds of public policy, the legal effectiveness of certain types of contracts will be restricted or negated. In the same way, in certain situations, principles of public policy will negate the legal effectiveness of consent in the context of sexual assault. In particular, in certain circumstances, consent will be considered legally ineffective if it can be shown that there was such a disparity in the relative positions of the parties that the weaker was not in a position to choose freely.

. . . .

APPLICATION TO THIS CASE

The trial judge held that the appellant's implied consent to the sexual activity was voluntary. Dr. Wynrib, he stated, exercised neither force nor threats of force and the appellant's capacity to consent was not impaired by her drug use. The Court of Appeal agreed that the appellant voluntarily engaged in the sexual encounters. However, it must be asked if the appellant was truly in a position to make a free choice. It seems clear to me that there was a marked inequality in the respective powers of the parties. The appellant was a young woman with limited education. More important, she was addicted to the heavy use of tranquillizers and painkillers. On this ground alone it can be said that there was an inequality in the position of the parties arising out of the appellant's need. The appellant's drug dependence diminished her ability to make a real choice. Although she did not wish to engage in sexual activity with Dr. Wynrib, her reluctance was overwhelmed by the driving force of her addiction and the unsettling prospect of a painful, unsupervised chemical withdrawal....

. . . .

On the other side of the equation was an elderly, male professional — the appellant's doctor. An unequal distribution of power is frequently a part of the doctor-patient relationship. As it is stated in the *Final Report of the Task Force on Sexual Abuse of Patients*, An Independent Task Force Commissioned by the College of Physicians and Surgeons of Ontario (November 25, 1991) (Chair: Marilou McPhedran), at p. 11:

> Patients seek the help of doctors when they are in a vulnerable state — when they are sick, when they are needy, when they are uncertain about what needs to be done.
>
> The unequal distribution of power in the physician-patient relationship makes opportunities for sexual exploitation more possible than in other relationships. This vulnerability gives physicians the power to exact sexual compliance. Physical force or weapons are not necessary because the physician's power comes from having the knowledge and being trusted by patients.

In this case, Dr. Wynrib knew that the appellant was vulnerable and driven by her compulsion for drugs. It is likely that he knew or at least strongly suspected that she was dependant upon Fiorinal before she admitted her addiction to him. It was he who ferreted out that she was addicted to drugs. As a doctor, the respondent knew how to assist the appellant medically and he knew (or should have known) that she could not "just quit" taking drugs without treatment....

. . . .

The respondent's medical knowledge and knowledge of the appellant's addiction, combined with his authority to prescribe drugs, gave him power over her. It was he who suggested the sex-for-drugs arrangement.

. . . .

To summarize, in my view, the defence of consent cannot succeed in the circumstances of this case. The appellant had a medical problem — an addiction to Fiorinal. Dr. Wynrib had knowledge of the problem. As a doctor, he had knowledge of the proper medical treatment, and knew she was motivated by her craving for drugs. Instead of fulfilling his professional responsibility to treat the appellant, he used his power and expertise to his own advantage and to her detriment. In my opinion, the unequal power between the parties and the exploitative nature of the relationship removed the possibility of the appellant's providing meaningful consent to the sexual contact.

. . . .

DISPOSITION

I would allow the appeal and enter judgment for the plaintiff against the defendant. The plaintiff is entitled to aggravated damages in the amount of $20,000 and punitive damages in the amount of $10,000, the whole with costs throughout.

[McLACHLIN J.:]

I have had the advantage of reading the reasons of my colleagues Justice La Forest and Justice Sopinka. With respect, I do not find that the doctrines of tort or contract capture the essential nature of the wrong done to the plaintiff. Unquestionably, they do catch aspects of that wrong. But to look at the events which occurred over the course of the relationship between Dr. Wynrib and Ms. Norberg from the perspective of tort or contract is to view that relationship through lenses which distort more than they bring into focus. Only the principles applicable to fiduciary relationships and their breach encompass it in its totality. In my view, that doctrine is clearly applicable to the facts of this case on principles articulated by this Court in earlier cases. It alone encompasses the true relationship between the parties and the gravity of the wrong done by the defendant; accordingly it should be applied.

. . . .

It is not disputed that Dr. Wynrib abused his duty to the plaintiff. He provided her with drugs he knew she should not have. He failed to advise her to enrol in an anti-addiction program, thereby prolonging her addiction. Instead, he took advantage of her addiction to obtain sexual favours from her over a period of more than two years.

The relationship of physician and patient can be conceptualized in a variety of ways. It can be viewed as a creature of contract, with the physician's failure to fulfil his or her obligations giving rise to an action for breach of contract. It undoubtedly gives rise to a duty of care, the breach of which constitutes the tort of negligence. In common with all members of society, the doctor owes the patient a duty not to touch him or her without his/her consent; if the doctor breaches this duty he or she will have committed the tort of battery. But perhaps the most fundamental characteristic of the doctor-patient relationship is its <u>fiduciary</u> nature. All the authorities agree that the relationship of physician to patient also falls into that special category of relationships which the law calls fiduciary.

The recent judgment of La Forest J. in *McInerney v. MacDonald*, a case recognizing a patient's right of access to her medical records, canvasses those authorities and confirms the fiduciary nature of the doctor-patient relationship. I can do no better than to quote the following passage from his judgment:

> A physician begins compiling a medical file when a patient chooses to share intimate details about his or her life in the course of medical consultation. The patient "entrusts" this personal information to the physician for medical purposes. It is important to keep in mind the nature of the physician-patient relationship within which the information is confided. In *Kenny v. Lockwood*, Hodgins J.A. stated, that the relationship between physician and patient is one in which "trust and confidence" must be placed in the physician. This statement was referred to with approval by LeBel J. in *Henderson v. Johnston*, who himself characterized the physician-patient relationship as "fiduciary and confidential", and went on to say: "It is the same relationship as that which exists in equity between a parent and his child, a man and his wife, an attorney and his client, a confessor and his penitent, and a guardian and his ward". Several academic writers have similarly defined the physician-patient relationship as a fiduciary or trust relationship [...] I agree with this characterization.

So do I. I think it is readily apparent that the doctor-patient relationship shares the peculiar hallmark of the fiduciary relationship — trust, the trust of a person with inferior power that another person who has assumed superior power and responsibility will exercise that power for his or her good and only for his or her good and in his or her own best interests. Recognizing the fiduciary nature of the doctor-patient relationship provides the law with an analytic model by which physicians can be held to the high standards of dealing with their patients which the trust accorded them requires....

The foundation and ambit of the fiduciary obligation are conceptually distinct from the foundation and ambit of contract and tort. Sometimes the doctrines may overlap in their application, but that does not destroy their conceptual and functional uniqueness. In negligence and contract the parties are taken to be independent and equal actors, concerned primarily with their own self-interest. Consequently, the law seeks a balance between enforcing obligations by awarding compensation when those obligations are breached, and preserving optimum freedom for those involved in the relationship in question. The essence of a fiduciary relationship, by contrast, is that one party exercises power on behalf of another and pledges himself or herself to act in the best interests of the other.

Frankel, in "Fiduciary Law", compares the fiduciary relationship with status and contract relationships, with both of which fiduciary relationships may overlap. Like a status relationship (the relationship of parent and child is perhaps the archetypical status relationship), the fiduciary relationship is characterized by dependency, but the scope of that dependency is usually not as all-encompassing and pervasive as that obtaining in a status relationship. The beneficiary entrusts the fiduciary with information or other sources of power over the beneficiary, but does so only within a circumscribed area, for example entrusting his or her lawyer with power over his or her legal affairs or his or her physician with power over his or her body. Although fiduciary relationships may properly be recognized in the absence of consent by the beneficiary — the consent of a child to his or her parents' acting in a fiduciary capacity for the child's benefit is not required — they are more typically the product of the voluntary agreement of the parties that the beneficiary will cede to the fiduciary some power, and are always dependent on the fiduciary's undertaking to act in the beneficiary's interests. In this respect fiduciary relationships resemble contractual relationships. In contrast to both status and contract relationships, however,

> ... fiduciary relations are designed not to satisfy both parties' needs, but only those of the entrustor. Thus, a fiduciary may enter into a fiduciary relation without regard to his own needs. Moreover, an entrustor does not owe the fiduciary anything by virtue of the relation except in accordance with the agreed-upon terms or legally fixed status duties. Therefore, in a fiduciary relation, the entrustor is free from domination by the fiduciary, although he may still be coerced in parallel status relation. Thus, fiduciary relations combine the bargaining freedom inherent in contract relations with a limited form of the power and dependence of status relations.
>
> Accordingly, the law of fiduciary relations should, if possible, preserve the best aspects of status and contract relations. It is desirable for the entrustor to depend on the fiduciary to satisfy certain needs. But it would not be desirable for fiduciary law to impose the relation on either party or to allow the fiduciary to abuse his power. Therefore, fiduciary law should permit the parties to enter into the relation freely and ensure that the fiduciary will not coerce the entrustor.

The fiduciary relationship has trust, not self-interest, at its core, and when breach occurs, the balance favours the person wronged. The freedom of the fiduciary is limited by the obligation he or she has undertaken — an obligation which "betokens loyalty, good faith and avoidance of a conflict of duty and self-interest": *Canadian Aero Service Ltd v. O'Malley*. To cast a fiduciary relationship in terms of contract or tort (whether negligence or battery) is to diminish this obligation. If a fiduciary relationship is shown to exist, then the proper legal analysis is one based squarely on the full and fair consequences of a breach of that relationship.

. . . .

Dr. Wynrib was in a position of power *vis-à-vis* the plaintiff; he had scope for the exercise of power and discretion with respect to her. He had the power to advise her, to treat her, to give her the drug or to refuse her the drug. He could unilaterally exercise that power or discretion in a way that affected her interests. And her status as a patient rendered her vulnerable and at his mercy, particularly in light of their addiction. So Wilson J.'s test appears to be met. All the classic characteristics of fiduciary relationship were present. Dr.

Wynrib and Ms. Norberg were on an unequal footing. He pledged himself — by the act of hanging out his shingle as a medical doctor and accepting her as his patient — to act in her best interests and not permit any conflict between his duty to act only in her best interests and his own interests — including his interest in sexual gratification — to arise. As a physician, he owed her the classic duties associated with a fiduciary relationship — the duties of "loyalty, good faith and avoidance of a conflict of duty and self-interest".

. . . .

If we accept that the principles can apply in this case to protect the plaintiff's interest in receiving medical care free of exploitation at the hands of her physician, as I think we must, then the consequences are most significant. As we have just seen, the defences based on the alleged fault of the plaintiff, so pressing in tort, may carry little weight when raised against the beneficiary of a fiduciary relationship. This is because the fiduciary approach, unlike those based on tort or contract, is founded on the recognition of the power imbalance inherent in the relationship between fiduciary and beneficiary, and to giving redress where that power imbalance is abused. Another consequence that flows from considering the matter on the basis of breach of fiduciary obligation may be a more generous approach to remedies, as I will come to presently. Equity has always held trustees strictly accountable in a way the tort of negligence and contract have not. Foreseeability of loss is not a factor in equitable damages. Certain defences, such as mitigation, may not apply.

But the most significant consequence of applying the doctrine of fiduciary obligation to a person in the position of Dr. Wynrib is this. Tort and contract can provide a remedy for a physician's failure to provide adequate treatment. But only with considerable difficulty can they be bent to accommodate the wrong of a physician's abusing his or her position to obtain sexual favours from his or her patient. The law has never recognized consensual sexual relations as capable of giving rise to an obligation in tort or in contract. My colleagues, with respect, strain to conclude the contrary. La Forest J. does so by using the contractual doctrine of relief from unconscionable transactions to negate the consent which the plaintiff, as found by the trial judge, undoubtedly gave. The problems inherent in this approach have already been noted. Sopinka J., at p. 317, finds himself tacking damages

for the sexual encounters onto the breach of the duty to treat on the ground that "[t]he sexual acts were causally connected to the failure to treat and must form part of the damage suffered by the appellant". But can damages flow from acts the law finds lawful simply on the ground they are "connected" to damages for an actionable wrong? And what of the patient whose medical needs are fully met but who is sexually exploited? On Sopinka J.'s reasoning she has no cause of action. These examples underline the importance of treating the consequences of this relationship on the footing of what it is — a fiduciary relationship — rather than forcing it into the ill-fitting molds of contract and tort. Contrary to the conclusion of the court below, characterizing the duty as fiduciary <u>does</u> add something; indeed, without doing so the wrong done to the plaintiff can neither be fully comprehended in law nor adequately compensated in damages.

. . . .

DAMAGES

. . . .

My colleague La Forest J. refers to a number of decisions which have considered the quantum of damages for rape and sexual assault. While one must be cautious in making such comparisons, particularly given the somewhat arbitrary basis upon which damages have been assessed in some sexual assault cases, I find the trauma caused to Ms. Norberg as a consequence of the sexual acts in many respects similar to that in *Harder v. Brown*. There the plaintiff, a minor, was assaulted a number of times over a seven-year period by the defendant, an elderly friend of her grandfather. As here, the acts consisted of kissing, fondling and attempted intercourse. The defendant also caused the plaintiff to undress and be photographed. As a result, the plaintiff suffered lasting psychological trauma, including a diminished sense of self-worth and difficulty in forming intimate relationships. Wood J., as he then was, awarded general damages in the sum of $40,000. Ms. Norberg has suffered similar consequential trauma, but bearing in mind the shorter period during which the sexual abuse occurred here, I would award $25,000 in damages for sexual exploitation.

Finally, this is in my opinion an appropriate case in which to make an award of punitive damages. In so far as reference to tort principles may be appropriate I note that punitive damages have been awarded in several sexual assault cases: see, for example, *Myers v. Haroldson*, ($40,000); *Harder v. Brown, supra* ($10,000).

Quite apart from analogies with tort, punitive (or exemplary) damages are available with respect to breaches of fiduciary duty, and in particular for breaches of the sort exemplified by this case....

I find Ellis' statement, found in his text *Fiduciary Duties in Canada*, as to the circumstances which will constitute the conditions precedent for awarding punitive damages for a breach of fiduciary duty both helpful and applicable to the facts of this case:

> Where the actions of the fiduciary are purposefully repugnant to the beneficiary's best interests, punitive damages are a logical award to be made by the Court. This award will be particularly applicable where the impugned activity is motivated by the fiduciary's self-interest.

I do not think it can be seriously questioned that Dr. Wynrib's activities were both purposefully repugnant to Ms. Norberg's best interests, and motivated entirely by his own self-interest.

Punitive damages are awarded, not for the purpose of compensating the victim for her loss, but with a view to punishing the wrongdoer and deterring both him and others from engaging in similar conduct in the future. Dr. Wynrib's conduct is sufficiently reprehensible and offensive to common standards of decency to render him liable to such a punitive award. While, given his age, it is unlikely that such damages will have much utility in terms of specific deterrent effect, concerns for general deterrence militate in favour of their being granted. The Report of the Task Force of the Ontario College of Physicians and Surgeons makes it clear that the sexual exploitation of patients by physicians is more widespread than it is comfortable to contemplate. Its damaging effects extend not only to those persons who are directly harmed, but also to the image of the profession as a whole and the community's trust in physicians to act in our best interests. In this context punitive damages may serve to reinforce the high standard of conduct which the fiduciary relationship between physicians and patients demands be honoured. This is completely in keeping with the law's role in protecting beneficiaries and promoting fiduciary relationships through the strict regulation of the conduct of fiduciaries: on this point see Frankel, *supra* at p. 816. An award of punitive damages in the present case would signal the community's disapprobation of the sexual exploitation of vulnerable patients, and for that reason ought to be made.

. . . .

Although the circumstances of the present case are quite different from those in *Myers v. Haroldson, supra*, I find guidance in that case. The factors referred to by Osborn J. — blameworthy conduct, prevalence of conduct necessitating deterrence, lack of empathy for the victim and lack concern for the consequences to the victim — are present. Most important in this case, as in *Myers*, is the need for deterrence. Dr. Wynrib is not alone in breaching the trust of his patient through sexually exploiting her; physicians, and all those in positions of trust, must be warned that society will not condone abuse of the trust placed in them. I would award punitive damages against Dr. Wynrib in the amount of $25,000.

In the result I would allow the appeal and award the plaintiff judgment for $70,000....

(c) *Guerin v. Canada*†

[This case was previously considered in Chapter of this volume. Only those portions of the judgment dealing with the fiduciary obligation of the crown are reproduced here.]

---

† [1984] 2 S.C.R. 335.

[WILSON J.:]

The appellant, Delbert Guerin, is the Chief of the Musqueam Indian Band, the members of which are descended from the original inhabitants of Greater Vancouver. The other appellants are Band Councillors. In 1955 there were 235 members in the Band and they lived on a reserve located within the charter area of the City of Vancouver which contained approximately 416.53 acres of very valuable land.

The subject of the litigation is a lease of 162 acres of the reserve land entered into on January 22, 1958 on behalf of the Band by the Indian Affairs Branch of the federal government with the Shaughnessy Heights Golf Club as lessee. The trial judge found that the Crown was in breach of trust in entering into this lease and awarded the Band $10 million in damages. The Crown appealed to the Federal Court of Appeal to have the trial judgment set aside and the Band cross-appealed seeking an increase in the award of damages.

By a unanimous judgment [(1982), 143 D.L.R. (3d) 416] the Crown's appeal was allowed and the cross-appeal dismissed. The Band sought and was granted leave to appeal to this Court.

There are four main grounds on which the appellants submit that the trial judge's finding of liability should have been upheld in the Court of Appeal. I paraphrase them from the appellants' factum as follows:

1. Section 18(1) of the *Indian Act*, R.S.C. 1952, c. 149, imposes a trust or, at a minimum, fiduciary duties on the Crown with respect to reserve lands held by it for the use and benefit of Indian Bands. This trust or those fiduciary duties are not merely political in nature but are enforceable in the courts like any other trust or fiduciary duty.
2. The Federal Court of Appeal should not have allowed the Crown to put forward the concept of "political trust" as a defence to the Band's claim since, as the learned trial judge pointed out, it was not specifically pleaded as required by Rule 409 of the *Federal Court Rules*.
3. The leased lands were surrendered by the Band to the Crown in trust for lease to the Golf Club on very specific terms and those terms were not obtained. The terms which were obtained were much less favourable to the Band and the Band would not have surrendered the land for lease on those terms.
4. The Crown, by misrepresenting the terms it could and would obtain on the lease, induced the Band to surrender its land and thereby committed the tort of deceit.

In any case of alleged breach of trust the facts are extremely important and none more so than in this case. We are fortunate, however, in having very careful and extensive findings by the learned trial judge and, although counsel on both sides roamed at large through the transcript for evidence in support of their various propositions, I have considered it desirable to confine myself very closely to the trial judge's findings.

1. THE FACTS

There can be little doubt that by the mid 1950's the Indian Affairs Branch was well aware that the appellants' reserve was a very valuable one because of its location. Indeed, offers to lease or buy large tracts of the reserve had already been received. We know this from a report dated October 11, 1955 made by Mr. Anfield who was in charge of the Vancouver agency at the time to Mr. Arneil, the Indian Commissioner for British Columbia. Both these men are since deceased which is unfortunate since Mr. Anfield played a lead role in the impugned lease transaction. In a later report to Mr. Arneil, Mr. Anfield suggested that a detailed study should be made of the Band's requirements of its reserve lands so that the surplus, if any, could be identified and turned to good account for the Band's benefit. He suggested that not only should they obtain an appraisal of land values but that a land use planning survey should be prepared aimed at maximum development in order to provide long-term revenue for the Band.

He continued:

> It seems to me that the real requirement here is the services of an expert estate planner with courage and vision and whose interest and concern would be as much the future of the Musqueam Indians as the revenue use of the lands unrequired by these Indians. It is essential that any new village be a model community. The present or any Agency staff set up could not possibly manage a project like this, and some very realistic and immediate plans must be formulated to bring about the stated wish of these Musqueam people, the fullest possible use and development for their benefit, of what is undoubtedly the [potentially most]

valuable 400 acres in metropolitan Vancouver today.

Mr. Anfield went on to speak in terms of "another potential 'British Properties'" and suggested that all parties interested in the land should be advised that the land not required by the Band for its own use, when defined and surrendered, would be publicly advertised.

About this time the Shaughnessy Heights Golf Club was looking for a new site. Its lease from the Canadian Pacific Railway was due to expire in 1960 and the club had been told that it would not be renewed. The club turned its attention therefore to the Musqueam Reserve. At the same time an active interest in the reserve was being displayed by a representative of a prominent Vancouver real estate firm on behalf of a developer client interested in a long-term lease. Although his contact had been directly with the Indian Affairs Branch in Ottawa, Messrs. Arneil and Anfield were both aware of it. Indeed, when he suggested to them that he meet with the Chief and Councillors of the Band to try to work out some arrangement, he was told by Mr. Anfield not to do so but to deal only through Indian Affairs personnel. That he followed this advice is made clear from the evidence of the Band members who testified. They were told of no interest in their land other than that expressed by the golf club.

The learned trial judge dealt specifically with the issue of the credibility of the members of the Band because he was very conscious of the fact that neither Mr. Arneil nor Mr. Anfield was alive to testify. He found the Band members to be "honest, truthful witnesses" and accepted their testimony.

The Band agreed that its surplus land should be leased and authorized a land appraisal to be made and paid for out of Band funds. In fact the appraisal was done by Mr. Howell of the Veterans Land Act Administration. Although he was a qualified appraiser, he was not a land use expert. He divided the reserve for valuation purposes into four areas, the first of which included the 162 acres leased to the golf club. This area comprised 220 acres classified by Mr. Howell as "First Class Residential area" and valued at $5,500 per acre making a total of $1,209,120. The other three areas which were all low lying he valued at $625 per acre. The Band was not given a copy of his report and indeed Mr. Arneil and Mr. Anfield had difficulty getting copies. They were very anxious to get the report because they were considering a lease of

150 acres to the golf club at "a figure of say $20,000 to $25,000 a year". The documentary evidence at trial showed that meetings and discussions had taken place between Mr. Anfield and the president of the golf club in 1956 and in the early part of 1957. It is of interest to note that Mr. Anfield had told the president of the golf club about the appraisal which was being carried out and had subsequently reviewed Mr. Howell's report with them. The golf club was, of course, advised that any proposal made by it would have to be laid before the Band for its approval.

On April 7, 1957 the Band Council met, Mr. Anfield presiding. The trial judge found that the golf club proposal was put to the Chief and Councillors only in the most general terms. They were told the lease would be of approximately 160 acres, that it would be for an initial term of fifteen years with options to the club for additional fifteen year periods and that it would be "on terms to be agreed upon". In fact the rent that had been proposed by the club was $25,000 a year for the first fifteen years with the rent for each successive fifteen-year period being settled by mutual agreement or failing that by arbitration. However, under the proposal the rent for the renewal periods was subject to a ceiling increase of 15 per cent on the initial rent of $25,000.

The learned trial judge found that when Mr. Bethune, the Superintendent of Reserves and Trusts in Ottawa, was advised of the $25,000 rental figure he questioned its adequacy and suggested to Mr. Arneil that he consult with Mr. Howell, the appraiser, as to what a proper return on the 160 acres would be. Unfortunately, Mr. Howell was not given all the facts. He was not told of the 15 per cent ceiling on rent increases. He was not told that the golf club would have the right to remove all improvements on termination of the lease although he was told that the club proposed to spend up to a million dollars in buildings and improvements on the leased land. Mr. Howell therefore recommended acceptance of the gold club's offer stating: "These improvements will revert to the Band at the end of the lease" and "the Department will be in a much sounder position to negotiate an increase in rental in fifteen years time when the club will have invested a considerable amount of capital in the property which they will have to protect." Mr. Howell testified at trial that he would not have recommended acceptance of the golf club's offer had he known that the improvements would not revert to the Band and that the rental on renewal periods was subject to a 15 per cent ceiling increase.

Mr. Howell's letter was forwarded to Ottawa with the request that surrender documents be prepared for submission to the Band and this was done. It is interesting to note, however, that in the letter forwarding the surrender documents Mr. Bethune indicated to Mr. Arneil that he would like to see the 15 per cent ceiling on rent removed and rent for subsequent periods established either by mutual agreement or by arbitration.

A Band Council meeting was held on July 25, 1957 again with Mr. Anfield in the chair. There was further discussion of the proposed lease to the golf club and two Councillors expressed the view that the renewal period should be at ten year intervals rather than fifteen. It was at this meeting that the resolution was passed to hold a general meeting of Band members to consider and vote on the surrender of the 162 acres to the Crown for purposes of the lease. The meeting of the Band was held on October 6, 1957 but prior to that there was another meeting of Councillors on September 27, 1957. Mr. Harrison and Mr. Jackson of the Shaughnessy Golf Club attended this meeting and Mr. Anfield, who had in the interval been promoted to Assistant Indian Commissioner for British Columbia, was there along with a Mr. Grant who was described as "Officer in Charge — Vancouver Agency". In the presence of the golf club representatives Chief Sparrow took issue with the $25,000 per annum rental figure and stipulated for something in the neighbourhood of $44,000 to $44,500 per annum. The golf club representatives balked at this and they were asked to step outside while the Band Council and the Indian Affairs personnel had a private discussion.

Mr. Anfield expressed the view that the $44,000 figure was unreasonable and suggested $29,000 to which the Councillors agreed on the understanding that the first lease period would be for ten years and subsequent rental negotiations would take place every five years. Mr. Grant testified that Mr. Anfield advised the Council to go ahead with the lease at the $29,000 figure and in ten years demand a healthy increase from the golf club. Mr. Grant also testified that the Council objected to any ceiling on future rental and Mr. Anfield said that he would convey their concern to the Department of Indian Affairs. On that basis the Council, according to Mr. Grant, reluctantly accepted the $29,000 figure.

At the meeting of the Band on October 6, 1957 ("the surrender meeting") Chief Sparrow was present along with the Councillors and members. Mr. Anfield presided as usual. The learned trial judge made specific findings as to what occurred at the meeting and I reproduce them from his reasons:

(a) The golf club lease would be, aside from the first term, for 10-year periods, not 15 years.

(b) Before the Band members voted, those present assumed or understood there would be no 15% limitation on rental increases.

(c) The meeting was not told the golf club proposed it should have the right, at any time during the lease and for a period of up to 6 months after termination, to remove any buildings or structures, and any course improvements and facilities.

(d) The meeting was not told that future rent on renewal periods was to be determined as if the land were still in an uncleared and unimproved condition and used as a golf club.

(e) The meeting was not told that the golf club would have the right at the end of each 15-year period to terminate the lease on six-month's prior notice.

Neither (d) nor (e) were in the original golf club proposal and first appeared in the draft lease following the surrender meeting. They were not brought before the Band Council or the Band at any time for comment or approval. The Band voted almost unanimously in favour of the surrender.

By the surrender document the Chief and Councillors of the Band acting on behalf of the Band surrendered 162 acres to the Crown:

TO HAVE AND TO HOLD the same unto Her said Majesty the Queen, her Heirs and Successors forever in trust to lease the same to such person or persons, and upon such terms as the Government of Canada may deem most conducive to our Welfare and that of our people.

AND upon the further condition that all moneys received from the leasing thereof, shall be credited to our revenue trust account at Ottawa.

AND WE, the said Chief and Councillors of the said Musqueam Band of Indians do on behalf of our people and for ourselves, hereby ratify and confirm, and promise to ratify and confirm, whatever the said Government may do, or cause to be lawfully done, in connection with the leasing thereof.

It will be noted that there is no reference in the surrender to the proposed lease to the golf club. The position of the Crown at trial was that once the surrender documents were signed the Crown could lease to anyone on whatever terms it saw fit.

After the surrender there was considerable correspondence between Mr. Anfield and personnel in the Indian Affairs Branch in Ottawa particularly over the more controversial provisions of the lease but none of this correspondence was communicated to the Band Council nor were they given a copy of the draft lease which would have drawn these controversial provisions to their attention.

The trial judge states at p. 409:

> Put baldly, the band members, regardless of the whole history of dealings and the limited information imparted at the surrender meeting, were not consulted. But it was their land. It was their potential investment and revenue. It was their future.

The learned trial judge accepted that the Chief, the Councillors and the Band members were wholly excluded from any further discussions or negotiations among the Indian Affairs personnel, the golf club officers and their respective solicitors with respect to the terms of the lease. The trial judge found an explanation, although not a justification, for this in the possibility that Indian Affairs personnel at the time took a rather paternalistic attitude towards the Indian people whom they regarded as wards of the Crown.

I turn now to the essential terms of the lease as entered into in January 22, 1958 as described by the learned trial judge at p. 412:

1. The term is for 75 years, unless sooner terminated.
2. The rent for the first 15 years is $29,000 per annum.
3. For the 4 succeeding 15-year periods, annual rent is to be determined by mutual agreement, or failing such agreement, by arbitration ... such rent to be equal to the fair rent for the demised premises as if the same were still in an uncleared and unimproved condition as at the date of each respective determination and considering the restricted use to which the Lessee may put the demised premises under the terms of this lease....
4. The maximum increase in rent for the second 15-year period (January 1, 1973 to January 1, 1988) is limited to 15% of $29,000, that is $4,350 per annum.
5. The golf club can terminate the lease at the end of any 15-year period by giving 6 months' prior notice.
6. The golf club can, at any time during the lease and up to 6 months after termination, remove any buildings or other structures, and any course improvements and facilities.

Mr. Grant stated in evidence that the terms of the lease ultimately entered into bore little resemblance to what was discussed and approved at the surrender meeting and the learned trial judge agreed. He found that had the Band been aware of the terms in fact contained in the lease they would never have surrendered their land.

So much for the facts as found by the learned trial judge. What recourse in law, if any, does the Band have in such circumstances?

2. SECTION 18 OF THE *INDIAN ACT*

The appellants contend that the Federal Court of Appeal erred in failing to find that s. 18 of the *Indian Act* imposed on the Crown a fiduciary obligation enforceable in the courts. The section reads as follows:

> 18.(1) Subject to the provisions of this Act, reserves shall be held by Her Majesty for the use and benefit of the respective bands for which they were set apart; and subject to this Act and to the terms of any treaty or surrender, the Governor in Council may determine whether any purpose for which lands in a reserve are used or are to be used is for the use and benefit of the band.

. . . .

6. THE MEASURE OF DAMAGES

. . . .

The position at common law concerning damages for breach of trust and, in particular, the difference between the principles in trust law from those applicable in tort and contract, are well summarized in the following passages from Mr. Justice Street's judgment in the Australian case of *Re Dawson; Union Fidelity Trustee Co. v. Perpetual Trustee Co.*:

> The obligation of a defaulting trustee is essentially one of effecting a restitution to the estate. The obligation is of a personal charac-

ter and its extent is not to be limited by common law principles governing remoteness of damage.

...

Caffrey v. Darby is consistent with the proposition that if a breach has been committed then the trustee is liable to place the trust estate in the same position as it would have been in if no breach had been committed. Considerations of causation, foreseeability and remoteness do not readily enter into the matter.

...

The principles embodied in this approach do not appear to involve any inquiry as to whether the loss was caused by or flowed from the breach. Rather the inquiry in each instance would appear to be whether the loss would have happened if there had been no breach.

...

The cases to which I have referred demonstrate that the obligation to make restitution, which courts of equity have from very early times imposed on defaulting trustees and other fiduciaries, is of a more absolute nature than the common-law obligation to pay damages for tort or breach of contract. It is on this fundamental ground that I regard the principles in *Tomkinson's* case [*Tomkinson v. First Pennsylvania Banking and Trust Co.*, [1961] A.C. 1007] as distinguishable. ...

. . . .

This statement of the law has been cited with approval in Underhill's *Law of Trusts and Trustees* (13th ed. 1979), and was also recently adopted by Brightman L.J. in *Bartlett v. Barclays Bank Trust Co. (No. 2)*: see also Waters, *Law of Trusts in Canada* (1974).

In this case the Band surrendered the land to the Crown for lease on certain specified terms. The trial judge found as a fact that such a lease was impossible to obtain. The Crown's duty at that point was to go back to the Band, consult with it, and obtain further instructions. Instead of doing that it went ahead and leased the land on unauthorized terms. In my view it thereby committed a breach of trust and damages are to be assessed on the basis of the principles enunciated by Mr. Justice Street. The lost opportunity to develop the land for a period of up to seventy-five years in duration is to be compensated as at the date of trial notwithstanding that market values may have increased since the date of breach. The beneficiary gets the benefit of any such increase. It seems to me that there is no merit in the Crown's submis-

sion that "if a trustee is under a duty to alienate land by lease or otherwise, the date to assess compensation for breach of that duty is the date when the alienation should have taken place not the date of trial or judgment". Since the lease that was authorized by the Band was impossible to obtain, the Crown's breach of duty in this case was not in failing to lease the land, but in leasing it when it could not lease it on the terms approved by the Band. The Band was thereby deprived of its land and any use to which it might have wanted to put it. Just as it is to be presumed that a beneficiary would have wished to sell his securities at the highest price available during the period they were wrongfully withheld from him by the trustee (see *McNeil v. Fultz*) so also it should be presumed that the Band would have wished to develop its land in the most advantageous way possible during the period covered by the unauthorized lease. In this respect also the principles applicable to determine damages for breach of trust are to be contrasted with the principles applicable to determine damages for breach of contract. In contract it would have been necessary for the Band to prove that it would have developed the land; in equity a presumption is made to that effect: see Waters, *Law of Trusts in Canada*.

. . . .

[DICKSON J.:]

. . . .

(c) The Crown's Fiduciary Obligation

The concept of fiduciary obligation originated long ago in the notion of breach of confidence, one of the original heads of jurisdiction in Chancery. In the present appeal its relevance is based on the requirement of a "surrender" before Indian land can be alienated.

The *Royal Proclamation of 1763* provided that no private person could purchase from the Indians any lands that the Proclamation had reserved to them, and provided further that all purchases had to be by and in the name of the Crown, in a public assembly of the Indians held by the governor or commander-in-chief of the colony in which the lands in question lay. As Lord Watson pointed out in *St. [Catharine's] Milling, supra*, this policy with respect to the sale or transfer of the Indians' interest in land has been continuously maintained by the British Crown, by the governments of the colonies when they became responsible for the administration of Indian affairs, and, after 1867, by the federal government of Canada. Successive federal statutes, predecessors to the present *Indian Act*, have all provided for the general inalienability of Indian reserve land except upon surrender to the Crown, the relevant provisions in the present Act being ss. 37–41.

The purpose of this surrender requirement is clearly to interpose the Crown between the Indians and prospective purchasers or lessees of their land, so as to prevent the Indians from being exploited. This is made clear in the *Royal Proclamation* itself, which prefaces the provision making the Crown an intermediary with a declaration that "great Frauds and Abuses have been committed in purchasing Lands of the Indians, to the great Prejudice of our Interests, and to the great Dissatisfaction of the said Indians ...." Through the confirmation in the *Indian Act* of the historic responsibility which the Crown has undertaken, to act on behalf of the Indians so as to protect their interests in transactions with third parties, Parliament has conferred upon the Crown a discretion to decide for itself where the Indians' best interests really lie. This is the effect of s. 18(1) of the Act.

This discretion on the part of the Crown, far from ousting, as the Crown contends, the jurisdiction of the courts to regulate the relationship between the Crown and the Indians, has the effect of transforming the Crown's obligation into a fiduciary one. Professor Ernest Weinrib maintains in his article "The Fiduciary Obligation", that "the hallmark of a fiduciary relation is that the relative legal positions are such that one party is at the mercy of the other's discretion." Earlier, he puts the point in the following way:

> [Where there is a fiduciary obligation] there is a relation in which the principal's interests can be affected by, and are therefore dependent on, the manner in which the fiduciary uses the discretion which has been delegated to him. The fiduciary obligation is the law's blunt tool for the control of this discretion.

I make no comment upon whether this description is broad enough to embrace all fiduciary obligations. I do agree, however, that where by statute, agreement, or perhaps by unilateral undertaking, one party has an obligation to act for the benefit of another, and that obligation carries with it a discretionary power, the party thus empowered becomes a fiduciary. Equity will then supervise the relationship by holding him to the fiduciary's strict standard of conduct.

It is sometimes said that the nature of fiduciary relationships is both established and exhausted by the standard categories of agent, trustee, partner, director, and the like. I do not agree. It is the nature of the relationship, not the specific category of actor involved that gives rise to the fiduciary duty. The categories of fiduciary, like those of negligence, should not be considered closed.

It should be noted that fiduciary duties generally arise only with regard to obligations originating in a private law context. Public law duties, the performance of which requires the exercise of discretion, do not typically give rise to a fiduciary relationship. As the "political trust" cases indicate, the Crown is not normally viewed as a fiduciary in the exercise of its legislative or administrative function. The mere fact, however, that it is the Crown which is obligated to act on the Indians' behalf does not of itself remove the Crown's obligation from the scope of the fiduciary principle. As was pointed out earlier, the Indians' interest in land is an independent legal interest. It is not a creation of either the legislative or executive branches of government. The Crown's obligation to the Indians with respect to that interest is therefore not a public law duty. While it is not a private law duty in the strict sense either, it is nonetheless in the nature of a private law duty. Therefore, in this *sui generis* relationship, it is not improper to regard the Crown as a fiduciary.

Section 18(1) of the *Indian Act* confers upon the Crown a broad discretion in dealing with surrendered land. In the present case, the document of surrender, set out in part earlier in these reasons, by which the Musqueam Band surrendered the land at issue, confirms this discretion in the clause conveying the land to the Crown "in trust to lease ... upon such terms as the Government of Canada may deem most conducive to our Welfare and that of our people". When, as here, an Indian Band surrenders its interest to the Crown, a fiduciary obligation takes hold to regulate the manner in which the Crown exercises its discretion in dealing with the land on the Indians' behalf.

I agree with Le Dain J. that before surrender the Crown does not hold the land in trust for the Indians. I also agree that the Crown's obligation does not somehow crystallize into a trust, express or implied, at the time of surrender. The law of trusts is a highly developed, specialized branch of the law. An express trust requires a settlor, a beneficiary, a trust corpus, words of settlement, certainty of object and certainty of obligation. Not all of these elements are present here. Indeed, there is not even a trust corpus. As the *Smith* decision, *supra*, makes clear, upon unconditional surrender the Indians' right in the land disappears. No property interest is transferred which could constitute the trust *res*, so that even if the other indicia of an express or implied trust could be made out, the basic requirement of a settlement of property has not been met.

Accordingly, although the nature of Indian title coupled with the discretion vested in the Crown are sufficient to give rise to a fiduciary obligation, neither an express nor an implied trust arises upon surrender. Nor does surrender give rise to a constructive trust. As was said by this Court in *Pettkus v. Becker*, "The principle of unjust enrichment lies at the heart of the constructive trust." Any similarity between a constructive trust and the Crown's fiduciary obligation to the Indians is limited to the fact that both arise by operation of law; the former is an essentially restitutionary remedy, while the latter is not. In the present case, for example, the Crown has in no way been enriched by the surrender transaction, whether unjustly or otherwise, but the fact that this is so cannot alter either the existence or the nature of the obligation which the Crown owes.

The Crown's fiduciary obligation to the Indians is therefore not a trust. To say as much is not to deny that the obligation is trust-like in character. As would be the case with a trust, the Crown must hold surrendered land for the use and benefit of the surrendering Band. The obligation is thus subject to principles very similar to those which govern the law of trusts concerning, for example, the measure of damages for breach. The fiduciary relationship between the Crown and the Indians also bears a certain resemblance to agency, since the obligation can be characterized as a duty to act on behalf of the Indian Bands who have surrendered lands, by negotiating for the sale or lease of the land to third parties. But just as the Crown is not a trustee for the Indians, neither is it their agent; not only does the Crown's authority to act on the Band's behalf lack a basis in contract, but the Band is not a party to the ultimate sale on lease, as it would be if it were the Crown's principal. I repeat, the fiduciary obligation which is owed to the Indians by the Crown is *sui generis*. Given the unique character both of the Indians interest in land and of their historical relationship with the Crown, the fact that this is so should occasion no surprise.

The discretion which is the hallmark of any fiduciary relationship is capable of being considerably narrowed in a particular case. This is as true of the Crown's discretion vis-à-vis the Indians as it is of the discretion of trustees, agents, and other traditional categories of fiduciary. The *Indian Act* makes specific provision for such narrowing in ss. 18(1) and 38(2). A fiduciary obligation will not of course, be eliminated by the imposition of conditions that have the effect of restricting the fiduciary's discretion. A failure to adhere to the imposed conditions will simply itself be a prima facie breach of the obligation. In the present case both the surrender and the Order in Council accepting the surrender referred to the Crown's leasing the land on the Band's behalf. Prior to the surrender the Band had also been given to understand that a lease was to be entered into with the Shaughnessy Heights Golf Club upon certain terms, but this understanding was not incorporated into the surrender document itself. The effect of these so-called oral terms will be considered in the next section.

(d) Breach of the Fiduciary Obligation

. . . .

... [T]he Crown, in my view, was not empowered by the surrender document to ignore the oral terms which the Band understood would be embodied in the lease. The oral representations form the backdrop against which the Crown's conduct in discharging its fiduciary obligation must be measured. They inform and confine the field of discretion within which the Crown was free to act. After the Crown's agents had induced the Band to surrender its land on the understanding that the land would be leased on certain terms, it would be unconscionable to permit the Crown simply to ignore those terms. When the promised lease proved impossible to obtain, the Crown, instead of proceeding to lease the land on different, unfavourable terms, should have returned to the Band to explain what had occurred and seek the Band's counsel on how to proceed. The existence of such unconscionability is the key to a conclusion that the Crown breached its fiduciary duty. Equity will not countenance unconscionable behaviour in a fiduciary, whose duty is that of utmost loyalty to his principal.

While the existence of the fiduciary obligation which the Crown owes to the Indians is dependent on the nature of the surrender process, the standard of conduct which the obligation imports is both more general and more exacting than the terms on any particular surrender. In the present case the relevant aspect of the required standard of conduct is defined by a principle analogous to that which underlies the doctrine of promissory or equitable estoppel. The Crown cannot promise the [B]and that it will obtain a lease of the latter's land on certain stated terms, thereby inducing the [B]and to alter its legal position by surrendering the land, and then simply ignore that promise to the [B]and's detriment.

In obtaining without consultation a much less valuable lease than that promised, the Crown breached the fiduciary obligation it owed the Band. It must make good the loss suffered in consequence.

(d) *Frame v. Smith*[†]

[WILSON J. (dissenting):]

The central issue in this case is whether the courts should recognize a common law parental right of access to children or, alternatively, a right to recover damages for interference with an order for access made by a court pursuant to statutory authority. The issue arises in the context of an application to strike out the plaintiff's state of claim as disclosing no reasonable cause of action. Because this is the context there is no evidence in the record to support the allegations made in the statement of claim but, in accordance with well-established principles, the facts as pleaded must for this limited purpose be taken as proved.

1.   THE FACTS

In September, 1962, the appellant (plaintiff) and the respondent Eleanor Smith were married in Winnipeg. In the ensuing years they had three children. The eldest, Richard, was born in 1963; Kathleen was born in 1967 and the youngest, Diane, was born in 1969. In November, 1970, Eleanor Smith left the appellant to live with another man. She subsequently returned to the matrimonial home in Montreal for a brief period of time. However, she left again, ostensibly to stay with her parents in Winnipeg and to seek counselling. She took the children with her. Once in Winnipeg she instituted proceedings for their custody. At some stage — it is not clear from the pleadings precisely when — the appellant took similar steps in Manitoba. On August 12, 1971, a judge of the Family court in Winnipeg awarded Eleanor Smith custody of the three children. The appellant was awarded "generous visiting privileges".

Some time around February, 1972, Eleanor Smith and the co-defendant Johnston Smith began living together. During 1973 they left Winnipeg and took the children with them. They did not tell the appellant that they were leaving the city. After several months of searching the appellant managed to locate his children who were with the respondents in Toronto. He was prevented from seeing his children. The respondents told him "You are not their father. Stay away from them." So the appellant applied to the Ontario courts to spell out his access rights more specifically. On November 22, 1974, Master Davidson of the Supreme Court of Ontario ordered Eleanor Smith to provide specified access to the appellant so that he could see and spend time with his children. A further order for access was made by Master Davidson in January, 1975. In October, 1976, the appellant went to Toronto to see his children but found the house deserted and no indication where the children or the respondents had gone. The respondents knew the appellant was coming to Toronto to see his

---

† (1987), 42 D.L.R. (4th) 81 (S.C.C.) at 84–85, 88–94, 97–105, 108.

children on that occasion. It took the appellant six months of searching to find them. They were living with the respondents in Denver, Colorado. On being discovered there, they all moved back to Toronto.

The appellant pleads that from 1972 on the respondents made it extremely difficult, if not impossible, for him to have any contact with his children. They deliberately limited or prevented telephone contact. They diverted the letters and gifts he sent them. They also instructed the children not to attempt to contact the appellant. The children were told not to use their real surname, Frame; they were to use the surname, Smith. Against the express wishes of the appellant the children's religion was changed by the respondents. Throughout the years the respondents told the children that the appellant was not their father, that they were to regard Johnston Smith as their father.

The appellant has since 1972 expended considerable amounts of money trying to maintain his relationship with his children. He has sought the assistance of the courts to no avail. The respondents' behaviour has frustrated him at every turn. Moreover, since 1977 the appellant has had to seek medical treatment for severe depression resulting from the respondents' conduct. They have effectively deprived him of a normal, meaningful parent-child relationship or, indeed, of any relationship at all with his children.

In April, 1982, the appellant issued a writ against the respondents in the Supreme Court of Ontario. A statement of claim was filed some months later. It contained several allegations concerning the respondents' interference with the appellant's access to his children and identified a number of heads under which the cause of action might be subsumed including wilful infliction of harm on the appellant, intentional interference with a legal right of the appellant and conspiracy to do either or both. The appellant sought general damages of $1,000,000, punitive damages of $500,000 and special damages estimated at $25,000. He did not seek access to his children as they were by that time all over fifteen years of age and his relationship with them had been completely destroyed.

. . . .

3. THE ISSUE

. . . .

(ii) Possible Causes of Action

The appellant correctly notes that s. 69(4) of the *Family Law Reform Act* abolishes the old actions of enticement, harbouring or seduction and loss of services. As well, is should be added that this court has already unanimously rejected "alienation of affections" as a separate head of liability: see *Kungl v. Schiefer*. In that case [Cartwright] J. held that there was no separate action for alienation apart from an action for criminal conversation or enticement. Now that these causes of action have been abolished by the *Family Law Reform Act*, clearly no recovery can be permitted for "alienation of affections" in respect of these causes of action. The appellant advances a number of other causes of action.

(a) Conspiracy

Counsel for the appellant submitted that the tort of conspiracy was available to the appellant. This court in *Canada Cement LaFarge Ltd. v. B.C. Lightweight Aggregate Ltd.*, while conceding that "the law concerning the scope of the tort of conspiracy is far from clear", held that the law of torts recognizes a conspiracy claim against two or more defendants if:

(1) whether the means used by the defendants are lawful or unlawful, the predominant purpose of the defendant's conduct is to cause injury to the plaintiff; or,

(2) where the conduct of the defendants is unlawful, the conduct is directed towards the plaintiff (alone or together with others), and the defendants should know in the circumstances that injury to the plaintiff is likely to and does result.

This case would seem to fit within either of these two branches. The plaintiff may well be able to establish at trial that the predominant purpose of the defendants' conduct was to cause injury to the plaintiff. In addition, since the defendants' conduct in violating the court order was unlawful, if it is proved at trial that the conduct was directed at the plaintiff and that the defendants should have known that injury to the plaintiff was likely to and did result, this case would fall squarely within the second branch. In my view, therefore, given this court's holding in *Canada Cement LaFarge Ltd. v. B.C. Lightweight Aggregate Ltd.*, this tort is capable of extension to the family law context. The real question is whether such an extension should be permitted.

It would be my view that the tort of conspiracy should not be extended to the family law context ... the criticisms which have been levelled at the tort give good reason to pause before extending it beyond the commercial context. As was said by Estey J. in *Canada Cement LaFarge Ltd.*:

> The tort of conspiracy to injure, even without the extension to include a conspiracy to perform unlawful acts where there is a constructive intent to injure, has been the target of much criticism throughout the common law world. It is indeed a commercial anachronism as so aptly described by Lord Diplock in *Lonrho*.... In fact, the action may have lost much of its usefulness in our commercial world, and survives in our law as an anomaly.

. . . .

But the paramount concern in extending the tort of conspiracy into the family law context is, I think, that such an extension would not be in the best interests of children. If the tort only applies to conduct in combination it would do little to encourage the maintenance and development of a relationship between both parents and their children. Yet it would be tailor-made for abuse. It would lend itself so readily to malicious use by one spouse against the other. The fact that the action is against not only the ex-spouse but also his or her "friend" may well provide an incentive to the plaintiff to litigate. Moreover, a single "agreement" to deny the plaintiff one visitation would be actionable and the success of that action would depend largely on uncertain evidence of agreement and intention as to which each party might be expected to take a fundamentally different view. These factors — incentive to litigate, low threshold for actionability, uncertainty of success and issues of credibility with respect to the crucial evidence — suggest frequent resort to this cause of action as a "weapon" with little possibility of amicable settlement. These concerns are aggravated by the fact that, if the tort of conspiracy were introduced into the family law context, it would be difficult to restrict it to the area of custody and access. Acts which contributed to marriage breakdown would also be actionable as conspiracy and the potential for detrimental impact on the children could be substantial. Having regard to the overriding concern for the best interests of the children, I am not persuaded that the tort of con-

spiracy should be extended to encompass the claim of the plaintiff.

(b) *Other Torts*

Counsel for the appellant submitted that the torts of intentional infliction of mental suffering and unlawful interference with another's relationship could cover the facts as pleaded. It may well be that the tort of intentional infliction of mental suffering could be extended to cover the facts alleged by the appellant. The requirements of this cause of action were set out in the case of *Wilkinson v. Downton*. In that case the defendant as a "practical joke" told the plaintiff that her husband had been involved in an accident and had broken his legs. The plaintiff believed the defendant and as a result suffered nervous shock and a number of physical consequences. In granting recovery, Wright J. stated:

> One question is whether the defendant's act was so plainly calculated to produce some effect of the kind which was produced that an intention to produce it ought to be imputed to the defendant, regard being had to the fact that the effect was produced on a person proved to be in an ordinary state of health and mind. I think that it was. It is difficult to imagine that such a statement, made suddenly and with apparent seriousness, could fail to produce grave effects under the circumstances upon any but an exceptionally indifferent person, and therefore an intention to produce such an effect must be imputed, and it is no answer in law to say that more harm was done than was anticipated, for that is commonly the case with all wrongs. The other question is whether the effect was, to use the ordinary phrase, too remote to be in law regarded as a consequence for which the defendant is answerable.

In this case, the conduct of the respondents may have been "plainly calculated to produce some effect of the kind which was produced". Certainly the conduct appears to be of the extreme and outrageous character which was held in *Wilkinson v. Downton* to be required before this cause of action exists. But there are a number of disadvantages associated with this tort which make me reluctant to extend it to the facts of this case. One such disadvantage is that a visible and provable illness caused by the defendant's action must be present for tort to be actionable: see *Guay v. Sun Publishing Co.* This requirement is based on the need to discourage spurious claims — an especially pressing need in the family law context where unnecessary and vexatious litigation is to be discouraged. Another disadvantage associated with this tort is that, even if it were extended to cover the case at bar, it might not provide the plaintiff with the compensation that he wishes. According to John G. Fleming, *The Law of Torts*, 6th ed. (1983), "our courts, while at last admitting that injury to the nervous system is capable of causing recognizable physical harm, are not yet prepared to protect emotional security as such". If such a cause of action were extended to the facts of this case the appellant would only be entitled to recover damages stemming from recognizable physical or psychopathological harm caused by the actions of the defendant. This would include only the damages stemming from the appellant's treatment for mental depression. In my view, if another cause of action better vindicates the plaintiff's interest and is in the best interests of the children, this particular cause of action should not be recognized.

. . . .

There would appear to be no generalized tort of "wrongful interference with another's relationship" as the appellant submits. The law of torts up to this point has protected only certain types of relationships from interference. Relief has been granted for interference with contractual relationships (e.g., *Lumley v. Gye*, interference through intimidation and unlawful means (e.g., *Rookes v. Barnard*, and interference with economic relations through injurious falsehood (e.g., *Ratcliffe v. Evans*). The common denominator of these torts is that they constitute wrongful interference with economic relationships and I do not think they should be extended to a non-economic relationship such as the one under review. As in the case of the tort of intentional infliction of mental suffering, if they were extended to the area of custody and access, there is no rational basis upon which their extension to other areas of family law could be resisted. They would be available in respect of all inter-spousal conduct both before and after marital breakdown and torts grounded in intimidation and injurious falsehood would again seem to be tailor-made for spouses, so motivated, to use against each other. Their extension to the family law area would not, it seems to me, be in the best interests of children.

But there are two other causes of action which could loosely be said to fall within the rubric of

"wrongful interference with another's relationship" and which may well cover the case at bar. There are (a) a cause of action for interference with a right of access founded on the common law or the court order, and (b) a cause of action for breach of a fiduciary duty owed by the custodial to the non-custodial parent to respect the latter's relationship with the child. As neither has traditionally been regarded as a "tort", I shall deal with them under separate headings.

. . . .

(d) Breach of Fiduciary Duty

The final cause of action to be considered is breach of fiduciary duty. This possibility was not advanced by counsel in his original material but, since the issue before the court was whether the statement of claim should be struck out "as disclosing no reasonable cause of action", the court was of the view that it should be addressed. Counsel was accordingly invited to file written submissions of which we have had the benefit.

In the past the question whether a particular relationship is subject to a fiduciary obligation has been approached by referring to categories of relationships in which a fiduciary obligation has already been held to be present. Some recognized examples of these categories are relationships between directors and corporations, solicitors and clients, trustees and beneficiaries, agents and principals, life tenants and remaindermen, and partners. As well, it has frequently been noted that the categories of fiduciary relationship are never closed.... An extension of fiduciary obligations to new "categories" of relationship presupposes the existence of an underlying principle which governs the imposition of the fiduciary obligation.

However, there has been a reluctance throughout the common law world to affirm the existence of and give content to a general fiduciary principle which can be applied in appropriate circumstances. Sir Anthony Mason is probably correct when he says that "the fiduciary relationship is a concept in search of a principle". As a result there is no definition of the concept "fiduciary" apart from the contexts in which it has been held to arise and, indeed, it may be more accurate to speak of relationships as having a fiduciary component to them rather than to speak of fiduciary relationships as such. Perhaps the biggest obstacle to the development of a general fiduciary principle has been the fact that the content of the fiduciary duty varies with the type of relationship to which it is applied. It seems on its face therefore to comprise a collection of unrelated rules such as the rule against self-dealing, the misappropriation of assets rule, the conflict and profit rules and (in Canada) a special business opportunity rule. The failure to identify and apply a general fiduciary principle has resulted in the courts relying almost exclusively on the established list of categories of fiduciary relationships and being reluctant to grant admittance to new relationships despite their oft-repeated declaration that the category of fiduciary relationships is never closed.

A few commentators have attempted to discern an underlying fiduciary principle but, given the widely divergent contexts emerging from the case-law, it is understandable that they have differed in their analyses.... Yet there are common features discernible in the contexts in which fiduciary duties have been found to exist and these common features do provide a rough and ready guide to whether or not the imposition of a fiduciary obligation on a new relationship would be appropriate and consistent.

Relationships in which a fiduciary obligation have been imposed seem to possess three general characteristics:

(1) The fiduciary has scope for the exercise of some discretion or power.
(2) The fiduciary can unilaterally exercise that power or discretion so as to affect the beneficiary's legal or practical interests.
(3) The beneficiary is peculiarly vulnerable to or at the mercy of the fiduciary holding the discretion or power.

Very little need be said about the first characteristic except this, that unless such a discretion or power is present there is no need for a superadded obligation to restrict the damaging use of the discretion or power....

With respect to the second characteristic it is, of course, the fact that the power or discretion may be used to affect the beneficiary in a damaging way that makes the imposition of a fiduciary duty necessary. Indeed, fiduciary duties are frequently imposed on those who are capable of affecting not only the legal interests of the beneficiary but also the beneficiary's vital non-legal or "practical" interests. For example, it is generally conceded that a director is in a fiduciary relationship to the corporation. But the corporation's interest which is protected by the fiduciary duty is not

confined to an interest in the property of the corporation but extends to non-legal, practical interests in the financial well-being of the corporation and perhaps to even more intangible practical interests such as the corporation's public image and reputation. Another example is found in cases of undue influence where a fiduciary uses a power over the beneficiary to obtain money at the expense of the beneficiary. The beneficiary's interest in such a case is a pecuniary interest. Finally, in *Reading v. Attorney-General*, [1951] A.C. 507 (H.L.), a British soldier who was unable to smuggle items past Egyptian guards because these guards excused uniformed soldiers from their inspections was held to be a fiduciary. The Crown's interest was a "practical" or even a "moral" one, namely that its uniform should not be used in corrupt ways. The solider-fiduciary had no power to change the legal position of the British Crown, so how could the Crown's legal interests have been affected by the soldier's action? The same can be said of the Crown's interest in *Attorney-General v. Goddard* (1929), 98 L.J.K.B. 743, where the Crown was able to recover bribes which had been paid to its employee, a sergeant in the Metropolitan Police. In my view, what was protected in that case was not a "legal" interest but a vital and substantial "practical" interest.

The third characteristic of relationships in which a fiduciary duty has been imposed is the element of vulnerability. This vulnerability arises from the inability of the beneficiary (despite his or her best efforts) to prevent the injurious exercise of the power or discretion combined with the grave inadequacy or absence of other legal or practical remedies to redress the wrongful exercise of the discretion or power. Because of the requirement of vulnerability of the beneficiary at the hands of the fiduciary, fiduciary obligations are seldom present in dealings of experienced businessmen of similar bargaining strength acting at arm's length: see, for example, *Jirna Ltd. v. Mister Donut of Canada Ltd.* The law takes the position that such individuals are perfectly capable of agreeing as to the scope of the discretion or power to be exercised, *i.e.*, any "vulnerability" could have been prevented through the more prudent exercise of their bargaining power and the remedies for the wrongful exercise or abuse of that discretion or power, namely damages, are adequate in such a case.

. . . .

A similar formulation of the principle was enunciated in at least one Canadian case. In *H.L. Misener & Son Ltd. v. Misener*, Macdonald J.A. enunciated the principle in this way:

> The reason such persons [directors] are subjected to the fiduciary relationship apparently is because they have a leeway for the exercise of discretion in dealing with third parties which can affect the legal position of their principals.

. . . .

In my view, the relationship between the custodial parent and the non-custodial parent fits within the fiduciary principle I have described. There is no doubt that prior to the custody and access order the parent who will become the non-custodial parent has a very substantial interest in his or her relationship with the child. The granting of the access order confirms that the relationship between the non-custodial parent and the child is of benefit to the child and therefore worth preserving. That relationship pre-dated the access order and it continues to subsist after the access order is made. It is not itself created by the access order. But the custody and access order, by splitting access from custody, puts the custodial parent in a position of power and authority which enables him or her, if so motivated, to affect the non-custodial parent's relationship with his or her child in an injurious way. The selfish exercise of custody over a long period of time without regard to the access order can utterly destroy the non-custodial parent's relationship with his child. The non-custodial parent (and, of course, the child also) is completely vulnerable to this. Yet the underlying premise in a grant of custody to one parent and access to the other is that the custodial parent will facilitate the exercise of the other's access rights for the sake of the child. This is reflected s. 16(10) of the *Divorce Act, 1985*, which provides:

> **16.**(10) In making an order under this section, the court shall give effect to the principle that a child of the marriage should have as much contact with each spouse as is consistent with the best interests of the child and, for that purpose, shall take into consideration the willingness of the person for whom custody is sought to facilitate such contact.

The custodial parent is expected to act in good faith not only towards the non-custodial parent but also towards the children. Section 16(10) makes it clear that this is one of the qualifications of a good custodial parent.

It seems to me that the three underlying characteristics of relationships in which fiduciary duties are imposed are present in the relationship under review. The custodial parent has been placed as a result of the court's order in a position of power and authority over the children with the potential to prejudicially affect and indeed utterly destroy their relationship with their non-custodial parent through improper exercise of the power. There can be no doubt also that the requisite vulnerability is present and that in practical terms there is little that the non-custodial parent can do to restrain the custodial parent's improper exercise of authority or to obtain redress for it. The options open to an aggrieved non-custodial parent in the face of a campaign by a custodial parent to cut the non-custodial parent off from the child are exceedingly limited....

. . . .

It is sometimes suggested that transferring custody is an appropriate means of punishing the custodial parent for an ongoing denial of access: see, for example, the suggestions made in *Woodburn v. Woodburn*; *Jones v. Jones*; *Currie v. Currie*; *Donald v. Donald*. And indeed this is being done; see *Nayar v. Nayar*, and *Fast v. Fast*. But again, because of the bonding that takes place between the custodial parent and his or her child over a period of time, such a step may not be in the child's best interests. In *Racine v. Woods*, a case involving a custody dispute between an Indian child's cultural parents and the child's adopted parents, this court stressed the need for children to have continuity of relationships. It held that, while an Indian child's cultural heritage and background were important factors to be considered by the court in applying the best interests doctrine, these factors had declined in importance in light of the degree of psychological bonding which had developed with the foster parents. Because of this psychological bonding a transfer of custody may not be a suitable remedy. Finally, as has been indicated above, there are good reasons for not extending common law causes of action in tort in order to permit the non-custodial parent to obtain redress for the custodial parent's denial of access.

I have already indicated that substantial nonlegal, practical interests are protected by the imposition of fiduciary duties in appropriate cases. It cannot be denied that the non-custodial parent's interest in his or her child is as worthy of protection as some interests commonly protected by a fiduciary duty. For example, just as a corporation has a substantial interest in its relationship to corporate opportunities and customers that is worthy of protection (see, for example, *Canadian Aero Service Ltd. v. O'Malley*) it can be said that a non-custodial parent has a substantial interest in his or her relationship with his or her child that is worthy of protection. However, one salient distinction between the non-custodial parent-child relationship and the corporation-customer relationship is that the former involves a substantial non-economic interest of the parent while the latter normally involves a substantial economic interest of the corporation. But I believe that this distinction should not be determinative. The non-custodial parent's interest in the relationship with his or her child is without doubt of tremendous importance to him or her. To deny relief because of the nature of the interest involved, to afford protection to material interests but not to human and personal interests would, it seems to me, be arbitrary in the extreme. In contract law equity recognizes interests beyond the purely economic when, instead of awarding damages in the market value of real estate against a vendor who has wrongfully refused to close, it grants specific performance. Other non-economic interests should also be capable of protection in equity through the imposition of a fiduciary duty. I would hold, therefore, that the appellant's interest in a continuing relationship with his or her child is capable of protection by the imposition of such a duty.

Before a cause of action for breach of fiduciary duty can be said to exist in this limited area within the field of family law, it is necessary to ask the same question as was asked in the context of the various torts proposed by the appellant, namely, should existing fiduciary principles be extended? In examining this question it will again be necessary to consider the possibility that this cause of action might be used as a weapon by vindictive spouses and, more important still, it is necessary to consider whether or not the extension of fiduciary principles to this particular relationship would be in the best interests of children.

This cause of action has, in my view, a number of significant advantages over the others. First, it arises only in one particular circumstance, the circumstance of vulnerability created by the splitting of the custody and access of children by the issuance of a court order. Unlike some of the torts examined this action would not be available in any other family law context. This is a very important consideration in light of the possible detrimental impact on children of recurring lawsuits by one parent against the other.

Second, the cause of action for breach of fiduciary duty creates a very strong incentive to custodial parents to exercise their custodial rights so as to further the best interests of their children, to recognize that their children are entitled to an ongoing relationship with their other parent and that it is a serious matter to use the authority confided in them by an order of the court to deprive their children of this other dimension in their lives. I believe that this cause of action will help to promote a healthy and beneficial relationship between a child and both parents and is, in this respect, much more conducive to the best interests of the child than the tort actions previously considered.

Finally, unlike the cause of action in tort, the cause of action for breach of fiduciary duty allows the court to take into account conduct of a non-custodial parent (whether related to custody and access issues or not) which might be contrary to the best interests of children. When considering breaches of equitable duty and awarding equitable remedies the court has a wide scope for the exercise of discretion which does not exist in respect of common law causes of action. In the context of breach of fiduciary duty this discretion would allow the court to deny relief to an aggrieved party or grant relief on certain terms if that party's conduct has disabled him or her from full relief, e.g., non-payment of spousal support or previous abuse of access rights. There is neither precedent nor historical basis for the exercise of such a discretion in the case of the common law tort action. The tort would be actionable regardless of the inequitable conduct of the plaintiff.

. . . .

Accordingly, it would be my view that the cause of action for breach of fiduciary duty should be extended to this narrow but extremely important area of family law where the non-custodial parent is completely at the mercy of the custodial parent by virtue of that parent's position of power and authority over the children. If this is a situation which for very good reason the common law is ill-equipped to handle, resort to equity is entirely appropriate so that no just cause shall go without a remedy. The breach will be actionable only when judgment recovery will not impair child support and when the non-custodial parent-child relationship has been so severely damaged by the custodial parent's conduct as to make it highly unlikely that the action brought by the non-custodial parent would be the cause of any conflict of loyalties in the children. Such a cause of action, properly tailored as only equity can do and has done in other contexts, will create a strong incentive to further the best interests of children while eliminating the more harmful effects commonly associated with inter-spousal litigation.

One word of caution may be in order. At times, a perfectly legitimate exercise by the custodial parent of his or her custodial rights or custodial obligations will result in an individual denial of access to the other parent. It is not the role of the court to review this sort of exercise of discretion with respect to the child. It is only when a sustained course of conduct designed to destroy the relationship is being engaged in that there is a breach of the duty. If and when a custodial parent comes to believe that continued access to the child by the other parent is not in the child's interests or is harmful to the child, the proper course for the custodial parent to follow is not to engage in ongoing wilful violations of the access order but to apply to the court to vary or rescind it.

(e)   *M.(K.) v. M.(H.)*†

[La FOREST J.:]

This case concerns the procedural obstacles facing victims of childhood incestuous abuse who attempt to vindicate their rights in a civil action for damages against the perpetrator of the incest. While the problem of incest is not new, it has only recently gained recognition as one of the more serious depredations plaguing Canadian families. Its incidence is alarming and profoundly disturbing. The damages wrought by incest are peculiarly complex and devastating, often manifesting themselves slowly and imperceptibly, so that the victim may only come to realize the harms she (and at times he) has suffered, and their cause, long after the statute of limitations has ostensibly proscribed a civil remedy. It has been said that the statute of limitations remains the primary stumbling block for adult survivors of incest, and this has proved to be the case thus far for the appellant in the present action. The appellant commenced this action for damages occasioned as a result of recurrent sexual assaults between the ages of eight and sixteen when she was twenty-eight. A jury found that the respondent committed sexual assault upon the appellant and assessed damages at $50,000, but her action was dismissed on the basis of a statute of limitations.

BACKGROUND

The appellant testified at trial that the abuse began when she was eight when the respondent, her father, asked her about her knowledge of the female genital and breast areas and the male genital area. It progressed to the respondent's touching her body and telling her that "if he played with [her] breasts that they would grow big". Intercourse began when she was between ten and eleven and continued thereafter two or three times a week. Her cooperation and silence were elicited by various means: the respondent reportedly threatened that disclosure would cause her mother to commit suicide, the family would break up, nobody would believe her, and finally that he would kill her. The appellant had good reason to take these threats seriously, inasmuch as she was told that her mother had been hospitalized for attempting to harm her when she was an infant by cutting her wrists; her father pointed out the scars on her wrist as proof. The appellant's mother, who was also named as a defendant in the action, confirmed the incident, but

---

† [1992] 3 S.C.R. 6 at 17–20, 23–24, 59, 61–66, 80–82, 85–86.

attributed it to depression. The appellant also gave evidence that her mother regularly exhibited irrational behaviour when she was upset, such as pulling her hair and screaming.

In addition to the threats, the respondent induced his daughter to submit to the abuse silently; he rewarded her with pop, potato chips and money. In time, he gave her the responsibility for initiating sexual contact. She was instructed to leave her bedroom light on when she wanted him, and she complied out of fear that he would turn to her younger sister for gratification. Eventually, she turned on the light because "that was the way for [her] to do it". Her mental process during the act of intercourse was to imagine herself as an inanimate object, for example a door handle or carpet. This process took place against an emotional backdrop of fear — fear of him and fear of discovery.

At the age of ten or eleven the appellant tried to tell her mother what was occurring by obliquely referring to a white substance that appeared on her genital area, but she testified that her mother ignored the complaint. Her mother denied that she was unresponsive, and testified that she gave her daughter a book on menstruation. When the appellant was sixteen she told a high school guidance counsellor that her father was having sex with her. She made the disclosure because she thought she could trust the counsellor and that she would be removed from the home so as to be "safe" from her father. Although she was not certain that having sex with her father was wrong, she knew she did not want him to do it to her any more. She was ultimately referred to a psychologist at the Kitchener-Waterloo Hospital, Dr. McKie, and she recalls that he seemed to disbelieve her complaint since he kept sending her home. His report, dated July 16, 1973, indicates that after interviewing the appellant and respondent separately, both came to see him and told him that "it was all a lie and things are fine now", whereupon no further steps were taken. The appellant does not remember this, but testified that her father brought her to see a lawyer for the local school board and forced her to tell the lawyer that she had been lying about her allegations of incest.

Later that year the appellant left home to live with another family as their babysitter. She told her employer of the incest, but nothing came of it. The following year she obtained employment as a waitress, where she met Steven. They were married a short while later. Her evidence was that she married him so that she could visit her siblings at the family home without being assaulted by the respon-

dent. She harboured the belief that she was protected from further incestuous abuse because she thought her husband now "owned" her and therefore enjoyed an exclusive right to have sex with her, and that he had thus replaced her father as her owner. She also disclosed the incest to her husband, and although there was some conflict in the evidence as to what his response was, the matter went no further.

Over the next few years the appellant had three children and continued to work at a series of low-paying jobs. In the fall of 1982 the appellant and her husband separated because she could no longer tolerate sexual relations with him. She sought counselling for depression and her marital problems in the spring of 1983, and was referred to Dr. Voss, a psychologist at the Kitchener-Waterloo Hospital. He read the hospital file on her consultation with Dr. McKie in 1973, and the subject of incest was accordingly raised during one of their sessions. However, the appellant did not want to talk about the incest and Dr. Voss did not feel it prudent to pursue the subject, in light of his professional opinion that the requisite degree of trust between patient and therapist had not been established to deal effectively with the problem, and because her current problems did not appear to be directly connected to her history of incest.

Later in 1983 the appellant met Peter, to whom she became engaged to be married. Shortly after they met, she told him of the incestuous abuse because, in her words, she "didn't want to lose him and I wanted him to know right away what I had done". As a result of their discussion, she made enquiries about self-help groups for incest victims and found one in Kitchener. It was during the course of attending meetings of this group in 1984 that the appellant began to recall many of her childhood experiences and to make the connection between that history and her psychological and emotional problems. Until then she believed that her phobias, including a fear of strangers and difficulties coping with her children, were attributable to her own stupidity. She was only able to overcome her overwhelming feelings of guilt for causing the incest once she came to the realization that it was her father who was responsible for the abuse. Beginning in 1985 she has continued in therapy with a marital and family therapist, Ms. Pressman, who also testified at the trial.

. . . .

In 1985 the appellant sued her father for damages arising from the incest, or in the alternative for the infliction of mental distress. Further damages were claimed for breach of a parent's fiduciary duty to care for and minister to his child. The claims of mental distress and breach of fiduciary duty were also made against the appellant's mother....

. . . .

ISSUES

Several issues were argued by the appellant, and for the sake of completeness, I will enumerate them all here: (1) incest is a separate and distinct tort which is not subject to any limitation period; (2) incest constitutes a breach of fiduciary duty by a parent and is not subject to any limitation period; (3) if a limitation period applies, the cause of action does not accrue until it is reasonably discoverable; (4) the appellant was of unsound mind pursuant to s. 47 of the *Limitations Act*; (5) the tort is continuous in nature and the limitation period does not begin to run until the plaintiff is no longer subjected to parental authority and conditioning; and (6) the equitable doctrine of fraudulent concealment operates to postpone the limitation period.

For the reasons that follow, I am of the view that this appeal should be allowed. Incest is both a tortious assault and a breach of fiduciary duty. The tort claim, although subject to limitations legislation, does not accrue until the plaintiff is reasonably capable of discovering the wrongful nature of the defendant's acts and the nexus between those acts and her injuries. In this case, that discovery took place only when the appellant entered therapy, and the lawsuit was commenced promptly thereafter. The time for bringing a claim for breach of a fiduciary duty is not limited by statute in Ontario, and therefore stands along with the tort claim as a basis for recovery by the appellant. As for the other issues raised by the appellant, I am of the view that incest does not constitute a distinct tort, separate and apart from the intentional tort of assault and battery, and the continuous nature of the tort need not be decided in this case. Similarly, I do not find it necessary to deal with the question of whether the appellant was of unsound mind, although it seems to me that such a pejorative term is inappropriate in this context. Fraudulent concealment

was not considered by the courts below, and the respondent argued that additional evidence might have been adduced had the issue been raised in those courts. As such, I make no finding on that issue, but I would not foreclose considering its availability for postponing limitation periods in other cases.

. . . .

RECOVERY FOR BREACH OF FIDUCIARY OBLIGATION

The appellant argues that incest constitutes not only the tort of assault and battery, but is also a breach of the fiduciary relationship between parent and child. The appellant submits that Ontario's *Limitations Act* does not apply to fiduciary duties, and as such the plaintiff's delay is no defence to the fiduciary action. I agree. Incest is a breach of both common law and equitable duties, and the latter claim is not foreclosed by the Act. Certain equitable defences may, however, be available to the respondent.

. . . .

Consequently, it is left to this Court to consider the question of fiduciary duty. In my view, the issue must be addressed even though the tort action has survived the limitations defence. It was fully argued by the parties, and there may well be cases where the limitations statute cannot be circumvented but where the fiduciary claim is unaffected by the statute. Moreover, the equitable remedy available to the appellant may vary from the common law award established by the jury. The importance of considering any equitable cause of action has recently been stated by Justice McLachlin in *Norberg v. Wynrib*, [1992] 2 S.C.R. 226, at pp. 290–91:

> These examples underline the importance of treating the consequences of this relationship on the footing of what it is — a fiduciary relationship — rather than forcing it into the ill-fitting molds of contract and tort. Contrary to the conclusion of the court below, characterizing the duty as fiduciary does add something; indeed, without doing so the wrong done to the plaintiff can neither be fully comprehended in law nor adequately compensated in damages. [Emphasis in original.]

In *Norberg*, McLachlin J. and I differed on the path to be followed in upholding recovery. She chose the route of the fiduciary claim whereas I preferred the route afforded by common law tort of battery because in the circumstances of that case there might be difficulties concerning the applicability of fiduciary obligations, an issue I did not find it necessary to decide. I could do this because I did not consider the common law molds to be ill-fitting in that case. Nor, as I will attempt to demonstrate, do I think they are ill-fitting in the present circumstances. Nonetheless, I agree with my colleague that a breach of fiduciary duty cannot be automatically overlooked in favour of concurrent common law claims. The point is simply stated by Cooke P. of the New Zealand Court of Appeal in *Mouat v. Boyce*: "For breach of these duties, now that common law and equity are mingled the Court has available the full range of remedies, including damages or compensation and restitutionary remedies such as an account of profits. What is appropriate to the particular facts may be granted."

In the present case, the lower courts have not ruled on the question of fiduciary obligation. As such, this Court must assume the role of finder of fact in equity, but in this case that burden poses no difficulty. We have a jury's verdict on the fact of sexual assault, and it is easy enough to apply that finding to the equitable claim. What remains is the legal issue of whether the assaults constitute a breach of fiduciary duty. I turn now to that issue.

Fiduciary Obligation of a Parent

It is intuitively apparent that the relationship between parent and child is fiduciary in nature, and that the sexual assault of one's child is a grievous breach of the obligations arising from that relationship. Indeed, I can think of few cases that are clearer than this. For obvious reasons society has imposed upon parents the obligation to care for, protect and rear their children. The act of incest is a heinous violation of that obligation. Equity has imposed fiduciary obligations on parents in contexts other than incest, and I see no barrier to the extension of a father's fiduciary obligation to include a duty to refrain from incestuous assaults on his daughter.

Over the past decade, this Court has explored the scope of fiduciary obligations, and we have perhaps reached the point where a "fiduciary principle" can be applied through a well-defined method. The process was started in *Guerin v. The Queen*,

supra, where Dickson J. (as he then was) found that certain obligations owed by the federal government to an Indian Band were fiduciary in nature. In the course of his reasons, Dickson J. confirmed certain broad principles with respect to fiduciary obligations, at p. 384:

> Professor Ernest Weinrib maintains in his article *The Fiduciary Obligation* (1975), 25 U.T.L.J. 1, at p. 7, that "the hallmark of a fiduciary relation is that the relative legal positions are such that one party is at the mercy of the other's discretion." Earlier, at p. 4, he puts the point in the following way:
>
> > [Where there is a fiduciary obligation] there is a relation in which the principal's interests can be affected by, and are therefore dependent on, the manner in which the fiduciary uses the discretion which has been delegated to him. The fiduciary obligation is the law's blunt tool for the control of this discretion.

I make no comment upon whether this description is broad enough to embrace all fiduciary obligations. I do agree, however, that where by statute, agreement, or perhaps by unilateral undertaking, one party has an obligation to act for the benefit of another, and that obligation carries with it a discretionary power, the party thus empowered becomes a fiduciary. Equity will then supervise the relationship by holding him to the fiduciary's strict standard of conduct.

It is sometimes said that the nature of the fiduciary relationship is both established and exhausted by the standard categories of agent, trustee, partner, director, and the like. I do not agree. It is the nature of the relationship, not the specific category of actor involved that gives rise to the fiduciary duty. The categories of fiduciary, like those of negligence, should not be considered closed.

I would go one step further, and suggest that fiduciary obligations are imposed in some situations even in the absence of any unilateral undertaking by the fiduciary. In the present case, however, it is sufficient to say that being a parent comprises a unilateral undertaking that is fiduciary in nature. Equity then imposes a range of obligations coordinate with that undertaking.

The next step in the evolution of the fiduciary principle came with *Frame v. Smith*. In this case the dissenting judgment of Wilson J. elaborates on the approach established by Dickson J. in *Guerin*. Although the majority held that the remedy of fiduciary obligation did not apply in the circumstances of that case, Wilson J.'s mode of approach was later held to apply in the circumstances that arose in *Lac Minerals Ltd. v. International Corona Resources Ltd.*; see also the concurring reasons in *Canson Enterprises Ltd. v. Boughton & Co., supra*. Recognizing that the categories of fiduciary relationships are not closed, Wilson J. proposed the following approach for their identification, at p. 136:

> Relationships in which a fiduciary obligation have [sic] been imposed seem to possess three general characteristics:
> (1) The fiduciary has scope for the exercise of some discretion or power.
> (2) The fiduciary can unilaterally exercise that power or discretion so as to affect the beneficiary's legal or practical interests.
> (3) The beneficiary is peculiarly vulnerable to or at the mercy of the fiduciary holding the discretion or power.

Even a cursory examination of these *indicia* establishes that a parent must owe fiduciary obligations to his or her child. Parents exercise great power over their children's lives, and make daily decisions that effect their welfare. In this regard, the child is without doubt at the mercy of her parents.

. . . .

It is this first usage of the term "fiduciary" which arises in the present case. The inherent purpose of the family relationship imposes certain obligations on a parent to act in his or her child's best interests, and a presumption of fiduciary obligation arises.

In *Lac Minerals* I stressed the point, which also emerges from *Frame v. Smith*, that the substance of the fiduciary obligation in any given case is not derived from some immutable list of duties attached to a category of relationships. In other words, the duty is not determined by analogy with the "established" heads of fiduciary duty. Rather, the nature of the obligation will vary depending on the factual context of the relationship in which it arises. Recently, I had occasion to return to this point in the context of a doctor-patient relationship in *McInerney v. MacDonald*. I there stated:

> In characterizing the physician-patient relationship as "fiduciary", I would not wish it to be thought that a fixed set of rules and principles apply in all circumstances or to all obligations arising out of the doctor-patient relation-

ship. As I noted in *Canson Enterprises Ltd. v. Boughton & Co.*, not all fiduciary relationships and not all fiduciary obligations are the same; these are shaped by the demands of the situation. A relationship may properly be described as "fiduciary" for some purposes, but not for others.

In certain parent-child contexts, equity has recognized a parental duty to protect the <u>economic</u> interests of his or her child. However, this case law does not limit the range of the obligations that may attach to other aspects of the parent-child relationship.

. . . .

REMEDIES

The jury in this case found that the respondent had sexually assaulted the appellant, and assessed general damages of $10,000 and punitive damages of $40,000. Though the punitive damages are within the general range of such awards, the general damages seem rather low. The jury, however, had the whole matter before it, and its award should not lightly be disturbed. At all events, the quantum was not disputed on this appeal. However, as I have found that a breach of fiduciary duty has also occurred, it raises the issue whether some additional remedy in equity is necessary to compensate the appellant fully and properly.

Recently, I have had occasion to consider the relationship between equitable and common law remedies, and in particular compensation for breach of fiduciary obligation; see *Canson Enterprises Ltd. v. Boughton & Co., supra*. In equity there is no capacity to award damages, but the remedy of compensation has evolved. The distinction between damages and compensation is often slight, and as I noted in *Canson*, the courts have tended to merge the principles of law and equity when necessary to achieve a just remedy. There I was speaking of the relationship between remedies for tortious misstatement and breach of fiduciary duty, but the underlying principles are equally applicable in this case. Of particular relevance are my comments beginning at p. 581, and particularly the following passages at pp. 581 and 586–87 respectively:

> The truth is that barring different policy considerations underlying one action or the other, I see no reason why the same basic claim,

whether framed in terms of a common law action or an equitable remedy, should give rise to different levels of redress.

...

Only when there are different policy objectives should equity engage in its well-known flexibility to achieve a different and fairer result. The foundation of the obligation sought to be enforced ... is "the trust or confidence reposed by one and accepted by the other or the assumption to act for the one by that other." That being so, it would be odd if a different result followed solely on the manner in which one framed an identical claim. What is required is a measure of rationalization.

The question in this appeal is whether there are different policy objectives animating the breach of a parent's fiduciary duty as compared with incestuous sexual assault. In my view, the underlying objectives are the same. Both seek to compensate the victim for her injuries and to punish the wrongdoer. The jury award of general damages was made with full knowledge of the injuries suffered by the appellant and her rehabilitative needs. The same concerns would apply in assessing equitable compensation, and as such I would decline to provide any additional compensation for the breach of fiduciary obligation. The punitive damages award should also not be varied in equity. Of course, equitable compensation to punish the gravity of a defendant's conduct is available on the same basis as the common law remedy of punitive damages; see *Aquaculture Corp. v. New Zealand Green Mussel Co.*

In the result, I am of the view that the jury award of $50,000 is an appropriate remedy for both the equitable and the common law claims.

. . . .

[McLACHLIN J.:]

I agree with the reasons of my colleague Justice La Forest, subject to the following comments.

. . . .

Third, I would not wish to be taken as sharing the view that the award which the jury made was adequate. The jury was asked only to assess damages for the tort of battery and assault. It did so, and the appellant has not appealed from that award, asking only that the jury's award be reinstated. In these circumstances the question of whether the award was appropriate or not does not arise on this appeal. I would dispose of the appeal as proposed by La Forest J., but on the ground that the question of the quantum of the award was not before us.

Having said that, I add that were I to enter on the matter of the quantum of damages, I would find myself unable to agree that the measure of damages for battery and assault would necessarily be the same as compensation for breach of fiduciary duty. As I see it, the question is whether the wrong encompassed by the cause of action is the same. The wrong encompassed by the torts of battery and assault may be different from the wrong encompassed by the action for a breach of fiduciary duty. The latter encompasses damage to the trust relationship, for example, which the former does not. The action for breach of fiduciary duty may also be more concerned with imposing a measure which will deter future breaches; as I noted in *Canson Enterprises Ltd. v. Boughton & Co.*, trustees have always been held to highest account in a manner stricter than that applicable to tortfeasors. In short, while agreeing with my colleague that where the same policy objectives underlie two different causes of action similar measures of compensation may be appropriate, I would not conclude that the policy objectives or the wrong involved in breach of fiduciary duty of this nature are necessarily the same as those which underlie the torts of battery and assault.

Subject to these observations, I concur in the reasons of La Forest J.

(f) Lac Minerals Ltd. v. International Corona Resources Ltd.†

[SOPINKA J. (dissenting in part):]

This appeal and cross-appeal raise important issues relating to fiduciary duty and breach of confidence. In particular, they require this Court to consider whether fiduciary obligations can arise in the context of abortive arm's-length negotiations between parties to a prospective commercial transaction. Also at issue are the nature of confidential information and the appropriate remedy for its misuse.

THE FACTS

The facts are fully developed in the reasons for judgment of the trial judge, R. Holland J. My recital of them, here, will therefore be skeletal in nature. From time to time in these reasons, some of the facts relating to specific issues will be examined in greater detail.

The parties to these proceedings are International Corona Resources Ltd. (which I will refer to as either "Corona" or the "respondent") and Lac Minerals Ltd. (which I will refer to as either "Lac" or the "appellant"). Corona, which was incorporated in 1979, was at material times a junior mining company listed on the Vancouver Stock Exchange. Lac is a senior mining company which owns a number of operating mines and is listed on several Stock Exchanges. This action arises out of negotiations between Corona and Lac relating to the Corona property, the Williams property and the Hughes property, all of which are located in the Hemlo area of northern Ontario.

The Corona property consists of 17 claims with an area of approximately 680 acres. The Williams property consists of 11 patented claims, covering a total of about 400 acres, and is contiguous to the Corona property and to the west. The Hughes property consists of approximately 156 claims and surrounds both the Corona and Williams properties, except to the north of the Williams prop-

erty. It is now in the names of Golden Sceptre Resources Limited, Goliath Gold Mines Limited and Noranda Exploration Company, Limited.

. . . .

[La FOREST J.:]

INTRODUCTION

The short issue in this appeal is whether this Court will uphold the Ontario Court of Appeal and trial court decisions ordering Lac Minerals Ltd. ("Lac") to deliver up to International Corona Resources Ltd. ("Corona"), land (the Williams property) on which there is a gold mine, on being compensated for the value of improvements Lac has made to the property ($153,978,000) in developing the mine.

. . . .

THE ISSUES

Three issues must be addressed:

1. What was the nature of the duty of confidence that was breached by Lac?
2. Does the existence of the duty of confidence, alone or in conjunction with the other facts as found below, give rise to any fiduciary obligation or relationship? If so, what is the nature of that obligation or relation?
3. Is a constructive trust an available remedy for a breach of confidence as well as for breach of a fiduciary duty, and if so, should this Court interfere with the lower courts' imposition of that remedy?

. . . .

---

† [1989] 2 S.C.R 574.

FIDUCIARY OBLIGATION

Having established that Lac breached a duty of confidence owed to Corona, the existence of a fiduciary relationship is only relevant if the remedies for a breach of a fiduciary obligation differ from those available for a breach of confidence. In my view, the remedies available to one head of claim are available to the other, so that provided a constructive trust is an appropriate remedy for the breach of confidence in this case, finding a fiduciary duty is not strictly necessary. In my view, regardless of the basis of liability, a constructive trust is the only just remedy in this case. Nonetheless, in light of the argument, I think it appropriate to consider whether a fiduciary relationship exists in the circumstances here.

There are few legal concepts more frequently invoked but less conceptually certain than that of the fiduciary relationship. In specific circumstances and in specific relationships, courts have no difficulty in imposing fiduciary obligations, but at a more fundamental level, the principle on which that obligation is based is unclear. Indeed, the term "fiduciary" has been described as "one of the most ill-defined, if not altogether misleading terms in our law": see Finn, *Fiduciary Obligations*, at p. 1. ...

. . . .

Much of the confusion surrounding the term "fiduciary" stems, in my view, from its undifferentiated use in at least three distinct ways. The first is as used by Wilson J. in *Frame v. Smith, supra*. There the issue was whether a certain class of relationship, custodial and non-custodial parents, were a category, analogous to directors and corporations, solicitors and clients, trustees and beneficiaries, and agents and principals, the existence of which relationship would give rise to fiduciary obligations. The focus is on the identification of relationships in which, because of their inherent purpose or their presumed factual or legal incidents, the courts will impose a fiduciary obligation on one party to act or refrain from acting in a certain way. The obligation imposed may vary in its specific substance depending on the relationship, though compendiously it can be described as the fiduciary duty of loyalty and will most often include the avoidance of a conflict of duty and interest and a duty not to profit at the expense of the beneficiary. The presumption that a fiduciary obligation will be owed in the context of such a relationship is not irrebuttable, but a strong presumption will exist

that such an obligation is present. Further, not every legal claim arising out of a relationship with fiduciary incidents will give rise to a claim for breach of fiduciary duty. This was made clear by Southin J. (as she then was) in *Girardet v. Crease & Co.* (1987), 11 B.C.L.R. (2d) 361 (S.C.), at p. 362. She stated:

> Counsel for the plaintiff spoke of this case in his opening as one of breach of fiduciary duty and negligence. It became clear during his opening that no breach of fiduciary duty is in issue. What is in issue is whether the defendant was negligent in advising on the settlement of a claim for injuries suffered in an accident. The word "fiduciary" is flung around now as if it applied to all breaches of duty by solicitors, directors of companies and so forth. But "fiduciary" comes from the Latin "fiducia" meaning "trust". Thus, the adjective, "fiduciary" means of or pertaining to a trustee or trusteeship. That a lawyer can commit a breach of the special duty of a trustee, e.g., by stealing his client's money, by entering into a contract with the client without full disclosure, by sending a client a bill claiming disbursements never made and so forth is clear. But to say that simple carelessness in giving advice is such a breach is a perversion of words.

It is only in relation to breaches of the specific obligations imposed because the relationship is one characterized as fiduciary that a claim for breach of fiduciary duty can be founded. In determining whether the categories of relationships which should be presumed to give rise to fiduciary obligations should be extended, the rough and ready guide adopted by Wilson J. is a useful tool for that evaluation. This class of fiduciary obligation need not be considered further, as Corona's contention is not that "parties negotiating towards a joint-venture" constitute a category of relationship, proof of which will give rise to a presumption of fiduciary obligation, but rather that a fiduciary relationship arises out of the particular circumstances of this case.

This brings me to the second usage of fiduciary, one I think more apt to the present case. The imposition of fiduciary obligations is not limited to those relationships in which a presumption of such an obligation arises. Rather, a fiduciary obligation can arise as a matter of fact out of the specific circumstances of a relationship. As such it can arise between parties in a relationship in which fiduciary obligations would not normally be expected. I agree with this comment of Professor Finn in "The Fiduciary Principle", supra, at p. 64:

> What must be shown, in the writer's view, is that the actual circumstances of a relationship are such that one party is entitled to expect that the other will act in his interests in and for the purposes of the relationship. Ascendancy, influence, vulnerability, trust, confidence or dependence doubtless will be of importance in making this out. But they will be important only to the extent that they evidence a relationship suggesting that entitlement. The critical matter in the end is the role that the alleged fiduciary has, or should be taken to have, in the relationship. It must so implicate that party in the other's affairs or so align him with the protection or advancement of that other's interests that foundation exists for the "fiduciary expectation". Such a role may generate an actual expectation that that other's interests are being served. This is commonly so with lawyers and investment advisers. But equally the expectation may be a judicially prescribed one because the law itself ordains it to be that other's entitlement. And this may be so either because that party should, given the actual circumstances of the relationship, be accorded that entitlement irrespective of whether he has adverted to the matter, or because the purpose of the relationship itself is perceived to be such that to allow disloyalty in it would be to jeopardise its perceived social utility.

It is in this sense, then, that the existence of a fiduciary obligation can be said to be a question of fact to be determined by examining the specific facts and circumstances surrounding each relationship; see Waters, *Law of Trusts in Canada* (2nd ed. 1984). If the facts give rise to a fiduciary obligation, a breach of the duties thereby imposed will give rise to a claim for equitable relief.

The third sense in which the term "fiduciary" is used is markedly different from the two usages discussed above. It requires examination here because, as I will endeavour to explain, it gives a misleading colouration to the fiduciary concept. This third usage of "fiduciary" stems, it seems, from a perception of remedial inflexibility in equity. Courts have resorted to fiduciary language because of the view that certain remedies, deemed appropriate in the circumstances, would not be available unless a fiduciary relationship was present. In this sense, the label fiduciary imposes no obligations, but rather is merely instrumental or facilitative in achieving what appears to be the appropriate result. ...

. . . .

In my view, this third use of the term fiduciary, used as a conclusion to justify a result, reads equity backwards. It is a misuse of the term. It will only be eliminated, however, if the courts give explicit recognition to the existence of a range of remedies, including the constructive trust, available on a principled basis even though outside the context of a fiduciary relationship.

To recapitulate, the first class of fiduciary is not in issue in this appeal. It is not contended that all parties negotiating towards a joint venture are a class to which fiduciary obligations should presumptively attach. As will be clear from my discussion of the third usage of the term fiduciary, I am not prepared to hold that because a constructive trust is the appropriate remedy a fiduciary label therefore attaches, though I will deal later with why, even if the relationship is not fiduciary in any sense, a constructive trust may nonetheless be appropriate. The issue that remains for immediate discussion is whether the facts in this case, as found by the courts below, support the imposition of a fiduciary obligation within the second category discussed above, and whether, acting as it did, Lac was in breach of the obligations thereby imposed.

. . . .

While it is almost trite to say that a fiduciary relationship does not normally arise between arm's length commercial parties, I am of the view that the courts below correctly found a fiduciary obligation in the circumstances of this case and correctly found Lac to be in breach of it. I turn then to a consideration of the factors which in this case support the imposition of that duty. These can conveniently be grouped under three headings, (1) trust and confidence, (2) industry practice and (3) vulnerability. As will be seen these factors overlap to some extent, but considered as a whole they support the proposition that Corona could reasonably expect Lac to not act to Corona's detriment by acquiring the Williams land, and that Corona's expectation should be legally protected.

TRUST AND CONFIDENCE

The relationship of trust and confidence that developed between Corona and Lac is a factor worthy of significant weight in determining if a fiduciary obligation existed between the parties. The existence of such a bond plays an important role in determining whether one party could reasonably expect the other to act or refrain from acting against the interests of the former. ...

In a claim for breach of confidence, Gurry tells us (*Breach of Confidence*, at pp. 161–62):

> ... the court's concern is for the protection of a confidence which has been created by the disclosure of confidential information by the confider to the confidant. The court's attention is thus focused on the protection of the confidential information because it has been the medium for the creation of a relationship of confidence; its attention is not focused on the information as a medium by which a pre-existing duty is breached.

However, the facts giving rise to an obligation of confidence are also of considerable importance in the creation of a fiduciary obligation. If information is imparted in circumstances of confidence, and if the information is known to be confidential, it cannot be denied that the expectations of the parties may be affected so that one party reasonably anticipates that the other will act or refrain from acting in a certain way. A claim for breach of confidence will only be made out, however, when it is shown that the confidee has misused the information to the detriment of the confidor. Fiduciary law, being concerned with the exaction of a duty of loyalty, does not require that harm in the particular case be shown to have resulted.

There are other distinctions between the law of fiduciary obligations and that of confidence which need not be pursued further here, but among them I simply note that unlike fiduciary obligations, duties of confidence can arise outside a direct relationship, where for example a third party has received confidential information from a confidee in breach of the confidee's obligation to the confidor: see *Liquid Veneer Co. v. Scott*. It would be a misuse of the term to suggest that the third party stood in a fiduciary position to the original confidor. Another difference is that breach of confidence also has a jurisdictional base at law, whereas fiduciary obligations are a solely equitable creation. Though this is becoming of less importance, these differences of origin give to the

claim for breach of confidence a greater remedial flexibility than is available in fiduciary law. Remedies available from both law and equity are available in the former case, equitable remedies alone are available in the latter.

. . . .

INDUSTRY PRACTICE

Both courts below placed considerable weight on the evidence of Allen to the effect that there was a "duty" not to act to the other party's detriment when in serious negotiations through the misuse of confidential information. ...

. . . .

Undoubtedly experts on mining practice are not qualified to give evidence on whether fiduciary obligations arose between the parties, as the existence of fiduciary obligations is a question of law to be answered by the court after a consideration of all the facts and circumstances. Thus, while the term "fiduciary" was not properly used by the trial judge in this passage, the evidence of the experts is of considerable importance in establishing standard practice in the industry from which one can determine the nature of the obligations which will be imposed by law.

. . . .

... In any event, it is not, in my opinion, necessary to determine if the practice established by the evidence of Lac's executives and experts amounts to a legal usage. It is clear to me that the practice in the industry is so well known that at the very least Corona could reasonably expect Lac to abide by it. There is absolutely no substance to the submission of Lac that this practice is vague or uncertain. It is premised on the disclosure of confidential information in the context of serious negotiations. I do not find it necessary to define "serious", and will not interfere with the concurrent findings of the courts below. The industry practice therefore, while not conclusive, is entitled to significant weight in determining the reasonable expectations of Corona, and for that matter of Lac regarding how the latter should behave.

VULNERABILITY

As I indicated above, vulnerability is not, in my view a necessary ingredient in every fiduciary relationship. It will of course often be present, and when it is found it is an additional circumstance that must be considered in determining if the facts give rise to a fiduciary obligation. I agree with the proposition put forward by Wilson J. that when determining if new classes of relationship should be taken to give rise to fiduciary obligations then the vulnerability of the class of beneficiaries of the obligation is a relevant consideration.

. . . .

Persons are vulnerable if they are susceptible to harm, or open to injury. They are vulnerable at the hands of a fiduciary if the fiduciary is the one who can inflict that harm. It is clear, however, that fiduciary obligations can be breached without harm being inflicted on the beneficiary. *Keech v. Sandford* (1726), Sel. Cas. T. King 61, 25 E.R. 223, is the clearest example. In that case a fiduciary duty was breached even though the beneficiary suffered no harm and indeed could not have benefitted from the opportunity the fiduciary pursued. Beneficiaries of trusts, however, are a class that is susceptible to harm, and are therefore protected by the fiduciary regime. Not only is actual harm not necessary, susceptibility to harm will not be present in many cases. Each director of General Motors owes a fiduciary duty to that company, but one can seriously question whether General Motors is vulnerable to the actions of each and every director. Nonetheless, the fiduciary obligation is owed because, as a class, corporations are susceptible to harm from the actions of their directors.

. . . .

I conclude therefore that Corona was vulnerable to Lac. The fact that these are commercial parties may be a factor in determining what the reasonable expectations of the parties are, and thus it may be a rare occasion that vulnerability is found between such parties. It is, however, shown to exist in this case and is a factor deserving of considerable weight in the identification of a fiduciary obligation.

CONCLUSION ON FIDUCIARY OBLIGATIONS

Taking these factors together, I am of the view that the courts below did not err in finding that a fiduciary obligation existed and that it was breached. Lac urged this Court not to accept this finding, warning that imposing a fiduciary relationship in a case such as this would give rise to the greatest uncertainty in commercial law, and result in the determination of the rules of commercial conduct on the basis of ad hoc moral judgments rather than on the basis of established principles of commercial law.

I cannot accept either of these submissions. Certainty in commercial law is, no doubt, an important value, but it is not the only value. As Grange J. has noted:

> There are many limitations on the freedom of contract both in the common law and by statute. Every one of them carries within itself the seeds of debate as to its meaning or at least its applicability to a particular set of facts.

In any event, it is difficult to see how giving legal recognition to the parties' expectations will throw commercial law into turmoil.

Commercial relationships will more rarely involve fiduciary obligations. That is not because they are immune from them, but because in most cases, they would not be appropriately imposed. I agree with this comment of Mason J. in *Hospital Products Ltd. v. United States Surgical Corp.*, *supra*:

> There has been an understandable reluctance to subject commercial transactions to the equitable doctrine of constructive trust and constructive notice. But it is altogether too simplistic, if not superficial, to suggest that commercial transactions stand outside the fiduciary regime as though in some way commercial transactions do not lend themselves to the creation of a relationship in which one person comes under an obligation to act in the interests of another. The fact that in the great majority of commercial transactions the parties stand at arms' length does not enable us to make a generalization that is universally true in relation to every commercial transaction. In truth, every such transaction must be examined on its merits with a view to ascertaining whether it manifests the characteristics of a fiduciary relationship.

. . . .

REMEDY

. . . .

The issue then is this. If it is established that one party, (here Lac), has been enriched by the acquisition of an asset, the Williams property, that would have, but for the actions of that party been acquired by the plaintiff, (here Corona), and if the acquisition of that asset amounts to a breach of duty to the plaintiff, here either a breach of fiduciary obligation or a breach of a duty of confidence, what remedy is available to the party deprived of the benefit? In my view the constructive trust is one available remedy, and in this case it is the only appropriate remedy.

In my view the facts present in this case make out a restitutionary claim, or what is the same thing, a claim for unjust enrichment. When one talks of restitution, one normally talks of giving back to someone something that has been taken from them (a restitutionary proprietary award), or its equivalent value (a personal restitutionary award). As the Court of Appeal noted in this case, Corona never in fact owned the Williams property, and so it cannot be "given back" to them. However, there are concurrent findings below that but for its interception by Lac, Corona would have acquired the property. In *Air Canada v. British Columbia*, I said that the function of the law of restitution "is to ensure that where a plaintiff has been deprived of wealth that is either in his possession or <u>would have accrued for his benefit</u>, it is restored to him. The measure of restitutionary recovery is the gain the [defendant] made at the [plaintiff's] expense." [Emphasis added.] In my view the fact that Corona never owned the property should not preclude it from [] pursuing a restitutionary claim. Lac has therefore been enriched at the expense of Corona.

That enrichment is also unjust, or unjustified, so that the plaintiff is entitled to a remedy. There is, in the words of Dickson J. in *Pettkus v. Becker*, an "absence of any juristic reason for the enrichment". The determination that the enrichment is "unjust" does not refer to abstract notions of morality and justice, but flows directly from the finding that there was a breach of a legally recognized duty for which the courts will grant relief. Restitution is a distinct body of law governed by its own developing system of rules. Breaches of fiduciary duties and breaches of confidence are both wrongs for which restitutionary relief is often appropriate. It is not every case of such a breach of duty, however, that will attract recovery based on the gain of the defendant at the plaintiff's expense. Indeed this has long been recognized by the courts. ...

. . . .

In breach of confidence cases as well, there is considerable flexibility in remedy. Injunctions preventing the continued use of the confidential information are commonly awarded. Obviously that remedy would be of no use in this case where the total benefit accrues to the defendant through a single misuse of information. An account of profits is also often available. Indeed in both courts below an account of profits to the date of transfer of the mine was awarded. Usually an accounting is not a restitutionary measure of damages. Thus, while it is measured according to the defendant's gain, it is not measured by the defendant's gain at the plaintiff's expense. Occasionally, as in this case, the measures coincide. ...

. . . .

The trial judge assessed damages in this case at $700,000,000 in the event that the order that Lac deliver up the property was not upheld on appeal. In doing so he had to assess the damages in the face of evidence that the Williams property would be valued by the market at up to 1.95 billion dollars. Before us there is a cross-appeal that damages be reassessed at $1.5 billion. The trial judge found that no one could predict future gold prices, exchange rates or inflation with any certainty, or even on the balance of probabilities. Likewise he noted that the property had not been fully explored and that further reserves may be found. The Court of Appeal made the following comment, at p. 59, with which I am in entire agreement:

> ... there is no question but that gold properties of significance are unique and rare. There are almost insurmountable difficulties in assessing the value of such a property in the open market. The actual damage which has been sustained by Corona is virtually impossible to determine with any degree of accuracy. The profitability of the mine, and accordingly its value, will depend on the ore reserves of the mine, the future price of gold from time to time, which in turn depends on the rate of exchange between the U.S. dollar and Canadian dollar, inflationary trends, together with myriad other matters, all of which are virtually impossible to predict.

To award only a monetary remedy in such circumstances when an alternative remedy is both available and appropriate would in my view be unfair and unjust.

. . . . .

Having specific regard to the uniqueness of the Williams property, to the fact that but for Lac's breaches of duty Corona would have acquired it, and recognizing the virtual impossibility of accurately valuing the property, I am of the view that it is appropriate to award Corona a constructive trust over that land.

(g) *Canada Aero Service Ltd. v. O'Malley*†

[LASKIN J.:]

This appeal arises out of a claim by the plaintiff-appellant (hereinafter referred to as Canaero) that the defendants had improperly taken the fruits of a corporate opportunity in which Canaero had a prior and continuing interest. The allegation against the defendants O'Malley and Zarzycki is that while directors or officers of Canaero they had devoted effort and planning in respect of the particular corporate opportunity as representatives of Canaero, but had subsequently wrongfully taken the benefit thereof in breach of a fiduciary duty to Canaero. The defendant Wells, who had been a director of Canaero but never an officer, was brought into the action as an associate of the other individual defendants in an alleged scheme to deprive Canaero of the corporate opportunity which it had been developing through O'Malley and Zarzycki; and the defendant Terra Surveys Limited was joined as the vehicle through which the individual defendants in fact obtained the benefit for which Canaero had been negotiating.

. . . .

Canaero was incorporated in 1948 under the *Companies Act* of Canada as a wholly-owned subsidiary of Aero Service Corporation, a United States company whose main business, like that of Canaero and other subsidiaries, was topographical mapping and geophysical exploration. In 1961,

the parent Aero and its subsidiaries came under the control of another United States corporation, Litton Industries Inc. O'Malley joined Aero Service Corporation in 1936 and, apart from army service, remained with it until 1950 when he became general manager and president of Canaero whose head office was in Ottawa. He returned to the parent Aero company in 1957, but rejoined Canaero in 1964 as president and chief executive officer, and remained as such until he resigned on August 19, 1966. Acknowledgement and acceptance of the resignation followed on August 26, 1966.

Zarzycki, who attained a widely-respected reputation in geodesy, joined Canaero in 1953, soon becoming chief engineer. He was named executive vice-president in 1964 and made a director in March 1965. He resigned these posts on August 22, 1966, and received the acknowledgment and acceptance of his resignation in a letter of August 29, 1966.

. . . .

The defendant Terra Surveys Limited was incorporated on August 16, 1966, following a luncheon meeting of O'Malley, Zarzycki and Wells on August 6, 1966, at which the suggestion to form a company of their own was made by Wells to O'Malley and Zarzycki. To Wells' knowledge, the latter were discontented at Canaero by reason of the limitations upon their authority and the scope of independent action imposed by the Litton

---

† [1974] 1 S.C.R. 592 at 594–602, 604–10, 613–20 (On Appeal from the Court of Appeal for Ontario).

company, and they also feared loss of position if Canaero should fail to get contracts. Nominal directors and officers of the new company were appointed, but O'Malley and Zarzycki became major shareholders when common stock was issued on September 12, 1966. One share was issued to Wells at this time but he made a further investment in the new company on November 6, 1966. There is no doubt that Terra Surveys Limited was conceived as a company through which O'Malley and Zarzycki could pursue the same objects that animated Canaero. O'Malley became president of Terra Surveys Limited and Zarzycki became executive vice-president shortly after its incorporation.

The legal issues in this appeal concern what I shall call the Guyana project, the topographical mapping and aerial photographing of parts of Guyana (known as British Guiana until its independence on May 25, 1965) to be financed through an external aid grant or loan from the Government of Canada under its programme of aid to developing countries. Terra Surveys Limited, in association with Survair Limited and another company, succeeded in obtaining the contract for the Guyana project which Canaero had been pursuing through O'Malley and Zarzycki, among others, for a number of years. There is a coincidence of dates and events surrounding the maturing and realization of that project, and the departure of O'Malley and Zarzycki from Canaero, their involvement with Wells in the incorporation of Terra Surveys Limited and its success, almost immediately thereafter, in obtaining the contract for the project. The significance of this coincidence is related, first, to the nature of the duty owed to Canaero by O'Malley and Zarzycki by reason of their positions with that company and, second, to the continuation of the duty, if any, upon a severance of relationship.

. . . .

Canaero's interest in promoting a project in Guyana for the development of its natural resources, and in particular electrical energy, began in 1961. It had done work in nearby Surinam (or Dutch Guiana) where conditions were similar. It envisaged extensive aerial photography and mapping of the country which, apart from the populated coastal area, was covered by dense jungle. Promotional work to persuade the local authorities that Canaero was best equipped to carry out the topographical mapping was done by O'Malley and by another associate of the parent Aero. A local

agent, one Gavin B. Kennard, was engaged by Canaero. In May 1962, Zarzycki spent three days in Guyana in the interests of Canaero, obtaining information, examining existing geographical surveys and meeting government officials. He submitted a report on his visit to Canaero and to the parent Aero company.

Between 1962 and 1964 Canaero did magnetometer and electromagnetometer surveys in Guyana on behalf of the United Nations, and it envisaged either the United Nations or the United States as the funding agency to support the topographical mapping project that it was evolving as a result of its contacts in Guyana and Zarzycki's visit and report. Political conditions in Guyana after Zarzycki's visit in May 1962 did not conduce to furtherance of the project and activity thereon was suspended.

. . . .

Zarzycki returned to Guyana on July 14, 1965, and remained there until July 18, 1965. By July 26, 1965, he completed a proposal for topographical mapping of the country, a proposal that the Government thereof might use in seeking Canadian financial aid. Copies went to a Guyana cabinet minister, to the Canadian High Commissioner there and to the External Aid Office in Ottawa. Zarzycki in his evidence described the proposal as more sales-slanted than technical. The technical aspects were none the less covered; for example, the report recommended the use of an aerodist, a recently invented airborne electronic distance-measuring device. ...

A few days earlier, on July 10, 1966, to be exact, an internal communication to the acting director-general of the Canadian External Aid Office, one Peter Towe, informed him that the Governments of Guyana and Canada had agreed in principle on a loan to Guyana for a topographical survey and mapping. The Prime Minister of Guyana had come to Ottawa early in July, 1966, for discussion on that among other matters. O'Malley had felt that if the assistance from Canada was by way of a loan Guyana would have the major say in naming the contractor, and this would make Canaero's chances better than if the assistance was by way of grant because then the selection would be determined by Canada. ... Towe was informed by departmental letter of August 18, 1966, of a recommendation that Canaero, Lockwood Survey Corporation, Spartan Air Services Limited and

Survair Limited be invited to submit proposals for the project. There was a pencilled note on the side of the letter, apparently added later, of the following words: "general photogramy Terra Ltd.".

The Canadian External Aid Office by letter of August 23, 1966, invited five companies to bid on the Guyana project. Survair Limited was dropped from the originally recommended group of four companies, and Terra Surveys Limited and General Photogrammetric Services Limited were added. A briefing on the specifications for the project was held by the Department of Mines and Technical Surveys on August 29, 1966. Zarzycki and another represented Terra Surveys Limited at this briefing.

O'Malley and Zarzycki pursued the Guyana project on behalf of Canaero up to July 25, 1966, but did nothing thereon for Canaero thereafter. On July 9, 1966, they had met with the Prime Minister of Guyana during his visit to Ottawa, and on July 13, 1966, they had met with Towe (who had previously been informed of the intergovernmental agreement in principle on the Guyana project) and learned from him that the project was on foot. O'Malley had written to Kennard, Canaero's Guyana agent, on July 15, 1966, that he felt the job was a certainty for Canaero. ...

Thereafter the record of events, subject to one exception, concerns the involvement of O'Malley and Zarzycki with Wells in the incorporation of Terra Surveys Limited, their resignations from their positions with Canaero and their successful intervention through Terra Surveys Limited into the Guyana project. As of the date of O'Malley's letter of resignation, August 19, 1966, Terra Surveys Limited had a post office box and a favorable bank reference. Zarzycki had then not yet formally resigned as had O'Malley but had made the decision to do so. ...

. . . . .

Despite having lost O'Malley and Zarzycki and also a senior employee Turner (who joined the Terra venture and attended the briefing session on August 29, 1966, on its behalf with Zarzycki), Canaero associated itself with Spartan Air Services Limited in the latter's proposal on the Guyana project which was submitted under date of September 12, 1966. Prior to this submission, representatives of these two companies visited Guyana to assure officials there that Canaero was involved in the preparation of the Spartan proposal and was supporting it.

Terra Surveys Limited submitted its proposal on September 12, 1966, through Zarzycki, having sent a letter on that date to the External Aid Office setting out its qualifications. A report on the various proposals submitted was issued on September 16, 1966, by the Canadian government officer who had visited Guyana and had prepared the specifications for the project. He recommended that Terra Surveys Limited be the contractor ... :

. . . .

The proposal submitted by Terra Surveys Limited covered the operation in much greater detail than might normally be expected. However, the suggestions put forward indicate that all aspects of the operation have been most carefully reviewed and the plan of operation well thought out. The sections of the Terra proposal dealing with Aerodist indicate a more complete understanding of the problems in the field and subsequent operations than the other two proposals.

The treatment of many aspects of the project varies very little in the three proposals. However, appreciable differences do appear in the key phases of aerial photography and Aerodist control as explained in the preceding paragraphs. My assessment is that Terra Surveys Limited, in combination with Survair Limited and General Photogrammetric Services Limited, is best fitted to undertake this very difficult operation.

In the result, Terra Surveys Limited negotiated a contract with the External Aid Office, and on November 26, 1966, entered into an agreement with the Government of Guyana to carry out the project for the sum of $2,300,000. This was the amount indicated in the proposal of July 26, 1965, prepared by Zarzycki on behalf of Canaero.

. . . .

There are four issues that arise for consideration on the facts so far recited. There is, first, the determination of the relationship of O'Malley and Zarzycki to Canaero. Second, there is the duty or duties, if any, owed by them to Canaero by reason of the ascertained relationship. Third, there is the question whether there has been any breach of duty, if any is owing, by reason of the conduct of O'Malley and Zarzycki in acting through Terra to secure the contract for the Guyana project; and, fourth, there is the question of liability for breach of duty if established.

... What is not in doubt is that they acted respectively as president and executive vice-president of Canaero for about two years prior to their resignations. To paraphrase the findings of the trial judge in this respect, they acted in those positions and their remuneration and responsibilities verified their status as senior officers of Canaero. They were "top management" and not mere employees whose duty to their employer, unless enlarged by contract, consisted only of respect for trade secrets and for confidentiality of customer lists. Theirs was a larger, more exacting duty which, unless modified by statute or by contract (and there is nothing of this sort here), was similar to that owed to a corporate employer by its directors. I adopt what is said on this point by Gower, *Principles of Modern Company Law*, 3rd ed. as follows:

> ... these duties, except in so far as they depend on statutory provisions expressly limited to directors, are not so restricted but apply equally to any officials of the company who are authorized to act on its behalf, and in particular to those acting in a managerial capacity.

The distinction taken between agents and servants of an employer is apt here, and I am unable to appreciate the basis upon which the Ontario Court of Appeal concluded that O'Malley and Zarzycki were mere employees, that is servants of Canaero rather than agents. Although they were subject to supervision of the officers of the controlling company, their positions as senior officers of a subsidiary, which was a working organization, charged them with initiatives and with responsibilities far removed from the obedient role of servants.

It follows that O'Malley and Zarzycki stood in a fiduciary relationship to Canaero, which in its generality betokens loyalty, good faith and avoidance of a conflict of duty and self-interest. Descending from the generality, the fiduciary relationship goes at least this far: a director or a senior officer like O'Malley or Zarzycki is precluded from obtaining for himself, either secretly or without the approval of the company (which would have to be properly manifested upon full disclosure of the facts), any property or business advantage either belonging to the company or for which it has been negotiating; and especially is this so where the director or officer is a participant in the negotiations on behalf of the company.

An examination of the case law in this Court and in the Courts of other like jurisdictions on the fiduciary duties of directors and senior officers shows the pervasiveness of a strict ethic in this area of the law. In my opinion, this ethic disqualifies a director or senior officer from usurping for himself or diverting to another person or company with whom or with which he is associated a maturing business opportunity which his company is actively pursuing; he is also precluded from so acting even after his resignation where the resignation may fairly be said to have been prompted or influenced by a wish to acquire for himself the opportunity sought by the company, or where it was his position with the company rather than a fresh initiative that led him to the opportunity which he later acquired.

.   .   .   .

This Court considered the issue of fiduciary duty of directors in *Zwicker v. Stanbury*, where it found apt for the purposes of that case certain general statements of law by Viscount Sankey and by Lord Russell of Killowen in *Regal (Hastings) Ltd. v. Gulliver*. These statements, reflecting basic principle which is not challenged in the present case, are represented in the following passages:

Per Viscount Sankey:

> In my view, the respondents were in a fiduciary position and their liability to account does not depend upon proof of *mala fides*. The general rule of equity is that no one who has duties of a fiduciary nature to perform is allowed to enter into engagements in which he has or can have a personal interest conflicting with the interests of those whom he is bound to protect. If he holds any property so acquired as trustee, he is bound to account for it to his *cestui que trust*. The earlier cases are concerned with trusts of specific property: *Keech v. Sandford*. The rule, however, applies to agents, as, for example, solicitors and directors, when acting in a fiduciary capacity.

Per Lord Russell of Killowen:

> In the result, I am of opinion that the directors standing in a fiduciary relationship to Regal in regard to the exercise of their powers as directors, and having obtained these shares by reason and only by reason of the fact that they were directors of Regal and in the course of the execution of that office, are accountable for the profits which they have made out of them. The equitable rule laid down in *Keech v. Sandford [supra]* and *Ex p. James*, and similar authorities applies ... in full force. It was con-

tended that these cases were distinguishable by reason of the fact that it was impossible for Regal to get the shares owing to lack of funds, and that the directors in taking the shares were really acting as members of the public. I cannot accept this argument. It was impossible for the *cestui que trust* in *Keech v. Sandford* to obtain the lease, nevertheless the trustee was accountable. The suggestion that the directors were applying simply as members of the public is a travesty of the facts. They could, had they wished, have protected themselves by a resolution (either antecedent or subsequent) of the Regal shareholders in general meeting. In default of such approval, the liability to account must remain.

. . . .

The reaping of a profit by a person at a company's expense while a director thereof is, of course, an adequate ground upon which to hold the director accountable. Yet there may be situations where a profit must be disgorged, although not gained at the expense of the company, on the ground that a director must not be allowed to use his position as such to make a profit even if it was not open to the company, as for example, by reason of legal disability, to participate in the transaction. An analogous situation, albeit not involving a director, existed for all practical purposes in the case of *Phipps v. Boardman*, which also supports the view that liability to account does not depend on proof of an actual conflict of duty and self-interest. ...

What these decisions indicate is an updating of the equitable principle whose roots lie in the general standards that I have already mentioned, namely, loyalty, good faith and avoidance of a conflict of duty and self-interest. Strict application against directors and senior management officials is simply recognition of the degree of control which their positions give them in corporate operations, a control which rises above day-to-day accountability to owning shareholders and which comes under some scrutiny only at annual general or at special meetings. It is a necessary supplement, in the public interest, of statutory regulation and accountability which themselves are, at one and the same time, an acknowledgment of the importance of the corporation in the life of community and of the need to compel obedience by it and by its promoters, directors and managers to norms of exemplary behaviour.

. . . .

That the rigorous standard of behaviour enforced against directors and executives may survive their tenure of such offices was indicated as early as *Ex p. James* where Lord Eldon, speaking of the fiduciary in that case who was a solicitor purchasing at a sale, said:

> With respect to the question now put whether I will permit Jones to give up the office of solicitor and to bid, I cannot give that permission. If the principle is right that the solicitor cannot buy, it would lead to all the mischief of acting up to the point of the sale, getting all the information that may be useful to him, then discharging himself from the character of solicitor and buying the property.... On the other hand I do not deny that those interested in the question may give the permission.

The same principle, although applied in a master-servant case in respect of the use to his own advantage of confidential information acquired by the respondent while employed by the appellant, was recognized by this Court in *Pre-Cam Exploration & Development Ltd. v. McTavish.*

The trial judge appeared to treat this question differently in quoting a passage from *Raines v. Toney*, a judgment of the Supreme Court of Arkansas, at p. 809. The passage is in the following words:

> It is, however, a common occurrence for corporate fiduciaries to resign and form a competing enterprise. Unless restricted by contract, this may be done with complete immunity because freedom of employment and encouragement of competition generally dictate that such persons can leave their corporation at any time and go into a competing business. They cannot while still corporate fiduciaries set up a competitive enterprise ... or resign and take with them the key personnel of their corporations for the purposes of operating their own competitive enterprises ... but they can, while still employed, notify their corporation's customers of their intention to resign and subsequently go into business for themselves, and accept business from them and offer it to them ... but they can use in their own enterprise the experience and knowledge they gained while working for their corporation.... They can solicit the customers of their former corporation for business unless the customer list is itself confidential.

. . . .

The view taken by the trial judge, and affirmed by the Court of Appeal (which quoted the same passage from the reasons of Lord Russell of Killowen in *Regal (Hastings) Ltd. v. Gulliver*), tended to obscure the difference between the survival of fiduciary duty after resignation and the right to use non-confidential information acquired in the course of employment and as a result of experience. I do not see that either the question of the confidentiality of the information acquired by O'Malley and Zarzycki in the course of their work for Canaero on the Guyana project or the question of copyright is relevant to the enforcement against them of a fiduciary duty. The fact that breach of confidence or violation of copyright may itself afford a ground of relief does not make either one a necessary ingredient of a successful claim for breach of fiduciary duty.

. . . .

Again, whether or not Terra was incorporated for the purpose of intercepting the contract for the Guyana project is not central to the issue of breach of fiduciary duty. Honesty of purpose is no more a defence in that respect than it would be in respect of personal interception of the contract by O'Malley and Zarzycki. This is fundamental in the enforcement of fiduciary duty where the fiduciaries are acting against the interests of their principal. Then it is urged that Canaero could not in any event have obtained the contract, and that O'Malley and Zarzycki left Canaero as an ultimate response to their dissatisfaction with that company and with the restrictions that they were under in managing it. There was, however, no certain knowledge at the time O'Malley and Zarzycki resigned that the Guyana project was beyond Canaero's grasp. Canaero had not abandoned its hope of capturing it, even if Wells was of opinion, expressed during his luncheon with O'Malley and Zarzycki on August 6, 1966, that it would not get a foreign aid contract from the Canadian Government. Although it was contended that O'Malley and Zarzycki did not know of the imminence of the approval of the Guyana project, their ready run for it, when it was approved at about the time of their resignations and at a time when they knew of Canaero's continuing interest, are factors to be considered in deciding whether they were still under a fiduciary duty not to seek to procure for themselves or for their newly-formed company the business opportunity which they had nurtured for Canaero.

. . . .

... Accepting the facts found by the trial judge, I find no obstructing considerations to the conclusion that O'Malley and Zarzycki continued, after their resignations, to be under a fiduciary duty to respect Canaero's priority, as against them and their instrument Terra, in seeking to capture the contract for the Guyana project. They entered the lists in the heat of the maturation of the project, known to them to be under active Government consideration when they resigned from Canaero and when they proposed to bid on behalf of Terra.

In holding that on the facts found by the trial judge, there was a breach of fiduciary duty by O'Malley and Zarzycki which survived their resignations I am not to be taken as laying down any rule of liability to be read as if it were a statute. The general standards of loyalty, good faith and avoidance of a conflict of duty and self-interest to which the conduct of a director or senior officer must conform, must be tested in each case by many factors which it would be reckless to attempt to enumerate exhaustively. Among them are the factor of position or office held, the nature of corporate opportunity, its ripeness, its specificness and the director's or managerial officer's relation to it, the amount of knowledge possessed, the circumstances in which it was obtained and whether it was special or, indeed, even private, the factor of time in the continuation of fiduciary duty where the alleged breach occurs after termination of the relationship with the company, and the circumstances under which the relationship was terminated, that is whether by retirement or resignation or discharge.

236

(a)   Compensation for Damage Caused by Government†

Peter W. Hogg, Q.C.

2.   A UNIVERSAL REGIME OF NO-FAULT GOVERNMENTAL LIABILITY?

Should governments be subjected by statute to a universal no-fault regime of liability?

There is a large body of respectable opinion in favour of such a change. This is usually premised on a theory of "risk", involving an obligation on the part of government to pay compensation where its action (or inaction) has created unusual risks to private persons. A similar proposal has been based on a theory of "entitlement," involving an obligation on the part of government to pay compensation where its action (or inaction) has resulted in the denial of some public benefit to which a private person was entitled. The advantages that are claimed for these regimes are considerable. First, the regime could be better tailored to the special characteristics of government than is possible when government liability depends on the application of the general law of torts. Secondly, the regime could provide compensation for those unfortunate victims who (like Lapierre) cannot establish fault on the part of the government. Thirdly, the imposition of a broader liability on government would enable the cost of the damage caused by government to be distributed to the community at large.

The trouble with these regimes is that the controlling concepts of "risk" or "entitlement" are exceedingly vague. If we were to shift to a regime of no-fault public liability, the central issue would be the definition of the losses that are compensated. Can the concepts of risk or entitlement be used to develop a definition of the losses caused by government that should be compensated? The difficulty is that the task of government inevitably imposes costs of infinite variety on those who are governed. Any universal scheme of compensation would obviously be unacceptable, because the cost would effectively destroy the capacity of government to regulate in support of public purposes, such as[] health, safety or the environment.

The objection to a universal scheme of compensation goes beyond cost. Much regulation has a redistributive purpose: it is designed to reduce the rights of one group (manufacturers, employers, for example) and increase the rights of another (consumers, employers, for example). A compensation regime should not work at cross-purposes to the redistributive choices that are made by democratic legislative bodies. Indeed, any regime that did so would be met with legislative reversal. It follows that limits would have to be placed on the kinds of government activity that give rise to compensable risks, or the kinds of losses (unusual, exceptional) that are compensable, or both. But it is not easy to see how the idea of risk or entitlement would enable us to frame appropriate limits, or what agency (the courts?) would be competent to undertake the task.

† (1996) 6 N.J.C.L. 7 at 10–19. [Notes and/or References omitted.] Reproduced with permission of Peter W. Hogg, Scholar In Residence, Blake Cassels & Greydon LLP, Toronto, Canada.

3. PROGRAM-SPECIFIC REGIMES OF NO-FAULT GOVERNMENTAL LIABILITY?

Many statutes do of course provide for compensation to private persons who have been harmed by a government program. For example, all jurisdictions provide compensation for property expropriated by a public authority, and for injuries caused by criminal acts (failures of the criminal justice system). It ought to be a routine part of the planning for a new government program to undertake an analysis of the private losses that might be caused by the program. The planners obviously ought to design the program so as to minimize those losses, but they ought also to give consideration to the provision of compensation for the losses that cannot be avoided. Of course, where the program has a redistributive purpose it would make no sense to negate the purpose by restoring the position of those whose rights have been limited. But the predictable, undesired side effects of a program could and should be analyzed with a view to considering making legislative provision for private compensation, which would then become part of the cost of the program.

Where no provision for compensation has been made, the government may still choose to make ex gratia payments to persons who have been harmed. Indeed, in cases of serious harm, the government will come under political pressure from the opposition and the press to provide relief on an ex gratia basis, and perhaps to develop a formal policy for the identification and payment of deserving claims.

Returning to the *Lapierre* case, is there any reason why a person who suffers personal injury as the result of a public immunization program should not be compensated? The compensation would be a cost to the government, of course, but an immunization program entails many costs and the payment of compensation to accidental victims should surely be treated as one of those costs. Like the cost of vaccine, needles, clinics, nurses, publicity and the like, the cost of compensation should be distributed to the community at large which benefits from the program. The definition of the injuries that are to be compensated does not seem difficult, and the administration of claims (which would not be numerous) would also not be difficult. In fact, after the *Lapierre* case, Quebec amended its *Public Health Protection Act* to provide no-fault compensation for any person who suffered personal injury resulting from a public immunization program. The effect of this legislation (which

applied retroactively so as to benefit Lapierre himself) was to recognize belatedly that the compensation of innocent victims ought to be treated as a cost of any public immunization program. In my view, that was the appropriate outcome.

4. A NO-LIABILITY REGIME FOR GOVERNMENT?

Should governments be exempt from the general law of torts, and *only* be subject to program-specific regimes of liability for the losses caused by governmental action (or inaction)?

An affirmative answer to this question is the conclusion of David Cohen in two articles that appeared in 1990 in the University of Toronto Law Journal. Writing from a law-and-economics perspective, he argues that a government is fundamentally different from a private person in two respects. First, the government, unlike a private firm, is established to accomplish social objectives, and does not need tort law to force it to take account of the social costs of its actions. Secondly, the government, unlike a private firm, will not change its behaviour in order to avoid tort liability for the accidents it causes. For these two reasons, he concludes that tort law will not have appropriate incentive effects on government, and "the optimal liability rule applicable to state action is a 'no liability' rule."

Cohen would also abolish the individual tort liability of government employees, as well as that of the government itself. His reasoning is that individual liability is likely to produce overly cautious, risk-averse behaviour by government employees. The risk of personal liability would have a chilling effect on government employees, leading to inefficiency in the discharge of their regulatory responsibilities. (It is a paradox in his argument that individual immunity is said to be desirable because tort liability would influence the behaviour of individual officials, while government immunity is said to be desirable because tort liability would not influence the behaviour of government.)

Cohen's regime of "no-liability" is not literally one in which government is immune from all liability for losses caused by its action (or inaction). He argues that government should develop "adjustment policies," by which he means policies to compensate for losses, on a program-specific basis. At least in an ideal world, there would be a compensation program to cover many losses caused by government. However he rejects the notion that tort law should operate as a default system until a program-specific compensation policy had been developed, or that tort law should operate simultaneously with or as an alternative to program-specific compensation mechanisms. This is because of his main thesis that governmental liability should not be determined by "a system designed to define relations between individuals," which is "precisely what tort law represents."

In my opinion, it is unsafe to assume that government's concern to maximize social welfare would lead to the voluntary development of adjustment policies that would fairly treat all accident victims. That might or might not happen, but as long as no-liability was the default rule, the phenomenon of inertia would likely keep the no-liability rule in a prominent place. Where no adjustment policy had been developed, a person injured by government, in circumstances that would lead to liability in any other defendant, would be without a remedy.

What of the theory that government does not respond to the normal incentives of tort liability, and will grind relentlessly on in blind indifference to damages awards for its negligent acts and omissions? First, the theory is implausible. It is hard to believe that public officials would not usually take corrective action after being found, perhaps repeatedly, to be guilty of negligence. Secondly, the indifference theory seems inconsistent with the chill theory, which is that individual government employees will be deterred from doing their duty by the risk of tort liability. Thirdly, even if the indifference theory were correct, it would not provide a sufficient basis to eliminate tort liability. It could as easily be argued that tort liability "should be strengthened — for example, with punitive damages — to bring forth the appropriate response."

I conclude that the case has not been made for the radical transformation of our legal system that would be entailed by the removal from government of liability under the general law of torts.

5.   DICEY'S IDEA OF EQUALITY

It remains to deal with the "symbolic and legitimating authority" of the regime of governmental liability. The proposals for universal, no-fault governmental liability (perhaps, based on a theory of risk) or only program-specific government liability (as advocated by Cohen) have this feature in common: they reject the general law of torts as the law governing the liability of government. I have already given specific reasons for rejecting either of the proposed alternatives. But there is also a principle involved here which, in my view, makes it undesirable to construct a special tort regime for government. That principle is that the same law should be applied to government and its officials as is applied to private citizens. This was Dicey's "idea of equality," which was one of the elements of Dicey's "rule of law."

The principle that Dicey defended was not merely that government should be under the law, but that government should be under the same law as applies to everyone else. In that way, government is denied the special exemptions and privileges that could lead to tyranny. Moreover, the application of the law to government is placed in the hands of the ordinary courts, which are independent of government, and which can be relied upon to award an appropriate remedy to the citizen who has been injured by illegal government action. This is the rosy picture that led Dicey to make his famous boast that "every official, from the Prime Minister down to a constable or collector of taxes, is under the same responsibility for every act done without legal justification as any other citizen."

A variety of criticisms can be levelled at Dicey's notion of the equal treatment of government and citizen. One is that it was an inaccurate description of the legal system of the United Kingdom in 1885, when it was written, because of the extensive immunities and privileges that the Crown enjoyed at that time. That is a fair criticism, but statutory reform starting with the United Kingdom's *Crown Proceedings Act* of 1947, and judicial developments since then, have brought the law much closer to Dicey's ideal — and indeed have been driven by Dicey's ideal. A second criticism is that it ignores all the special powers that a modern government needs in order to govern. In carrying out those powers, it is plain that government officials are not subject to the same law as everyone else, but by a body of constitutional and administrative law that is particular to the operations of government. This is also a fair criticism, which greatly restricts the scope of Dicey's idea. Finally, there is the alternative model of the European legal systems, where there is typically a special regime of public law administered by special administrative courts. Dicey abhorred these systems, but it seems likely that he did not understand them very well, and that he exaggerated the differences between the European systems and that of the United Kingdom. Other scholars have usually concluded that the European systems succeed in controlling the government and compensating for losses at least as well as the British-derived systems.

It is not surprising that many public law scholars have entirely rejected Dicey's idea of equality. In their view, relations between government and subject ought to be governed by a distinctive body of public law, which would be more sensitive to the unique characteristics of government. This insight leads commentators in a variety of directions, each of which has been briefly described earlier in this paper. While I have given my reasons for disagreeing with the various models, I acknowledge that a public-law model of liability (or no-liability) is obviously a defensible policy choice. What can be said, I think, is that Dicey captured, articulated and reinforced a fundamental attitude towards government which, at least in common law jurisdictions, is widespread both in the legal profession and in the community at large. A special regime of public liability, especially if it were administered by special courts, would lack an important symbolic and legitimating authority. In other words, at least for a common lawyer, I believe that some notion of equality with the citizen is embedded in our notion of a fair regime of public liability.

Another, strictly practical, point can be made in favour of Dicey's idea of equality. A special regime of liability would create enormous definitional problems, as courts struggled to determine which acts of which bodies were subject to the public law, as opposed to the ordinary private law. In many cases where allegations of negligence are made against government, the plaintiff (or the defendant government) will also implead private firms whose products or services may have contributed to the plaintiff's injury. An aircraft accident,

for example, may have been contributed to by government's negligent air traffic control, but may also involve pilot error (the airline), inadequate maintenance (a service company), poor design of the aircraft (the aircraft manufacturer) and a defective engine (the engine manufacturer). Each of these potential defendants may be held to be negligent, and damages will need to be apportioned among them. To determine the government's liability or the measure of its damages by a different set of "public" rules from those applicable to the other defendants (or third parties) would be an outrageous complication in what is already a complex legal situation.

If the government's liability had to be determined by a special administrative court, which is the French model, the multi-defendant lawsuit would require more than one set of proceedings, causing a great increase in costs, the possibility of inconsistent verdicts and the impossibility of a judicial apportionment of blame among all defendants. Indeed, we endured this nightmare in Canada when the government of Canada could be sued only in the Federal Court of Canada and private defendants could be sued only in the appropriate provincial court. That problem was alleviated in 1990 when the Federal Court's jurisdiction over the government of Canada was amended by statute to become concurrent rather than exclusive. What the pre-1990 cases showed was that if claims against government are tried in a different forum than claims against private parties, there is much wasteful litigation over jurisdiction, not only in multi-defendant cases (although these are the worst), but also in simpler cases where litigants will attempt to position themselves in the forum perceived most favourable to success.

(b) *Kamloops v. Nielsen*[†]

[WILSON J.:]

This case raises the rather difficult question whether a municipality can be held liable for negligence in failing to prevent the construction of a house with defective foundations. It also raises a number of ancillary questions, such as whether such a liability, assuming it exists, extends to third

---

† [1984] 2 S.C.R. 2 at 5–13, 21–25.

party purchasers, what sort of damages are recoverable, and when the limitation period starts to run.

1.   THE FACTS

Since the facts are of vital importance I set them out in some detail. Mr. Hughes Jr. set out to build a house on a hillside for his father who was an alderman in the City of Kamloops. To this end he submitted plans to the city's building inspector. The plans were approved, subject to the requirement that the footings were to be taken down to solid bearing, and a building permit was issued. Mr. Hughes did not take the footings down to solid bearing; instead he set the foundations on piles which were set into loose fill. He then requested an inspection of the foundations. When one of the city's building inspectors arrived to make his inspection on December 18, 1973, he realized that the foundations were not in accordance with the plans but he was unable to check whether they were adequate to support the building because the concrete had been poured. Accordingly on his own initiative the building inspector followed up with two further inspections on December 23, 1973 and January 2, 1974, and sent a letter to Mr. Hughes on the latter date indicating that a stop work order had been placed on the site and would not be lifted until new plans had been submitted showing how the structural defects were going to be remedied. Mr. Hughes retained a firm of professional engineers to prepare the new plans and on receipt of their proposal the building inspector lifted the stop work order. Mr. Hughes, however, did not co-operate with the engineers on the required changes but continued with the construction of the house on the original plans. The engineers, disavowing all liability, notified the building inspector.

On February 27, 1974, two building inspectors attended at the site. This was followed next day by a registered letter from the building inspector to Mr. Hughes telling him that the stop work order would remain in effect until he submitted a report from a structural engineer. Mr. Hughes ignored this communication and carried on with the building. Various further inspections were made by building inspectors who reported to their superior, the building inspector, that construction was continuing despite the stop work order.

On April 9, 1974, Mr. Hughes Sr. and his wife purchased the property from his son. The city solicitor wrote to them on April 22, 1974, advising them of the city's concern over the structural integrity of the building and that the stop work order which was currently in force would not be lifted until the city was provided with complete structural drawings from an engineer verifying the adequacy of the proposed construction. Mr. Backmeyer, director of planning for the city, became involved at this stage but no resolution to the problem was effected. The dialogue moved into the council chamber and Mr. Backmeyer testified that Mr. Hughes Sr.'s plea to his fellow council members was that this was his retirement home and, since he was going to live in it, any problems that arose would be his and his alone. It was therefore no-one's business but his and why was he being subjected to this kind of harassment?

At this point a strike of city employees broke out and the director of planning and the building division administrator were left to run the building division by themselves until the strike ended some time in July. No further inspections were made after the strike and no occupancy permit was ever issued. A plumbing permit was, however, issued in August, 1974. The house was completed and the Hughes moved in in February, 1975. In December, 1977, they sold the property to the present plaintiff who was told nothing of its chequered history. Before purchasing the house the plaintiff had taken a contractor with him to advise him on the cost of some renovations and also to make a general inspection of the house. The contractor did not see anything to alert him to a potential problem with the foundations but he did not crawl under the house to examine them. Accordingly, the first the plaintiff knew of the defective foundations was when they were drawn to his attention in November, 1978, by a plumber called to attend to a burst pipe. The plumber discovered the situation when he went into the four-foot crawl space under part of the house and saw that the foundations had subsided.

The plaintiff issued his writ in January, 1979, alleging against his vendor (1) fraudulent misrepresentation; (2) breach of contract; and (3) negligence in the construction of the house. He alleged negligence also against the City of Kamloops for failing to enforce the stop work order or, alternatively, for failing to condemn the building as unfit for habitation.

Andrews J. found both defendants liable and apportioned fault between them, 75% against the Hughes and 25% against the city. No appeal was taken by the Hughes. The city's appeal to the Court of Appeal of British Columbia was dismissed.

But for the issue of limitations which I will deal with later, the city's grounds of appeal to this court were substantially the same as those presented to the Court of Appeal and rejected by it. The first was that no duty of care was owed by the city to the plaintiff and, absent such a duty, no liability in negligence could be incurred.

2. THE DUTY OF CARE

The leading English authority favouring the existence of a duty of care owed by the city to the plaintiff is the decision of the House of Lords in *Anns v. Merton London Borough Council*. The facts, in brief, were that the borough council in February, 1962, approved plans for the creation of a two-storey block of flats. The plans called for the foundations to be "three feet or deeper to the approval of local authority". In fact the foundations were only two feet six inches deep. By February, 1970, cracks had appeared in the walls of the flats and the floors had begun to slope. Two of the plaintiffs were original lessees; the others were assignees from original lessees. All claimed against the borough for the negligence of the council surveyor in approving foundations that were inadequate.

The relevant English legislation was the *Public Health Act*, 1936 (U.K.), c. 49, s. 61, which empowered council to make by-laws to regulate the construction of buildings. By-law 18(1)(b) provided that the foundations of every building should be taken down to such depth or be so designed as to safeguard the building against damage caused by swelling and shrinking of the subsoil. The builder was under a statutory duty to notify the local authority before covering up the foundations and the local authority had at that stage the right to inspect and to insist on any correction necessary to bring the work into conformity with the by-laws.

Lord Wilberforce pointed out that the local authority is a public body whose powers and duties are definable in terms of public rather than private law. However, in some circumstances the law could impose over and above, or perhaps alongside, these public law powers and duties a private law duty towards individuals enabling them to sue the authority for damages in a civil suit. The difficulty was to determine when such a private law duty could be imposed. The first step, Lord Wilberforce said, is to analyse the powers and duties of the authority to determine whether they require the authority to make "policy" decisions or "operational" decisions. He said at p. 754:

Most, indeed probably all, statutes relating to public authorities or public bodies[] contain in them a large area of policy. The courts call this "discretion" meaning that the decision is one for the authority or body to make, and not for the courts. Many statutes also prescribe or at least presuppose, the practical execution of policy decisions: a convenient description of this is to say that in addition to the area of policy or discretion, there is an operational area. Although this distinction between the policy area and the operational area is convenient, and illuminating, it is probably a distinction of degree: many "operational" powers or duties have in them some element of "discretion." It can safely be said that the more "operational" a power or duty may be, the easier it is to superimpose upon it a common law duty of care.

His Lordship then adverted to the fact that frequently policy decisions are affected by budgetary considerations. It is for the local authority to decide what resources it should make available to carry out its role in supervising and controlling the activities of builders. For example, budgetary considerations may dictate how many inspectors should be hired for this purpose, what their qualifications should be, and how often inspections should be made. He approved the statement of du Parcq L.J. in *Kent v. East Suffolk Rivers Catchment Board*, that public authorities have to strike a balance between the claims of efficiency and thrift and whether they get the right balance can only be decided through the ballot-box and not in the courts. He then dealt with the argument that where the local authority is under no duty to inspect but merely has a power to inspect, it can avoid liability for negligent inspection by simply deciding not to inspect at all. He pointed out that this overlooks the fact that local authorities are public bodies operating under statute with a clear responsibility for public health in their area. They must, therefore, make their discretionary decisions responsibly and for reasons that accord with the statutory purpose. They must at the very least give due consideration to the question whether they should inspect or not and, having decided to inspect, they must then be under a duty to exercise reasonable care in conducting that inspection.

Lord Wilberforce rejected the notion that a distinction was to be made in this context between statutory powers, the former giving rise to possible liability and the latter not. Such a distinction, he says, overlooks the fact that parallel with public law duties owed by local authorities there may co-exist private law duties to avoid causing damage to other persons in proximity to them. The trilogy of House of Lords cases — *M'Alister (or Donoghue) v. Stevenson*; *Hedley Byrne & Co. Ltd. v. Heller & Partner Ltd.*, and *Dorset Yacht Co. Ltd. v. Home Office* — clearly established that in order to decide whether or not a private law duty of care existed, two questions must be asked:

1. is there a sufficiently close relationship between the parties (the local authority and the person who has suffered the damage) so that, in the reasonable contemplation of the authority, carelessness on its part might cause damage to that person? If so,
2. are there any considerations which ought to negative or limit
   (a) the scope of the duty and
   (b) the class of persons to whom it is owed or
   (c) the damages to which a breach of it may give rise?

These questions, Lord Wilberforce said, must be answered by an examination of the governing legislation.

Lord Wilberforce categorized the various types of legislation as follows:

1. statutes conferring powers to interfere with the rights of individuals in which case an action in respect of damage caused by the exercise of such powers will generally not lie except in the case where the local authority has done what the Legislature authorized but done it negligently;
2. statutes conferring powers but leaving the scale on which they are to be exercised to the discretion of the local authority. Here there will be an option to the local authority whether or not to do the thing authorized but, if it elects to do it and does it negligently, then the policy decision having been made, there is a duty at the operational level to use due care in giving effect to it.

Lord Wilberforce found that the defendant in *Anns* was under a private law duty to the plaintiff. It had to exercise a *bona fide* discretion as to whether to inspect the foundations or not and, if it decided to inspect them, to exercise reasonable skill and care in doing so. He concluded that the allegations of negligence were consistent with the council or its inspector having acted outside any

delegated discretion either as to the making of an inspection or as to the manner in which the inspection was made.

Following the path charted by Lord Wilberforce and directing myself to the governing legislation, s. 714 of the *Municipal Act* of British Columbia, R.S.B.C. 1960, c. 255, as amended, now R.S.B.C. 1979, c. 290, provides in part as follows:

> **714.** The Council may, for the health, safety, and protection of persons and property, and subject to the *Health Act* and the *Fire Marshal Act* and the regulations made thereunder, by by-law
> (a) regulate the construction, alteration, repair, or demolition of buildings and structures;
>
> ...
>
> (k) require that, prior to any occupancy of a building or part thereof after construction, wrecking, or alteration of that building or part thereof, or any change in class of occupancy of any building or part thereof, an occupancy permit be obtained from the Council or the proper authorized official, which permit may be withheld until the building or part thereof complies with the health and safety requirements of the by-laws of the municipality or of any Statute.

It would appear from the use of the word "may" in s. 714 that the council has a discretion under the statute whether to regulate the construction of buildings by by-laws or not. However, in fact council decided to exercise its regulatory power and passed By-law No. 11–1. The by-law prohibited construction without a building permit, provided for a scheme of inspections at various stages of construction, prohibited occupancy without an occupancy permit and, perhaps most important, imposed on the building inspector the duty to enforce its provisions. It should be noted, however, that the by-law also imposed a duty on the owner of the building or his agent to give notice to the building inspector when the building reached the various stages at which inspection was called for under the by-law.

It seems to me that, applying the principle in *Anns*, it is fair to say that the City of Kamloops had a statutory power to regulate construction by by-law. It did not have to do so. It was in its discretion whether to do so or not. It was, in other words, a "policy" decision. However, not only did it make the policy decision in favour of regulating construction by by-law, it also imposed on the city's building inspector a duty to enforce the provisions of the by-law. This would be Lord Wilberforce's "operational" duty. Is the city not then in the position where in discharging its operational duty it must take care not to injure persons such as the plaintiff whose relationship to the city was sufficiently close that the city ought reasonably to have had him in contemplation?

. . . .

5. THE NATURE OF THE ALLEGED BREACH

Two important questions that must be answered in the present case are: (1) What was it that the building inspector failed to do in this case that is alleged to have contributed to the plaintiff's damage?; and (2) Was he under a duty to do that thing? If the building inspector was under a duty to do the thing he failed to do, then it seems to me that Seaton J.A. was right in *McCrea* when he stated that the non-feasance/misfeasance dichotomy becomes irrelevant. He is in breach of a duty and, if his breach caused the plaintiff's damage, liability must ensue. If, however, he is under no duty to do the thing he failed to do, there can be no liability. Again, the nonfeasance/misfeasance dichotomy is irrelevant.

Lambert J.A., speaking for the Court of Appeal, found that the building inspector was under a public law duty to prevent the continuation of the construction of the building on structurally unsound foundations once he became aware that the foundations were structurally unsound. He was also under a public law duty to prevent the occupancy of the building by the Hughes or the plaintiff. He failed to discharge either of those public law duties. Lambert J.A. then went on to discuss the nature of the private law duty he was under. He said:

> I turn now to the private law duty. The conduct of the building inspector in response to the public law duties involved decisions on alternative courses of conduct which were, in my opinion, operational in character. The building was a danger to the occupant of the house and to adjoining property owners. It may have been a danger to anyone in the house. Policy decisions could have confronted the city as to whether to prosecute or to seek an injunction. There may have been other policy choices. But a decision not to act at all, or a failure to decide to act, cannot be supported by any reasonable policy choice. That decision

or failure was not "within the limits of a discretion bona fide exercised", using again the words of Lord Wilberforce. It was certainly open to the trial Judge to reach that conclusion. Indeed, having regard to the evidence of Mr. Backmeyer, it was open to the trial Judge to conclude that the decision not to act or the failure to decide to act, was influenced by the pressure exerted by Mr. Hughes, Sr. in his capacity as alderman.

> I would follow the reasons of Lord Wilberforce in *Anns* in concluding that a private law duty was owed to Mr. Nielsen as the owner and occupier of the house at the time when the defective foundations first became apparent by causing actual subsidence and damage. [My emphasis.]

It seems to me that Lambert J.A. was correct in concluding that the courses of conduct open to the building inspector called for "operational" decisions. The essential question was what steps to take to enforce the provisions of the by-law in the circumstances that had arisen. He had a duty to enforce its provisions. He did not have a discretion whether to enforce them or not. He did, however, have a discretion as to how to go about it. This may, therefore, be the kind of situation envisaged by Lord Wilberforce when, after discussing the distinction between policy decisions and operational decisions, he added the rider [[1978] A.C. 728 at p. 754):

> Although this distinction between the policy area and the operational area is convenient, and illuminating, it is probably a distinction of degree; many "operational" powers or duties have in them some element of "discretion." It can safely be said that the more "operational" a power or duty may be, the easier it is to superimpose upon it a common law duty of care.

It may be, for example, that although the building inspector had a duty to enforce the by-law, the lengths to which he should go in doing so involved policy considerations. The making of inspections, the issuance of stop orders and the withholding of occupancy permits may be one thing; resort to litigation, if this became necessary, may be quite another. Must the city enforce infractions by legal proceedings or does there come a point at which economic considerations, for example, enter in? And if so, how do you measure the "operational" against the "policy" content of the decision in order to decide whether it is more "operational" than "policy" or vice versa? Clearly this is a matter of very fine distinctions.

Mr. Justice Lambert resolves this problem, as I apprehend the passage already quoted from his reasons, by concluding that the city could have made a policy decision either to prosecute or to seek an injunction. If it had taken either of those steps, it could not be faulted. Moreover, if it had considered taking either of those steps and decided against them, it could likewise not be faulted. But not to consider taking them at all was not open to it. In other words, as I read his reasons, his view was that the city, at the very least, had to give serious consideration to taking the steps towards enforcement that were open to it. If it decided against taking them, say on economic grounds, then that would be a legitimate policy decision within the operational context and the courts should not interfere with it. It would be a decision made, as Lord Wilberforce put it, within the limits of a discretion *bona fide* exercised.

There is no evidence to support the proposition that the city gave serious consideration to legal proceedings and decided against them on policy grounds. Rather the evidence gives rise to a strong inference that the city, with full knowledge that the work was progressing in violation of the by-law and that the house was being occupied without a permit, dropped the matter because one of its aldermen was involved. Having regard to the fact that we are here concerned with a statutory duty and that the plaintiff was clearly a person who should have been in the contemplation of the city as someone who might be injured by any breach of that duty, I think this is an appropriate case for the application of the principle in *Anns*. I do not think the appellant can take any comfort from the distinction between non-feasance and misfeasance where there is a duty to act or, at the very least, to make a conscious decision not to act on policy grounds. In my view, inaction for no reason or inaction for an improper reason cannot be a policy decision taken in the *bona fide* exercise of discretion. Where the question whether the requisite action should be taken has not even been considered by the public authority, or at least has not been considered in good faith, it seems clear that for that very reason the authority has not acted with reasonable care. I conclude, therefore, that the conditions for liability of the city to the plaintiff have been met.

It is of interest to note in this connection that other courses were open to the city. It could have posted warning notices on the building and it could have condemned it. In fact, it did neither even although it knew that work was continuing despite the stop work order and that the house was being occupied without any occupancy permit. Indeed, it issued a plumbing permit in August, 1974, before the Hughes moved in.

(c) *Just v. British Columbia*†

[CORY J.:]

This appeal puts in issue the approach that should be taken by courts when considering the liability of government agencies in tort actions.

FACTUAL BACKGROUND

On the morning of January 16, 1982 the appellant and his daughter set out, undoubtedly with high hopes and great expectations for a day of skiing at Whistler Mountain. As a result of a heavy snow fall they were forced to stop in the northbound line of traffic on Highway 99. While they were waiting for the traffic to move forward a great boulder weighing more than a ton somehow worked loose from the wooded slopes above the highway and came crashing down upon the appellant's car. The impact killed the appellant's daughter and caused him very serious injuries. He then brought this action against the respondent contend-

---

† [1989] 2 S.C.R. 1228.

ing that it had negligently failed to maintain the highway properly.

Highway 99 is a major commuter road between Vancouver and the major ski resorts located at Whistler Mountain. The appellant alleged that there had been earlier rock falls near the scene of the tragedy. As well it was said that the climatic conditions of freezing and thawing, coupled with a heavy build up of snow in the trees and resulting tree damage created a great risk of rock falls. Trees were said to be a well-known factor in levering rocks loose. It was contended that inadequate attention had been given to all these factors by the respondent and that a reasonable inspection would have demonstrated that the rock constituted a danger to users of the highway.

At the time of the accident the Department of Highways had set up a system for inspection and remedial work upon rock slopes particularly along Highway 99. At the apex of the organization was a Mr. Eastman, the regional geotechnical material engineer. He is a specialist in rock slope maintenance and together with another engineer was responsible for inspecting rock slopes and making recommendations regarding their stability.

The Department contained a rock work section which included Mr. Oliver, the rock work engineer responsible for rock stabilization and inspections on Highway 99. The section also included a rock scaling crew which was formed in 1971 to perform remedial work on the slopes. This crew serviced the entire province. The crew's function was to remove potentially dangerous rocks by prying them loose using a crowbar. As well, they removed trees that were considered a hazard to the safety of those using the highways. Mr. Oliver was required to inspect rock cut areas to assess the stability of the slope and to determine whether there was a risk that a rock might fall on the highway. His inspection duties extended to the entire slope from which such a danger might arise.

When the rock work engineer inspected the rock slopes on Highway 99 he would report his findings and recommendations to the district highways manager responsible for the area. The district manager in turn through the regional geotechnical material engineer submitted requests for the services of the rock scaling crew. The rock scaling crew itself had no discretion as to where and when it worked; its schedule was determined by the requests for remedial work made to the rock work section.

Prior to the accident the practice had been for the Department of Highways to make visual inspections of the rock cuts on Highway 99. These were carried out from the highway unless there was evidence or history of instability in an area in which case the rock engineer would climb the slope. In addition there were numerous informal inspections carried out by highway personnel as they drove along the road when they would look for signs of change in the rock cut and for rocks in the ditch.

.   .   .   .

TEST TO BE APPLIED

In cases such as this where allegations of negligence are brought against a government agency, it is appropriate for courts to consider and apply the test laid down by Lord Wilberforce in *Anns v. Merton London Borough Council*, he set out his position in these words:

> Through the trilogy of cases in this House — *Donoghue v. Stevenson, Hedley Byrne & Co. Ltd. v. Heller & Partners Ltd.*, and *Dorset Yacht Co. Ltd. v. Home Office*, the position has now been reached that in order to establish that a duty of care arises in a particular situation, it is not necessary to bring the facts of that situation within those of previous situations in which a duty of care has been held to exist. Rather the question has to be approached in two stages. First one has to ask whether, as between the alleged wrongdoer and the person who has suffered damage there is a sufficient relationship of proximity or neighbourhood such that, in the reasonable contemplation of the former, carelessness on his part may be likely to cause damage to the latter — in which case a prima facie duty of care arises. Secondly, if the first question is answered affirmatively, it is necessary to consider whether there are any considerations which ought to negative, or to reduce or limit the scope of the duty or the class of person to whom it is owed or the damages to which a breach of it may give rise: see *Dorset Yacht* case. [Emphasis added.]

That test received the approval of the majority of this Court in *City of Kamloops v. Nielsen*. As well it was specifically referred to by both Beetz and L'Heureux-Dubé JJ. in *Laurentide Motels Ltd. v. Beauport (City)*. It may be that the two-step approach as suggested by Lord Wilberforce should not always be slavishly followed, see *Yuen Kun Yeu v. Attorney-General of Hong Kong*. Nevertheless it is a sound approach to first determine if there is a duty of care owed by a defendant to the plaintiff in any case where negligent misconduct has been alleged against a government agency.

In the case at bar the accident occurred on a well used major highway in the Province of British Columbia. All the provinces across Canada extol their attributes and attractions in the fierce competition for tourist business. The skiing facilities at Whistler are undoubtedly just such a magnificent attraction. It would be hard to imagine a more open and welcoming invitation to use those facilities than that extended by the provincial highway leading to them. In light of that invitation to use both the facilities and the highway leading to them, it would appear that apart from some specific exemption, arising from a statutory provision or established common law principle, a duty of care was owed by the province to those that use its highways. That duty of care would extend ordinarily to reasonable maintenance of those roads. The appellant as a user of the highway was certainly in sufficient proximity to the respondent to come within the purview of that duty of care. In this case it can be said that it would be eminently reasonable for the appellant as a user of the highway to expect that it would be reasonably maintained. For the Department of Highways it would be a readily foreseeable risk that harm might befall users of a highway if it were not reasonably maintained. That maintenance could, on the basis of the evidence put forward by the appellant, be found to extend to the prevention of injury from falling rock.

Even with the duty of care established, it is necessary to explore two aspects in order to determine whether liability may be imposed upon the respondent. First, the applicable legislation must be reviewed to see if it imposes any obligation upon the respondent to maintain its highways or alternatively if it provides an exemption from liability for failure to so maintain them. Secondly, it must be determined whether the province is exempted from liability on the grounds that the system of inspections, including their quantity and quality, constituted a "policy" decision of a government agency and was thus exempt from liability.

THE APPLICABLE LEGISLATION

The *Highway Act*, R.S.B.C. 1979, c. 167, ss. 8, provides for construction and maintenance of highways in these words:

> **8.** The minister may ... maintain a highway across any land taken under the powers conferred by this Act....

and the *Ministry of Transportation and Highways Act*, R.S.B.C. 1979, c. 280, s. 14, as follows:

> **14.** The minister has the management, charge and direction of all matters relating to the acquisition, construction, repair, maintenance, alteration, improvement and operation of ... highways....

The liability of the respondent in respect of the exercise of these powers is limited by ss. 2 and 3 of the *Crown Proceeding Act*, R.S.B.C. 1979, c. 86, in this manner:

> **2.** Subject to this Act,
>
> ...
>
> (c) the Crown is subject to all those liabilities to which it would be liable if it were a person, ...
>
> **3.**
>
> ...
>
> (2) Nothing in section 2
>
> ...
>
> (f) subjects the Crown, in its capacity as a highway authority, to any greater liability than that to which a municipal corporation is subject in that capacity.

On their face these statutory provisions do not appear to absolve the respondent from its duty of care to maintain the highways reasonably. Rather, by inference they appear to place an obligation on the province to maintain its highways at least to the same extent that a municipality is obligated to repair its roads.

WAS THE DECISION OF THE ROCK SECTION AS TO THE QUANTITY AND QUALITY OF INSPECTIONS A "POLICY" DECISION EXEMPTING THE RESPONDENT FROM LIABILITY?

The respondent placed great reliance on the decision of this Court in *Barratt v. District of North Vancouver*, [1980] 2 S.C.R. 418. In the *Barratt* case injury occurred as a result of a pothole on the road. It was established that the City of North Vancouver had a policy of inspecting its roads for potholes every two weeks. Indeed it had inspected the road where the accident occurred one week earlier and found no pothole. It was found that the inspection policy established by the municipality was a reasonable and proper one. However, Mr. Justice Martland in giving the reasons for this Court went on to express an opinion that the municipality could not be held negligent for formulating one inspection policy rather than another. He put it this way at pp. 427–28:

> In essence, he [the trial judge] is finding that the Municipality should have instituted a system of continuous inspection to ensure that no possible damage could occur and holds that, in the absence of such a system, if damage occurs, the Municipality must be held liable.
>
> In my opinion, no such duty existed. The Municipality, a public authority, exercised its power to maintain Marine Drive. It was under no statutory duty to do so. Its method of exercising its power was a matter of policy to be determined by the Municipality itself. If, in the implementation of its policy its servants acted negligently, causing damage, liability could arise, but the Municipality cannot be held to be negligent because it formulated one policy of operation rather than another.

This statement was not necessary to the decision as it had already been determined that the system of inspection established by the municipality was eminently reasonable. Neither was there any serious question raised that there had been any negligence in carrying out the system of inspection. The finding that a reasonable system of inspection had been established and carried out without negligence constituted the basis for the conclusion reached by the Court in that case. With the greatest respect, I am of the view that the portion of the reasons relied on by the respondent went farther than was necessary to the decision or appropriate as a statement of principle. For example, the Court would not have approved as "policy" a system that called for the inspection of the roads in a large urban municipality once every five years. Once a policy to inspect is established then it must be open to a litigant to attack the system as not having been adopted in a *bona fide* exercise of discretion and to demonstrate that in all the circumstances, including budgetary restraints, it is appropriate for a court to make a finding on the issue.

The functions of government and government agencies have multiplied enormously in this century. Often government agencies were and continue to be the best suited entities and indeed the only organizations which could protect the public in the diverse and difficult situations arising in so many fields. They may encompass such matters as the manufacture and distribution of food and drug products, energy production, environmental protection, transportation and tourism, fire prevention and building developments. The increasing complexities of life involve agencies of government in almost every aspect of daily living. Over the passage of time the increased government activities gave rise to incidents that would have led to tortious liability if they had occurred between private citizens. The early governmental immunity from tortious liability became intolerable. This led to the enactment of legislation which in general imposed liability on the Crown for its acts as though it were a person. However, the Crown is not a person and must be free to govern and make true policy decisions without becoming subject to tort liability as a result of those decisions. On the other hand, complete Crown immunity should not be restored by having every government decision designated as one of policy. Thus the dilemma giving rise to the continuing judicial struggle to differentiate between policy and operation. Particularly difficult decisions will arise in situations where governmental inspections may be expected.

· · · ·

Mason J., speaking for himself and one other member of the Australian High Court in *Sutherland Shire Council v. Heyman*, set out what I find to be most helpful guidelines. He wrote:

> *Anns* decided that a duty of care cannot arise in relation to acts and omissions which reflect the policymaking and discretionary elements involved in the exercise of statutory discretions. It has been said that it is for the authority to strike that balance between the claims of efficiency and thrift to which du Parcq LJ referred in *Kent v. East Suffolk Rivers Catchment Board*, and that it is not for the court to substitute its decision for the authority's decision on those matters when they were committed by the legislature to the authority for decision (*Dorset Yacht Co. v. Home Office; Anns*, at p. 754; *Barratt v. District of North Vancouver*. Although these injunctions have compelling force in their application to policymaking decisions, their cogency is less obvious when applied to other discretionary matters. The standard of negligence applied by the courts in determining whether a duty of care has been breached cannot be applied to a policy decision, but it can be applied to operational decisions. Accordingly, it is possible that a duty of care may

exist in relation to discretionary considerations which stand outside the policy category in the division between policy factors on the one hand and operational factors on the other. This classification has evolved in the judicial interpretation of the "discretionary function" exception in the United States Federal Tort Claims Act — see *Dalehite v. United States*; ... *United States v. Varig Airlines, supra*. The object of the *Federal Tort Claims Act* in displacing government immunity and subjecting the United States Government to liability in tort in the same manner and to the same extent as a private individual under like circumstances, subject to the "discretionary function" exception, is similar to that of s. 64 of the *Judiciary Act*, 1903 (Cth).

The distinction between policy and operational factors is not easy to formulate, but the dividing line between them will be observed if we recognize that a public authority is under no duty of care in relation to decisions which involve or are dictated by financial, economic, social or political factors or constraints. Thus budgetary allocations and the constraints which they entail in terms of allocation of resources cannot be made the subject of a duty of care. But it may be otherwise when the courts are called upon to apply a standard of care to action or inaction that is merely the product of administrative direction, expert or professional opinion, technical standards or general standards of reasonableness. [Emphasis added.]

The duty of care should apply to a public authority unless there is a valid basis for its exclusion. A true policy decision undertaken by a government agency constitutes such a valid basis for exclusion. What constitutes a policy decision may vary infinitely and may be made at different levels although usually at a high level.

The decisions in *Anns v. Merton London Borough Council* and *City of Kamloops v. Nielsen* indicate that a government agency in reaching a decision pertaining to inspection must act in a reasonable manner which constitutes a *bona fide* exercise of discretion. To do so they must specifically consider whether to inspect and if so, the system of inspection must be a reasonable one in all the circumstances.

For example, at a high level there may be a policy decision made concerning the inspection of lighthouses. If the policy decision is made that there is such a pressing need to maintain air safety by the construction of additional airport facilities with the result that no funds can be made available for lighthouse inspection, then this would constitute

a *bona fide* exercise of discretion that would be unassailable. Should then a lighthouse beacon be extinguished as a result of the lack of inspection and a shipwreck ensue no liability can be placed upon the government agency. The result would be the same if a policy decision were made to increase the funds for job retraining and reduce the funds for lighthouse inspection so that a beacon could only be inspected every second year and as a result the light was extinguished. Once again this would constitute the *bona fide* exercise of discretion. Thus a decision either not to inspect at all or to reduce the number of inspections may be an unassailable policy decision. This is so provided it constitutes a reasonable exercise of *bona fide* discretion based, for example, upon the availability of funds.

On the other hand, if a decision is made to inspect lighthouse facilities the system of inspections must be reasonable and they must be made properly. See *Indian Towing Co.*. Thus once the policy decision to inspect has been made, the Court may review the scheme of inspection to ensure it is reasonable and has been reasonably carried out in light of all the circumstances, including the availability of funds, to determine whether the government agency has met the requisite standard of care.

At a lower level, government aircraft inspectors checking on the quality of manufactured aircraft parts at a factory may make a policy decision to make a spot check of manufactured items throughout the day as opposed to checking every item manufactured in the course of one hour of the day. Such a choice as to how the inspection was to be undertaken could well be necessitated by the lack of both trained personnel and funds to provide such inspection personnel. In those circumstances the policy decision that a spot check inspection would be made could not be attacked. (See *United States v. S.A. Empresa De Viacao Aerea Rio Grandense (Varig Airlines)*.)

Thus a true policy decision may be made at a lower level provided that the government agency establishes that it was a reasonable decision in light of the surrounding circumstances.

The consideration of the duty of care that may be owed must be kept separate and distinct from the consideration of the standard of care that should be maintained by the government agency involved.

Let us assume a case where a duty of care is clearly owed by a governmental agency to an individual that is not exempted either by a statutory provision or because it was a true policy decision. In those circumstances the duty of care owed by the government agency would be the same as that owed by one person to another. Nevertheless the standard of care imposed upon the Crown may not be the same as that owed by an individual. An individual is expected to maintain his or her sidewalk or driveway reasonably, while a government agency such as the respondent may be responsible for the maintenance of hundreds of miles of highway. The frequency and the nature of inspection required of the individual may well be different from that required of the Crown. In each case the frequency and method must be reasonable in light of all the surrounding circumstances. The governmental agency should be entitled to demonstrate that balanced against the nature and quantity of the risk involved, its system of inspection was reasonable in light of all the circumstances including budgetary limits, the personnel and equipment available to it and that it had met the standard duty of care imposed upon it.

It may be convenient at this stage to summarize what I consider to be the principles applicable and the manner of proceeding in cases of this kind. As a general rule, the traditional tort law duty of care will apply to a government agency in the same way that it will apply to an individual. In determining whether a duty of care exists the first question to be resolved is whether the parties are in a relationship of sufficient proximity to warrant the imposition of such a duty. In the case of a government agency, exemption from this imposition of duty may occur as a result of an explicit statutory exemption. Alternatively, the exemption may arise as a result of the nature of the decision made by the government agency. That is, a government agency will be exempt from the imposition of a duty of care in situations which arise from its pure policy decisions.

In determining what constitutes such a policy decision, it should be borne in mind that such decisions are generally made by persons of a high level of authority in the agency, but may also properly be made by persons of a lower level of authority. The characterization of such a decision rests on the nature of the decision and not on the identity of the actors. As a general rule, decisions concerning budgetary allotments for departments or government agencies will be classified as policy decisions. Further, it must be recalled that a policy decision is open to challenge on the basis that it is not made in the *bona fide* exercise of discretion. If after due consideration it is found that a duty of

care is owed by the government agency and no exemption by way of statute or policy decision-making is found to exist, a traditional torts analysis ensues and the issue of standard of care required of the government agency must next be considered.

The manner and quality of an inspection system is clearly part of the operational aspect of a governmental activity and falls to be assessed in the consideration of the standard of care issue. At this stage, the requisite standard of care to be applied to the particular operation must be assessed in light of all the surrounding circumstances including, for example, budgetary restraints and the availability of qualified personnel and equipment.

Turning to the case at bar it is now appropriate to apply the principles set forth by Mason J. in *Sutherland Shire Council v. Heyman, supra*, to determine whether the decision or decisions of the government agency were policy decisions exempting the province from liability. Here what was challenged was the manner in which the inspections were carried out, their frequency or infrequency and how and when trees above the rock cut should have been inspected, and the manner in which the cutting and scaling operations should have been carried out. In short, the public authority had settled on a plan which called upon it to inspect all slopes visually and then conduct further inspections of those slopes where the taking of additional safety measures was warranted. Those matters are all part and parcel of what Mason J. described as "the product of administrative direction, expert or professional opinion, technical standards or general standards of care". They were not decisions that could be designated as policy decisions. Rather they were manifestations of the implementation of the policy decision to inspect and were operational in nature. As such, they were subject to review by the Court to determine whether the respondent had been negligent or had satisfied the appropriate standard of care.

At trial the conclusion was reached that the number and frequency of inspections, of scaling and other remedial measures were matters of policy; as a result no findings of fact were made on the issues bearing on the standard of care. Since the matter was one of operation the respondent was not immune from suit and the negligence issue had to be canvassed in its entirety. The appellant was therefore entitled to a finding of fact on these questions and a new trial should be directed to accomplish this.

It may well be that the respondent at the new trial will satisfy the Court that it has met the requisite standard of care. It is apparent that although the *Crown Proceeding Act* imposes the liability of a person upon the Crown, it is not in the same position as an individual. To repeat, the respondent is responsible not for the maintenance of a single private road or driveway but for the maintenance of many hundreds of miles of highway running through difficult mountainous terrain, all of it to be undertaken within budgetary restraints. As noted earlier, decisions reached as to budgetary allotment for departments or government agencies will in the usual course of events be policy decisions that cannot be the basis for imposing liability in tort even though these political policy decisions will have an effect upon the frequency of inspections and the manner in which they may be carried out. All of these factors should be taken into account in determining whether the system was adopted in bona fide exercise of discretion and whether within that system the frequency, quality and manner of inspection were reasonable.

To proceed in this way is fair to both the government agency and the litigant. Once a duty of care that is not exempted has been established the trial will determine whether the government agency has met the requisite standard of care. At that stage the system and manner of inspection may be reviewed. However, the review will be undertaken bearing in mind the budgetary restraints imposed and the availability of personnel and equipment to carry out such an inspection.

DISPOSITION

In the result, a new trial must be held to determine whether the respondent had in all the circumstances met the standard of care that should reasonably be imposed upon it with regard to the frequency and manner of inspection of the rock cut and to the cutting and sealing operations carried out upon it.

. . . . .

[SOPINKA J. (dissenting):]

This appeal raises the issue of the liability for negligence of a public body in the absence of the breach of a statutory duty of care. The facts are set out in the reasons of Justice Cory, which I have had the advantage of reading. Regrettably, I find that I cannot agree with his conclusion. In my opinion, the conclusion of the trial judge and a unanimous Court of Appeal was the correct one. This conclusion is expressed by Hinkson J.A., speaking for the court, affirming the following passage from the reasons of McLachlin J. (as she then was):

> ... I conclude that the decisions here complained of fall within the area of policy and cannot be reviewed by this court. The number and quality of inspections as well as the frequency of scaling and other remedial measures were matters of planning and policy involving the utilization of scarce resources and the balancing of needs and priorities throughout the province. Decisions of that nature are for the governmental authorities, not the courts.

In comparatively recent years the law of torts has evolved by imposing on public authorities a common law duty of care based on the neighbourhood or proximity principle, frequently called the *Anns* principle. This has resulted in substantially increasing their liability in negligence for activity which they are authorized to carry on by statute but in respect of which the statute imposes no duty of care. This change in the law was not brought about by legislation but through the evolution of the common law which has traditionally taken account of the changing views and needs of society. The expansion of liability by reason of this and other developments in the law of torts has created a crisis in this area of the law leading to demands for the fundamental reappraisal of the tort system itself. The basic premise of adjusting losses on the basis of fault is being subjected to intense criticism. In the United States there is a growing consensus that the tort system is responsible for the crisis in liability insurance. There is now substantial support for wholesale legislative reform of the tort system. These developments are discussed in the *Final Report of the Ontario Task Force on Insurance to the Ministry of Financial Institutions*. Reference is made to the study made by Professor Michael J. Trebilcock and entitled "The [Insurance-Deterrence] Dilemma of Modern Tort Law: Trends in North American Tort Law and Their Implications for the Current Liability Crisis". At pp. 53–54 of the *Report of the Task Force*, it is stated that:

> A crucial finding in the Trebilcock study was that the current "explosion" in American tort law was not the result of judicial extensions of already-advanced American strict liability doctrines but rather the judicial extension of traditional negligence liability and its application

to an ever-widening range of activities and injuries.

The Report goes on to state at p. 54:

There is every indication that similar tendencies exist in Canadian negligence law and that similar developments will occur in the future in Canada as well. The reason for this inevitable expansion of liability, even within the bounds of traditional negligence doctrine, is a matter that is intractably and unavoidably rooted in what we will later describe as the "insurance-deterrence dilemma" in modern tort law.

The insurance-deterrence dilemma is described in a study paper prepared by Philip Osborne for the Task Force and cited at pp. 61–62 as follows:

The massive transformation of the fault system ... is a change which is explicable only on the basis of liability insurance and judicial compassion for the victims of social progress. Judges who in their written judgments give no indication of the prevalence of liability insurance are in fact keenly aware that in almost all cases the defendant is not paying, and that they are in the last analysis deciding whether or not the plaintiff should be compensated from insurance monies.... The prevalence of liability insurance fundamentally altered the moralistic nature of the loss-shifting function of fault. The loss-shifting mechanism was converted into a loss-spreading mechanism and it became more realistic to speak of the fault system as a fault-insurance system. The punitive and deterrent aspects of fault were diminished and compensation became the predominant function of tort law.

Other commentators are generally in support of the above criticisms of the tort system....

I draw attention to these developments in order to emphasize that while the law of torts must move with the times, this is not a time to move. Yet, I am of the opinion that the reasons of my colleague would considerably expand the liability for negligence of public authorities by subjecting to judicial review their policy decisions which were hitherto not reviewable.

The starting point for the application of the *Anns* principle is that there is no statutory duty in favour of the plaintiff to do the thing the lack of which is alleged to have caused the injury to the plaintiff. Many public bodies have the power to carry out a function but no duty to do so. In these circumstances, they have a discretion whether to do

the thing or not. Conduct within the limits of that discretion gives rise to no duty of care. Conduct outside of these limits may attract a private law duty of care. ...

· · · ·

If a statutory duty to the plaintiff is breached, the private duty based on the neighbourhood principle is unnecessary. In *London Passenger Transport Board v. Upson*, Lord Wright stated:

The statutory right has its origin in the statute, but the particular remedy of an action for damages is given by the common law in order to make effective, for the benefit of the injured plaintiff, his right to the performance by the defendant of the defendant's statutory duty.

· · · ·

My colleague's reasons are based essentially on an attack on the policy of the respondent with respect to the extent and manner of the inspection program. In my opinion, absent evidence that a policy was adopted for some ulterior motive and not for a municipal purpose, it is not open to a litigant to attack it, nor is it appropriate for a court to pass upon it. As stated by Lord du Parcq in *Kent v. East Suffolk Rivers Catchment Board*:

... it must be remembered that when Parliament has left it to a public authority to decide which of its powers it shall exercise, and when and to what extent it shall exercise them, there would be some inconvenience in submitting to the subsequent decision of a jury, or judge of fact, the question whether the authority had acted reasonably, a question involving the consideration of matters of policy and sometimes the striking of a just balance between the rival claims of efficiency and thrift.

· · · ·

In the following passage, Lord Wilberforce makes it clear that a decision to inspect, and the time, manner and techniques of inspection, may all be within the discretionary power:

There may be a discretionary element in its exercise — discretionary as to the time and manner of inspection, and the techniques to be used. A plaintiff complaining of negligence must prove, the burden being on him, that action taken was not within the limits of a discretion bona fide exercised, before he can begin to rely upon a common law duty of care. But if he can do this, he should, in principle, be able to sue.

If, as here, the statute creates no duty to inspect at all, but simply confers a power to do so, it follows logically that a decision to inspect and the extent and manner thereof are all discretionary powers of the authority.

It is not suggested here that the respondent failed to consider whether to inspect or the manner of inspections. The trial judge and the Court of Appeal found that a policy decision was made that inspections would be carried out by a crew of men called the Rockwork Section. In view of the fact that the crew had responsibility for the inspection of the slopes of all highways, the extent and manner of the inspection was delegated to the Rockwork Section. While it might be suggested that guidelines for inspection should have been laid down for the guidance of the crew, this would be second guessing the policy decision and not a matter for the Court. The appellant's attack on the conduct of the respondent and its employees is an attack on the manner in which they carried out the inspection and scaling of the mountain. The Rockwork Section had decided it could not closely monitor all slopes at all times. Some slopes would only be visually inspected from the highway. The appellant contended that the slopes above man-made cuts should have been closely inspected and that the trees should have been removed within ten feet of a cut slope. The trial judge made the following important findings concerning the decision of the respondent as to the extent and manner of the inspection program:

> The question in the case at bar is thus whether the failure of the Crown to take the steps which the plaintiff says it should have taken to prevent the rock fall was a matter of policy or operational. In order to answer it, it is necessary to consider the nature of the decisions here in question. The Crown had never established as a matter of policy that all slopes above highways must be inspected for potential

rock fall. Nor had it laid out specific guidelines for dealing with problems if danger was perceived. What it had done was to establish a small crew of men (the rock scaling crew) to deal with problems arising on cliff faces throughout the Province. This crew responded to specific requests from various highway districts for inspection and scaling. For the most part, however, it developed and followed its own program. Given that it was responsible for inspection of slopes and appropriate remedial measures for all the highways in the Province, it could not closely monitor all slopes at all times. The slope here in question was visually inspected from the highway on a number of occasions. However, there had never been scaling or close inspection of the area above the cut because the rock scaling crew did not deem that work to be a priority.

. . . .

In this case, the extent of the inspection program was delegated to the Rockwork Section. The respondent acted within its statutory discretion in making that decision. It was a decision that inspections should be done and the manner in which they should be done. In order for a private duty to arise, it would have to be shown that the Rockwork Section acted outside its delegated discretion to determine whether to inspect and the manner in which the inspection is to be made.

. . . .

In order for a private duty to arise in this case, the plaintiff would have to establish that the Rockwork Section, having exercised its discretion as to the manner or frequency of inspection, carried out the inspection without reasonable care or at all. There is no evidence or indeed allegation in this regard. In this respect, the decision in *Barratt v. District of North Vancouver, supra*, is on all fours and ought to be applied here. I would therefore dismiss the appeal.

(d) *Jane Doe v. Metropolitan Toronto (Municipality) Commissioners of Police*[†]

[MacFARLAND J.:]

Jane Doe was raped and otherwise sexually assaulted at knife point in her own bed in the early morning hours of August 24, 1986, by a stranger subsequently identified as Paul Douglas Callow. Ms. Doe then lived in a second floor apartment at ... in the City of Toronto; her apartment had a balcony which was used by the rapist to gain access to her premises. At the time, Ms. Doe was the fifth known victim of Callow who would become known as "the balcony rapist".

Ms. Doe brings a suit against the Metropolitan Toronto Police Force (hereafter referred to as MTPF) on two bases; firstly she suggests that the MTPF conducted a negligent investigation in relation to the balcony rapist and failed to warn women whom they knew to be potential targets of Callow of the fact that they were at risk. She says, as the result of such conduct, Callow was not apprehended as early as he might otherwise have been and she was denied the opportunity, had she known the risk she faced, to take any specific measures to protect herself from attack. Secondly, she said that the MTPF being a public body having the statutory duty to protect the public from criminal activity, must exercise that duty in accordance with the *Canadian Charter of Rights and Freedoms* and may not act in a way that is discriminatory because of gender. She says the police must act constitutionally, they did not do so in this case and as the result, her rights under sections 15 and 7 of the *Charter*[] have been breached. She seeks damages against the MTPF under both heads of her claim.

The trial of this action took place over approximately eight weeks; some thirty witnesses were called and voluminous documentary evidence filed. Counsel have filed lengthy written argument and had two days in which to give an oral outline of their written submissions.

OVERVIEW

. . . .

The Specific Investigation

I am told that much of the MTPF documentation in relation to the investigation of the balcony rapist has been destroyed. All that remains are the occurrence reports and the officers' memo books for the most part. Additional documentation which was kept by officers working on the case while the investigation was active [has] been destroyed. While most of the officers were still in possession of their individual memo books, Staff Sgt. Duggan, who investigated the K.B. rape, was not; his memo books for this period were destroyed. So that it is perfectly clear, I should say there is no evidence that there was any deliberate destruction of records on the part of the MTPF. I point this out simply to record that by reason thereof the police were somewhat hampered in giving their evidence.

It is necessary in order to fully understand the investigation of the Jane Doe assault to also have reference to the investigations into the four other related assaults beginning with that of P.A. on December 31, 1985; B.K. on January 10, 1986; R.P. on June 25, 1986, and F.D. on July 25, 1986. Each of these women were victims of Paul Douglas Callow.

All of the attacks were within the geographical confines of what was known as 52 Division with the exception of the first attack which occurred within 51 Division of the MTPF. All were within very close proximity to the intersection of Church and Wellesley Streets in Toronto in an area known as the Church/Wellesley area.

---

† (1998), 160 D.L.R. (4th) 697 (Ontario Court (Gen. Div.)) at 701, 713–14, 721–40, 744–48.

. . . .

Jane Doe

Jane Doe lived at apartment ... Street East when she was attacked in the early hours of August 24, 1986, by Paul Douglas Callow. As he had with other victims, Callow covered Ms. Doe's eyes with a pillow case, threatened her with the knife he had in his possession and spoke conversationally with her during the attack. He raped her and otherwise sexually assaulted her before leaving her apartment via the front door. Entrance to Ms. Doe's apartment had been gained by means of a balcony window which she had left slightly ajar for ventilation. For the duration of the attack Callow disguised his own appearance by covering his face. Ms. Doe was interviewed at length by a number of police officers immediately following the occurrence at her apartment and at Women's College Hospital where she was taken for examination and completion of the customary rape kit.

. . . .

I accept that Sgt. Cameron told Ms. Doe that he believed she had been raped by a serial rapist and that four other women had been similarly attacked. While he may not have used the word "cyclical" I find it reasonable that he indicated there was a pattern of sorts to the attacks and accept that he likely indicated in Ms. Doe's case that the rapist had struck a day early. The R.P. and F.D. attacks (the 3rd and 4th), had taken place on the 25th day of the month and Ms. Doe was attacked on the 24th day of the month. That the officers in charge of this investigation believed that the suspect was likely to attack around the 25th of the month is borne out by the arrangements later made for a [stakeout] of the area to be carried out five days before and after September 25th, 1986. I accept that Ms. Doe was told all victims lived on 2nd and 3rd floors and entry had been via balconies.

Ms. Doe expressed shock that women in the neighbourhood had not been warned that a serial rapist was in their midst. Sgt. Cameron indicated, I find, that it was not the practice to issue warnings in such cases because women would become hysterical or panic (I do not see any real difference which word he used, the meaning is the same), the rapist would flee and the investigation would be compromised. Of course it was not true that it was not the policy of the MTPF to issue warnings

in such cases because it had been done in the Dawson Davidson case — just months earlier and in the very same division.

When Ms. Doe indicated that if the police were not prepared to warn area women she would, she was told that if she did, she may be considered to be interfering in a police investigation and she could be charged for doing so.

. . . .

By memorandum dated August 27, 1986, Sgts. Cameron and Derry for the first time requested the assistance of other officers and this, for the purpose of conducting a canvass of local apartment buildings. They requested that all apartments on the first, second and third floors of each building be checked. The additional officers were to be instructed to tell tenants only that there had been a number of break and enters in the area and specifically instructed NOT to mention the sexual assaults. They were to note any single females living in the apartments canvassed.

Later in a memorandum dated September 7, 1986, Sgt. Derry indicated to Staff Sgt. Bukowski as follows:

> It is important that the officers check each apartment in order to establish the hair colour of the women and receive information from the people interviewed regarding prowlers etc.

On that same day Sgt. Cameron by memorandum detailed to Inspector Cowling, the officer in charge of 52 C.I.B. office, his request for manpower and equipment necessary for a stakeout to be carried out the five days before and after September 25, 1986. The operation is detailed as follows:

> The operation would run as follows:
> 1) Using the streets as boundaries each group of apartments would be covered by two, three or four men.
> 2) Each group of men would have at least one unmarked car at their disposal in the event there is an attack and they have to move quickly.
> 3) Vans would be used as stationary observation points within the area.
> 4) The uniform cars would stay just outside of their designated area and would be used to seal off the area around the location of any attack and stop all persons on foot or in vehicles. They will be assisted by some of the old clothes men.

5) The remainder of the [old] clothes men would then enter the area of attack and search on foot for any suspect that may be hiding.

6) The radio room would be advised in advance of this operation and would be required to assist in sealing off the area.

7) Sergeants Cameron and Derry would be present and take charge of the scene and direct the operation for those ten days.

8) Attached hereto is a map indicating the area of concern. Further recording will be made to the map upon completion of the canvassing detail.

Respectfully submitted
William Cameron Sgt. 2887
Kim Derry Sgt. 3373

Sgt. Derry in a memorandum to Inspector Cowling dated September 7, 1986, again detailed the request for foot patrol and beat officers to canvass the first three floors of the apartment buildings identified by him and Sgt. Cameron to obtain the apartment numbers with single females and their description. This original request to the Staff Sgt. had apparently been cancelled. He noted:

If any chance at identifying possible targets through this method is not carried out, then the possibility of narrowing the surveillance cannot be done.

Once again the Staff Sgts. were advised that the officers conducting the canvass were "not to mention anything about sexual assaults which have occurred in the area but to advise people contacted that this is a crime prevention program and that single women are victims of break and enters and theft". Officers were to obtain the names and addresses of single women and note their hair colour.

The stakeout proceeded as planned. Unmarked vehicles were used and those participating were informed the only time the cover would be broken was in the event they observed someone attempting to climb a balcony in which event the person was to be stopped. The stakeout did not produce any useful information except that for all the covertness of the operation, crime in the area of the stakeout was almost entirely eliminated for its duration. Obviously the criminal element were aware of the police presence.

It has been suggested that the women who occupied these apartments were being used as "bait". The police adamantly denied the suggestion which they say implies that they knew who would,

and when an attack would occur, when in fact they had no idea who would, where, or even if an attack would occur. I can only conclude on the evidence that the police believed it to be a virtual certainty that there would be another attack and that it would be made against one of the women their canvass had identified as a potential target and in view of the fact that the last three victims had been attacked on the 24th or 25th of the month that the attack would likely take place during that general time period in the month — the entire stakeout operation was premised on the assumption of these factors.

The police were there to wait and watch for an attack to occur. The women were given no warning and were thereby precluded from taking any steps to protect themselves against such an attack. Unbeknownst to them they were left completely vulnerable. When all of these circumstances are taken and considered together, it certainly suggests to me that the women were being used — without their knowledge or consent — as "bait" to attract a predator whose specific identity then was unknown to the police, but whose general and characteristic identity most certainly was.

. . . .

Subsequent investigation would reveal that Paul Douglas Callow had, in May 1981, raped an elderly woman who resided in a 5th floor apartment at ... Street East. The circumstances of that rape — for which Callow was arrested by the MTPF [—] were hauntingly similar to the *modus operandi* employed by him in the five rapes with which this action is concerned. Charges were not proceeded with in that case because of the age and health of the victim.

Police at the time felt reasonably confident however that Callow was responsible for that rape and noted that the *modus operandi* was similar to that used by Callow in the Vancouver rape in 1978, for which he was convicted and sentenced to four years imprisonment.

Surprisingly, P.C. Ellis took it upon himself to contact Jackie Callow directly and speak to her about her husband. I say surprisingly because of Sgts. Cameron and Derry's evidence in relation to the "low key" approach they wished to take in this investigation in order that the offender not be tipped off or displaced.

Sgts. Cameron and Derry both indicated they did not want a media blitz alerting the public to this danger because they did not want their suspect to flee as Dawson Davidson had. The discussions, they say, which were ongoing in the 52 C.I.B. office where they worked, were to the effect that Dawson Davidson had left the jurisdiction because of the intense media coverage given to his criminal activity at the time. Additionally, they say the overwhelming and obvious police presence was a contributing factor in his departure. For these reasons Derry and Cameron adopted the "low profile" approach, next to no media coverage of the events, no community programs to specifically warn women in the area of the attacks and any additional police presence to be of a covert nature. This was also the reason that officers conducting the canvass were specifically told not to inform tenants about the sexual assaults. As Cameron and Derry said, they believed their suspect lived in the neighbourhood and they could be knocking on his door during the canvass or the door of his wife or girlfriend; he would then be tipped off that a manhunt was underway and be likely to flee because of it.

When cross-examined as to why police would not have similar concerns mentioning the break and enters [—] *i.e.* that the suspect would flee knowing police were looking for him in relation to those crimes — Sgt. Cameron gave a convoluted, and to my mind, simply an incredible explanation to the effect that any "time" (of incarceration) that a thief would get would be the kind of time this type of criminal could do "standing on his head" to quote Sgt. Cameron. In any event they thought there was no risk mentioning break and enters but was if the sexual assaults were mentioned.

I was given the clear impression from the evidence of Sgts. Derry and Cameron that these matters were topics of ongoing discussion within the 52 C.I.B. office and P.C. Ellis for one would be aware of them. I found it surprising in these circumstances that P.C. Ellis would then, immediately on learning of his identity, contact the suspect's wife.

In any event Callow was soon after put under constant surveillance and arrested October 3, 1986. He ultimately confessed to having committed all five rapes. After the commencement of the preliminary inquiry he pled guilty and was sentenced in total to a period of incarceration of twenty years.

CONCLUSIONS

Competency of the Investigation

It is suggested that the investigation into the balcony rapist was slipshod and incompetent. The plaintiff has criticized the documentary productions of the defendant and suggested they are incomplete. Professor Hodgson testified that every step in an investigation should be recorded on supplementary occurrence reports. In this way, he said, anyone picking up the file could be reasonably informed on the status of the investigation. While that may be the ideal I accept that it is not the reality. Often steps taken and information gathered were recorded on supplementary reports but often they were not. Officers differ in their manner and method of note and record keeping. I accept that there were numerous documents created in relation to this investigation which unfortunately were destroyed before the litigation was commenced.

I am not persuaded on the evidence that Callow would have been identified and apprehended any earlier because of documentary deficiencies.

I am satisfied that the officers ultimately assigned to this investigation had too many other urgent assignments ongoing at the same time which prevented them from devoting the necessary attention which this investigation required. At the critical time much of their energy and attention was directed to other matters — often for days at a time. They had no back up, no one else directly responsible for this investigation when they were otherwise engaged.

While it is true that there was no evidence called in relation to what other demands there may have been on the MTPF for manpower at this time, one must bear in mind that it is the evidence of the police that sexual assault is a very serious crime second only to homicide and then to consider the resources made available in the Annex Rapist investigation in this same division only a month or two before.

While the plaintiff submits that I must infer that Callow would have been apprehended sooner had greater resources been devoted to this investigation earlier on the theory — the sooner a job is started the sooner it is finished — I cannot agree. While one may say in that event Callow might have been apprehended sooner, it is to my mind equally probable that he might not have been.

. . . . .

Decision Not to Warn

As I have said Sgts. Cameron and Derry determined that this investigation would be "low key" compared to the investigation conducted into the "Annex Rapist" and no warning would be given to the women they knew to be at risk for fear of displacing the rapist leaving him free to re-offend elsewhere undetected.

I am not persuaded that their professed reason for not warning women is the real reason no warning was issued.

.   .   .   .

There was, I find, no "policy" not to issue warnings to potential victims in these cases — clearly warnings had been given in the Dawson Davidson Annex Rapist investigation — warnings which incidentally all defence expert witnesses agreed were appropriate in the circumstances.

I find that the real reason a warning was not given in the circumstances of this case was because Sgts. Cameron and Derry believed that women living in the area would become hysterical and panic and their investigation would thereby be jeopardized. In addition, they were not motivated by any sense of urgency because Callow's attacks were not seen as "violent" as Dawson Davidson's by comparison had been.

I am satisfied on the evidence that a meaningful warning could and should have been given to the women who were at particular risk. That warning could have been by way of a canvass of their apartments, by a media blitz, by holding widely publicized public meetings or any one or combination of these methods. Such warning should have alerted the particular women at risk, and advised them of suggested precautions they might take to protect themselves. The defence experts, with the exception of Mr. Piers, agreed that a warning could have been given without compromising the investigation on the facts of the case.

Even the experienced defence expert witnesses Det. Inspector Kevin Rossmo and former FBI special agent McCrary agreed that as Det. Inspector Rossmo said:

> The police have a responsibility to release a balanced volume of information to protect the community ... where that balance is will depend on the particular facts of the case.

In my view it has been conceded in this case clearly and unequivocally [—] by the Chief of Police at the time, Jack Marks — that no warning was given in this case and one ought to have been. His public response to the proposals of the group known as Women against Violence against Women in the aftermath of this investigation presented to the Board of Commissioners of Police could not in my view be any clearer when he said:

> I would concede that for a variety of reasons unique to the Church/Wellesley investigation, no press release in the nature of a general warning was issued and acknowledge that one should have been. This is not only a matter for concern and regret, but action has already been taken to prevent a similar breakdown from occurring in the future. Specifically, the Sexual Assault Co-ordinator who monitors all of these offences has been directed to ensure that members of the public are informed about such matters which may affect their safety. These warnings will be directed toward all potential victims with special attention given to members of the public who have been identified as most at risk, e.g. as in the case at hand, women living in high-rise buildings in the downtown area would be targeted as a high risk group and requiring extra efforts to bring the potential risk to their attention.

I accept and agree entirely with these remarks.

.   .   .   .

There are three other factors which have influenced my decision that a warning ought to have been given:

- the fact that Sgts. Cameron and Derry thought it appropriate to warn Ms. Samoluk and Ms. Martin, that they may be potential targets of the balcony rapist after they reported break-ins to their apartments in their absence.
- the fact that Dawson Davidson had been arrested in July 1986 received considerable publicity. Women living in the general vicinity may have felt some relief knowing that [the] serial rapist had been apprehended and let down their guard somewhat, completely unaware that another serial rapist was on the loose in their neighbourhood.
- the fact that Sgt. Hughes in his memo to his superior, Staff Sgt. Hein — both of 52 Division — dated July 29, 1986, thought that building superintendents should have been contacted and told to advise "trusted tenants", especially single women, to be aware of the occurrences and to

advise police of any person they feel may be suspect.

I am satisfied on Ms. Doe's evidence that if she had been aware a serial rapist was in her neighbourhood raping women whose apartments he accessed via their balconies she would have taken steps to protect herself and that most probably those steps would have prevented her from being raped.

Section 57 of the *Police Act*, R.S.O. 1980, c. 381 (the governing statute at the time these events occurred) provides:

> 57. ... members of police forces ... are charged with the duty of preserving the peace, preventing robberies and other crimes ...

The police are statutorily obligated to prevent crime and at common law they owe a duty to protect life and property. As Schroeder J.A. stated in *Schacht v. The Queen in right of the Province of Ontario*:

> The duties which I would lay upon them stem not only from the relevant statutes to which reference has been made, but from the common law, which recognizes the existence of a broad conventional or customary duty in the established constabulary as an arm of the State to protect the life, limb and property of the subject.

In my view, the police failed utterly in their duty to protect these women and the plaintiff in particular from the serial rapist the police knew to be in their midst by failing to warn so that they may have had the opportunity to take steps to protect themselves.

It is no answer for the police to say women are always at risk and as an urban adult living in downtown Toronto they have an obligation to look out for themselves. Women generally do, every day of their lives, conduct themselves and their lives in such a way as to avoid the general pervasive threat of male violence which exists in our society. Here police were aware of a specific threat or risk to a specific group of women and they did nothing to warn those women of the danger they were in, nor did they take any measures to protect them.

Discrimination

The plaintiff's argument is not simply that she has been discriminated against, because she is a woman, by individual officers in the investigation of

her specific complaint [] but that systemic discrimination existed within the MTPF in 1986, which impacted adversely on all women and, specifically, those who were survivors of sexual assault who came into contact with the MTPF — a class of persons of which the plaintiff was one. She says in effect, the sexist stereotypical views held by the MTPF informed the investigation of this serial rapist and caused that investigation to be conducted incompetently and in such a way that the plaintiff has been denied the equal protection and equal benefit of law guaranteed to her by s. 15(1) of the *Charter*.

. . . .

In my view the conduct of this investigation and the failure to warn in particular[] was motivated and informed by the adherence to rape myths as well as sexist stereotypical reasoning about rape, about women and about women who are raped. The plaintiff therefore has been discriminated against by reason of her gender and as a result the plaintiff's rights to equal protection and equal benefit of the law were compromised.

Security of the Person

I am satisfied that the defendants deprived the plaintiff of her right to security of the person by subjecting her to the very real risk of attack by a serial rapist — a risk of which they were aware but about which they quite deliberately failed to inform the plaintiff or any women living in the Church/Wellesley area at the time save only Gloria Samoluk and Lori Martin and where in the face of that knowledge and their belief that the rapist would certainly attack again, they additionally failed to take any steps to protect the plaintiff or other women like her. Clearly the rape of the plaintiff constituted a deprivation of her security of the person. As Madam Justice Wilson stated in *Singh v. Canada (Minister of Employment and Immigration)*:

> ... "security of the person" must encompass freedom from the threat of physical punishment or suffering as well as freedom from such punishment itself.

As I have indicated because the defendants exercised their discretion in the investigation of this case in a discriminatory and negligent way as I have detailed above, their exercise of discretion was thereby contrary to the principle of fundamental justice.

. . . .

In view of my findings the plaintiff is entitled under s. 24 to a remedy.

Negligence

My task has been rendered less onerous by the very thorough analysis of Henry J. of the issues raised by the pleading in this case [*Jane Doe v. Metropolitan Toronto (Municipality) Commissioners of Police*] reported at (1989), 58 D.L.R. (4th) 396 (H.C.J.), when the matter came before him on a motion to strike out the statement of claim and the succinct reasons of Moldaver J. (as he then was) on behalf of the Divisional Court (1990), 74 O.R. (2d) 225, 72 D.L.R. (4th) 580, when the decision of Henry J. went to that Court on appeal.

After citing section 57 of the *Police Act*, R.S.O. 1980, c. 381, and observing that by virtue thereof the police are charged with the duty of protecting the public from those who would commit or have committed crimes, Moldaver J. (as he then was) goes on at pp. 230–31 as follows:

> To establish a private law duty of care, foreseeability of risk must coexist with a special relationship of proximity. In the leading case of *Anns v. Merton (London Borough)*, Lord Wilberforce defined the requirements of this special relationship as follows:
>
> > "First one has to ask whether, as between the alleged wrongdoer and the person who has suffered damage there is a sufficient relationship of proximity or neighbourhood such that, in the reasonable contemplation of the former, carelessness on his part may be likely to cause damage to the latter — in which case a *prima facie* duty of care arises."
>
> This principle has been approved by the Supreme Court of Canada in *Kamloops (City) v. Nielsen*.

Do the pleadings support a private law duty of care by the defendants in this case?

The plaintiff alleges that the defendants knew of the existence of a serial rapist. It was eminently foreseeable that he would strike again and cause harm to yet another victim. The allegations therefore support foreseeability of risk. The plaintiff further alleges that by the time she was raped, the defendants knew or

ought to have known that she had become part of a narrow and distinct group of potential victims, sufficient to support a special relationship of proximity. According to the allegations, the defendants knew:

(1) that the rapist confined his attacks to the Church-Wellesley area of Toronto;
(2) that the victims all resided in second or third floor apartments;
(3) that entry in each case was gained through a balcony door; and
(4) that the victims were all white, single and female.

Accepting as I must the facts as pleaded, I agree with Henry J. that they do support the requisite knowledge on the part of the police sufficient to establish a private law duty of care. The harm was foreseeable and a special relationship of proximity existed.

Do the pleadings support a breach of the private law duty of care?

The law is clear that in certain circumstances, the police have a duty to warn citizens of foreseeable harm. See *Schact v. R.*, and *Beutler v. Beutler, Adams v. Beutler*. The obvious purpose of the warning is to protect the citizens.

I would add to this by saying that in some circumstances where foreseeable harm and a special relationship of proximity exist, the police might reasonably conclude that a warning ought not to be given. For example, it might be decided that a warning would cause general and unnecessary panic on the part of the public which could lead to greater harm.

It would, however, be improper to suggest that a legitimate decision not to warn would excuse a failure to protect. The duty to protect would still remain. It would simply have to be accomplished by other means.

In this case the plaintiff claims, *inter alia*, that the duty owed to her by the defendants required (1) that she be warned of the impending danger; or (2) in the absence of such a warning, that she be adequately protected. It is alleged that the police did neither.

Instead she claims they made a conscious decision to sacrifice her in order to apprehend the suspect. They decided to use her as "bait". They chose not to warn her due to a stereotypical belief that because she was a woman, she and others like her would become hysterical. This would have "scared off" the attacker, making his capture more difficult.

The evidence establishes that Det. Sgt. Cameron clearly had linked the four rapes which preceded Ms. Doe's by the early days of August in 1986, and he and Det. Sgt. Derry knew that the rapist would continue to attack women until he was stopped. They knew the rapist was attacking single white women living alone in second and third floor apartments with balconies in the Church/Wellesley area of the City of Toronto.

On the evidence I find the plaintiff has established a private law duty of care.

Det. Sgts. Derry and Cameron determined, in the context of their investigation, that no warning would be given to any women — let alone the specific target group they had identified — and among the reasons given for deciding not to warn was their view that women would panic and compromise the investigation. Det. Sgt. Cameron gave this as a reason to Ms. Doe when he interviewed her following her rape and she asked why women had not been warned.

In spite of the knowledge that police had about this sexual rapist and their decision not to warn, they took no steps to protect Ms. Doe or any other women from this known danger. In my view, in the circumstances of this case, the police failed utterly in the duty of care they owed Ms. Doe.

The decision not to warn women was a decision made by Sgts. Cameron and Derry in the course of their investigation. It was made on the basis of "shop talk" they had overheard or been a part of, according to them, in relation to the Dawson Davidson-Annex Rapist investigation. What is apparent is that neither Sgts. Cameron nor Derry made any real effort to look into that investigation and determine whether in fact it had been the publicity that caused Dawson Davidson to flee.

Their decision was based largely on rumour and "shop talk" essentially within the 52 C.I.B. and they said they relied on it alone in making the very serious decision not to warn these women of the risk they faced. This they did in the face of the almost certain knowledge that the rapist would attack again and cause irreparable harm to his victim. In my view their decision in this respect was irresponsible and grossly negligent.

There is simply no evidence before this court which could be interpreted as suggesting that no warning should have been given in the circumstances of this case. The only persuasive expert opinion called by the defence, in fact, suggests that a suitable warning could have been and should have been given. While the defence experts were careful in giving their evidence, when one looks at the totality of their evidence this conclusion is irresistible.

Sgts. Cameron and Derry made a decision not to warn women in the neighbourhood and did not do so. They took no steps to protect the women they knew to be at risk from an almost certain attack; in result, they failed to take the reasonable care the law requires and denied the plaintiff the opportunity to take steps to protect herself to eliminate the danger and ensure that she would not be attacked.

In this respect they are liable to her in damages.

Charter Law

In my view the decision of the Divisional Court in this matter has already determined that the Charter can apply, in the circumstances of this case, to the police conduct. The section 15(1) violation alleged relates to discriminatory conduct by state officials in the carrying out and enforcing of the law. In the view of Moldaver J. (as he then was) the pleadings supported a violation of the plaintiff's rights under section 15(1). At that time the plaintiff's pleadings were mere allegations. It is implicit in the court's decision — if the allegations were proved it would constitute a violation of rights.

For reasons given above I am satisfied on the evidence and the plaintiff has established that the defendants had a legal duty to warn her of the danger she faced; that they adopted a policy not to warn her because of a stereotypical discriminatory belief that as a woman she and others like her would become hysterical and panic and scare off an attacker, among others.

A man in similar circumstances, implicit from Det. Sgt. Cameron's comment, would have been warned and therefore have the opportunity to choose whether to expose himself to danger in order to help catch the attacker.

It is not necessary that their decision not to warn be based solely on discriminatory grounds. It is enough that one of the bases for it was as the plaintiff has submitted:

> It need not have been the only factor, nor even the major or primary factor, in order for discrimination to be found.

Counsel in this respect goes on to quote from the decision of Chief Justice Dickson in *Janzen v. Platy Enterprises Ltd.*.

In the result the plaintiff has established a breach of her section 15(1) right to equal benefit and protection of the law.

As for the breach of section 7 the decision of the Divisional Court in respect of the pleadings is:

> Section 7 reads as follows:
> "7. Everyone has the right to life, liberty and security of the person and the right not to be deprived thereof except in accordance with the principles of fundamental justice."

> The plaintiff claims that she was deprived of her right to security of the person. The defendants chose, or at least adopted a policy which favoured the apprehension of the criminal over her protection as a targeted rape victim. By using Ms. Doe as "bait" without her knowledge or consent, the police knowingly placed her security interest at risk. This stemmed from the same stereotypical and therefore discriminatory belief already referred to.

> According to the plaintiff, she was deprived of her right to security of the person in a manner which did not accord with the principles of fundamental justice. These principles, while entitled to broad and generous interpretation, especially in the area of law enforcement, could not be said to embrace a discretion exercised arbitrarily or for improper motives. See *R. v. Beare*; *R. v. Higgins*.

> As a result, the plaintiff claims that her rights under s. 7 of the *Charter* were violated. Again, in my opinion, these pleadings do support such a violation.

As I have found in relation to section 15, the plaintiff has established on the evidence, the factual foundation pleaded for reasons set out herein. In the result, I am of the view that the decision of the Divisional Court was that in that event a violation of section 7 is established. I agree with that determination but even if I did not, I would consider myself bound.

Section 24

I will deal with the plaintiff's claim for damages fully when I deal with that aspect of her case later in these reasons.

I am satisfied on the facts of this case that the plaintiff's damages are the same in respect of the two bases upon which her action is founded i.e. negligence and breach of *Charter* rights.

The result of the breaches which she has established are the personal repercussion to her having been raped at knife point by a stranger. They are profound.

It is the same conduct by the police which I have found supports and establishes both causes of action.

In such circumstances the plaintiff is entitled to one award of damages to compensate her for the damage she has suffered. She is not, in my view, in these circumstances, entitled to any additional or "extra" damages because the police conduct has breached her *Charter* rights. In this respect assuming she is otherwise fully compensated, a declaration will suffice.

DAMAGES

. . . .

That Ms. Doe has been profoundly affected by the events of August 24, 1986, in every aspect of her life cannot be doubted on the evidence. That she continues to suffer, albeit not to the extent she did in the two years immediately following the rape, to this day is agreed by all experts.

. . . .

Rape is unlike any other sort of injury incurred by accident or neglect. Survivors of rape must bear social stigmatization which accident victims do not. Rape is not about sex; it is about anger, it is about power and it is about control. It is, in the words of Dr. Peter Jaffe, "an overwhelming life event". It is a form of violence intended to create terror, to dominate, to control and to humiliate. It is an act of hostility and aggression. Forced sexual intercourse is inherently violent and profoundly degrading.

As Mr. Justice Cory stated in *R. v. Osolin*:

> It cannot be forgotten that a sexual assault is very different from other assaults. It is true that it, like all the other forms of assault, is an act of violence. Yet it is something more than a simple act of violence. Sexual assault is in the vast majority of cases gender based. It is an assault upon human dignity and constitutes a denial of any concept of equality for women.

It is not helpful to compare the assessments of damages in accidental injury cases nor to look to those cases for any sort of guidance in assessing damages for rape.

Ms. Doe's life has been affected by the events of August 24, 1986, in every respect, and while she has improved considerably in the eleven years since, she continues to experience symptomology related to the rape. She will never be free of the terror and the indignity that Paul Douglas Callow brought into her life and left at the very core of her being. Her condition is chronic and the persuasive evidence suggests that this is likely to continue.

In my view, damage awards in the $40–50,000 range are reflective of neither the horrific nature of the violation nor of the overwhelming and all-encompassing consequences of it.

In my view, an appropriate general damage award for Ms. Doe in all the circumstances of this case is $175,000.00.

. . . .

I should add that the Chief of Police is responsible to see the members of his force carry out their duties properly and will be vicariously liable when they fail to do so as will the Board of Commissioners of Police which is charged with the overall responsibility of policing and maintaining law and order within the Municipality of Metropolitan Toronto (as it then was).

(e) B.(W.R.) v. Plint†

[BRENNER J.:]

In these actions the plaintiffs seek damages for sexual assaults committed against them by the defendant Arthur Henry Plint. The plaintiffs, all of whom are Indians within the meaning of the *Indian Act*, were students or residents at the Alberni Indian Residential School ("AIRS") during various years between 1943 and 1970 when their ages ranged from 5 to 19.

In the late 1800's the Presbyterian Church founded a residential school at Port Alberni for the education of First Nations children. The school was operated by that Church with periodic financial assistance from the Federal Government. In 1911 the parties entered into a written agreement in connection with what was then known as the "Alberni Boarding School". In 1925 a portion of the Presbyterian Church in Canada combined with two other religious denominations to form, through an Act of Parliament, the United Church of Canada. The United Church was involved in the school from 1925 onwards.

In 1962 another written agreement relating to the school was entered into by Canada and the United Church. On April 1, 1969, Canada took over the complete operation of the residential school and operated it until it was closed in 1973.

PARTIES

Plint was employed as a dormitory supervisor at the school from 1948 to approximately 1953 and from 1963 to 1968. The dormitory supervisors, including Plint, worked in the residence at AIRS and were responsible for the daily care and well-being of the resident children including the plaintiffs. They reported to and worked under the direction of the principal of AIRS.

The defendants Caldwell, Dennys and Andrews were principals at AIRS during the periods the plaintiffs were in residence. Caldwell was principal from 1944 to 1959, Dennys from 1959 to 1962 and Andrews was the principal and residence administrator from 1962 to 1973. In the mid-1960's his title was changed to residence administrator to reflect the fact that the children no longer attended school at the AIRS but went instead to public school in Port Alberni.

The defendant United Church of Canada (the "Church") was incorporated in 1925. It was formed

---

† 161 D.L.R. (4th) 538 (B.C.S.C.) at 540–44, 546, 548–49, 560–72, 574.

as the result of a merger between the Methodist Church, Canada, the Congregational Union of Canada and approximately 70% of the Presbyterian Church in Canada.

The Church is the largest Protestant denomination in Canada and ministers to over 3.5 million people in 4,100 congregations. It is structured into four levels or "Courts":

(a) the local congregations;
(b) district presbyteries;
(c) the regional conferences; and
(d) the General Council.

The congregations are the local church pastoral charges. District presbyteries cover a geographical area including 20 to 50 pastoral charges. In 1992 there were 96 presbyteries. There are 13 conferences, 12 of which cover a much wider geographical area roughly contiguous with provincial and territorial boundaries. The 13th Conference is known as the All Native Circle Conference. Its jurisdiction includes all First Nations congregations. Each conference has its own executive secretary and staff. The General Council is the highest court in the Church and is composed of some 400 commissioners. It meets biennially. Between General Council meetings the national affairs of the Church are administered by the Executive of the General Council.

The defendant, Her Majesty the Queen in Right of Canada is represented by the Minister of Indian Affairs and Northern Development and is referred to as "Canada", the "Crown", or "Indian Affairs" as the context requires.

On the application of the plaintiffs, I directed that the following issue be tried in this portion of the proceedings:

> Are the Defendants Her Majesty the Queen and/or the Defendant United Church of Canada vicariously liable for the sexual assaults committed by the Defendant Arthur Henry Plint against each of the Plaintiffs while those Plaintiffs were students at Port Alberni Indian Residential School, which sexual assaults are set out in the Statement of Claim?

. . . .

THE ASSAULTS

The plaintiffs in these actions allege that they were sexually assaulted by Plint while they were minors and resident at AIRS. Virtually all of the assaults at the school are said to have occurred in the residence in Plint's bedroom and/or office. As is set out in the agreed facts, in 1995 and 1997 Plint was convicted of multiple counts of sexual assault involving many of the plaintiffs. He is presently incarcerated serving sentences totaling 12 years. The Church and Canada admit that Plint sexually assaulted those plaintiffs in respect of whom a criminal conviction has been entered.

In addition a number of plaintiffs for whom there is at present no criminal conviction against Plint testified as to the sexual assaults he committed against them. These are F.L.B., R.J.J., D.B.W., M.S.W., H.B. and M.B.W. For this vicarious liability phase of the trial the nature and frequency of the assaults need not be determined and the plaintiffs need only prove that there was at least one assault by Plint for each plaintiff who seeks judgment against the defendants.

After hearing their evidence and in view of the fact that neither the Church nor Canada argued that any of these plaintiffs had never been sexually assaulted by Plint, I find that these plaintiffs were in fact assaulted on at least one occasion by Plint. The issue of the frequency and severity of the assaults will be dealt with during the damages assessment phase of this trial. Accordingly in these Reasons I do not review the evidence given by the plaintiffs of the particulars of the assaults.

Accordingly to be decided is whether the Church or Canada or both are vicariously liable for the Plint assaults.

THE VICARIOUS LIABILITY OF PLINT'S EMPLOYER

The law in British Columbia dealing with the test for the vicarious liability of an employer in respect of a sexual assault perpetrated by a child care worker against children was set out by the Court of Appeal in *B.(P.A.) v. Children's Foundation*. In that case one of the Foundation's employees Leslie Charles Curry sexually abused children in a group home operated by the Foundation. Curry was employed as a child care counselor and he was expected to fulfill the duties of a parent to the children. He worked day (7 a.m. to 3 p.m.) and evening (8 p.m. to 11 p.m.) shifts.

. . . .

Accordingly I conclude that when the facts of this case are considered in the context of the tests outlined by the Court of Appeal in the *Children's Foundation* case, the employer of Plint is vicariously liable for the sexual assaults he committed.

WHO EMPLOYED PLINT?

The Church and Canada each contend that the other was the sole employer of Plint. It is clear that Plint reported to the principal of AIRS. The principal created the rules Plint was to follow and he had complete control over and responsibility for Plint's day-to-day activities. The principal determined Plint's salary within the appropriate budget category approved by Canada. The principal had the authority to hire and fire dormitory supervisors: this is just what Andrews did after his wife reported to him seeing one of the children in Plint's room which contravened the rules Andrews had put in place.

However in my view it is not accurate to characterize the principal as the "employer" of Plint. The principal was the chief executive officer at AIRS. If incorporated, AIRS would have been the employer of Plint. However AIRS did not exist as a legal entity and hence it is necessary to look beyond AIRS to the Church and Canada to try to answer the real question: Which one of the Church or Canada can be properly characterized as the directing or controlling entity of AIRS and consequently responsible in law for the conduct of Plint who was controlled and directed on a day-to-day basis through the office of the principal?

The resolution of this issue requires an analysis of the historical relationship between the Church and Canada with respect to AIRS and a consideration of the applicable legal principles of vicarious liability.

.   .   .   .

HISTORY OF AIRS

In 1891 the Presbyterian Church in Canada founded AIRS on land owned by the Church. Until 1911 the Church operated the school with periodic financial assistance from Canada. In 1911 the Church and Canada entered into an agreement formalizing their arrangement. The Church agreed to manage the school in accordance with regulations and standards prescribed by Canada. Canada [provided] the funding for the operation of the school on a per capita basis. Although that agree-

ment expired in 1916, AIRS continued to operate under the general principles set out in the 1911 contract with minor variations in, for example, the rate of payment.

In 1917 a fire destroyed the main buildings of AIRS. The Presbyterian Church proposed and Canada agreed to pay for the construction of a new school and residence. The Church conveyed to Canada 16 acres of land on which the new school was to be built and the remainder of the AIRS property of some 160 acres [composed] of buildings and cultivated farm land was retained by the Church. On December 1, 1920 the new school now owned by Canada was opened.

In 1925 the United Church was formed and it took over the Presbyterian Church's role with AIRS.

The AIRS building burned again in 1937 and was rebuilt at Canada's expense. The new school reopened in 1940 and the arrangement between Canada and the Church for the operation of AIRS continued.

In the late 1950's Canada changed its method of funding residential schools from a per capita basis to a cost-controlled basis. In 1962 it entered into a new agreement with the Church for AIRS (as it did with other religious organizations for other residential schools in Canada). Classroom instruction at AIRS with the exception of kindergarten ceased in 1965 after which all the students were bussed daily to attend schools in Port Alberni. In 1969 Canada assumed responsibility for the administration of AIRS which continued to operate until 1973.

.   .   .   .

THE RELATIONSHIP OF CANADA AND THE CHURCH TO AIRS

As stated at the outset of these Reasons, Canada takes the position that, as stated in the 1962 agreement, the Church was the "management" at AIRS, that the principal who was hired by the Church carried out this mandate and that Canada's role was limited to providing the funding and to having in place sufficient checks and reporting to ensure that public funds were spent appropriately.

The Church says that by controlling the funding, Canada effectively controlled every aspect of the operation at AIRS. The Church says that although it was labeled as the "management" in the 1962 agreement drafted by Canada, if one examines what was really going on, the only conclusion is that the Church was acting solely as the agent of Canada.

In my view what is clear is that for more than a hundred years Canada and the churches including the United Church after 1925 were jointly involved in the education of Indian children. Many of the schools were originally founded by the churches as part of their missionary work. By 1892 Canada was providing per capita grants and by 1894 Canada's responsibility for the education of Indian children was entrenched by statute.

The joint character of this relationship is reflected in many of the communications. In 1929 the Assistant Deputy Minister of Indian Affairs wrote as follows:

> I have your letter ... asking certain questions in connection with Indian schools on Vancouver Island. There are five residential schools and seven day schools for the Indian children on the Island. All are financed by grants from this Department, and all, with the exception of one day school, are managed by one or other of the churches that are co-operating with this Department in the education of Indian children.

"Co-operation" and a "co-operative spirit" are common themes in the documentary history of the relationship between the churches and Canada. In 1923 the Deputy Superintendent of Indian Affairs admonished the Indian Commissioner of B.C. when he said there was "no intention of altering cooperation between the government and religious denominations in Indian education".

In a 1935 meeting between Canada and the "Committee of Churches Cooperating with the Department of Indian Affairs in Indian Education", Canon Gould expressed the hope that the "co-operative spirit" that characterized the relationship might be renewed. That same Committee in a brief to Minister Crerar presented in 1943 said, in urging Canada to provide more funding:

> [Indian education] is a joint undertaking carried on under an agreement between the Government and the Churches ... The operation of Residential Schools is a partnership between the Government and the Churches.

In 1943 the Churches made another joint presentation to Minister Crerar on the ongoing problems of financing the Indian residential schools. In that presentation they reminded Canada that they were "partners" in the "great enterprise" of the schools and that the churches were involved in Indian education as part of their "missionary and humanitarian program" before the Government assumed any responsibility. They went on as follows:

> This is a joint undertaking carried on under an agreement between the Government and the Churches, which can shortly be summarized in this way:
>
> > The Churches agree to provide teachers and staff necessary to look after the needs of the children admitted to the schools by authority of the Government. These needs include moral and religious instruction, teaching, physical needs (food, clothing, shelter, etc.) — all those up to the standard required by the Government.
>
> The Government provides the buildings and physical properties necessary and pays each pupil a sum agreed on for each school.

The United Church continued to view the relationship as that of a partnership as late as October 27, 1993 when it submitted its brief to the Royal Commission on Aboriginal Affairs stating that it had a partnership relationship with Canada with respect to Indian education generally and the residential schools in particular:

> The Residential School period coincides with the general partnership which existed between the established Christian churches and the Canadian Government in the process of nation-building, particularly the expansion of European-based settlement of the west and north. Church participation could be described as an inadvertent and unfortunate part of that shared nation-building project. Since the 1960's, the churches, including the United Church, have moved a considerable distance from this partnership role.
>
> The Residential School experience clearly indicates that an uncritical partnership with government holds great dangers for the churches.

. . . .

Both Canada and the Church hired some School staff directly: Canada hired the teachers and guidance counselors (after 1949); the Church hired the Christian Education workers. Both Canada and the Church were involved in the appointment of the principal, who in turn hired the domestic workers. Both parties received reports [from] the principal and both inspected AIRS. Both Canada and the Church owned school assets: Canada owned the buildings and the land on which they were erected and most of the contents; the Church owned the farm land and buildings.

Canada controlled admissions but consulted with the Church about the admissions and policies. Standards and regulations for the operation of AIRS were established by Canada and communicated directly to the principal after some consultation with the Church. Canada set up and funded training programs for dormitory supervisors but the Church participated in the development of those programs.

I conclude that Canada did not effectively transfer all aspects of the operation of AIRS to the Church under the agreements and the practice both parties followed. Canada did not limit its communications to the Church with the expectation that the Church would take whatever steps it considered appropriate to forward these on to the principal at AIRS. Rather it is clear that Canada issued many instructions regarding the operation of AIRS directly to the principal. This is inconsistent with the purported transfer of all management responsibility to the Church as set out in the 1911 and 1962 agreements. Simply put, what the agreements say was not what the parties put into practice.

I also conclude that Canada was not the sole controlling entity of AIRS. Andrews considered Reverend MacKay to be his "boss". The Church's involvement at AIRS was not limited to simply carrying out the expressed requirements of Canada. The Church provided Christian education and it communicated frequently with the principal concerning a wide range of matters at the school. While many of the communications featured matters which could only ultimately be dealt with by Canada, it is clear in my view that the Church nevertheless had a role beyond that of being merely the conduit of money and messages between the principal and Canada. In fact to be found in the documents concerning the historical relationship between Canada and the Church are many references to their "partnership" and to this "joint undertaking".

In its submissions the Church conceded that there are various historical documents within the Archives at the Church which use language "suggestive of a management or controlling role by the United Church in the AIRS". However the Church says that these statements were not made in the context of an attempt to apply a legal definition to the role of the Church and it says that none of the

individuals using such language were qualified by training to arrive at any such legal definition.

However the words which the parties used to describe their historical relationship, although not conclusive on the point, must nonetheless be weighed when considering the status of the Church and Canada. In my view it is appropriate to consider terms such as "joint enterprise" and "partnership" found in the documents written by the parties not in their legal sense, but rather having regard to their ordinary meaning. When I do this I conclude that these words selected by the parties themselves accurately describe their historical relationship with respect to AIRS.

LAW ON VICARIOUS LIABILITY

The doctrine of vicarious liability is described by Professor Atiyah in *The Law of Torts* (London: Butterworths, 1967) at p. 1:

> Vicarious liability in the law of tort may be defined as liability imposed by the law upon a person as a result of 1) a tortious act or omission by another, 2) some relationship between the actual tortfeasor and the defendant whom it is sought to make liable, and 3) some connection between the tortious act or omission and that relationship. In the modern law there are three and only three relationships which satisfy the second requirement of vicarious liability[,] namely that of master and servant, that of principal and agent, and that of employer and independent contractor.

Vicarious liability is the imposition of liability without fault. It is entirely dependent upon the relationship between the wrongdoer and the person or entity to whom a party seeks to attribute vicarious liability. The ultimate question for determination in this phase of the trial is, under the doctrine of *respondeat superior*, who bears the vicarious responsibility for assaults committed by Plint against the plaintiffs while they were students at AIRS.

In sexual assault cases when determining this question, the Court will focus on the total and actual relationship between the parties. *(A.(C.) v. C.(J.W.)).*

When considering vicarious liability the Courts are reluctant to rely on only one test. In *Odin v. Columbia Cellulose Co.* this Court held:

> ... there is no single test and the whole of the circumstances must be considered to determine the relationship between the parties.

. . . .

In the case at bar I have found as a fact that the Church and Canada jointly controlled the activities of the dormitory supervisors including Plint at AIRS through the office of the Principal. The question then becomes whether two entities can be simultaneously in control of a single employee or agent, for the purposes of determining vicarious liability.

. . . .

As stated by Atiyah [in] *Vicarious Liability in the Law of Torts* at p. 149:

> There is, of course, no reason why two employers should not jointly employ a servant, and this would normally be the case with the employees of a partnership. Here the servant is the servant of each partner and of all jointly, and they are all jointly and severally liable for the servant's torts.

. . . .

Although there was no formal partnership in the case at bar, there was in my view at the very least an informal one. I have found that each of the parties exercised control over the activities of the dormitory supervisors through the office of the principal. "Partnership" was the word used by each of the parties from time to time to describe their relationship and in my view it was accurate. The decision in Sinclair was based on a finding that both companies exercised control over the employee and that both companies benefited from the arrangement. The facts in the case at bar are similar and hence support a conclusion that both Canada and the Church are vicariously responsible for Plint's activities.

CANADA'S VICARIOUS LIABILITY

Canada argues that the traditional "control" test ought to be used in the analysis as to who was Plint's superior and hence liable for his wrongful acts. Canada says that the Church selected and, with Canada's approval, hired the principal who directed Plint's activities. Canada says that as stated in the 1962 agreement, the Church was in fact the "management" and hence is the entity vicariously responsible for Plint's activities. It says that the Church had a great degree of freedom and autonomy in fulfilling its contractual obligations to the Crown and that the principal, as representative of the Church, had a high degree of control over Plint. Therefore says Canada, vicarious liability cannot flow through the Church to Canada.

However I do not think it accurate to characterize the principal as the representative of the Church alone. For the reasons earlier set out I consider that both the Church and Canada were directly involved with and exerted effective control over the principal's activities in the furtherance of their joint and several objectives.

Canada says that it is appropriate to "look upwards" to define the employer and that when one does so, it is clear that the employer was the Church. Canada says that the essential question to be asked is "Which of the two entities controls the method in which the wrongdoer performs his work or duties?" Canada also emphasizes *de jure* rather than *de facto* control.

However when one "looks up" in this case, one sees not only the terms of the 1962 Agreement defining the Church as the "Management" as stressed by Canada, but also the provisions of the *Indian Act* which casts a statutory duty on Canada for the education of Indian children. This is not a case where the Church was hired as an independent contractor and then left to manage the school subject only to periodic overview. The direct communications that passed between Canada and the principal are inconsistent with that type of relationship.

In this case, Canada exercised the degree of control over the principal and over the activities at AIRS necessary to support a finding of vicarious liability in law. It was not simply a *de facto* control arising from the direct communications that passed between the Crown and the principal; nor was it the *de jure* control flowing from the provisions of the *Indian Act*.

Rather, it was a combination of both. Canada's control over the manner in which Plint discharged his duties flowed from Canada's obligations under the *Indian Act* coupled with the purported exercise of that duty by issuing directives directly to the principal of AIRS in the form of correspondence, regulations, budget reviews, *etcetera*. In my view this degree of control distinguishes this case from cases such as *Mochinski v. Trendline Industries Ltd.*; and *Lewis (Guardian ad Litem of) v. British Columbia*, in which the Crown was relieved of vicarious (although not direct) liability because the Crown did not exercise the degree of control necessary to bring the independent contractor's employees into the ambit of service of the Crown.

Accordingly I conclude that under the "looking upward" control test it proposes, Canada had the authority to and did in fact exercise control over the manner of execution of the activity in question and hence is vicariously liable for the wrongful acts of Plint.

THE CHURCH'S VICARIOUS LIABILITY

The Church says that more than just "control" must be examined. It relies on the more complete test set out by the Privy Council in *Montreal v. Montreal Locomotive Works Ltd.*. That test requires the Court to examine, in addition to control, additional factors such as ownership of the tools of the business, the chance of profit and the risk of loss.

The *Montreal Locomotive* case involved a plant in Montreal that was used for war production. The issue before the Privy Council was whether the Montreal Locomotive Works Company was carrying on business on its own behalf and therefore subject to city taxes, or operating as merely a manager or agent of the Federal Government in which case no city taxes would be payable. Under their agreement Montreal Locomotive sold its property to the Crown and built at the direction and expense of the Crown a new plant for the production of war [matériel]. The Company was paid a fee for each item produced; quality control was at the sole discretion of the Crown which could reject any production or required it to be redone at the Crown's sole expense. In all of the contracts the company's obligations were referred to as "for and on behalf of the Government and as its agent".

The Privy Council specified a four-part test to be applied in determining the relationship between the parties:

(a) control;
(b) ownership of the tools;
(c) chance of profit; and
(d) risk of loss.

After setting out this test the Privy Council went on to state:

> In many cases the question can only be settled by examining the whole of the various elements which constitute the relationship between the parties. In this way it is in some cases possible to decide the issue by raising as the crucial question whose business is it, or in other words by asking whether the party is carrying on the business, in the sense of carrying

it on for himself or on his own behalf and not merely for a superior.

. . . .

In the case at bar the Church was never designated as Canada's "agent" in either contract. Neither did Canada ever agree to the type of indemnity seen in the *Montreal Locomotive* case. Finally the issue as to which party would have been liable for torts committed by employees did not arise in that case which had nothing to do with the issue of vicarious liability of either the Government of Canada or the company for the actions of employees in the factory.

However if one considers the *Montreal Locomotive* tests in the context of the case at bar, arguably only the "ownership of the tools" test supports the Church's position since the building and contents at AIRS were owned by Canada (leaving aside the agricultural land).

I have earlier made the factual finding that both the Church and Canada exercised control over AIRS through the principal. The chance of profit and risk of loss factors are of questionable application when considering institutions such as the Church or Canada. However when dealing with other than private sector organizations, these *Montreal Locomotive* tests can perhaps be restated as the chance of advancing or the risk of diminishing the interests of the institution.

Canada had a statutory obligation to educate Indian children. Leaving aside the question as to whether that statutory duty was delegable, Canada nonetheless chose the Church as its instrument to fulfill at least part of its statutory obligations. This arrangement clearly advanced Canada's interests.

The arrangement at AIRS also served to advance the interests of the Church. Beyond the rather obvious conclusion that the Church presumably would not have continued the arrangement with Canada for over 50 years unless it was beneficial to the Church's interests, the arrangement clearly allowed the Church to advance its ministry amongst the First Nations people. It allowed the Church to provide Christian education in parallel to the secular education being provided by the teaching staff in the direct employ of Canada.

And so I conclude that their participation in AIRS advanced the interests of both Canada and the Church and hence the chance of profit/risk of loss tests set out in *Montreal Locomotive* are satisfied. To the extent that the *Montreal Locomotive* tests apply they support a conclusion that both the Church and Canada are vicariously responsible.

. . . .

However in my view the careful monitoring of the manner in which public funds are expended cannot be necessarily equated with sole control. In the case at bar if one focuses on the "total relationship between the parties" as referred to by Allan J. in Critchley, it is clear that both the Church and Canada exercised control over the activities at AIRS through the office of the principal.

CONCLUSION

In my view there was sufficient joint control and a co-operative advancement of the respective interests of the parties in this case that the term joint venture is apt. This conclusion is not only supported on the facts and the law, but it also coincides with the language used by the parties themselves to describe their relationship. Accordingly I conclude that both the Church and Canada are vicariously liable for the sexual assaults committed against the plaintiffs by Plint.

Judgment accordingly.